and tools necessary for your organization to develop a strategy and process for maintaining data integrity, security, and permanence. Dorians' extensive experience and knowledge in this area really come through, but it is his "common-man" writing style that really allows you to Grok the concepts in the book.

Tom McBride
IT Director
Wicken International

Everyone knows to have data backup (thanks to Dorian's books from the 90's), but people aren't thinking about what they need to protect *today*. Email, remote access, web assets. Dorian takes you through what to do in a post 2K disaster, and how to keep your company up all of the time.

Mike Landman
President
3rd Wave

The Dorian has done it again. This book is going to be the absolute authority on backup. We can't wait to see it in print. We'll make every one of our clients read it—or else.

David N. Salav   Vincent DiSpigno
President, PWR Systems   CEO, PWR Systems & Vizacom
CIO, Vizacom

The "Backup Book" is the greatest thing since sliced bread! Whether you are a beginner or a long time professional in computer technology you will be delighted at how well written and informative this book is. The why, when and how of backup strategies are extremely well covered in this book. Thank goodness that someone wrote it ... this book will make a big difference in the computer backup world. I believe it will become the industry standard.

Joe Vulgan
President
MacSystems Plus, Inc.

It has been a joy reading your Backup book. I have been in information protection and security for more than seven years now. I truly believe that this will be my new go to guide for backup and recovery. I love how you get right to the point and there is no BS. I will highly recommend this resource to my colleagues and friends. I can't wait until it is hot off the press.

Wyatt Banks
Security Systems Engineer
Pacific Northwest, Los Angeles

Good resources that help IT managers ensure their data integrity are scarce. Most deal with security vulnerabilities and do not address the best practices for preserving data. The Backup Book: Disaster Recovery from Desktop to Data Center is an invaluable tool designed to help professionals keep their secured data available.

Scott Petry
Vice President of Products and Engineering
Postini, Inc.

Dorian Cougias continues to be the go-to authority on networking and backup solutions for Macintosh operating systems. His new The Backup Book goes global and is a 'must read' for any administrator of mixed environments, from workgroups to the enterprise, that is challenged to safely and economically manage, store and retrieve vast amounts of information from local or widely distributed sources. In this book, your backup options are explained and compared. Too little thought is given to protecting valuable business information before a tragedy strikes. Lost data will halt a company's cash flow, stop manufacturing lines, lose business opportunities and frustrate everyone involved. This book is dedicated to preventing those losses before they happen. The Backup Book is well researched and can be read cover-to-cover because Dorian tells this complex technical story in an entertaining way. Reading this book will save you and your company a lot of money in disaster avoidance, but this will also be a book regularly consulted for reference by the smart data administrator.

Mitch Krayton
Digital Resources * 1stKIOSK

This is the perfect book written for the managers who keep ignoring request for funds from the IT department and at the same time complain that their data is not available.

Joseph Farkas
Columbia Univ.

An excellent overview on the subject. Not only is this book desperately needed by the IT professional, it is also an essential reference for anyone interested in storage technology.

Mark Hurlow
President
FWB Software

I am impressed. A man once told me to speak, write, and act at a 9th grade level. This seems to work best for most people. I believe you have captured that for the most part. If I had more time I may pick it apart some but all in all it seems very well done. It seems as though this book will be an excellent and enjoyable primer for the curious and possibly, and with the details you've added, an excellent refresher for seasoned Network personnel.

Joel Faust

Dorian's strength lies not just in his in-depth understanding of backup software and strategies but also in his real life, hands-on experiences planning disaster recovery strategies and helping organizations of all sizes recover from disasters.

Craig Isaacs
President
Neon Software

Today, time and effort are measured in digital output and an employee without a working computer is only about 50% of an employee. Data backup architecture, implementation, and execution are the most important domain any company can invest in. Dorian Cougias is the master of this domain and the latest edition of his book is one of the most important survival guides any IT person will ever buy.

Jerry Pape, Founder
Excalibur Software Production and Testing

After reading just two chapters of the book, the author shows a very complete subject knowledge along with a remarkable gift for communicating that knowledge clearly and concisely.

Peter House
field editor

The best compliment I can give this book is that you searched out the best talent in the industry and verified all your facts. I have read many books on this subject and they have almost always been swayed by the contributing vendors, your book gives the facts without being biased. I believe this book will become required reading by all in the industry.

Daniel Gray
field editor

The Backup Book is the most in-depth comprehensive publication I have ever seen, covering every imaginable aspect of data backup and recovery. From applications to RAID to networks, it addresses every issue a backup administrator will ever encounter. A must-read for anyone who is responsible for a single computer to a medium sized business network.

John R. Shearer
Systems & Network Architect

When disaster strikes, and it will, there are two classes of DBAs; one says "Ok, but we've got a good backup," the other says "Oh sh_t." This book will put you in the first category.

Ira Solomon
field editor

The Backup Book is absolutely the best book ever written about keeping your data secure. Cougias hands over the tools and methodology to protect yourself from basic hard drive failure to a catastrophic network outage. This book is a must-read for all practitioners, students, and teachers. I teach with it myself.

Cihan Cobanoglu, PhD, CHTP
Assistant Professor of IT
University of Delaware

Once again Cougias takes dry-as-toast material and masterfully infuses it with a measure of detail and humor that makes it a pleasure to read. You'll buy this book because you need to, but you'll read this book because you want to!

Tom Dell
author, "AppleShare IP," "MCSE Core 2000," etc.

Hey, what are you doing there reading this part? You aren't going to learn anything by reading these quotes! Turn into the book about twenty pages and get learning! And if you are still in the bookstore deciding what to do, then buy the book already. Geez.

Dorian J. Cougias
author of the really heavy book you have in your hands

THE BACKUP BOOK

DISASTER RECOVERY FROM DESKTOP TO DATA CENTER

Network Frontiers Field Manual Series

Dorian J. Cougias • E.L. Heiberger • Karsten Koop • Laurie O'Connell (ed.)

Foreword by:

David Bell, CEO of Interpublic Group and member of the Homeland Security Council

Industry Forewords by:

Adam R. Dell (MessageOne), Jim Simmons (SunGard), and Gary Cotshott (Dell)

COPYRIGHT AND HOUSEKEEPING INFORMATION

Schaser-Vartan Books
US Offices:
5620 West Dayflower Path
Lecanto, FL 34461

SAN # 255-2582

ISBN 0-9729039-0-9

Library of Congress Catalog Card Number: 2001274299

Printed in the United States of America
10 9 8 7 6 5 4 3 2 1

Feedback: info@backupbook.com

For bulk orders: (800) 888-4741

http://www.backupbook.com

DORIAN'S DEDICATION

This book is dedicated to Dave and Vinny who survived being an Apple VAR during the worst possible years. Who survived being bought during the dot.com rush only to have to bring the whole thing back from the brink when the parent company disolved. Who survived the World Trade Center bombing by of a couple hundred feet of distance. And through it all, taught me that friendship, the type of freindship they have with one another, is stronger than anything.

And to my Dad Gust Cougias, my hero.

TABLE OF CONTENTS

FOREWORD BY DAVID BELL,

CHAIRMAN AND CEO,
INTERPUBLIC GROUP OF COMPANIES,
& A MEMBER OF
THE PRESIDENT'S HOMELAND SECURITY ADVISORY COUNCIL

Preparing for a potential disaster makes good business sense. Because of the uncertainty of the world situation, not only the federal government, but organizations across America are working hard to strengthen our security and hone our ability to respond quickly and decisively when the worst happens, and I've learned that first hand as a member of the President's Homeland Security Advisory Council.

As business leaders and professional IT staff, we must learn about potential threats so that we're better prepared to react in an emergency. And, while we can't predict what will happen, or when, we can take simple steps to prepare our organizations to react effectively in the event of a disaster:

- Create a plan

- Develop a "disaster kit" designed to support the plan, and then

- Stay informed, stay flexible, and be proactive.

Organizations today are hungry for leadership and action—eager to learn what to do to be more prepared, and to gain confidence that this preparedness will make a difference. Organizational leaders are more than willing to take responsibility in an emergency., but they need guidance and council from their CIOs, IT directors, and managers. Today's business leaders look to their IT departments to help them determine various rescue and recovery missions in the event of myriad disasters, from quotidian operating glitches to devastating building loss.

This ability to pre-plan and respond quickly becomes ever more important as your organization becomes ever more collaborative. During the time Dorian worked for me at True North Communications (which became a part of IPG), we created a culture of collaboration across our brands on behalf of clients seeking broader solutions. This collaboration significantly drove our organization's organic growth, yet necessarily put us at a higher risk for disaster—a risk that we accepted and then accommodated with careful research, assessment, planning, and quick reactions when anything went wrong.

As Dorian says at the outset of this book, we *do* live and work in a connected world. And because of that, the challenge to you, the IT staff, is to plan in advance for anything and everything that may go wrong, to quickly assess the situation when it does, and to use good, common business sense in reacting to each and every disaster. By planning for fault tolerance, high availability, and quick recovery, you can turn disaster into opportunity—for increased team cohesiveness, business flexibility, and fail-safe security.

Your planning will ultimately lead to the establishment of your disaster recovery kit. In this book, Dorian has analyzed the products and services that form your kit's components—more extensively than any author to date. While some of the specifics are beyond my technical grasp, he and I both share the same three-point focus: Re-establishment of communication, reconnection with clients, and normalization of collaborative work.

Whatever products and methods you choose, your first step must be the resumption of communication. As long as you can communicate, you're in business. Not only do you need to communicate with staff, you must communicate with clients, because without them, you have no reason to be in business.

While Dorian might have joked with us about some of the technology he inherited back at True North, we all knew he was deadly serious about never allowing our client-serving technology to fail. In your organization, be just as serious. The moment a disaster strikes, an invisible clock starts running in your clients' minds. You have to beat that clock and recover well ahead of their expectations.

Just as quickly, you must normalize your staff's ability to work collaboratively. Organizations are groups of teams, not merely a series of individuals. Therefore, your kit must expand its focus from restoring computers and information to recovering entire systemic and group functions so that teams can resume their normal work process as quickly as possible.

Because businesses evolve, and the way we collaborate and do business evolves with them, your plan should never get dusty. Your biggest challenge is to keep informed, to stay one-up on the bad guys and potential disasters. I'm awake every morning at 4:30A.M., reading the day's news and ingesting what's happening in the world, because I need that informed edge to stay ahead of the power curve. You may not need to set your alarm clock quite that early, but you do need to stay one step ahead in regard to your business, your business process, and your technology. Keep ahead of the game by determining and dealing with potential threats and the pitfalls of doing business in new and evolving ways. You're the voice of technology guidance for your business leaders, informing them of their choices, consequences, and necessary support budgets for new business processes—so be an educated voice.

As Dorian says in his conclusion, this book is a beginning—the future has yet to be written, for each and every company. To stay informed, you might want to take Dorian up on that offer to become one of his field editors, so that you can learn what's happening before it happens. Don't be the last one to find out that a certain technology could easily suffer a disaster and end your organization's relationship with a client, or even end your organization completely—that's a true disaster. Instead, with educated judgment and proactive planning, you can substitute action for anxiety, and feel confident that you've done all you can to ensure your company's security.

David Bell
CEO, Interpublic Group of Companies
New York City, 2003

David Bell, an industry leader in marketing communications and a strong advocate of collaborative work, is chairman and CEO of The Interpublic Group of Companies. Interpublic is one of the world's leading organizations of advertising agencies and marketing services companies. In addition, Mr. Bell is also currently the chairman of The Advertising Council, (a private, nonprofit organization that has been the leading producer of public service communications programs in the United States since 1942), and is one of 16 people appointed by President Bush to the Homeland Security Advisory Council.

Not only did I ask David Bell to write a foreword, but being inspired by what he wrote, I wanted to provide three different insights into this world of disaster recovery *from the viewpoint of industry insiders*. Therefore, I have asked three very distinguished industry leaders to expound upon what disaster recovery means to them in their world.

Read what they say, and heed their advice.

INDUSTRY FOREWORD BY ADAM R. DELL
FOUNDER AND CHAIRMAN, MESSAGEONE INC.
MANAGING GENERAL PARTNER, IMPACT VENTURES

David Bell, in his foreword, mentioned the establishment of a disaster recovery kit, and how this kit needs to help you regain your ability to work collaboratively as quickly as possible. With that in mind, Dorian asked if I would expound more on the topic of what should go into the kit from a communications perspective, and so I'll focus on that topic herein.

The underpinning of The Backup Book is correct—we work in a connected world. This is plainly evident by the fact that electronic mail has become such an intrinsic part of our organizational communication process that we are hardly aware of its existence. That is, we aren't aware of how weaved into our fabric it is until we try to communicate to the organization without it. Your organizational "workhorse" servers running in your data centers follow the same pattern. No one thinks about them until they aren't running. The problem with this scenario of the forgotten but all-important communications infrastructure is that if you do forget about planning for the failure of these systems, reacting to their failure puts you at a massive disadvantage in a crisis. If you want to find out how connected your organization is, unplug your communications infrastructure for a few minutes, and then you'll understand the important of pre-planning for a real disruption, no matter where it originates. It will help you decide what you are going to need to preserve; and how, with whom, and what, you are going to communicate in an emergency.

As is pointed out in the first chapter of this book entitled "When bad things happen to good computers," the threats to your computer systems are myriad, and unless you are in that lucky 2% of the population that nothing ever happens to you, you'd better heed these warnings. What isn't presented in the book's first chapter is that you can also be affected by what happens to supporting organizations around you. Many of the firms located in mid-town Manhattan, miles away from ground-zero during the 9/11 attacks lost complete connectivity to their organization when Verizon, their Internet Service Provider was brought down. Because they hadn't planned for this type of outage, all e-mail, all integrated systems were downed for up to a week for some organizations while they scrambled to react and re-connect through other service providers or at other locations. Some lost hundreds of thousands of dollars in revenue and opportunities. Why did it cost so much and take so long to recover?

The plain and simple fact of the matter is that planning for component failure such as a computer, hard drive, or a single server is completely different than planning for your communications infrastructure to fail. As many parts as there are in a single component, there are that many components in your communications infrastructure. Think of the way that your hard drives, memory, motherboard, and PCI cards have to work together to keep the computer running. That is how your DNS, Internet feeds, mail servers, fax servers, remote access serves, and key supply chain servers have to interact with each other to keep your company communicating within its own structure as well as outward to your clients and supporting vendors. And because you are using these systems to communicate both inside and outside of your organization, you are exposing your clients and suppliers to the risk of your failure as well.

Ask yourself these tough, hard questions today—if your building were lost, or your data center and therefore key communications equipment were lost, or your Internet Service Provider were suddenly unavailable; how would you communicate your emergency procedures with your staff, your suppliers, and your clients? Are you one of those companies that is mentioned in the book that has both of their authoritative DNS servers within their own LAN (and therefore would become invisible to the Internet)? If you knew you were going to lose your building tonight and could only take certain equipment out of it, what would you take, what would you preserve? Do you have any mechanism in place for emergency communications? Have you ever tested an emergency communications plan (other than within your own IT staff)? These are all "lifeboat drill" questions. They are questions designed to determine how well you've pre-planned for a communications emergency and what you would instinctively know to preserve in case of loss. They are questions designed to test your ability to communicate what is happening; what the staff, clients, and suppliers should do in the situation, and how and when you are going to restore normalized work.

You'll want to preserve your DNS presence on the Internet. You'll want to preserve some of your infrastructure support servers (like supply chain management, etc.). You'll want to preserve your e-mail servers as well. How much you want to preserve is up to you. Decisions about DNS are easy. Decisions about preserving contents of mailboxes (do you really need Tom the sales guy's birthday pictures?) aren't always that straightforward. You and the leadership of your organization are the only ones able to make your decisions. You and the leadership of your organization are the only ones able to conduct your lifeboat drills and decide what gets budgeted and what gets cut. This book, The Backup Book: Disaster Recovery from Desktop to Data Center has some great ideas about what might and might not work for you. Use the book as a planning tool. Use the book as an idea generator. Use the book as a brick to throw at anybody not paying attention to you when you say that establishing an emergency communications plan is vitally important to your organization.

And then make your own decisions. Create an emergency communications plan that works for you. Because we work in a connected world. And any time that we aren't connected and working is wasted time.

Adam R. Dell
Founder and Chairman, MessageOne Inc.
Managing General Partner, Impact Ventures

Austin, Texas, 2003

A former attorney at Winstead, Sechrest and Minick, Adam Dell serves as managing partner at Impact Venture Partners, is on the board of XO Communications and is an adjunct professor at the graduate business school at Columbia University.

Industry Foreword by Jim Simmons
Chief Executive Officer,
SunGard Availability Services

We didn't ask Dorian to write this book, though it might seem that way once you read all the gratifying things he's said about us!

At SunGard, we're in the business of educating business leaders, IT professionals, governments and others about the best ways to keep information available and up to date in this increasingly complex, connected world we live in.

I like to think of business systems the way we do the human body: Information is the lifeblood propelled through the veins and arteries of the organization – to keep it healthy, alert and in motion. When the blood vessels, your information systems, get clogged, unhealthy or vulnerable to disease, your entire enterprise is at risk.

Keeping the organizational body healthy is one of the most important functions of the IT professional. At SunGard, we call that healthy state Information Availability. Simply put, Information Availability is about connecting people to data, that is, to information – through hardware, software, and connectivity systems that transcend the main office, across state, regional and national boundaries.

But more than that, technology serves the people who use it: yourself, colleagues throughout your company, customers, vendors, shareholders. Whether you work with mainframes or microprocessors, the ultimate goal of your endeavor is to bring the next critical piece of information to the person who needs it… to keep those organizational blood vessels operating cleanly and smoothly.

What makes your job more exciting – and even more important – than ever before? Today, unlike any other time in history, your responsibility doesn't stop inside the walls of your own company. This has never been more true than it is now, thanks to the power of technology. Every company, from the largest multinational to the smallest mom-and-pop shop has access to customers, vendors, partners – that is, with anyone -- anywhere in the world.

And that brings up a brand-new concern. Open access to information means open access to problems. In December of 1999, people all over the world took extra money out of cash machines, stocked up on candles and flashlights, downloaded their hard drives and, in general, prepared for what some feared might be the worst computer outage in history. The fact that it didn't happen doesn't mean that we can be complacent. When one system fails it affects another, which was made infinitely clear in the days following September 11. In May 2003, just days before I write this, the Fizzer worm began spreading via e-mail and the KaZaa network. Not only can Fizzer knock out certain anti-virus programs, it can open a back door to servers for unauthorized access.

Bugs, worms, viruses -- and let's not forget power outages, fires, floods and other disasters -- can disable operations in any number of ways. Your systems can be down for minutes, hours or days; the financial impact can range from thousands to millions of dollars per minute. And your challenge? It's to expect – and prepare – for the unexpected… in order to protect your company's information against the most insidious electronic intruders as well as the gravest external threats.

It's not a job for the faint of heart.

Dorian, more than most people, knows that Information Availability is a philosophy, one which applies to every aspect of business and communications. Author Herman Melville once wrote that "A thousand fibers connect us with our fellow men; and among those fibers, as sympathetic threads, our actions run as causes, and they come back to us as effects."

Look at it this way: how long would you want to be without your cell phone, ATM access, GPS, EasyPass, e-mail? From the most mundane task to the most sophisticated process, information availability gives us what we need, when we need it, both as consumers and business professionals.

Your job is to make that happen. I think that's pretty terrific. Actually, I think it's invaluable.

Bobby Unser, auto racer and three-time winner of the Indy 500, once said that "Success is where preparation and opportunity meet." Dorian's tremendous knowledge and lively writing will help give you the preparation you need to become an expert in the vital field of Information Availability. The rest is up to you.

I wish you much success.

Jim Simmons
CEO
SunGard Availability Services
Wayne, Pennsylvania

May 2003

INDUSTRY FOREWORD BY GARY COTSHOTT
VICE PRESIDENT AND GENERAL MANAGER, DELL SERVICES
DELL COMPUTER

A wise man once said, "Knowledge is power." But an even wiser man said, "A little knowledge is a dangerous thing." Sometimes I wonder if they were both talking about backups and disaster recovery planning. In these crucial fields, what you don't know *will* hurt you. As a business technologist, you have to ask the tough questions: What are the ramifications to your bottom line if you can't access the information you need, when you need it? If the worst happens, are you prepared to recover from a disaster? What constitutes a disaster to your organization? You must ask these questions because you need the answers to protect and support your business.

Proper support for computers in today's organizations means supporting business continuity and high-availability needs, as well as planning for disaster recovery. Dell equipment the world over supports major organizational computing endeavors—everything from front-end Point of Sale (POS) cash registers through integration to back-end servers that tie data into Supply Chain Management (SCM) and Inventory Management (IM); data center servers and storage supporting mission critical Enterprise Resource Planning applications; and High Performance Computing Clusters performing the world's most complex supercomputing functions. At Dell, we don't consider these products a collection of systems—we see our hardware devices the same way you do: as tools to support people and processes. And as such, they must be supported before, during and after expected or unexpected disruptions. These disruptions can be as simple as performing routine maintenance, as complex as relocating your business unit to a new building, or as unexpected as dealing with a destroyed data center. When disaster can range so far and wide, what exactly do you need to know in order to provide proper support?

As David Bell noted in his foreword, you must know how to create a plan, understand what's appropriate to put in a disaster recovery kit, and stay abreast of changes, both in your organization and in technology.

The Backup Book divides what can go wrong into three categories (freezes, corruption and loss), explaining how those problems affect your computers, your data, your applications and even your building. Throughout the book, Dorian proposes remedies for each possible threat, to help you design a comprehensive, customized kit to help your business respond proactively to a bevy of disasters.

Similarly, our belief is founded within our own Dell-on-Dell experience wherein we lead through industry best practices. From its inception, Dell.com has been powered by our own self-supplied computing infrastructure. This means that we have had to discern what goes into *our own disaster recovery kit* from the perspective of hands-on experience. We've taken that knowledge and have created powerful partnerships, programs, and services to meet the real-world business challenges we all face.

From this experience, we've come to analyze business continuity at four levels, dealing with both high availability and disaster recovery at each level. Let's touch on these levels as they're explored in the course of this book.

Platform continuity

The first level of continuity begins at the platform level, with "in the box" availability features, such as redundant, hot-swappable components. And, when equipment is damaged beyond repair, you'll want to learn about rapid replacement programs that are designed to ship out preconfigured replacement systems faster than you could imagine. Dorian covers both of these issues thoroughly when he explains what to look for in storage enclosures, or how to pre-plan systems for drop shipping to recovery rooms.

Data continuity

Data continuity is divided into regular backup and restoration programs for disaster recovery and fault-tolerant storage for high availability. At a minimum, RAID (redundant array inexpensive disks) disk-level data protection on key systems should be required. As your quantity of information and data grows, external storage systems such as Direct Attach Storage (DAS), Network Attach Storage (NAS) and Storage Area Networks (SAN) offer higher performance and capacities with advanced management and recovery features. You'll find a comprehensive guide on fault tolerance and RAID in this book, covering everything from simple hard drive failure to complex server clusters, and NAS over SAN systems that provide the highest levels of availability.

Application continuity Application continuity means eliminating single points of failure in the overall system architecture. This helps ensure a continued pathway and working system that end users can access in the event of disaster. The tools in your kit should include application fail-over clustering, "snapshot copy," storage area networks (SAN) and redundant communications services.

Site continuity When it comes to site continuity, you have to think beyond the building to develop remote recovery systems and services in the event of a building, site or metropolitan disaster. This can be as simple as testing the efficacy of a restore-from-tape onto a brand-new piece of equipment at a remote location, or as complex as developing a world-wide "follow the sun" system of data centers (Dorian calls it the round-robin approach) with global fail-over capability. Commercial recovery services include offsite media storage, electronic vaulting (mirrored storage), application hosting, drop ship, mobile site, cold site, hot site and more. The concluding chapters on high-availability networks and building loss detail these options.

As you can see, to prepare for the myriad problems—from small mishaps to lost buildings—that arise in today's business environment, your kit must be comprehensive and flexible. In **The Backup Book**, you'll find the essential information that will help you protect and empower your business. When it comes to backup and disaster recovery planning, knowledge *is* power—and the more knowledge you have, the more secure your business will be. The collective expertise of **The Backup Book**'s authors and the engineers and field editors who assisted them comprises an indispensable road-map on your path to network security and professional peace of mind.

Gary Cotshott
Vice President and General Manager, Dell Services
Dell Computer

Austin, Texas, 2003

THANKS FROM THE STAFF AT NETWORK FRONTIERS

Thank you, David

I truly appreciate David taking time out of his hectic schedule to write the foreword to this book. I wanted it to come from a business person, not a technologist, so you'll understand that what you're protecting is your organization's business. Yes, you might focus on the computers, but what you're really protecting is the work produced in business functions and client endeavors. It's not about technology—it's about protecting people's work. Don't ever forget that.

Thank you, Adam Dell

In our industry, its great to meet folks who are on the track of The Main Thing as I like to call it. Adam Dell and his company MessageOne are on the right track when you think about where they are going with their Emergency Messaging Services product. We all know how important e-mail is to us—when we lose the use of it. And as Adam points out in his foreword, *that's not the time* to think about securing it. I was very pleased when this foreword was written. Thank you.

Thank you, Jim Simmons

I am very excited that Jim Simmons, CEO of SunGard's High Availability Services, offered his assistance and provided a foreword to this book. As you'll be able to tell from the chapters that include their products, I am very impressed with SunGard's stance on the need for high availability and very happy to work with them.

Thank you, Gary Cotshott

When most people think of Dell, they think of hardware. Dell is much, much more than that. Did you know that Dell provides services that help you develop an effective Business Continuity plan? Yep, that's a fact. And that's just one of the services that Gary Cotshott's group at Dell provides customers. Dell's server and storage consolidation (consolidation being one of the things I really believe in) planning services will not only help you with the plan, they will also help in quantifying your problem to support a proposed solution—and *that* helps a lot.

Thank you, Laurie

A book is penned by an author, but written by many—and this is no exception. This book is the first in our series to introduce our new editor, Laurie O'Connell. What we put down as mere explanations, she turned into something you'll want to read. She's a great addition to our team.

Thank you, field editors

This book continues our noble tradition of listening to the field. In this case, we've listened to more than 300 people. You'll find the complete list of field editors on our backupbook.com website. The most prolific of those field editors are listed throughout the book, and we thank them in each and every chapter they contributed to. If something's wrong in this book, don't blame them—blame us. We probably weren't listening as well as we should. If you'd like to become one of the field editors who get to "tell it like it is," feel free to drop by the same website (www.backupbook.com) and sign up. We'd love your input. We're limited by our own viewpoints and our own opinions—and we relish those from you, who know better than we do.

So, if you're wondering why some vendors get more space...

Wonder no more. You'll find that we reference a great many vendors throughout this book. I can't give them enough thanks. If you know of a vendor we haven't listed—tell them to get their act together. The only vendors that aren't listed are those that we don't know about, or those that gave us the cold shoulder. *We didn't write about any vendor who didn't get us product to test and engineers to quiz.* They got space in the book because they were (a) suggested as "good answers" to the problems we all find in the real world by our field editors, (b) gave us the time of day and helped us understand how their products solved our collective problems, or (c) assigned resources to this project to help pull it off. Think about it—and think about how you'd be treated by these companies, as well. That said, we do strive for objectivity. Bottom line, the products are puffed or panned based on quality, not P.R.

Thank you, VARs

Our most enthused thanks go to all of the VARs who are willing to support our theories—and your backup and recovery needs. We've gotta tell you that in this world, a great VAR is worth her weight in gold—maybe even platinum. If you get stuck—get a VAR. If you have a good question about what's right for your needs—get a VAR. By the way, we aren't a VAR, but our website does list the best VARs we know in each fields and in each state. If you get stuck, or better yet, *before* you get stuck—find a VAR from our website. You'll be glad you did.

If you're looking for a good VAR, go to:

www.backupbook.com

If you want to be a field editor, go to:

www.backupbook.com

If you want to take advantage of all of the free info and tools that just wouldn't fit into the measly page count our publisher allowed us, guess where you should go?

www.backupbook.com

What's a Disaster Without a Recovery?

We work in a connected world. Wow, there's a news flash, huh? Seriously—we work in a connected world. Think about it—"break it down," as they say.

We work in a connected world.

Let's break down the above sentence into its constituent parts. Doing so will give us a firm handle on what we need to think about when cooking up departmental or organizational backup and recovery plans. Let's start with our connectedness.

Connected. Almost 10 years ago I wrote my first backup book. Yes, I know this sounds like one of your father's "I walked uphill to school both ways" stories, but it's true. Back then, there were no such animals as client-facing applications, CRM systems, or supply chain management systems that actually *connected* with some other system outside the organization. Back then, we were measuring local area network connect times and comparing the difference between Apple's LocalTalk, Ethernet, and the "new" wireless connectivity that ran at about 1 MB. Wide Area Network connectivity between offices was at an average of 56 kbps. And now, 10 years later, everyone connects to almost everything. Bluetooth connects our toasters to our computers. Right now I'm sitting in Starbucks, surfing the Internet at 2.5 Mbps through my 802.11 wireless Ethernet card. My connection at home (cable modem) is every bit as fast as my connection at the office (T1).

> Whatever backup plan you create, it must reach out and touch each and every system that you need to protect.

Work is **connected**. Originally, networks were for printing. Originally, computers supported word processing, spreadsheets, graphic artists, layout folks, and simple research databases. Heck, even when I wrote that maiden backup book those 10 long years ago, workgroups weren't *really* workgroups in the sense that they are today. But today, this very book you're reading is sitting on a server as we write it, with a master document controlling the overall outline and formatting, with individual chapters written by myself, Karsten, and Lynn; then checked in and out of the master. We have a web server that connects to the world. As we near completion of chapters, we e-mail our field editors for their sage advice, tying information into the chapters directly from their field edits and comments in our forum.

> When you create your backup plan, understand that your work environment has three layers of connectedness: the individual user applications that aren't connected much at all, the workgroup applications that affect departments or teams, and the outward-facing applications and organizational applications that affect your entire company and its clients.

Work. It really *is* about protecting your work, not your computer. Forget the computer—save the work. Computers are cheap, but your creative effort is your lifeblood. And some systems, documents, and processes within your work comprise more of that vital ichor than others. One of our field editors, Joe Vulgan, put this well when he said, "Maintaining business continuity is a proactive process that is a key responsibility of a business organization. Taking this responsibility should be a direct business goal implemented with the proper planning and tools necessary to maintain and protect the company's data. Probably the most important factor in maintaining business continuity is to have a data backup system that's designed or scripted to fit the specific business data model, and, finally, to ensure that the equipment is up and running properly."

> Base your backup plan on your work's tolerance to downtime, and budget accordingly. It's all about saving the work—not the computers.

We work. When I write, I work. However, when I write, I work by walking next door to Karsten's office and bugging him. I work by coming up with ideas and then nagging our 350 field editors. I work by annoying the heck out of Lynn with inane questions (okay, you vendors can all include yourselves there, too). Even I, a writer, the most solitary creature since the noble wolf, work as a "we." Yep, Mr. Donne, I guess you were right: No man is an island. I'm pointing this out because you really *do* need to understand your organization's workflow. You need to understand how group work affects the tolerance to downtime of the information that flows through your company—and here, as in so many other endeavors, from soccer to stand-up comedy, timing is everything. At the project's inception, while everyone's getting their act together, pieces necessary to the final stage of production can probably be ignored for a few days, but as you near your goal—or punch—line, all essentials must be accounted for. Any piece of information's tolerance to downtime truly depends upon the workflow stage in which it occurs. Your backup plan must deal with that—to ensure that the work is both protected and restorable within the right time frame. The plan relies on an appropriate budget for each stage of the workflow.

> When creating your backup plan, take into account the workflow of the organization, department, or group that you're protecting. Ask yourself: Am I protecting the right information at the right time? If *any* point of failure can cause a workflow bottleneck, make sure that failure can be overcome quickly. If not, the costs of downtime will be multiplied by the number of people sitting around twiddling their thumbs.

We. People do the work. The company is made up not of systems, but of us living, breathing bits of humanity. And, oddly enough, the most frequent data loss problems on a network are caused directly by people. The "we" of your organization must believe in, and buy off on, your backup plan. So you have to understand the people you work with. How does the boss think? What's important to the boss in terms of you protecting the organization's work? What's important to the other key staff members? How do you present your budget—as a straight set of numbers or as an attachment to some specific and possibly favored program? Who can you trust to do their own local, critical backups—and who *can't* you trust?

> When writing your backup plan, keep your audience in mind. The story of recovery isn't a tale of you heroically saving a system: It's the odyssey of you saving a person's work—work they're proud of; work they do for a living. And if you're the protector of what someone does for a living, that's kind of important. You do have a good shot at being a hero here—if you remain mindful and, as Pat Fallon, CEO of the famed Fallon McElligott ad agency, used to say to me in critical times: "Don't blow it." Tailor your plan to the "we" of your organization.

Let's put this into perspective

We work in a **connected** world. Understand that. Understand the nature of it. Plan for it. Live by it. Here's a simple way to look at what's important within your organization: by connectedness and need for availability, as shown in Figure Intro-1. on page 4.

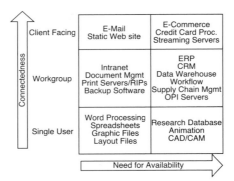

Figure Intro-1. Connectedness and need for availability

Think through the organization(s) you work with. How much of what you need to back up is in the single-user, low-need-for-availability category, and how much is in the client-facing, high-need-for-availability category? What you have, and how connected your group to be backed up is, will play a major part in determining the nature of your backup plan. One of our field editors, Ira Solomon, added this little tidbit: To find the right balance, you must attune yourself to the organization's grunts and groans.

Let's translate this into computer terms

Let's take the business processes that we were looking at above and put a more technical perspective on it for the purposes of this book. Because, for the purposes of this book, while you can't back up "word processing," you sure can back up Microsoft Office Suite documents. While you can't back up "workflow" or "supply chain management," you sure can back up the file servers' data and the databases that support supply chain management. To make it easier to understand what we're dealing with, we've created four basic icons to convey the three basic types of information that you need to protect: **documents**, **group work**, and **group communications**—and, of course, you need to protect your **hardware**, as well.

 This icon of a Microsoft Word document represents an individual's **documents**. Both the individual effort and the documents that need to be protected are part of disaster planning and backup operations. These documents are static in nature—simple to back up because they don't change unless the user hits the **Save** command. Keeping dated versions of these documents allows the user to restore a lost or corrupted document to any point in time.

An icon of a folder (a.k.a. **directory**) and a data storage container (a.k.a. **database**) is our symbol for **group work**. This can be as simple as a file server or as complex as a supply chain management system. These systems are more fluid, in that data flows into and out of them on a regular basis. At any given time, several or several hundred users can be simultaneously accessing this data. These files have a high propensity to be open—in-use/in-flux. Given the nature of this data (especially databases), it's much harder to protect them and even harder to maintain a historical record of dated versions.

 Our symbol for **group communications** is a cross between a postage stamp that represents electronic mail and a web page that represents transactional client-facing systems such as e-commerce, EDI, Point of Sale, etc. They have the same components of group work but support different processes. These systems produce records or documents that are *fleeting*, meaning that their importance lies in their flow within a time-sensitive communication pattern. It's no good to the organization if e-mail is backed up regularly when the mail server isn't stable and loses messages. However, it's just as bad if the organization has a very stable Point of Sale system, but doesn't protect the historical transaction records.

 Our generic symbol for all **hardware** is this picture of a hard drive, which represents the computer components of that which you need to protect. As we said in the paragraph above, if you protect the data for your Point of Sale system but forget about the hardware, that could be bad for your business. Your customers won't understand why they can't purchase something from you simply because the POS server or the communication link for their credit card transactions are down.

Protecting your organization's data and systems is a delicate balance of protecting the data and protecting the hardware that the data lives and runs on. You must find that balance in your protection plan.

The three basic types of protection

A backup and disaster recovery plan is a blend of protecting both data and hardware. Data and hardware protection falls into three basic categories: fault tolerance, mirroring or duplication, and archived backups.

Fault tolerance (not a part of backups) **Fault tolerance** is very much like having a quick-fix kit or spare parts available at all times, and is often coupled with mirroring or duplication, as well. *The goal of fault tolerance is either continuous operation or quick recovery.* Fault tolerance for hardware can be as simple as having two Ethernet cards, so that if one dies, the other continues working—or as complex as building a clustered server with duplicates of *everything.* Fault tolerance can be applied to some degree to individual

Fault Tolerance	Quick Recovery		Continuous operation

Table Intro-1. Fault tolerance

documents (as shown in the left cell of Table Intro-1. above) so that if they're trashed or deleted, they can be quickly recovered. Fault tolerance *should* be applied to group work and group communications systems to provide continuous operations in the event of hardware failure. In the center and right cells of Table Intro-1. we show group work and group communications coupled with fault-tolerant hardware to depict the fact that the fault tolerance is applied to the hardware, *not* to the data.

Duplication (a part of backups) & mirroring (for hardware)

Both of these processes aim at the same goal: creating an exact replica of the primary source and maintaining that replica on its destination. **Mirroring** pertains to hardware: The process of attaching a second drive so that the data written to the first is automatically written to the second. **Duplication** (a.k.a. **replication**)—the copying of files from a source computer to a protected destination computer—is an integral part of the backup process that pertains to all data types, whether the data is a document, a database, or an e-mail system. Pointing your backup software at your computer's hard drive and telling it to back up everything (create a full backup) to a tape is a form of duplication because the contents of both the computer and the tape contain the same thing.

The goal of duplicating and mirroring is quick recovery during a disaster.

The mirrored duplicate of a primary data source or an entire groupwork server exists solely to be put into play when the primary fails. Restoring data from a full backup is the fastest restoration from a tape backup. Both data and hardware can be mirrored or duplicated. In Table Intro-2. we depict the split nature of dupli-

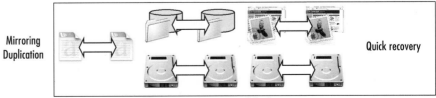

Mirroring Duplication		Quick recovery

Table Intro-2. Mirroring and duplication

cating data (all three cells) and mirroring hardware (the center and right cells). Whether the protection plan is to duplicate the data, mirror the hardware, or mirror the hardware *and* duplicate the data the goal is the same—quick recovery in case of failure or loss.

Archived backups take a "snapshot" of data and then place that snapshot in a safe destination. Every time you back up to tape, you copy the original source data onto that tape. Backing up a second time without erasing the tape (known as a **normal backup**) creates a second, dated copy of the original files. You now have a historical record—day one's files and day two's files. You can restore *either* day one's files *or* day two's files, depending upon your needs. This process is called **cre-**

Archived backups

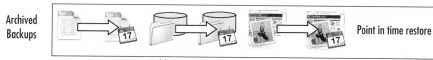

Archived Backups — Point in time restore

Table Intro-3. Archived backups

ating an archived backup and is different than a full backup in that it has a dated history of files instead of an exact replica. *Point-in-time restoration is the purpose of an archived backup.* You don't back up hardware systems; only the data that lives on them—hence, none of the cells in Table Intro-3. show any hardware.

Layered protection

Smart systems administrators layer their protection plans based on the needs of the individual or organization and the IT staff's budget constraints. With an

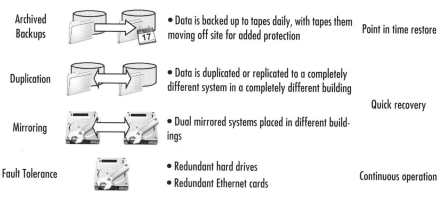

Archived Backups	• Data is backed up to tapes daily, with tapes them moving off site for added protection	Point in time restore
Duplication	• Data is duplicated or replicated to a completely different system in a completely different building	
Mirroring	• Dual mirrored systems placed in different buildings	Quick recovery
Fault Tolerance	• Redundant hard drives • Redundant Ethernet cards	Continuous operation

Table Intro-4. Layers of protection

unlimited, "battleship" budget, you could build a system that would protect you from pretty much every disaster that could happen. Let's look at what might be built for a file server that would be "totally protected." Begin by putting your hardware together in a fashion that provides fault tolerance *for that individual computer* as shown in the bottom row of Table Intro-4. on page 7. Next, add another layer of hardware protection by mirroring your hardware so that you have two exact sets (second row from bottom in Table Intro-4. on page 7)—preferably in two different buildings in case the first building is lost. Next, add a layer of data protection on top of that by duplicating your data (second row from top in Table Intro-4. on page 7) to a *completely different system* than the mirrored system. With this layer, even if the complete mirrored set of computers is lost, you'll still have an exact copy of the data. Your icing-on-the-cake is creating a daily backup to tape of the data to create a daily point-in-time snapshot of your data, in case you need to "roll back" your information to a specific date (top row of Table Intro-4.). Feeling invincible? Well, that can be quickly cured with a look at your budget—the only failure of this supersystem. Nobody can afford to build this level of protection in the real world—if you can, we'd like to sell you our company for a ton of money.

Creating a balance for when bad things happen

Your organization is humming along quite nicely. And then, *KABLOOEY!* During a windstorm, lightning strikes a century-old oak tree a block away. The oak falls onto the power lines, dropping power to your building and sending sparks across your neighbor's roof—which then catches fire. And since it was a sweatshop packed full of polyester hip-hop apparel, the whole shebang goes up like the proverbial Christmas tree. Flames cascade through your open windows, torching your building just seconds after the last worker dashes to the street to take digital disaster shots for the company scrapbook. The Worst has happened.

In situations like this, an event (I call it the Kablooey! event) is triggered, and data (therefore, somebody's work), productivity, or computers are lost—sometimes, all of the above. Your restoration timer is ticking away, and your data protection plan (and spending budget) is now being tested.

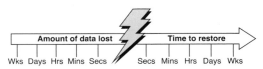

Figure Intro-2. When "Kablooey!" happens

When Kablooey! happens, time becomes your enemy in two ways: You have to fight loss of productivity by reducing the time to restore your systems, and you have to hope that your backup plan captured as much data as possible so that minimal time is spent on document re-creation. You must create a balance between the need for protecting people's documents (amount of data lost) and reducing business downtime due to systems failure (time to restore). When Kablooey! hap-

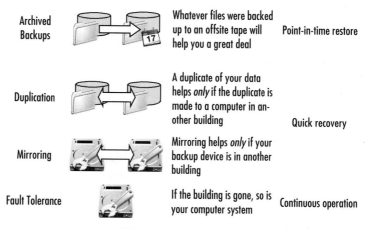

Archived Backups	Whatever files were backed up to an offsite tape will help you a great deal	Point-in-time restore
Duplication	A duplicate of your data helps *only* if the duplicate is made to a computer in another building	
		Quick recovery
Mirroring	Mirroring helps *only* if your backup device is in another building	
Fault Tolerance	If the building is gone, so is your computer system	Continuous operation

Table Intro-5. Layers of protection

pens and you lose your building, certain aspects of a "battleship" disaster recovery plan become moot. The extra parts of your fault-tolerant systems have now melted and are no good to anybody. However, if you mirrored your system or duplicated your data to a computer in a different building (which didn't get hurt), you'd be fine. You'd be able to "bring the mirror live" and be back in business within minutes, as shown in Figure Intro-3.

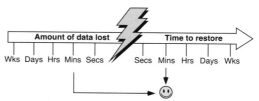

Figure Intro-3. Data loss & recovery with a mirrored system

What would have happened if you had spent all of your money building a fault-tolerant, mirrored system and put the mirror in the building that was lost, or in a local building that was *also* lost? That would mean that you hadn't prepared for the problems a lost building would cause you, and therefore you weren't prepared with any offsite hardware or any place offsite to *put* your hardware. At that point, while you might have up-to-the minute data protection, it could take you *days* to get new hardware in so that you have something to put the data on during restoration—not a career-enhancing move.

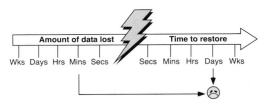

Figure Intro-4. Way too long to restore

On the other hand, if your tactics have a total hardware focus, you'll spend your budget on redundant, clustered hardware systems and CD- and network-based imaging, and you'll ensure that you have mirrored systems offsite in case your building goes down. But you won't have much of a budget left for building in document replication, versioning, and tape backup libraries that deliver document history to your end users. Yes, your servers will be well protected and will probably never be out of commission. But if Sandy down in accounting loses her revenue projection spreadsheets because of a virus, hacker, or just an "uh-oh," you might not have backed it up for more than a week, thus saying sayonara to the week's worth of changes that will have to be laboriously re-created.

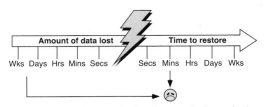

Figure Intro-5. Hardware-redundant focus might forego backups

Which tactic is correct? Neither: You must balance disaster recovery for catastrophic events with backup for disruptive events. One puts you out of business, and the other is a pain in the patoot. If you can throw people at document re-creation, feel free to spend your budget on clustered hardware. If everyone can go on a two-day coffee break but you could never re-create the data that could be lost, spend your time and effort on the data backups. Only you can say where the balance lies for your organization and its particular challenges. And don't make the mistake of picking your hardware and software first—before you go shopping, develop your philosophy (or strategy, as some might call it) based on your organizational needs and budget. And since we're talking philosophy here, Socrates' *sophrosyne*, the principle of self-control and balance, has stuck around all these centuries for a reason: It makes sense.

The fundamental rule of balance? Don't spend more on a backup system than the cost of the data or systems that you're backing up. If the data you're backing up is worth $10,000, your budget-conscious CFO isn't going to fork over $10,000 or more. Even if the data is your company's primary asset, your backup budget will be only a percentage of the overall IT budget.

You've developed a well-balanced backup plan? *Respect it, but don't set it in stone:* As time goes on, your needs—and your center of balance—will change. Your backup and recovery plan can't be an inflexible document—instead, it should serve as an active philosophy. And, as with all philosophies, it must accommodate change as you, and your business needs, mature.

But, before you can begin building your backup plan, you need to know what's most likely to break, and where to direct your maiden efforts.

Security is job 1...

I thought I'd throw this in because I had a blank page to fill, it's humorous, and provides some insight on my thinking. The drawing on this page was done by the same brilliant artist who draws those funny bugs getting zapped by the RAID bug spray. It was presented to me at one of our Management Executive Committee meetings while I was the CIO of True North Communications, one of the largest ad agencies in the world (now IPG—*the* largest ad agency in the world).

"DORIAN, SECURITY IS JOB 1"

During my first MEC meeting, I reported on the health of our organization's IT infrastructure. I was visibly shaken because I had just found our key servers that purchased and then billed for all of our clients' ads. It was in the basement of our building. A leaky basement. Next to a sewer system that often overflowed. Ouch.

In typical ad agency fashion we fixed the problem immediately and then made fun of the situation for the next two years. Hence the picture (the original is in color).

By the time I left, we had mirrored systems that were geographically dispersed by hundreds of miles, multiple data feeds to every key location, and (thanks to Scooter) a WAN that just didn't ever go down. A great finish after a lousy start.

Section 1.
The problems &
the costs

Get your head together when you read this section.

Wake up and smell the coffee.

And prepare yourself and your organization for what can go wrong.

Then figure out the value of your computers and their processes so that you can construct an argument for your backup and disaster plan budget.

Because whatever you don't plan for might—and probably will—happen. And if you aren't ready, the chances are slim that you'll get through the problem in one piece.

By that time, the argument for budgets will be long past, but the responsibility will still rest securely on your shoulders.

CHAPTER 1:
WHEN BAD THINGS HAPPEN TO
GOOD COMPUTERS

What, me worry? That's the mantra of Alfred E. Neuman, poster child of *Mad* magazine[1]. Alfred never seems to worry about anything. That's probably because he's a comic book character—only fictional folks can manage to pull off that level of detachment. But, come to think of it, I know some comic book characters in business who don't worry about anything, either. I don't know if I should emulate or pity them—because in business, worrisome things *do* happen. They happen all the time. I wouldn't have had an audience for the first *or* second version of *The Backup Book* if bad things didn't happen to good computers.

And bad things come in three flavors: freezes that lock up the computer, forcing you to restart; corruption of your files, applications, and hard drive; and loss due to theft, fire, outages, etc. What these three flavors *affect* ranges from individual documents all the way to the loss of your building(s).

I'm including this chapter to give you an idea of what *can* go wrong, as well as the chance that it can happen to you and to the assets of your organization. I'll walk you through what can go wrong by pairing each of the three flavors of what can

---

1. http://www.madmagazine.com. I love *Mad* magazine, absolutely love it. Best rag on the racks.

happen with each of the organization's key assets. And to bring it home, I've added a survey we took that asked folks how often each of these things have happened to them over a three-year period.

	Documents	Applications	OS	Storage	CPUs	Network	Power	Building
Freeze		✔	✔					
Corruption	✔	✔	✔	✔		✔		
Loss	✔	✔	✔	✔	✔	✔	✔	✔

Table 1-1. What can go wrong

If you think none of this will happen to you, think again. You have a 2 percent chance of being in that miraculous minority—the fortunate few who've never had a bad thing happen.

I've never been so lucky.

THE MAIN THING

The Main Thing in this section is to familiarize yourself with the key assets your company has—and what can happen to them.

This should give you a starting point for the areas in which your organization should focus its efforts in creating a backup and disaster plan.

*The nitty-gritty you need to understand is the cold, hard fact that you **are** at risk— and to protect yourself against that risk, you must take preventative measures within certain cost boundaries to limit the impact of downtime.*

FROM MACRO TO MICRO—A QUICK LOOK AT THE STABILITY OF ASSETS

 Okay, let's start with your building. Every company exists in one—except, of course, those that are in boats, tents, yak caravans, or the last few extant VW microbuses. Buildings are very robust, for the most part.

 Every building is powered by electricity. This is necessary for seeing what in the world you're doing and for powering your computer system. Some buildings (very few) are powered by solar energy (like in Berkeley, California). Electricity is, for the most part, pretty dependable. Since electrical failure (too little or too much) is a cause of hard drive crashes, etc., we figured we'd leave it out of the survey.

 Most companies inside buildings have their computer systems tied together with Local Area Networks (LANs). The computers use these networks to yak to each other and then talk to the rest of the world through The Network: the Internet. Networks are, for the most part, pretty secure and reliable. Because a downed network doesn't affect the data on your hard drive much (if at all), we chose to leave it out of the survey.

 Sitting on the networks are lots and lots (okay, not so many lots, if you're a small company) of computers. Big ones, small ones, fast ones, slow ones. Now we're starting to get to the real meat of the digital asset world. Normally computers either break immediately upon arrival, one day after their initial warranty is up, or not until they're well beyond their usefulness.

 Each computer has one or more storage devices, such as hard drives, Zip drives, CD drives, flash drives, etc. This storage space is where the information lives. Okay, some of it lives in the heads of the people who go home at night, but this isn't a book about employee retention, so we'll let that part slide. Storage devices are rated in "mean time between failure rates"—which means that they're destined for failure in your lifetime. So count on it.

 Operating systems hold the software that is the engine of your computer. The main flavors are Windows (pick a variety from 95, 98, NT, 2000, XP, blah blah blah), Macintosh (OS 8 through X), and a gazillion flavors of Unix (Unix, Sun Solaris, the Linuxes, etc.). Operating systems—as they're shipped by the manufacturer—are pretty robust and very reliable. However, once installed, users generally gunk them up with their own extensions,[2] quickly making them less reliable.

Operating systems are also a favorite target for the cretins who write viruses. The good news is that most users have only a single operating system on their computer that they can screw up.

Applications (such as Microsoft Word) are the individual productivity tools that each user spends most of their time working on within their computer. My own computer has 92 different applications on it, and normally I use about eight of them at a time[3]. Most applications are installed and used as suggested by the publisher. However, others can be quite extensible. (On my computer, Dreamweaver has an additional 29 extensions.) Because applications are what users operate day in and day out, they're the whipping boys that bear the brunt of a computer's corruption and loss problems. When users freeze the computer, they're usually freezing an individual application. When viruses attack a computer, they attack the open (in-use) applications. Therefore, because of outside influences, applications are prone to problems.

Aside from sports-betting pools, documents are a company's most-frequently produced asset[4]. Documents are also *the* usual suspects when it comes to getting into trouble—like the time my dog ate my research report in college. How it got into my hard drive, I'll never know—the dog, that is. Documents get corrupted. Get erased. Get all sorts of havoc wreaked upon them. Documents are about as unstable as me taking a bottle of red wine on a visit to my mother-in-law.

---

2. Hey, I know what I'm talking about here. My own computer takes about five minutes to boot while loading the 23 additional system extensions I stuck on it.

3. As I'm writing this, I have MS Word, Internet Explorer, Canvas, Fetch, Dreamweaver, and two databases open at once.

4. A friend once told me that Hughes Aircraft really makes documents. Every so often, they manage to miraculously create an airplane, but that isn't their real focus.

FREEZES, CORRUPTION, AND LOSS—THAT WHICH CAN GO WRONG

Now let's put what can happen into perspective. Based on our international backup survey taken over a one-month period with more than 300 respondents in seven countries, here's how often things can go wrong over a three-year period.

 Luck of the Irish: Some people have it; most of us non-Celtic types don't. Of those surveyed, 2 percent stated that over a three-year period, nothing had ever happened to their computer systems or the data on it. Wow, some people have all the luck in the world. That means that the *other* 98 percent of us are prey to evil leprechauns. Back to reality.

First stop, the frozen section.

Freezes

When freezing occurs, the computer simply "locks up" or stops working. The lights are on, but nobody's home. You type on the keyboard; nothing happens. You move the mouse on the desk; it doesn't move on the screen. When a personal computer hangs, it often offers no indication of what caused the problem; it's just sort of stuck in freeze-frame mode, affecting both the application and OS.

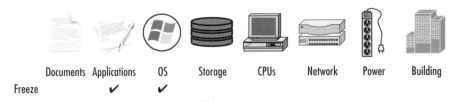

	Documents	Applications	OS	Storage	CPUs	Network	Power	Building
Freeze		✔	✔					

Table 1-2. Freezes

Frozen applications

Normally, frozen applications such as Microsoft Word affect only the document you're working on. When the application freezes, it can no longer access the document, and therefore whatever was added to the document since the last time it was saved will be lost. Sometimes application freezes can corrupt the application itself and you'll have to either restore or reload it. No big whoop. However, when the chilled-out application is your web server, your database server, or your e-mail server (you get the point), it affects communications and productivity. Then it becomes a much bigger deal to bring the computer back to normal.

Frozen operating systems

A frozen application isn't the same problem as a frozen operating system. With a frozen application, the user can normally "force quit" the affected application and continue working because the operating system is unaffected.

When the operating system freezes, *everything* on the computer is locked down tighter than the cockpit of an Al Qaeda–chartered airplane. Whatever you were working on in your document—*from the last time you saved until the computer froze*—is forever lost. There's nothing there to restore—empiricist philosopher John Locke's *tabula rasa*. It's like having your short-term memory zapped.

When the operating system freezes, the only choice for the user is to restart the computer and hope for the best. Optimism is sometimes the only way to deal with cold, cruel reality.

How do freezes happen?

When a personal computer freezes, it often gives you no indication of what caused the problem. The computer could have crashed, or it could be something simple, such as the printer running out of paper. Usually a freeze is caused by input or data presented to a computer that is beyond its ability to cope (like asking it to do too many things at once, or aborting an operation at a critical stage). If a freeze happens in a single-task program (like MS-DOS, Windows, or Mac OS 9), the machine will cease to take input ("lock up") and must be restarted ("rebooted"). If a freeze happens in a multitasking operating system like Unix, Linux, or Mac OS X, the user can force-quit the offending application and continue working. Sometimes.

Corruption

We're not talking the House or the Senate here—we're discussing what happens during excessive freezes or when viruses attack good computer systems. They become corrupted. The other day, I was working on a different (more boring) version of this chapter. I bombed the computer twice. When I reopened the chapter, it was completely rearranged for me. Too bad the arrangement was worse than the one I created myself. But that's what corruption does: It moves things around in an order you (or your spouse) didn't create.

Corruption affects not only software, but can affect your storage devices and your network, as well.

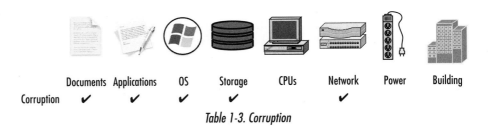

	Documents	Applications	OS	Storage	CPUs	Network	Power	Building
Corruption	✔	✔	✔	✔		✔		

Table 1-3. Corruption

Document corruption

Document corruption usually happens after a couple of computer or application freezes in a row. When your document becomes corrupted, the only thing you can do about it is either restore the document (if you backed it up) or re-create the document. Survey Sez:

	Files that were corrupted
85%	chance it could happen to **you** over a 3-year period
30%	chance it could happen to **you** once in a year
15%	chance it could happen to **you** 3 times in a year
12%	chance it could happen to **you** 5 times in a year
8%	chance it could happen to **you** 10 times in a year
6%	chance it could happened to **you** more than 10 times in a year

Table 1-4. Corruption probabilities

Application corruption

Every so often, after I've bombed an application repeatedly, it becomes corrupt. The only other way applications become corrupt is if they get hit by a virus. Either way, you get to restore the document from your backup system, or you get to re-create it from original disks and downloads of new "updates," not to mention replacing all those additional extensions the user tacked on along the way[5].

Now, when an application such as a database server becomes corrupt, it could corrupt or even overwrite the data it's working with. This is because data is updated in a database server's cache first. It's transferred to its target memory or disk only at certain times. Therefore, when the database application becomes corrupt, the chance of data corruption in its files is pretty good, too. Survey Sez:

Corrupted Applications	
55%	chance it could happen to **you** over a 3-year period
26%	chance it could happen to **you** once in a year
7%	chance it could happen to **you** 3 times in a year
6%	chance it could happen to **you** 5 times in a year
4%	chance it could happen to **you** 10 times in a year
3%	chance it could happened to **you** more than 10 times in a year

Table 1-5. Corrupted application probabilities

Operating system corruption

In its quick-fix amenability, operating system corruption is worse than either document or application corruption. If the operating system becomes corrupt, you can't even access the computer. When this happens, you're facing a bit of time before the system is back in operation, unless you wipe the drive and start again.

Operating systems can become corrupt due to virus attacks, freezes, or upgrades performed either by an individual who is "adding some special extension or control panel" or through an actual patch from the manufacturer. When Apple shipped an upgrade to its System 9.2 software, one of the upgrades was *much* worse than the preceding version. The patch wouldn't allow the end user to return to the previous state (without restoring the computer from backup or completely re-creating the system from scratch).

The problem isn't limited to just Apple, either. Some software manufacturers ship their software buggy as all get out, and it takes a while to figure out that it really

---

5. Okay, there's another type of application corruption that usually happens after you talk to an imbecile in Technical Support, like the guy my dad talked to at Kodak, who told him to remove part of his software package. However, we can't cover *all* of the bases, or idiots, here, so we'll leave the human-I-know-more-than-you-even-though-I-can't-spell-tech-support type of corruption out of it.

isn't your fault that nothing works. Karsten's experience with Windows NT 4 was a very interesting one...

I was assigned a project in Hong Kong installing the Quark Publishing System (QPS) at a business magazine. Everything went smoothly until we started working with QPS. The editors were happily typing their stories into the Windows text editor; graphics artists grabbed the finished stories and placed them into the layout. Suddenly everything froze, and all the applications connected to QPS stopped. In a frenzy, I asked everybody to stop working. I began rebooting every single machine, rebooted the QPS server, and checked all network connections, but found nothing. I exchanged the QPS server for a new machine, but no success.

Finally I turned on the monitor of the file server that holds all layout data—and found that the server had died, simply showing the Blue Screen of Death (BSOD). I restarted the file server, and everybody started working—until the file server died again. Suspicious now that this phenomenon somehow had to be connected to the graphics people, I asked one of the guys to drag a file from his desktop to the file server. Bang!—it died again. So I started downloading and applying bug fixes (yeah, MS calls them "Service Packs") from the MS website. What can I say—after installing the fourth Service Pack, it all worked just fine.

Survey Sez:

	Corrupted Operating Systems
65%	chance it could happen to **you** over a 3-year period
26%	chance it could happen to **you** once in a year
10%	chance it could happen to **you** 3 times in a year
5%	chance it could happen to **you** 5 times in a year
8%	chance it could happen to **you** 10 times in a year
4%	chance it could happened to **you** more than 10 times in a year

Table 1-6. Corrupted OS probabilities

Storage corruption

Storage corruption happens when the drive's logical system of arrangement or the physical drive gets messed up.

Each and every drive maintains a hierarchical system of organization. Sometimes those directories and pointer files become corrupted during a freeze, through a virus, or just plain old extended usage. If the drive's logical system is corrupted, the computer can't be accessed at all, very much like if the operating system goes down until the drive is completely reconstructed through restoration or simply wiping it and starting completely fresh.

Survey Sez:

	Corrupted Hard Drives
71%	chance it could happen to **you** over a 3-year period
32%	chance it could happen to **you** once in a year
10%	chance it could happen to **you** 3 times in a year
7%	chance it could happen to **you** 5 times in a year
5%	chance it could happen to **you** 10 times in a year
5%	chance it could happened to **you** more than 10 times in a year

Table 1-7. Corrupted hard drive probabilities

Network corruption

Many networks can become corrupt over time—especially large networks that become larger. We once had a client whose network was so vast and so corrupt that "storms" of bad information would fly through every so often—so often that the client called them "the pause that refreshes," because the users would simply get a cup of coffee until it was over[6]. Network corruption causes "slowness" in computing, and can actually corrupt files as they're transferred across the network.

How do you corrupt your computer?

Teach it to smoke at an early age. Okay, I'm kidding. Sometimes, in the case of newly released software and hardware, it's shipped to you corrupted. In one case that we know of, a Sun UltraSparc III workstation was shipped to a university medical lab wherein the new 64-bit processor was causing data corruption in their medical experiment results. After losing about a week's worth of work—and *finally* being informed by Sun that a download was available, the Sun guys said, "We've identified a very rare occurrence in the SunBlade 1000 that occurs only

---

6.   True story, that one. Absolutely true. Hard to believe—but true.

when running floating-point applications, like science and engineering applications. It is one of those far-corner occurrences where certain things have to occur in certain sequence for this [problem] to happen." The guys at the university must have had that sequence down pat.

Viruses are a great system corrupter. Our website at Network Frontiers wasn't up one day when it started getting hit with the NIMDA virus. Thank the Lord we were running a Unix-based server instead of NT. And sometimes, even if the virus doesn't corrupt your system, applications, or documents, the virus cleaner may not be too particular with the files *it* attacks, and *it* can cause corruption, as well— talk about the cure being worse than the disease! Here are a couple of download.com comments about a particular anti-virus program:

> After install I did not establish a Restore point, and I kept experiencing lockups after I downloaded. I ended up doing a complete F-disk and fresh install of XP. Second time, I established a Restore point, and again I experienced lockups.

> This software detected the virus that had infected my computer, but in an attempt to cure it, sent my computer on a downward spiral that made it restart over 30 times. Now I have to open a program the minute Windows opens to trick my computer into not restarting. Even though I uninstalled the software, this bug persisted.

Software programs can corrupt your hard drive as well as themselves. There's a certain indexing application that offers to "find anything, anywhere within the files of your computer." Supposedly it works by indexing each and every file on the computer as well as the contents within each and every file on your computer. However, in reality, after a couple of hours of grinding through your computer's files, the indexing engine goes crazy, getting stuck in a deranged loop, indexing and re-indexing everything on the computer over and over again. When I contacted the company, their official statement read in part, "You may experience a corrupt index file that will use up most of the available space on your local drive. This will cause your system to function below its capacity." Actually, it uses up so much space that the hard drive seizes up and dies. "You will notice delays executing programs, and will not be able to copy large files to your computer." In reality, if it doesn't kill the drive completely, it causes the system to go so slowly that it becomes unusable. The entire hard drive has to be reformatted, and the entire operating system has to be reloaded—without the software, of course.

Loss

In its simplest form, loss is not having access to something. "I lost the keys in my house" could mean anything from the dog ate them to my wife moved them (again) to they fell off my desk into the garbage and are now very, *very* gone. Loss in the computer world means various things, based upon what is lost. You don't really *lose* electricity, but rather the use of it. You don't really *lose* a building (unless you're in California, where they're known to slide a few blocks downhill every rainy season). Let's look at loss as it applies to corporate assets.

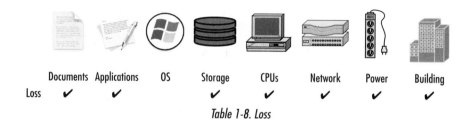

	Documents	Applications	OS	Storage	CPUs	Network	Power	Building
Loss	✔	✔		✔	✔	✔	✔	✔

Table 1-8. Loss

Document loss

You could have accidentally erased it. Or purposefully erased it but wanted to "undo" the erasure, only to find out you can't undo that kind of thing. Or you could have created a completely new document named exactly the same thing and stored it in exactly the same folder as the opus you just finished writing—thus erasing the opus and replacing it with pretty much nothing. Survey Sez:

Trashed or deleted files	
90%	chance it could happen to **you** over a 3-year period
21%	chance it could happen to **you** once in a year
18%	chance it could happen to **you** 3 times in a year
12%	chance it could happen to **you** 5 times in a year
10%	chance it could happen to **you** 10 times in a year
11%	chance it could happened to **you** more than 10 times in a year

Table 1-9. Trashed files probabilities

Those are pretty high numbers for trashed files, but that's an accurate reading of the situation. Here are the numbers (which aren't as high) for the probabilities of what can happen to you when files are accidentally overwritten—as I've done to myself twice so far this book.

Files that were overwritten	
77%	chance it could happen to **you** over a 3-ear period
24%	chance it could happen to **you** once in a year
12%	chance it could happen to **you** 3 times in a year
9%	chance it could happen to **you** 5 times in a year
5%	chance it could happen to **you** 10 times in a year
9%	chance it could happened to **you** more than 10 times in a year

Table 1-10. File overwrite probabilities

Application loss

It's kind of hard to lose an entire application, but people have done it. As a matter of fact, I've been asked "What happens if I delete my hard drive?" It's a truism that while computers have gotten bigger and faster, users remain a little "challenged" at times—right, Gerron?

Trashed applications can also arise from people playing games at the expense of someone else's computers. At a New York university, joking crossed the line into hazing. A female computer science undergraduate who declined to be named found herself the object of a hacker's hazing rituals. "They trashed my computer, uploading non-lethal programs that would flash dirty pictures every thousand keystrokes, reset my configurations, and rearrange and delete my files. I was in tears. The guys thought it was a riot," she says. Yeah, very funny.

Again, if the applications are "lost," you have to either restore them or reload them from the original CDs or downloads.

Storage loss

One day, your hard drive will fail and you won't be able to do anything about it. Unless you've planned for this event, you will lose all your data. If you didn't plan, there's nothing you can do—the data is gone forever. The following illustrations depict a few of the problems your drives can encounter. Although some of these problems relate specifically to drives with "open" formats, such as Zip and Jaz cartridges, others are universal.

Hard drives are basically racks of spinning aluminum platters that are approximately .075 inches thick. These platters have a 50-microinch-thick coating of oxide for the reading and writing of information. Information is written to these platters by small read/write heads that pass over the drive platters but don't touch them. Information is passed back and forth via electrical current and magnetism.

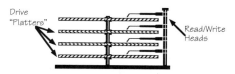

Figure 1-1. Hard drive platters and read/write heads

In the following picture, we show a drive platter and read/write head along with various particles that can cause problems.

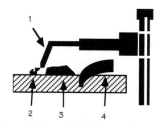

Figure 1-2. Particles and their relative sizes

This is the read/write head of the hard drive mechanism, and it isn't supposed to touch the disk. This allows very small dust particles to fit between the disk's surface and the read/write head without causing any problems. Sometimes, however, it just doesn't work that way.

1. This item shows the relative size of a smoke particle. These are usually 250 microinches thick—large enough to cause interference between the read/ write head and the disk's platter.

2. These items show the relative sizes of fingerprints and dust, which can cause even more interference problems.

3. A human hair is 3,000 microinches thick (yes, even you folks with "thin" hair). A hair causes extreme problems immediately.

4. Even if your disks are kept free of these hazards (that is, they're hard drives and are therefore sealed), general usage over time causes the disk to fluctuate and begin to have problems.

Performance is at its best when the read/write head is hovering over the disk at 100 microinches. Over time, "stuff" builds up on the disk's surface, and the read/write head begins to hover higher in the areas of more buildup and lower in the areas of less buildup.

Thus, the read/write head hovers in an erratic pattern. Sooner or later, the head comes in contact with the recording area of the disk and a head crash results. When a head crash results, it creates a dimple in the surface of the drive. And whatever info was there (where the dimple is now) is obliterated. If the crash is hard enough, it causes the oxide to flake off and you'll begin to lose a *lot* of data.

Computers

Computers either work or they don't. And it doesn't matter if the memory is bad, the motherboard, daughterboard, or poor cousin-in-law-board is broken—the whole thing is out of commission until it's fixed.

And that means that whatever was on the computer is now unavailable until either the computer is replaced or the information is restored to another working computer (or completely rebuilt from scratch). Survey Sez:

	Broken Computer
64%	chance it could happen to **you** over a 3-year period
35%	chance it could happen to **you** once in a year
5%	chance it could happen to **you** 3 times in a year
5%	chance it could happen to **you** 5 times in a year
5%	chance it could happen to **you** 10 times in a year
3%	chance it could happened to **you** more than 10 times in a year

Table 1-11. Broken computer probabilities

Baggage handlers   I once watched a baggage handler (mauler is a better word) toss my computer onto a ramp when an air carrier forced me to check it because of limited storage space. It was gone forever. Even worse, I had to wait to put my drive in a new container.

Thieves   Twice while I was CIO of a company, someone posed as a maintenance person— and stole two of our computers right off the desks of people in the office. How do we know? We caught the person on his third attempt.

Survey Sez:

	Having to replace a lost or stolen computer
28%	chance it could happen to **you** over a 3-year period
19%	chance it could happen to **you** once in a year
2%	chance it could happen to **you** 3 times in a year
2%	chance it could happen to **you** 5 times in a year
0%	chance it could happen to **you** 10 times in a year
0%	chance it could happened to **you** more than 10 times in a year

Table 1-12. Lost computer probabilities

Network

Yes, you *can* lose your network, or at least network connectivity within your organization or out to the "real world." As we state elsewhere in this book, during our first online survey about backup, Excite@Home decided to go belly up. AT&T, who was licensing the service through them, assured us that we'd be operational within three days. Ha! The system came back up after four days, but the services we had contracted with them haven't come back up yet. We had to move our equipment to another location in order to reestablish connectivity.

If you lose connectivity, you haven't necessarily lost data—unless you have a split system in which part A is on one side of your lost connectivity system, and part B is on the other side, with no way to share data. We'll talk more about that when we cover the loss of organizational functions and systems.

Power

Yep, it goes away sometimes—especially in San Francisco. Many years ago, while we were writing the second edition of this book, they were building a McDonald's on the same location where Dirty Harry saved the coffee shop. And as chance had it, during the writing of the book, the electric company knocked out the power seven times. Ouch.

When the power goes out, it can cause document and computer corruption for any computer that isn't on an alternate power source. If you're wondering, that's a bad thing.

Too much power creates electrical surges. Too little power creates brownouts. No power is a blackout. None of the three are welcome. Here's what can cause them:

Transformer Failure

Nobody in Chicago ever planned for emergencies caused by floods. What could flood in Chicago? The lake has never risen above normal levels, and the Chicago River is fully regulated by the locks and dams of the Chicago River Trade Authority. Nevertheless, in 1992, Chicago did flood. Somehow, the river leaked into the old coal tunnels that run beneath most of Chicago. These tunnels were used back in the early 1900s to deliver coal for furnaces in the larger buildings and had since been abandoned. When the river poured into these tunnels, it also poured into the basements of most of the downtown buildings, causing the electrical systems to send high-voltage energy throughout the buildings before being destroyed. Many companies had to temporarily relocate while the entire electrical system for these buildings was rewired. Some companies survived; others didn't.

Small brown-outs, sags, and surges

Over 90 percent of all electrical problems are associated with power fluctuations that drop (brownouts and sags) or rise (surges) too much and too quickly for the computer system to accommodate. However, power outages in commercial buildings are usually both sporadic and short-lived, and can be worked around fairly easily.

Building

All references to September 11th aside, buildings fall down, burn, etc. This doesn't happen that often, but it does occur. When you lose the building, you lose access to all computer systems in it. And if this is where you were keeping your backup tapes, guess what? You lost access to them, too.

Cuban cigars

Lighted tobacco products are on fire, even though the burning is usually contained to the end of the cigar or cigarette. The smoke can be a potential hazard, too, as was the case in this story I heard. A well-liked corporate MIS director's wife had just had a baby. The excited new father, who had just come back from overseas with a stash of smuggled Cuban cigars, passed them out to everyone in the office. A few of the "old boys" gathered at one of the desks, lighting up en masse. Now, I don't really know how this happened, but supposedly it was the combination of all eight men smoking in one small space that caused the sprinkler system to activate. Since it was an old building, water, instead of Halon, shot out of the sprinklers, drenching two computers on the desk and blowing out the monitors. Because the monitors' power cords were connected to the backs of the computers, one of those was lost, too.

Construction dust

One day, a client called to ask me about a certain type of hard drive's reliability. Apparently, half a dozen of them at his site had broken recently. I told him that the optical drives were normally very reliable, but that all things wear out over time. I asked how long the client had owned those hard drives, thinking that the mean-time-between-failure rate might have been reached, but two were new and the rest hadn't been around for long. After further questioning, I found out that a construction project was going on in their area. When the drive manufacturer's service representative opened the hard drives, he found the culprit: They were caked with construction dust.

Plumbing leaks If you're in an old building, it might behoove you to check on your upstairs neighbor. In Chicago, there are a great many old buildings that have been rehabbed. I worked in one of these. In my office, there was a hole in the floor big enough for a ping-pong ball to drop through. Next door was a service bureau operating several film-processing devices. Often, as they were changing the highly acidic fluids in these devices, some of those fluids spilled onto the floor and consequently down to the office below. I'll leave the gory results up to your imagination.

Survey Sez:

	Having to recover from a Disaster
31%	chance it could happen to **you** over a 3-year period
17%	chance it could happen to **you** once in a year
5%	chance it could happen to **you** 3 times in a year
2%	chance it could happen to **you** 5 times in a year
0%	chance it could happen to **you** 10 times in a year
0%	chance it could happened to **you** more than 10 times in a year

Table 1-13. Building loss probabilities

PUTTING IT INTO PERSPECTIVE

In the second edition of our backup book, we used a pyramid we stole[7] that I really like and that we've since modified. Based upon Maslow's hierarchy of human needs, this pyramid shows the hierarchy of loss—or, as seen differently—potential risks. At the nitty-gritty, risk analysis is really about continually asking the question "To what degree can the company tolerate the loss of information or networking systems ordinarily provided?" Here's what you *can* lose (the most important is on the top, but if you couldn't figure that out, you'd better head out of the computer aisle and limp over to the self-help section).

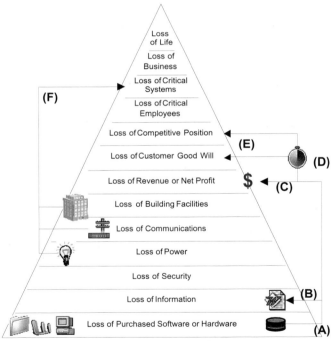

Figure 1-3. Hierarchy of loss

---

7. *Disaster Recovery Planning: Networks, Telecommunications, and Data Communications,* by Regis J. Bates (McGraw-Hill, 1992).

Different labels are associated with a few levels of loss on this diagram (A through E, and F). Before we cover A through E, I want to cover F, as F really isn't in the purview of this book.

F. If you lose power or communications, or if you lose access to your building's facilities, there's a good chance that you'll lose access to your critical systems, as well. Losing all power or all communications access to your data (or the data center itself) will automatically cause you to lose the use of your company's critical systems. Since this is a book about backup and we have only limited information in our power outage section, we can't cover all of the things that are necessary for continued power use, communications use, or building use. Call us and we'll refer you to other writings or consulting services.

If, however, you're concerned with hardware loss that causes information loss, you're in the right place. You want to stop this chain of events from occurring:

A. You lose your computer system or hard drive or operating system (to a virus or attack of some sort). Whatever happens, the net result is that you can't access whatever data you had on the system.

B. If you can't access the data on the system, you've effectively lost that data, and it has to be re-created somehow. If you have a backup, re-creation of that data is done through restoration and making any changes necessary to bring the data back to the point it was at the latest backup.

C. If you can't restore the data, you'll have to re-create it. Re-creating the data costs time—which, as we all know, is money. At best, the additional time it takes to re-create the data will affect the bottom line—and not in a nice way. At worst, you won't have time enough to re-create the data, and the client will leave a cooling breeze in his wake after he shuts the door behind him.

D. If you can't re-create the data in the time frame necessary to meet your client's demands, you'll—at minimum—not only lose revenue (or net profit) on this project, you'll lose client goodwill. If your tardiness on projects continues, and you lose enough client goodwill, you'll lose the client.

E. If you lose enough clients, you'll lose competitive position. If you're wondering, losing competitive position because the network administrator didn't create a good backup plan usually provides the network administrator the opportunity of seeking alternative employment—yep, you're history.

In this book, we offer a simple way for you to calculate the costs of downtime and create a backup plan budget based upon cold, hard bottom-line numbers. Using our forms (found on the website), you can easily identify costs associated with downtime and come up with some pretty straightforward budgets.

Throughout, remember to balance your budget with the value of that which you are protecting. While the topic is backup and disaster recovery, the theme is based upon solid business decisions and not the hottest, coolest technology available.

CHAPTER 2:
COST JUSTIFYING YOUR BACKUP
PLAN

There are many methods for coming up with backup-plan cost justifications. What makes this one different? It's "CFO Approved"—we've run it by our favorite CFO, to his resounding approval. It's also been approved by quite a few insanely smart business and finance folks. All this means it will be much easier for you to get your budget approved because we've already come up against some of the arguments and questions you'll have to answer.

That doesn't mean moving your backup plan through the budget process is going to be a breeze—getting companies to part with the green stuff is never easy.

However, we will provide you with language and spreadsheet calculations that translate CIO-speak into the obscure CFO dialect. And hopefully, that will make the process a bit simpler.

THE MAIN THING

The Main Thing is that you understand the nature of your business well enough to translate technical problems—like computer loss—into organizational costs and benefits. If you can't do that, you won't be able to defend your backup plan's expenses.

In short, learn the business. And then learn how to translate your pain into their pain. Nothing like a toothache in common to draw folks together.

Special thanks

I was that kid in school who always thought that 2 + 2 = 457.345782.3. Therefore, this chapter never would have been possible without the direct help of Joe Benway (my favorite CFO), Fred Heiberger (Exeter, Harvard, Kellog, etc.), Mitch Krayton, Karen Stella, Kent Jenkins, Joe Vulgan, and Jeff Witzke.

TYPES OF CALCULATIONS

In working through downtime cost calculations with a few fellow field editors, Mitch Krayton wrote, "The biggest cost factors [in tolerance to downtime] are 1) time to recover; 2) the value of the time lost to market; and 3) value/worth of lost or unrecoverable data." Karen Stella agreed that you have to look at "the impact that not delivering your product has down the food chain... if the designer doesn't produce the ad in time, you pay rush fees [to get it to press]; if it [completely] misses the deadline, you pay for a blank page ad in the magazine. And then you have all the other people standing around waiting..."

As Kent Jenkins, another field editor, said, "If I can't produce a product on time, I'm out of business. In our business, while product quality is very important, timeliness is a key factor."

So we know that to be in business, your systems must be running. Of course. But *not all systems are created equal.* The loss of Joe's computer affects Joe and anyone in the production cycle waiting for whatever Joe produces. The loss of the print server affects everyone trying to print, which in turn could affect the timely completion of many client projects. The loss of the inventory database could shut down the only store, directly and immediately affecting hundreds of Internet shoppers.

The costs associated with a single user losing access to a computer are different than those associated with a file server going down, because a file server holds the data of a great many people, thus affecting them all. The costs of losing a client-facing system such as a web-based storefront are also different than the costs of losing a server or a user's word processing files. Let's look at each one individually and examine the types of costs related to each scenario.

Which brings me to the three levels of availability and understanding the costs of downtime. On the following page, Figure 2-1. illustrates this triumvirate, breaking down the different computing environments in an organization into single user, workgroup, and client-facing systems, with their respective levels of need for availability.

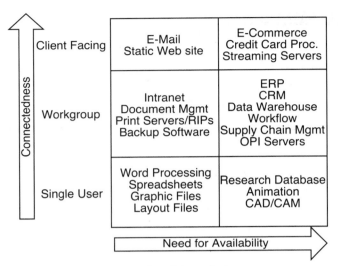

Figure 2-1. "Uptime" needs by application segment

If you're wondering where to aim your first backup-budget dollars, start with the upper-right quadrant and then work your way down to the lower-left quadrant. If you run out of money along the way, at least your key servers and shared systems will be protected.

BUSINESS CONTINUITY WHEN DATA LOSS OCCURS = RE-CREATION COSTS

Joe Vulgan, one of our field editors, put this much better than I could:

> Maintaining business continuity is a proactive process that is a key responsibility of a business organization. Taking this responsibility, then, should be a direct business goal implemented with the proper planning and tools in place to maintain and protect the company's data.
>
> When implementing and managing the protection of a system's data, you're minimizing data loss and maximizing business continuity, since the data loss is directly related to the loss of business continuity. So just what factors are involved in maintaining this continuity? And just what losses can be incurred to the business because of data loss?
>
> Probably the most important factor to maintaining the company's continuity is to have a data backup system in place and to ensure the system is designed or scripted to fit the specific business data model and to ensure the equipment is up and running properly. That said, just what are the latent business losses that can be incurred that cause the business continuity system to fail or break?

Job re-creation cost variables

As far as we're concerned, a job is that which an employee uses a computer for. If you're the bookkeeper, the job is keeping the books. If you are a writer, the job is the story you're writing. A graphic designer, programmer, whatever—all use the computer to create something: their jobs. Five basic variables come into play when dealing with the job re-creation costs used in our calculations.

Active jobs

This is the total number of active jobs the user has on her computer at the time of the system crash and data loss. An **active job** is one that is being worked on for a client (or the company), and that has a due date.

Creation time

This is the **time in hours** it took (on average) to originally create each of the currently active jobs. Whether the job is finished or not, you want to know how long it took to get to the loss point. You already know about some jobs being done and some not being done—but you also need to know how far you got in hours spent *before* the loss.

Re-creation time

The theory goes that re-creating a job takes less time than it did to create it in the first place. Numbers bandied about by those we interviewed hover around 75 percent (.75) of the original amount of time. Our calculation figures that if it took you 10 hours to get as far as you *did get* (factor X), it will take you less time (factor Y) to get to the same place. So we calculate it X*Y, or 50 Hours * 75%—but you can certainly use your own factor.

Percent lost

When Mr. Murphy visits, he visits at the worst time you could imagine. When a system goes down, there's a distinct chance that it will *not* go down when your organization has plenty of time to recover—it will probably go down at a point in time wherein even if you could re-create some of the files, you wouldn't be able to re-create *all* of them in time to meet your client's deadlines. Sometimes, you won't have time enough to re-create *any* of them—but that's not usually the case.

Rate

How much does the person who lost the documents cost the company per hour? This rate gives us the monetary definition we need to build our case, because it's the cost of their time that we have to calculate.

A few of our field editors, like Fred Heiberger, suggested two ways to assign an hourly rate. One is by "loading" the rate through calculating office space consumed, benefits, etc. The other is based on the person's gross salary. "As worded [now in the survey], people will probably fill out the sheets on a gross salary basis. Your average knowledge worker's loaded rate is more likely twice his salary. You're probably keeping it conservative to appease a fussy CFO. I personally wouldn't change it—the conservative approach makes the financial case that much more defensible," he pointed out.

The form

We've put all this together in an online form that anyone can fill out. By walking through the above five questions, you can see how the numbers quickly add up.

Recreation Questions	
When the system "went down," how many **active jobs** were you working on at the time?	10
What is the hourly rate that you get paid?	$ 25
How many hours, on average, did it take you to complete each of those jobs?	6
What percentage of the original time it took you to create the jobs do you think it will take to **re-create** the jobs? (An average is 75% of the original time)	.75
Loss Questions	
If the system crashed at the "worst possible time," what percentage of the **active jobs** you were working on would you **not** be able to re-create in time enough to meet client expectations? (An average is around 10%)	.10

Answers	
You will lose 1 jobs that can't be recreated in time, costing:	$ 150
You will need to recreate a total of 9 jobs, costing:	$ 1012.5
Therefore, your **data backup breakeven budget** is roughly:	$ 1162.5

Figure 2-2. Cost recreation form

This person had a total of 10 active jobs on the crashed system, with each job taking roughly six hours to complete at $25 per hour.

Because of time constraints when the system crashed, the user couldn't re-create 10 percent of the jobs—thus, one job was totally lost. The cost to originally create this job (6 hours @ $25 per hour), which the company can no longer bill for, is **$150**.

This leaves the user with nine other jobs to re-create. Since the re-creation time is only 75 percent of the original time, it takes the user 40.5 hours of re-creation time (versus the original 60) to reconstruct the documents. The cost of document reconstruction is a total of **$1,012.50**.

Therefore, you can spend up to **$1,162.50** on data backup measures, because at that point, the cost of restoration and the cost of data loss prevention are equal.

DOWNTIME FOR AN INDIVIDUAL IS *MUCH* DIFFERENT THAN DOWNTIME FOR A WORKGROUP

Gee, that should go without saying. But this is a book, and if it went without saying, we wouldn't be saying much and therefore wouldn't have a book (how's that for logic?). If your liability on an individual basis depends on what an individual has on their computer and how that affects *that person's* contribution to client billings, imagine your liability if an organizational process, such as the e-mail, inventory management, or billing system, takes a dive. Avert your eyes—it's not a pretty sight.

Figure 2-3. Individual loss vs. organizational loss

Here's a story about organizational loss from one of our field editors, Joe Vulgan (it's not about a crashed machine, but *is* about the cost of entire-office downtime):

> At a law-firm client's office, some dummy brought in a diskette to play games while waiting for his wife—and wiped out the office for two days. They had to reformat 15 Macs and reinstall all software. Fortunately, they had backed up all their data on a central hard disk, which was not affected by the virus. Now, I assure you it cost them far more in downtime than the puny $120/hr. I charged to restore their systems—they figured the total recovery cost was $20,000. Anyway, my story encompasses an entire office—not a single machine; and a virus, not a crashed program.

The point here is that when the office gets infected by a virus or affected by a downed inventory management server or downed major-league process, the costs go real high, real fast. Here's a look at how re-creation costs are extended when a server instead of a single user's computer goes down.

First, we'll walk through the form with some basic sample data. Then we'll analyze the costs of a real-world organization—the old Chicago office of Organic Online.

Extending the argument to analyze the effects of a server crash

Extending our basic argument that the budget for data backup can be determined by calculating the cost of re-creation (and adding in the cost of documents that can't be re-created in time), to get the server-wide picture, we include the numbers of people who store their documents on a file server that has crashed.

By adding a single field to our form (the number of users associated with a crashed file server) and changing the text from "you and your" to "the users," as well as ensuring that numbers are averaged and generalized across the board, we get the figure below, a quick view of the scope of costs associated with losing the data on a server.

Recreation Questions	
When the system "went down," how many **active jobs** were the users working on at the time?	10
What is the average hourly rate that the users get paid?	$ 25
How many hours, on average, did it take the users to complete each of those jobs?	6
What percentage of the original time it took the users to create the jobs do you think it will take to **re-create** the jobs? (An average is 75% of the original time)	.75
Loss Questions	
If the system crashed at the "worst possible time," what percentage of the **active jobs** the users were working on would you **not** be able to re-create in time enough to meet client expectations? (An average is around 10%)	.10
How many users of this server were affected?	25
Answers	
You will lose 25 jobs that can't be recreated in time, costing:	$ 3750
You will need to recreate a total of 225 jobs, costing:	$ 25312.5
Therefore, your **data backup breakeven budget** is roughly:	$ 29062.5

Figure 2-4. Server loss form

With 25 users, the organization can now lose 25 documents that can't be re-created, costing the organization **$3,750** instead of $250.

And instead of the $1,025 in re-creation costs, the organization gets hit with **$29,062.50**. Ouch.

Yep, the numbers jump up a little, don't they? And here's an interesting note: The numbers we come up with time and again correlate equally to the cost of protecting six individual workstations versus one server storing the information for six individual workstations.

Then there's the ripple effect...

When you drop a stone into a pool of water, it causes small waves to radiate outward, and when those waves bounce against something else, they in turn cause more small waves, and so on. This is the definition of the **ripple effect**: One action causes other like actions.

Idle time

In the case of a server going down, some people having to re-create their work isn't the only ripple in the pool. Remember, we work in a connected world. In today's offices, most workers' timelines are dependent upon others. A layout artist can't finish the layout if the writers have to rewrite the articles and the graphic artist has to redraw the art. While the layout artist can probably spend some time taking care of other tasks that need doing, there will come a time when she's idle until the others have finished their work.

Because of this, we've added a section to the backup cost form called the Ripple Effect Questions. The first three have to do with the amount of re-creative work that must be done that will cause coworkers to become temporary thumb-twiddlers.

Not all work that has to be re-created will cause others down the project flow line to twiddle. We start out by estimating that 10 percent of the total number of jobs that must be re-created cause workflow scheduling conflicts.

You'll also want to list the number of people these scheduling conflicts will affect, and what percentage of their overall time they'll be idle while the files are being re-created.

Fines

Idle costs aren't the only ripple effect costs that you might have to endure. Clients usually aren't too happy about the fact that you aren't going to deliver what you promised to them when you promised it.

Every single network design contract that we write for our clients stipulates that if the wiring contractor goes "past the due date, a fine will be levied per day." And you'd better believe that we cling tightly to that clause.

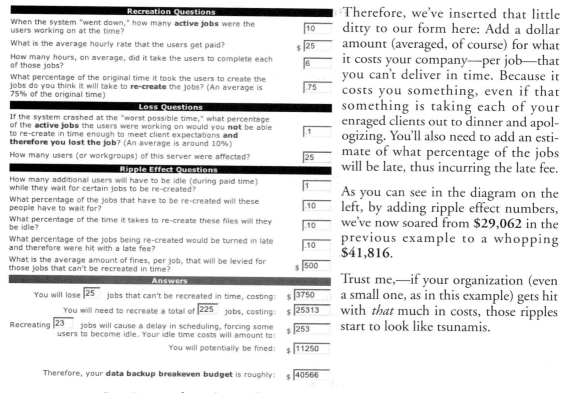

Figure 2-5. Server form with ripple effect

Therefore, we've inserted that little ditty to our form here: Add a dollar amount (averaged, of course) for what it costs your company—per job—that you can't deliver in time. Because it costs you something, even if that something is taking each of your enraged clients out to dinner and apologizing. You'll also need to add an estimate of what percentage of the jobs will be late, thus incurring the late fee.

As you can see in the diagram on the left, by adding ripple effect numbers, we've now soared from **$29,062** in the previous example to a whopping **$41,816**.

Trust me,—if your organization (even a small one, as in this example) gets hit with *that* much in costs, those ripples start to look like tsunamis.

Real-world example

Here's a real-world example from the old Chicago-based Organic Online office from E.L. Heiberger, the office's founder and original managing director. She went through the entire form for us and then let us sit down for an in-depth chat. We added italics throughout the quote in an attempt to convey the emphasis in her voice and tone during the interview.

Re-creation questions

"At any given time, we had only two or three large projects going at once. We weren't a small job shop—we handled large accounts that took an incredible amount of time to accomplish per project," Heiberger explained. Therefore, her numbers showed only two total active jobs, but each job took around 1,200 hours to complete. "If we had to do them all over again, it would take us about 75 percent of the original time it took to create them" she mused.

Loss questions

On the subject of whether or not the projects had to be abandoned if they couldn't get finished in time, Heiberger said, "Unequivocally, no way. We'd never not finish a job. In the worst instance, a job would be really late—and we'd be hit with huge late fees. But to *not* finish a job? No way."

As to the number of users working on a project, she said, "We worked as a team. You'd have one or two jobs with everybody adding to the job itself. Therefore, you'd have to put us down for a '1' in the users/workgroup space."

Ripple effect questions

"Because of the way we worked," said Heiberger, "we'd have around five folks who would finish up jobs. If the jobs had to be redone, those five folks would have their thumbs up their you-know-what about half of their day." And no, they wouldn't have to wait for both jobs to be completely finished; they could pick up percentages of the job and finish them as the rest came in.

"As far as fines go, this is where we'd get hit hardest. We would always have to agree up front that we'd pay a 10 percent late fee on all jobs that didn't come in on time," she explained, working the numbers on a piece of scratch paper. "When you think that we'd only be making around 15 percent net profit on any given job, being hit for 10 percent late fees was pretty devastating."

The form

Here's the server form, Figure 2-6. on page 49, as she filled it out.

Recreation Questions	
When the system "went down," how many **active jobs** were the users working on at the time?	2
What is the average hourly rate that the users get paid?	$ 30
How many hours, on average, did it take the users to complete each of those jobs?	1200
What percentage of the original time it took the users to create the jobs do you think it will take to **re-create** the jobs? (An average is 75% of the original time)	.75
Loss Questions	
If the system crashed at the "worst possible time," what percentage of the **active jobs** the users were working on would you **not** be able to re-create in time enough to meet client expectations **and therefore you lost the job**? (An average is around 10%)	0
How many users (or workgroups) of this server were affected?	1
Ripple Effect Questions	
How many additional users will have to be idle (during paid time) while they wait for certain jobs to be re-created?	5
What percentage of the jobs that have to be re-created will these people have to wait for?	.1
What percentage of the time it takes to re-create these files will they be idle?	.50
What percentage of the jobs being re-created would be turned in late and therefore were hit with a late fee?	1
What is the average amount of fines, per job, that will be levied for those jobs that can't be recreated in time?	$ 21600
Answers	
You will lose 0 jobs that can't be recreated in time, costing:	$ 0
You will need to recreate a total of 2 jobs, costing:	$ 54000
Recreating 0.2 jobs will cause a delay in scheduling, forcing some users to become idle. Your idle time costs will amount to:	$ 13500
You will potentially be fined:	$ 43200
Therefore, your **data backup breakeven budget** is roughly:	$ 110700

Figure 2-6. Real-world server form

I've got to say, **$110,700** is one heck of a backup budget—and a staggering amount of loss for only two projects in a small office.

COMMERCE SYSTEMS LOSS = SALES NET PROFIT LOSSES

When you're calculating the backup budget for a commerce system, you aren't going to calculate loss based on just the re-creation of a job. Instead, to get a rough estimate of a commerce system site's loss per day, you must take into account how many orders per day run through the system, the average cost, and the average markup per item. Because if the system isn't up, you can't take orders. And more than likely, your erstwhile customers will not hesitate to traipse off to your competitor. And because you weren't able to "capture" their information, you have nothing to re-create.

Sales questions

You need to ask three sales questions:

First: How many items are sold on the system per day? Second: What's the average price paid per item? Once you know that much, you have your basic volume down pat.

Third: What's the net profit? You can't base your backup budget on the total number of sales made per day. If you sell $1,000 in goods per day, but it costs you $999 to produce, sell, and ship those goods, your daily net profit is a measly $1. Therefore, to round out your backup budget numbers, you need to determine the percentage of net profit.

Downtime questions

You also need to know this: If the server dies, how long it takes to get a new server, install all the software, and get the new server up and talking with the rest of the system.

Downtime isn't measured in how long it takes to get another computer from your friendly neighborhood Robert Beaven, or Dave and Vinny. It's how long it takes to get it to your door, installed, up, tested, and running—because that's how long you'll be out of business.

Ripple effects

Commerce servers are subject to ripple effects, too. Foremost among them? The possibility of fines associated with your server's temporary demise. We know that the iPrint service contracts with third parties all over the United States to provide localized printing services. Their agreement with the local printers is that if the printers are down for a certain amount of time (thus making iPrint unavailable in that area), the local service is fined $X during the downtime.

The form

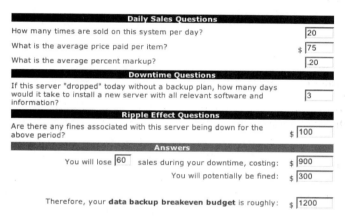

Our form for commerce servers isn't as long or as complicated as the first server form—this one has only five total fields to fill out. We've plugged in some numbers we got from a friend who runs a boutique website. As with all of reality, your numbers will probably differ.

Figure 2-7. Commerce server form

WHEN TIMING IS EVERYTHING, COSTS ARE ASSOCIATED WITH THE EVENT

Sometimes, you can't build your backup plan budget on the costs of re-creating the data. When I showed the above re-creation cost scenario to Karsten, his first question was "What if you *can't* re-create the data?" After immediately telling him that all data can be re-created, I started thinking about that. A long time ago, when the Berlin Wall was coming down, one of my gigs was to transmit pictures being taken of marathon runners as they raced through the Brandenburg Gate. If for some reason I couldn't get the files transferred from Berlin back to the States to run in the papers *right then*, and the papers ran without the pictures of the winner racing through the gate, I would have been looking for another job. Nobody wants yesterday's news tomorrow. In cases like these, no re-creation budget in the world will suffice, because there's nothing to re-create.

Same thing with an old (and still favorite) client of mine, Payless Cashways in Kansas City, Missouri. It was my pleasure to work with their advertising department, which created all of the Sunday paper inserts for the ads for their various lumber yards around the country. I was told on a regular basis that if the ads they created weren't finished by Thursday at 10A.M. and ready for pickup by the guy who made the plates for the papers, they wouldn't be printed in time to make the Sunday paper (which actually ships on Friday, but that's another story). And, as Barb and Cello used to say, "If the ads don't run, we lose more than $2.4 million in income (for that week alone) that the ads would have generated by bringing the people into the stores." This is one of those "timing" events wherein if the system fails, re-creating the data does *absolutely no good* because the Sunday paper is already in the hands of people across the country—thus, the company would simply lose that week's ad-driven revenue.

The easy thing about budgeting for these types of events are that they're usually so front-and-center and cut-and-dried that the numbers are obvious.

Monetary questions

There are two simple questions concerning money. The first is how much, and the second is how that translates into net profit. Again, if you're getting paid $100 and your net profit is $10, you have a 10 percent net profit (.10). A net profit of around 15 to 20 percent is a good target.

Why don't you add in your time to create the documents as an additional item? Because you've presumably already covered the costs of creation when you estimated your net profit margin.

Downtime questions

Usually, when you're planning the backup of this type of system, you don't have to keep it "live" throughout—much of the time, you can still recover from loss by re-creating the data. However, you'll eventually reach that critical point wherein you won't have time to re-create the data, thereby losing the whole project (or a significant part). In this section, you need to fill in the point in time when you'll cross that "no data can be lost" mark.

Ripple effect

Again, don't forget the ripple effect. For most folks who work with time-based schedules, there's the issue of additional fines and levies associated with not delivering on time. At Payless Cashways, Barb let me know that if my backup plan didn't work and the ads didn't run, the fine levied against me was a complex process involving stout ropes in uncomfortable proximity to the nearby train tracks at switching time—with no Dudley Do-Right in sight.

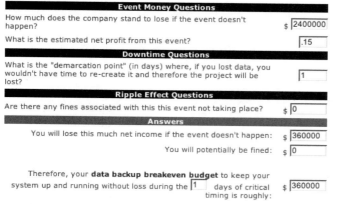

The form for this scenario is very simple, and is presented at left.

Figure 2-8. Event-driven loss form

Sometimes, it's simply cheaper to do things with a computer

The one set of calculations that we didn't put on our website are those based upon the costs of performing tasks and procedures with a computer system versus without a computer system. Why don't we have a form? Because there are three fields; the "this is how much it costs to do it with computers" field (we'll call this field X), the "this is how much it costs if we don't have the computers" field (we'll call this field Y), and the calculation of Y - X = cost savings.

Sometimes, those cost savings come in the form of price breaks. Not so long ago, we began researching the material we're going to use for the Contingency Plan Pro application we are creating with Palo Alto Software. We started talking to various folks in the restaurant and retail industry about their Point of Sale systems, supply ordering systems, and so on. We wanted to get a handle on what costs were involved if one of those systems went down. A CIO we talked with (who'd rather remain anonymous) stated that their supply chain ordering system saved them an average of about $20,000 per week because they're able to standardize their orders and send them all at once directly to each vendor's system. If this CIO's system failed for any reason, and the orders had to be placed manually on a store-by-store basis (they have over 200 stores), the costs would skyrocket because of each vendor's higher handling costs for manual orders. Simply put, it's less expensive for them to order everything through a computer system than to order everything over the phone.

Section 2.
Putting a Stop to
Mr. Freeze

Freezing occurs when the computer simply "locks up" or stops working. The lights are on, but nobody's home. You type on the keyboard—nothing happens. You move the mouse on the desk—it doesn't move on the screen. You might even see the dreaded Windows Blue Screen of Death (BsoD). When a personal computer hangs, there's often no indication of what caused the problem; it's just sort of stuck in freeze-frame mode. Either an application has frozen, or the operating system has frozen, or both.

How prevalent is this sudden drop in temperature? Here's a chapter from our own problem files. We had moved our servers to a temporary hosting location as we moved offices. We put our server up there, secured it, and went home. Before we got back to the office it had crashed, and the local guys restarted it for us. Then it crashed during the middle of the night—and again two days later. So we attached it to a small APC uninterruptible power supply (fearing power problems), and also attached the Kick-off! hardware/software monitoring tool to look for application and computer crashes. Within three days, we had a Kick-off! problem log longer than a drug dealer's rap sheet. It seems that our survey application massively crashed each time a large group of users hit it (we looked at the web logs and the crash logs next to each other to make that determination). The good news? With Kick-off! installed, the server didn't freeze when the application went down.

Kick-off! was able to restart the database (quite regularly, in fact) without having to restart the server. A quick call to the survey vendor found our real problem: We needed about four more boxes to handle the number of simultaneous survey users hitting our site. At least with Kick-off!, the entire server (which was also our main web server and e-mail server) wasn't taking a dive due to the survey overload.

And as we started doing more research on the subject of computer or application freezing, we found out that this is a very prevalent problem: Applications freeze "quite regularly". How often that is, we don't really know. But for many folks we've talked to, it's more than once a month; for "heavy" users, it's many times a week.

Frozen applications

Frozen applications such as Microsoft Word normally affect only the document you're working on. When the application freezes, it can no longer access the document, and therefore whatever was added to it since the last time it was saved is lost. Sometimes application freezes can corrupt the application itself, and you'll have to restore or reload it. No big whoop.

However, when the application freezing is your web server, your database server, your e-mail server (you get the point), it affects communications and productivity. Then it becomes a much bigger deal to bring the computer back to normal.

Frozen operating systems

A frozen application isn't the same problem as a frozen operating system. With a frozen application, the user can normally "force quit" the affected application and continue working because the operating system is unaffected.

When the operating system freezes, *everything* on the computer is locked down tighter than Hannibal Lecter's jaws. Whatever you were working on in your document—*the last time you saved until the computer froze*—is forever lost. There's nothing there to restore—it's like having your short-term memory zapped.

When this happens, the user's only choice is to restart the computer and hope for the best.

CHAPTER 3:
PROTECTION FOR APPLICATION
FREEZES

Yes, this is a bit of a misnomer—you really can't stop application freezes. Either they freeze or they don't. However, you can protect yourself from application freezes by ensuring that your software automatically backs up your files often, and in more places than one. As we already covered in *The three basic types of protection*

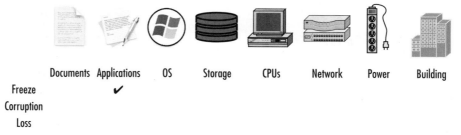

	Documents	Applications	OS	Storage	CPUs	Network	Power	Building
Freeze		✔						
Corruption								
Loss								

Table 3-1. Application freezes

on page 5, application freeze protection falls into the mirroring and backup levels of data protection.

FREEZE *LOSS* PREVENTION—SORT OF

There's nothing you can do between the time a person saves and the time he loses his data to a freeze. However, you *can* set certain application preferences to automatically make backup copies or to auto-save the files in use. Microsoft Office is one of those application suites with the auto-save feature built into each application's preferences. Below (Figure 3-1.) is a screenshot from my Microsoft Word application wherein I've set the Save AutoRecover info every 30 minutes preference.

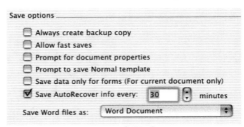

Figure 3-1. Microsoft Word save options

By setting this option, I've ensured that the most data I'll lose will be 30 minutes' worth. If a freeze or crash *does* happen, the next time Word opens, a "recovered" file will also open—with the last changes that Word saved for that file.

DoubleSaveXT ⊗

DoubleSave XT is a QuarkXPress extension that supersedes that program's implemented backup function in many ways. It was developed for those who store their documents on a file server first, and then on their local computer.

DoubleSave XT saves a copy of your XPress document to any location on your hard drive or the network whenever you execute the **Save** command. The DoubleSave XTsettings are saved in every XPress document that uses it, so different documents can be saved to different locations. Let's look at a sample three-step workflow (Figure 3-1.) using DoubleSave XT.

DoubleSave XT was originally developed for a large magazine publisher in the Netherlands (former VNU Magazines). In their workflow, they create different folders per article or spread on the file server.

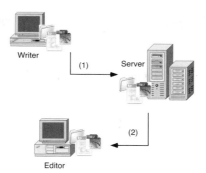

Figure 3-2. DoubleSaveXT workflow

1. Editors put articles in the appropriate article folder. Then the layout artist drags the article folder to his local hard drive and adds images and a QuarkX-Press layout to the article folder. On opening the layout for the first time, DoubleSave asks for the backup folder: the article folder on the server. The chosen path is stored within the QXP document. When the layout artist saves the document, DoubleSave XT automatically saves a backup copy to the backup folder. When the layout is finished, a print is created and handed over to the editor.

2. The editor drags the article folder to her local hard drive and opens the layout in QXP. After working on the text, she saves the document, DoubleSave XT automatically saves a copy of the updated file to the correct article folder on the file server. The editor creates a print and hands it over to the layout artist, who drags the update article folder to his hard drive and prepares the layout for the service bureau.

DoubleSave's interface is simple enough. Through the standard Open File dialog box, you navigate over to a shared directory on your server and tell the utility that is where you'd like your files saved. Other than that, the user simply tells the application which preferences they want, including

*   Remove old backup after completing... makes DoubleSave wait to complete the saving tasks before it removes the previous version.

*   Always check backup folder... checks for the backup folder when a document is reopened. If there is none, DoubleSave displays the Select Backup Folder dialog.

*   Copy in background... hides the dialog that shows that files are being copied.

- Copy imported pictures… copies all pictures that have been imported into the XPress document into the backup folder.

Proactive network backups with Retrospect ⓧ ⓑ ⊞

You can protect documents, application files and settings that are key assets in your network (i.e., production system computers, etc.) that *don't* have automated backup capabilities either built in or added on, through a network-based backup solution from Dantz Development. As far as we can tell, Dantz Retrospect (server version) is the only product that we know of that allows the end user to say to the backup server "Hey, back me up *NOW!*" And we *know* it's the only product that supports Mac OS X, Windows, and Linux end-user clients to this extent.

What's a proactive network backup? Glad you asked. There are two types of network backup: First, the one we all know so well—where the network administrator builds a backup server, loads client software on each and every key computing device to be backed up, and then enters those devices into a backup schedule whereby on Tuesday at 2:00P.M. (it can be any time; this is merely a humble homage to an old Carl Reiner joke), the schedule kicks off and backs up each device on the list in order. That's *not* proactive—rather, it's as scheduled as your Monday-morning garbage pickup.

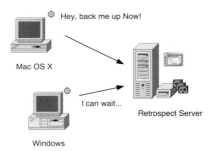

Mac OS X

Windows

A proactive system is different. Build the backup server as you normally would, but once you've loaded the clients, you then add them to a listing of devices to back up on an ad hoc basis, point to the location you want to store the information (anything from a CD/RW through a server volume to a tape backup). Voilà! The backup is up and running. No scripts; just a backup server that now polls each computer looking for it, asking if it should back it up yet, as shown in Figure 3-3. And, of course, a bit of end-user education is in order, too.

Figure 3-3. Proactive backup server

This end-user education comes into play when you're teaching them about their responsibilities for such a system. Unlike a fully automated process in which every time the end user saves the document, it's backed up to a different location, a proactive backup system isn't that intuitive. The end user has to *do* something other than merely hit the **Save** button. In the case of Retrospect's end-user software (Retrospect Client), the end user must open up the client software and set the backup schedule request from its normal rotational schedule to either ASAP or a time-based kick-off[1]. Figure 3-4. shows the Mac OS X version of the client software. The Linux and Windows versions contain the same information as the Macintosh version.

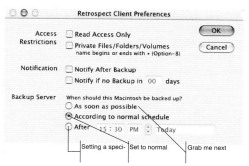

Figure 3-4. Retrospect client preferences

Is proactive backup as good as auto-save? Sort of—with two drawbacks: It's not built into a key application so that it occurs simultaneously with saving, and it doesn't save the files into a directory on a server in native-file format. Can a special backup process be run to back up each computer in the list every hour? Yep. That's pretty cool in and of itself. Is this better than working with key workstations that freeze often and not having anything? You betcha. Will this system be improved so that it ties directly into applications in the future, or ties into a backup in native file format in the future? Couldn't tell you, but you can bet one thing for sure— if this *does* happen, we'll be covering the changes on our backupbook.com website, www.backupbook.com, and we'll keep you posted.

---

1. Even though a user may say "Back me up at 2:00P.M. on Wednesday," if another device's backup is still taking place at that time, that job will continue, and the end user's computer will be backed up as soon as possible after the original backup has completed.

Chapter 4:
Protection for computer freezes

When your computer freezes, there's nothing much you can do other than restart it. When the computer freezes in a wiring closet at 2:00A.M. (which is when they normally freeze, just to tick you off), you can drag yourself out of bed, scrape the ice off your windshield, drive 10 miles through the snow to your office, and restart the miserable machine, or you can have software on the computer that does that for you automatically. Lazy slackers that we are, we prefer the latter approach.

The best protection for computer freezes we know of is Sophisticated Circuits': Kick-off! computer and application monitoring system. Kick-off! is a comprehensive system that automatically monitors and then automatically recovers your computer when common system failures like power loss occur, and application/operating systems freeze occur—and trust me, they will.

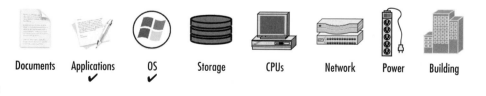

	Documents	Applications	OS	Storage	CPUs	Network	Power	Building
Freeze Corruption Loss		✔	✔					

Table 4-1. Computer freezes

The Kick-off! system comprises a power cable that connects to your computer for monitoring purposes through a USB interface, and the associated software that you install to run in the background for Macintosh, Linux, and Windows operating systems.

Figure 4-1. The Kick-off! USB and power cable system

How it works

Because the Kick-off! system is comprised of both hardware and software, it reaches deep within your computer and communicate with running applications, asking them if they're "alive" enough to keep going.

While the applications in your computer are ticking away normally, the Kick-off! software is in constant communication with the computer and its associated hardware cable. If the desired application doesn't respond to the Kick-off! software's enquiry, the Kick-off! software will force the application in question to restart, or, in the case of a total system failure, the hardware will notice that it's no longer in contact with the Kick-off! software and will then force the entire computer to restart.

Installation

Installation is quick and straightforward. Once you shut your computer down, connect your current power cable into the Kick-off! power cable, and connect the Kick-off! power cable into your computer. You also need to connect the USB cable into one of your USB ports[1]. The software installs onto your computer with a few clicks and is loaded during the startup process. I'll show the Macintosh OS 9 interface in the subsequent figures, as the Windows, Mac OS 9, and Mac OS X interface are all pretty much exactly the same (and I already had it running for awhile under OS 9).

Setup

Setup is done in four steps, the most important of which is the attention paid to system and application crashes and freezes.

System crashes   Monitoring for **system crashes** is the first phase of the setup process and the primary window tab that appears when the application is launched (Figure 4-2.). The default setup (what most of us need) makes the system restart if it doesn't respond within five minutes, attempting up to five restarts, waiting five minutes each time for full restart.

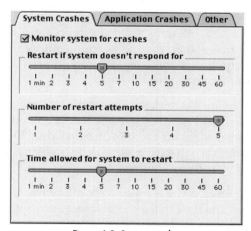

Figure 4-2. System crashes

Leaving these defaults set as they are gives the unattended computer enough time to restart, go through any automatic disk-related repair processes and reboot any long-process applications, such as database servers, DNS servers, etc.

Application crashes   The second tab in the setup window relates to **application crashes**. The defaults monitor for application crashes as well as timers in supported applications (we'll talk more about the timers in a minute).

---

1.   Re: the USB cable—if you're out of ports, you'll need a *powered* USB hub, as the cable needs power.

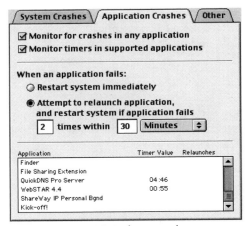

Figure 4-3. Application crashes

The Kick-off! software/hardware combo is big on multilevel communication with your computer. Beyond watching out for running appplication failure and entire computer failure, Kick-off! determines if the applications are having difficulty *restarting* when they do fail.

In Figure 4-3. note the two settings detailing action options for when an application fails. The first restarts the entire computer if a key application fails—not such a great idea, for the most part. If your DNS server software fails and you can restart the software again with no problems, why go through the process of restarting your entire computer?

However, if you set your Kick-off! system to restart your DNS server software if it fails, and the DNS server software attempts to relaunch a couple of times and continues to fail, that's another story. At that point, you can assume that there's either a corrupted bit of memory in the computer's RAM or a problem with your DNS server software. Restarting the computer will take care of the RAM issue—and if your DNS server software continues to fail, you should look elsewhere for your problem spot. For that, peruse some good logs to find out when the problem began and how pervasive it is.

Other settings Kick-off! also writes a log file of what's happening to your computer while it's monitoring it. In the Macintosh OS 9 version of the software, Kick-off! writes its log to a small application called MonoLog (which we won't cover here, as everyone is migrating away from OS 9). Messages are sent to the Windows logging client for all versions of Windows, and to the SysLog for Macintosh OS X.

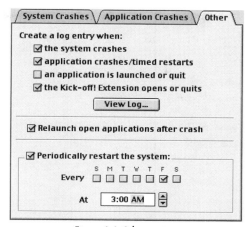

Figure 4-4. Other settings

Log all entries in the top logging section except when applications are launched and quit. Why not this one? Because each time a process launches in the background, however mundane that process is, Kick-off! thinks it's an application launch. Know the phrase "too much information"? You don't need to know that much about your computer system, but you will want to relaunch any applications that are open when the system crashes (and must be restarted).

And it's really up to you if you want to periodically restart your system "just because." We've found that restarting your system about once a week (we do it early in the morning when nobody cares) keeps it in the pink and prevents it from becoming sluggish.

W*API timers

For users who have WebSTAR servers and other applications that support the W*API (WebSTAR API) programming plug-in language, Sophisticated Circuits offers a plug-in to their Kick-off! software. The W*API AppTimer Plug-in adds support for the "application timer" technology that enables Kick-off! to monitor the application for failures, offering your server additional reliability. The W*API AppTimer Plug-in supports web-based configuration on server platforms that provide that capability. The URL that you access to open the plug-in's configuration page differs from server to server. What's important is that you can set specific timers for each application that you're running—a great feature, especially for non-multithreaded applications like FileMaker (for both Mac and Windows) that can cause time-out problems when running massive database jobs.

 While you can't stop your applications or computers from freezing, you *can* do something about it.

If Chicago's motto is "Vote early, vote often," the computer user's motto is "Save early, save often."

And, it seems to me, if you're putting up a server somewhere in a "headless," no-monitor environment, you might just want to have Kick-off! running on it to ensure its longevity.

SECTION 3.
WILL THE CORRUPTION
NEVER END?

What is corruption? The dictionary describes it as the process of *tainting* something. I like that word. What's the difference between corruption and loss? Let's say your car gets in an accident. You're driving down the road, spill coffee in your lap because you aren't paying attention (you were probably on your cell phone to your bookie) and hit a tree—your car is either "tainted," or "lost." If you hit the tree at 15 m.p.h., chances are you can fix the damage. If you hit the tree at 50 m.p.h., chances are you'll be getting a different car. In essence, corruption is a measure of what you can fix. If you can fix it, it's only corrupted. If you can't fix it and have to replace it, it's lost.

Documents, applications, and operating systems have two things in common. At the computer level, they're all simply files. This book is a collection of documents. The application I'm writing it in (Word) is a collection of documents. And, of course, my operating system is a collection of documents. That's the first thing they have in common. The second commonality? They can become corrupt over time due to applications and operating systems unexpectedly quitting (thus leaving fragments of data in the wrong place in the file), or viruses or hackers altering data in the file. At some point, enough corruption of the document causes document **loss**.

Corruption can also be defined as decay or decomposition. Therefore, corruption (through wear and tear) happens as a normal part of using your hard drive. As David Lethe reminded me, "You can corrupt your drive just by turning it off without shutting it down properly."

And your hard drive isn't the only storage media that can become corrupted. If you want to see quick corruption on a backup tape, put a new DLT tape into a DLT tape system that hasn't been cleaned in a couple of months. After a few runs, your brand-new tape will have errors throughout, caused by dirty write heads on the tape system.

And finally, yes, Roger, your network can become corrupted, as well, and that corruption can, and does, affect the computers attached to it. Here's a real-world complaint from a guy on a large corporate network about the network corruption affecting his computers:

> Every Monday for the last three weeks, I come in to work to find any number of our 12 new Sun Blade 100 workstations "kicked out" of NIS+. I have to Stop-A and sync to get them back. After they reboot, they're fine.
>
> The Sun Infodocs say that this is caused by network corruption. I called the network guys and they confirm that they had network problems shortly before these messages start getting logged…

What causes network corruption? It can be introduced with a new driver from a vendor, such as the past drivers that Netware has introduced. It can be caused by adding a group of new networking devices that all come predefined with the same IP address for SNMP management (and the hapless admin, not knowing that, puts them all on the same network at once without changing the address, causing a *huge* address resolution protocol error storm). Hooking up networking devices the wrong way can cause it. And, of course, some moron hacker can cause it, too.

CHAPTER 5:
DOCUMENT CORRUPTION

Generically, there are two types of files: workstation-application-driven and database-driven. Files like those created by Excel, Word, PowerPoint, and Photoshop are usually opened and worked on by one person at a time on an individual computer. Files like those created by Microsoft Access, FileMaker, MySQL, Ingris, Oracle, etc., and certain e-mail applications are database-driven and therefore network-driven, with multiple continuous users and complex file structures. Want to guess which are more prone to corruption? So what can you do about it? File cor-

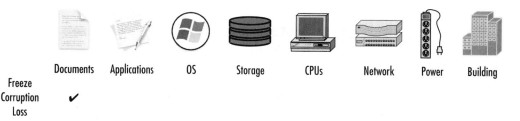

	Documents	Applications	OS	Storage	CPUs	Network	Power	Building
Freeze								
Corruption	✔							
Loss								

Table 5-1. Document corruption

ruption can't be prevented with mirroring, duplication, or replication. Whatever is being written to the file that would cause it to become corrupted would also be immediately written to the mirrored, duplicated, or replicated file. Other than end-user education, there are no preventative measures per se. Depending upon the types of documents in question, you can either use tools that provide a level of fault tolerance or you can be very proactive in your point-in-time backups so that you can restore the uncorrupted version of a file.

THE MAIN THING

The Main Thing here is to realize that users are the biggest causes of file corruption. To counter this, you need to employ tools to fix the corruption in their documents, or be religious about document backups from the desktop level.

One (of many) bane of your existence is the myriad small, ad hoc databases that crop up like so many weeds—but you can't kill these with Roundup; instead, you must back them up properly with open-file backup tools and backup software that supports open file backups.

Backing up an e-mail server—especially dealing with individual mailboxes—presents its own special challenges. While we touch on this subject here, we'll cover mail server backups more thoroughly in a chapter by itself.

And last but not least, you'll want to only employ operating system software that allows you to "fix what ails it" using an Emergency Repair Disk (ERD). Any operating system (like some home versions of Microsoft's products) that doesn't come with an ERD should be ruled out.

Special thanks...

I don't know where I'd be without the field editors for this chapter, who include:

Terry Calvert, Bill Carn, John Shearer, Ira Solomon, Mitch Krayton, Cherie Nickell, Roger Royce, and Paul Schauble.

WORD (AND OTHER STAND-ALONE DOCUMENTS) FILE CORRUPTION

The longer they get, the more susceptible to corruption Word files become. I speak from bitter experience: I've written more than a few books and have sent many curses to the heavens in this regard. This type of file corruption is caused by the application unexpectedly quitting and leaving bits of code strewn throughout the document that shouldn't be there—sort of like confetti on the morning after.

What can you do about this? Pretty much nothing (other than copying and pasting the document into itself to reduce its size). This is a part, albeit unpleasant, of working with computers. However, some firms out there specialize in building tools to fix these problems when they occur, before the document is completely lost. DocXtools from MicroSystems[1] is one of those solutions. Though this applies only to Microsoft Word documents (we use this one as an example), you should be able to get the drift—there are tools to help the end user fix corrupted documents before they vanish into the ether.

The only other thing that can be done to remedy this situation is to back up the in-progress, important end-user files on a regular basis. We'll cover that aspect in great detail in the desktop backup chapter of the book.

 Surely, if there are tools that will fix your corrupted documents, have a copy of them on hand. Why bother performing a data restoration if your document can be fixed by a faster method?

With that said, ensure that you're backing up critical information on your users' computers. We cover how to target and back up (on a timed or regular basis) specific types of files in the Document Loss chapter later on (see *Documents that don't die* on page 261). You'll want the peace of mind that comes with essential document backup. Remember, if you don't back it up, you can't restore it in times of trouble.

---

1.   http://www.microsystems.com/docxtools/

ENTRY-LEVEL DATABASE CORRUPTION

The active database document[2] is a second type of document. Beyond the corporate CRM and inventory management databases there lie a thousand little databases strung all through the organizational network, creating a cacophony of network traffic, like blue jays squawking on a telephone wire. Do these databases get corrupted? You betcha. Much more than the big corporate systems, because there's really nobody minding the farm—er, aviary—so good data practices are never really put into use. But God forbid you lose data on one of these things—especially if it's the CEO's pet database.

Corruption in these types of databases in the early stages of their use is mainly caused by a network error or a workstation crash; particularly while data is being updated. As Terry Calvert, one of our field editors, points out, "Data files may *appear* to be corrupted if the index files become corrupt. With Access [and File-Maker as well], all the eggs are in one basket (e.g., all parts of the application are found in one file). When Access [and FileMaker] fails or freezes, the basket is munched, and the data, application programs, reports, and queries are all toast." The diagram at left, below, shows two computers accessing the same FileMaker file. Terry's right: The single file being accessed is the one that can corrupt, for any number of causes.

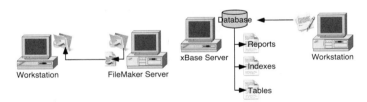

Figure 5-1. FileMaker sharing (left) vs. xBase database structure (right)

I'm show that diagram to set you up for its partner on the right, and I'll explain it in Terry's words. "With other databases, such as Advantage or xBASE, the data is in one physical file, indexes in another physical file, reports in another physical

---

2.   No, this is not an active endorsement of either Access or FileMaker. We cover them because we've "heard enough already" about them corrupting on a regular basis.

file, etc. If a report is munched, only that single report is lost and must be re-created or restored. If an index file is corrupted, the data are OK (usually), and the index can be re-created."

Low-level database servers are often blamed on faulty networks. Yes, sometimes flaky network cards send out bursts of bad packets, and you may occasionally find that users you thought were knowledgeable are turning off their computers at the end of the day without closing access or shutting down Windows properly.

However, before you look too hard for a network-based corruption problem, another of our field editors, Paul Schauble, reminded me of something very important to investigate. Writing a database application that can run multi-user services, he explained, requires a certain degree of skill to correctly handle conflicts between users (regarding record-locking issues)—and all too frequently, these pet database applications are constructed by someone lacking that skill. These applications may work correctly for a long time until they become popular enough that conflicts start to happen. Then the database falls apart. These problems are often, and incorrectly, blamed on the machine or on the network.

 The only real recovery method for a downed database of this ilk is to have backed it up so that you can restore it to its pre-corrupt level. Backing up database files is different than backing up regular documents because database files are more than likely to be open and in use during the backup process—which would normally cause the backup software to skip those files. To perform a backup of a live database, you'll need backup software that backs up open files during the backup process. Retrospect, NovaStor, Computer Associates, and VERITAS back up open files through special settings or additional software we cover in the section on *Open file backup for databases* on page 339. However, backing up the database won't actually fix the problem—it'll just ensure that you're covered when it happens (and, believe me, it'll happen again and again if you don't fix it).

We're dealing with two distinct problems here: network corruption and end-user sloppiness. Let's tackle end-user sloppiness first.

The only real way to deal with this is education. A quick look through the database's "who's connected" list will reveal your potential perpetrators: an automatic attendee roster for a quick class on database etiquette. Chances are that these same people who hit the "power off" button on their computers, thus corrupting the database, are also muddling up their hard drives at the same time.

The second problem is caused by network corruption or by having placed the database server on the wrong machine or the wrong location. Having a database server on a very slow or overworked machine causes problems. Check the load of the server (you can find a gazillion load-analysis tools on the Web for this). Having a database server on a network segment that is itself corrupted also causes database problems (see *Wh t d d you s y?* on page 176). Having the database server on the wrong network segment also causes problems. You're on your own there.

OUTLOOK AND ENTOURAGE E-MAIL CLIENTS CORRUPTION

Here's an e-mail that came in asking for help with Outlook Express. The same thing can be said for a few other e-mail applications that work the same way.

> It started with Outlook Express... every now and again, the e-mail files would get corrupted and I would lose e-mail... could not be repaired. Happened too many times, so I switched to Outlook to see if it could do a better job. Corruption occurred today in Outlook, but I was able to retrieve the e-mail, using the Inbox Repair Tool. I would really like to find out what the cause of this problem is...

The underlying structure of Outlook is a cross between regular documents and a one-user database (the message database). If the message database is continually corrupting, something's wrong, either with the drive, the network, or the software. Outlook Express's message database can be corrupted more easily than Outlook's, but that shouldn't happen very often. For infrequent crashes, Outlook and Eudora share the same capability of rebuilding their own internal data structures.

The anatomy of the situation

With e-mail corruption, you're dealing with a more complex set of circumstances than when you were dealing with a simple Access or FileMaker database corruption. (Figure 5-2.) is a diagram that shows an Exchange server on a network with a local client, that's also connected through a firewall to a home e-mail user. We've numbered the potential trouble spots 1 through 6 in the order that they should be examined when problems occur.

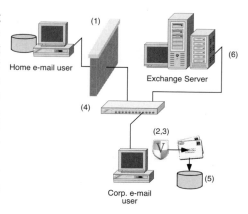

Figure 5-2. Exchange setup and points of failure

1. If you're having problems with e-mail continually corrupting when being sent to home users, first check your firewall configuration. More often than not, settings for port filters can get "confused" and dynamically reallocated away from control of the Exchange server.

2. Note that I said *users* above. That's plural. If you're talking about just one user, that's a different story—you should be troubleshooting that individual's computer, setups, and anti-virus programs.

3. However, if the same problem is happening on end-user computers in the office, next, try checking for interfering anti-virus software running on the local computer. All too often, we've heard about outdated or misconfigured anti-virus software corrupting incoming e-mail messages. The best place to run anti-virus software for e-mail is outside the company or at the e-mail server.

4. If you have checked for virus scanning and have eliminated that possibility as a problem, and are still having problems with several users on the LAN, check the network for corruption. Chances are that's the culprit.

5. If you're having spotty e-mail problems on only one or two computers, check the hard drive of each user as the last resort. Because e-mail applications create small databases for the inbox and other mailboxes on the local computer, and these database files just get bigger and bigger and bigger, they're very susceptible to being corrupted by hard drive problems. Not only is defragmentation of the hard drive a good idea, but running drive anti-corruption software like that from Norton, FWB, and others can help, too. Keeping software that detects potential problems on an ongoing basis on the local computer is also recommended.

6. Of course, if everyone on the network connected to this server is having problems, check the e-mail server itself. More than likely, the e-mail server's hard drive is acting up and needs to be replaced. This is a good time to check your backup files for the server, as well. If the clients are having problems *and* the backup is having problems, don't waste your time trying to back up the server again: Either reformat the drive and restore your system, or get a new drive and restore your system.

 Because e-mail applications are a hybrid of regular documents and active, open file databases, you'll need to install backup software on each computer you want to back up that can handle open file backups; if you have Exchange, you'll want to have backup software that directly supports it. Again, Retrospect, NovaStor,

Computer Associates, and VERITAS all handle open file backups, but only certain ones support Exchange. This ensures that the end users' e-mail files are backed up—but it doesn't fix the problems.

To do that, you must understand your firewall setup. This isn't the book for working with firewalls, but if you want to get our opinion, e-mail us and we'll give you some good recommendations on where to start.

And finally, you'll want to ensure that you're either running defragmentation software on a semi-regular basis for your user's computers, or have hard drive monitoring software installed that can actively look for potential trouble spots within the hard drives.

Chapter 6:
Application & operating system corruption

An application or an operating system can become corrupted in four basic ways:

1. Through users adding or deleting something they shouldn't.

2. Through the software vendor creating a version that "didn't quite work."

3. As a part of the hard drive becoming corrupted.

4. Through a virus or hacker attack.

Any of these four methods of distortion will leave a portion or all of the application or operating system corrupt, tainted, or just plain missing (Figure 6-1.).

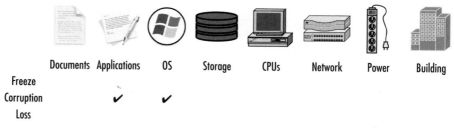

	Documents	Applications	OS	Storage	CPUs	Network	Power	Building
Freeze								
Corruption		✔	✔					
Loss								

Table 6-1. Application and opeating system corruption

The problem with applications and operating systems versus straight documents? Because they're more complex than mere documents, you're at a loss for real tools to "uncorrupt" them if they go south for any reason. What you're left with, for all intents and purposes, is something *worse* than the garden-variety lost application or operating system: An application or OS tailored to the user's own idiosyncrasies in order to be "more productive"—and the tailored version is now corrupt.

Recovering from a Windows OS crash (a true Karsten Tale...)

You're probably not working with the first and original version of your operating system; instead, it's been updated and modified in order to fix security holes and be customized for your daily use. In fact, it'll probably be very different from the creature you originally installed from the operating system CD. If you work in a Windows environment, you might be familiar with the term "Service Pack"—a friendly euphemism for "bug fix." As we write this b ook, for Windows NT 4, Service Pack 6a is available; officially the seventh big Service Pack since the original release, determined to track down and clean up all the little bugs and security holes that the previous releases had created. In addition, there are service packs for Internet Explorer, and all the little applications and services that Windows shepherds.

On the Macintosh, you see something very similar. While I'm writing this book, my iBook has miraculously been updated to Mac OS X 10.2.4—the umpteenth update since OS X was originally released. Then, of course, there are system utilities like ATM, fonts, a virus scanner, drivers for printers, display adapters and sound cards, Acrobat Reader, and a gazillion other gizmos that make working with your computer fun. Now imagine that one tiny virus attacks your computer and shreds all your system files, forcing the computer to reboot and then letting the PC hang with a blue screen. Do I hear laughter? Well, stifle the snickers: That's exactly what happened to me last week. Of course, I constantly back up my files,[1] but opted to skip the boot volume. How do I restore my operating system? Do I still have the CDs and disks with all the nifty tools I use everyday? What kind of display adapter am I using? Do I have the serial numbers of all my applications somewhere? So the grueling odyssey began. I rebooted my computer from the Windows 2000 CD, reformatted the hard drive, and began installing. The Win-

---

[1.] Actually, I always keep a complete backup of my hard drive in a folder on our backup server. In this case, though, I didn't want to restore the whole hard drive—the virus might have gotten into those files, too.

dows installation took about an hour and a half. Next came the security updates. Fortunately, both Microsoft and Apple have an automated way of updating your system. For Windows, you simply need a reasonably fast Internet connection and a web browser. Next, you go to their website and select **Windows Update**. Their smart little tool checks the status of your operating system and recommends downloads. They even promise not to spy on your computer…

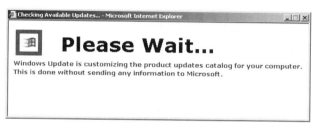

Figure 6-1. Windows update dialog

On the Macintosh, this is even simpler: Select **Software Update** from the **System Preferences** and click **Update Now**. Basically, this *sounds* simple, but the bitter truth is that this can take you a few more hours, depending on the speed of your Internet connection and your level of frustration. A search for updates since Windows 2000 has been released revealed a listing of 208 update packages, the largest a whopping 308 MB. Just imagine downloading roughly 200 gigantic files and installing them in the right order. Fortunately, many of them are grouped in later updates, but it still took two more hours to finish this task—and it might have taken a whole lot longer had I not shared a blistering fast T1 line with Dorian— and nobody else. Now, I faced the task of installing my everyday bread-and-butter software: Microsoft Office, ScreenPrint, ATM, fonts and Photoshop. Fortunately, we have a well-filled software rack, with every box bearing a sticker of the machine it belongs to, so after another hour, my PC was almost ready for work again. Still, the monitor showed only 16 colors at an 800x600 resolution. The box for my display adapter had long since disappeared, and I had no idea who had manufactured it. The only way I could find out what was in my PC was to open it, remove the adapter, and check for traces of a product or manufacturer. Fortunately, after I cracked open the case, there it was, in bold relief: NVidia. I went to their website, downloaded the drivers, and installed them.

Days later, though, I realized here and there that I was missing a few things. I didn't have Acrobat Reader, my ScreenPrint version reverted to a 30-day trial, and a few fonts had disappeared on me. This will even out, though, as I continue to add those nifty little tools that make working with my PC so much fun.

Windows doesn't start for a number of reasons; the most common ones involving drivers or services that block it from starting or even exiting into the infamous Blue Screen of Death (BSoD); or corrupted registries. Alas, unless you start Windows in safe mode, you have no means of interaction to stop certain functions from being executed. Macintosh users have it easy: They can just plug an external drive into any connection—USB, FireWire or SCSI—and boot from that device. PCs can't do this, as the current generation of FireWire and USB cards doesn't provide INT13[2], and therefore drive boot support. The only bootable options are those that are known to the BIOS of your PC[3]. Depending on the way your PC is equipped, you'll probably find the following options in there: drive A: as the floppy drive; drive C: as the primary bootable disk; and drive D: to Z: for any other drives in your computer. In addition, one of the available drives is probably a CD or DVD drive. These are the only weapons in your arsenal—so use them wisely.

---

[2]. To be precise: Interrupt 13 is being used to make a call to the BIOS to negotiate bootable drives.

[3]. There is an exception: If your PC has a SCSI interface card, you have more options. We'll talk about that later.

REPAIRING YOUR WINDOWS OPERATING SYSTEM

For starters, it's always a good idea to create an emergency recovery disk (ERD), as recommended by Microsoft. This option is available in every Windows version but XP Home. In its infinite wisdom, Microsoft probably assumed that home users don't create valuable data, so a fresh Windows installation would do no harm. Hmm...

The most obvious situation that screams for an ERD occurs when your PC hangs on startup, displaying the infamous blue screen—a sure sign of a Windows installation that has gone down the drain. Other glum scenarios come to mind, too; for example, Windows rebooting constantly without ever finishing the boot process. To get around this, use your Windows CD as a startup disk, wait for the Windows installation to load, and select the Repair option to repair the Windows installation. In the following screen, you have two options: Either let Windows repair your installation or use the ERD. Using the ERD is the better choice because it has the most recent information about your PC. Insert the disk on request and let Windows work its miracle.

You can create an ERD anytime from within Windows by selecting the **Start** menu and choosing **Programs** > **Accessories** > **System Tools** > **Backup**. In this dialog, click the **Emergency Repair Disk** button and follow the instructions. It's generally a good idea to include the registry[4] on this disk. During this process, Windows saves the current system state to the floppy disk. In case of OS corruption, this information helps Windows to identify corrupted files and settings and to restore them from the installation CD.

The whole process takes less than a minute, but saves you hours of valuable time if your boot disk ever gets corrupted. Store this disk in a safe place and create a new disk from time to time as the registry changes when you change settings in Windows or install new software.

---

[4] The registry is the central location in which all Windows applications and Windows itself save their settings. If the registry gets corrupted, applications or even Windows itself become instable or might even refuse to run.

Remember: Don't use this disk on a different computer. You need one disk for each PC. If you restore the registry from one PC onto another, you might destroy more than you save.

The alternatives

Several products on the market promise an easier way to repair a defunct Windows installation. Instead of using the DOS command prompt after booting into repair mode, they present you with a graphical interface and several tools to repair your Windows installation and to reset the password if you've lost it, or if the PC has become inaccessible, for some obscure reason[5]. The repair tools currently on the market tackle different aspects—from recovering deleted files to repairing your Windows installation—so make sure to choose the right tool to tackle your problem. However, if the diagnostic tools don't even recognize the hard drive anymore, you're out of luck, and should consider a new career. Wouldn't it be fun to be a singing waiter?

Winternals ERD Commander

ERD Commander is a better substitute for the Emergency Recovery Disk. Use it when your PC doesn't boot anymore due to software-related problems. It comes on a bootable CD with a Windows-like interface that's basically a stripped-down Windows XP version with a handful of very useful tools. From the start menu, you can select the tools and repair your system. If you like, you can even start programs from your hard drive or copy files to other drives.

If you forgot the administrator's password, for example, or had it changed by a hacker who broke into your system[6], you can use the Locksmith tool to reset the password. Simply start Locksmith, choose the account whose password you want to change, and enter the new password. On reboot, you can use the new password to log in.

---

5. True story: As we're writing this book, a Norwegian educational center asked hackers on the Internet for help with opening their database on ancient Norwegian languages. The professor working on the files had died, taking the password with him to Valhalla. Five hours later, the password was cracked—it was the professor's name spelled backward.

6. I hate to admit it, but that happened to me.

The Registry Editor that looks and works like the Microsoft version is another nifty tool (Figure 6-2.). Use it to edit the registry[7], which might become necessary when an application or a system extension prevents the PC from booting. This is serious stuff, though—before you start tinkering with the registry, you should certainly have read appropriate literature; otherwise you might end up reinstalling Windows from scratch—a delightful way to spend your summer vacation.

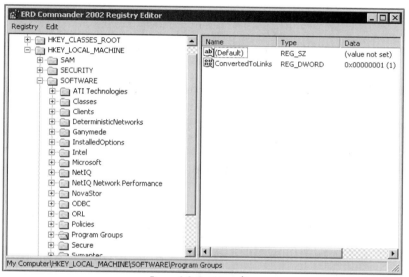

Figure 6-2. Registry editor

Consider calling ERD Commander to your aid when corrupt or outdated drivers let Windows struggle. This scenario becomes very obvious when you've just installed the drivers for your new steering wheel, reboot your PC to start the game —and Windows hangs. The Computer Management tool, again very similar to the Windows version, lets you remove every single installed driver until you have a working PC again.

---

7.   With the arrival of Windows 98, Microsoft introduced the registry, replacing the win.ini file that most applications used to store their settings. Those of you who have been around long enough to have used Windows 1.0 (yes, I still have a copy) might remember the dreadful experience of editing the win.ini file for adding fonts or modifying an application's behavior, in sheer terror that Windows might not work after the edits…

Norton Utilities

Probably the veteran among disk repair tools, Norton Utilities comes with a bootable CD containing all your old pals like SpeedDisk, UnErase, Disk Doctor, WinDoctor, and many more. As stated before, aside from faulty drivers and services, the most common cause of frozen Windows is a corrupt registry. WinDoctor (Figure 6-3.) can warm up the patient by checking the registry for faulty or obsolete entries and removing them.

After you've booted your PC from the CD, start the WinDoctor Wizard and let WinDoctor do the repair work on your Windows installation. You can see it move through each of the registries, analyzing them one by one.

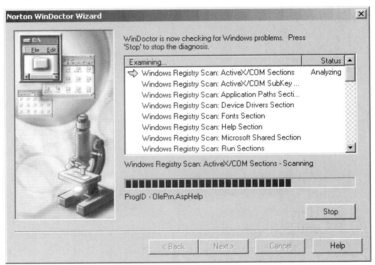

Figure 6-3. WinDoctor checking the Registry

If there's a problem, WinDoctor will find and fix it—you can trust it on this one. I've deliberately messed up the registry a few times, and WinDoctor always came through. After repairing the registry, you'll have to reboot your PC from your hard drive to put your newly healed registry back on duty.

Drive 10 Ⓧ

In the Macintosh world, Drive 10 (Figure 6-3.) is the predominant application for raising a corrupted Mac OS X hard drive from the netherworld. Norton and Disk Warrior might have more bells and whistles, but Drive 10 does the job better.

Figure 6-4. Drive 10 Interface

Hint here: If the results say that a section failed, run the test(s) again (and again) until the results all say "passed." Sometimes you've got more problems than Drive 10 can fix in a single pass—or two or three.

Forget your OS X user passwords?

You can insert the OS X install CD into the drive, restart, hold down the C key, and let the installer come up. Click on **Installer** > **Reset Password** in themenu list. The software will direct you through the process, and this works for any of the base users (Root, admin, etc.), as well as defined users (like Dorian). Restart, log in with new password, and you're back in business.

CAN YOU *STOP* APPLICATION AND OS CORRUPTION?

No, not entirely. Look at the four root causes again. The first two deal with users doing something they shouldn't. People have been doing something they shouldn't since the beginning of time, so *that* ain't gonna change. The third root cause is the vendor. Some vendors, Microsoft more than others, seem to be guilty of sending out software that just doesn't work too well. Are you going to stop them? Fat chance.

The remedy we suggest for adding new applications? Add them in a "quarantined" environment before you roll them out to the whole workgroup or enterprise. It just makes plain old sense that before you add anything completely new, you test it out first. When we moved some of the computers in our little 15-computer network over to Microsoft X for Mac OS X, we first tested it out—and found that the printing within Word X was just plain horrible. We had to rely on printing long documents or documents with tables and pictures in them from Word's Mac OS 9 version. Had we just made a blanket switch, we would have had to restore each and every copy of the older version of Word back onto each person's computer. Joy. So, if an application or operating system on a user workstation corrupts, you're left with four choices;

1. Repair the operating system with either Windows ERD, Winternals ERD, or Norton for the Windows world, and Drive 10 for the Mac OS X world—if you can.

2. Restore a backed-up version that has all of the tailoring the user added.

3. Restore a corporate "image" of the application or operating system that it would equate to as an off-the-rack version of the application or operating system.

4. Allow the user to restore the application from the original CD or network-mounted application-installation directory.

Chapter 7:
Storage corruption

Remember: Corruption is a form of "tainting," decay, and decomposition. In the case of hard drives, corruption happens as normal wear and tear. Therefore, you've got to know when your drives are heading down the path of corruption beyond recovery, so you can plan for redundancy, with a spare handy; or closely monitor your drives, so that you swap them out before corruption becomes loss.

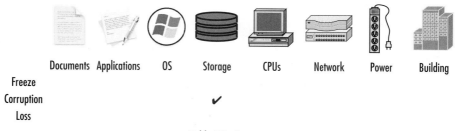

	Documents	Applications	OS	Storage	CPUs	Network	Power	Building
Freeze								
Corruption				✔				
Loss								

Table 7-1. Corruption

And your hard drive isn't the only storage media that can become corrupted. If you want to see quick corruption on a backup tape, put a new DLT tape into a DLT tape system that hasn't been cleaned for a couple of months. Within a few runs, your brand-new tape will have errors throughout, caused by dirty write heads on the tape system. So it's important to understand the nature of corruption and how to deal with it as it happens.

THE MAIN THING

Corruption happens—my drive is laced with "Word Work" files that pop up whenever Word unexpectedly quits—and that's just one example. You can shun wine, women, and song—but in case that doesn't work, let's examine some other methods to keep corruption in check relative to your documents, applications, and operating system.

Because of inevitable corruption due to wear and tear, you can't *prevent* drive failure, but you can *lessen* its impact on business continuity by creating redundant drive systems for your key computers using RAID. And because there are a gazillion variations, you might want to pay attention during that part of the chapter.

Also, understand that some drives are SMARTer than others and will predict when they're going to fail.

The Main Thing is to build redundant systems and then heed their warning *before* your drives break, be proactive in your backups, and be ready for restoration.

Special thanks

Wow, this one took a *lot* of input from a *lot* of people. First, this section was written with David Lethe of SANtools, Inc., who spoon-fed me with most of the information about SMART drive tools. Alex Grossman and Tom Goguen at Apple for talking to us about Apple's Xserve. I thank Mike Hall and Alan Dunton of Adaptec for the use of their equipment and all of their (read Alan's) direct input on RAID systems. Kate Phillips of RaidTec Corporation gave me the use of their White Paper on when to use Fibre Channel instead of Parallel SCSI.

And I don't know where I'd be without the field editors for this chapter, who include:

Terry Calvert, Bill Carn, John Shearer, Ira Solomon, Mitch Krayton, Cherie Nickell, Roger Royce, and Paul Schauble.

STORAGE FORMATS AND STORAGE CORRUPTION

Storage corruption doesn't really equate to total loss of all information stored on the drive. Often, only a small subset of all files stored on a hard drive are affected when the drive becomes corrupted. Have you ever really thought about how information is stored to the hard drive? Okay, so your life isn't *that* boring—I'm jealous. But there *are* some things you might want to know about your drives—things that you may not be aware of or take for granted that *someone* is going to fix.

A brief overview of your hard drives (and what goes wrong with them)

The hard drive is to your computer what the data center is to your organization—the nerve center where all things important are stored. Your operating system is there. Your applications are there. Your résumé for your next job is there. And, of course, the work you're doing for your boss at *this* job is there.

The platters A hard drive uses round, flat disks called **platters**. A magnetic alloy is bonded onto both sides of the hard drive platter, which, by its name, tells you that it's ferromagnetic material designed to store information in the form of magnetic patterns.

Figure 7-1. Hard drive platters

Your drive works because of magnetic writing. If you expose ferromagnetic material to a magnetic field, it's semi-permanently magnetized by the field[1], giving hard drives two of their major features:

1. You can record whatever you want on to the surface, and then

---

[1] The hard drive will "remember" the magnetic flux patterns that have been written to each disk block for a *very* long time, or until you run a magnet over the drive—whichever comes first.

2. You can rerecord whatever you want on to the surface.

In time, the ferromagnetic surface wears away, and your hard drive will die. RIP.

The spindle The platters are mounted through a hole in the center and stacked (anywhere from three to a much larger quantity) onto a **spindle**. Rotating at high speed, the platters are driven by a special **spindle motor** connected to the spindle. Eventually, the spindle system (which usually sits on a set of mini–ball bearings) begins to wear out, lengthening the spin uptime (the time it takes to get the drive moving at full speed). When the spin uptime takes too long, the system sends another "spin try" signal to it. After a certain number of spin-tries, the CPU thinks the drive is dead. You can do nothing to stop spindle wear and tear—but you can, and should, monitor the drive and replace it when it gets old.

The sliders and heads Special electromagnetic read/write devices called **heads** are mounted onto **sliders** and used to either record information onto the disk or read information from it. Through bumps and abrasions on the heads, the ferromagnetic surface can chip off, leaving potholes in your drive. When you run diagnostic software on the drive, you should run a **Rezero Unit test** to determine the drive's ability to resynchronize and re-zero the read and write heads.

Most hard drives have multiple platters on which to write their information. The data is stored on the surface of each of the platters in **sectors** and **tracks.** The tracks are the concentric circles, and the sectors are the pie-shaped wedges within the tracks, as shown in Figure 7-2. my poorly drawn diagram, below:

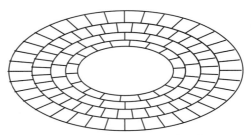

Figure 7-2. A drive's sectors and tracks

A sector contains a fixed number of bytes[2]. When you write a file to a disk, the file is written to a certain number of sectors based on the size of the file. In our example and Figure 7-3. on page 95, the diagram below (both of which are very,

very simplistic), we show our drive with two files written to it, with each file taking up the same number of sectors.

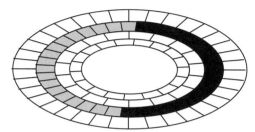

Figure 7-3. Drive with two files

The *good* news is that if (maybe *when?*) a write head bumps into the hard drive, causing a pothole, the lost information can be contained to a certain sector or certain track. Because in drives, as in blacktop, potholes are all-too-common events, mechanisms are built into the drive system to reroute the data intended for that sector and track to a new sector and track. Those areas are then sort of "roped off" —like a crime scene with caution tape—so you can't write data to them as shown in Figure 7-4.

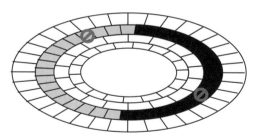

Figure 7-4. Potholes in your drive

When a utility like Norton fixes your drive, the "fix" actually blocks out the bad sectors and then reallocates the sector counts to match the fewer available sectors on the drive—think seats in a movie theatre here. If you were running a movie theatre like a hard drive, whenever a seat broke, you'd use Norton to simply block out the seat so that nobody could perch in it; then you'd adjust the reduced rate

---

2.   The size of each sector is determined by how you format your drive for your operating system. Windows has three formats (FAT32, FAT, and NTFS); the Mac OS has two (HFS and HFS+).

of available tickets by the number of seats you've blocked out. With enough blocked-out seats, you won't make any money running the theatre. With enough reallocated sectors, your drive's performance will degrade dramatically. Therefore, when completing a drive diagnostic , you'll want to perform a **Space sector check**, to see ifenough service tracks remain to isolate spare blocks for block repairs.

The arms, actuator, and logic board

The sliders are mounted onto **arms**, all of which are mechanically connected into a single assembly and positioned over the surface of the disk by a device called an **actuator**. A **logic board** controls the activity of the other components and communicates with the rest of the PC. With power spikes, the logic board can blow. A **Seek test** will check the initiator's ability to position the device heads in preparation for access to a particular logical block.

The drive's extra memory cache

Each drive has its own memory cache where certain portions of the drive are held until they can be written to the drive later. When people don't shut down their PC properly, the drive's cache doesn't get flushed the right way. In the Unix world, the write cache and the write buffer are turned off before you shut down. Enough turn-offs or power failures resulting in awkward shutdowns, and your drive's cache and buffers go Kablooey! and start causing *real* problems. Conducting **Read** and **Write Buffer tests** will check the drive's buffer cache and bus integrity.

The enclosure and cooling system

Of course, all of this activity occurs inside of a standard enclosure that has a power supply and a fan to keep it cooled. Drives can operate in outside temperatures as extreme as –30°F to 150°F, with drive operating temperatures as low as 40°F and as high as whatever the manufacturer suggests. If the cooling system (read fan[s] here) ever goes out, the drive overheats due to the spindle and electric motor creating heat within the system.

The best thing you can do on a regular basis is test your hard drives for wear and tear—and while you're at it, you might as well defragment them at the same time. No, fragmentation isn't really corruption per se, but, if it isn't kept in check, it sure can cause you pain and suffering.

FRAGMENTATION MAY NOT BE CORRUPTION...

...but it's just as bad if you let it get out of hand. When you delete applications or files from your computer, hard drive space opens up. Your computer sees a space here and a space there within your hard drive and figures that it'll store new files in whatever number of open spaces are available (as in Figure 7-5.), because it knows it can track the location of a non-contiguous file through the **Master File Table (MFT)**.

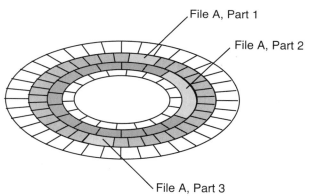

File A, Part 1

File A, Part 2

File A, Part 3

Figure 7-5. Non-contiguous file storage

When an application creates a file, the file system looks for a place to put the file, making a file entry in the Master File Table (MFT). The MFT contains pointers indicating the starting **Logical Cluster Number (LCN)** for the file, and the file length. If the file is fragmented, the MFT has a series of pointers with a starting LCN and a length for each fragment. The file is then physically written to the disk by the disk controller. With a new drive, the mapping between the file system's LCN and the **Physical Cluster Number (PCN)** is probably a one-to-one relationship. However, as a disk ages and develops bad sectors, the mapping between LCN and PCN will change.

Over time, as more and more of your files are strewn about your hard drive like empty beer bottles in a frat house, reassembling those fragmented files takes longer and longer.

How bad can the fragmentation get?

Well, Ohio Savings Bank found that if they ran a defragmentation program called PerfectDisk once a week on their computer systems, it would improve that computer's performance by 30 percent, and would save them about three hours per reported trouble ticket on tech support calls for "slow computers.[3]" Sources can be found all over the Microsoft website as to why and when you'd want to defragment your computers' hard drives[4], and, as stated on the Microsoft site in numerous places, fragmentation begins almost immediately after you fire up your hard drive. Raxco Software, the makers of one of the better Windows-based defragmentation tools, conducted a test scenario in which they installed Windows NT 4 and its Service Packs, Internet Explorer, and Microsoft Office on a new drive. There were 4,747 files on the disk, and 399 of these files were fragmented. The Master File Table (MFT) was in 95 fragments; the registry in 325 fragments, and the MS Office Program Files folder was in 267 fragments[5]. That's a lot of fragments.

A couple of years ago, IDC (International Data Corporation) conducted defragmentation tests on selected Windows NT and Windows 2000 workstations and servers[6]. Here's what they found:

- 74 and 80 percent performance boosts respectively on two separate Windows NT workstations.

- 19 and 56 percent performance improvements, respectively, on two separate Windows NT servers.

[3.] "Defragmenting Workstation Disks Boosts Ohio Savings Bank System Performance 30 Percent." (2002). Raxco Software.

[4.] Go to http://support.microsoft.com and type in *defragment* in their search field. Because the number of documents is so numerous, we've chosen to give you the directions to find them instead of listing them here.

[5.] "Six Reasons You Need Defragmentation Software on Windows NT/2000/XP." (2002). Raxco Software.

[6.] "Defrag Disks for Real Savings. Info-Tech Advisor, and Disk Defragmentation for Windows NT/ 2000: Hidden Gold for the Enterprise." (2000). IDC.

- Even higher performance improvements on Windows 2000 servers and workstations. A 4 GB drive on a 400 MHz Pentium II workstation saw improved performance of 219 percent.

What does this cost your organization?

There are a lot of theories on the cost of fragmentation. We know that fragmentation *definitely* affects the backup process, because the more fragmented the hard drive, the slower the backup. We know that fragmentation slows down server access, database access, and general computer access. Here's what we consider the most reasonable fragmentation cost analysis (Figure 7-6.). You can find the actual form on our backupbook.com website.

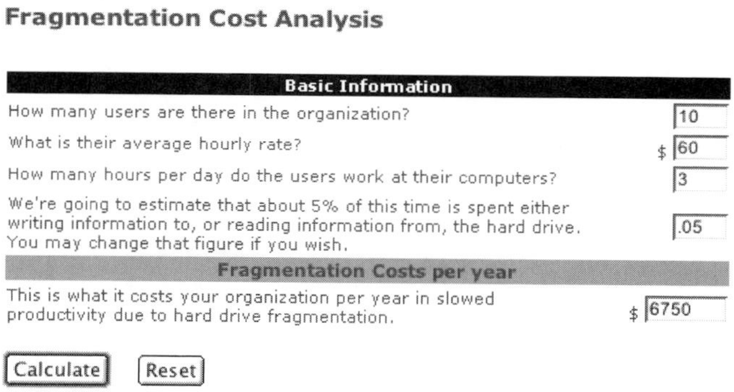

Fragmentation Cost Analysis

Basic Information	
How many users are there in the organization?	10
What is their average hourly rate?	$ 60
How many hours per day do the users work at their computers?	3
We're going to estimate that about 5% of this time is spent either writing information to, or reading information from, the hard drive. You may change that figure if you wish.	.05
Fragmentation Costs per year	
This is what it costs your organization per year in slowed productivity due to hard drive fragmentation.	$ 6750

[Calculate] [Reset]

Figure 7-6. Fragmentation cost analysis

The calculation for the above form is as follows for a 250-day year, assuming that defragmentation is going to speed up the computer system by 30 percent (which is what all reports state).

$$\left(\left(\text{Users} \times \frac{\text{Rate}}{\text{Usage}}\right) \times \text{Access}\right) \times 250$$

Figure 7-7. Fragmentation calculation

We've calculated the cost for a small workgroup of 10 users who work at their computers about three hours per day (Figure 7-6.). With a very average base pay, and the users either hitting the Save button or launching new files about 5 percent of the three hours they spend at their computer per day, the cost of fragmentation for this group runs about $6,750 per year. This isn't taking into account heavy users or lost time due to help-desk support calls, either.

Tools

Windows 95/98 included a disk defragmentation utility, but Windows NT 4 did not. Windows 2000 includes the capability again, but its implementation is underwhelming at best. Apple has never included a disk defragging tool. Unix has one built into the operating system. On the whole, the Unix system works great, but you'll need third-party tools

Drive 10 ⓧ

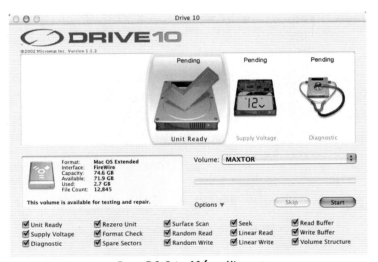

Figure 7-8. Drive 10 from Micromat

There's really only one tool for the Macintosh OS X market: Micromat's Drive 10. Micromat's original monitoring and diagnostic utility, MacEKG, was used by NASA on space-shuttle flight STS-51 to test the effects of microgravity on digital electronic equipment in space—the first such experiment in history—and it worked flawlessly. Back on Earth, the Micromat folks have worked up a nice package in the form of Drive 10.

Sporting a sleek Aqua interface (Figure 7-8. on page 100), this advanced disk repair and recovery product has been designed exclusively for Mac OS X. As well as repairing drives and recovering data, Drive 10 provides automatic, regular backups of important volume structure data. The Mac OS X file system uses a variety of invisible files, settings, and parameters to locate files, free disk space, and for other maintenance and management routines. These are known collectively as the **volume structure**. The Catalog and Disk Directory are parts of the volume structure. Damage to these and other critical structures can result in lost or damaged data that could require a complete reformat of the media. Reformatting a drive destroys *all* data on the media.

Drive 10 can scan your drives and repair problems related to the numerous structures necessary for the volume to operate correctly. If problems are found, Drive 10 can often repair these problems and resurrect your drive. When Drive 10 finds a problem, it builds a new set of volume structures instead of patching the old structures, as other utilities do. This is the surest and safest method of recovering your valuable data. Drive 10 can also be utilized for drive optimization. Figure 7-9. depicts the analysis of my iPod's drive. The bubbly, dark areas are the used space, and the little bubbles within them are the disk and file fragments.

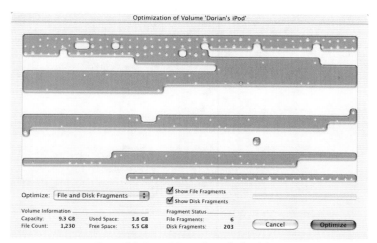

Figure 7-9. Drive 10's analysis of a hard drive

Diskeeper Server and Workstation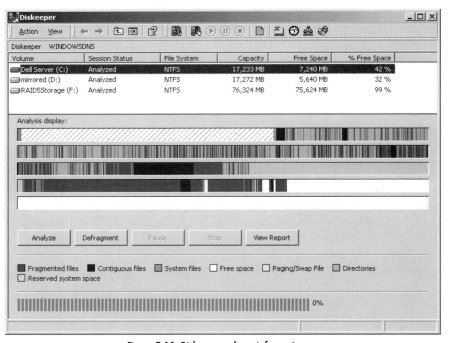

Diskeeper from Executive Software comes in two flavors—Server and Workstation. With this combination of products, the network manager can manage the schedules of a full site deployment in just a few clicks (we know because we tested it).

We installed Diskeeper on our Windows 2000 server (Figure 7-10.) to examine our three logical volumes. Our boot drive is the one highlighted showing massive fragmentation.

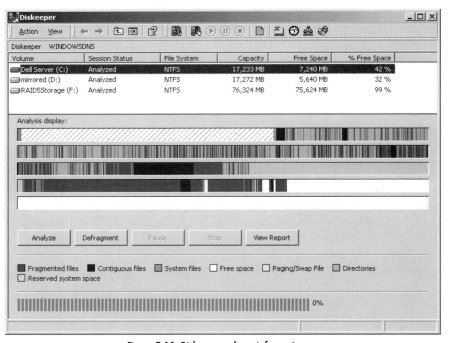

Figure 7-10. Diskeeper volume information

Here's the report in a nutshell: Total fragmentation for our boot volume was 20 percent, with 31 percent of our files fragmented; 7 percent of our free space fragmented; and 7 percent of our directories fragmented, as well. Defragmentation was set to run in the background and took about about 35 minutes.

Setting a schedule

Setting an automatic schedule for our networked workstations to defragment themselves was a three-click process. First, I clicked the main screen to get to the window shown below. The second click selected the individual computers (okay, so I fudged the numbers a bit, because you have to click each computer you want to select). The third click, on the **Set Schedule** button, selected the "smart schedule" to run every day (it's the default).

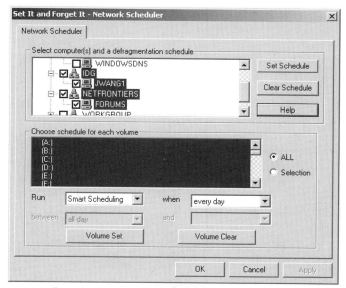

Figure 7-11. Setting a networked defragmentation schedule

After examining all of the scheduling options available (you know, those scintillating morning staff meetings, lunch, whatever), we decided on Diskeeper's Smart Scheduling feature (Figure 7-11.). With Smart Scheduling enabled, Diskeeper keeps track of the number of files that are moved around the drive each time it runs its defragmentation operations. Once it spots a trend—say, an increased amount of drive activity—Diskeeper automatically schedules itself to run more often. As it sees a decrease in activity, it'll shift its schedule to run less often. Very smart, this tool.

Smart Scheduling can also be set to run in an "enveloped window" so that it runs only on certain days and between certain time periods. This great feature ensures that Smart Schedule isn't running when your backups are running—now *that* would be bad.

PerfectDisk ⊞

Like its competitor, Executive Software's Diskeeper, PerfectDisk uses the hard drive defragmentation APIs built into Microsoft Windows NT, Windows 2000, and Windows XP. These APIs ensure that no data is lost in the defragmentation process, even if several other programs are using the hard drive at the same time. The APIs let users defragment drives on file and application servers without taking the servers offline.

PerfectDisk includes a scheduler feature that automatically defragments your drive at predetermined intervals. As with Diskeeper, a network administrator can schedule defragmentation sessions on client PCs strewn across the network. Diskeeper includes this feature only in its more expensive network version; Raxco offers network scheduling in all versions of PerfectDisk.

PerfectDisk uses a patented disk-optimization strategy that keeps track of file usage over time. If a group of files doesn't change over the course of several PerfectDisk sessions, the program doesn't try to move those files during subsequent defragmentation sessions. Consequently, frequent defragmentations take less time.

For best results when you defragment volumes, follow these tips:

- Analyze volumes regularly and defragment them only when your disk defragmenter recommends it, or set your system to autopilot and have it run once a week in server environments. If you seldom need to defragment volumes, analyze volumes monthly instead of weekly.

- Defragment a volume before you add a large number of files to the volume; for example, before you install programs. If you do so, the files occupy contiguous space and don't become fragmented after you add them.

- Defragment a volume after you delete a large number of files from the volume. Because they might become excessively fragmented when you add a large number of files or folders, make sure to analyze volumes after you add a large number of files or folder. Generally, you should defragment volumes on busy file servers more often than volumes on single-user workstations.

- Defragment a volume after you install programs on it. Volumes often become fragmented after you install software. Disk Defragmenter helps to ensure optimal file system performance.

- Defragment the system and boot volumes after you install Windows 2000 or after you perform Windows upgrades.

- Defragment volumes during periods of low system activity. Defragment file server volumes during low-volume usage periods to minimize the effect that the defragmentation process has on file server performance. The time that Disk Defragmenter takes to defragment a volume depends on several factors, including the size of the volume, the number of files on the volume, the number of fragmented files, and the available system resources.

By the way, some errors are normal

I'm a pretty fast typist. About 100+ words per minute. That's because I type a *heck* of a lot (seven books now, including this one) *and* because I use Microsoft Word, which has *automatic error correction* built into the system. As I type misspelled words, Word automatically changes them so that I don't have to (*thik* automatically changes to *think*, for example). Same thing with hard drives.

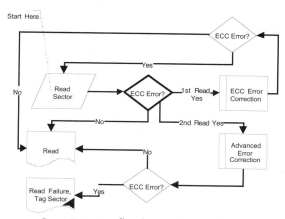

Figure 7-12. Error flow diagram for a hard drive

Errors that occur when reading information from a hard drive are very common. So common, in fact, that hard drive manufacturers have built error management logic into the devices' logic boards. It looks something like the flow diagram (Figure 7-12. on page 105) above.

Of course, if these read failures start to happen more frequently, chances are that something bad is happening to the drive platter(s)—maybe one of the read/write heads crashed, causing a pothole, or two or three. Just as the manufacturers have built in error detecting and handling logic, they've also built certain types of hard drives with the capability of monitoring *and reporting* a whole host of errors that drives typically encounter. However, what the drive can monitor and report depends upon whether it's a SCSI drive (more expensive) or a EIDE/ATA drive (less expensive). Let's take a quick look at some of the differences between SCSI and EIDE/ATA drives, and the ways that two server vendors (Dell and Apple) have approached the mid-range server line using SCSI (Dell) and EIDE/ATA (Apple).

Hard drive interfaces—differences between SCSI and EIDE/ATA

Let's interface, you know? Let's talk. Let's connect. I'll call you. While these familiar phrases are reminiscent of Hollywood doubletalk, they're far more straightforward than that—they're the way computers talk to their drives. In compuspeak, the way a CPU and operating system *interface* with a drive or drive-set is the way they *communicate* with that drive. For hard disk drives, several interfaces are currently popular: the IDE family (IDE, Enhanced IDE, and ATA), the SCSI family (Ultra SCSI, Ultra2 SCSI, Ultra160 SCSI), SSA, and Fibre Channel. Each has its own peculiarities and advantages. Sometimes the interface is like a phone call (two-way simultaneous communication) and sometimes like a walkie-talkie (one-way, non-simultaneous communication). For our purposes, we'll cover the main differences between SCSI and ATA (which is another name for EIDE).

You need to know the basics of these interfaces so that you can understand the differences in operation (and cost), in how long they'll probably live before dying on you, and in how well they can perform self-diagnostics so that they can predict what's wrong with them and how soon they are going to die. Making a choice between these interfaces may not seem obvious at first glance, but looking further into the matter should make it clearer, as structural differences between the two alternatives influence the system throughout its lifetime. Below we show how to vendors, Dell and Apple, have deployed servers for the same market. Dell chose the traditional SCSI route, and Apple the ATA route. We present this information solely so that you can see that, while everyone might argue the merits for or against SCSI or ATA, if properly configured and used right, either of them will work for you.

SCSI drives

There are two types of SCSI: Serial, which includes Fibre Channel, FireWire, and Parallel SCSI (the most common SCSI). Most of this section concerns Parallel SCSI.

The **Small Computer Systems Interface (SCSI)** has a controller with its own bus and set of instructions that make SCSI an intelligent interface that hides a device's physical format from the computer's processor. You can mix and match all kinds of devices on one Parallel SCSI controller: Up to 15 SCSI IDs plus the SCSI adapter can be attached to a single-wide SCSI bus (and up to seven on a standard SCSI bus).

Unlike EIDE devices, SCSI devices can also be attached to the computer externally through a direct cable connection[7]. In Figure 7-13. , we show a Dell PowerEdge 1650, 1U[8] rack-mount server's backside. Internally, this server can hold three SCSI drives in its bay. However, the device also has two PCI slots that you can plug SCSI cards into in order to attach additional drives, such as a whole box of drives in a RAID bank.

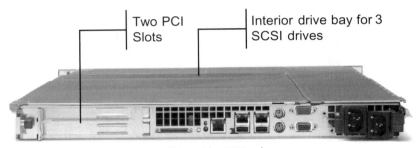

Two PCI Slots

Interior drive bay for 3 SCSI drives

Figure 7-13. Dell PowerEdge 1650 rack-mount server

Expandability isn't the most important difference between SCSI and EIDE. Most significant is the ways the two accept requests for processing. EIDE acts on requests in the order in which they're received, processing and completing one task at a time (hey, it's very single-minded). Very much like a walkie-talkie conversation, in which one person speaks and the other listens, and vice versa. SCSI, on the other hand, supports the multithreading capabilities available in the Microsoft Windows 2000 and Unix worlds. Windows and Unix are optimized to support multitasking so that applications can share resources equally and run concurrently, eliminating the I/O bottleneck created by traditional single-tasking as is found in Windows 95 or Macintosh OS 9. This interface is much like a two-

---

7. While you *can* attach IDE drives externally, there is no such thing as an IDE cable connector. You have to use a USB, FireWire, SCSI, or Fibre Channel cable to connect to an external drive enclosure, and then a SCSI, FireWire, USB, or Fibre Channel to IDE bridge to connect to the drive inside of the enclosure.

8. *1U* refers to how many units of rack space a server takes up. A *U* equals 1.75 inches (height) in size. Hence, a 1U takes up one server space, and a 2U takes up two spaces (3.5 inches).

way telephone conversation wherein both people can speak at once, just like my sister and mother do when they are on the phone (I've always wondered how they understand each other).

In addition, Windows 2000, Unix, and SCSI also support multithreading. **Multithreading** allows multiple applications to conduct multiple I/O transactions simultaneously. The application can accomplish other work while it's waiting for the result of a prior task. A very simple example is a user who saves a document to the local disk drive while printing the same document in the background.

IDE, EIDE/ATA

IDE stands for Integrated Drive Electronics. Drives capable of bus mastering are **EIDE** drives. This is the common name given to the **ATA** disk drive format popularly used in PCs today. Usually, an ATA drive connects directly to the motherboard.

Enhanced IDE (EIDE) improves upon its predecessor by offering greater support in demanding environments, supporting faster data transfer rates with up to 66 MBps burst rate—and higher disk capacities—with capacity up to 137 GB. Most of today's EIDE drives support Ultra DMA Mode 2 at 33 MBps, and are called various names, including Ultra ATA.

EIDE enjoys a considerable price advantage over SCSI because the interface and electronics are simpler and the hard drives sell in much higher volume, with many more competing suppliers. EIDE satisfies the price and performance requirements of most desktop and mobile computing environments, and now, with the introduction of Apple's Xserve box and its innovative use of EIDE, ATA drives will undoubtedly show up in more servers.

Apple's Xserve implementation of ATA

Think different—think ATA. Most of Apple's competitors turned to the Ultra-SCSI drive buses in their servers because an ATA bus technology laden with multiple drives simply can't handle the kinds of simultaneous access that SCSI is designed to handle. However, Ultra-SCSI is more expensive than ATA. Not opting for the "Sophie's Choice" of the high price of SCSI or low performance of a single ATA bus, Apple has outdesigned their competitors by putting each of the drives on their *own independent bus*, much as the folks at Adaptec and others do with their RAID ATA cards. The Xserve can thus hit full ATA performance without the slow-down problems associated with high-use ATA systems, thus keeping costs down and performance high (a first in the server world).

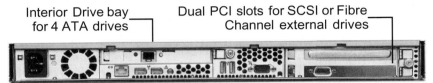

Figure 7-14. Rear view of Apple's Xserve

Alex Grossman, hardware director for the Xserve box (Figure 7-14.), gave me this input:

> While Dell offers an optional Hardware RAID solution based on ROMB[9] technology, they offer only three SCSI hard drives in the 1U form factor. In that configuration, they employ a single SCSI 160 bus (their second bus is external). This bus has good bandwidth for three drives, but offers limited use for HW RAID, as sophisticated and expected options such as hot sparing aren't practical with only three drives. The use of SCSI drives today limits their capacity to 3x73 or 219 GB versus Xserve's 480 GB capacity. With a single SCSI bus, they have little bus isolation, and it's possible to hang the bus with a drive failure, resulting in inaccessibility of the remaining drives until the failed drive can be removed.
>
> Xserve's unique quad independent ATA drive subsystem provides up to four independent ATA-100 hard drives with dedicated controllers providing drive isolation and throughput superior to Ultra 160 SCSI (400 MB/s at the controllers and 266 MB/s at the dedicated Storage subsystem PCI bus). The implementation of RAID 0 and RAID 1 in software with dual processors essentially has little or no impact on processor performance, and helps to keep Xserve cost-effective, with high throughput. Another way to look at this is that ATA, which is normally single-threaded (in a master/slave configuration), is now multithreaded by using four independent buses that can be communicated with simultaneously by both processors.

When asked about how Apple overcomes the multithreading limitation of ATA (it doesn't do it, while SCSI does), Alex stated, "Using the four-bus technology,

---

9. *ROMB* stands for *Raid On Mother Board*, the same thing as Adaptec's zero channel RAID.

you can send multiple commands to all of the hard drives on the channel in a [parallel] fashion, and then each drive will go off, get its data, and be prepared to send it off to the channel." The information will be "stacked up and ready to go" as it returns. To put things in perspective, he gave this insight: "We effectively have multithreading through the use of multiple [four] channels. We have multiple single-threaded channels." In theory, this should provide the same throughput as a single multithreaded channel. In reality, according to Apple, they have the advantage over a single-channel system if a drive fails and hangs the entire bus, thus hanging the entire computer, because nothing can get through to the rest of the drives. For external drive connectivity, Apple has two full-length PCI cards. Therefore, you can connect through either a SCSI interface or Fibre Channel interface.

What these comparisons fail to mention...

What these two simplistic descriptions of SCSI, ATA, and the ways they can be deployed in a server environment fail to mention is legion. We're not trying to dump a textbook on you—just the basics about both options, and the fact that, despite its limitations, ATA can be implemented in a mid-range server environment. As field editor Roger Royce pointed out so aptly in an e-mail to me:

> IDE requires step-by-step control of [the] hard drive physical function through software drivers (an IDE drive is really very dumb), whereas SCSI is off loading the CPU of almost all the overhead of access. The OS just says to SCSI "Give me a file," and SCSI delivers it, whereas with IDE, the OS (through the IDE driver) must micromanage the entire access process of the drive (including handling fragmentation, etc., for example). CPU cycles *do* count—and there are only so many of them. That's why there are such things as performance monitoring software and tools in operating systems like Win 2000, XP, Unix, etc.

> But there's so much more [to know about SCSI versus ATA], about how SCSI reorders seeks, generally has some type of hardware data cache to boost performance, has drivers specifically oriented toward network server needs, has higher reliability in its drives (versus ICE), etc. More reading is in order to get a fuller understanding of these and other concepts.

Pick up a copy of Alting Mees' *Hard Drive Encyclopedia* (Annabooks, 1991). It'll tell you everything that you've ever wanted to know about hard drives.

SMART PRECLUDES DUMB...

Wouldn't it be nice to have an automated system telling you that your head is flying too high, that your spin count is way low, and that your seek and throughput performance is off—for your hard drive, at least? Believe it or not, such a system has been in place since 1996, but most of us haven't enabled it on our computers[10]. The technology that allows this type of automated monitoring is called **SMART (Self-Monitoring, Analysis, and Reporting Technology)**, and it's a diagnostic method and technology originally developed by IBM for mainframe drives.

Compaq then created a full specification based upon that IBM initiative so that it could be used with a variety of drives from a variety of manufactures at the PC level. They then submitted their specification to the ATA/IDE standards committee, and the SMART standard was created (after a great deal of haggling and angst, I suspect). Below is an excerpt from the official ATA-4 specification[11] (with some editorializing from us):

> 5.10 Self-monitoring, analysis, and reporting technology feature set
>
> The intent of self-monitoring, analysis, and reporting technology (the SMART feature set) is to protect user data and minimize the likelihood of unscheduled system downtime that may be caused by predictable degradation and/or fault of the device. By monitoring and storing critical performance and calibration parameters, SMART feature set devices attempt to predict the likelihood of near-term degradation or fault condition.

Okay, there are two types of reporting: predictable (that which degrades over time) and "out of the blue" faults (like the time the janitor kicked the drive at midnight during cleaning operations, knocking it over and crashing the heads before he sneaked it back on the shelf). SMART will report on both (well, it won't tell

---

10. This is only *just* becoming a part of the Macintosh world, with the introduction of Apple's Xserve Unix-based Enterprise server.

11. (ANSI X3T13/1153D Revision 8).

you that the janitor did it, but that a massive problem happened, and when). The definition says further:

> Providing the host system the knowledge of a negative reliability condition, allows the host system to warn the user of the impending risk of a data loss and advise the user of appropriate action...

The SMART specification is a way to enable early warning of some hard disk drive failures. When the SMART hard disk drive detects drive errors that indicate an impending failure, a warning message is sent to either the end user, management application or SNMP monitoring tool, so data can be backed up and the drive replaced, thus avoiding the necessity for significant data recovery efforts. *Even though your computer and drive (or even backup software) is SMART-aware, you have to implement software to continually monitor for messages and alerts.*

There's *really* SMART and then *not so* SMART

SMART drives won't read the data on your disk to inform you that you forgot today's "to do" (flowers for your wife's birthday) and that she's awaiting you at the front door with a hatchet in lieu of a kiss. And they won't be able to predict upcoming power failures, election results in Argentina, or that glorious day America will win the World Cup—these things are too unpredictable. However, the SMART technology can and does look for a great many *predictable* failures. Predictable failures can be characterized by the degradation of an attribute over time—before the drive has a chance to fail.

If a drive attribute can be monitored and compared against a drive's specification (such as seek time or throughput), a predictive failure can be analyzed and reported over time. Mechanical deviations due to continual normal use (head flying height, spin uptime, spin retry count, drive calibration) account for approximately 60 percent of all known failures. Disk drives equipped with SMART make a status report to the host (or other monitoring software) when they detect degradation with these drive attributes. SMART drives have a massive amount of generic reporting categories; too many to name here.

However, not all drives report the same information. IDE drives use internal registers. The base registers monitored and reported by SMART firmware in IDE disks are shown on the left in Table 7-2. below:

Description	Number
Raw Read Error Rate	1
Throughput Performance	2
Spin Up Time	3
Start/Stop Count	4
Reallocated Sector Count	5
Read Channel Margin	6
Seek Error Rate	7
Seek Time Performance	8
Power On Hours Count	9
Spin Retry Count	10
Calibration Retry Count	11
Power Cycle Count	12

Description	Number
Reallocation Description Event Count	196
Current Pending Sector Count	197
Off-Line Scan Uncorrectable Sector Count	198
Ultra DMA CRC Error Count	199

Table 7-2. SMART firmware IDE descriptors (left) and additions from IBM (right)

In addition, vendors are free to add their own. For example, David's IBM Travelstar disk also reports additional information as shown on right in Table 7-2. above.

SCSI drives use sense keys, codes, and SMART information (divided into the categories of **keys (K)**, **additional sense codes (ASC)**, and **additional sense qualifiers (ASQ)**, as well as vendor-specific information (such as shown in the table below), but because each drive manufacturer handles commands differently, don't expect consistency in their different command sets. Table 7-3. is an excerpt from one manufacturer's key, code, and qualifier listing, depicting four different qualifiers for the Track Following Error qualifier.

K	ASC	ASQ	Vendor		Comments
1	09	00	-	-	Track Following Error.
1	09	00	02	60	Servo error - Excessive Runout - recalibrate requested from Servo.
1	09	00	02	61	Servo error - Timed out waiting for PES interrupt.
1	09	00	02	62	Servo error - Settle timeout.
1	09	00	02	63	Servo error - Three consecutive bad SIDs (track follow).

Table 7-3. Sample IBM tools

Why should you give a hoot about these tables? Look at them again. Notice something? Again, SCSI is at the top of the heap because its table can convey extremely detailed information about the state of your hard drive. You get what you pay for. If you want limited information about the drive going bad, get an ATA drive. If you want to know the minutest details about which elements could be degrading, get SCSI. In my humble opinion, people using very intensive drive operations should never use ATA.

SMART drives on your computer

While SMART Drives are made by the big five: IBM, Seagate, Western Digital Corporation, Quantum, and Maxtor, and are present in a great many Windows, Mac, and Unix boxes, as of this writing, these companies aren't wearing themselves out to enable this feature on the computer or to allow software companies to take advantage of it. To implement SMART, the host computer must have a device driver in the BIOS and/or application software capable of sending SMART commands to and from the disk and the disk's firmware.

Many motherboards (such as those from Dell and Compaq) have the ability to check for SMART information. However, they check only during the boot process, and if the computer's drive runs into a problem after it boots (say a week later, in the case of a server), you're out of luck.

When you get your computer out of the box, if you do nothing else, it will check for SMART pre-failures at boot time only, so if you don't reboot your system every day, you get no further information. However, if you put additional software on your computer (such as SMARTmon from SANtools[12]), you'll get full-time monitoring and reporting.

SMART drives on the Apple Xserve

Apple's new SMART hard drive management system is able to leverage the Unix operating system to *fully* connect with their hardware. Unix admins running automatic notification get an e-mail, page, or phone message that a drive is heading for failure *before* it happens, so they can respond *proactively.*. Starting with IBM's and Seagate's pre-fail hard drive standards, Apple asked, "What are the typical pre-fails that they have and how would that apply in the use of a server?" Once they had their data set, Apple then processed this information into an XML file as a set

12. http://www.santools.com

of management rules. "As soon as a drive meets the standards for a pre-fail bit at any one of the SMART data points, we announce that information to the SNMP MIB and management software" explained Tom Goguen, director of software development for Apple's Xserve box. Because of the tight integration between Unix software and Apple hardware, notification lights are set on both levels, and XML data is written not only to the log file, but to the hard drive itself.

It should be noted, though, that while Apple is seemingly aware of the fact that "on head 4 of track 71, the drive had 10 retries," all they announce and show in management software is "the yellow light," indicating a predictive failure notice from the drive.

How much pre-alert time is there?

The vendors are shooting for a minimum of around 48 hours before the disk fails. They *try* to hit this mark, but cold, cruel reality can vary greatly. "You really don't know if you have minutes or days," says field editor David Lethe, "I once had a PC that would boot or wouldn't. It turns out after I wrote some code, I found it had a SMART error that had been going on for months."

Being SMART isn't everything

Ich glaube ich bin im film![13] There are two types of server admins, and you can figure out which one you are by taking this simple one-question test. You're in a deserted house with three friends when you hear a chainsaw roaring behind you. Two of your friends, mute with fear, start pointing over your shoulder. The other friend faints dead away in sheer terror after managing to utter a frenzied "Watch out!" Do you A) Turn around and scream as the bad guy cuts you up into bite-sized chunks, or B) Heed the warning and flatten Mr. Meanie with a roundhouse back kick, sending his lower parts into his upper parts? If you're of the *B* ilk, you're a good candidate for SMART drives because you'll heed their warnings and do something about them. If you chose *A*, SMART will simply beget DUMB (Disasters Usually Motivate Backups).

- SMART will tell you to back up your drive because something bad is imminent (if it's hooked up to your backup software).

---

13. That's a contribution from Karsten that means "I think I'm in a horror movie!"

- SMART will tell you to take the drive offline and fix it.

That is, *if* you have the software enabled and the software knows what to do with a SMART declaration from the drive. We cover that below.

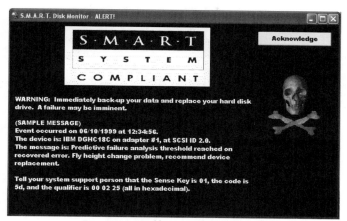

*Figure 7-15. Would **you** ignore this warning?*

Since this is an overview of SMART only, we don't show actual setup info here. Be patient, though: We cover that in detail in the hands-on sections to follow.

When it comes to drive enclosures, it's better to be SES/SAF-TE than sorry

Okay, that was bad—but I couldn't help myself. I've been writing this bloody chapter now for about 20 days, and I'm going batty. And, since I'm a generous guy, I must share all—even awful puns—with you, dear readers. But back to the Main Thing—which is discussing why monitoring external drive enclosures (we cover these in the hardware loss chapter) is a good thing. They have parts that break—like their cooling systems—and parts that don't break very often—like their power supplies. But, inevitably, break they will. And you'll want to know about it when (and hopefully before) that blessed event occurs.

SAF-TE-based intelligent controllers provide indicators about the health of the enclosure and its key components, including the state of the RAID drives in the enclosure, as well as failure and maintenance information. This information is provided through SES for Fibre Channel and SAF-TE for SCSI.

Companies like Granite Digital have created external hard drive kits that feature SMART technology, such as their FIREVue case kit, shown in Figure 7-16. below, which houses an external FireWire-driven IDE hard drive.

Figure 7-16. Granite Digital's FIREVue SMART case kit

While Granite Digital claims that FIREVue will "tell you everytyhing you wanted to know" about your hard drive, it will tell you only what it *can* tell you. Basically, the information that can be reported is as follows for SES: Disks (called **devices** in the spec); power supplies; cooling elements (fans); temperature sensors; door locks; audible alarms; services electronics; SCC electronics; non-volatile caches; uninterruptible power supplies; displays; keypad entry devices; SCSI port/transceivers; language defined; communication ports; voltage sensors; current sensors; SCSI target ports; and SCSI initiator ports.

The information for SAF-TE-enabled devices is a bit slimmer: It supports power, cooling, door locks, temperature, and device status. Doesn't SMART report that information? Yup, you betcha. *Good* SMART-disk software will know that, reporting a disk error only once instead of twice (once using SMART and once using SES/SAF-TE). Figure 7-17. on page 119 shows a single window from SANtools' S.M.A.R.T. Disk Monitor application depicting information from an SES/SAF-TE-compliant enclosure.

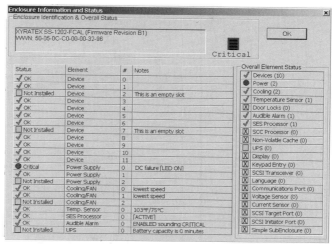

Figure 7-17. SES/SAF-TE reporting from S.M.A.R.T. Disk Monitor

 # The basics of enabling SMART monitoring

First, you must get your SMART drive set up and running. Next, figure out what your software will *do* with the warning messages, and what you'll do when you get them. *Remember, by default, even though your computer might support SMART monitoring, unless you have a specific tool for reporting, you won't know what's wrong until boot time.*

Adenix S.M.A.R.T. Explorer and SMART Indicator ⊞

Adenix S.M.A.R.T. Explorer is an application and underlying API that lets you monitor reliability and performance of SMART-compatible ATA/ATAPI devices installed on your local Windows computer. Adenix S.M.A.R.T. indicator is a *freeware* Windows (95-XP) shell extension that provides an interface to S.M.A.R.T. capabilities of IDE/ATAPI drives. A new sheet is added to the drive property page:

• Navigate explorer to "My Computer" and right-click a drive.

• Select Properties in the pop-up menu.

The S.M.A.R.T. tab pops up in the new window, which looks like the one in Figure 7-18. below.

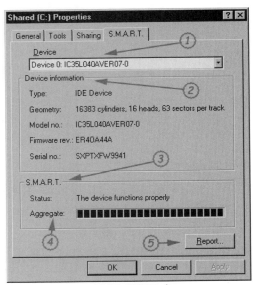

Figure 7-18. SMART Indicator

Here's what's happening onscreen:

1. IDE/ATAPI device. Note that in Windows 95/98/Me, all compatible devices are listed here. In Windows 2000/2K/XP, you'll see the device associated with the drive.

2. Drive information section shows generic information about the selected device.

3. S.M.A.R.T. section displays S.M.A.R.T.-related information .

4. Aggregate bar displays reliability rating for the device. Full bar means "reliable" and empty bar means "pre-failure/advisory" warning.

5. Report button generates HTML report containing S.M.A.R.T.-related information on the devices installed in your system.

FWB SMART Toolkit ⓧ

FWB has entered the fray with its SMART Toolkit, the first general-purpose Mac OS X software for SMART alerts. This very simple software has the potential to grow as the Mac market accepts SMART monitoring and seeks more information and reporting. The application has two windows. One, shown below (Figure 7-19.), is the drive view window, which shows the status of the drives and notes whether or not they're supported for SMART monitoring. The other, a preferences window, allows the user to set an e-mail address for receiving SMART alerts and opt whether or not to receive additional regular reporting. Reports can also be sent to a web page on the local computer (handy for running SMART Toolkit on web servers).

Figure 7-19. SMART Toolkit window

SANtools S.M.A.R.T. Disk Monitor ⊞ ⚙

This is the best program we've found so far for monitoring and reporting on system-wide SMART disks, because, while it's enabled on a local computer, it has e-mail notification capabilities so that you can let the backup administrator know if a drive is having *particular* problems—problems that you've set thresholds for yourself. If I were running an important server that shipped with ATA drives (and many of them do these days), I'd absolutely make sure I was running this software because of ATA drives' short life span compared to SCSI drives' longevity.

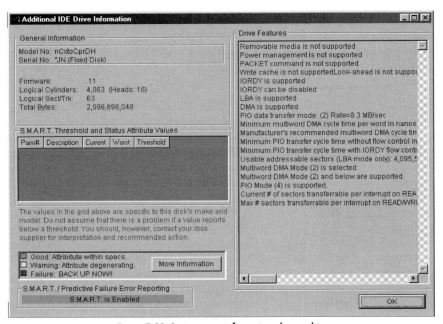

Figure 7-20. Seeing more information about a drive

Once you've installed SANtools on your computer, you can set it to open into the normal size mode, or have it auto-launch and open in minimized mode so that you see only the icon in the tools section of the bottom-right side of your window—which is what we recommend. To see a drive's SMART reporting capabilities, a pop-up window (different for IDE than for SCSI and Fibre Channel), shows specific information about the drive and its features. Looking at Figure 7-20. , you can tell if SMART is enabled for this drive by the green "enabled" indicator or the red "not enabled" notice in the bottom-left window.

Setting up alert rules

Once you've configured the alert status e-mail services (under the **Alert** menu), you need to set alert rules. This is where the rubber meets the road. You can use the default rules that come with the program (they're different for every drive type) or you can modify the rules already present, tailoring them to your own business needs. I tend to be more aggressive than the folks who made the software when it comes to sending out predictive failures for drives on servers—especially on the ATA drives that are now widespread throughout the industry. I'd rather endure a dozen false alarms than have to spend the wee hours calling computer catalog companies in search of a new drive.

To set your alert rules, check the **Alert Rule Set** by selecting **Alerts>Maintain Rulesets for Displaying and Sending Alerts**. When you select this menu item, the window shown below (Figure 7-21.) will appear, showing your basic pre-defined alert rules.

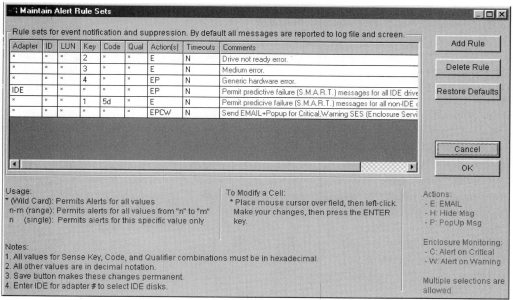

Figure 7-21. Alert rule set

The basics are enough to get you going and notify you of the worst types of failures. Once you're comfortable with the basics, you might want to do some further reading (a quick Google search will kick-start your syllabus) to become a SMART expert.

Setting up statistical alerts (pre-pre-fail alerts)

Whenever data is returned by SMART devices to the SMARTmon software, that data is filtered through the rule sets (Figure 7-22. on page 124). If the rule sets allow the error to pass (which means that the drive isn't about to fail), the message is forwarded to reporting logic and logged. You can choose to ignore this information (as most folks do), or you can set your own filters so that you'll be notified when the software picks up the specific thresholds you've defined (such as read or write errors that would cause a problem, but not a pre-failure notification).

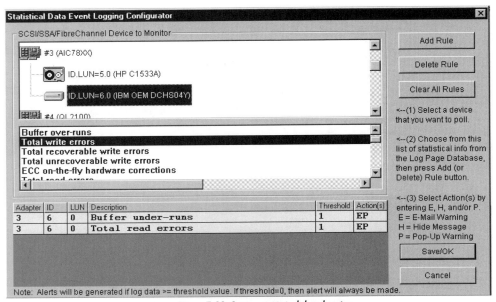

Figure 7-22. Setting statistical data logging

With access to these lower-threshold statistics *before* a drive registers a fail, you'll be armed and ready for potential faulty devices when the alert comes. This is particularly useful in the audio/video world, where failure thresholds are significantly lower than those in other fields.

CHAPTER 8:
NETWORK CORRUPTION

What is corruption? The dictionary describes it as the process of *tainting* something. I really do like that word. When you talk about network corruption, you aren't talking about the network vanishing (as if somebody stole its parts), you're talking about something happening during the movement of data from point A to point B wherein the data becomes *tainted,* and parts of it arrive at the destination no longer in their original condition.

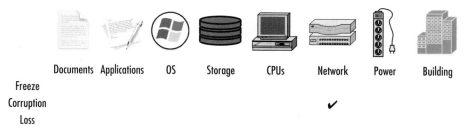

	Documents	Applications	OS	Storage	CPUs	Network	Power	Building
Freeze								
Corruption						✔		
Loss								

Table 8-1. Network corruption

You can corrupt your network by hooking up too many Ethernet hubs in a row, by using cables that are too long. or, as in the case of my former assistant, running over your network cable with your chair every day. Unfortunately, network corruption isn't as easy to spot as, say, hard drive corruption. If your hard drive is corrupted, you look to your hard drive. If your network is corrupted, you look where? The hub? The cable? The router? The switch? Sometimes, you actually have to do a fair amount of troubleshooting to pinpoint the problem. *However, note this caveat: This section doesn't even attempt to make you a terrific troubleshooter, dear reader—it merely presents some tools, options, and opinions as a way to get started with troubleshooting a corrupted network.*

It seems odd to talk to backup administrators about network monitoring and troubleshooting, but it shouldn't. Network corruption poses a major problem for them, as it's one of the root causes of file corruption in the first place, and it can also hamper the ability to back up files from one point on the network to another. Over the years, I've learned that network corruption can be the downfall of many a backup administrator's plans. Why? *Because if the network is corrupt, your backups are probably corrupt, too—and a corrupt backup file isn't any good to anybody.* That said, given this short list of tools and troubleshooting methodologies, you'll be able to discover what's causing your network's hiccups, so that you can either fix it yourself if it's simple (holding your breath and swallowing three times), or hire an expert to fix it, without going broke from exorbitant diagnostic fees.

THE MAIN THING

Test your network connections *before* you decide to conduct a backup from point A to point B.

Baseline your network's performance *before* something breaks, so that *when* it breaks (corrupts), you have some "normal" numbers to compare to the corrupted ones.

Start with a network map *before* you start having problems with your network. You must know how the network looks in its normal state to understand the difference when something goes wrong.

Special thanks...

Thanks very much to my great friends over at Neon Software, Craig Isaacs and Michael Swan, as well as my great friends over at WildPackets: Janice Spampinato and Mahboud Zabetian. Without their software, help, and guidance, along with some material copped directly from their own writing, this book would be a mere figment—and I wouldn't know a bloody thing about network management or troubleshooting.

And I don't know where I'd be without the field editors for this chapter, who include:

Mitch Krayton, and Roger Royce.

HOW DOES MY ETHERNET WORK?

Before we can learn how to track down and cure network hiccups, let's get back to basics. Because Ethernet is currently the most common Local Area Network (LAN) technology, that's the one we'll cover here.

Ethernet provides simple and cost-effective networking to all types of computer equipment. In the 1970s, Dr. Robert M. Metcalf invented it at the Xerox Palo Alto Research Center. His goal was to support research on the "office of the future," based on individual workstations with the ability to communicate through a shared network over the ether; hence, the name. Further developed jointly by Digital Equipment Corporation, Intel Corporation, and Xerox Corporation, Ethernet was unveiled back in 1980. Ethernet outdistanced the competition of its time with its high speed (back in those days, sonny, 10 million bits per second *smoked!*), its unusual signaling methodology, and the physical medium on which it ran: a thick coaxial cable. Ethernet now runs on a wide variety of physical media, from the original thick coaxial cable to thin coaxial (neither of which is used much anymore), to twisted-pair wires (shielded and unshielded), to fiber optic cables, and radio waves, among others. Two direct developments of Ethernet are Fast Ethernet (at 100 Mbps) and Gigabit Ethernet 1000 Mbps).

So? The good news, kids, is that Ethernet is Ethernet; whether it runs at 10, 100, or at gigabit speeds; or on copper, fiber, or wireless transmission media. Once you understand the principles, you can apply them to all of your local area networking setups.

The basics—a layered approach

Okay, this part's important: TCP/IP, the networking language used by most of the computer universe, employs a **layered approach** to send messages from sending applications such as your Exchange e-mail server out across the network to receiving applications such as your Entourage e-mail client software. To isolate and fix the corruption that plagues your network, you must understand a bit of what each of the layers does.

As I said, TCP/IP delivers data from one device to another through transmission paths, including both software and hardware components, based on a layered design model. Specific protocols delineate the ways that the networking software or hardware must implement the functions of each particular layer. These protocols are set up so that each layer communicates with its peer in the other system: When two computers communicate, each layer within the TCP/IP protocol stack talks with the same layer on the other computer's protocol stack.

What the heck is a protocol?

If you're wondering what a protocol is, you aren't alone. A **protocol** is a set of rules governing the format of messages exchanged between computers and people. It defines the procedure for adding order to the data exchange, acting as a specific set of rules, procedures, or conventions relating to the format and timing of the data transmission between two network devices. In a sense, a protocol acts as a standard procedure that the two data devices must accept and use to be able to understand each other—sort of like the tea ceremony in Japan, or the executive golf game in corporate America.

Protocols break a file into equal parts called **blocks** (otherwise known as **packets**). After a packet is sent, the receiving computer checks the arriving packet and returns an **acknowledgment (ACK)** to the sending computer. But, as with our own postal service, networks are *never* error-free. When a packet is damaged in transit, or the sending computer sends faster than the receiving computer can process incoming packets, an error occurs. Here, the protocol kicks in, setting up a mathematical way of measuring if the packet came through intact—and, if it didn't, asking the sender to re-transmit the packet until it gets it right.

We're all peers here; it's just that some of us are higher up the ladder

If a protocol is a specific set of rules, procedures, or conventions relating to format and timing of transmission between two devices, a **protocol stack** is a collection of software modules that combine to produce the software that enables the protocol to work—TCP/IP has a **stack** of these protocols piled one on top of the other—and each layer of protocols in the stack is a **peer** to the layer just above and just below it.

The **OSI (Open Systems Interconnect)** networking model was designed to delineate a layered system with certain specific functions at each layer. With peer-to-peer networking, each layer provides a service to the layer above it, as defined by the OSI networking model[1]. By dividing the system into multiple layers, the OSI sets rules by which the individual layers communicate with each other, and describes how each protocol should behave within the layered-model framework. Figure 8-1. shows the OSI model layers that apply to TCP/IP and the protocols that fall within each layer. Because TCP/IP was developed before the OSI model existed, it doesn't even *have* protocols in the bottom two layers—instead, it uses whatever protocols are available).

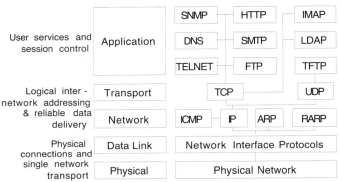

Figure 8-1. OSI model and TCP/IP protocols

Without having to know everything about protocols[2], let's walk through the way each layer sends a bit of information and then receives and processes the information. You know that a web page uses the HTTP protocol (at least I *hope* you know that a web page uses the HTTP protocol). As shown in Figure 8-1. it's part of the Application layer. When a sending application sends a bit of a web page, this HTTP protocol then connects to the TCP protocol below it (see it in the transport layer?). As you can see, HTTP connects directly to TCP. To send the data on its merry way, TCP then reaches down a level to connect to IP, which itself connects down to the Network Interface Protocols (the drivers on your computer), which then connect to the physical network you're attached to. Of course, to receive the bit of data, everything on the receiving computer works exactly opposite as the information travels back up to the Application layer and HTTP.

---

1. The OSI model of network was created by the International Organization for Standardization (IOS) and the International ElectroTechnical Commission (www.iso.ch). It set the standard for the way most modern protocols work.

2. If you *really* want to know a lot about protocols and computer networks, *the* book to read is A.S. Tannenbaum's *Computer Networks* (Prentice Hall, 1988).

To better explain this, in Figure 8-2. , we show how a packet of information from an Apache web server is sent onto the network by one device and then received by another. As the data is created and "packaged" to be sent out onto the network, the Transport layer presents the data to the Network layer, which then encapsulates the data and adds its own header and addressing information.

The Data Link layer then encapsulates the information passed to it by the Network layer into a frame, adding a frame header that contains the physical address information for the sender and receiver. Finally, the Physical layer encodes the information sent to it by the Data Link layer into the necessary patterns of 1s and 0s for transmission across the wire.

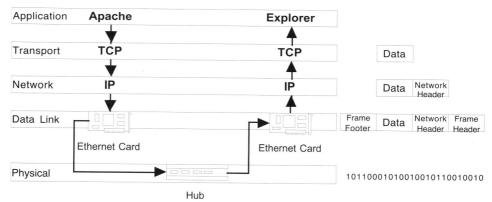

Figure 8-2. Information moving up and down a protocol stack

On the receiving side, the transfer takes the opposite course. The Physical layer receives the information, and each layer above it reads and strips off the appropriate encapsulating information until the data reaches its destination.

Enough mumbo jumbo—what does this have to do with troubleshooting?

Ethernet uses a layered approach. You can use this structured, layered approach as a natural warning mechanism for potential corruption spots. Four sets of natural indicators on your network will pretty much tell you when the network is having problems and becoming corrupted—all you have to do is start from the bottom and move to the top, heeding their warnings.

If the bottom (Physical) layer is corrupt, there's no hope that the top layer will work. Fortunately, idiot lights on the Ethernet cards and hubs are good indicators, but to find subtle corruption, you still need a professional-level tool called a **cable tester**, which we'll cover in depth later on).

If the Data Link layer is corrupt, you won't get an address, or your addressing will be as wacked out as a garden mole on Phen-phen, making sending or receiving messages all but impossible. Network mapping tools will help you root out this problem pretty quickly.

If you've made it to the Network layer before corruption seeps in, **ICMP (Internet Control Message Protocol)** will become your best buddy. ICMP performs services for TCP/IP, including flow control, detecting unreachable destinations, redirecting routes, and checking remote hosts. What's that all about, Alfie? IP has a flow control mechanism that monitors the destination computer to determine if the packets are being received properly. If the transmission is too fast for the packets to be processed, a message is sent to the originating computer, begging it to temporarily stop sending packets.

If the destination is unreachable, the system detecting the problem sends a message to the originating computer to let it know that. A gateway may send a redirect message to a host computer, to inform it that an alternate gateway is the preferred route for this delivery. A host computer can send an ICMP echo message to determine if the remote computer is on the network. The remote computer returns the same packet to indicate reception of the packet, which is referred to as a **ping**. The ability to use ICMP pings to create network maps gives a troubleshooter an outstanding edge, as you'll see in our next segment on creating and viewing logical network maps. If, in troubleshooting, you can "talk" to ICMP and ping the device, you know that you're not having cable, network card, or basic network address problems. If you can't ping the device, you've immediately nailed down the problem's location of to the cabling layer or the network cards, drivers, and addressing layer!

And finally, if you're still having problems but can communicate with the top of the ladder, SNMP will help you out. **SNMP (Simple Network Management Protocol)** is the most common method by which network management applications can query a management agent on a network device. This IP-based protocol forms the basis of most network management software, to the extent that today the phrase "managed device" implies SNMP compliance.

Data is passed from SNMP agents, which are hardware or software processes reporting activity in each network device (hub, router, bridge, computer, printer, server, etc.) to the workstation console used to oversee the network. These agents return information contained in a **MIB (Management Information Base)**, which is a data structure that defines what's obtainable from the device and what can be controlled (turned off, on, etc.). Since SNMP sits at the top of the TCP/IP stack, if you can get basic information out of the SNMP module on the device, you're communicating all the way to the top of the TCP/IP stack—which means, alas, that your problem is subtler than you might suspect. Figure 8-3. should put this into perspective:

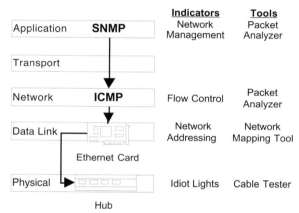

Figure 8-3. Network management layers, indicators, and tools

FIRST STOP ON THE CORRUPTION EXPRESS: YOUR CABLING

As I was writing this chapter, one of our field editors, Roger Royce, pointed out that any talk of network corruption should begin with cabling. "I certify cable already installed and find lots of problems that may not keep a network from working totally, but do cause network corruption and disruption: for example, cable that was installed and worked fine at 10 Mbps but not fine as new 100 Mbps network speeds. Many installers don't certify their installations or do only basic tests, leaving the problems to be found later," he pointed out. And he's right.

The three major causes of network corruption can be blamed on cabling. First, point that accusing finger at your cable installer. I don't know the percentage of incompetence in that field, but it seems awfully high to me. For one of my clients, an installer promised that AT&T would actually come out and "certify" the network cabling installation. I was there when this guy who was an AT&T sales rep came out, peeked at the cabling plant in the wiring room to verify that it composed of all AT&T parts, and then "certified" that it was up to speed—without deigning to put a cable tester on the system to see if the darn thing worked.

The second cause of cabling problems lies under most of your user's desks: the dreaded patch cable. This is the cable that connects from the back of the computer to the wall plate—you know, the one that gets stepped on, run over, kinked, bent, smushed, and broken on a regular basis because it's "in the way" of somebody's big, fat Doc Martens, needle-sharp Manolo Blahniks, or, worst of all, as field editor Mitch Krayton reminded me, the cleaning lady's dripping mop.

The final culprit is the "steady migration" corruption plan:

- A long time ago the organization moved to Ethernet and built a 10 Mbps system using standard methods.

- Then 100 Mbps Ethernet cards, hubs, and switches came out. So, *without* ripping out the old cable and putting in new cable, the organization simply swapped out the 10 Mbps cards, hubs, and switches for 100 Mbps cards, hubs and switches. And, since the cable installer didn't come back in, the old wires were never tested to determine if they were good enough to support the 100 Mbps system.

Why is this problem important to you? If you're a migratory victim, you're having major cabling problems and you probably don't even know it. And, as I write, many of us have already migrated from 100 Mbps systems to 1000 Mbps systems—and migrating to 1000 Mbps networking without switching the basic underlying cabling structure from 100 Mbps cabling to 1000 Mbps cabling causes just as many problems as migrating from 10 Mbps cabling to 100 Mbps cabling.

Just like TCP/IP, cabling has its own set of rules and regulations. Let's take a quick glance at them.

Who makes the rules

Who are the demigods with the authority to create a standard? The **EIA (Electronics Industry Association)** is just one of many U.S. bodies issuing standards that evolve through an interactive committee process. You should become familiar with some other organizations, as well—the **Telecommunications Industry Association (TIA)** and the **IEEE (Institute of Electrical and Electronic Engineers)** chief among them. Although these organizations depend somewhat on each other's standards, both have their own independent agendas. If you think of the IEEE as the architects and the EIA as the contractors, you'll understand the basic differences between the two. The IEEE puts forth the concepts that enable networking; the EIA creates a standard to enable the planning and installation of a structured cabling system. Different categories of network speed demand different standards. The most widely recognized categories of cabling are as follows:

- Category 3: 16 MHz

- Category 5: 100 MHz

- Category 6: 1000 MHz

While we're on the subject, **MHz** is a unit of frequency equal to 1 million cycles per second. This term relates to an electronic signal traveling down a cable; data or otherwise. **Mbps** (megabits per second) is the number of 1024-bit groupings that can be sent per second. This term relates to data transfer rates. Since data transfer rates are different than frequencies, the categories state frequencies of signal running over the wire versus data transfer rates. You can always run a 10 Mbps computer on a category 6 cable. Or, to think of it another way, you couldn't drive a Ferrari (1000 Mbps network card) very fast down a dirt road (Cat 3 cable system), but there's no law against a granny in her '60 Cadillac (10 Mbps network card) zooming down Route 66—unless she flouts the speed limit (Cat 6 cable system).

What are the parts that you have to worry about?

Figure 8-4. helps us run through the parts of an average network. We'll refer to the numbers when going over the parts.

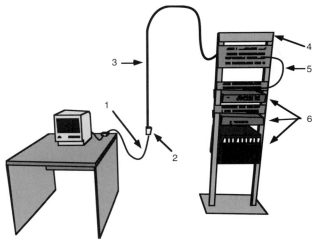

Figure 8-4. Wiring parts

Cables – 1, 3, and 5

Cables come in many forms and can be used for many purposes.

Home-run cables (3 in the diagram) go from the jack to the patch panel. They need to be fitted with a jack at one end and be punched down at the other end. These are never longer than 295 foot.

Patch cables (1 and 5 in the diagram), sometimes called **drop cables**, are the cables that go from the workstation to the wall jack, or from one patch panel to another in the wiring closet. Patch cables are already outfitted with plugs at each end. They should have CAT5 stamped on them for 100 Mbps networks, and CAT 6 for 1000 Mbps networks.

Cable types   The patch cables go from the front of the patch panel to the hub or distribution panel. If there is a distribution panel, the cables go from there to the patch panel. The combined length of all these cables (1 + 3 + 5) is the **run length** of the cable from the computer back to the network hub or switch. In your testing, make sure this length doesn't exceed 328 feet—a total run length exceeding 328 feet is out of spec and can cause network corruption.

The most common, affordable, and easiest cable to manage is four-pair 100ʃ **unshielded twisted pair** (**UTP**), which is used for 100 Mbps networks. This consists of four unshielded, individually twisted pairs of cable enclosed by a PVC (polyvinyl chloride) thermoplastic jacket. Two-pair 150ʃ **shielded twisted pair** (**STP**) has two individually twisted pairs of 22 AWG thermoplastic, insulated, solid conductors enclosed by a shield and an overall thermoplastic jacket. It's less common in the U.S., but widely used in Europe.

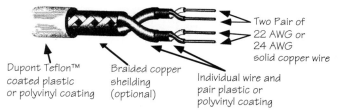

Figure 8-5. Two-pair twisted-pair cable

Two-fiber 62.5/125 μm **optical fiber** has two 62.5/125 μm (known as **multimode**) optical fibers enclosed by a protective sheath. It's used primarily for jumper and horizontal cables. Multimode fiber cable can come in configurations exceeding 144 strands.

Jacks – 2

Jacks go on the end of cable runs (the cable that goes from the patch panel in the wiring room out to the office), where the cable terminates in each person's office. If the cable system is CAT5 system, the jack has to be a CAT5 jack.

Okay, it's time for a little fun fact: Did you know that the *RJ* in RJ45 (what a CAT5 jack is called) stands for *Registered Jack?* Way back when the phone company owned your phone (ask Mom and Dad if you don't know what I'm talking about), the phone was a "registered jack" because it was registered with the phone company. We still use this outdated nomenclature in these modern times.

Patch Panels — 5

If a jack is the mechanism by which the cable terminates at the user's office, the other end of the cable is connected to a patch panel in the wiring room. **Patch panels** come in many sizes and shapes. Most have data receptacles on one side (on the right, in Figure 8-6.) and the termination blocks on the opposite side. Depicted below is a Homaco Patch panel that we like:

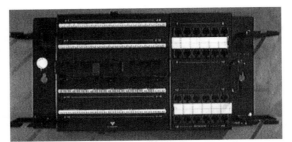

Figure 8-6. Category 5 Homaco patch panel

Is a patch panel just an array of jacks? Yes and no. Cables terminate in a patch panel before they are connected to a network hub so the cables can be grounded. Patch panels are grounded to the wiring rack (see below). The wiring rack is then itself grounded to the building ground system, so that when the Wrath of God hits your office, the hub and all of the computers aren't immediately zotzed by high-voltage spike.

Racks — 4

Racks hold the patch panels and hubs. Most standard racks are 19 inches wide. That's why it is important to make sure your hubs are 19 inches wide. Racks should be grounded. The easiest way to find a ground is to go to the electrical closet, which, by code, must have a ground. A ground wire or bus bar is then run to the rack in the wiring closet. Grounding the rack does some good. In addition, some hubs have a connection for a ground. If this is the case, a 6 AWG (American Wire Gauge) copper cable can be run from the ground on the rack to the hub requiring a ground wire.

Hubs, Switches, & Routers – 6

There's not much you need to know about your hubs, switches, and routers other than this if you have a 100 Mbps hub connecting to a 100 Mbps computer on the other end, *all* of the cabling parts in between (items 1, 2, 3, & 5) must meet 100 MHz (CAT5) specifications, or your network is doomed to corruption.

If you have a 1000 Mbps hub connecting to a 1000 Mbps computer on the other end, *all* of the cabling parts in between (items 1, 2, 3, & 5) have to meet 1000 MHz (CAT6) specifications or your network is doomed to corruption.

If you have a 1000 Mbps hub connecting to a 100 Mbps computer on the other end, the 1000 Mbps hub will *downgrade* its speed to 100 Mbps for that computer (same thing with 100 Mbps hub and 10 Mbps computer). In these instances, you need to have cabling parts in between the hub and computer (items 1, 2, 3, and 5) that meet the **lowest common denominator,** because that's the speed at which the network connection between the two devices will run.

How do you know if your cabling is up to speed?

The answer is, you *won't* unless you have an active cable management and test plan. Here's a really abbreviated methodology you can use.:

First, get the original drawings. They'll probably have been done on a Unix box or PC, and come in a format called **DXF, Direct eXchange Format.** Where do you get them? Building management usually has a copy. Somebody had to have a copy to draw up the emergency evacuation plan that's required in each of the meeting rooms of the building. While they may be a pain to ferret out, you *can* get them for most buildings.

Once you have them, try opening the document in whatever blueprint management program you have. A 2 Mbps file should open in about 10 seconds running on a good (500 MHz processor or better) machine. If your blueprint application chokes, try Canvas (X $\blacksquare$), Visio ($\blacksquare$), or Adobe Illustrator (X $\blacksquare$). They'll translate just about anything, but make sure it's time for a coffee break. Canvas can take about 10 minutes to translate a large DXF file. Visio takes about half that. To explain the three things we need to create for documentation, we'll work from the following drawing (Figure 8-7.) of a typical high-rise floor.

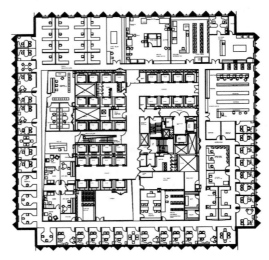

Figure 8-7. A typical high-rise floor

Drop location identification

Here's what a single room in this building would look like if blown up to its normal size. First, the little triangles are the data drops on the walls. A circle with a triangle in it represents the floor-mounted drops. The numbers by the triangles within the room coordinate to your database of jack labels.

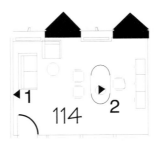

Figure 8-8. An office on the floor plan

Let's do an example; there are two wall plates in room 114 in Figure 8-8. . One is wall-mounted (left) and one is floor-mounted. We need to refer to our database to see how many phone and/or data jacks are in the drop.

A drawing can save a lot of time for anyone who is responsible for identifying the physical pathway, providing a *current* record of what your network looks like and where your network cabling can be found.

Next, use this information to test *each and every full run on your network—if you haven't already done so.*

Testing and troubleshooting

In this section, let's talk testing and troubleshooting. In the world of networking today, we have the older 10 Mbps networks that can run on Category 3 cabling. We have the 100 Mbps networks that must run on Category 5 or better cabling. And we have the 1000 Mbps, or gigabit networks, which must run on Category 6 cabling. Of the three testing standards, I chose the Category 5 standards for the purpose of this discussion. Why? Because 100 Mbps networks are the predominant networks right now. And because testing standards for Cat 5 and Cat 6 don't differ much, but differences in the testing standards between Cat 3 and Cat 5 are *huge*. The only *real* differences are in the settings on your cable testing equipment—*what* you're testing *for* is the same.

This section shows you how to install cable according to EIA/TIA CAT5 standards, and how to pass a CAT5 inspection. Why? Because you have to know a bit about how it was *supposed* to be installed if you're going to test for correct installation. Even if you do everything by the rules, you may have a non-CAT5 network. As with everything touched by human hands, the possibility for error runs rampant.

To check for errors, obtain a TDR (Time Domain Reflectometer) and make sure you know what you're looking for and what your measurements mean. Every test discussed here isn't vendor-specific—it's EIA/TIA 568A specific. If you need a TDR, you can either buy one or you can rent one from companies like Graybar Electrical, which are scattered all over the country.

What are a TDR and an OMNIScanner?

A **Time Domain Reflectometer (TDR)** is 10 steps up in the test-equipment kingdom from the tone generator your wiring contractor probably used to "certify" that the cables were installed correctly. Yes, voice circuits require only something like a tone generator to ensure that the cable has no breaks in it. However, data cables are much more susceptible to problems than are voice cables, and data signals require far better conductivity than voice signals. Therefore, a TDR is one of the best investments you can make. Microtest (which has been acquired by Fluke) makes a really good model: the OMNIScanner.

The OMNIScanner allows you to scientifically check your work. The tests networking cables must pass boil down to an analysis of signal propagation on cable. In layperson's terms, in addition to *looking* good, your cabling system must *sound* good. OMNIScanner checks for all the qualities a good, clean signal should have.

Every day, you need to run the following tests on each and every cable in your system. Remember to run the test starting with the patch cable that goes into the back of the computer and concluding with the patch cable that goes from the punchdown block into the hub, switch, or router.

Wire map tests

To work properly, the wires, connectors, and jacks all must have two matching pin locations. If an installation (a.k.a. **punchdown**) was sloppy, you may be missing a connection on a pin. This is not related to a measurement, and is the most self-explanatory test. Pin 1 of the jack must match pin 1 of the patch panel, and so on down the line. If the wires of your pairs are mismatched, re-punch them down so that 1 goes to 1, 2 goes to 2, and so on.

CAT5 cables have eight wires (four pairs). Only two of these pairs are actually used to transmit the signal. The 802.3i committee has designated where these cables should be placed on the RJ45 or RJ11 jack, as shown in the Figure 8-9.

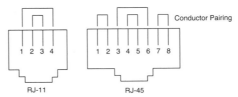

Figure 8-9. RJ45 and RJ11 cable placement

The TDR should have a line on top showing all eight connections, and a line below showing where the cables on the opposite end match up (See the left side of Figure 8-10.). On OMNIScanner, the cables should look like the right side of Figure 8-10. :

Figure 8-10. Straight-through pairing

If you have "rolled" cables—put different cables into different jacks—you might see something like this (Figure 8-11. left). The right side of Figure 8-11. shows how it might look on OMNIScanner:

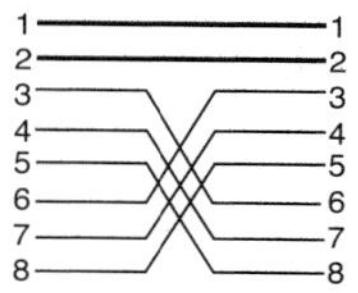

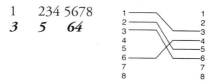

Figure 8-11. Rolled-over pairing

I've seen some strange things in the last couple of years. At a recent client site, I saw the setup shown in the diagram below. When I asked the wiring contractor why she wired it that way, she informed me that "another consultant" had told her this was a better way to connect the wires. Notice that two pairs aren't even wired into the jack! Figure 8-12. right shows how it would look on OMNIScanner:

```
1    234 5678      1 ─────╮    1
3    5   64        2      ╲──  2
                  3 ─────╯ ╲   3
                  4      ╱   ╲ 4
                  5 ────╯  ╱ ─5
                  6 ──────╱    6
                  7           7
                  8           8
```

Figure 8-12. Crossed-over pair

Nope, it didn't work. If you receive nothing at all, there's a good chance that the wiring contractor either mismarked the room's location number or the room's jack in the wiring closet—or, as I recently discovered, just left the wires dangling *next to* the wall jack. I guess he thought the data would transfer by osmosis.

Split-pair errors **Split pairs** occur when, instead of a single twisted pair, the two-wire circuit uses one wire from one pair and another wire from another pair. The original pairs are separated, causing significant noise levels (enough to halt network transmissions). The resulting pair does provide a DC circuit for the two wires, but the wires aren't from the same pair and therefore don't cancel out the EMI fields through coupling. Because of this, a tone generator will show that the electrical connection can be made and that the computer might "see" the network. However, all pair-twisting benefits are lost. If you test for near-end crosstalk (NEXT), you'll see poor NEXT characteristics, usually less than 20 dB.

Split pairs are very probable with 10BaseT cable installations using different types of wiring systems, especially when the AT&T Premises Distribution System wiring scheme and the Universal Service Order Code (USOC) wiring scheme are intermixed.

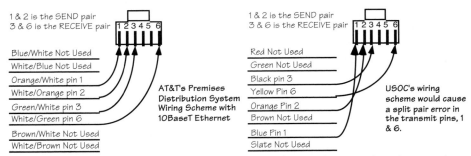

Figure 8-13. AT&T Premises Distribution System wiring scheme / Universal Service Order Code wiring scheme

Split pair errors aren't easily detected (other than cases in which the node doesn't come up on the network). The only way to detect them is to visually inspect both ends of the cable to ensure that they're properly connected to the right pins.

Reverse polarity problems **Reverse polarity problems** occur when one or more of the wires in the pair are reversed in order. Both Token Ring and 10BaseT Ethernet networks require a transmit (Tx) and receive (Rx) wire pair to carry a positive (Tx+, Rx+) and negative (Tx-, Rx-) voltage signal. The Tx+ transmitter wire must connect to the Rx+ receiver wire. A simple handheld scanner should be able to tell if the Tx and Rx pairs are correct, or if one or both are swapped.

Length

The **velocity of propagation (VP)**—the speed of a signal as it travels down the wire—is used to determine cable segment length. Velocity of propagation is used with delay measurements to compute the length of a cable segment, and is measured as a percentage of the speed of light in a vacuum.

Cable length comprises more than physical length alone: It also represents the length of cable that the signal actually travels. The total lengths of the patch and run cables should be no longer than 328 feet. If the cable length read is shorter than the physical length of the cable, check for breaks in the cable measured at the distance noted by the scanner. If your cable length fails due to cable lengths in excess of 328 feet, either the jack or the patch panel has to move.

How does the TDR check for a short?

TDRs send an electronic radar-like pulse signal to scan cables for open ends or faults. This is more than a simple tone-generated continuity test: the radar pulse injected into a cable is sensitive to impedance changes, whether they register as higher (opens) or lower (shorts) than the cable's characteristic impedance. When a radar pulse is reflected back to the TDR at the same polarity it was sent, it registers as an "open at X ft." When a radar pulse is reflected back to the TDR at a lower impedance, it registers as a "short at X ft."

Solving length problems

Table 8-2. shows how to solve your length problems:

Problem	Solution
Intermediate reflection	Punchdown blocks or other intermediate connections may cause a reflection before the end of the cable. If other test parameters are within limits, it may not cause a problem.
Length exceeds limits	Check for excess cable coiled in walls or ceilings. This may not be a problem if attenuation and NEXT readings are within specifications.
Length measured inaccurately	Verify VP in scanner is set correctly for the cable being tested. Also, check for excess cabling in walls and ceilings.
Can't trace cable to find location of short or open	Use a toner to trace the path from the source to the point of the break.

Table 8-2. Causes and solutions for length problems

Near-end crosstalk (NEXT)

Crosstalk is a measurement of the noise coupled from one wire pair to an adjacent wire pair in the same cable, and is measured in dB.

Crosstalk occurs in twisted pair cabling as an unwanted signal in one wire pair that comes from another wire pair in the network cable. The cable's electrical parameters have a significant effect on the amount of crosstalk present in the adjacent wire pairs.

The twists in the wires themselves provide what is known as **coupling**. As a network signal passes through the cable, it creates an electromagnetic field. The electromagnetic fields of the two wires have opposite polarities and intensities. These opposite polarities and intensities of the electromagnetic field created by the network signal moving across the twisted pair of wire cancel out magnetic flux in the cable.

Near-end crosstalk occurs when the signal being sent across the transmit pair from the network card causes noise in the receive pair of the same cable. Inferior cable, poor installation practices, and poor RJ45 connectors are the usual suspects when it comes to crosstalk, but other culprits include too few twists per foot, incorrect wire sizes, worn coverings, careless installation, and poor quality control.

If your problem isn't the cable itself, check the punchdown block and the jack. The cable was probably terminated too far away from the place the jacket was trimmed back, thus creating an exposed length of untwisted cable exceeding a half inch.

Solving NEXT problems

Table 8-3. shows you how to solve your NEXT problems:

Possible Cause	Solution
Use of couplers	Elimination of couplers can reduce NEXT. The fewer the total number of connections in the link, the lower the total NEXT.
Grade of cable	Verify that the grade of cable is suited to the application.
Multiple applications	Use of additional pairs to carry data for other applications can affect NEXT. Ensure that wiring is used for hub-workstation communication only. Reroute other traffic to different cables.
Substandard components	The overall quality of the link is determined by the quality of its weakest component. For CAT5 links, all components—cables, patch cords, terminations, connectors, patch panels, and punch-down blocks—must be CAT5.
Patch cables	Where patch cables are necessary, use high grade cables of the minimum possible length. The use of untwisted-pair patch cables, as in silver satin, adversely affects NEXT.
Split pairs	Ensure that logical pairs are twisted together. USOC wiring causes split pairs.

Table 8-3. Causes and solutions for NEXT problems

Attenuation

Attenuation is the deterioration of signals as they pass through the cable; it's measured in dB/Kft (decibels per 100 or 1000 ft.). It's a measurement of power loss as the signal travels the length of a network cable. Attenuation and mutual capacitance combined have the greatest effect on signal quality. Attenuation in Unshielded Twisted Pair (UTP) media is greater than that in coaxial cable. Figure 8-14. shows a 1-byte signal being sent through a network cable (from Bill Woodcock's *Networking the Macintosh* [McGraw Hill, 1993]). Ideally, the computer generates a 5 V signal and sends that signal to the receiving computer.

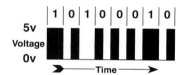

Figure 8-14. One-byte signal sent over a network cable

As the signal travels down the cable, it deteriorates. If it deteriorates too much, the computer at the other end won't understand whether it's a computer-generated signal or simply "noise." OMNIScanner can send from 1 through 100 MHz signal frequencies through the cable. Check the entire bandwidth, as a cable can be within specifications for one frequency and not the other.

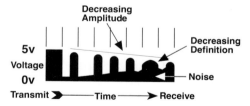

Figure 8-15. Noise on the network

When the frequency is 100 MHz, attenuation must not exceed 22 dB. When the frequency is .772 MHz, attenuation must not exceed 2 dB. The standard frequently refers to .772 MHz as a common parameter; however, OMNIScanner will automatically compare the test results against the appropriate standards and provide a pass or fail result. Potential problems are bad connections and impedance mismatches.

Solving Attenuation Problems

Table 8-4. shows you how to solve your attenuation problems:

Possible Cause	Solution
Cable grade unsuitable for data rate, as in using CAT3 for TP-PMD applications that need CAT5	Replace the cable with the appropriate grade.
Excessive length	Is length within manufacturer's guidelines for your network type? Move user to a closer hub or replace the cable with a higher grade of cable.
Untwisted or poor-quality patch cable, as in silver satin	Replace with CAT5 patch cables.
Poor punch-down block connections	Check and reconnect, if necessary. The 66 blocks typically exhibit much greater loss than 110 or Krone blocks.
Poor RJ45 connections or other terminations	Verify that conductors are seated properly. Check for tight wire twists at all termination points.

Table 8-4. Causes and solutions for attenuation problems

ACR

The **attenuation-to-crosstalk ratio (ACR)** is a measurement of how much larger the received signal is compared to the noise (NEXT) on the same pair. It's measured in dB.

Because of attenuation, the signal weakens as it travels down the cable. Therefore, it's weakest at the receiver's end. At the same time, this is where NEXT is the strongest. This presents a problem, as signals that are still strong enough after the effects of attenuation must now pass through the gauntlet of NEXT to make it into the receiving computer. Therefore, ACR is really what is called a **test of merit**, measuring how much overhead is left after the signal travels down the wire and through all the crosstalk noise. The greater is the ACR, the better.

As far as cable standards are concerned, ACR is computed simply by subtracting the attenuation from the NEXT number in dB. ACR requirements, however, are dictated by the individual applications and vary for ATM, 100BaseT, 10BaseT, etc.

Effects of noise on the cable

Noise is ever-present on your network—like a long-suffering parent of a teenager, you'll never be totally free of it. No rules are written in stone about how much noise can be tolerated by a network's computers. Measure for noise when the network is *not* in use. When the computers are off, you should detect no electrical signals being sent across the cables. If you find any signals, *that's noise!*

Electrical noise is caused by fluorescent lights, electric motors, coffeepots, microwaves, photocopiers, garage bands—er, sorry—and other electrical equipment. Different noise is transmitted on different bands, or frequencies. Therefore, you should measure for noise on different frequencies.

- **Low-band noise** Low-band noise (10-150 KHz) comes from fluorescent lights, AC power lines, or video signals.

- **High-band noise** High-band noise (10-100 MHz) comes from police stations, radio antennae, television transmitters, and the like.

- **Impulse noise** Impulse noise comes from copiers; heating, ventilation, and cooling systems; machinery; and electric motors (like ones that lift elevators). Handheld testers and oscilloscopes easily measure noise levels.

- **Jitter** The deterioration of the network signal from crosstalk and signal distortion combined, jitter manifests itself as a signal being missed or being out of phase with the Network Interface Card (NIC). The signal can either arrive too early or too late, causing the NIC to improperly read it. Figure 8-16. depicts a signal affected by jitter:

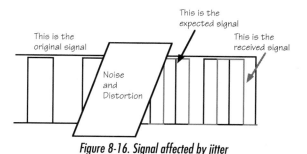

Figure 8-16. Signal affected by jitter

When both shielded and unshielded twisted-pair cables are mixed together, jitter most definitely takes place. It becomes worse as the cable lengths reach maximum distances.

Of all of the problems we've encountered, noise is the most prevalent because of what lurks between the drop ceilings and actual ceilings within today's work environments. *Anything* can be up there, from air pumps to elevator motors to entire HVAC systems.

Solving noise problems

Table 8-5. will help you solve your noise problems:

Possible Cause	Solution
AC lines, light fixtures	Do not put data cables alongside power cables. Move data cables away from power sources and light fixtures, especially fluorescent light fixtures.
Machinery and other impulse noise-generating equipment	If possible, move data cables away from the source of noise. If this is not possible and the noise is excessive (for example, a factory environment), you may need to replace UTP with STP or fiber.
RFI sources	Move the data cable away from the source of noise. If this is not possible, you may need to replace UTP with STP or fiber.

Table 8-5. Causes and solutions for noise problems

Characteristic impedance

Characteristic impedance is a measurement, in ohms (∫), of the total opposition the circuit offers to the flow of alternating current at a particular frequency in a cable.

Every cable has a value for impedance. You head into trouble when cables on the same run have different impedances. Impedance is best illustrated with the big and little pipe analogy. If water travels from the big pipe into the little pipe, eventually, the little pipe will lack the capacity to take in all the water coming out of the big pipe. In essence, the water will wash back into the big pipe, disturbing the flow of water—or, in our case, the flow of information. For CAT5, the impedance value is 100 ± 15 percent.

To avoid impedance problems, ensure that all your network cable runs come from the same spool of cable. When a large job requires more than one spool of cable, buy all the cable from the same manufacturer. If you 're adding cable to an already existing network, obtain the make of the cable originally used and try to match the cable's specifications as closely as possible.

If you have bad impedance readings, make sure the wire's characteristics are the same for your patch cables and run cables. Patch cables are normally stranded, and cable runs that go from patch panel to office jack are normally solid. Stranded cables can withstand bending and being stepped on better than solid can. However, solid cables have lower impedance. Check for number of pairs, solid copper versus stranded, and wire gauge. If they're not within tolerance to each other, you'll have to trade off more malleable patch cables for solid ones made from the same spool that don't cause impedance problems.

Structural Return Loss (SRL) is related to impedance changes and the impedance value of a cable. If a cable has been manufactured improperly or has been stretched so that the conductors are disfigured, the SRL will have a lower dB reading. Changes in the structure or the impedance values result in loss of signal strength. The measurement is the logarithm 23 -10 log ($f/20$), where f is the frequency in MHz. Remember that delightful trig class back in high school? The fun never ends.

DC loop resistance

DC loop resistance is the measure of the linear DC (direct current) loss of a conductor.

Solving resistance problems
DC loop resistance tests determine whether the cable length has exceeded 100 meters. Directly related to the length of the cable, it's measured in ohms; the measure should not exceed 9.38f. Table 8-6. on page 151 should help you solve some of your resistance problems:

Possible Cause	Solution
Excess length	See table on Solving Length Problems.
Poor connections	Poor connections at punchdown blocks or RJ45 connectors can cause excessive resistance and signal loss. Inspect all termination points for good contact on connections. Inspect all contact surfaces of connectors and reseat all connections.

Table 8-6. Causes and solutions for resistance problems

Capacitance

Capacitance is a measure of the electrical energy that the dielectric between the cables picks up and stores as a result of network signals flowing through the cables. Capacitance is measured in nF/kft, or nanofarads per thousand ft.

In other words (how 'bout English, anyone?), capacitance is the measure of how much energy is absorbed by the cable as the signal passes through it. A cable's capacitance is determined by its dialectical constant, distance between the cable conductors, and the total cable length as specified in picofarads per foot or meter.

Capacitance causes signal distortion, resulting in nodes losing the ability to distinguish a network signal from common network "noise" as shown in Figure 8-17.

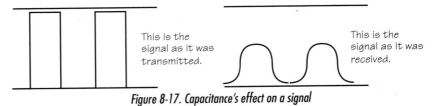

Figure 8-17. Capacitance's effect on a signal

The mutual capacitance of any pair should not exceed 5.6 nF per 100M.

The capacitance of a cable is directly related to electrical crosstalk, where the signal on one twisted pair overpowers or corrupts the signal on an adjacent pair.

Solving capacitance problems

Table 8-7. should help you solve some capacitance problems:

Possible Cause	Solution
Lower than expected capacitance	Check for a broken conductor in the cable, split wire pairs in the near end connector, the wrong type of cable, or excessive noise on the cable.
Higher than expected capacitance	Check for shorted conductors or shielding, wrong type of cable (using RadioShackNet), open cable terminations, or excessive noise on the cable.

Table 8-7. Causes and solutions for capacitance problem

Once you've ensured a full cable test of your network, you can store the information in a database. All of the TDRs we've worked with in the last 10 years or so allow a direct text file export from their system so that you can load it into a database. This database is outstanding for use when troubleshooting the Physical layer for potential network corruption.

If you're *sure* that the corruption you face isn't caused by the Physical layer, your next step is to make a different kind of map that uses your network language to create a picture of what the network looks like from the *computer's point of view*. This is extremely useful, because if the map created doesn't show all of the computers you expect to see, or doesn't show them in the locations you thought they existed in, you have a good idea where (which network segments) some of the problems are.

THE COMPUTER'S-EYE VIEW OF YOUR NETWORK

There's a series of network tools that don't cost an arm or a leg that will give you a picture of your network from the vantage point of the network itself—how the network looks from the point of view of a computer on the network. A logical network map utilizes SNMP (Simple Network Management Protocol) and ICMP to create the map. *If you create a network map and you don't see computers that you know are there (and turned on), you know that you have a network cabling, network addressing, or network computer card problem with those computers.* You know that because you know that TCP/IP is a layered protocol. And you know that if your mapping software isn't getting information back from the ICMP protocol on the computer, for some reason, the connection to that layer of the computer isn't happening. If, on the other hand, you map your network and find *all* the computers you thought you should see, you have basic connectivity to them and the problem is more subtle, requiring further intervention. The products we like the best (and that we feel give the best bang for your buck) are Intermapper and LANsurveyor.

Intermapper ⓧ

Intermapper is a network mapping tool that originated from Dartmouth University a bunch of years ago and has evolved into a professional tool. It's a Macintosh OS–only product, and even ships on the Xserve box. It's a pretty decent package for monitoring overall network traffic. You can find out more about Intermapper at their website (www.intermapper.com).

LANsurveyor ⊞ ⓧ

LANsurveyor is a network monitoring package from Neon Software that originated on the Macintosh and, by the time this book is published, will have successfully migrated to the Windows platform. I like Neon's LANsurveyor more than any of the other tools simply because it's on both platforms, and because of its IP auto-discovery features for specific software services running on TCP/IP-based computers. IP auto-discovery includes services such as Netopia's Timbuktu, Dantz Development's Retrospect backup software (client) nodes, SNMP and ICMP nodes. LANsurveyor automatically maps a customizable variety of IP services to provide a complete view of the network. I'll be using LANsurveyor to create the network map that we'll use for our discussions.

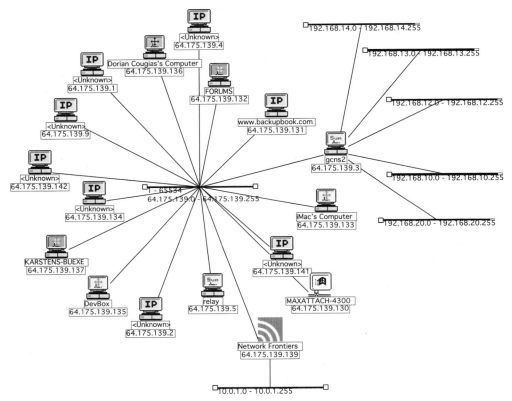

Figure 8-18. Our network segment

Network mapping software like LANsurveyor searches for nodes that respond to the ICMP ping protocol. Since nearly every node that implements IP will respond to ICMP ping, this will find nearly all IP devices within a specified IP address range. When you're creating your network map, the mapping software will ask how many router "hop counts" it should look for beyond your specified address range. Use the Search *x* hops from IP address range option to increase the range of IP addresses that your mapping software searches *only if* you're mapping more than one subnet. For example, if you set your hop value to 0 mapping, software like LANsurveyor will search only within the specified IP address range. Changing the hop value to 1 causes LANsurveyor to search the specified IP address range plus any other IP address range connected to any IP router found in the specified IP address range. That is, LANsurveyor will search any IP address range one hop, or separated by one router, from the specified IP address range. LANsurveyor uses the SNMP in order to determine hop counts because that's where the router stores its routing tables.

Figure 8-18. on page 154 shows the map for our network here at Network Frontiers, LLC, which contains three types of network objects: networks, routers, and end nodes.

- The straight lines with their network range addresses attached below them depict the networks, or **subnets,** as they're also called. The port on the router they connect to defines each of these networks.

- A **router** is a device that allows the transfer of network data between IP networks. LANsurveyor represents a router by displaying an icon with lines drawn to the networks to which the router is directly connected. In the map below there are two routers shown, one is 64.175.139.3, and the other is our Ethernet to Wireless router, 64.175.139.139.

- An **end node** is any device that doesn't behave like a router. Examples of end node objects are Mac OS computers, PCs or Unix workstations running IP, printers, switches, and hubs that use the SNMP protocol for management reasons[3], and even networked soft-drink machines. LANsurveyor represents an end node by displaying an icon with a line drawn to the network to which it is connected and then lists the device's IP address below its icon.

Within the map, you'll notice a grouping of computers off of one subnet, and then six other subnets with *nothing* listed on them at all. These subnets are connected via a device called a **Network Address Translator (NAT).** Why is nothing listed? That's simply the way NAT works: It creates a single exterior "address" that is the access point for all nodes behind the NAT device. Someone like me mapping from the exterior side of the NAT device sees the NAT device and may see the NAT address range returned by the NAT device (if it has SNMP, as in the example of the network map above), but any addresses (and therefore, computers) in the NAT range are invisible to a network map and the outside world. Why use NAT? Privacy, security, and not enough network addresses to go around for everybody

---

3. Many switches and hubs today are completely invisible to the network because they operate in a non-managed method. When these switches or hubs don't have management software running on them, they become invisible to the network and therefore invisible to network mapping software.

in the company—and many other reasons, none of which we're going to get into here.

What are some other reasons that devices don't show up on a network map? Simple—the network is somehow corrupted at the network cabling, network address, or network card layer.

If you map your network and computers don't show up...

Okay, so you know that you have 120 computers on your network. You scan your network with a network map, and a bunch of computers fail to show up on it. Uh-oh—something's missing, and you have to find out what, where, and why.

Are all of the idiot lights on?

Thank the Lord that Ethernet cards (10, 100 as well as 1000 Mbps) all have idiot green lights on them to show a connection between the card and the hub. If you don't have this connection, you have a cabling problem. At this point, go back and troubleshoot the cable with a TDR, as we discussed earlier.

Are the missing computers on one subnet?

If all the computers are on one subnet, chances are somebody made a mistake in network addressing, thus allowing network corruption to creep in. For instance, let's say that some schmoe on your network decides to update the DHCP server. Of course, not paying attention while wolfing down his piping-hot Krispy Kremes, he adds the DHCP network address range intended for router port B onto the network segment attached to router port A. This will, of course, wreak havoc on your network. And of course, when you ran LANsurveyor, all the affected nodes just disappeared off the map. Why? LANsurveyor won't see any of those bogus nodes with subnet B addresses because they don't know how to send to subnet A or elsewhere off subnet B—they'll be trying to send to the router address on subnet B, which they think is a local subnet address, the Address Resolution Protocol (ARP) request[4] would fail, and they'd be unable to send the response. If LANsurveyor were sitting on subnet B, the bogus nodes would attempt to send to the LANsurveyor address *directly* because they think it's on the

---

4.   This is a request a computer sends out when it's confused about a local computer's IP address.

same subnet as they are, and would ARP for LANsurveyor (which would never respond because it's on the other side of the router). When the ARP fails, the response wouldn't get sent. Thus, the nodes become "invisible" to the mapping software and the rest of the network.

Did your computers shift to a different subnet (part A)?

Here's a real-life problem solved by a network mapping package for you. The backup software package was set to scan subnet 1 for computers A, B, and C—all three computers in a research lab. Everything worked fine for the first couple of months. Then computers B and C weren't backed up anymore, because the backup software claimed it couldn't find them on the network, yet the users were using the network without problem, sending e-mail and being productive. Their network addresses were (and had always been) assigned dynamically through the router port's DHCP server, and neither user B nor C had changed offices, computers, or even their socks.

Beginning with an original version of the logical network map, the administrator asked the package to rescan the network, logging all changes. Sure enough, computer A was still where it should have been, but B and C were on a different subnet altogether, getting their new address from the DHCP server on *that* subnet.

Noticing on the *physical* map that all three computers were in room 42, we checked it out. Connecting the computers was one of those little NetGear 10/100 Mbps Ethernet hubs. One cable was connected to computer A, another to B, and a third to C. A fourth cable connected the unit to the wall jack leading back to the main switch and the router port for subnet 1. However, a fifth cable was connected to a wall jack on the *other* side of the room. Looking into our Physical layer database, we saw that the other wall jack led to a different switch and the router port for subnet 2! The hub, connected to two different router ports, created a loop in the network that allowed the computers to get their DHCP address from *either* the DHCP server on subnet 1 *or* the DHCP server on subnet 2.

If we hadn't had both a logical network map and a physical network map, we would have almost certainly *never* found that problem so quickly.

Did your computer shift to a different subnet (part B)?

Okay, here's another one for you. The client *knew* that all of the addresses were being handed out by DHCP, so when moving a computer from subnet 1 to subnet

2, he couldn't understand why it didn't get an address and was invisible on the network map. Upon further examination, it turned out that the network that had four different subnets, 1 through 4, with one DHCP server, a Windows 2000 server servicing each of the different subnets (Microsoft would call each setup a scope). Even though the user's computer was attempting to get the address from the DHCP server, nothing was happening.

Now, a network map isn't going to tell us what's wrong here. We have two choices at this point: Either use our much-vaunted intuition, or use a software package called a **packet analyzer**. Intuition told me that either there weren't enough addresses to go around, or that the user's Network Interface Card had been entered into the DHCP server so that the user could have a "static" IP address. Turns out to be the latter problem—intuition saved the day. Would a packet analyzer have caught that? It would have nabbed the conversation between the client computer and the DHCP server, where the client computer was asking for an address that was no longer valid, and the DHCP server was denying the request. Right now, you must be thinking, "Aha! In my toolkit, I might need one of these packet analyzers." But what's a packet analyzer, and more importantly, what's a packet? Well, read on—the next section's just for you.

Did somebody move the network?

True story: While I was at True North Communications (read *really big ad agency* here), one of our branch offices was moving into a new building. No, they didn't need help; they had it under control. However, come Monday morning after the weekend move, nobody was receiving e-mail from outside the office. Strange, they thought. They sure could *send* to outside folks. Since it was the president of the office calling me, I asked him to send me a message. I told him that as soon as I got it (while we were still on the phone together), I'd send him a reply and we'd see what happened.

Well, he said he sent it. So we waited. And chit-chatted. And waited—for nothing. So I dispatched an IT guy from one of our other local offices to see what was up. As soon as he got there, he called me. Sure enough, everything had been moved. The wiring rack was in place; the server room was all nice and shiny. However, not only had the Wide Area Network (WAN) router *not* been plugged into a Wide Area Network, they'd never even *provisioned* for an outside line and therefore could connect only with themselves.

Of course, their "sending" of e-mail to the outside world went only as far as the mail server.

Trouble spots on the Local Area Network

 Network corruption is more than bad cabling and bad addresses. Network corruption also enters the picture when you have multiple applications that are all CPU intensive running on the same computer, causing contention[5] on the device. It also happens when you have a misbehaving Ethernet card on a device...and so on. The only way to determine these types of problems is with a **packet analyzer**: a tool that examines the packets of information on a network.

The smallest unit of information on Ethernet is a packet—as we've discussed earlier, packets are discrete units that are containers for information. By today's information standards, packets are very small. The Ethernet Frame type controls their size, which is typically 1500 bytes (not K bytes, but raw bytes). Therefore, when computers exchange information over a network, they typically use a stream of multiple packets called a **session**. Think of it this way: When you use the phone, the phone call itself is the session, and the various bits and pieces of conversation shared between you are the packets.

How do packets on an Ethernet network work?

On Ethernet networks, one computer doesn't send a packet exclusively to another computer. When a device sends a packet (in this instance, computer A), each network node on the same network segment receives the packet and examines its destination address to determine if that node should process it.

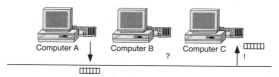

Figure 8-19. Ethernet network

5.　Contention occurs when more requests vie for the attention of a server or application than it can handle. This can be caused by either a heavy load on the receiving device or too many processes running on the CPU. I've seen servers have contention problems *before* users caused a heavy load, simply because the server was staggering under the weight of too many software apps.

If the packet was intended for a particular computer (in this instance, computer C), that machine captures it, puts it in memory, and then passes it to the next layer of the protocol software for processing. While Figure 8-19. on page 159 shows a single cable connecting all devices, most networks are strung together through a series of individual cables leading to Ethernet hubs of one sort or another. To a packet on an Ethernet network, a hub is completely transparent. The packet passes in one port and out all of the other ports. In effect (at least to the packet), the network might as well be one big cable.

But because each computer on the network gets to listen to *all* of the network traffic for that network segment, Ethernet networks are generally cordoned off through a switch or router to control the amount of traffic flowing on any one segment.

How do packet analyzers work?

As we said earlier, a packet analyzer is a device (either a hardware/software combination, or special software running on a local computer like WildPackets' EtherPeek, or Neon Software's NetMinder Ethernet) that captures network packets and analyzes them for potential problems and other information. I like EtherPeek NX( ) because it uses what WildPackets calls NetSense Expert Technology. NetSense Expert Technology provides a mechanism to automatically isolate and describe a variety of network problems so that you as a backup administrator don't need to know as much about troubleshooting as diagnostics guru Kurt Vandersluis. EtherPeek NX assesses and evaluates all seven layers of the OSI Model in all network conversations and behaviors. When situations or behaviors indicative of a network, client, server, router, or infrastructure problem are observed, the NX component of EtherPeek records the error, displays the packets that caused the error, and provides a textual explanation of why the error occurred (and more importantly, what can be done to correct it). Better yet, it extracts salient packet data and then bases ongoing, real-time analysis on multiple events within a conversation on the network segment being analyzed. While some problem diagnoses are discrete events, such as a transport retransmission, others are based on traffic characteristics, not just the packet. A threshold-based system says: Event x happened y times within time period z. This type of analysis may be important for some event types, but some events become significant only when paired with others, or based on an event response. To diagnose problem areas, EtherPeek NX examines several packets in relation to each other.

When EtherPeek ( ) or NetMinder Ethernet ( ) runs on a workstation, the software puts the Ethernet hardware in **promiscuous mode**, a state that prevents any packet from being ignored. In this mode, the workstation running the packet analyzer accepts every packet, whether or not it's addressed to that workstation. Think of a packet analyzer as a network vacuum cleaner: It sucks up everything that it sees and stores it for later analysis (okay, so maybe your vacuum cleaner doesn't exactly analyze your dirt...).

On an Ethernet network connected by a hub, because all the packets are being sent to all ports of the hub, you can place your EtherPeek workstation on any port of the hub and capture all the packets for that network.

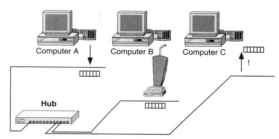

Figure 8-20. EtherPeek on an Ethernet network

Traffic routing & the ability to sense a trouble spot

The most obvious method of routing network traffic is through—what else?—a network router. If a hub is completely transparent to a packet, a router is completely opaque to the packet. The packet doesn't pass through the router unless the router determines that the intended device for the packet lives on a certain port of the router. Nothing passes through a router unless the router deigns to forward it on. You can think of a firewall as a one-way router.

Less opaque and more transparent than a router is a **switch** (they used to be called **bridges**, but that's ancient history). Switches are completely transparent to some types of traffic: multicast and broadcast. They forward these packets on without hesitation because most of these packets are used for looking up the services of computers on the network. If the switch didn't pass them on, computers wouldn't be able to find the addresses for other computers on the network.

That said, switches keep a list of Ethernet card (a.k.a. **Network Interface Card**, or **NIC**) addresses, and examine regular packets to decide whether or not the packet should be passed from one port to another. Let's expand on our first scenario, where computer A is sending a packet to computer C. In the scenario below (Figure 8-21.), each computer (A, B, and C) is a switch's individual port. Remember, it's the switch's job to segregate traffic for each of its ports, so it knows that computer A lives on one port, B on another, and C on a third. When computer A sends out its packet destined for computer C, the switch will pick up the computer C's hardware address from the packet and forward the packet on to the appropriate port, where computer C will pick it up.

Computer B will be completely spared the hassle of even having to look at the packet because it'll never reach its network segment, because the switch determined that the packet wasn't destined for any computer on that port and therefore didn't forward the packet on to computer B's port.

Are you still with me? Well, networking gets dicey if you don't think about where you're placing your packet analysis computer—if you stick it in the wrong spot, you might not be able to pick up the conversation. In Figure 8-21. we've swapped out the hub for a switch. The switch would *not* put any packets on computer B's segment if the conversation were between computer A and computer C.

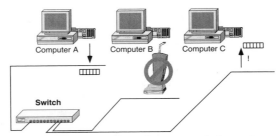

Figure 8-21. No packet analysis on a switched network

In the situation above, computer B would see nothing of the conversation between computer A and C. Therefore, for the packet analyzer to do its job, it would have to be on the same cabling segment as computer A or computer B—I may sound like a traffic cop, but it's good to keep all this back-and-forth in mind.

 ## How do I use a packet analyzer to find network corruption?

You can deploy a packet analyzer in two basic ways: First, the proactive method, which is used by some—and should be used by all. This method requires a spare computer on your network to be used for nothing but traffic monitoring. Like a roving traffic cop, you station the computer here and there on the network, usually in the wiring closet so that nobody futzes with it. Most packet analyzers will alert you through e-mail if a problem arises, and will also post their graphs to the Web, so you don't have to lurk around just to watch the pretty pictures go by.

The second method is what most folks use: Wait until someone gets cranky about the network's performance, and then plug the packet analyzer into that segment of the network to see what the problem is—more or less like a detective on the prowl.

The difference between cops and detectives? Cops have a day-to-day handle on the norm in their beat, and detectives are usually brought in after the murder's been committed. Make up your own mind about which of the two you'd rather emulate. For now, let's cover the types of problems you'll see through the eyes of a packet analyzer, starting with the network layer and proceeding up to the application layer.

Network layer problems

Network layer problems show up as CRC frame check errors, fragments, checksum errors, or ICMP errors. If you aren't the proactive type, you'll hear about this type of corruption being reported as applications quitting (bombing) or throwing up error dialogs or error logs stating that the network process (whatever it was) couldn't be completed because of too many errors.

CRC frame check errors

CRC (**Cyclical Redundancy Checking**) is an error-checking technique used to ensure the accuracy of transmitting digital data. The transmitted messages are divided into predetermined lengths divided by a fixed divisor. The remainder of the calculation is appended onto and sent with the message. At the receiving end, the computer recalculates the remainder. If it doesn't match the transmitted remainder, an error is detected, indicating one or more corrupted bits in the frame.

This is more or less indicative of a bad network card, sloppy cabling installations, or migrating to a 100 Mb network with 10 Mb network cabling (the same dismal result can be achieved by migrating to 1000 Mb networks with 100 Mb cabling).

The bad news? For each CRC error, the sending device must send another packet to make up for the corrupted one. This slows down transmission time, and enough fragments in a row can cause your network transaction to stop because of errors.

The good news? If you're seeing these errors, you're in the right spot, and the problem is local to where you've placed the packet analyzer. For each port on the hub connected to this segment of the network, check wiring with a good cable tester; then check the hub itself.

What's a fragment? A **fragmented packet** occurs when a piece of the packet has been dropped by a switch or router on its way from point A to point B.

For each fragment, like each CRC error, the sending device must send another packet to make up for the lost one. This slows down transmission time, and enough fragments in a row can cause your network transaction to stop because of errors.

The bad news? If you're seeing these fragments, they aren't coming from the hub segment you're on. Since there's no way to find the missing piece (it's not lying around the Ethernet somewhere, waiting to be scooped up), you have to map out the number of switches or routers between the sender at point A and the recipient at point B. Then you'll need to physically move your packet-capturing software so that you can capture the dropped packets at other points in the path between their source and destination. Once you're on a segment where the packets are still okay, you'll know the culprit is the switch or router ports between your current segment and the one you just left.

Checksum errors A **checksum** is created by calculating the binary values in a block of data using some algorithm and storing the results with the data. When the data is received at the other end of a network, a new checksum is computed and matched against the existing checksum. A non-match indicates an error: One or more bits within the packet have changed. Oops.

Just try backing up a computer where the data sent doesn't match the data received. Nope, it doesn't work.

Usually, the enemy is a store-and-forward device such as a switch or router that may have corrupted the packet. Troubleshoot this problem the same way you troubleshoot frame errors, by moving your analyzer to the other "side" of the switch or router and testing again. You'll know you've found the spot once you get to the point where the packets are free of checksum errors.

By the way, these errors can happen not only at the Network level as IP header checksum errors, but at the TCP and UDP levels, as well, which reside in the Transport layer.

ICMP errors If you remember that far back into this chapter (there's a midterm at the end, so you'd better!), ICMP is used by TCP/IP to report processing errors. Usually, the ICMP error reports that it can't reach a host, port, or protocol on the destination computer.

Most of the time, you'll already know that there are ICMP errors because Johnny down the hall called you, whimpering, "I can't see device blah blah blah." Or your backup server can't see some device it was backing up anymore. A quick look at your ICMP messages will merely confirm what folks are already crabbing about, but at least now you've got it in writing.

As in the hunt for the device that caused the fragment, you'll need to move progressively closer to the device until you can ping it to discover where the blockage is coming from.

Transport layer corruption

Transport layer problems are usually reported by users as "Boy, is that process slow!" or "Our $#@!! database got corrupted again," or by your backup software's log noting midstream failures. When you put your packet analyzer on the segment, Transport layer problems show up as "window size" errors, slow acknowledgment errors, retransmissions, and reset connections,

Zero window size The recipient's TCP receive buffer is full; therefore, the application isn't keeping up with incoming TCP packets. This is caused by inefficient applications, CPU contention, or inefficient adapter/drivers.

Check to see if the application in question, or other applications running simultaneously, is CPU intensive. If too many applications are running at once, break them apart and put them on different servers. If that's not the case, check for driver efficiency, or even consider upgrading the computer to a newer model or faster network card.

Low window size The recipient's TCP receive buffer is filling up, which isn't as bad as having a zero window size. Although the application isn't overloaded, it may be one or more packets behind in processing incoming TCP segments. This is caused by inefficient applications, CPU contention, or inefficient adapter/drivers.

As with zero window size, check to see if the application in question, or other applications running simultaneously, is CPU intensive. If too many applications are running at once, break them apart and put them on different servers. If that's not the case, check for driver efficiency, or even consider upgrading the computer to a newer model or faster network card.

Slow acknowl-edgment

The receiver is drunk or sleepy. Just kidding—it really means that the receiver of these packets is slow to process the data, because of too much latency between point A and point B, or because the CPU of the receiver is being bombarded with requests and is therefore busier than a one-armed paper hanger.

At the end of this section, we discuss software that specifically checks for latency problems. Either use that or your mapping software to test the end-to-end latency.

If latency isn't the issue, put a cheap-and-easy CPU load analyzer on the computer to dig out the problem.

TCP retransmissions

The source node is sending yet another TCP packet with a sequence number that matches a previously sent TCP packet to the same server and socket number. Sort of like when I'm driving down the road in my Miata with the top down, trying to listen to my wife beside me. Before I can process her dulcet words (because I'm imbued with the beauty of driving through California's great outdoors with the top down), she says the same thing over again—only not quite so dulcetly this time. Yeesh.

Back on the network side, retransmissions occur when the packet being retransmitted may not have reached the destination, a returning acknowledgment may not have reached the source, or the latency or congestion is so high that by the time a response *does* come, the packet has already been retransmitted.

If the receiver is way on the other side of your Wide Area Network, or is a home user, you'll first want to check the round-trip packet delay (latency) to see if it exceeds your timeout norm—we'll show you how to do that later.

If that's not the problem, check network traffic (also below) to ensure that your network has adequate bandwidth. If *that's* not the problem, deal with it just as you would a reset (see the next paragraph), because that's what will inevitably happen.

Reset connections

You'll see a reset connection when the RST flag in the packet has been sent. This is usually preceded by repeated retransmission of TCP data (see below) with no acknowledgment until the sender gives up and resets the connection.

What's happening here? Well, the packets being retransmitted may not be reaching the destination because they were held up by highwaymen (or by Bess, the landlord's daughter—apologies to Alfred Noyes). Or, if you look at it the other way, the returning acknowledgments may not be reaching the originating source. The only way to check? Put the packet analyzer on the segment of the original recipient, see if the packets are reaching the that far, and ensure that the recipient is acknowledging these data packets. If they did get there, reverse the process to check and see where the returning acknowledgments are being stopped.

By the way, a reset can also occur when a server times out an inactive connection, such as the doofus who just turns off the computer instead of quitting the network database and shutting down completely, or the geek who doesn't know his laptop is being backed up and unplugs midstream to take it home (Who, *me?*).

The various-and-sundry department

All of the above is good stuff to know. However, in the case of most network corruption, no single problem is detected—rather, a host of other problems muddies up the pond. Here, a tool like EtherPeek NX comes in handy. It can analyze the network and tell you when you have inefficient clients, when your server is busy, etc. When I ran a test of moving files between an older Mac and a new NAS box, EtherPeek NX recorded 3,118 problem packets during transmission, labeling them as indicative of an inefficient client.

Within EtherPeek NX's window is an Expert tab, which brings the user to the Expert Problem Finder window, which has already decoded the network conversations and arrived at its own conclusions. For example, the Expert Problem Finder describes an Inefficient Client as a "chatty" conversation between two devices in which data packets from a server have small average packet sizes. Instead of putting more payload into each packet, more packets are used to send the same amount of data with much greater overhead. As potential causes, Expert Problem Finder suspects that the client may be asking for small amounts of data from the server. The suggested remedy that EtherPeek's database presents is to discover the application and potentially optimize the application (if possible), so that it can handle larger quantities of data per packet. Well, the *real* problem in this instance is that AppleShare's running on a Mac OS X computer—it *can't* be optimized. However, since this is an OS X computer, the user has the choice of employing other protocols to send data to the NAS server, including SMB, FTP, and NFS— all of which are *much* more data intensive and network savvy than AppleShare running on TCP, and all of which are supported by the MaxAttach NAS box.

Here's the big question: Is this normal or broken? If you don't have a baseline set of statistics to begin with, you're just guessing. To be an effective troubleshooting tool, the packet analyzer needs a set of **baseline capture files** that can be used to compare to problem situations. These files should be generated regularly and at every critical point on a network: on the outbound leg of the network's Internet connection, inside a firewall if one is present, on segments with critical servers, and on heavily utilized segments such as backbones. Typically, a baseline file is created by capturing for five to 10 minutes and at different times of the day. These files are your record of normal network activity, so your network must be monitored frequently enough to determine what normal activity really looks like.

Like backup files, baseline files should be stored for later comparison. If these files aren't of a sensitive nature, they can be stored locally, as backup files may be stored. Removable media is a good storage choice since it allows fast access to the files without having to go through a restore process.

The first baseline should be the amount of traffic that is "normal" for *your* network. As our esteemed field editor Mitch Krayton points out, the choice is between "two hours to test and record a baseline versus one lost weekend without air conditioning trying to trap an elusive network flap." Me? I'd opt for the two hours of baselining.

 ## How's the traffic?

After a first glance at a network traffic meter to make sure everything is normal, most managers scan key indicators, seeking signs of current or impending trouble. Error packets in themselves are normal for Ethernet networks, but some patterns of errors aren't. User complaints of an unavailable or malfunctioning service are a common starting point for quick investigations. A faulty NIC often announces its failure with a barrage of **runt packets**[6]. A failing card may have difficulty accurately detecting other data on the wire—when this happens, it just starts jabbering, which may register as runt packets. Concentrators and switches can also

---

6.   Ethernet-compliant packets are at least 64 bytes long. Packets under that size are considered runt packets, and are reported and flagged as errors. These undersized runts comprise a certain number of packets on any network, but when their number increases dramatically, you've got a clear indication of trouble. Runts typically indicate a Physical layer problem.

generate runts. Fixing concentrator or switch-generated runt packets may be as simple as power-cycling the device.

High volumes of network traffic comprise one of the most significant contributors to network data corruption. Even worse? A low volume of network traffic combined with a high volume of errors. You can use several good tools to monitor network traffic. In this section, we write about EtherPeek NX's ability to monitor basic traffic information because we also discuss this tool for packet analysis troubleshooting methodologies, and it's easiest to nab two birds... However, it's not the only good tool in the aviary.

CyberGauge ⊞ Ⓧ

CyberGauge is an easy-to-use utility for monitoring network and device utilization and bandwidth from Neon Software. It works with any SNMP-enabled device, including routers, gateways, NAS (Network Attached Storage), servers, printers, and more. CyberGauge features e-mail and pager alerts for both nonresponsive devices and for interface traffic thresholds—great for notification when something on your network starts to wig out. All the information gathered can also be viewed, printed, exported, or saved for long-term trend analysis. We cover CyberGauge in the section on Internet backups, so you'll learn much more about it there. This is a great product for any small to midsized network that needs to monitor network bandwidth utilization—and a *must* for anyone managing high-usage Internet connections.

NetEnforcer (hardware) ⊞

The NetEnforcer family of hardware products is designed to be installed at the WAN boundary or central router boundary of your LAN network to enforce administrator defined policies through advanced Quality of Service traffic-shaping rules.

Figure 8-22. NetEnforcer

This device (see Figure 8-22. on page 169) is exemplary for creating a tiered user-services network management plan. Tiered services are necessary when you have to segregate the delivery of multimedia applications from normal network traffic, or provide network behavior–aware performance guarantees and Service Level Agreements (SLA) for Voice-over IP (VoIP) or any other application services delivered over your LAN or WAN. Since this is such a sophisticated system, we don't go into that here. If you want to know more about it, just contact us, or them[7].

After tossing a few glitches into our network system, I created some network traffic and launched the EtherPeek NX product. Before I even turned on the packet-capturing capability of the software, an instant network meter started to show me statistics of the traffic it saw zooming by.

Figure 8-23. Network traffic indicators

The three dial indicators in the picture above show 15 percent network utilization (pretty low), but 125 errors per second (pretty high). Well-designed networks can handle up to 60 percent utilization before their error rate should creep that high. So what's the problem? Look at the dials again—notice something? While the network has ample room for more utilization (more users talking at the same time), shown by the left dial, the middle dial shows a high rate of transfer—1,800 packets per second—happening somewhere. If that high rate of transfer corresponds to the higher-than-expected error rate—Eureka! We may have found the cause of a potential network corruption problem.

Before you ever delve deeper into potential network corruption problems, place a packet analyzer on the network's problem segment and let the device do your homework—never fear, I won't squeal to your teacher. Traffic levels are an outstanding indicator of what can be wrong. High utilization coupled with high error rates suggests one type of problem, while low utilization coupled with high error rates suggests a completely different animal.

---

7.   http://www.allot.com/html/products_main.shtm#netenforcer

SEARCHING OUT LATENCY AND THROUGHPUT TROUBLE SPOTS

Remember the punch line to that old joke about getting directions from point A to point B: "You can't get there from here"? In the world of backing up one device to another, such as a client to a backup server's tape drive, to a Network Attached Storage (NAS) device, or to an Internet backup service provider; you must know about the route you are going to take, and how much data you can send from point A to point B at any given time—so first, check your route and your speed from point A to point B—or you really *won't* be able to get there from here.

Discovered by Austrian physicist Christian Doppler, the **Doppler effect** is a change in electromagnetic frequency that occurs when the source of two objects move toward or away from each other. From that discovery, Doppler radar was created to measure the speed of one object either approaching or retreating from another. The folks at WildPackets—good friends of ours for quite some time, and makers of EtherPeek NX, which we've discussed at length on these pages—have also used this theory (and borrowed its name) to create their NetDoppler product.

NetDoppler ( ) utilizes a combination of ICMP Echo (the ability to ping one device from another) and the Domain Name Service (DNS) protocols to perform route discovery, latency test, and throughput tests from one computer to another.

We are here—where are you?

Figure 8-24. NetDoppler traceroute

NetDoppler works by first building an IP-node route tree that represents the path packets take from point A to point B. In the Figure 8-24. , there are actually only two routes: the first nested-upon-nested tree is the route between our backup server (computer at the very top) and the web server that hosts the WildPackets website; and the second route is to the Network Frontiers web server. Notice the *direct connection* (no in-between routers) from the backup server to the Network Frontiers web server. However, sitting between our backup server and the Wild-Packets server about 30 miles away are 12 routers.

The more network segments you have between point A and point B, the more likely it is that something will go wrong—and the more places you've got to investigate when that something *does* go wrong.

How long does it take to get there?

Latency is a measurement of the time it takes for data to go from the sending computer to a receiving computer, for the receiving computer to process the information, and then send a response back to the sending computer. It's kind of like an echo: You shout, it bounces off a far wall, and then returns. The farther the wall, the longer the latency. In the computer world, longer latency times are created by slow network connections, network congestion, overburdened routers, gateways, or switches, or a slow or overburdened receiving computer.

Let's look at two real-world examples. The first (Figure 8-25.) depicts the latency (or relative lack thereof) between the backup server and my web server on the same 100 Mbps network.

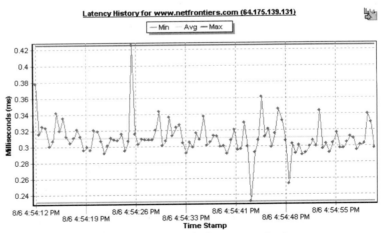

Figure 8-25. Latency between backup server and web server

Now let's compare that information to the latency between my backup server here and the WildPackets web server 30 miles and 12 Internet routers away (Figure 8-26.):

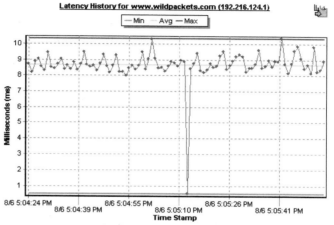

Figure 8-26. Latency between backup server and WildPackets web server

The average latency on my own network was .31 milliseconds, and the average latency between here and WildPackets was 8.7 milliseconds. That's a *very* large difference, equating to a major slowdown in throughput, as we shall see in a second.

How big is the pipe?

Now you know how to get from point A to point B. You know how long each round trip takes. The last major question you want to ask yourself, is how much data can you transfer from point A to point B at any given time? While the truest test of throughput will be conducted when you move backup files from point A to point B (since that tests application layer to application layer throughput instead of network layer to network layer throughput), there *are* two tests that you can pre-run using NetDoppler. NetDoppler calculates throughput by measuring the round trip time it takes for data to be sent and received over the ICMP protocol (throughput = data / time) through performing two types of tests (streaming and single packet throughput). To understand the differences, let's take a step back and chat for a second about the way computer systems divide up data and send it out over the network.

Computer systems speak over the network using a system built on layers—remember the OSI layers we talked about earlier? Within any given networking system, each layer is assigned to a specific function. Within TCP/IP, for what we care about right now, you must understand the fundamentals of three layers.

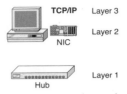

Figure 8-27. Layered networking

Layer one (cabling system) is concerned with cabling and the electrical attributes of the signal that's sent through the network.

Layer two (Ethernet, FDDI, etc.) governs how data is formatted into bite-sized chunks called **frames**[8] to be passed from one computer to another .

Layer three (TCP/IP, IPX, AppleTalk) extracts information to be sent from the host application (your backup software), asks the Layer two protocol for the largest frame size that can be transmitted, and breaks the message into fragments to fit the frame size of the Layer two protocol. The **Maximum Transmission Unit (MTU)** is a measure of the largest frame size that can be transmitted over the particular Layer two protocols in use.

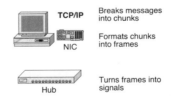

Figure 8-28. Layered networking explained (simply)

Streaming throughput tests send the entire data chunk in a single ICMP packet, which will be fragmented if it's greater than the Maximum Transmission Unit (MTU). Therefore, all the data goes to the destination before the destination returns a reply.

---

8. The more common name, even though it is technically incorrect, is *packet*, and since we've been using *packet* throughout this section, we'll continue to do so.

Single packet tests send data over one MTU chunk at a time. In this test, a single MTU chunk is sent to the destination, to which the destination replies; then another MTU chunk is sent, and so on.

So, streaming tests measure achievable throughput for bursting protocols such as TCP, while single packet tests measure achievable throughput for ping-pong protocols such as NCP. Streaming tests are directly affected by the amount of data used for testing; the more data you send, the better your throughput. In other words, since it's incurred only once, the more data you send in one fell swoop, the less negative impact your round-trip latency will have. Compare this to single packet tests, in which round-trip latency is incurred for every single command/ reply pair. Therefore, single packet tests are bound by latency, and the amount of data doesn't affect the results.

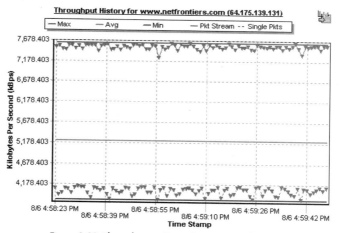

Figure 8-29. Throughput to Network Frontiers web server

You'll see the huge differences in throughput between the backup server to the Network Frontiers web server (5,229 KBps), shown in Figure 8-29. ; and the backup server to the WildPackets.com web server (110 KBps) shown below in Figure 8-30. on page 176.

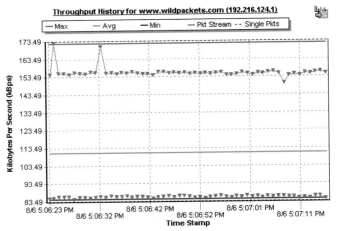

Figure 8-30. Throughput to WildPackets.com web server

Let's run a quick backup calculation. Let's say that I was backing up an average hard drive of a web server, about 5 Gb of data, from point A to point B, where point A will first be the Network Frontiers web server and then the WildPackets web server. The internal backup takes about 25 minutes. The backup over the Internet to WildPackets at that speed takes about 11 hours—now *that's* an increase, and *not* a good one![9]

Wh t d d you s y?

A fw lttrs mssng, ys? Here's how NetDoppler found the reason why the backups from a home worker (using a high-speed ATT cable modem and up-to-date hardware) to the corporate site were corrupted. Mind you, the home user's computer is six miles from the network site backing it up. From the window of the organization's office, you can *see* the AT&T local office through which the home user connects. But, alas, real distance and computer distance are so seldom the same.

---

9.   To test our throughput calculator, find it on our website in the forms section of *The Backup Book*. Give it any calculation you want, and it will spit back your transmission time for most network connection speeds.

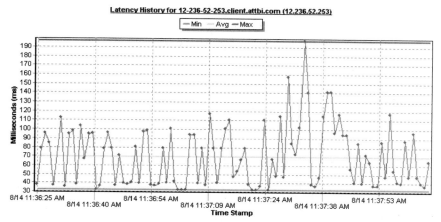

Figure 8-31. Latency between backup server and home user

Let's start with the latency test (Figure 8-31.). The latency test for the connection between backup computer and this device revealed an average **70**-millisecond delay between the two points. If you remember the average latency between our office and WildPackets (8.7) you'll realize that this is almost *10 times* the Wide Area Network (WAN) latency to that device. Yep, that's a whole lot of latency going on. And, more than likely, that much latency is going to cause a few problems—which is where the throughput test comes into play.

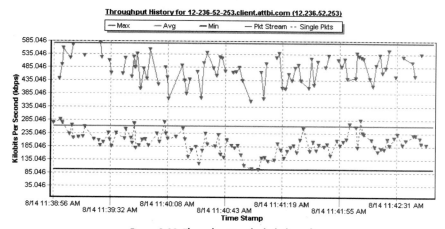

Figure 8-32. Throughput (or the lack thereof)

Remember the throughput to the WildPackets server from the backup server? Around 110 Kbps. The graph (see Figure 8-32. on page 177) shows us the average throughput to this particular home user: around 435 Kbps—much faster. But—*aha!*—the graph below reveals something different that wasn't present in the other throughput graphs!

Notice the gaps between the lines in the top set of throughput numbers in Figure 8-32. —gaps that indicate the difference between the number of packets sent out and the number of packets received. In other words, packets were dropped in the conversation between points A and B. While computer networking languages such as TCP/IP allow for a certain number of packets to be dropped and get picked up again, after a certain point they throw up their metaphorical hands, and corruption of the transferred file(s) sets in. This becomes very evident in backup software, when the backup verification routine states that what was *to be* backed up and what actually *was* backed up differ.

Putting this into perspective

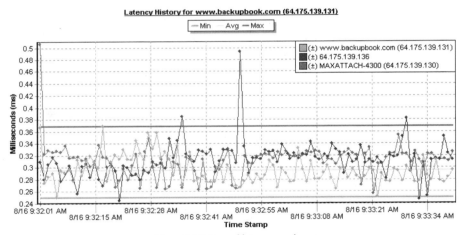

Figure 8-33. Normal latency envelope

We've talked about latency and throughput and how that can affect network corruption and backup corruption. We've gone through a couple of graphs to show you what you might see. Now let's wrap this up by putting a few things into perspective. The easiest way to see which devices are out of line is to create a quick latency test between them(y do the same with throughput if you want).

Figure 8-33. on page 178 depicts a NetDoppler latency test for three devices on our network: a laptop, our web server, and our NAS box. With the solid straight red and green lines across the top and bottom, the graph reveals that all three devices are more or less within the same latency envelope.

This is what you're aiming for in terms of network latency: All of your devices more or less in tune with each other and cozying up inside the same envelope. The graph that follows this paragraph (Figure 8-34.) depicts a device that's slightly out of the normal envelope set by the first set of devices. Note that the straight envelope lines across the whole graph have moved to bracket the top set of numbers, revealing that the envelope for this device is very different than those of the other three. This device (our e-mail server) is about twice as slow on the uptake as the others, showing an average latency of around .62 milliseconds versus the .28 milliseconds of the first set of devices measured.

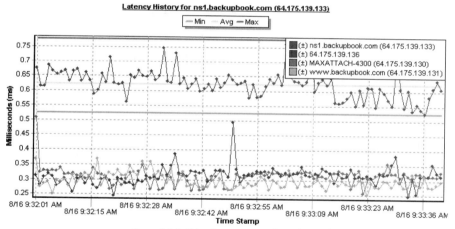

Figure 8-34. Older device is "out of envelope"

Why this extra latency? The e-mail server is one of our network's grandpas: an older computer running an older version of the Macintosh operating system, on a 10 MB Ethernet card versus a 100 MB Ethernet card, so naturally it is going to be slower. Okay, that's a given. Even with everything against the device, the latency histogram (see Figure 8-35. on page 180) reveals that all devices measured to this point are still within the 1-millisecond time frame.

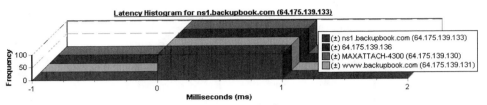

Figure 8-35. Packet histogram

Even with the slower device, the latency window is still within 1 millisecond—a normal reading. But if this is normal, what's *ab*normal? Check out the following chart (Figure 8-36.). We've now measured the home user's latency (between the backup server and the home user) and added that to our chart.

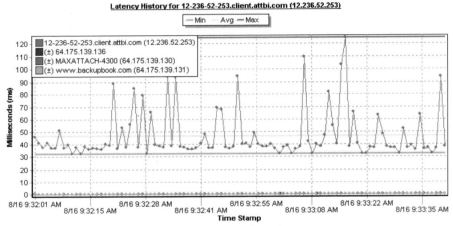

Figure 8-36. Way-out-of-spec device

Note that all of the other devices' chart lines are now scrunched down around the 0 line, because, in relation to this new device's ultra-high latency, the amount of fluctuation among the other devices was entirely negligible. Looking at Figure 8-36. we're talking latency of anywhere from 30 to 120 times that of the other devices. Get the picture?

First thing you do on your network for backups is to create a NetDoppler-type baseline for each connection route. Then measure the throughput and latency of each and every major type of device you're backing up. And do it before you have problems, so that you know what the basic connectivity to each device should be.

If you find that your connectivity to such a device has high latency or low throughput, move your backup server's physical location so that it has fewer network segments to span when traversing over to the device, or move your device so that it can get cozy with your backup server, or create another backup server on a network segment local to the device to support backup operations for that device.

If you find that latency is bad all over the network, then call us—we need the network redesign business. Alternately, you might also want to look into a packet analysis and network troubleshooting training class. I don't know about other packet analysis companies, but I do know that the folks over at WildPackets (www.wildpackets.com) offer an outstanding training course. After training, you might find that the culprit is bad equipment, normal wear and tear, or simply a network that has outgrown its original design. You won't know until you examine the problem from the network's point of view.

THE *REAL* ROOT CAUSE OF ALL NETWORK PROBLEMS?

The real root cause of all network problems can be found in the way network design is parlayed into organizational networks. If you look at the seven-layer networking model below, you'll notice that it has nine layers. The top two layers, Dorian Theory Eight and Nine, usually come into play in a corrupted network.

Layer 9	Politics	Inserts technologically challenged business leaders who negatively impact network design, maintenance, and ongoing development
Layer 8	Money	Delivers gradual network corruption due to the direct influence and interference of layer 9
Layer 7	Application	Software that utilizes the network, such as print drivers, databases, etc.
Layer 6	Presentation	Formats and standardizes the presentation of information to applications
Layer 5	Session	Manages sessions between network applications and devices
Layer 4	Transport	Provides end-to-end data error detection and correction
Layer 3	Network	Sets up and manages connections across the network
Layer 2	Data Link	Provides reliable data delivery across the physical network
Layer 1	Physical	Defines the physical characteristics of the network

Table 8-8. The 7-Layer OSI model + 2

If you can eliminate layers eight and nine, and reduce the number of end users on the network to around zero, I suspect that you'll have absolutely no problems. You'll also have no traffic, no users, and no productivity, but that's beside the point.

And if you didn't think that this little "root cause" piece was silliness, you've read *way* too much about network corruption and lost your sense of humor along the way as well—alas, I've somehow managed to corrupt your funny bone. For that, there is no analyzer save Freud.

CHAPTER 9:
KEEPING THE ALLIGATORS OUT OF THE SEWER

The backup administrator's guide to securing your network from hackers and viruses

When I was a kid, I heard a lot of stories about New York City and Chicago sewer workers who would encounter the occasional alligator lurking in the city sewer system, evoking the question, "How did an alligator get into the sewer system of such a big city?"

I knew—the Huber brothers, that's how. More than once, they'd return from a Florida vacation, pockets bulging with baby alligators. And as soon as Mrs. Huber wasn't looking, they'd toss the little monsters into the toilet or a local storm drain. When I asked them why in the world they were doing that, they replied coolly, "We wanna see how big they'll get and if they'll eat anybody."

The world is full of goofballs like the Brothers Huber. Somewhere, sometime, some goofball is going to hack your network "just because." They're going to hack it or send you a virus "just because" they want to see what happens or "just because" they intend you harm. And if you don't believe it can happen to you, scan these news briefs for a little enlightenment:

> MSNBC's Bob Sullivan reported on a company that got hacked, sustaining an 80 percent probability that all of the credit card data in its system had been compromised. More than 2,000 unsuspecting clients may face inflated bills this month—because someone might have lifted their information.

> The *San Mateo County Times* announced that many Silicon Valley businesses would be under siege from a perilous virus and Trojan horse attack by—believe it or not—the Russian Mafia.

> Robert Lemos of ZDNet reported "Microsoft spreads virus—by accident." Unbeknownst to Microsoft, the Korean language versions of Visual Studio .NET sent to their South Korean developers harbored an unwelcome guest—the virulent Nimda worm.

> Robert Lemos (again) reported on a new type of attack: the JPEG worm, which is breaking new ground in virus attacks. This virus infects and attaches itself to images on the system as they're opened and viewed.

All this mayhem happened just last week—and I found these stories without really looking. I'm sure a lot more stories are out there, but I just can't bear to read them. So the question becomes, how much of this do you have to worry about, how can you protect yourself—and what does this have to do with backup? In short, how do you keep those pesky alligators out of the sewer?

Let's take the first one last: What does this have to do with backup? In a word, *EVERYTHING*. If you back up a file that's infected with a virus, you've now stored the virus, as well. When you restore the file, the virus gets restored, too. If someone hacks your company's website and defaces several pages, you'll be restoring those files—that is, unless you caught it before you backed them up again.

Try this, just for fun: Run an attack and virus test on your computer systems, just to see what will happen. You can run these tests without harming anything on your system—except for your false sense of security, which may never recover. But that's part of what this chapter is about: the process of testing for basic hacker vulnerabilities in your systems and then passing that information on to the security folks to so that you and they can implement some *real* security. Because at the end of the IT day, it's your job to restore lost data, no matter who lost it.

THE MAIN THING

The threat to your system? The loss of data and of service availability (like Web, e-mail, and databases) through corruption, theft, or erasure. You've got to protect against the loss or corruption of data due to hacking and virus attacks. You've got to restore your data from its most recent uncorrupted version. Your network hacker and anti-virus protection program must encompass these four elements:

1. Prevention through firewalls, anti-virus measures, regular, ongoing anti-hacking analysis, and policies that are taught and enforced.

2. An intrusion detection system that will monitor your computers and notify you when something happens.

3. A quick-reaction team and quick-reaction plan for the time you do get hit with a virus or hack attack. You have to be ready with a plan to quarantine, wipe clean, and restore any computer that is attacked by a virus or hacker.

4. An after-action routine that will allow you to examine what happened and the holes in your security plan when bad things do happen to your system, so that you can patch those holes against future attacks.

Special thanks...

This chapter was derived from a vast array of material, but I'd like to personally thank:

Peter Coffee, Timothy Dyck, Jim Rapoza, and Cameron Sturdevant of Ziff Davis, for writing *eWeek*'s 2001 series, "5 Steps to Enterprise Security," whence we extracted the security research site list[1].

Jean-Baptiste Hervet, of Lagoon Software, for help on defining what should be scanned and how often (as well as for his wonderful MacAnalysis program).

---

[1]. The entire series is much more comprehensive than the material we present here, and can be found at www.eweek.com/category2/0,3960,3647,00.asp.

Also, Merche Shannon and Wyatt Banks from NetIQ, for all their help with intruder analysis and intrusion detection systems.

Caveat emptor

Very much like the network troubleshooting chapter (see *Network corruption* on page 125), we aren't trying to turn you into a security specialist here. Reading and following the guidelines set by this chapter will give you the bare basics of what it takes to secure your system.

This is not the place to go into a play-by-play description of what ports to leave open in firewalls, SNMP devices, and key services.

This *is* the place for backup administrators to discover where they and their actions fall in the general realm of hacker and virus defense management.

In the chapter appendix, we've provided a list of various website resources for you to choose from to learn more about security (see *Security research sites* on page 257). We've also provided a "How hackers hack" segment (see *How does a hacker hack? What does he look for?* on page 246).

Finally, if you search Amazon.com for *security*, you'll find a plethora of books to help you. Macintosh users should turn to www.opendoor.com, for a book specifically about securing Macintosh systems: Alan B. Oppenheimer and Charles H. Whitaker's *Internet Security for Your Macintosh* (Peachpit Press, 2001).

That said, let's proceed. If you aren't the security administrator, go see him or her with this chapter and a box of hot Krispy Kremes with a nice, big cup of coffee, and beg for assistance in scanning—and then plugging—all the holes you find on your network. If you've just become the security administrator, here's a quick rundown on the process you need to run through: Scan, Protect, Assign, Fix, Verify.

"I'M GOING TO IGNORE THIS CHAPTER BECAUSE I HAVE A FIREWALL."

Uh, better not! Two basic types of firewalls are in service in computer networks today. The first is the software-based firewall usually loaded onto a server that connects on one port to the Internet, and on the other to the rest of the computer network as shown at the bottom-left of Figure 9-1. This could be as simple as a built-in firewall that comes with some servers or as complex as Check Point's Firewall-1.

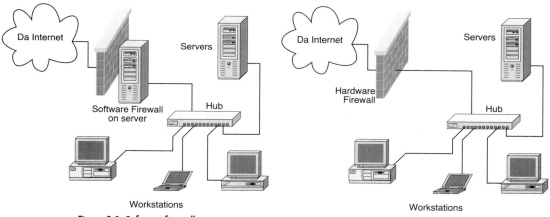

Figure 9-1. Software firewall   Figure 9-2. Hardware firewall

Then there's the hardware firewall that's a stand-alone device that separates the Internet from the rest of the network as shown at the top right of Figure 9-2. This could be as simple as the firewalls built into a cable router or as complex as a Cisco Pix.

Many people think that once they put up a firewall and create corporate security standards for what can go in and out, All Is Well—they're safe from those nasty things that go bump in the night. If think that way, the 49 percent of the hackers who come from *inside* the organization will love you for it. Ever wonder *why* those organizational security software makers like NetIQ, Foundstone, and others focus their efforts on scanning network *systems*? Because there are a whole lot of hackers who know how to get around the firewall, that's why. Just because you have a firewall doesn't mean that it's going to stop anyone from hacking your system. No one's invulnerable—even Superman was laid low by those nasty green rocks.

In a real security test we conducted for a company in Silicon Valley, we were in their meeting room discussing why my security audit was "over the top," as they put it. While they pooh-poohed my "ludicrous" proposal, one of our staff members, dressed in coveralls, brought in a fake work order and proceeded to detach a database server from the network, jam it in a box, and lug it out the front door. Outside the building, he knocked on the window as if on cue, proudly displaying the company's server, strapped to a dolly. Although that beautiful bit of guerilla theatre didn't get us the gig, the company did get the point: Security doesn't stop at the firewall.

During another audit, this time of my own company, a prankster simply walked into a conference room, hooked up his laptop to one of the available network ports (DHCP was running, so he could get an address), and right in the middle of a conversation, he scanned the network and interrupted services. Since there was no "map" of where DHCP was giving out addresses (at the time, it was set up for all eight floors of the building), the security person couldn't find the prankster—though he was hacking away right under our noses (we caught him the next time around).

In an article by Sharon Gaudin of *Network World*[2], the dangers of insider attacks were presented by the U.S. Secret Service. James Savage, deputy special agent in charge of the Secret Service's financial crimes division, was quoted as saying, "The insider poses the greatest threat because they know where the most critical information is kept and how to bypass the safeguards on the system." He further added that "information data is the new currency of choice in the criminal community. Our dollars are best spent on prevention."

Back to the backup administrator's home front. You decide that you're running out of storage room, so you buy one of those easily-secured Network Attached Storage devices you hear about. You got it out of a catalog, from Dell, Quantum, Linksys, or Iomega—good stuff. You install it and set up passwords, maybe even tie it into your Windows domain controller for added security. You're set, right? Wrongo, Bucko. You might as well have gotten the model with the concentric-circles target painted on it. Curious? *Read the appendix to this chapter.*

---

2.   "Study looks to define 'insider threat," *Network World*, 3/4/2002.

TESTING (SCANNING) YOUR NETWORK

You might want to use several methods to scan your systems for possible attacks. You can scan from the outside of your organization, testing to see how much gets through your firewall. You can scan from inside your organization, without the benefit of the firewall. I suggest that you run your tests from both directions—and take the inside attack just as seriously as the outside attack.

A host of available products conduct vulnerability assessment scans. Symantec's NetRecon (http://enterprisesecurity.symantec.com/), the open source–based Nessus (http://www.nessus.org/), and MacAnalysis (http://www.macanalysis.com/) are three very solid tools for small to medium-sized organizations.

The only two tools we recommend for larger organizations are FoundScan from Foundstone (http://www.foundstone.com/), and our company's favorite, Security Analyzer from NetIQ (http://www.netiq.com/).

Each of these packages scans either individual devices or your network, and prods the devices being scanned for open holes and potential vulnerabilities. Good stuff, these tools. But, as the immortal Jacqueline Susann taught us, once is not enough: You need to use these tools often, on a regular basis, to ensure that your software updates aren't cracking open any crevices for creepy-crawlies to slither through.

NetRecon

Symantec NetRecon utilizes a root-cause and path-analysis engine to illustrate the sequence of steps taken to uncover vulnerabilities. It tests the entire network infrastructure for security vulnerabilities and provides repair recommendations. It also learns as it scans, so if it cracks a password on one system, that password is then tried on others. Administrators can schedule repeating scans, as well. Management reports can be tailored for a range of audiences both technical and executive, and can be exported to a variety of formats including Microsoft Word, Excel, and HTML.

Shields Up! ⊞ Ⓧ ⚉

The simplest scanner of all is a website dedicated to Internet security testing, featuring the web-based program, Shields Up! To use it, simply click their "Test My Shields" or "Probe My Ports" buttons, and the system scans your computer (this works only on the computer you're testing) for open holes in your system.

It's a great start, but doesn't cut the mustard for a workgroup or an organization[3].

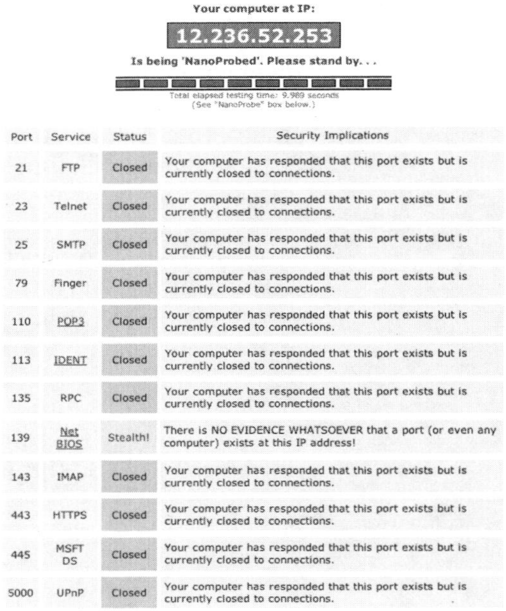

Figure 9-3. Shields Up! test

Your computer at IP:

12.236.52.253

Is being 'NanoProbed'. Please stand by. . .

Total elapsed testing time: 9.989 seconds
(See "NanoProbe" box below.)

Port	Service	Status	Security Implications
21	FTP	Closed	Your computer has responded that this port exists but is currently closed to connections.
23	Telnet	Closed	Your computer has responded that this port exists but is currently closed to connections.
25	SMTP	Closed	Your computer has responded that this port exists but is currently closed to connections.
79	Finger	Closed	Your computer has responded that this port exists but is currently closed to connections.
110	POP3	Closed	Your computer has responded that this port exists but is currently closed to connections.
113	IDENT	Closed	Your computer has responded that this port exists but is currently closed to connections.
135	RPC	Closed	Your computer has responded that this port exists but is currently closed to connections.
139	Net BIOS	Stealth!	There is NO EVIDENCE WHATSOEVER that a port (or even any computer) exists at this IP address!
143	IMAP	Closed	Your computer has responded that this port exists but is currently closed to connections.
443	HTTPS	Closed	Your computer has responded that this port exists but is currently closed to connections.
445	MSFT DS	Closed	Your computer has responded that this port exists but is currently closed to connections.
5000	UPnP	Closed	Your computer has responded that this port exists but is currently closed to connections.

Nessus ⚉ ⊞

Nessus is an open source project, which means that more programmers are working on and making it better than any proprietary program. And in its open fashion, it has a plug-in architecture. Each security test is written as an external plug-in, so that you can easily add your own tests without having to read the code of the Nessus engine.

The Nessus Security Scanner includes NASL (Nessus Attack Scripting Language) a language designed to write security tests easily and quickly. The Nessus Security Scanner is made up of two parts: a server, which performs the attacks; and a client, which is the front end. You can run the server and the client on different systems

---

3. The site can be found at https://grc.com/x/ne.dll?bh0bkyd2.

so that you can create your reports on your personal computer while the server performs its attacks from the Unix mainframe upstairs.

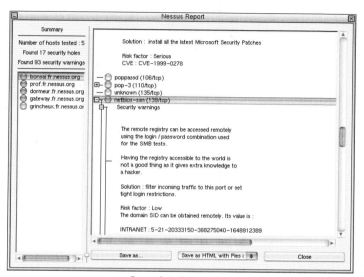

Figure 9-4. Nessus report

There are several clients: one for X11, one for Win32, and one written in Java. Nessus will not only tell you what's wrong on your network, but will, most of the time, give you the risk level of each problem found (from *Low* to *Very High*) and tell you how to prevent crackers from exploiting the security holes found.

The Unix client can export Nessus reports as ASCII text, LaTeX, HTML, "spiffy" HTML (with pies and graphs) and an easy-to-parse file format. And, given the power of your server, it can test a great many hosts at once.

MacAnalysis ⊗

The principal behind MacAnalysis is simple: It hacks your server (Unix, NT, Mac) as any experienced hacker would, informing you what it did and how to efficiently fix the vulnerabilities it exposed. MacAnalysis recognizes specific versions of specific daemons; for example, it knows the distinction between SendMail 8.8.2 and SendMail 8.8.3's vulnerabilities. Then, MacAnalysis offers a detailed description of the issues it discovers on your server.

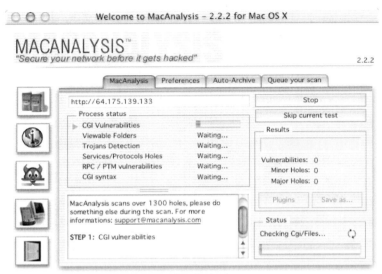

Figure 9-5. MacAnalysis

It doesn't provide path analysis like NetRecon, nor does it create fancy-schmancy graphs like Nessus. However, it does self-update its hack database and can run repeatedly scheduled tests on more than 1,300 holes to date. While it doesn't test multiple devices simultaneously, it lets you create a test schedule queue so that you can run multiple, scheduled tests. The tests we ran on our servers were done by MacAnalysis.

Corporate scanning with reporting

Corporate scanning systems should scan not only a single computer, they should run automatically and scan the entire network (adjusting for new nodes before each scan) on a regular basis. Since you're working with large-scale systems, they should include not only scanning, but problem reporting and courses of action planning, as well. And of course, with this kind of power and all-encompassing security testing you'll probably have to set aside a stand-alone computer just to run one of these babies. But trust me, they're worth it.

Security Analyzer

Another product in the same genre is Security Analyzer from NetIQ (the same folks who make WebTrends). While this isn't as heavy on business logic reporting capabilities as FoundScan, it is an *industrial-strength* product that does the job. NetIQ's Security Analyzer is a flexible, enterprise-scale vulnerability assessment product for Windows, Solaris, and Linux platforms. Security Analyzer scans computers in your network for vulnerabilities, providing reports that help you correct the problems it finds. Security Analyzer supplies detailed correction instructions, helping you close the door on attackers and prevent expensive outages. And it keeps itself up to date in its testing and corrective instructions. *As a technologist, I like this product immensely.*

Security Analyzer's security analysis report is broken down into a summary page, general statistics (how many hosts were scanned, a breakdown of high to low vulnerabilities found, etc.), host vulnerabilities, service vulnerabilities, the test policies put into play during the scan, and inventories of both the number and types of hosts found, as well as number and types of network services found.

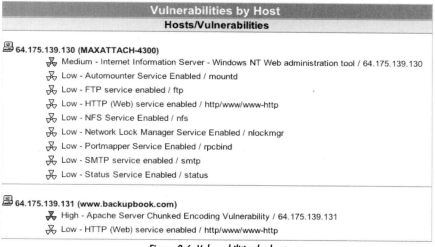

Figure 9-6. Vulnerabilities by host

The Host Vulnerabilities Report (Figure 9-6.) provides a visual breakdown of the high, medium, and low vulnerabilities *per device* that were found in the network scan. This graph shows a total of eight computers spanning a range of vulnerabilities.

While all of this is nice and scary enough to separate your CFO from some bucks for upgrades and patches, the product's real strength becomes evident at the end of the vulnerability report, when it gives instructions on *what to do* to fix the problems found.

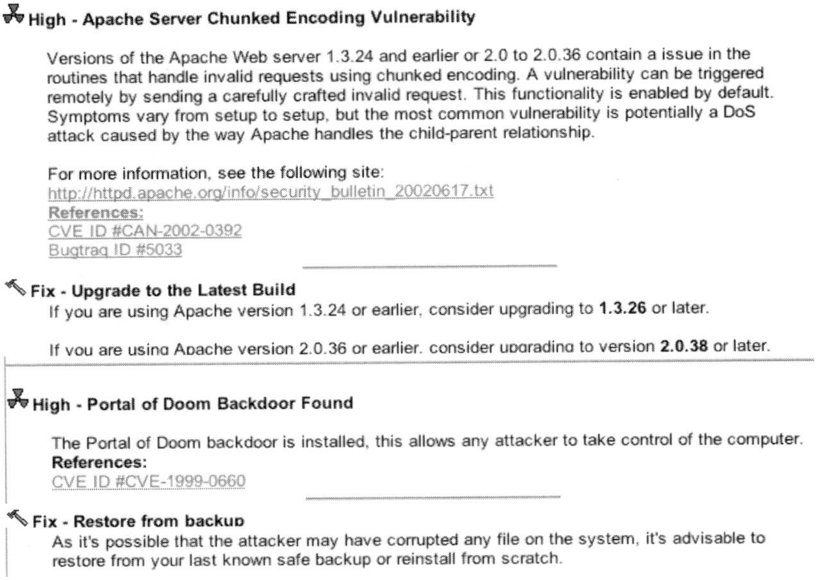

High - Apache Server Chunked Encoding Vulnerability

Versions of the Apache Web server 1.3.24 and earlier or 2.0 to 2.0.36 contain a issue in the routines that handle invalid requests using chunked encoding. A vulnerability can be triggered remotely by sending a carefully crafted invalid request. This functionality is enabled by default. Symptoms vary from setup to setup, but the most common vulnerability is potentially a DoS attack caused by the way Apache handles the child-parent relationship.

For more information, see the following site:
http://httpd.apache.org/info/security_bulletin_20020617.txt
References:
CVE ID #CAN-2002-0392
Bugtraq ID #5033

Fix - Upgrade to the Latest Build
If you are using Apache version 1.3.24 or earlier, consider upgrading to **1.3.26** or later.

If you are using Apache version 2.0.36 or earlier, consider upgrading to version **2.0.38** or later.

High - Portal of Doom Backdoor Found

The Portal of Doom backdoor is installed, this allows any attacker to take control of the computer.
References:
CVE ID #CVE-1999-0660

Fix - Restore from backup
As it's possible that the attacker may have corrupted any file on the system, it's advisable to restore from your last known safe backup or reinstall from scratch.

Figure 9-7. Fixit instructions

How smart is this "what to do" advice? I've spent hours talking to the engineers at NetIQ, ISS, Citadel, MacAnalysis, and other software vendors, and have come to realize that these guys are deadly serious about what they do. They're even more serious about the very best methods to handle the viruses, Trojan horses, and open security holes they find: They create a fix, attempt to hack the fix, and re-create and re-test until they get it right. The best move you can make is to follow their instructions directly and promptly.

Internet Security Systems Internet Scanner

Founded in 1994, Internet Security Systems (ISS) (Nasdaq: ISSX) is a world leader in software and services that protect critical online resources from attack and misuse. Their vulnerability assessment tool, Internet Scanner, performs scheduled or event-driven probes of network communication services, operating systems, routers, e-mail, web servers, firewalls, and applications to identify weaknesses that could be exploited by intruders to gain access to the network. Their SmartScan security data correlation detects interrelated network-based vulnerabilities, learns from vulnerabilities detected in previous scans, and builds on this knowledge to discover additional vulnerabilities that would otherwise go undetected. The additional FlexCheck capability provides additional coverage by allowing customers to write updates for custom applications.

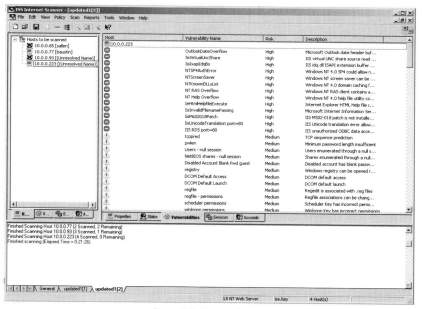

Figure 9-8. Internet Scanner

At this point, you can either remediate the problem manually, or you can turn to a remediation product—which we just happen to know about; read on.

QualysGuard Intranet Scanner

This product is the only hardware-based security scanner that we mention in our book. It's a pretty darn cool product. The device hooks into the network like any other computer and continuously monitors the goings-on, producing a web page front-end report that is clean and very usable.

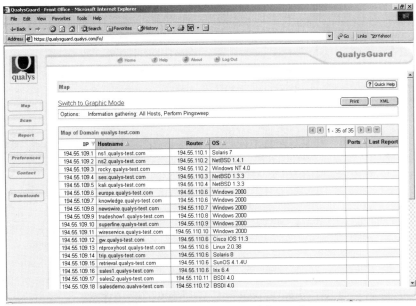

Figure 9-9. QualysGuard Intranet Scanner

Just minutes after turning it on, connecting it to the network, and entering a username and password (for getting updates from the parent company), administrators can begin assessing their networks for vulnerabilities. If you're looking for an appliance to run your security tests, this is a great device.

Figure 9-10. Intranet Scanner web front end

FoundScan

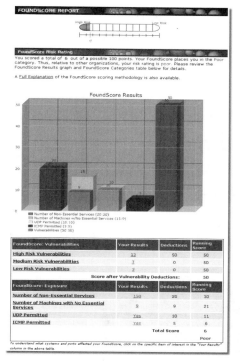

Foundstone's FoundScan application is one of the best scanning and reporting tools we've seen. We like FoundScan so much because of FoundScore, its reporting capabilities that rate an organization's vulnerability status from 0 to 100. These reports are powerful enough to get the job done, and easy enough to interpret so that you can present them to the CEO and CFO at your corporation's executive management meetings.

Trying to explain security issues to non-technical audiences can be frustrating. The *lingua franca* of CFOs is *not* patches, service packs, and upgrades—it's "What's the bottom line?" FoundScore levels this playing field nicely. Based on exposure risks (firewall policies and Internet architecture) and vulnerabilities discovered during its assessments, FoundScore is a quantitative gauge of the organization's success at securing their systems. Most usefully, the Long-Term Trend Report tracks an organization's FoundScore over the last 10 scans, graphically depicting improvements to the organization's risk profile so that the CFO can see the value of the security investment. Figure 9-11. shows a sample FoundScore report.

Figure 9-11. FoundScore

Immediate remediation

While I was giving a presentation in Orlando not so long ago, I met two very bright senior-level IT staff members, who asked me about immediate remediation products and whether or not I'd heard of them. Until that very moment, I had to admit that I hadn't. Soon after returning from the show, I was contacted by the folks at Citadel Security Software regarding Hercules—no, not the Greek hero; their vulnerability remediation product. I was impressed—so much so that I just *had* to call this chapter back from the editor to add this product to the list.

What does Hercules do, when it's spruced up those filthy Augean stables? Its labors, like those of its eponym, are simple, yet quite complex.

	Without Hercules		With Hercules
1.	Assign the vulnerability to a staff member	1.	Import Security Scan into Hercules
2.	Locate the machine/device		
3.	Research the vulnerability	2.	Review the vulnerability/remediation
4.	Research the remediation		
5.	Acquire & test remediation		
6.	Apply remediation to each system	3.	Click a button to remediate
7.	Hope for overtime or comp time	4.	Drink coffee and eat Krispy Kremes

Table 9-1. Manual remediation process vs. Hercules automated remediation process

Hercules is a classic case of swapping the cost of time with the cost of hardware and software. How much time is that? More than two hours a day, when scans are

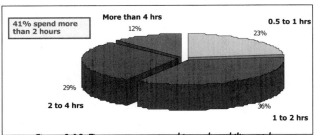

Figure 9-12. Time spent on researching vulnerability patches

happening for researching the patches alone, that's how long. Figure 9-12. shows a chart from a recent survey asking folks how much time they spend on researching vulnerability fixes (around one to four hours of research per patch). However, that's only a part of the manual-fix picture. Let's run a hypothetical scan of your system for vulnerabilities; say, 250 computers on the network and nine servers. The first time you run your scans (if you're a normal person and you've not been as security conscious as you should), you'll find a lot of patches and security updates that need changing. I'm not going to even try to guess how long that would take—probably as long as the original Hercules' 12 labors put together.

- Once you've cleaned up the system, and scan once a month, you find an average of three patches per server and one patch per computer. There are nine different patches for the servers, and six different patches among the 250 workstations.

- Research time for each patch is about two hours on average. That makes nine plus six patches times two hours, for a total of 30 hours of vulnerability research.

- With the network down for maintenance on a Friday night, the tech comes in and patches five devices simultaneously. At this rate, five patches can be done in half an hour, or one patch in six minutes. With three patches times nine servers and one patch times 250 workstations, that's 277 patches * 6 = 1,662 minutes, or 27.7 hours.

- (30 hrs. research + 27.7 hours updating/patching) = 57.7 hours * $30 an hour (that's for your cognitive IT professional) = $1,731 month in time costs.

- $1,731 a month * 12 months = $20,772 per year.

I'm sorry, but when I can have a computer assigned to do the legwork of securing other computers for me, I don't even think twice—that's where Citadel's Hercules comes in. Let's look at the process.

Importing a security scan

The first step is to run your security audit with your favorite tools, such as Nessus, etc. You then import your security scan into Citadel's Hercules. Hercules maps the information from the security scanner into its own format, examines its own templates and profiles, and then presents you with a window like the one shown inFigure 9-13.

The mapped vulnerabilities show up as a two-part window. The left windowpane reveals the list of computers that have vulnerabilities; the right windowpane shows the vulnerabilities that the system found on those computers, with some basic information such as the vulnerability's name, severity, and CVE reference number (CVE.mitre.org is an outstanding reference site and clearinghouse for vulnerability assessment).

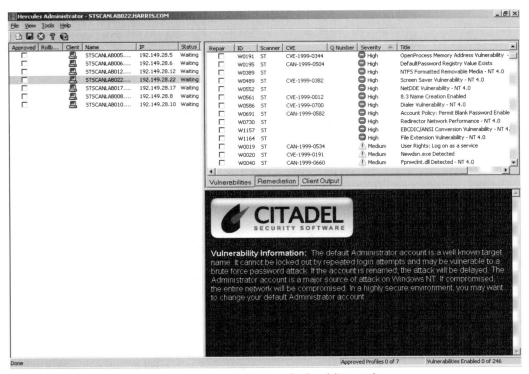

Figure 9-13. Mapped vulnerabilities window

In the Hercules system, every vulnerability has a description as well as a signature (think of this as the DNA of the vulnerability). The vulnerability's signature includes whether or not the patch can be uninstalled (which is very important if you find out that the patch causes more problems than the vulnerability), and where the patch can be found. It also includes the registry information for where the patch will be placed, along with other registry data and values.

Double-click on one of the vulnerabilities in the right pane of the mapped vulnerabilities window to get a dialog showing you the vulnerability's signature and giving you three distinct options. You may either chose to fix the vulnerability, ignore it, or (I really like this) roll back a previously fixed vulnerability. Some patches are best roll backed, because the patch turns out to be worse than the vulnerability. Knowing which *can* be rolled back and which *can't* be is a major plus—and doing it automatically is even better. Ever try sending out a tech back to each computer that he installed a patch on and ask him to roll the device back to the way he found it? Yeah, like *that's* going to happen sometime soon. But even if it does, you'll be the new target on his dartboard. But back to the main thing: fixing vulnerabilities. Once you set the property to **Repair**, you go through the window again and instruct Hercules to repair all or any subset of devices that had this vulnerability.

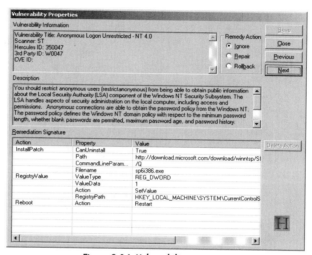

Figure 9-14. Vulnerability properties

You can even create custom fix signatures so that you apply one set of rules for servers, another set for end users, and a third set for those kind folks in HR who scotched your last pay raise.

Reporting

I've gone through Hercules' reports, which are quite nice and can be customized. However, as a former executive committee member of a publicly traded company, I'm going to tell you a little secret: The best report you can ever present is the **before-and-after report**. You take your first Nessus scan, all 160 pages of it, and put it in a three-ring binder. You then use Hercules to fix all of your problems. Run another Nessus scan, and take that beautiful, blank single page with nothing on it and put *that* in a binder of the same size by itself. Then, ta-daa! You present the "before" and "after" binders as your full presentation to the audit committee, while saying no more than "Here's where we *were*, and here's where we *are*." You'll get that next pay raise.

How Hercules works and what you'll need

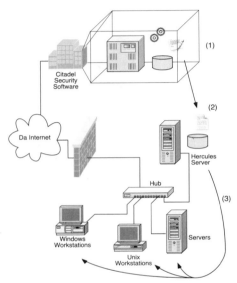

The Hercules system works in three distinct steps, and you need to run it on a server class machine. If you have a server with enough processing power and disk available, use that. If not, add another machine to your network, and enough bandwidth to send the patches across (which really doesn't take much bandwidth at all).

Citadel's offices keep constant watch on the CVE list and others,continually updating their master database of all known common vulnerabilities and exposures.

In step one of the process, all incoming intelligence is scrubbed and then added to their database, where a combination of their proprietary signature creation software and their engineers build and then test the constantly updated list of vulnerability and patch signatures.

Figure 9-15. The Hercules process

In the second step, the local Hercules server resident on your network downloads those signatures into its database so that they'll be ready as soon as you are. Once you have the most up-to-date information in the server, you're ready to load in your scans and then patch your devices.

The third and final step, of course, is the patching of your devices while you're gulping Jamaican Blue Mountain coffee and hot Krispy Kremes.

Politics and other issues of computer-driven security systems

Okay, we've now run through the process of including a semi-automatic security remediation system in your security plan. You're probably wondering if your company will buy off on it and what the fallout might be. Let's go through a couple of issues that can hit you, do you'll be prepared to dodge.

This is an expense. Sure is. The price might be coming down as they grow and gain marketshare, but whatever the price, *somebody* is bound to balk at it. You've gotta be persuasive here. I'd balance an argument for this product against the argument of hiring additional staff to keep up with security threats. Ask for the staff first, and then add (once you get them going on the exorbitance of buying fresh bodies) that you *have* found a device that'scheaper and easier to manage and maintain than a human being—that might clinch the deal.

And, since you're replacing bodies with machinery, there's bound to be a bit of a turf war in larger organizations. Decentralized companies like restaurant chains or store chains won't offer that argument because they don't have the decentralized IT staff to begin with. However, larger organizations with their own IT fiefdoms may put up a security turf barrier or two. That's where "approval" teams come into the picture.

When I was CIO of True North Communications, I dealt with about a dozen "local-division" CIOs across the world. With those based in the U.S., I held a monthly meeting to "decide" where we were going. It was like the President wrangling with Congress—but it worked, and I recommend it as a turf-war-deflection tactic. At monthly meetings, you can turn the territorial instinct aside by presenting the most current security scans along with the most current Hercules-suggested remedies. Letting folks "decide" which updates should be run gives them a voice in the system, and enables to you get their backing and, potentially, some bucks if you need more budget—which you *are* going to need for this system.

PROTECTION: SET UP AN INTRUSION DETECTION SYSTEM (IDS)

In tandem with assigning responsibilities and fixing problems, you need to set up a proper intrusion detection system so that if you get hit again mid-fix, you'll know who's hitting you and how they' re hitting you. What you do *not* want to do is to back up systems that have been hacked! This is one time you don't want a new backup. Think of it: If you back up a back-door operation like the Doom back door, you've effectively put a back door into your offsite storage—not good[4].

The best thing to do? Immediately erect an **intrusion detection system** while you're assigning responsibilities and conducting the fixes that the security analysis software found. There are two good, basic choices for this, and one *outstanding* choice in software.

Snort and HenWen Ⓧ Ⓧ

Snort is an open source network intrusion detection system, capable of performing real-time traffic analysis and packet logging on IP networks. It performs protocol analysis and content searching/matching and can be used to detect a variety of attacks and probes, such as buffer overflows, stealth port scans, CGI attacks, SMB probes, OS fingerprinting attempts, and much more.

Snort uses a flexible rules language to describe traffic that it should collect or pass, as well as a detection engine that utilizes a modular plug-in architecture.It has a real-time alerting capability, as well, incorporating alerting mechanisms for syslog, a user-specified file, a UNIX socket, or WinPopup messages to Windows clients using Samba's SMB client.

Named after the ancient Welsh sow goddess and Lloyd Alexander's temperamental oracular pig (check out *The Book of Three* for a great all-ages read), HenWen is a network intrusion detection package for Mac OS X that makes it easy to configure and run Snort. HenWen simplifies setting up and maintaining software that scans network traffic for undesirables that a firewall may not block. Everything you need is bundled in, with no compiling or command-line use necessary.

---

4.   See *Responding to a hacker attack or other security breach* on page 216for more info.

Security Manager

NetIQ's Security Manager takes over where Security Analyzer leaves off by creating a system for automated response, host-based intrusion detection, event log consolidation, and security configuration management. The automatic response portion of this product is amazing. Security Manager provides more than 30 out-of-the-box responses, ranging from administrative tasks, including enabling or disabling user IDs, to operations tasks that include starting and stopping services and terminating applications and processes. Security Manager is more than an intrusion detection system, it's a defense intelligence system.

You're probably wondering what exactly constitutes a defense intelligence system for a network. Chances are, you've already encountered one in your childhood. What am I talking about? Actually, it's a who—every bad kid's nightmare, Sister Mary Knucklebuster of the School of Perpetual Sorrows, that's who. She's the nun who just sorta Knew All about your every questionable deed. No matter what you did, she knew it—and then *whack!* Sore knuckles for a day. It didn't matter if you screwed up in gym—*whack!* The lunch hall—*whack!* Putting prickles in Janey-Sue's pigtails—*whack!* She had eyes *everywhere.* How? Because each and every person around you was snitching, that's how. She *knew* because she had her tentacles wrapped tightly around every kid-snitch, teacher, and assistant in school, that's how. Very, *very* effective. Now think about Sister Mary's effectiveness if the only person in school who reported on your misbehavior was the principal—you'd be sailing off scot-free.

A network defense intelligence system is Sister Mary Knucklebuster's mechanical doppleganger. The heart of any defense intelligence system is the security auditing console—probably a SQL server running on your network somewhere that gathers all your security logs from the different security monitoring silos, such as your corporate firewall logs, your network intrusion detection system reports, each key user's personal firewall logs, etc. NetIQ's Security Manager is such a device.

The defense intelligence system gathers all the various security reporting tools' logs mentioned above, and puts the pieces of each individual security audit into their proper place in the puzzle. Recently, Wyatt Banks of NetIQ was up at the office, and we were discussing the role of such a system. As he pointed out, "It isn't that situation A being reported by audit software is bad in and of itself. Nor is it that situation B is very bad in and of itself. However, when situation A happens in tandem with situation B, you might have an attack on your hands." And the only way to build a secure system is to make all of your tools work *in concert* with each other. Let's walk through what it takes to build such a system.

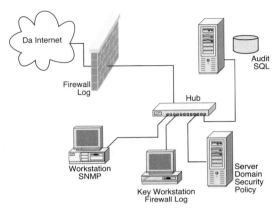

Figure 9-16. Security audit system

Know what is where

As we've stressed in our network corruption chapter, in *The computer's-eye view of your network* on page 153, one of the most critical baselines of networking is the name game: You must name your computers so that you can find them and differentiate them from each other. If you need to know how to do that, go back to the network corruption chapter (see *Network corruption* on page 125) and follow those directions.

Set local security policies

You can set the local security policy on Windows NT, 2000, and XP computers by enabling Windows security auditing, which enables the operating system to send security-specific events to the security event log on your computer, which is picked up by the security audit console. You can set these security audit settings in **User Manager** in NT and **Local Security Policy** in 2000 and XP. Both are in the **Start > Programs > Administrative tools folder**. Keep at least 20 MB of space for your logs.

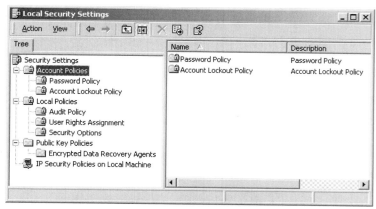

Figure 9-17. Windows 2000 Local Security Settings

Ⓧ While Mac OS X does indeed have a firewall system built into each computer (you can access its setting through the Sharing folder in System Preferences), it's not entirely clear whether or not any attempts or breaches are logged to the syslog file on the computer. As we learn more about this operating system, we'll update our information on our www.backupbook.com website. Even if the firewall isn't logging information that the audit console can read, it won't hurt to turn the firewall on anyway—but you'd do well to get additional computer-based security tools like BrickHouse or FireWalk for OS X.

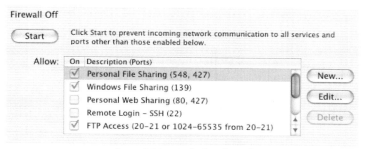

Figure 9-18. OS X built-in firewall

🐧 For Linux, you'll be working with ipfwadm. No, I didn't abandon spellcheck: **ipfwadm** is a utility to administer the IP accounting and firewall services offered by the Linux kernel. Firewall rules can be created or deleted via the **setsockopt(2)** system call. Via the same mechanism, a filter's default policy can be changed. Filters can be inspected by reading the following pseudo-files in the proc file system:

/proc/net/ip_input /proc/net/ip_output /proc/net/ip_forward

Each of these files lists the default policy, followed by the details of all rules (if any) belonging to that filter, in a compact format. The **ipfwadm** command provides a command-level interface for managing the Linux firewall facilities, and can be used to change or inspect all aspects of the kernel filters.

Standardize your security policies beforehand, document and then post them somewhere in your intranet for your security team to read and review on a regular basis. They'll be a bit different for each OS, but that's par for the course.

Set domain security policies

You'll need to set your **domain security policies** on the Windows 2000 domain controller (this isn't available in Windows NT 4.0). Domain security policies override local security policies and allow you to use the policy to enable security auditing[5]. In Microsoft Windows NT Server 4.0, *domain security policy* referred to an associated group of items considered critical to the secure configuration of a domain. These include:

- Audit Policy to control what types of events are recorded in the security log. User Password, or Account Policy to control how passwords are used by user accounts.

- User Rights are applied to groups or users and affect the activities permitted on an individual workstation, a member server, or on all domain controllers in a domain.

---

5.   This and other security information can be found on Microsoft's support website, and in more detail in their white paper: "Introduction to Windows 2000 Group Policy," http://www.microsoft.com/windows2000/techinfo/howitworks/management/grouppolicyintro.asp.

In Windows 2000, Microsoft has reconfigured these components into one consistent hierarchy or tool, the Security Settings snap-in in the Group Policy Editor. This may be useful if you want to know the proper group policy object to change.

To configure security settings intended to span a domain, use the Group Policy Editor snap-in, with its focus set to the "Default Domain Policy" Group Policy object (GPO):

1. Click **Start**, point to **Programs**, point to **Administrative Tools**, and then click **Active Directory Users and Computers**.

2. Right-click the appropriate domain object, and then click **Properties**.

3. Click the **Group Policy** tab to view currently linked group policy objects.

4. Click the **Default Domain Policy** GPO link, and then click **Edit**.

After you start the Group Policy Editor snap-in, you can gain access to domain security policies from the following node:

Console Root\"Default Domain Policy" Policy\Computer Configuration\Windows Settings\Security Settings

At this point in the hierarchy, you have access to both the account policies and the local policies.

When a computer is joined to a domain with the Active Directory and group policy implemented, a local **Group Policy Object** is processed. The Windows Group Policy is administered through the use of these Group Policy Objects, data structures that are attached in a specific hierarchy to selected Active Directory objects, such as sites, domains, or organizational units. These GPOs, once created, are applied in a standard order: LSDOU, which stands for (1) Local; (2) Site; (3) Domain; and (4) OU; the later policies are superior to the earlier applied policies.

Set Windows group policy

Windows 2000 domain controllers pull some security settings only from Group Policy objects linked to the root of the domain (the domain container). These settings from Group Policy Objects are not applied on the domain controller's organizational unit, because a domain controller can be moved into a different

ASSIGN RESPONSIBILITIES & CREATE YOUR TEAM

Once you've got your intrusion detection or defense intelligence system running, assign the hacker or virus attack fixes to the most likely candidate in your organization—probably the individual server's administrator, and, in the case of workstations with holes and vulnerabilities, whoever takes care of network security.

By assigning the various fixes for each box to the person responsible, you have now set a date by which the hole should be fixed, and you can later verify that those fixes have been accomplished. Yes, you must continue to set update dates frequently, making sure that each of your patches is both current and correct.

For a team effort, share the responsibility for security-hole-testing any new platform you add to the network with the security administrator. Before you back up the new device, check off on whether or not it is secure. The security administrator must keep current on patch updates for software for each of the platforms in your system. The security admin should then communicate which patches are available for which applications to both the backup admin and the training coordinator (who should be teaching a security class to folks who run network services on their computers). While the security admin runs monthly scanning probes on the network (and full-time monitoring programs), emergency response to a hack attempt should be shared with the backup administrator.

	Equip. Testing	Updating Patches	Monthly Testing	Response Tm	Comm. & Training
Backup Admin	Yes			Yes	
Security Admin	Yes	Yes	Yes	Yes	Yes
Help Desk Admin				Yes	Yes
Training Coordinator					Yes
VAR	Yes			Yes	

Table 9-2. Responsibilities list

Why should an emergency response to a hack attempt be shared with a backup administrator? Think of it this way—if someone were to deface your website, unless the defacement was obvious, how would you know? The easiest way to find defaced pages on a website is to create a backup report. Your backup software can and will quickly tell you which pages of the website are *newer* than the last ones it backed up. A quick coordination check with the webmaster will reveal which page changes are from your staff—and which are courtesy of the hacker.

We've also listed your VAR in the group. If your VAR is building and prepping your systems for you before they're sent to your organization, you'll want to keep her in the loop about the newest builds, images, and security patches you're working with. And, if you keep her in the loop at the best of times, your VAR might be able to come to the rescue at the worst of times with a loaner machine or other valuable services—but if it comes down to the tumbril, I wouldn't count on her pulling a Sidney Carton for you.

 For everyone in your team, make sure you know whether or not they can be contacted in the evenings and on weekends, and keep multiple methods of contact on file.

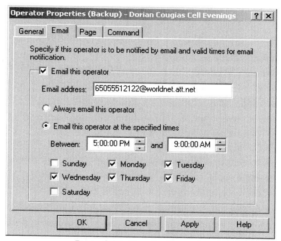

Figure 9-19. Operator Properties

As with the settings for configuring the notification groups of NetIQ, set up the user twice: for business-hours and for after-hours contact. In the window depicted in Figure 9-19. I've set myself up for evenings. I've added my cell phone number, which is set up by AT&T so that it can receive short (255 characters) text-based e-mail messages called SMS messages; this works great for evening calls when I'm not going checking regular e-mail. I then set up another account for myself during the day to send messages directly to my normal e-mail address.

Fixing the holes

Plain and simple: Fixes should be done as quickly and painlessly as possible. Your scanning software should include not only the problems it's discovered, but the recommended solutions to those problems, as well. Several Internet databases archive security vulnerabilities, but Cisco's Secure Encyclopedia (CSEC)[6] actually helps security personnel prioritize potential problems by relating security faults to specific industries. The service is free, but you do have to sign up for a Cisco ID to use it.

A quick tour of their headlines at the site turned up this little tidbit (Figure 9-20.), which not only describes the problem, but details its severity, its consequences—and its fix.

Multiple Vulnerabilitiesfound in Microsoft IIS

Severity:Vulnerability Type:Exploit Type: High SeverityNetwork Access

Description
Microsoft advisory MS02-0018 describes ten vulneralilities related to the IIS HTTP / FTP server component of Windows NT / 2000 / XP.

The vulnerabilities included in the Microsoft advisory are:
- Buffer overrun in Chunked Encoding mechanism
- Microsoft-discovered variant of Chunked Encoding buffer overrun
- ...

Consequences
A remote attacker may be able to execute arbitrary code on the web server with varying degrees of privilege depending upon the version of IIS. Denial of service attacks could render the IIS service unavailable. Cross site scripting issues could lead to the exposure of sensitive information such as HTTP session cookies.

Countermeasures
Apply the cumulative patch listed in the referenced Microsoft advisory for your particular platform(s).

Access Required:Network connectivity to the vulnerable web server.

Access Gained:Ability to execute arbitrary code or denial of service depending on the vulnerability exploited.

Figure 9-20. CESC vulnerability report

As you download your patches and apply them to the boxes on your network, communicate with your team members to coordinate your applied patches so that you don't have multiple people doing the same research.

 If you're using Citadel's Hercules system, you don't have to worry about much of the above, as it's done automatically for you (and within minutes versus hours).

---

6.   http://www.cisco.com/pcgi-bin/front.x/csec/csecHome.pl

All you have to do is import the security scan into their system (as mentioned earlier in *Immediate remediation* on page 197), decide which of the updates to apply, and then apply them. No fuss, no muss.

Verify that the holes are fixed

The best way to verify the efficacy of the fixes? Rerun the tests on the computers and check your original scores against the after-patch-and-repair scores.

If the same holes remain, someone has dropped the ball (Security Analyzer lets you run a comparison report to tell the difference between two scans).

If you can get in through a new hole, go back and put new patches in.

 Once you've verified that your holes are fixed:

1. Re-image the system, and then

2. Back up the system, so if something gets hit and you have to restore, you can restore to the last known level of security before adding additional patches. If you don't, you could lose some patches you've already applied.

RESPONDING TO A HACKER ATTACK OR OTHER SECURITY BREACH

You're the backup administrator, and you're at lunch. Your feet are propped up on your desk, and you're scarfing a sloppy sub, chuckling at the latest *Mad* magazine. All is well—until you glance at your security management console and see 30 new breaches!

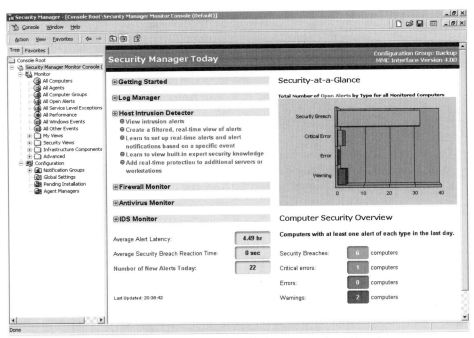

Figure 9-21. Security Manager console showing more than 30 breaches

Once you've swallowed hard and your pulse returns to somewhere near normal, if you're using NetIQ, you'd simply click the **Security Breaches** button below the bar chart to get a list of all six computers with breaches. Accessing the list, you see individual devices and then open up each of the alerts to assign them to someone to fix one-by-one. If you're using an intrusion detection system like HenWen or Snort that doesn't provide a console, you'd walk into the office and scan 30+ e-mails with the same information. Because it presents the most consolidated front and has the better interface of the three products we've reviewed, we'll use NetIQ's Security Manager to demonstrate how to examine a condition, assign the fix, and then find a resolution. With this product, you can select each breach and open the property for that alert, as shown in the window below (Figure 9-22.).

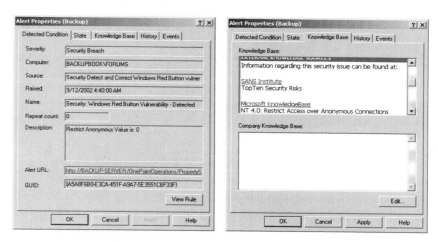

Figure 9-22. NetIQ's alert properties window showing Condition (left) and KnowledgeBase (right)

Before you assign someone in the team to fix the alert (assuming the "team" isn't just you) check the KnowledgeBase to find out more about the alert and how to fix it. As we've noted above, any intrusion detection worth its salt gives you a location to find out more about the alert and ways to fix that specific security breach. In this case, the window (right side, Figure 9-22.) reveals two locations the administrator can examine to sniff out more about this specific problem.

This particular alert sends the administrator off to the SANS Institute as well as the Microsoft website, in search of very specific answers. Once you know what in the world has happened to the device, you can assign fixing the problem to the particular person or group responsible for this aspect of your security management arena.

If you're using NetIQ, move over to the **State** tab of the dialog, assign the problem to an owner to be alerted, and then fix the problem (Figure 9-23. on page 218).

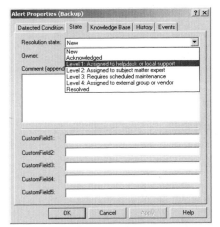

Figure 9-23. Assigning the security breach to an owner

If you're using Snort or HenWen, simply forward the e-mail notification to the appropriate person with your own notes on what to do.

Quarantine the device

The next step? *Immediately* quarantine your device. Any attacked system, especially if attacked by a virus or Trojan horse, must be taken off the normal network to stop the spread of the attacking program. Quarantining your device means *taking it completely off of the network* so that you can make a disk image of the hard drive to send to the authorities or your security personnel for analysis.

Restore the backed-up contents to a temporary replacement server

If the quarantined system is a key element in the work process, you, as backup administrator, must get a secondary computer up and running to take its place by swapping computers and doing an emergency restore of the backed-up data to the new or temporary box taking Device X's place.

This might mean moving a "hot" swap box into place, or doubling up another server to act as two for the time being. Whatever your decision, use your own business continuity plan for disaster recovery in this instance. It's one heck of a way to test your theories, but they should work, and you should be in business as soon as you can restore the data of Server X to your temporary location on Server Y.

Now, *before* you decide to restore any of the data, check which files were modified by the hacker, virus, or Trojan horse. Also, check which methodology your backup software uses when backing up and restoring files. Knowing which methodology your backup software uses to back up files is important—especially if your system is one like Retrospect,which backs up the first instance of a file it sees (this is called **single-instance storage**), and then *doesn't* back up any other file with the same metadata (name/modify date/creation date/byte size/host file system, etc.), but merely creates a pointer to the file on the tape or disk backup.

Let's say that there are two computers being backed up: a workstation and a server. When it comes to backing up common files, such as dlls that have the same meta-data, Retrospect and other backup software like it backs up the first instance of the file (in the case of Figure 9-24. , the workstation version) and then, instead of backing up the same file again, the next computer has a *pointer* to the place on the tape (or disk) where the initial file was backed up.

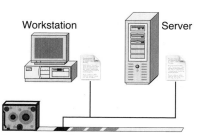

Workstation   Server

Figure 9-24. Backing up the .dll file once and then using a pointer to it afterward

So, let's say that on day 1 of the backup, everything was hunky-dory and went smoothly. But on day 4 , a hacker hits the server right before it's backed up so that you can't get there and stop the process quick enough. You have now successfully backed up a hacked file. The *good news*? As long as any piece of the metadata has changed (for example, the file has a new modification date and its size is different), the file will be different enough that no other device (unless it, too, was hacked) will have a pointer to this file. The server's snapshot of day 4's backup points to the newly backed-up (hacked) version of the dll (Figure 9-25. on page 220).

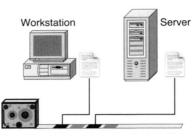

Figure 9-25. Backing up a hacked dll

You can see from the above that restoring using the day 4 snapshot of the server will restore the hacked file. So what you *don't* want to ever do after an attack is to set your backup software's preferences to restore *the most recent* version of the backup. First, you must find out when you got hit and restore the information that was backed up before that date. You won't have to worry about other restores to other computers—they'll use the undamaged file. Using snapshots, you never get a different file from one that originally resided on a given machine at that date and time. In the case of Retrospect, the program doesn't use a newer date to decide that the file is "better"—it's completely date-agnostic, treating older or newer dates as different, but never preferring one to the other.

Allow limited access to this information and plan for a separate backup

Once you've the restored data onto a working substitute server, if that server is one that you've had to double-up on, make sure that you keep your backup of this data separate from the rest of the server's normal data, so if you have to restore that server, you won't accidentally put these documents back on the substitute computer at a later date.

And since this is a temporary home for your data, treat it like a *good* friend's house: Don't invite all of your rowdy pals over to have at the data. Based on this server's new load, you might want to restrict access to those who need immediate access to the data, and have the others in the organization tackle something else on their busy schedules for the day.

Wipe the system

You'd be just plain old goofy to want to put the infected Server X back onto your network. *Wipe the system completely.* Reformat the hard drives and reinstall the system, either from your drive image or from the backup files themselves.

 Don't waste your time with cleaning systems, virus removers, etc. Sterilize that baby and start from scratch. You won't have to worry about having missed something. And then don't bring the system back online until you've found how the hacker entered the system in the first place and you've found and applied the patches that close that open door the hacker crept in through.

Because you're probably rebuilding the system from an image, and then updating your image for new security patches, this is a great time to update the drive image master, as well.

Change your address

I know this sounds hokey, but you might want to change the address of the affected system, too. This makes it just a few minutes harder for the hacker to find it again, but at least you'll have those few minutes to spot the incoming attack while Mr. Creepo's rummaging around looking for the new address.

If your backup of the old server was "hard coded" to an IP address, make sure that you have the new address and you've tested your new address in the backup system.

Run another backup

Before you put the new system live on the network again, back it up once more. It's now spanking clean, and having one full backup in this state sure won't hurt your chances for future survival.

A SECURITY CHECKLIST FOR BRINGING A NEW SYSTEM ONLINE

1. Change the defaults for your device as much as you can. Ensure that the default user names are changed to something else that fits your naming strategy, as discussed earlier. Doubly ensure that all default passwords are changed to something other than their "boxed" version. Change the root directories of your web server's files. People attack what they know. If you've moved things, the hacker will be like a blind person navigating a stranger's house.

2. Build computer-based defense systems around the computer you're going to deploy. Does the device need a "personal" firewall? How will anti-virus software work with this computer? Have you installed *all* of the known patches for the system—you've checked them out at Cisco's CSEC site? Should this device be monitored by the organization's defense intelligence system?

3. Run a penetration scan using the tools you've run on the network or individual devices, on this one. If you've run an up-to-date vulnerability scan on the device and everything is clean, you're ready for a full backup and image creation.

4. Image the device—or, if you aren't into imaging your devices, get ready for failure in whatever fashion you so choose for your network. Have the information "locked and loaded," as they say in the military, so that when something hits, you're ready for the bombardment.

5. Plan for failure. If this device gets hit and you have to take it offline, how will you replace it? Will you replace it with a spare computer? Will it stay offline until you've wiped it and then restored it? Will this device be "doubled up" onto another device—if so, have you tested your theory to see if it'll work?

6. Test your recovery theory. If you don't test it in the absence of panic, when there *is* a panic, it's likely that you won't be ready and you'll flub the recovery effort. Always test when you have time to think through issues that come up at the last second. To test the theory, once everything is set up, bring the box down and then move the data over to whatever your plan suggests. Get it working, and time how long it takes. This will be useful if something really does go wrong: You'll be able to say (with confidence) that you'll be up and running again within the time-frame you already tested. Make sure you add

15 minutes to your estimate, so that when you finish early, everyone will realize your true genius.

7. Bring the system fully online and then run one more test hit against it. Did the Intrusion Detection System (IDS) pick up the hit? Did you get notified? If so, you're finally ready. If not, make sure that a hit to the system can get picked up by your IDS and that you get notified in whatever fashion you've set.

8. Then go get some Krispy Kremes and relax. You deserve it. You are ready. And send us an e-mail. We want to know how it all worked out.

SETTING UP AN E-MAIL DEFENSE SYSTEM

An **e-mail defense system** is a bit different than a hacker defense system, as you don't have to scan the entire network to find the point of failure. It's simple—it's your e-mail server and the content that comes in through it. E-mail resources have never been more vulnerable, and the incidence of hostile attacks continues to climb. More than 90 percent of all viruses can be attributed to e-mail, and who knows how many new viruses are unleashed each month? Here are some interesting numbers about SPAM and e-mail viruses:

650 – The percent of increase in spam during 2001. Source: SurfControl

$2,000 – The amount that a Washington State small-claims court awarded Bennett Haselton, who sued spammers over four messages they sent him. Each spammer had to pay $500. Source: Spamcon Foundation (www.spamcon.org)

15 – The age of "suid," the Israeli kid who admitted writing the "Pentagone" virus, which attacked millions of Windows users through Outlook and ICQ. Masquerading as a screensaver, the program deleted anti-virus software and installed a Trojan horse that allowed remote control via Internet Relay Chat (IRC). Source: McAfee

Spam is getting so bad that some ISPs[7] have begun issuing ultimatums to corporate customers: Meet baseline standards or take your business elsewhere. Whether they're successful or not (most service providers have not yet created a formal list of security requirements), many have some kind of policy that attempts to dictate what companies can and can't do as customers, and the kinds of security systems that must be in place before they can purchase services. These service providers want to see IT managers install encryption and authentication products, firewalls that interact with intrusion detection software, dedicated servers, and VPN links to secure data. They also want IT shops to use tools such as anti-virus software, specified intrusion detection systems, and anti-spam content filtering[8]. In this sec-

---

7. Service providers that have such a policy include Ameritech, AT&T and CTC Communications, and national ISPs, EarthLink, Exodus Communications, and PSINet.

tion, we'll describe the things you need to know about anti-spam content filtering and anti-virus software for your e-mail server.

Simple mail server anti-virus defense

I followed a recent discussion in Google Groups among a bunch of friends who had encountered a new and interesting e-mail-borne virus. I've gotten their permission to give you details, but have taken their names and most of the rest of the conversation out of the loop. This is more or less what was said:

Friend 1   I tried to open an attachment today that was labeled !"#$. It wouldn't open, but later in the day, I got an e-mail saying that I had a virus. It's called sulfnbk.exe. I did a search and found it in the WINDOWS\COMMAND folder. So, if anyone gets that attachment in their mail (mine was from *Friend X*), DON'T OPEN IT!

Friend 2   Note to everybody: You might not get sulfnbk.exe as the attachment. The actual virus/worm is called Magistr and it sends out a variety of infected .exe files. cfgwz32.exe is another of its victims (I got an e-mail with this one from Friend X myself, but I didn't run the attachment). Note that these are *real* Windows files (sulfnbk is for managing long file names, for instance), and if you delete the infected versions, it would be a good idea to replace them from your original Windows installation disks. You don't have to worry about replacing anything if you just delete the e-mails and their attachments without running the attachments.

I got 2 e-mails this morning from *Friend 1's* address with a stars.exe and sulfbnk.exe. I deleted the 2 e-mails and didn't attempt opening the files. I also got an e-mail from *Friend X* yesterday with sulfbnk.exe too. Ugh! I hate viruses.

Friend 3   This was my first experience with a virus, and I've sure learned my lesson! I hardly ever open attachments. Unfortunately, with all the e-mails going back and forth about *Friend Y*, I thought the attachment "from *Friend X*" had something to do with him. So I naively clicked on it.

It turns out that this virus is smart enough (once activated) to enter a user's address book, get the list of names in the address book, grab *one* of the names in the address book, and set it as the outgoing e-mail address (whether it was that user's

8.   "Security Strategies: Get serious about security—ISPs are demanding that IT shops get their security policies in order, and companies are complying," by R. Tadjer, *InternetWeek* (2001).

particular computer or not), and then send itself to all other users in the address book. In reality, it wasn't *Friend X* who had sent those two e-mails—it was another friend not even mentioned in this dialog. Ouch. I asked him directly if I could interview him for this book. What I learned was (as usual)…

- The Windows machines are at *great* risk, there's *some* risk to the Macintosh machines, and little risk to the Linux machines.

- Some of the mail servers and users in question had anti-virus software running on them, and some of those were completely up-to-date with the latest virus definitions.

- Each of the users whose computers had become infected indeed lost the Windows files that the virus attacked. There's no fix for this other than restoring the files from original CD, disk image, or backup application.

What are we to conclude? At minimum, you'll need anti-virus software on your mail server, such as Norton's AntiVirus for Microsoft Exchange for Windows, or the built-in McAfee Virex for 4D (Webstar) Mail. *This doesn't obviate the necessity of running anti-virus software on your desktops and other servers, as well.*

Norton AntiVirus for Microsoft Exchange secures your Microsoft Exchange environment against virus attack by monitoring all public folders and mailboxes on your Exchange servers, scanning the body and attachments of e-mail messages, including files in compressed and encoded formats. The Auto-Protect feature of Norton AntiVirus detects viruses in real-time, managing them according to your specifications. You can configure Norton AntiVirus to repair, quarantine, delete, or log detected viruses and send e-mail alerts to selected administrators and users to keep them informed of virus activity. You can use LiveUpdate to keep virus protection current. With LiveUpdate, Norton AntiVirus for Microsoft Exchange connects *automatically* (which is great, because you don't have to worry about keeping it up-to-date) to special Symantec sites and determines if virus definitions need updating. If updates are needed, the required files are downloaded and installed in the proper location.

4D Mail provides support for virus scanning through McAfee Virex. If the administrator enables this feature, 4D Mail passes all incoming mail for local addresses to the virus scanner. The server immediately refuses to accept a message that Virex flags as infected, sending an error to the sending SMTP server explaining the failure. Administrators can choose to keep a copy of rejected messages in the Quarantine folder. Administrators are not notified, since the message is automatically rejected (and the sender is aware of the problem), but they can review the Quarantine folder for troubleshooting purposes. Just like Norton's, McAfee Virex's virus definitions can be automatically updated to ensure your safety from any new virus attacks.

In essence, both programs work the same way. The application intercepts all incoming e-mail and then checks it and all its attachments for viruses. If a virus is detected, the message is rejected, returning an error to the sender or sending SMTP server and then putting the offending message into a quarantine directory on the mail server for troubleshooting or legal purposes. If, on the other hand, the message has no viruses in it or attached to it, it's forwarded to the mail server's normal operations, and all is fine in the world.

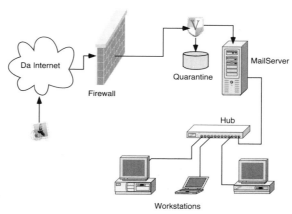

Figure 9-26. Direct Server-based protection

The advantage of adding anti-virus capabilities to your organization's mail server is that the mail server–based anti-virus program doesn't care whether the sender or receiver's computer is a Mac, Windows, or Linux computer. At the mail server level, a known virus is a known virus. This is not always the case on the end user's computer. Some programs check for viruses for only the particular workstation OS that the program is running on—some Mac software checks for Mac-only viruses; Windows for Windows-only, etc., which means that a Mac user could pass on a virus to a Windows user, and vice versa.

Perimeter protection for your e-mail server

To be honest with you, putting e-mail anti-virus protection on the e-mail server itself is very much like having a guard dog that lets thieves into the building but doesn't let them leave. Call me silly, but I'd much rather keep the bad guys out of the building completely than let them into a quarantined room of the building. By moving your protection to a perimeter service, you can set up your anti-spam mechanism much more effectively than if you ran it from your own servers.

In establishing a well-protected e-mail system, you also have to guard against server misuse by hackers and spammers. Spammers are not only bothersome, but the spam that comes through the mail server hogs mail server processes as well as network bandwidth.

One type of spam/hacking, the **Directory Harvest Attack (DHA)**, is designed to obtain valid e-mail addresses in the organization to send members of the organization more spam. In a DHA, spammers attempt to deliver messages to multiple addresses, such as johndoe@yourco.com, jdoe@yourco.com, and john@yourco.com. Addresses that aren't rejected by the receiving mail server are determined valid, compiled into lists and repeatedly sold to other spammers. A successful DHA can net a spammer thousands of corporate e-mail addresses in just a few minutes. Users whose addresses are harvested quickly begin receiving an ever-growing amount of junk e-mail, as spammers resell and exchange lists of known valid addresses[9].

To further complicate issues, e-mail servers overloaded by DHA traffic may be unable to accept legitimate incoming traffic, thus appearing unreachable to customers and business partners who are attempting to send real business-related messages. Sure, it's possible to identify DHA hackers by manually examining e-mail server logs. However, attackers aren't stupid—just lazy and unprincipled—they frequently switch IP addresses to stay under the detection radar. And by the time a DHA hacker is identified through log file analysis, the horse already done run outa the barn: Your organization's addresses are in the spammer's database, and they've moved on to the next mark.

---

9. "Directory Harvest Attacks Pose Significant Security Threat to Corporate E-mail Systems," Postini, http://www.postini.com/press/pr/pr081302.html (2002).

The best thing to do? Identify these attacks in real-time, and on a server other than yours, so that your organization can proactively protect the proprietary personnel list stored on your e-mail systems using a pertinacious approach. (My apologies: I adore alliterative excess!) Oh, by the way, this is a good way to get rid of general spam, as well.

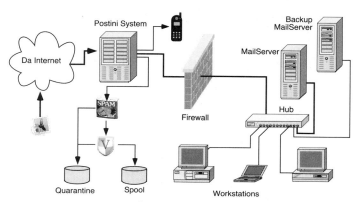

Figure 9-27. E-mail system perimeter protection by Postini

The Postini service is the best we've seen. They set up their server so that it's a "bump in the road" of the flow of e-mail traffic—*before* the e-mail hits your server (they call it an inline SMTP utility service). Figure 9-27. shows the Postini system setup, in which all e-mail (good, bad, and indifferent) hits the Postini service first, filtering out unwanted spam as well as viruses and DHA attacks, before the mail you want is then forwarded through to your company. The small phone on the top of the diagram above indicates that Postini can even contact you via wireless cell phone, blueberry, blackberry, raspberry, whateverberry, to tell you if your e-mail service can't be reached and is therefore "down" for some reason. The thick line in the diagram follows the route that "good" mail takes through the system as it passes through the Content Manager and then Content Filter of the Postini perimeter protection system.

As you can see in Figure 9-27. , I've also placed a *backup* e-mail server. When you move your e-mail gathering and filtering system outside your network, you can also use the Postini service as a mail spool, so that if your mail server dies, you can quickly bring a secondary server online and have Postini redirect e-mail to *it*, ensuring that you keep your e-mail downtime to a minimum. A very nice service to have at the ready, it makes e-mail backup and recovery that much easier.

Setting up the Postini system

As you can see from the form below that shows the organizational information, and Figure 9-29. on page 231 on the following page, the Postini setup is quite detailed. New service, junk-mail notification, virus suspicion, and virus alert e-mails for the organization are set up (so that the user gets a custom message that fits the organization's personality). At the same time, an initial list of "approved" junk-mail senders and blocked senders can be added. Once that's done, it's time to configure the attack-blocking mechanisms (which is the real reason you've chosen this service).

Postini Internal Mail → Network Frontiers Account

Organization Identification

Postini customer name	Network Frontiers
Organization ID	100029453
Organization Name	Network Frontiers Account
Parent	Postini Internal Mail
Support Contact	dcouglas@netfrontiers.com — This is the email address for support inquiries.
Default User	postinidefault@netfrontiers.com
Mail Host	Select from the list of email servers in the left side navigation, then select the Delivery Manager tab. Default Message Limit is located at the bottom of this page. All CC addresses must be deliverable through the same mailhost that the orginal message was routed to.
Virus alert CC	
Detailed Reporting	on

User Notifications

All user notifications include default branding with the name of your organization in the text. In most cases, you will not need to modify this text. However, you may choose to customize the following notifications:

Welcome notification	on
New service welcome	None. You may add one.
First-time junk email alert	None. You may add one.
Junk email alert	None. You may add one.
Suspension alert	None. You may add one.
Notification Interval	7 days
Virus alert	None. You may add one.

Applications

User access — Enable end-user control over applications

Junk Email

Approved Senders — Enter a specific address or an entire domain to explicitly allow email from a sender to pass through Postini filters for this organization, regardless of junk email charicteristics (Note: users may override organizational settings within their personal configurations.)

Example: user@domain.com or domain.com

postini.com
postinicorp.com
1.digital.cnet.com
2.digital.cnet.com
123greetings.com

Add this item to list — Select item(s) to remove

Blocked Senders — Enter a specific address or an entire domain to explicitly block email, regardless of legitimate email characteristics. Any message from the sender will be held in quarantine for this organization's users until manual deletion by the user or expiration. (Note: users may override organizational blocked senders within their personal configurations.)

Example: user@domain.com or domain.com

Add this item to list — Select item(s) to remove

Virus Cleaning	on
Max Message Size	MB. If specified, must be between 1 - 300 MB. Default value is 200 MB (when left blank).
Default Message Limit	Number of messages per day. User settings override organization settings.

Figure 9-28. Organizational management setup

To identify attacks, Postini's system performs statistical and content analysis. They wouldn't tell us the syntax or threshold values of the rules definitions, because we're writing a book and they want to keep the spammers guessing.

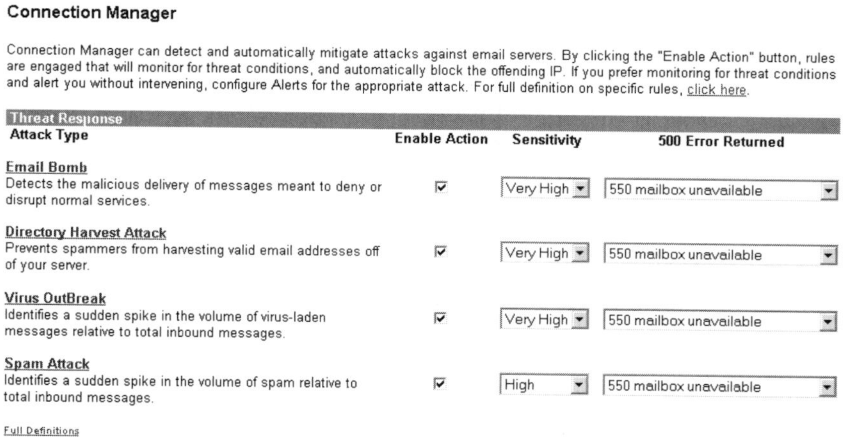

Connection Manager

Connection Manager can detect and automatically mitigate attacks against email servers. By clicking the "Enable Action" button, rules are engaged that will monitor for threat conditions, and automatically block the offending IP. If you prefer monitoring for threat conditions and alert you without intervening, configure Alerts for the appropriate attack. For full definition on specific rules, click here.

Threat Response

Attack Type	Enable Action	Sensitivity	500 Error Returned
Email Bomb Detects the malicious delivery of messages meant to deny or disrupt normal services.	☑	Very High ▾	550 mailbox unavailable ▾
Directory Harvest Attack Prevents spammers from harvesting valid email addresses off of your server.	☑	Very High ▾	550 mailbox unavailable ▾
Virus OutBreak Identifies a sudden spike in the volume of virus-laden messages relative to total inbound messages.	☑	Very High ▾	550 mailbox unavailable ▾
Spam Attack Identifies a sudden spike in the volume of spam relative to total inbound messages.	☑	High ▾	550 mailbox unavailable ▾

Full Definitions

Figure 9-29. Blocking attacks through Postini

A Very High sensitivity triggers a particular rule when the standard deviation from normal traffic characteristics is low. Conversely, a Very Low sensitivity requires a more substantial change in the characteristics of the traffic to trigger a rule. Normal is the recommended setting, recognizing the majority of attacks. The Normal setting is calibrated on the ongoing analysis of threat conditions across the nearly 20 million messages that Postini processes each day. Here are their targets:

E-mail bomb

E-mail bombs are denial of service attacks in which unusually large messages or an unusually high volume of messages are sent repeatedly. Postini's Connection Manager identifies spikes in message volume that violate standard variance in message traffic. Similar messages sent repeatedly, messages of particular size characteristics, and a high ratio of suspect to valid e-mail are classified as e-mail bombs.

Directory harvest attack

A **directory harvest attack**, also known as an **e-mail harvest attack**, is a series of delivery attempts that result in 550 errors. Your e-mail server happily responds to each request, issuing potentially thousands of 550 errors. When the spammer lucks into a valid address, a spam may be delivered, and the address is logged as valid. Sensitivity allows a variance in the ratio of valid to invalid messages per session or per source IP. Very Low sensitivity doesn't block the IP if a single valid address is in the session. Very High sensitivity ranges up to a ratio of 1:5 valid addresses.

Virus outbreak To identify this type of attack, Postini looks at a number of criteria. A **virus outbreak** is tracked by monitoring both the ratio of infected messages to valid e-mail and the total volume of infected messages from the network connection during a specific interval. If the ratio changes in a statistically significant manner, the network connection will be blocked for several hours.

Spam attack To identify this type of attack, Postini examines a number of criteria. A **spam attack** is tracked by monitoring both the ratio of spam to valid e-mail, as well as the total volume of spam from the network connection during a specific interval. If the ratio changes in a statistically significant manner, the network connection will be blocked for several hours.

Allowing individual user preferences for filters

Once you've set up your organizational information, you need to set up your user accounts. These can be automatically gleaned from Postini's surveillance of who is getting e-mail, or manually entered into the system through uploading a spreadsheet. Either way is effective.

One of the great things about the Postini system is that each user can set individual thresholds for five different categories of e-mail: bulk, sexually explicit, get-rich-quick schemes, racially insensitive, and special offers.

Figure 9-30. Filter categories

Reporting

After it's set up, the system does some nice reporting—one of the parts of the system that I really, *really* like, because it gives me visual evidence of what Postini does for me every day. Postini will report on everything from normal mail processes through amount of spool activity (they can spool your mail for you so that if your server goes down, nobody in the outside world will know), and the number of attacks blocked on a daily or weekly basis.

The daily address information shows you who got what mail. This is a great place to notice the fact that folks who aren't even at your organization anymore (like our editor, Cass) are still getting mail (four years post-departure!). It's also a pretty decent indicator of where your staff members are spending their time. One of our clients' staff members usually gets a ratio of 85 spam and virus-laden messages to every single good message. A quick check over his shoulder proves that he spends *a lot of time* on the Internet visiting all sorts of various and sundry sites.

Traffic by Domain - Daily for 09-11-2002
For Domain: netfrontiers.com

Recipient	Messages	Bytes	Account Messages	Forwarded	% of Msgs	% of Bytes	Quarantined	% of Msgs	% of Bytes
lheiberger@netfrontiers.com	55	444,582	0	55	--	--	0	--	--
lynn_heiberger@netfrontiers.com	15	59,370	0	15	--	--	0	--	--
heiberger@netfrontiers.com	10	59,739	0	10	--	--	0	--	--
dcougias@netfrontiers.com	10	30,400	10	9	90.0	82.6	1	10.0	17.4
cass_kovel@netfrontiers.com	4	15,715	0	4	--	--	0	--	--
dorian_cougias@netfrontiers.com	4	10,883	0	4	--	--	0	--	--
kkoop@netfrontiers.com	2	987,030	0	2	--	--	0	--	--
dcougias@netfrontiers.com	1	18,324	0	1	--	--	0	--	--
Grand Total	101	1,626,043	10	100	90.0	82.6	1	10.0	17.4

Figure 9-31. Daily e-mail traffic flow

You can also use this information to see how people are misaddressing mail to your users. Once you know how folks on the outside are misaddressing your mail, you can set up aliases of the misspellings and have the mail forwarded to the right person in the organization.

For those of us who like graph views of the same information, Postini provides graph views, as well, as shown in Figure 9-32. on page 234. We've highlighted two lines in the graph for you. The gray bars represent the total number of messages that have hit the system. The top line shows directory harvest attacks, e-mail bombs, etc. The line slightly below it shows the number of spam blocks that are currently running. Over to the right, we've highlighted the event tracker list that shows when the directory harvest attacks hit. You can use that list to back-track to those domains that are continuously attacking you, and then add them to your black-hole list of mail that never goes through.

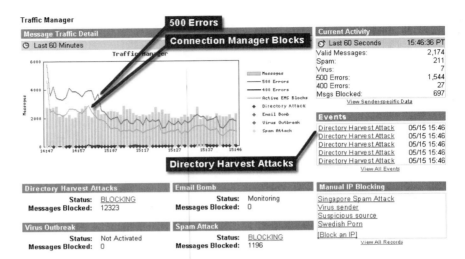

Figure 9-32. Traffic Manager reports

DNS SECURITY

During its most recent DNS health survey[10], Men & Mice found that 13 percent of the Fortune 1000 companies were running with *known* security vulnerabilities that could lead to denial-of-service attacks in their BIND (Berkeley Internet Name Domain) DNS software. Exploiting this vulnerability would cause the BIND server to shut down and leave the Internet blind to the location of the organization's client-facing servers.

An attacker can cause shutdown by sending a specific DNS packet designed to trigger an internal consistency check. However, this vulnerability doesn't allow an attacker to execute arbitrary code or write data to arbitrary locations in memory. The internal consistency check that triggers the shutdown occurs when the rdataset parameter to the dns_message_findtype() function in message.c is not NULL as expected. The condition causes the code to assert an error message and call abort() to shut down the BIND server[11]. It's also possible to accidentally trigger this vulnerability using common queries found in routine operations, especially queries originating from SMTP servers.

Exploitation of this vulnerability causes the BIND server to abort and shut down. As a result, the BIND server won't be available unless it is restarted.

And that's only the most current problem

Security holes in BIND have been found since hackers have found BIND. One of the interesting things that we've found regarding DNS security is that many DNS managers don't take security as serious as they should. A case in point is the *last* known security bug that was announced back in 2001.

After a major press run about the security bug in 2001 that affected roughly 17 percent of all companies, only about 5 percent of those affected fixed the bug![12]

---

10. "Domain Health Survey for .COM," http://www.menandmice.com/6000/61_recent_survey.html, Men & Mice (August 2002).

11. http://www.kb.cert.org/vuls/id/739123

The majority of news coverage of the bug list (there were four major bugs) focused on only the most serious of them[13]. Why so little attention to DNS security? It just isn't sexy, and there's not a lot anyone can do about it. It's not a big splash when it gets hit, and it isn't huge news unless it's a huge hacker attack. And the way to fix the attack is simply to upgrade the DNS server to a version that is patched for the attack: no packet analyzer teams swooping in, no intrusion detection system's bells and whistles blaring; simply a CERT warning that needs to be heeded and a patch that must be applied.

What can happen?

Hackers utilize BIND vulnerabilities to gain root access to the host or to turn the host into a launching platform for DOS attacks. An improper or insufficiently robust BIND configuration can also "leak" information about the hosts and addressing within the intranet. Miscreants can also take advantage of an insecure BIND configuration and poison the cache, thus permitting host impersonation and redirecting legitimate traffic to black holes or malicious hosts. Let's look at what can happen.

DNS spoofing and triggered cache poisoning

Triggered cache poisoning happens when a hacker induces a name server, either directly or indirectly, to query another name server under the hacker's control and then cache the bogus records. In July 1997, Eugene Kashpureff used an indirect triggered cache poisoning attack against the InterNIC's website. By poisoning the InterNIC's name servers' cache, he was able to spoof his alternic.net websites onto InterNIC's DNS system.

---

12. "Domain name system security still lax," http://www.cnn.com/2001/TECH/internet/03/02/lax.on.DNS.idg/index.html, CNN.com (2001).

13. "Fix for DNS software hole released," http://www.infoworld.com/articles/hn/xml/01/01/29/010129hnhole.xml?0129mnpm, *InfoWorld* (2001).

"Sleep tight, don't let the BIND bugs bite," http://www.thestandard.com/article/display/0,1151,21785,00.html, *The Standard* (2001).

"Software flaw may mean more Web outages," http://news.cnet.com/news/0-1003-201-4638816-0.html?tag=mn_hd, CNET (2001).

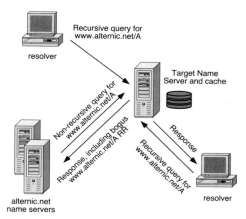

Figure 9-33. Kashpureff's attack

When spoofing, attackers can use the recursive mechanism described in the recursive call commands within legitimate DNS procedures by predicting the request that a DNS server will send out, and then replying with false information before the real reply arrives, as shown in the diagram above (Figure 9-33.). Each DNS packet has an associated 16-bit ID number that DNS servers use to determine the identity of the original query. In the case of BIND, the prevalent DNS server software, this number increases by 1 for each query, making the request easier to predict[14]. By providing false host name and mapping information, the attacker can misdirect name-resolution mapping while exposing network data to the threat of corruption. DNS involves a high trust relationship between client and server, and it is this trust that makes DNS vulnerable to spoofing.

After recursive querying, a second DNS vulnerability lies with DNS caching, which can be exploited through triggered cache poisoning. DNS servers cache all local zone files (hints file, and information for all zones the DNS server authorizes) and the results of all recursive queries they've performed since their last startup, to save time should they receive a similar query again. The length of time that recursive query results are held in the DNS cache (TTL–time to live) is configurable. The default is for a RR (resource record) to inherit the TTL of the zone (name domain) it's in.

---

14. This has been fixed in the later versions of BIND, in which DNS packets are assigned random numbers.

DNS cache poisoning involves sending a DNS server incorrect mapping information with a high TTL. The next time the DNS server is queried, it replies with the incorrect information. DNS cache poisoning occurs when malicious or misleading data received from a remote name server is inadvertently saved (cached) by another name server. This "bad" data is then made available to programs that request the cached data through the client interface. It's possible to limit exposure to this DNS cache poisoning attack by reducing the time that information is stored in the cache (the TTL), but this makes a negative impact on the server's performance.

Denial-of-Service attacks

Simple **denial-of-service attacks** can come in two forms. The first exploits DNS implementation flaws by responding to name server responses with parroted responses.

Figure 9-34. DNS denial-of-service parrot response attack

The second method overwhelms the server with zone name transfer requests. A **zone (name domain) transfer** is the transfer of the DNS database to a secondary server. It allows name servers that are authoritative for the same domain to stay in sync with each other. DNS servers should be configured to allow zone transfers between primary and secondary DNS servers only, because the information in a zone transfer, such as the IP addresses of important hosts, is very attractive to a hacker. Zone transfer attempts are often the first indication that a network is being probed.

Takeovers

Another attack involves breaking into the target network's DNS server per se; for example, the buffer overflow vulnerabilities of earlier BIND versions allowed root access to attackers. Once attackers gain control of the underlying DNS platform, they have control of the network environment.

Security measures you need to take

Let's walk through setting up DNS security for an organization laid out like the one in the following diagram that has two offices, with the main office in Ogunquit, Maine (with two subnets), and the branch office in Pismo Beach, California (with a single subnet).

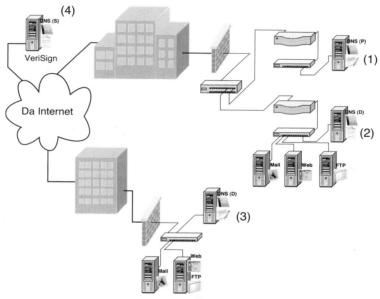

Figure 9-35. Two office organization

In this diagram, we show four name servers:

1. This is the Primary, or WhoIs listed authoritative server for the myco.com network. This server is a Unix box running BIND.

2. This is a Windows 2000 Server running Active Directory and Windows DNS. It has a delegated zone ogun.myco.com.

3. This is a Windows 2000 Server running Active Directory and Windows DNS. It has a delegated zone pismo.myco.com.

4. The organization has chosen to partially outsource DNS slave services to a third party (in this case, VeriSign) to protect the organization in case of disaster at either or both of their locations.

Setting up the firewall

First, restrict the number of services running on the name server itself and then restrict access to the servers at your border router and bastion host. Eliminating unnecessary network services reduces the potential holes in your server's security. Limiting protocol delivery sets up strong anti-spoofing measures.

From	Source Port	To	Dest. Port	Protocol	Purpose
Any	Any	Name Server (1)	53	UDP or TCP	Queries from the Internet
Name Server (1)	53	Any	Any	UDP or TCP	Name Server responses
Name Server (1)	Any	Any	53	UDP or TCP	Queries from your name server
Any	53	Name Server (1)	Any	UDP or TCP	Responses from your name server

Table 9-3. Firewall setup for name servers

Set this up for all firewalls that have name servers behind them so that the "public" queries are delivered only to your primary name server and not to any of the "local" delegated name servers, such as name servers 2 and 3.

Setting up an offsite name server

Because your building(s) can fall down, you need to find an offsite slave name server for one or more of your zones. Far too many organizations have a single point of failure (their own network) in their DNS infrastructure. Get into the habit of moving at least one of the authoritative name servers offsite in case your primary site has problems.

You can ask your local ISP whether or not slave name service is included (or at least available) in their package. Companies such as Nominum[15], SecondaryDNS[16], and VeriSign[17] offer secondary slave name server services. VeriSign's High-Availability service provides companies with robust DNS support for Inter-

---

15. http://www.nominum.com/.

16. http://www.secondarydns.com/

net systems (like websites and e-mail) through VeriSign's substantial investment in DNS infrastructure. VeriSign name servers are located around the globe and currently support the .com, .net, and .org domains. As such, they respond without interruption to more than 6 billion queries per day. Companies can now be sure their websites, e-mail, and other online systems are supported by the most robust and reliable DNS infrastructure available.

Or you can ask your local VAR who supplies your computer equipment for a slave name server service. Partnering with a local VAR whom you already trust is a really, *really* good idea.

TSIG

With BIND 8.2 and later name servers, you can use **transaction signatures** (**TSIG**) to cryptographically authenticate and verify zone data. TSIG uses shared secret codes and a one-way hash function to authenticate DNS messages such as updates. For this to work properly, you must configure a key on your primary master name server (as well as all slave name servers) and instruct them to use the key to sign communication with each other[18]. In essence, this means that you have to set the primary master's named. conf as well as synchronizing the time between all name servers involved.

Once TSIG is configured correctly, the name server (or client attempting to update its own record) adds a TSIG record to the additional data section of a DNS message, thus "signing" the DNS message to indicate that it isn't forged by some assailant to the system.

Set this up for all of your name servers running BIND. Windows 2000 DNS servers aren't TSIG compliant, so they should be relegated to specific zone services such as dynamic user zone services.

---

[17]. http://www.verisign-grs.com/mdns/ha/

[18]. This is covered thoroughly in pages 145–147 of C. Liu's "Defining a TSIG Key," *DNS and BIND Cookbook* (O'Reilly, 2002).

Limiting queries

Next, make sure you limit the devices from which your name servers accept queries. Accepting recursive queries from the Internet makes your name servers vulnerable to spoofing attacks, wherein your server is forced to query their server, which then sends back bogus data that could end up in your cache. Disabling recursion puts your name servers into a passive mode, telling them never to send queries on behalf of other name servers or resolvers. To deal with this, restrict recursion as well as the addresses the name server responds to when receiving queries. A non-recursive name server is very difficult to spoof.

A caching-only name server should accept queries *only* from the IP addresses of resolvers it serves. You can't disable recursion on a name server if any legitimate resolvers query it, or if other name servers use it as a forwarder.

An authoritative-only name server must accept queries from any IP address, but shouldn't accept any recursive queries.

And then you need to black-hole (deny) any private, experimental, or multicast networks. Rob Thomas maintains an outstanding list of those sites[19].

In our example (Figure 9-35. on page 239), you'd set up your Primary DNS server (1) to accept queries from any IP address, not *not* to accept recursive queries.

Restricting zone transfers

You must restrict zone transfers only to slave name servers and other authorized software. This prevents others from taxing your name server's resources, and prevents hackers from listing the contents of your zones to identify such targets as mail servers and other name servers, or even gaining "host demographic" information such as the number and models of your computers and their device names.

- In our example, you should restrict zone transfers from name server 1 to *only* name servers 2, 3, and 4.

---

19. "Secure BIND Template," Rob Thomas, http://www.cymru.com/Documents/secure-bind-template.html (2002).

- Name servers 2 and 3 should be able to copy information from name server 1, giving them a local copy of the master zone data.

- Name server 4 *should not* be allowed to transfer any of these zone's data files at all, since it's a slave server of 1 through 4. It's easy to forget that you also need to restrict zone transfers from your slave name servers, but it's just as simple to transfer a zone from a slave as it is from the primary master name server.

Setting the rules for Windows 2000 and BIND to play nicely

Next, you need to restrict dynamic updates, because they have near-complete control of the name server. To do this, you must set up an organizational policy and DNS structure for end-user machines such as Windows 2000 devices.

By default, each Windows 2000 client tries to update its own name-to-address mapping on the DNS server. If your organization has a small, trusted group of people and you want to permit these updates, simply allow dynamic updates to your forward-mapping zone (the zone that contains your hosts' A records) from any IP address that a Windows 2000 client might have in your network address range. A small, trusted group reduces the chance that some malcontent will meddle with your DNS system. But since this kind of meddling is an easy task, we don't suggest this method for most organizations for that simple reason.

The better approach is to configure the DHCP server to handle updating the client's name-to-address and address-to-name mappings on the DNS server. Since all dynamic updates come from the DHCP server's address, you can allow *that one* address (the DHCP server) to create dynamic updates in your DNS system. However, pay attention to this caveat: First, set an organizational policy that defines which zones can be updated dynamically and which cannot.

The diagram immediately to the right depicts the DNS hierarchy and pinpoints where we believe that you should allow dynamic updating of DNS records.

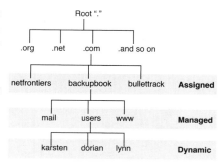

Figure 9-36. Dynamic range of DNS entries

Now that you've set the rules for who gets to be "king of the naming pile," it's time to build the sandbox that the Windows devices can play in. Unfortunately, the DHCP server simply accepts the information from a client when it specifies its fully qualified domain name. In other words, if JoeBo considers it a riot to name his Windows 2000 client with the domain name www.backupbook.com, the DHCP server will delete any conflicting address record at that domain name and add a record pointing www.backupbook.com to that Windows device's IP address—and that ain't good. To construct this sandbox, you create your own domain zone for the Windows devices themselves. By default, Windows 2000 assumes that the domain name of your device's forward-mapping zone is the same as the name of the Windows 2000 domain they belong to. However, Windows 2000 also allows you to specify the domain name of the zone independently.

Right-click on **My Computer** and choose **Properties**. Then navigate to **Network Identification** > **Properties** > **More…** to bring up the dialog below.

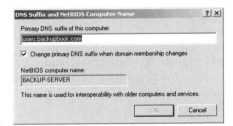

Figure 9-37. More… info for setting up a domain zone

Notice that we added the "users" label to the backupbook.com domain. By adding this new zone, the computer's address will be backup-server.users.backupbook.com. This new subzone, "users", is just for the Windows 2000 devices on the network.

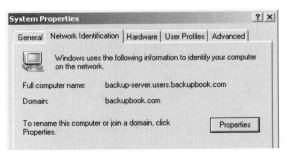

Figure 9-38. Windows client name in its own user zone

Thus, we'd configure the organization's Windows 2000 DNS/Active Directory servers (servers 2 and 3) to accept dynamic updates to that zone from only the DHCP server that's giving out their addresses, effectively building them their own little sandbox to play in. This can either be done directly through the DNS MMC in the Windows 2000 DNS server, by right-clicking on the properties of the zone and setting the **Allow dynamic updates** pop-up to **Yes**; or through Men & Mice's QuickDNS for Active Directory software.

Once you've done this, of course, since they are progeny of Mr. Bill, the Windows 2000 devices will more than likely trash each other's names, address records, etc. But at least they're limited to their own sandbox with their own king of the hill.

Run named as a user instead of root

To ensure that a vulnerability in BIND doesn't give a hacker root access to your hosts, you need to run *named* as a user instead of root on your BIND name servers (in our diagram, that's name server 1)[20]. Ensure that *named* can read your named.conf and zone data files, and if you use dynamic updates for your user zones, can write those zone data files. You'll also need to ensure that the user can write to *named*'s PID file. To make doubly sure that even if you *do* get hacked, your hacker doesn't get far, you'll want to run your BIND name server in a chroot() jail so that the hacker has very limited access to the host's file system[21].

Aggregate your logs to your IDS system & test your name servers

Use log file monitoring tools like NetIQ's Security Manager to alert your staff when hack attempts happen. Then sign up for services like Men & Mice's DomainHealth service[22], which monitors the health of your name servers.

---

20.   "Running a Name Server as a user other than Root," *DNS & BIND Cookbook*, by C. Liu, pp. 144–145 (O'Reilly, 2002).

21.   "Running a Name Server in a chroot() Jail," *DNS & BIND Cookbook*, by C. Liu, pp. 143–144 (O'Reilly, 2002).

22.   http://www.menandmice.com

Chapter Appendix

How does a hacker hack? What does he look for?

Holes. Like well-trained infantrymen on the front lines, they've learned to scout, scan, and detail their prey (read *you*). What hackers look for is an open door[23]. According to a "white hat" hacker[24] who sports the grandiose alias of Epic, "90 percent of all attacks stem from poor configuration and administrators who do not consistently update the software they use." The same article quoted a hacker by the nickname Hackah Jak, who stated, "I can in minutes code a scanner to scan the Internet for two-year-old known vulnerabilities... I've hit a lot of workstations this way and then worked my way through the network to the server." In addition to making simple configuration mistakes, most administrators don't keep up with the updates and patches released by software vendors. Doors open when administrators don't update services running on the system, or set up permissions and software settings the wrong way on the web server.

Let's walk through this so that you know what might happen to you and how it might happen.

The scouting process

Scouting, **profiling**, and **footprinting** are all the same terminology for one process: Gathering basic information about a potential target. When a hacker scouts a site, he's looking for infrastructure information, knowledge of the network, and the physical environment. Let's take a quick look at what a hacker can find out about you just from common tools on the Internet.

---

23. "Hackers Find Open Doors," by Dan Verton, *Computerworld*, 7/22/2002.

24. The terms "white hat" hackers and "black hat" hackers recall old cowboy movies in which the good guys wore white hats, and the bad guys wore —you guessed it—black. White hats hack into companies on the company's behalf or just for research, but black hats do this maliciously. Unconscious racism—or archetypal imagery? You decide.

Whois.net   The Whois database maintained on all domains allows you to get information about the owner of a domain name and its DNS servers. The default Whois server is whois.net. When searching for Network Frontiers information, we discovered our address, one of our staff's *real* e-mail addresses (instead of an alias such as host-master), and direct phone lines to our support staff (instead of general numbers).

```
Registrant:
Network Frontiers, Inc. (NETFRONTIERS-DOM)
   155 Bovet Road, #101
   San Mateo, CA 94402

   Domain Name: NETFRONTIERS.COM

   Administrative Contact:
     Gila, Joy (NUCDRNKGGI)jgila@INTERPUBLIC.COM
     The Interpublic Group of Companies
     676 St. Clair St.
     Chicago, IL 60611
     US
     312.425.6926 312.425.6924
   Technical Contact:
     Interpublic Hostmaster (NISGZUDGXO)hostmaster@INTERPUBLIC.COM
     The Interpublic Group of Companies, Inc.
     676 St. Clair St.
     Chicago, IL 60611
     US
     312.425.6926

   Record expires on 28-Feb-2003.
   Record created on 27-Feb-1995.
   Database last updated on 3-Aug-2002 09:55:30 EDT.

   Domain servers in listed order:

   NS1.TRUENORTH.COM        199.221.98.5
   NS2.TRUENORTH.COM        204.149.81.10
```

Figure 9-39. Whois registration info

However, around 50 percent of all hackers are *insiders*[25], so much of the work is already done. They know where the data center is, they know where the server room is, they have an up-to-date user list, and they know the address to the fire-wall. Scouting the target point isn't hard, nor is it time consuming. To start the process, the outside hacker is looking for a single IP address—which can be found easily enough at the www.netcraft.com website.

---

[25].   According to the 2001 Computer Security Institute/FBI Computer Crime and Security Survey. Before 2001, this was as high as 80 percent, so it's dropped significantly.

Netcraft Netcraft is supposedly a website "uptime" monitoring service that checks pretty much any site on the Internet that it can (we never asked them to check ours). According to their own website, "We report a site's operating system, web server, and netblock owner together with, if available, a graphical view of the time since last reboot for each of the computers serving the site.[26]" However, while this might be useful to some, to a hacker, it's a candy store. Just a quick trip to Netcraft can determine the make and model of a server for a planned attack. A quick check at Netcraft (by typing in www.netfrontiers.com) gives me *much* more information about the server itself:

OS	Server	IP address
MacOSX	Apache/1.3.23 (Darwin) DAV/1.0.2	64.175.139.131

Table 9-4. NetCraft info

Within three minutes of search, we now know that Network Frontiers is located in Los Altos, is running Apache on a Mac OS X box, and the server's address is 64.175.139.131. The hacker can now fine-tune the method to our specific vulnerabilities. Great. Just wonderful.

The scanning process

Hackers scan the network to create a list of network devices that are active and that have services that are potentially exploitable. Again, this is a three-minute process. It starts with matching names to addresses and then scanning each named entity on the network for service ports.

Name scan Name-scanning software uses a starting and ending TCP/IP address, and then performs a DNS query to find out what you've named your computers. Hackers look for things like "www" for web server, "intranet" for intranet server, "pop, smtp, mail" for mail server, and so on.

IP	Name
64.175.139.131	www.netfrontiers.com
64.175.139.132	Mail.netfrontiers.com
64.175.139.148	Surveys.netfrontiers.com

Table 9-5. Name Scan info

---

26. http://uptime.netcraft.com/up/graph/

The above list is just a small sampling of the information that can be found. So, now the hacker has a *list* of computers that might be running something fun. It's time to find out what kind of services and running ports are active on the computers in the list above.

Port scan Once the hacker knows what type of computer he's dealing with, he looks for each of the software services—called **ports** in the IP world—running on each individual computer. Here's a list of network services running on of *one* of the computers that was in the original list:

Port	Service Running
25	smtp - Simple Mail Transfer
53	domain - Domain Name Server
80	www-http - World Wide Web HTTP
110	pop3 - Post Office Protocol - Version 3
143	imap2 - Interim Mail Access Protocol v2
389	ldap - Lightweight Directory Acess Protocol
497	retrospect - Retrospect Backup software
548	AppleShare IP Server

Table 9-6. Port Scan info

Port scanning software like **7thSphere** or **nmap** then begin to fingerprint devices based on how they register their services, and provide the same type of information about the operating system software as Netcraft provides: Identifying a Mac OS X box, Windows 2000 box, Sun Solaris box, etc. This gives hackers the basic information about the network, its devices, and the software available to target on each of those devices.

Now it's time for the hacker to go to work and create a detailed exploitable plan of ways to hit each of these computers and software processes in their vulnerable spots. They focus on four "biggie categories" of network service vulnerabilities: CGI vulnerabilities, unshielded directories, Trojan horses, and service protocols that are left wide open.

The detailing process

The **detailing process**, or, as some call it, the **enumeration** process, involves accessing the different software processes running on each machine that might allow a way into documents, databases, file systems, or the web server per se.

A greater number of applications do this type of thing than you think. The information below has been compiled by Jean-Baptiste Hervet of Lagoon Software, makers of the great Macintosh analysis program called MacAnalysis that we mentioned earlier, the folks at Foundstone who make FoundScan, the gang at Security, and the team at Common Vulnerabilities and Exposures (CVE) who provide a list of standardized names for vulnerabilities and other information security exposures[27]. In reality, there are around 1,000–1,500 different tests that should be run *against each machine* to thoroughly scan.

CGI vulnerabilities

One of the first scans you undertake should be the available CGIs on your server, warning you about possible security holes if they're exploited. The CGI Syntax should then try to exploit every security hole found in "services/protocols holes" and "CGI vulnerability". If your software displays "Vulnerability Syntax Found: / scripts/test.idq?/../../ ," someone could exploit the hole in their very own browser by typing "http://www.yourserver.com//scripts/test.idq?/../../".

Unshielded directories

Many types of computers ship with certain folders pre-shared so that anybody in the world can gain access to them. It's common to see directories whose content is not viewable by everybody, like private folders, scripts, systems, etc (ex : /script, /private). Know that unprotected directories can compromise your server's security, because they can reveal precious information and allow anybody to see information you would not want exposed.

Installed Trojan horses

The most dangerous thing that can compromise your server is a Trojan horse, which allows anybody to remotely connect to your computer and execute network administrator (root) tasks. If, during a scan, your tool finds an installed Trojan, double-check that you haven't mistakenly launched a service on that port because your tool may interpret your daemon as a Trojan horse.

Enabled service protocols

Some tools have the ability to match a service protocol to a particular server. The software must first determine if the server is enabled, and then look in its database to find a relationship between the version of your service and a known security hole.

The two best sites for finding information about this type of detailing and exploiting are www.packetstorm.org, and the Common Vulnerabilities site, cve.mitre.org.

---

27. CVE provides a full list of all known vulnerabilities and exposures at their website, cve.mitre.org.

To determine your company's vulnerabilities, you must run your own tests, up to the point of actual exploitation. I decided to hit my own computer first, to see how things were configured and running. Why not start at home, hmm? So I ran the test, thinking that nothing would happen, and voilà! The software found two shared folders I didn't know I had and a CGI syntax that could hit me. Ouch! Taking my own medicine, I hit a standard Apple OS X file/web/mail server that we set up—again, directly out of the box and following their instructions. Only one hole—but a very high–risk hole. Apple zealot that I am, I decided to test the Windows server configured for running Windows 2000 and a very popular PHP/SQL-based forum package. The system was set up by direction, and we'd applied all of the security patches that we could from the Microsoft website. The last set of tests was run against a Network Attached Storage (NAS) box fresh out of the shipping container and set up according to the manufacturer's own guidelines for security. You aren't going to *believe* the holes in this thing! We've italicized Web:80 below because of the nature of its importance and the number of attacks that can run through it.

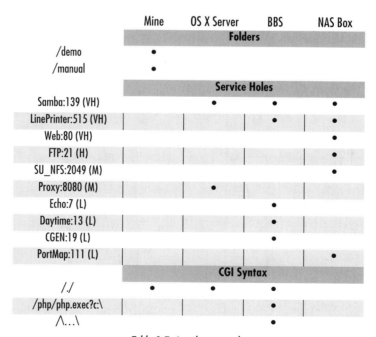

	Mine	OS X Server	BBS	NAS Box
Folders				
/demo	●			
/manual	●			
Service Holes				
Samba:139 (VH)		●	●	●
LinePrinter:515 (VH)			●	●
Web:80 (VH)				●
FTP:21 (H)				●
SU_NFS:2049 (M)				●
Proxy:8080 (M)		●		
Echo:7 (L)			●	
Daytime:13 (L)			●	
CGEN:19 (L)			●	
PortMap:111 (L)				●
CGI Syntax				
/./	●	●	●	
/php/php.exec?c:\			●	
/\...\			●	

Table 9-7. Attack test results

Notice that the *NAS box has three very high–risk holes!* Think of it: You buy a NAS box because it's a "simple" way to add quantities of storage to your network. You believe in the manufacturer, so you follow their instructions and set it up according to their manual, only to find out that the thing has three *very* vulnerable security holes from the moment you turn it on. Yeow—that smarts! Let's examine how these holes could be exploited and what can happen to your system.

Service/Protocol holes found in common systems

While having folders open and available isn't great, and having CGI syntaxes available and open is bad, having service holes open can go from negligible to very high risk. Here's a rundown of the very high–risk service holes we found, and what could happen to your system if they were exploited.

Samba:139 is active (Risk: Very High)

Some buffer overflows can be used to gain root access.

The fix: Disable the service or upgrade the version.

LinePrinter:515 is active (Risk: Very high)

Various buffer overflows exist in implementations of the line printer daemon, especially under Linux, BSD, and IRIX, which can lead to a root compromise. Linux lpd has proven to be exploitable to spawn a root shell.

The fix: upgrade to the latest lpd version; disable the service.

WEB:80 is active (Risk: Very High)

There are about two pages of things that can happen to the server when this port is wide open. We'll just go through a few of them, so that you get the idea.

It has been reported that the authentication methods supported by a given IIS server can be revealed to an attacker through the inspection of returned error messages, even when anonymous access is also granted.

Vulnerability has been discovered in Microsoft IIS that may disclose the internal IP address or internal network name to remote attackers. This vulnerability can be exploited if an attacker connects to a host using HTTPS (typically on port 443) and crafts a specially formed GET request. Microsoft IIS will return a 302 Object Moved error message containing the internal IP address or internal network name of the server.

A flaw exists in version 5.0 of Microsoft IIS that makes it subject to a potential denial of service attack. The problem occurs when the server is preparing the MIME headers for the response to an HTTP request for a certain type of file

The server doesn't restrict access to certain types of files when their parent folders have less restrictive permissions.

There you have it—that's how they get in.

Setting Windows Group Policies

Normally, administrators use a Windows 2000 Active Directory to distribute Group Policy settings. In this situation, the administrator creates Group Policy objects that contain policy settings, and then uses Active Directory to target the delivery and application of these settings. When you use Windows 2000 clients in an environment where there is no Active Directory, you can distribute policy settings using Windows NT 4.0-style system policies or Local Group Policy[28].

- If the needed settings are available for editing with the Poledit.exe tool, administrators can create a policy on a Windows 2000–based server with the Poledit tool and save it as a Ntconfig.pol file. On the user's workstation, the administrator must modify the NetworkPath registry value in the following location:

    HKEY_LOCAL_MACHINE\SYSTEM\CurrentControlSet\Control\Update\NetworkPath

If this value doesn't exist, the value must be added as a REG_SZ data type. For example, if the policy file is named Ntconfig.pol, and it's saved in the shared Directory \Policies on a Windows NT server, the value of NetworkPath should contain the following universal naming convention (UNC) path: \\Servername\Policies\Ntconfig.pol.

---

28. This information is courtesy Microsoft, and can be found on their website, at http://support.microsoft.com/default.aspx?scid=kb;en-us;Q274478

After adding the above registry entry, modify the registry entry Update-Mode(same location in the registry) to a value of 2. This sets the workstation to Manual Update mode, which is what you're setting by specifying the registry information above. If this entry, UpdateMode, is *not* changed, the workstation stays in Automatic mode, which means that it will look for the NTCONFIG.pol file in the default location instead of in the location you've specified.

When the users log onto the workstation, Windows 2000 can read the policy file specified by NetworkPath, and then apply the appropriate policy to the computer or user.

- If the settings that the administrator wants to enable are available on the user and computer level from the Group Policy Microsoft Management Console (MMC) snap-in, the administrator should use Local Machine policies. Since it may be difficult to visit each client to distribute and configure Local Group Policy, you can use the following two methods to configure Local Group Policy on multiple clients:

- Local Group Policy can be configured for a single system; then it can be cloned. The Microsoft System Preparation (Sysprep) tool can be used in conjunction with other third-party software to clone the computers. The cloned computers can retain the settings.

- Administrators can also configure a Local Group Policy on one client computer, and then copy the associate's pieces that make up the Local Group Policy Object (LGPO) to other clients.

Note that the only settings you can transfer from one client to another are those from Administrative Templates.

To edit the LGPO and to configure Local Group Policy settings on a local computer, and then to distribute to other computers, perform the following steps:

1. At the client requiring the policy settings, log on as an administrator and run the Group Policy snap-in (the Gpedit.msc file). Then focus the Group Policy snap-in on the Local Group Policy of the client.

2. Configure the LGPO on the client.

3. Edit and configure the policy settings you require.

4. Take the entries found in the Local Group Policy Object that are stored in the %Systemroot%\System32\GroupPolicy folder, and copy them to other clients where you also want to apply these Local Group Policy settings.

5. The settings under User Configuration normally take effect the next time the user logs on, and the settings under Computer Configuration normally take effect when you restart your system.

6. It may be necesary to edit the %systemroot%\system32\grouppolicy\gpt.ini and change the version entry so that the policy gets applied.

The preceding settings are stored in the LGPO on that client. If this client later joins a Windows 2000 Active Directory, Active Directory can override the settings in the LGPO using Group Policy distributed from Active Directory.

Security permissions on this folder can be changed to deny access to administrators to ensure that the policy does not apply to the local administrators.

If you use the preceding method, you must exercise much care because anything set on the original system that is specific to that particular computer is unsuccessful on the new target computer. In particular, many of the security settings for the computer should be avoided. If you're interested in only the administrative templates settings, copy the Registry.pol file to the target computer.

Setting the access control lists (ACLs) on the folder to prevent the local administrators from being affected works with any local built-in group, as well. When a change to the policy settings is required, the local administrator must take ownership, change the ACLs, make the change to the LGPO, and then change the ACLs back to *deny* for the local administrator. Combined with a certain set of policies, a failure to do this could render any further changes impossible.

Consider, for example, if the "Disable registry editing tools" or "Take ownership of files or other objects" policy is set and the "Deny access to this computer from the network" policy is set. This can lead to a situation in which administrators are locked out of a system.

In general, to avoid problems, be aware of the following suggestions:

• Each setting variance needs to be methodically tested prior to implementation.

- An administrator's strategy must be based on all clients having remote network access with Windows 2000.

If you wish to delegate the authority

Here are the steps to do so[29]:

1. Create an organizational unit (OU) and create a new GPO directly linked to this OU, by clicking **Properties** on the context menu of the OU, clicking the **Group Policy** tab in the Properties dialog box, and clicking the **New** button. Once the GPO has been created, launch the Delegation Wizard. The Delegation Wizard provides a step-by-step process in which specific functionality may be delegated easily, with a high degree of detail.

2. To start the Delegation Wizard, select the OU and right-click it. Then select Delegate Control. This starts the Delegation of Control Wizard.

3. Directly access the security settings for the GPO itself, by clicking **Properties** on the context menu of the specific GPO, and clicking the **Security** tab. Add your non-administrator user to the list of users for whom security is defined.

4. Provide your user **Full Control - Allow** privilege. Full Control gives the user the ability to write to the GPO, and also to change security permissions on the GPO. If you want to prevent this user from setting security, you may decide to give her only the **Write - Allow** permission. You may also decide that the user should be exempt from the application of this policy, and this may be accomplished by clearing the **Apply Group Policy - Allow** privilege.

To simplify administration for the user, launch the management console (Mmc.exe) and add the **Group Policy** snap-in. Browse for and add the GPO that you're configuring for delegation. Once this MMC session is appropriately configured, save the MMC session and give it to the user. The user can now utilize and administer her GPO with no additional setup.

---

29. http://support.microsoft.com/default.aspx?scid=kb;en-us;Q221577

SECURITY RESEARCH SITES

cve.mitre.org Common Vulnerabilities and Exposures, the authoritative list of vulnerability definitions

icat.nist.gov The National Institute of Standards and Technology's search engine for the CVE database

project.honeynet.org The Honeynet Project: Learn how to do detailed forensics after a compromise

www.2600.com Home of the venerable *Hacker Quarterly* magazine

www.atstake.com/research/advisories/index.html Formerly LOpht Advisories, this is an excellent list of advisories that often covers applications skipped by other lists

www.cert.org The CERT Coordination Center at Carnegie Mellon provides one of the best resources for security advisories and best-practices information

www.cisco.com/pcgi-bin/front.x/csec/csecHome.pl Cisco Secure Encyclopedia, a central warehouse of security knowledge

www.insecure.org Home of the definitive port scanner nmap, plus a great list of security tools

www.linuxsecurity.com All things Linux security

www.microsoft.com/technet/security Microsoft Product Security Notification Service and Microsoft's security vulnerability mailing list

www.ntbugtraq.com A Windows-specific vulnerability website and mailing list

www.sans.org Includes the SANS Institute's vulnerability list, white papers, and port scan statistics from monitors spread around the Internet

www.securityfocus.com Home of the Bugtraq mailing list archive, plus a good source of security white papers

www.securityportal.com Security news and commentary

www.wiretrip.net/rfp/ The "skinnable" home of Rain Forest Puppy provides detailed information on exploits and has been first to list several prominent vulnerabilities

Figure 9-40. I should have never turned off that spam filter!

SECTION 4.
DEALING WITH LOSS

I've seen two versions of dealing with computer or data loss in organizations. In those happy companies where everyone knows that their data is safe because it's backed up, alternate connectivity plans are in place, and there's even a plan in case the building falls down, I hear folks say, with marked insouciance, "Cool—now I can get a faster one with a bigger hard drive!" However, in those organizations that aren't quite up to snuff, aren't backing up, and don't have a continuity plan, a computer loss is usually met with knitted brows and a certain *angst und drang*.

Angst und drang is an obscure Swiss/German term that refers to an anxious pushing forward, a lack of resolution that evokes an effort—more forceful than necessary—to achieve that much-desired closure. And that's not good. Pushing too

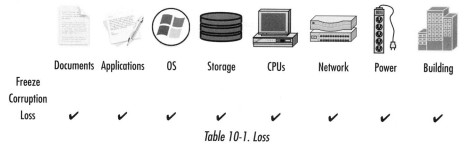

	Documents	Applications	OS	Storage	CPUs	Network	Power	Building
Freeze								
Corruption								
Loss	✔	✔	✔	✔	✔	✔	✔	✔

Table 10-1. Loss

hard usually means that you tend to forget a step here or there, especially if you're pushing under the burden of high anxiety. This lethal combination produces tun-

259

nel vision, the disease of focusing too intently on one subject while forgetting the all-important pieces on the periphery. Simply put, if you aren't prepared for loss, you can't cope because you aren't in a "transition" mind-set.

Which brings me to that very mind-set you must achieve: the "transition" state that enables you to tackle issues that come about in a certain order. *All transitions have this order*—whether you lose your computer, your network, or your building.

Disengagement and initial disorientation

This will happen first. Your computer dies (disengagement) and at first, you try to figure out what's wrong with it (disorientation) before you grasp the reality of rigor mortis. The line to the Internet goes out (disengagement), and you troubleshoot everything from the firewall through the router and MUX and cables (disorientation) until you realize that your service provider just went belly-up and you're now an island unto yourself. Or, the building burns down and you aimlessly walk the perimeter, tripping up the frustrated firefighters, snatching at charred scraps of paper fluttering out of what's left of the windows.

Float time

Float time occurs when the old system dies and the new system hasn't been installed yet—that twilight zone between the time the old building burned down and the new office springs up. To defray downtime and salvage morale in this period, you must create some short-term goals for your people. If you've simply lost an individual's computer, you can suggest that the user do something non-computer-related for awhile. If you've lost the building, you must be a bit more creative. The key to float time is to create short-range goals with checklists for each step so that people can perceive some forward momentum, diminishing their anxiety. This applies to administrators, as well. If you give your bosses your checklist for "coming back up to speed" and show some steady progress toward a defined goal, they too will be less anxious. In the absence of anxiety, confidence can bloom again.

Clarifying and communicating the new beginning

This is the transition process's final step. I've never been involved in a system that didn't change after a disaster. If a computer dies, you get a new one, with, most likely, a new operating system and some other differences. If a building dies, you get a new one. If you're recovering from a hacker or virus attack, the organization will have stricter access rules. Not everything will be the same, and the old problem, along with the new solution, must be dealt with and communicated to others. Understanding the transition process helps to fill the void of loss by painting a picture of the new reality to come. It also helps to assuage angst und drang, helping your organization take the first step on the road to recovery.

Chapter 10:
Documents that don't die

Like Old Soldiers, documents don't die, they just slowly fade away. Their names and indexes might be replaced, and finding them might be difficult, but banishing them completely is even harder.

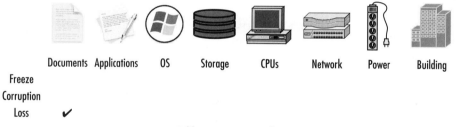

Table 10-1. Document loss

Think about it: Accidentally being trashed. Being written over. Lost, due to a bad drive, stolen computer, or misplaced Zip disk. I'm telling ya, the forces of Murphy must truly be marshalled against documents on a network, so you must protect them as well as you can.

Mirroring your hard drive's server volume doesn't really cut it, either. If you don't believe me, you can ask Zeke (real name withheld to protect the guilty). It seems that ol' Zeke's backup plan was simply to put a RAID5 system on his server—but a malicious coworker (who was on the way out the door—permanently) decided to trash the production folder the day before the clients came to see their new proofs. RAID systems are great for protecting a document from a hard drive's corruption—but they do nothing for all of the other perils, such as a malicious or accidental deletion, that a document must face daily. What happened to Zeke, you ask? Well, let's put it this way: He's now occupationally challenged.

The best way to protect your documents is to proactively back them up to a different location.

To protect a valuable document, you must back it up—that is, create a second (or third) copy to a different location, so that if the primary copy gets destroyed, you can replace it with the backup copy (well, actually a *copy* of the backup copy). However, when dealing with lost documents, you have other options than merely backing them up. These options follow the data protection layering discussed in our introduction (see *The three basic types of protection* on page 5), and comprise fault-tolerant, duplication, and archival backup solutions.

Fault-tolerant solutions
- Set up an undelete system on the user's computer if she's losing documents because she trashes them too often.

Duplication solutions
- Set up a network-based file replication system for the user so that his local work is automatically put onto a remote location in a fashion that allows him to retrieve the files for himself.

Archival backup solutions
- Set up a user-driven document backup system that makes copies of the files the *user* feels are most important, placing them in a remote location or burning them to a removable media.

- Set up a network-driven document backup system that moves the files to a remote location in a fashion that doesn't allow the user to automatically retrieve the files herself.

- And, last but not least, protect your open file documents such as databases completely differently—we'll discuss that, as well.

We'll walk through each of the methods in this and the next two chapters.

THE MAIN THING

It all comes down to productivity and document survivability: You must be able to restore your users' data if they lose it.

- If you have the best chance of keeping a user's documents alive and kicking by adding undelete software, do it.

- If users are losing scads of documents and need a lot of document retrieval, either a document duplication system, a document replication system, or a self-serve backup application should do the trick and keep them out of the administrator's—that's *your*—coiffure.

- If your users are road warriors, you must back them up in a manner that lets them restore the files—or lets you restore the files for them—wherever they happen to be and whenever they happen to need them. This can be dicey, so take care when setting up backup systems for travelling users.

- And last, people's personalities, technological capabilities, and politics play a significant role in the recovery process. Remember, backups are for users, not backup administrators.

Special thanks...

Most grateful thanks go to Colleen Toumayan of Executive Software for her outstanding help with Undelete, and for letting me steal wholeheartedly from their manual. In the same category is Jennifer Watson of Aladdin Systems, who rushed a copy of FlashBack off to me.

I am humbled by all of the help I received from Jon Burgoyne of EverStor, makers of Replicator; and Connie Chronis a wonderful woman who has *all* the right connections over at VERITAS.

Fault tolerance = Bringing files back from "gone"

Anyone remember Oliver North's problem with e-mail not *really* being gone? How about all of those old e-mails that put a few nails in the coffin of Microsoft's case? If these high-profile court cases have taught us anything, it's that files on a computer aren't *really* gone until the drive is burned or smushed. Which is good news for more than a few of us who, on a regular basis, do something stupid to our files that we wish we hadn't. To rescue "gone" files, you must understand how they're stored in the first place because, in the case of document loss, fault tolerance deals with bringing back lost, deleted, or damaged files.

What's put where on your drive

Oh, man, this is like learning to swim by being thrown in the deep end by your mean cousin Ritchy. If you get this section, you'll *really* understand it, but it's not easy, and you might go under a few times. If you prefer, skip it and mosey on down the road a few pages to learn about backups. But if you want to understand how undeleting files works, so that you can protect files before you have to restore them, you've gotta tread water here with me for a bit—I promise not to let you drown.

To understand how deleted files are recovered, you must know how files are stored on disk. On Windows platforms, three file systems are commonly used:

1. FAT (file allocation table);

2. FAT32 (32-bit file allocation table); and

3. NTFS (NT File System).

In the Macintosh world, there are two:

1. Macintosh HFS (Hierarchical File System); and

2. HFS+ or Mac OS Extended.

And Unix has one: UFS (Unix File System).

Under the FAT file system and HFS, every disk is divided into fixed-size clusters. The minimum cluster size is 512 bytes, and each larger size is twice the previous, to a maximum of 32 K. An **index**—a unique, 16-bit number—identifies each cluster. Because there are only 65,536 distinct 16-bit numbers, both FAT and HFS partitions can have no more than 65,536 clusters. That limitation, combined with the 32 K maximum cluster size, is the source of the 2 GB limit for FAT partitions and HFS files. FAT entries link the clusters that comprise a file, and the file's directory entry includes the index of the first cluster. That cluster's FAT entry contains the index for the next cluster, and so on. The FAT entry for the file's last cluster holds a special end-of-file code. Unused clusters and defective clusters are marked with their own special codes. The FAT32 file system is almost the same, but clusters are smaller, and because FAT entries are 32 bit, there can be more than 4 billion, theoretically.

NTFS is a substantially more advanced file system. Its Master File Table (MFT) is a full-blown database that indexes every file on the disk. Each MFT entry, usually 1 K in size, records a wide variety of file information. NTFS may store a very small file entirely in the file's MFT entry; for a larger file, the entry identifies the clusters that contain the file's data.

Unix UFS is arranged on a disk partition using a linked list of pointers to data. The structure of a partition begins with, or is defined by, the **superblock**: a data structure that includes information about the file system type (i.e., UFS, ext2FSs, etc.) and size and modification time; a list of free and allocated blocks; and the first inode (see below), which points to the root directory, /. The superblock is always replicated to provide fault tolerance against disk failure in the first superblock.

Files are stored in the file system in two pieces: (1) a chunk of data somewhere in the file system; and (2) a data structure that contains information about the location, size, creation/modification/access times, ownership, access attributes of and links to the file.

This data structure is called an **inode**. The only part of the file it doesn't include is the file name. This is important, both to the concept of links and to disentangle it from directory management.

Finally, directories bring the organization to a close, providing the linked list referred to above. A **directory** is a binary file containing the name/inode pair mappings for files "contained" within it. Thus, the superblock provides the mapping to the root directory, and from there, one can find any other file on the file system.

(X) Certain aspects of the Mac OS X file system are derived from UFS. From an architectural perspective, Mac OS X implements multiple file systems; most importantly, Mac OS Extended (HFS+), Mac OS Standard (HFS), UFS, ISO 9660, NFS, and AFP. But from a user perspective, the file systems are monolithic; when users copy, move, or drag files and folders, there is (or seems to be) one file system.

The physical organization of volumes is somewhat different than that which the Finder presents to the user. Looking at the directory structure using the Terminal application, you see that the boot volume is mounted at the root level (/), and non-boot volumes are located in /Volumes/. The Finder provides this abstraction to offer a more traditional Mac OS interface on top of the underlying UNIX system. The Mac OS X extended format and UFS have six major differences:

1. **Case sensitivity**–UFS is sensitive to case; although HFS+ is case-insensitive, it's case-preserving.

2. **Multiple forks**–HFS+ supports multiple forks (and additional metadata), whereas UFS supports only a single fork (Carbon simulates multiple forks on file systems that don't support them, such as UFS).

3. **Path separators**–HFS+ uses colons as path separators, whereas UFS follows the convention of forward slashes. The system translates between these separators.

4. **Modification dates**–HFS+ supports both creation and modification dates as file metadata; UFS supports modification dates, but not creation dates. If you copy a file with a command that understands modification dates but not creation dates, the command might reset the modification date as it creates a new file for the copy. Because of this behavior, it's possible to have a file with a creation date later than its modification date.

5. **Sparse files and zero filling**–UFS supports sparse files, which are a way for the file system to store the data in files without storing unused space allocated for those files. HFS+ doesn't support sparse files and, in fact, zero-fills all bytes allocated for a file until end-of-file.

6. **Lightweight references to file-system items**–These are file references for aliases that the HFS+ system supports and UFS doesn't.

In Mac OS X, the type of a file is identified using two techniques: file types and filename extensions. **File types** are common to Mac OS 9 and are stored as file metadata. **Filename extensions** are commonly used on Windows and UNIX operating systems, and are supported by Mac OS X to provide maximum compatibility with other operating systems. However, to preserve the Macintosh user experience, Mac OS X provides a way to hide file extensions on a per-file basis.

Each file in the file system now has a special flag identifying whether the file's extension is hidden or shown. This setting affects only the way the file is displayed; it doesn't physically change the name of the file in the file system. Users can change this setting for individual files from the file's Info panel, and can also hide all filename extensions by modifying the Finder preferences. We'll tell you more about filename extensions in the chapter on network backups (see *Painting the target* on page 701).

About file deletion

Regardless of the file system, when you "Trash" or "Recycle" a file, your operating system doesn't remove the file at all. Instead, it moves the file's directory entry and original location information into a hidden folder that represents the Recycle Bin or Trash directory. The data clusters for the file aren't deleted or even moved— only the location of the directory entry changes.

In Windows, when the Recycle Bin fills up, the oldest files are truly deleted, and when you empty the bin, they're all deleted. In the Mac world, the Trash doesn't "fill up;" it merely sits there waiting for you to empty it some day.

Although you can bypass using the Recycle Bin or Trash by holding down the Shift key in Windows or the Control key for Mac OS X when deleting a file, even then, the file's data remains. In all OSes, the file's name, index entry, or directory is changed to indicate that it should no longer be visible to the user and that the space is now available for reuse. The file's data remains, though, until the space on the drive gets recycled to store some other file. At that point, the drive then overwrites the available space with new information.

This means that if you aren't importing the video edition of *War and Peace* to your computer, you have a pretty good chance of recovering the data that you just deleted—which brings us to a few of the tools that allow you to resurrect your long-lost nearest and dearest—files, that is.

File recovery tools

The first step toward file recovery is simple: Check your Trash or your Recycle Bin to see if you've just put the file there—or if you put the file there and actually deleted it. Double-click the Recycle/Trash icon on your desktop or dock and look for your file on the list that appears. If it's there:

Right-click on the file and select Restore from the pop-up menu; and

Drag the file where you want it.

The sooner you do this, the better, so that you don't accidentally *really* delete it.

Recycle Bin and Trash utilities

The Recycle Bin has limitations—no, you don't have to sort plastic and aluminum, but, for example, it doesn't catch files deleted from DOS programs, from other nodes on the network, or from Windows programs that don't request deletion to the Recycle Bin. Some utility programs provide a second level of protection, snagging files that the Recycle Bin misses, and hanging onto files when they leave the Recycle Bin. The Norton Protected Recycle Bin, found in Symantec's Norton Utilities 2001, is one such program; the Fix-It Deleted Files Bin from Ontrack's Fix-It Utilities 3.0 is another. Of course, to help you, the utility must be running at the time the file is deleted.

For the life of me, I can't find a Trash utility for the Macintosh OS X platform—plenty of applications to help OS X delete files, but not recover them. If you know of any, e-mail us and we'll cover them in our updates to this book.

Undelete utilities

Remember that part about "Even when you really, *really* delete, it's still there?" Good—because the tools listed here take advantage of that fact. These utilities locate and reassemble the clusters that held the file's data. Remember, you can reconstruct only those files that haven't already been overwritten, so it's important to avoid writing to the disk at the same time you're trying to undelete files. Here's my point: If you don't already have an undelete utility installed, now's not a good time, as you just might overwrite the file you're trying to recover. The way around this? Buy one more copy of the undelete software and install *that* copy on your buddy's computer. You'll then open up sharing on the computer in question, mount the entire volume (you have to get the Trash), and run the utility from your buddy's computer, if you can.

On a FAT-based file system, an undelete utility uses low-level disk access to read the deleted directory entry, extracting the index of the original first cluster of the file and the file size. The utility then attempts to locate the rest of the clusters and, if successful, asks you to supply the filename's first letter, which was wiped out by the flag character. The equivalent process under NTFS is substantially more complicated; Microsoft goes so far as to state that it's "not possible to perform an undelete under Windows NT on any of the supported file systems[1]."

Undelete For the Windows world, only one product really works great: Executive Software's aptly named Undelete. We *love* it because it comes in all three flavors: home user, desktop user, and server version (which protects the shared Recycle Bin of a mapped network volume).

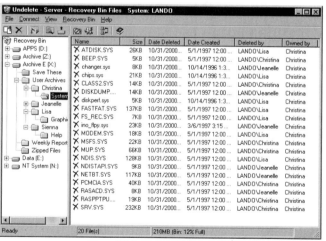

Figure 10-1. Recovery Bin interface

---

1.   http://support.microsoft.com/default.aspx?scid=kb;en-us;Q100108

With Undelete, deleted files aren't *really* deleted—the deletion request is intercepted by Undelete and the deleted files are actually stored in another location, called the Recovery Bin—so recovering these deleted files is only a few mouse-clicks away. The Recovery Bin interface (see Figure 10-1. on page 269) contains pull-down menus and a toolbar. A tree view of available disk volumes and folders is displayed on the left, and a list of files that were removed from the selected volume or folder but were saved in the Recovery Bin takes up the rest of the window.

The Recovery Bin isn't magic—here are a few limitations and important points:

- In keeping with NTFS file security, you must have sufficient file permissions and ownership to recover a file from the Recovery Bin.

- You can adjust the size of the Recovery Bin by using the Recovery Bin Properties option.

- You can drag and drop files from your desktop or from Windows Explorer into the Recovery Bin icon, but not into the main Recovery Bin interface.

- By default, when the Recovery Bin reaches the size you've specified, it's automatically partially purged to make room for newly deleted files. For this reason, files once stored in the Recovery Bin can become no longer available from the Recovery Bin (although they may still be recoverable with the Undelete From Disk feature). This default can be changed with the Recovery Bin Properties option, but changing this default can cause the Recovery Bin to fill completely, and additional file "deletions" won't be moved to the Recovery Bin.

- If a file of the same name exists in the "deleted" file's previous location, the "deleted" file can't be recovered. Undelete won't overwrite an existing file while recovering a "deleted" file. In that case, you must first rename the existing file before recovering the "deleted" file.

And, even though files might have been *deleted* deleted (versus just plain *deleted*), there's still a chance to recover them using Undelete. When you delete a file in Windows, the system doesn't remove it from the disk, but instead marks the space the file occupies as free space. When you recover a file with Undelete From Disk, a new file is created and the old file data is then copied into the new file[2].

The Undelete From Disk feature allows you to recover files that have really been deleted, such as files purged from the Recovery Bin, or files that were deleted when the Recovery Bin was not enabled. Undelete From Disk can also be used to recover files from volumes or directory folders that have been excluded from Recovery Bin processing[3].

That said, here are the limitations of undeleting a file from disk.

- For best results in recovering files that have really been deleted, use the Undelete From Disk feature as soon as possible after deleting the file. This increases your file recovery attempt's chances for success.

- In keeping with NTFS file security, you must be a member of the Administrators group and have sufficient file permissions and ownership to recover a file directly from the disk[4].

- The Undelete From Disk feature can recover files purged from the Recovery Bin (using the Empty Recovery Bin button or menu option), files deleted from directory folders that have been excluded from Recovery Bin processing (using the Recovery Bin Exclusion button or menu option), or files deleted from drives on which Recovery Bin processing is disabled (using the Recovery Bin Properties option).

- The Undelete From Disk feature can even undelete files that were deleted before you installed Undelete. However, be aware that simply installing an application (including Undelete) can overwrite the same files you want to recover. For this reason, Emergency Undelete on the installer disk is the recommended tool for recovering files that have been accidentally deleted. You can use this before you install Undelete.

- When a file is really deleted, the space it occupied on the volume is marked as available free space, but the file data remains on the volume until the space is used to store another file. Therefore, in some cases, the Undelete From Disk feature may not be able to recover the deleted file, or may be able to recover only a portion of it. As a rule, the more disk activity that occurs after a file is

---

2. We recommend that you recover the file to a volume other than the one from which the file was deleted. This prevents the old file data from being overwritten by the new file, which would render it unrecoverable.

3. This operation can succeed only if the space occupied by the file that is to be undeleted hasn't been overwritten during the time it was marked as free space.

4. A file recovered with the Undelete From Disk feature defaults to the security attributes of the user (Administrator) doing the file recovery.

deleted, the higher the chance that new or modified files will overwrite the file information.

- When a deleted file has been partially overwritten with new data, the Undelete From Disk feature may report successfully undeleting the file when in fact a portion of the file has been overwritten and is thus corrupt. At that point, you need to start typing, or hope that you have a backup of the file.

- When undeleting fragmented files on FAT volumes, the Undelete From Disk feature may undelete only the first contiguous portion of the file. Partial recovery of a text file can be better than none, but partial recovery of an executable file (an application) won't be of much help. For this reason, it's important to keep your files defragmented (particularly files on FAT volumes).

- Files removed from the Recovery Bin have a unique file identification number added to the original filename. (This prevents undeleted files of the same name from overwriting each other.) For example, after a file named *MyDocument.doc* is removed from the Recovery Bin, it might appear in the Undelete From Disk file listing as *MyDocument(01BF72299FB8019A).doc*. We therefore recommend that after you undelete a file that was previously removed from the Recovery Bin, you rename the file its original name, or any name that will be better understood.

- Files removed from the Recovery Bin are listed with the Recovery Bin location as their "Original Location," since that's where they resided before they were really deleted. This is a directory folder named \RecoveryBin\ on the volume(s) where you have specified Recovery Bins should reside on your system. Also, due to the unique file identification number assigned by the Recovery Bin, when attempting to use the Undelete From Disk feature to recover a file that has been removed from the Recovery Bin, use the asterisk (*) wildcard character in combination with the filename to narrow down the search. For example, to recover *MyDocument.doc* after it has been removed from the Recovery Bin, add an asterisk wildcard character in this manner: *MyDocument*.doc*.

- Note that when files are deleted from the Recovery Bin when the SecureDelete feature is enabled in the Recovery Bin properties, the deleted files aren't recoverable with the Undelete From Disk feature.

Speaking of unrecoverable things (no, not your eccentric Aunt Estelle's reputation), you probably don't want to worry about those cached pictures from Internet Explorer that you'd be embarrassed to have your spouse happen upon. You can set Undelete to ignore certain files or directories, and sometimes, that's a good thing;

for example, those temporary files you really do want to delete. These annoyingly ubiquitous files often have a .tmp file extension, but many other extensions are also used, depending on the applications you're running. A number of common temporary file types are excluded from Recovery Bin processing by default.

More candidates for the barrel room? The temp files created during an application's installation process. When you install an application, a number of temporary files are created and then eventually deleted by the installation program. Also, compilers and web browsers often create a large number of temporary files. There's little chance you'll ever need to recover these files, so by excluding them from being processed by the Recovery Bin, the program really will delete them, and they won't hog your Recovery Bin space. The graphic at right (Figure 10-2.) depicts an example of the Recovery Bin Exclusion List dialog box.

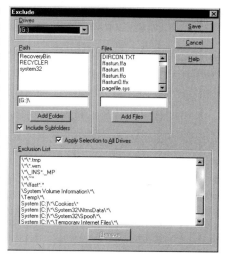

Figure 10-2. Exclusion list

Major surgery and DriveSavers

Once the disk clusters that were occupied by a deleted file have been overwritten with new data, the file is gone forever—or is it? In fact, the old data may still be present on the magnetic media, as a kind of wiggle in the waveforms that represent the data. Using intricate, high-tech equipment, technicians first copy the exact waveform recorded on an area of the disk, without translating the signal into bits and bytes. They then generate a perfect waveform representing the corresponding data bits, subtract the perfect waveform from the actual waveform, and amplify the differences. When successful, this process recovers the data previously stored in the specified area of the disk. Theoretically, you can even repeat the process, obtaining yet an earlier chunk of data. Physical limitations preclude more than seven repetitions of the recovery process. That doesn't mean you can recover seven layers of data; only that you can't recover more than seven. This level of recovery must be performed by experts, and is painstaking and expensive. In most cases, re-creating lost data from scratch is more cost-effective.

We think the big winners in this world are the folks over at DriveSavers. The following (Figure 10-3.) is an image of a computer that was burned to a crisp in 1700°F temperatures. If DriveSavers could restore the information from this drive within 24 hours, you can pretty well bet that they can restore the information from your drive, if at all possible.

Figure 10-3. A drive that DriveSavers recovered

Their proprietary technology and custom solutions have earned them the authorization of all drive and storage media manufacturers, and have delivered an industry-leading success rate of over 90 percent—which means that 10 percent of you could still be out in the cold—or, as with the above drive, the inferno. So don't even *think* of skipping your backups.

The cost for each of these types of restorations is something that has to be negotiated with the DriveSavers folks. Trust me on this one when I tell you it's cheaper to back up the data than it is to call DriveSavers.

Recovered data can be placed on any type of backup media, including hard drives, CDs, DVDs, tape, Jaz or Zip; or the recovered information (depending upon its size) can be downloaded back to you through FTP over the Internet.

And if you're worried about confidentiality, they're more than willing to sign a confidentiality agreement (some of their engineers have U.S. government security clearances).

Limitations of these tools

These tools' biggest limitation is that none are backup or file replication tools. In other words, yes, they'll *absolutely* help end users with file "oopses" on their local computers. Yes, they'll help bring back seemingly "dead" files or prevent mistakes. But if the drive goes, so do the files. If the computer is lost, so are the files. If the building burns down... you get the picture.

Does that mean that you shouldn't use them? *I couldn't live without them.* At the same time, I also back up my files to multiple locations (Internet, tape, CD, and my iPod), and our team replicates our working directories of the books and articles in production. Bottom line? These tools should work in concert with—not in lieu of—backup and file replication tools.

FILE AND DIRECTORY DUPLICATION AND REPLICATION

Duplication is one layer higher in the protection realm (see *Layered protection* on page 7) than fault tolerance. Document or directory **duplication** is very simple: merely the process of picking up the files or directory from a source device and then making an exact copy of those files or that directory on the destination volume. Basically, this is a fancy-schmancy, automated way of dragging your favorite work from one drive to another, onto a CD for safekeeping, or to a network volume, as shown in Figure 10-4. below.

Figure 10-4. Duplication

Replication is the process by which a file, a database, or some other computer information in one location is continually updated to match a mirrored version on another computer in another location, either on a scheduled basis or immediately as the file data is changing. Related to data, replication is a far more complex process than its dictionary definition (to wit, making copies of itself). Data replication is the coordination, updating, and reconciling of constantly changing datasets from one (or more) location to another (or multiple) location. In Figure 10-5. below, we show the process of replicating files from multiple clients (location A) to a server with the replication process running on it (location B).

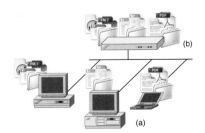

Figure 10-5. Replication

Replication systems operate by taking point-in-time data snapshots of the desired data and transferring the updated information to a replica volume. Even though our simple diagram shows files being replicated, replication can be file- or volume-based. If it's file-based, the data is examined at the file level and then updated from the source to the destination in whole or with the delta transfer method (See *Should the file, or only changes in the file, be backed up?* on page 302 for more information on this method). If the replication system is volume-based, the volume is examined block by block, and the replica is updated by that method.

 Replication differs from traditional backup by allowing the user to use the files from the destination volume or retrieve the replicated information without any action whatsoever by the backup administrator or the backup software.

Thus, the end user can recover the data by merely mounting the volume in which the data is stored in location B and then dragging the files or folders back to their original location, or simply by using the files *from* the destination volume. Some duplication and replication systems also provide their own front end to make the navigation and security management of retrieving files and folders much easier.

As opposed to replication, duplication offers you only the choice of moving this data to that place at certain times. Normally, duplication is used by individual computer users to make copies of their important files on a regular basis—usually to another hard drive or to a CD/DVD or other removable media. Both duplication and replication can play significant roles in the backup process. However, since replication normally involves a network-based solution (i.e., replicating data from one computer to another), let's hold off on further definitions of the replication process, software, and hardware until we can cover this information in its own chapter (see *Replication* on page 497).

That said, let's proceed to specific instances of duplication and then duplication software.

Document and directory duplication

In its simplest form, **duplication** is the moving of a set of directories or individual files from a source location to a destination location. This is usually a "push" process from the source computer to the destination computer or a "pull" process from the destination server. Or, as with Retrospect's backup server, the duplication engine resides on the backup server and then sends a command to the client computer, telling it to copy its files from the local source volume to a remote destination volume, as shown in Figure 10-6. .

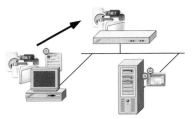

Figure 10-6. Network-based duplication

Since the replication application moves the files from one place to another in native file format, there isn't much else to explain. The directory structure that applied to the original set of files also applies to the replicated set of files on the remote device.

The only caveat? Ensure that the user has access privileges to that volume limited to *reading* the files that you've placed there. You don't want the user to have enough privileges to *write* files to the directory, lest he delete files on the replicated volume.

 Three different duplication tools are covered below: Retrospect from Dantz Development Corporation, Synchronize! Pro from Qdea, and Apple's Backup software (which is really duplication software, but they've named it Backup).

Retrospect

Dantz Retrospect is a full-fledged backup application with a fringe benefit of duplicating volumes of information from point A to point B.

For the purpose of duplication, Retrospect can run in server mode or desktop mode. If, however, you want to duplicate a Linux volume, you must run the Retrospect server software, because the Linux product is only a client product and thus must tie into the network-based backup solution. In the example below

(Figure 10-7.), Retrospect is running from a server, duplicating a specific directory on a client computer over to the backup server.

The Retrospect duplication process is a breeze: To launch it, the administrator chooses **Backup > Duplicate** from the main window. At this point, a dialog asks you to select the source volume (Figure 10-2. below left). In Retrospect parlance, a **source volume** is either the computer's entire hard drive or a single directory (with, of course, files and subdirectories inside).

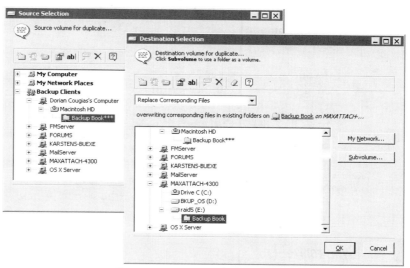

Figure 10-7. Retrospect's duplicate function

In this diagram (Figure 10-7.) we've selected the Backup Book directory that holds not only this copy of the book that you're reading, but the previous version, as well. Pretty hefty—about 500 MB of data, and that doesn't even include the research files that took up another 1.2 GB.

Next, select the destination volume and directory in which to place the duplicate files (Figure 10-7. , right side dialog). In this case, we navigated over to the Network Attached Storage (NAS) device, found the user's folder, and created another folder called *Backup Book* inside it.

Marking that directory as the subvolume to use, we then had one more instruction for Retrospect: **Replace Corresponding Files**. The other option, **Replace Entire**

Volume, replaces the entire contents of the destination volume with the selected files and folders of the source volume—identical files already present on the destination are not duplicated. **Replace Corresponding Files** overwrites any matching files existing on the destination volume that correspond to the selected files of the source, *even if the destination files are newer.* Retrospect leaves files untouched if their names and locations don't correspond to those files marked for duplication.

Once you've determined your source and destination, Retrospect presents you with the immediate duplicate window, where you can duplicate the source to the destination one time if you click the **Duplicate** button on the bottom right of the window.

If you want Retrospect to create a repeating duplicate option, simply click the small clock on the upper-left of the window to save the duplicate function as a script, and then set the time and date for the duplicate function to occur (mine kicks in every morning at 10A.M. and every evening at 5P.M. to ensure that updated documents are duplicated regularly).

 This is important: Retrospect's duplicate feature literally duplicates whatever's on the source location to the destination location—it doesn't matter if the file on the destination is newer or older than on the source. Whatever is on the source is on the destination.

Synchronize! Pro Ⓧ

Qdea's Synchronize! Pro X is backup software for OS X systems that not only backs up files, but allows full computer restoration. However, it's primariily intended to duplicate the most recent versions of your documents on more than one disk. Since there's not a lot to cover, we'll show you the entire duplication process. Once you've launched Synchronize! Pro, select **New** from the **File** menu to open an untitled backup window. By default, the pop-up in the window is set for Synchronization, so you'll have to change it to read **Backup,** as shown in Figure 10-8. on page 281.

The easiest way to select what to back up is to simply drag the source directory onto the left **Folder A** (source) side of the window, and then drag the mounted volume, secondary drive, or removable media directory onto the right **Folder B** (destination) side of the window, as shown in the following diagram (left dialog,

Figure 10-8.), where we've backed up the directory that holds the book you're reading.

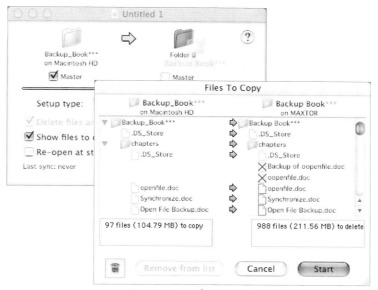

Figure 10-8. Synchronize Pro!

From here on out, Synchronize! Pro treats the source volume as the master and the destination as the slave. When you're ready, finishing the process of creating an immediate backup is as easy as clicking the **Start** button.

If the two directories are initially out of synch (as they are in Figure 10-8. on the right), Synchronize! Pro will present you with *X*es over the files that will be deleted during the backup process (as long as you've selected the **Show files to copy** check box).

Once you click the **Start** button, if you have files that need to be deleted, Synchronize! Pro warns you before letting you proceed. When you do finally proceed, the application presents you with a rather unique progress indicator.

Setting backup options

You can set a plethora of options in Synchronize! Pro (shown at right).

- You can **Auto-Connect** to a mounted server if you're backing up across the network.

Figure 10-9. Auto-Connect

If you're backing up automatically to a server and setting an automatic connection, you should know that, because of security or other policy reasons, some servers on your LAN might not be available to you once you leave your LAN.

- Qdea is even thoughtful enough to allow you to automatically un-mount any network-mounted backup destination volume—an outstanding security feature, as you'll probably be mounting your server or NAS box volume, and don't want it mounted on your computer once the backup is finished, if you aren't there.

Figure 10-10. Completion Options

- You can set your **Start Options**

to one of many features, including backing up on a regularly scheduled basis. Their schedule will let you set the number of minutes between backups—a pretty cool feature that can be useful in some circumstances—like allowing yourself time for a coffee-and–Krispy Kreme break.

- When copying the files from the source to the destination over a network, Synchronize! Pro copies the privileges exactly or sets specific user and group rights for the directories and files once they're on the remote location.

Figure 10-11. Users and groups privileges

- You can also set both **Copy** and **Don't copy** options (the dialogs look the same) so that you can eliminate backing up those invaluable Weird Al Yankovic MP3 files collected on your drive.

  You also have more or less the same options with folders.

- I've never seen any other software with such a detailed **Copy files if** selector set (other than Retrospect, which is industrial strength).

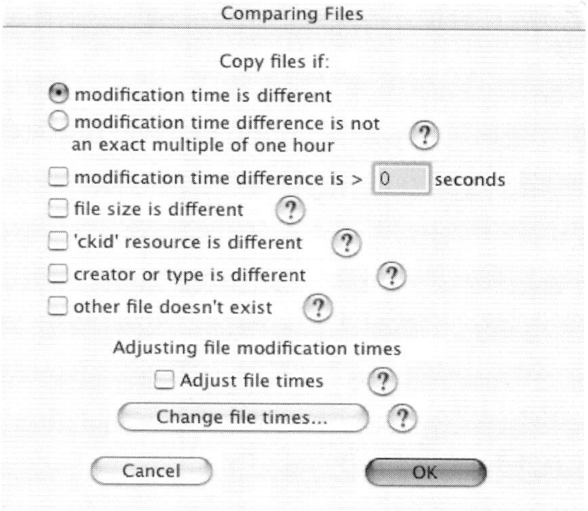

Figure 10-12. Comparing Files (copy if)

Since this software duplicates the directories and files from the source to the destination location, there's no need for any special restoration or retrieval process: All the directories and files in question are at the destination in their native file format.

Apple's Backup software (X)

Apple Computer's Backup software is really duplication software in that it stores information in native file format to either CD or the Internet. This software is available only for OS X 1.2 and greater operating systems, and only if the user is a member of the .Mac online community. The software is basically a very simplistic backup utility that offers backup capability to CDs or DVDs, and a duplicate function to the user's iDisk account.

Using a combination of predetermined items that Apple has created (backup "packages") and an interface that's basically a drag-and-drop, this is a pretty simple package to use.

Figure 10-13. Apple's Backup software

Because the iDisk storage space is a part of a web service, the user views a thermometer-type gauge showing how much iDisk space is currently in use (dark green) and how much space the new backup takes (light green). If the backup material takes more space than the user has allocated, the bar turns red and the user is asked to either **Buy Storage** or to reduce the amount of data being duplicated.

A simple once-daily (the most frequently a backup can happen) scheduler automates the process. The files can then be retrieved by the software, or the iDisk can be mounted to the desktop, and the user can simply drag the files and folders back to the computer.

As noted earlier, the user doesn't have enough permissions to make changes to the iDisk backup volume—only enough to see the files and directories and download them to the local computer.

Versioning utilities

Versioning utilities are different than duplication utilities in that they intercept the file's **Save** command and ensure that each and every time you save the file, the changes are put onto the disk in their format, and controlled and tracked by the versioning utility. They're a cross between duplication and archived backups in that they can maintain a history of documents (creating a new version on each subsequent **Save** command), much like a backup can.

GoBack and SecondChance

WildFile's GoBack utility takes over a chunk of each drive, using the space to record all changes to the drive. From the stored change records, you can roll back all changes, restoring the disk to its exact state at a chosen time. If a virus wipes out your operating system or an inept employee deletes the personnel files, you can simply roll the system back to an hour ago, yesterday, or any other time. PowerQuest's SecondChance works in a similar fashion, but stores disk changes at specified times, called **checkpoints**. The System Restore applet in Windows Me also lets you roll your disk back to a previously saved point.

FlashBack

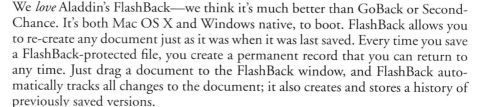

We *love* Aladdin's FlashBack—we think it's much better than GoBack or Second-Chance. It's both Mac OS X and Windows native, to boot. FlashBack allows you to re-create any document just as it was when it was last saved. Every time you save a FlashBack-protected file, you create a permanent record that you can return to any time. Just drag a document to the FlashBack window, and FlashBack automatically tracks all changes to the document; it also creates and stores a history of previously saved versions.

Since FlashBack records only the changes you made since the last time you saved the file, you don't waste a lot of valuable hard disk space with a collection of slightly different documents. Instead of cryptically named documents, each "FlashBacked" document is clearly labeled with a time and date stamp, to provide even easier access to saved versions.

FlashBack can track revisions of any file. To keep revisions of a file, you must add it to the FlashBack window. To add a document, drag it into the FlashBack window. You can hold down the Shift key to select multiple items to drag into the FlashBack window (on Windows, use the Control key to select multiple items not in a row).

The FlashBack window (Figure 10-14.) stores items in three main categories: applications, files, and revisions. When you add a file to the FlashBack window, if there's no category for the application, one is created. A file category is created for each item made by an application and is stored alphabetically within the application category. The revisions are sorted chronologically in the file category. The oldest is at the top, and the newest is at the bottom.

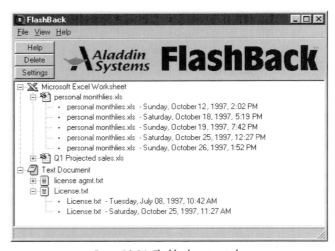

Figure 10-14. Flashback main window

You can choose to remove a single revision, a file and all its revisions, or an application category (and all its related items). When you use the **Delete** button to remove an application category or file from the FlashBack window, it still exists on your hard drive—you can add it to the FlashBack window again later. When you delete a revision, however, it's no longer accessible.

You've got a few things to remember when setting up FlashBack, and they have to do with thinking through how often you want revisions saved, and how many revisions you want to have saved. The **Save trigger** (Figure 10-15.) determines when FlashBack saves a revision of your files. To select the appropriate setting, consider how often you revise or save a file and how many revisions of a file you want to keep.

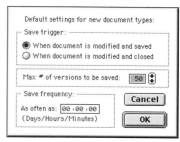

Figure 10-15. The Save and Versions settings

- Select "When document is modified and saved" to save a revision each time you modify and save the document. This will save more revisions and give you more flexibility in finding the "right" document, but will also take up more disk space. Now, if you're like me, and you "save early and save often," you'll have about five revisions per page written. While this gives you the most copies of a single document, it's great for short documents, but not so great for long ones. You can override this setting by changing the **Save frequency** to something like the 15-minutes setting so that even if you save your document every three minutes or so, FlashBack will track the Saves only every 15 minutes.

- Select "When document is modified and closed" to save a revision only when you modify and close the document. This saves fewer revisions and lets you access only the last revision prior to each close, but it takes up less hard disk space. This setting is independent of the number of times you save a document prior to closing, so beware: If you do something stupid to the document and then hit **Save**, whatever you did won't be recorded and you'll have to revert to an older version of the document; not simply an older version of your **Save** command.

- The last setting determines how many versions you want to track. The default setting is 50. Keep in mind that the more files and more revisions you save, the more hard disk space FlashBack requires. We recommend that you periodically check your hard disk to ensure the availability of disk space. If the revision being saved is over the limit set, the oldest revision is removed to make room. For instance, if you've selected a maximum of 35 revisions and are saving the 36th, the oldest (or first) will be removed to allow room for the newest revision.

WHAT'S A BACKUP?

 Data backup is a bit more complex than duplication and replication. As my buddy Craig Isaacs used to say, "To go forward, you must back up!" Of course, he said that when he was the marketing director for a backup software company. Now that he's head honcho of a network management software company, he's probably saying something like "To grow your network, you must first understand it!"—but I digress; we were talking about backups here. Simply put, as we stated in *Layered protection* on page 7, the process of backing up any given file or piece of data involves:

1. Making a copy of the source information; and

2. Transferring the copy of that information in a secure manner to the destination; and

3. Storing that copy in a format that the backup software creates (to maintain and track the information's history and versions for recovery purposes);

4. Which is usually in a compressed format, to save space on the destination's media; and

5. If the files are no longer in "native" file format (the user must access them with the backup software that created them), for retrieval purposes, the backup software createsa catalog of the files that have been backed up[5];

6. So that the same backup software can be used to restore the data to any backed-up point in time.

That's it—almost. This chapter offers a sort of explanation and glossary all in one. I use the term *glossary* because in reality, there are really only two types of backup procedures: full backups and changed-file backups (which I'll explain as we go along). However, each software vendor tries to put their own spin on what they're

---

5.   You'll really want to watch where the backup software keeps this catalog. As a good friend of mine reminded me when his business recently burned down, "If you don't have the catalogs of the backup files and you're having problems with the tapes, you're in deep [doo doo]."

doing, and it can get quite complicated trying to figure out who's saying what, and what that means regarding what's happening to your backup. It gets even more complicated when you think about the fact that there are backups to disk, backups to tape, and backups to the Internet. But first, we need to examine the three main components of any backup: the source being backed up, the destination the backup is going to, and the catalog that the backup software uses to manage the backup media and which files should be backed up.

The backup source

The source of a backup can be a partion, hard disk volume, a client computer's volumes, a network volume, the contents of a CD/DVD, or even a combination of multiple sources. In other words, what is being backed up is the logical contents of a computer.

You can't back up a "hard drive," but you can back up the partitions on a hard drive. Yes, some user's computers have a single partition, and therefore the entire contents of the hard drive are being backed up. However, backup software can't be pointed to a physical device and run a backup on, say, SCSI ID 1. Backup software can only be pointed at storage **volumes** (also known as **partitions**) that have been set up or individual **documents** (in this case, the backup software would treat an application as a document).

Backup media (backup sets)

Backup software copies files from a designated source and stores them on a designated destination in what we call a **backup set**.

The backup set at the destination can be saved on storage media including tapes (AIT, DAT, DLT, etc.), recordable disks (CD-R, CD-RW, DVD-R, DVD-RW, or DVD+RW), normal hard drives (internal or externally attached drives, Zip disks, or network volumes), an SQL database, or even a single file on a hard disk or server. We call what's stored on the destination a backup *set* because the *set* contains not only the data being backed up, but also a catalog, or index, of what has been backed up. Furthermore, we also use the term *set* to refer to the individual members, or pieces of media, that comprise the backup set.

If your backup set is to tape, CD, DVD, or a disk set (they can be removable disks, or even disks within a RAID system that are pulled out of the drawer and taken offsite), that means that the backups can *span* multiple pieces of media (another reason why we call the grouped pieces of media a backup *set*). Let's say that you're backing up your computer's hard drive to a DVD. Most likely, you don't have a hard drive that contains only 5 GB of data (roughly what a DVD can hold). To back up all of the contents of your computer, the backup software must back up some of it to DVD disk 1 and the rest to successive DVD disks. Each successive media storage container (tape, CD, DVD, disk) is merely a media asset in the backup set. The backup set that holds this book contains three CDs.

The catalog

Carl Reiner and Mel Brooks used to do a skit called "The 2,000-Year-Old Man." Mel Brooks was this ancient fella who was being interviewed by Carl Reiner. Reiner asks, "In your 2,000 years of existence, what is the most impressive technological advancement you've seen?" Brooks thinks about it, and then with a straight face, replies "The *thermos*." "The *thermos*?" asks Reiner incredulously. "How can that beat going to the moon or human cloning?" Brooks looks unabashed and replies, "For six bucks, you get a container that keeps hot things hot and cold things cold." "So?" asks Reiner. "So how does it know?" responds Brooks. *How does it know?* I love that one.

When you're backing up files that change on a regular basis, the backup software has to know which files have already been backed up, and where those backed-up files are located hin the different pieces of media in the backup set. *How does it know?* The backup software creates a **catalog** of what is backed up where. Different backup software applications call the catalog by different names: We've seen it called the *catalog file*, the *storage management database*, the *share resource library*, and even just *library*. But, as the ineffable Ms. Stein told us, "Rose is a rose is a rose"—and we call this rose a catalog.

The catalog holds the master list of all the files that have been backed up to date, where they came from, and where they're located in the backup media.

This catalog is very, *very* important. Why? Because it's used to track all known information about any given file, such as:

*   Its name, to include its file name extension;

- Creation, modification date, archive bit setting; and

- Size.

Each file also stores metadata, such as the names of each of the source computers associated with the file, the location of the file on each of those source computers, and the date that the file was backed up—based on each of the source computers.

Let's say that we have three computers: A, B, and C. Each has the very same file on it, called File1 (a PDF file). The file's name, filename extension, creation and modification date, and size are all exactly the same—so the backup software will treat it as the same file on all three computers. The backup software is smart enough to know that it should copy this file only once to the backup destination. Once the file has been copied (for computer A), when the next instance of this same file is encountered, the backup software does not copy it again. Instead, it enters into the backup catalog a placeholder and pointer to the location where the file exists on the tape.

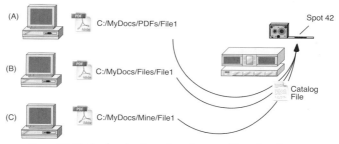

Figure 10-16. Catalog showing pointer for same file in three locations

The catalog now contains three instances for the same file. However, in each instance, even though the catalog points to the same spot on the tape, it knows that the restored file goes in a specific directory for each of the source computers.

 Without the catalog, the backup software can't create any more backups to or restore any data from the backup set. If a catalog is lost or damaged, the catalog must be rebuilt by reading the backup set data into the backup software, so that the backup software can re-create the catalog from scratch.

Two types of backup servers are on the market today: console coordinated backup servers and individual backup servers. **Console coordinated backup servers** can be controlled from a single computer, usually with a web interface. In such a coordinated environment, the catalog is shared among each backup server connected by the console. This provides the least amount of redundancy among files, as a single catalog can be used for all of the backup servers. **Individual backup servers,** which don't share a console, must maintain their own catalog. Some backup servers require that a catalog be maintained per backup set.

Software packages that require a separate catalog for each backup set place the catalog in certain places, depending on the type of backup media being used.

- If the backup is to tape, CD, DVD, or disk set (including mounted volumes) the catalog is created as a stand-alone file or database on a locally mounted volume.

- If the backup is to a single file or to an SQL database, the catalog is normally saved as a part of the file or SQL database.

These catalogs can get rather large at times. However, you can safely predict catalog size and storage requirements by using the following calculation, where N = number of files, and I = instances of any given file.

$$(N \times 128 \text{bytes}) + (I \times N \times 40 \text{bytes}), \textbf{ or } (100000 \times 128) + (25 \times 100000 \times 40) = 108\text{MB}$$
Figure 10-17. Calculations for sizing a catalog file

One of your big questions? Where to store your catalog files. Remember, each backup server that uses the file must have constant access to it. If you have multiple servers accessing the same catalog file, store the catalog file on a networked volume with easy access—like the console management workstation or the workstation that sits and monitors the network. Putting it on an IT admin's laptop is a bad idea.

Also, ensure that wherever you put this catalog file, you back it up offsite as often as possible. Remember, all backup and restore operations come to a screeching halt if this catalog file is missing or corrupted. Get it off site as quickly and as often as possible.

Backup types

There are really only two types of backups: Those that copy everything in the source to the destination, and those that copy only the files that have changed. However, the marketing folks at the various backup software companies have been running amok for the last bunch of years, deciding that it would be a great idea to give various and sundry names to those two operations. We're left with an assortment of vendor-driven gobbledygook that says either "Hey, we're now going to back up everything from this thing here and put it over there," or "Hey, we're now going to copy a bunch of stuff that has changed from this thing here and put it over on that thing there." (Our reinterpretation back into simple backup language of what they're doing during these various backup processes). First, let's run through backups to tape and then we'll look at backups to disk.

Full backups (a.k.a. recycle backups) to tape

A full backup and a recycle backup are the same thing. Each time a **full backup** happens, the tape set is erased and retentioned, the catalog is emptied, and the backup begins at the very beginning of the tape set. The full backup process doesn't really examine the contents of the computer—it simply begins copying everything from the source to the destination tape set. In the diagram below we

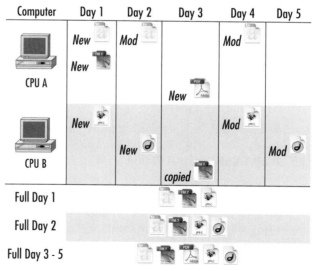

Table 10-2. 5-day full backup schedule

show two computers being backed up every day using a full backup method. For simplicity's sake, we'll count only the files we show here.

On day 1, computer A creates two files and computer B creates one file. The full backup process stores everything it finds on the tape; thus, three files are stored.

On day 2, computer A modifies a file and computer B creates a new file. Because this is a full backup, the backup software has completely erased the tape and writes every file it finds. Thus, since there are a total of four files on the two computers, there are four files on the backup tape.

On day 3, computer A creates a new file. Computer B copies a file from computer A. The backup software once again erases the contents of the tape, counts all of the files it finds, and thus now writes a total of five files to the tape. Yes, *I can count.* You smart alecks who have been paying attention say there should be *six* files on the tape—three from computer A and three from computer B? Ha! Listen closely: This is where that catalog concept comes in. The backup software compares each file it's about to back up to what's already listed in the catalog for this specific full backup. If the file matches all the necessary criteria (name, extension, creation, and modification date), the catalog merely sets a pointer to the file's preexisting location on the tape. This saves a lot of tape space.

On days 4 and 5, different files are modified, but the full backup doesn't really care, since it backs up everything it finds. There is a total of five distinct files on the two computers—and that's what is found on the backup tape.

Dantz Retrospect calls this a **recycle backup**, because each time it runs, both the catalog and tape are erased and the whole process starts from the beginning, reusing the tape and re-creating the catalog.

Full, or mirrored backups to disk

Some disk-based backup software calls a full backup a **mirrored backup**. In essence, this is more or less the same thing as a tape backup. When the backup begins, whatever *was* on the disk is erased, and the catalog file (stored separately) is erased, as well.

In Figure 10-18. on page 295 you'll see a hard drive with two directories (one enclosed within the other). During a full backup that happened on 5/1/02, the entire contents of the drive were copied to whatever backup hard drive you chose (an actual hard drive, a RAID bank, CD, DVD, etc.).

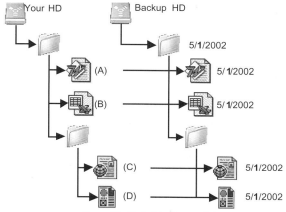

Figure 10-18. Full backup to disk

A full backup gives you the best ability to restore your computer easily when Kablooey! happens, because the information is in the exact same hierarchical structure (on disk) as it was when you backed it up. However, this approach sucks up the most capacity and the longest time, because each time a full (or mirrored) backup is undertaken, everything on the computer is transferred to the backup device.

Restoring from a full backup

Restoring from a full backup is the fastest possible way to restore, because most of the files that are being restored to any one computer are stored on the tape in linear, contiguous fashion. However, there's no "history" with a full backup—whatever was last backed up is what can be restored. Remember the above scenario, wherein computer A created the Word document on day 1 and then modified it on day 2 and again on day 4? If the file were lost or corrupted, the only version that could be restored is the last version that was backed up. This presents some real problems for us humans, because a great many of the files that we need to restore are the result of "uh-ohs"—we accidentally save over a file, and "uh-oh," better call the IT folks and get an older version restored. But you can't do that with only full backups. This is where incremental backups come into play.

 You should perform at least milestone full backups before and after dangerous or important events, such as office moves, power outages, or employee reviews.

Incremental backups (a.k.a. normal backups) to tape

A **normal**, or **incremental backup** is a bit different than a full backup. As you'll see below, some disk-based backup software packages also call this a *changed file, evolutive,* or *evolutionary* backup—all of which are simply other names for the incremental backup process. Incremental backups don't back up every file every time—they back up only those files that have changed. But how does the backup software know that a file has changed?

All files on all computers have certain metadata appended to the file that helps the operating system manage those files. One of those chunks of metadata is called the file's **archive bit** (a.k.a. **modified bit**). Whenever a file is created or modified, the operating system sets the file's archive bit to "on" status. Backup software uses this bit to determine whether or not a file has been backed up. During a full backup, the backup software backs up the files and then sets their archive bit to "off."

During the incremental backup process, the backup software examines the archive bit, and if it's on, it backs up the file. After the file has been backed up successfully, the backup software turns the archive bit off, and it remains off until the file is modified at some point, at which time, the operating system turns the archive bit on once again.

Let's go through the same two computer, five-day backup cycle again. This time we will only perform a full backup on day 1, and then incremental backups for the files that are being added and changed on days 2 through 5. With a full backup, all three files are backed up to the tape on the first day, as shown in Table 10-3. on page 297. Each time a file is backed up with a full backup, the backup software resets the file's archive bit to "off."

During the second day, computer B modifies the Word file. The operating system on the computer then sets the Word file's archive bit to "on." The backup software examines the archive bit, and the modified Word document and computer B's new Dreamweaver file are backed up again to the tape. Both files' archive bits are then set to "off" by the backup software.

On day 3, only the new PDF is backed up to the incremental tape backup because it's new, and its archive bit has been set by the operating system. Even though computer B has copied the FrameMaker file, the catalog handles that issue, and adds a pointer to the tape backup instead of the actual file.

On day 4, the Word file on computer A is modified again, as well as the picture file on computer B. Both files' archive bits were set by the operating system. Therefore, the backup software appended both of those files to the backup tape.

Finally, on day 5, computer B modifies the Dreamweaver file again, so it too is now appended to the backup tape.

Table 10-3. 5 day incremental backup schedule

The tape now has a daily historical record of all of the files that were changed. The total contents of the tape now contain three copies of the Word document (the original and the modified versions), two copies of both the Dreamweaver and picture documents, and individual copies of all of the other documents.

Incremental backups (a.k.a. normal, changed file, evolutionary) to disk

Believe it or not, all of the above names equal the same thing: backing up those files that have changed since the last backup—an incremental backup in our parlance.

One of the problems with changed-file backups? Restorations take longer, as the most current files usually end up on different tapes or the files are strewn throughout multiple iterations of the backup hard drive. Let's examine our test scenario to see how it would be backed up during a changed-file backup and where the files would be stored on a hard drive or *rewriteable* CD/DVD.

Changed-file backups to disk: Method 1

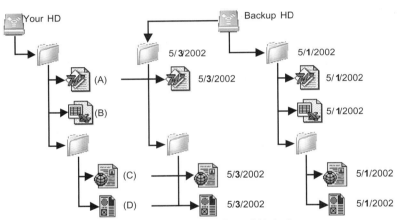

Figure 10-19. Disk-to-disk changed-file backup

What happens with changed file disk-to-disk backups reminds me of a magic show. There, what you see is what the magician *wants* you to see (the good-looking brunette who replaced the elephant didn't really just appear there, so don't get your hopes up, Marla). The same is more or less true with disk-to-disk backups: When you look at the backup destination, you might see all of your files up to date, but what you *don't see* is the files' real hierarchical format. In Figure 10-19. , we show what a real structure looks like during a disk-to-disk changed-file backup operation.

On the left is the original hard drive with its data in two directories (one inside the other). On the right is the original backup, where all of the files were moved to the backup location because that's what happens the first time a backup of this type is run. In the middle are the files that changed since the first backup.

Since looking at something like this is confusing (it confuses even me), most backup software applications mask this and show you a single directory structure as you'd normally encounter it—and that's a good thing for our meagre brains.

Changed-file backups to disk: Method 2 and 2a

There's another method of backing up to disk that doesn't involve moving actual files from the source to the destination; instead, it creates a single large file on the destination volume, and as the backup proceeds, the backup software copies the files on the source and then places their contents into the backup file itself. We represent this process below in Figure 10-20. with all of the original file's arrows pointing to the single destination backup file.

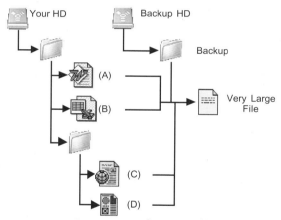

Figure 10-20. Backing up to a file

The limitation of this type of backup is set by the limitation of the filing system on the destination computer, differing with each filing system you use (HFS+, FAT32, NTFS, UFX). To learn more about the filing systems, go back to the beginning of this chapter (*What's put where on your drive* on page 264).

Another variant of this (Method 2a) is to back up all of the files to an SQL database instead of a large file. This has a few advantages over backing up to a file in that (a) there are no backup-file-size limitations, as SQL databases can grow to any size, and (b) sophisticated catalogs can be employed to reduce the overall number of files in the database.

Changed-file backups to disk: Method 3 Instead of putting a single file in the destination, the backup software creates multiple files as necessary, allowing much more data to be backed up to the destination so that the native file system isn't the limitation.

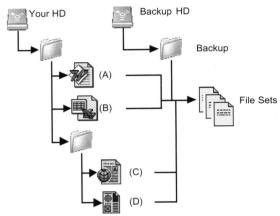

Figure 10-21. Disk backup

And, because this isn't a single file, the backup software should be able to span multiple hard drives during the backup process if it runs out of room on the first hard drive. Remember, the catalog that the backup software creates is the key, because it remembers the drive on which the backup software has placed the individual file you want to restore. Figure 10-20. shows all of the original file's arrows pointing to the destination backup file set.

Restoring from an incremental backup

The administrator can now restore any of the three versions of computer A's Word document, and either of the two versions of computer B's picture file or Dreamweaver document. This **point-in-time** (a.k.a. **snapshot**) restoration capability is great if you need individual files back. However, if you need to restore all the files on a computer, this type of backup makes restoration much slower than a full backup.

To restore the full three files for computer A, the backup software must rewind the tape to the second file in the list (FrameMaker file), copy it back to computer A, and fast-forward past the picture and second Word file, so that it can restore the

PDF file and then restore the latest version of the Word file. Obviously, the more files appended to the incremental tape backup, the longer the restoration process will take.

Differential backups

Differential backups ignore the archive bit and instead examine the creation and modification date of the files. They work the same whether you're backing up to disk or tape, so we'll explain them once using tape as the example. Differential backups back up all files created or modified since the last full backup, comparing the file's modification date to that of the modification date stored during the last full backup. If a file has been modified or created after the last full backup, it's then appended to the differential backup. Differential backup restores files faster than

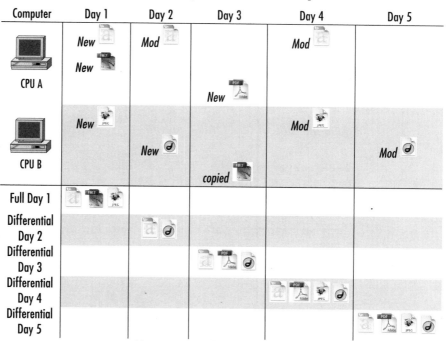

Table 10-4. 5 day differential backup schedule

incremental backup. Because differential backup appends every changed file since the last backup to the tape, on each and every backup session, it tends to use a *lot* of tape. On the other hand, since all the modified files have been grouped together contiguously on the tape, restorations of differential backups are much faster than restorations of incremental backups.

In our scenario shown in Table 10-4. on page 301, the first day's backup is a full backup. Three files exist between the two computers and are therefore backed up.

On day 2, the Word file is modified, and the Dreamweaver file is created. Thus, since both of these files fit the "new and modified since the last full backup" criterion, they're appended to the backup tape set.

On day 3, the PDF file is created. Along with the Word and Dreamweaver files, it too fits the "new and modified since the last full backup" criterion, and so all three are now appended to the backup tape set.

Day 4 sees changes to the Word file, and the picture file is modified, as well. There are now four files that are "new or modified since the last full backup" and are therefore appended to the tape backup set.

Day 5 sees the Dreamweaver file modified. It was appended before because it was "new" since the last full backup. It is appended still because it now fits the modified category of the rule.

The good and bad of differential backups

The good part about the differential backups is that the restore can begin at the front of the tape and restore only files that were existing but never modified. It can then skip over everything else and go to the back of the tape and restore the most recent contiguously spaced files in a much quicker fashion than parsing through the whole tape finding a file here and there. The bad part? This uses a lot of tape.

Should the file, or only changes in the file, be backed up?

When backing up a document, you might think that when the document changes, the best thing to do is back up the entire document to your backup media. While this is indeed the most obvious way of getting the document from point A to point B, sometimes it just doesn't make sense—especially in the case of differential backups.

Let's say that I have two documents I want to back up on my computer: a text document and an art document as shown in Figure 10-22. The text document is 100 K in size, and is a "why I should be promoted" letter that I'm writing to my boss. The JPEG is a picture of my boss that I've enhanced with a mustache and devil horns (a vast improvement, I must say). It's 2.5 MB.

Figure 10-22. Text document and art document

Normal backup software would back the files up to the destination, and then monitor if these files changed. Let's say that I decided to add a sentence to the letter and a goatee to the picture. Normally, the backup software would see that both files had changed and would then copy both files from their destination to the backup source media. Total space taken up would be 100 K + 2.5 MB.

Delta block backup

The next innovation beyond backing up changed files is in the **delta block backup**. The delta block process evaluates changed data by breaking each file down into discrete blocks of information (we show you a crude approximation in Figure 10-23.) that are anywhere from 4 to 32 K in size. The software can then utilize a cyclical redundancy check (CRC) mechanism to compare each block of the modified file with the corresponding block that has already been backed up. When the software detects a difference in the block, it will back up those blocks that have changed insted of backing up the entire file. Thus, changing a sentence in the text document might change a block or two, and adding that goatee might change quite a few blocks. However, unless the entire file has changed, you can pretty well bet that backing up the delta block changes will save time and space on your backup media.

Figure 10-23. files segmented into blocks

The only problem with delta block backup methods is that many changes *per block* don't take up the block's entire contents. In other words, let's say that all I did in the text document was change a period to an exclamation point. That wouldn't take up either 32 *or* 4 K in size (the smallest size of a block). So while delta block backups are better than copying the entire file, they lack a certain granularity.

FastBit patching

The only real difference between FastBit patching and delta block is that FastBit Patching examines the files at the binary level instead of the block level, so the level of extraction is much more precise, as shown in Figure 10-24. FastBit backup methods can yield backups that are half the size of the delta block method, which is insanely smaller than the space needed to back up the whole file.

Figure 10-24. FastBit patching

THE BASICS OF INTERNET BACKUP SERVICES

An **Internet**, or **online backup service** (we prefer to call it the former) allows computer users to back up the data on their computer to a server located somewhere on the Internet, as opposed to on a local hard drive, tape drive, or server in their company's Local Area Network.

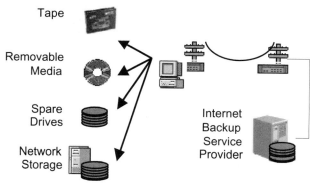

Tape

Removable
Media

Spare
Drives

Internet
Backup
Service
Provider

Network
Storage

Figure 10-25. Internet backup service as separate from local backups

Many backup software companies such as Dantz (makers of Retrospect) and NovaStor (makers of NovaNet-WEB and NovaBACKUP), which make individual workstation and network backup software, have now added the feature of backing up information to an Internet backup service. With both the Dantz and NovaStor products, the end user can back up to the Internet instead of or in addition to backing up to a local device. Other companies that offer Internet-based services, such as BackJack and SkyDesk, have developed software applications specifically for backing up to *their* Internet backup service.

Whichever approach you take, the idea is the same: *Internet backup services exist to provide a simple backup solution wherein the backed-up files are always available over the Internet without the need to contact the backup administrator.* We call this *geographical dispersal of critical data.*

When setting up your computer system for Internet backup, four factors are crucial: your connection to the Internet, the service being offered (and its price), the type of local application that sends your data to the service, and what you want to back up.

1a Your Internet connection

The speed of your connection to the Internet is of paramount importance: The slower your connection, the longer your backup and restoration will take. Let's take a few paragraphs to decode how fast you'll be able to run your Internet backups.

To make calculations easy, we've included a throughput calculator on our website (www.backupbook.com) in the forms area of *The Backup Book* (also shown below in Figure 10-26.). You can enter information in either KB, MB, or GB. (For fun, try entering the entire size of your hard drive and see how long it would take. Mine would take 16 hours over cable.)

I've entered the size of our test backup/restore file and folder (both are around 2.4 MB). We call this the **theoretical throughput calculator** because times vary according to your Internet backup service provider, the amount of compression your files are subject to before sending, and the nature of the software that your Internet backup service provider uses for backing up and restoring.

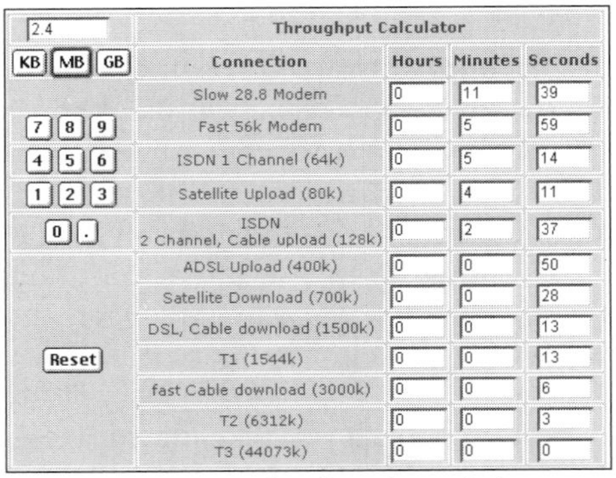

Throughput Calculator — input: 2.4 (KB | MB | GB)

Connection	Hours	Minutes	Seconds
Slow 28.8 Modem	0	11	39
Fast 56k Modem	0	5	59
ISDN 1 Channel (64k)	0	5	14
Satellite Upload (80k)	0	4	11
ISDN 2 Channel, Cable upload (128k)	0	2	37
ADSL Upload (400k)	0	0	50
Satellite Download (700k)	0	0	28
DSL, Cable download (1500k)	0	0	13
T1 (1544k)	0	0	13
fast Cable download (3000k)	0	0	6
T2 (6312k)	0	0	3
T3 (44073k)	0	0	0

Figure 10-26. Online throughput calculator

According to the calculator above, since I have AT&T cable service, my upload speed is around 128 Kbps, on average. Let's say that I want to back up a test directory made up of HTML files, images, and subdirectories (left window of

Figure 10-27.). The directory size will be about 2.4 MB. The second test is a single QuickTime movie of 2.4 MB (right side of Figure 10-27.).

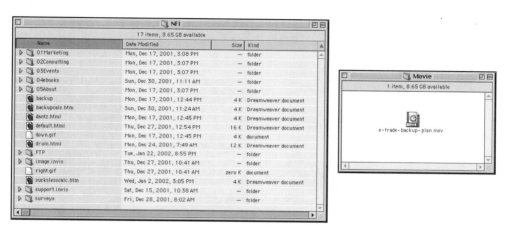

Figure 10-27. 2.4 MB test directory (left) and 2.4 MB quicktime movie (right)

Theoretically, since my upload speed is around 128 Kbps, my backup time should be about 2.5 minutes. And my restore time, since I'm running about 1500 Kbps, should be about 15 seconds.

Backup times To test these theories, we ran backups and restorations of our test files multiple times to each Internet location. We ran the WildPackets' Ether-Peek packet analyzer application during the process, capturing each and every packet that went by. The backup times for the movie and the directory were different for different backup methodologies, as shown in the chart and tables in Figure 10-28.

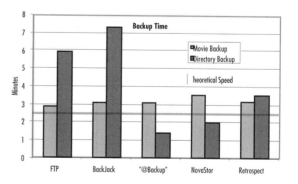

Figure 10-28. Backup time chart

307

Here are the tables for the Movie and Directory backups, with explanations.

Movie Backup	FTP	@Backup	BackJack	NovaNet-WEB	Retrospect
Original MB	2.4	2.4	2.4	2.4	2.4
Transferred MB	2.8	2.9	2.8	3.2	2.8
Kbps throughput	131	125	126	128	119
Duration (minutes)	2.9	3.1	3.	3.5	3.2

Table 10-5. Backup time table

Directory Backup	FTP	@Backup	BackJack	NovaNet-WEB	Retrospect
Original MB	2.4	2.4	2.4	2.4	2.4
Transferred MB	2.8	1.9	1.2	1.2	2.4
Kbps throughput	54	35	119	83	94
Duration (minutes)	5.9	7.3	1.4	2	3.5

Table 10-6. Directory backup

The differences are accounted for by the following:

• First is the amount of information transferred over the wires. While each of the backup test sets were about 2.4 MB, the different applications had different amounts of overhead and file compression for each. You'll notice during the directory backup that BackJack, @Backup, and NovaNet-WEB all sent *less* information across the wire than did FTP and Retrospect.

• The second discrepancy entails Kbps throughput. We know that the Retrospect server was running on a T1, as well as the FTP server (they're actually one in the same box). We don't know the theoretical speeds of the other servers, but we do know that none of them pushed the limit of our theoretical throughput during the directory backup process.

• Throughput was diminished in most instances by latency of the remote box during the send process.

• Throughput was also greatly diminished during directory backup for all applications *except* @Backup due to individual files being compressed before being sent. BackJack got nailed because it uses the third-party application, StuffIt Expander. FTP got nailed due to the overhead of creating multitudes of subdirectories—the latency during that process is amazingly high.

Throughput during the restore process was also pretty interesting. Only @Backup and NovaNet-WEB came close to hitting our theoretical ceiling of 1500 Kbps, scoring 1191 and 1354 Kbps, respectively, during the movie restore, as shown in Figure 10-29.

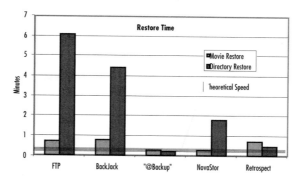

Figure 10-29. Restore throughput

The information table follows:

Movie Restore	FTP	@Backup	BackJack	NovaNet-WEB	Retrospect
Original MB	2.4	2.4	2.4	2.4	2.4
Transferred MB	2.8	2.7	2.8	3.2	2.7
Kbps throughput	540	476	1191	1354	562
Duration (minutes)	0.7	8.8	0.3	0.3	0.7

Table 10-7. Movie restore

Again, as with the directory backup, the directory restore really killed throughput. The speed differentials were measured as latency during directory and subdirectory the creation process, as well as decompression on the local computer. Again,

BackJack got murdered on the throughput issue because of its reliance on StuffIt Expander.

Directory Restore	FTP	@Backup	BackJack	NovaNet-WEB	Retrospect
Original MB	2.4	2.4	2.4	2.4	2.4
Transferred MB	2.4	1.7	1.2	1.2	2.2
Kbps throughput	54	52	932	92	582
Duration (minutes)	6.1	4.4	0.2	1.8	0.5

Table 10-8. Directory restore

To be safe when backing up and restoring large quantities of data in folders within folders, double your time calculations—a pretty good estimate of your realistic throughput speeds.

1b The nature of the file transfer mechanism

You must also understand the nature of the file transfer mechanisms that each application uses.

FTP, BackJack, and Retrospect all use the FTP protocol to send information over the Internet to the backup service. Therefore, if your firewall has the standard open port for FTP, you won't need to reconfigure it to use these applications.

Both @Backup and NovaNet-WEB use their own protocol for sending information over the Internet to their backup services. Therefore, to use these services, work with your network administrator to open that particular port in the firewall.

There's nothing wrong with either mechanism—it's just something you need to know.

2 The service being offered

Following are some questions to consider regarding any potential Internet backup service provider:

Security • What is their security policy for your information at their site? Can you read your policy?

• What are their password and login rules? Are they too strict, too loose, or just right?

• Do they keep their Internet backup servers in secure locations, with alarm systems and limited physical access?

• What is their security policy for protecting their service from hackers and denial of service attacks? Can you see any documentation of that plan?

• How is file encryption, such as DES or Blowfish, handled during transfer, and what overhead does that cost you in backup/restore speed?

Data protection • What software do *they* use for backups?

• Are they running their own backup plan that includes daily, rotating, offsite backups? Can you see any documentation?

Connectivity and server questions • What is the speed of the Internet connection on the server end?

• Does the Internet backup service have multiple Internet connection service providers, should one go off line?

Management • Are they able to monitor servers 24/7 for downtime and problems?

• Do they maintain UPS systems for continued service during power interruptions, and, if so, how long will those UPSes maintain Internet connectivity and server uptime in case of power failure?

• Are they available for phone support 24/7 in case you lose your password?

Economics • If they go out of business, can you get your data back?

• If you're backing up groups of computers, can you get bill-back information or a breakdown by user?

• If you think they're making money hand-over-fist, can you become an investor? Okay, we're just kidding with this one.

3 Proprietary or standard backup software

Next, you need to decide whether or not you want the Internet backup operation to be an integrated part of or mere appendage to your backup plan.

We state it this way because of the four Internet backup products we examined, two of them (Dantz' Retrospect and NovaStor's NovaNet-WEB software) integrate into an "all-around" backup solution as provided by the vendor.

While there's nothing wrong with @Backup and BackJack—as a matter of fact, we like both of them a lot—they're both stand-alone solutions and don't integrate with any one backup package. This can be a benefit: Stand-alone applications have developed some novel approaches that, quite frankly, the "solution" packages should implement, but don't.

If you're a small shop and Internet backup is your main methodology, there's no issue whatsoever.

4 That which you plan to back up and restore

You aren't going to be backing up your operating system to the Internet: It doesn't make sense because you can't restore it within any realistic timeframe, plain and simple. And, based upon the file types you have, you probably won't be backing up your massive "Terrentino dances the tarantella" file to the Internet, which is probably 6 GB or so—right, Dave? Everything else is up for grabs and therefore should be backed up according to cost and need.

The rule of thumb is that you'll want to back up the Users folder (Mac OS X), the My Documents folder (Windows 98), or Documents and Settings (Windows 2000) of your local computer, plus any specialized directories or files as necessary[6]. We'll explain how to gather that information in a section below.

When assessing each of the individual Internet backup services, you need to know whether you have to buy data in blocks, or as you use the space (in whatever increments). Because each company's billing methods differ, we won't cover them in-depth here.

---

6.   Which means, by the way, that you might want to tell your staff (or yourself) that you want to start *using* the My Documents folder to *store* your data that you are working on.

Internet backup software additional features tables

To help you select the right software and service to fit your needs, we present a few key product features, separated into four main categories: security, restoration, storage management, and a compression set.

Security

Obviously, you'll need both an ID and a basic password for security. However, you also need to know how the application is going to handle the DES, CAST, or Blowfish encryption for added security. Which, of course, gives you one more password or passphrase to remember.

Both BackJack and Retrospect require an additional password/phrase for added encryption. BackJack requires a passphrase of up to 100 characters. Retrospect requires a secondary password be added in its options tab when creating the backup set. The length of the passphrase and the tough-to-remember place the Retrospect password is set make both more tenuously recalled in times of crisis.

Security	@Backup	BackJack	NovaNet-WEB	Retrospect
ID	✔	✔	✔	✔
Password	✔	✔	✔	✔
Pass Phrase		✔		✔
DES	✔			✔
CAST-128		✔		
Blowfish			✔	

Table 10-9. Security

In case you care, Blowfish was written by Bruce Schneier; DES was written by committee at IBM, the National Bureau of Standards, and the National Security Agency, and CAST by Carlisle Adams/Stafford Tavares (hence *CAST*). Plain DES can accept up to a 56-bit key; Blowfish up to 448, and CAST uses a 128 Feistel cipher. DES is the current standard encryption algorithm. While DES was originally thought to be invincible, on July 17, 1998, the Electronic Frontier Foundation (EFF) announced the construction of a DES brute-force hardware cracker[7]. While Blowfish hadn't gained much acceptance earlier on and was thought to not be as secure as DES, it's now gaining a great deal of steam and momentum[8]. CAST is "resistant to both linear and differential crypt analysis—currently, there is no known way of breaking it short of brute force. There are no known attacks on CAST with reduced rounds—it looks incredibly secure. CAST is now the default cipher in PGP[9]."

You'll probably want to ask even more specific security questions than those we just suggested. If you do have questions that it seems we haven't even dreamed of, please give us a holler—we're always interested in learning something new.

Restoration

This is important: *You don't want to restore the entire contents of a computer from the Internet.* If you lose your operating system, you should first reinstall it from CD or other backup method. Then, once the computer is up and running again, and you've restored your backup software, you can reconnect to the Internet and perform your massive restore of everything you put up there.

There are basically two methods of restoring files and folders from Internet backup services: restoring the contents to a new folder created by the backup software, or restoring the files and folders back to their original locations. Both have advantages and disadvantages.

If you chose to restore your files and folders to a new location created by the backup software (usually a directory called "*x* restore," where *x* is the name of the software package), the advantage is that you can examine the files you've just restored before you put them back into their original directories. The disadvantage? If you don't put them back into their original locations, they won't be backed up anymore because the backup software won't know where to find them. Hence,

---

[7]. http://www.eff.org/descracker/

[8]. If you'd like to know more about Blowfish and DES, see http://www.netaction.org/encrypt/appendixb.html for some great articles.

[9]. PGP Diffie-Hellman vs. RSA FAQ, "What is CAST?" can be found at http://www.scramdisk.clara.net/pgpfaq.html#SubCAST

restoring in place ensures that the files you've brought back are in their original location and once you've modified them again, they'll remain a part of your regularly scheduled backup process.

Restoration	@Backup	BackJack	NovaNet-WEB	Retrospect
Custom Folder	✔	✔	✔	✔
In Place	✔		✔	✔
Web	✔		✔	
CD by Mail	✔	✔	✔	

Table 10-10. Restoration

At this writing, only @Backup and NovaNet-WEB allow you to restore your files directly from a web interface. This is a particularly outstanding feature for a couple good reasons: First, if you lose the entire computer and need that presentation back in a hurry, you can simply find another computer to use and download the files you need from the Web individually.

You can also use the web interface and Internet backup service as a "politically neutral" place for you and others working on a joint project to back files up. Once at the Internet backup service, your files can be downloaded by either party with the proper identification.

We at Network Frontiers think that web file restoration will be a major part of the future for Internet backup services. Wouldn't it be nice to have Internet backup integrated directly into your overall backup plan in such a way that your staff backs up their client reports directly to the intranet server? You could rest assured that the latest and greatest reports were always there, available for anyone to get their hooks on.

The last service available is CD by Mail. This isn't particularly useful if you are in a time crunch and need your files back by CD. However, it *is* particularly useful if you're looking for an archival solution in which you regularly schedule your files to be sent back to you via CD for your long-term records (just make sure you keep them offsite, for security reasons).

Storage management

Does the software allow you to incrementally back up files to the server so that you can restore the file backed up two days ago versus the same file backed up one day ago? @Backup maintains up to 90 versions of your files! That's right, count 'em, *ninety!* No other backup service can make this claim. With date-based file versioning, your @Backup account keeps a 90-day history of your backups. You can set BlackJack to maintain any number of copies (you enter the amount), or you can set it to maintain all copies of anything you've backed up. With Retrospect, we couldn't figure out how to tell it to only keep one copy.

Why is this important? Because, as Julie Hetherington of BackJack points out so succinctly, "When it comes down to it, each of the Internet backup services come down to one thing: *storage.*" Therefore, the way the combination of software and service handles storage is a biggie.

Storage Management functionality	@Backup	BackJack	NovaNet-WEB	Retrospect
Multiple File Versions		✔		✔
X Days worth of revisions	✔	✔		
Deletion of Files		✔	✔	✔

Table 10-11. Storage management

You should be allowed to overwrite all, some or none of your files each time you back up. You should be able to decide how many copies to keep—as with BackJack, which allows you to (file-by-file) set the number of versions of the file.

Or you should be allowed to keep the changes for how many days back (30 to 90) you want the change history to go, as @Backup and NovaNet-WEB allow you to do.

The lone standout for "bad file management" on an FTP site is Retrospect, because you can either back up all contents in an incremental fashion or delete all contents and start afresh. With this program, you can't have your cake and eat it too, alas.

Compression & storage space

There's more than meets the eye when you start thinking about compression and the amount of storage space you're using.

First-time backups

In our tests with compression *on* for each of the backup software products, none were able to compress the directory with a single QuickTime movie in it. That's because those file formats are already compressed, and since you're no Superman, your mere mortal—and technological—strength can't squeeze them any smaller.

When backing up the test directory of JPEGs, HTML files, subdirectories, GIFs, etc., both BackJack and Retrospect sent 79 percent of the original payload over the Internet for storage to the Internet backup service. In other words, both had a first-run compression rate of around 21 percent.

Both NovaNet-WEB and @Backup were able to compress their files by 50 percent before sending them up to the Web.

Incremental backups

Now comes the time for the Internet backup software to earn its stripes. We opened up the QuickTime movie and made one simple change: We altered the "poster" frame from a frame halfway down the movie's length to a frame more near the front. We then saved the file and closed it.

Retrospect, BackJack, and @Backup had to back up the entire movie again, so now there are two movies, both uncompressed and stored on the Internet backup site.

NovaNet-WEB, on the other hand, backed up only the changes in the file; thus, their speed was *really* fast.

AN OVERVIEW OF BACKUP TOOL OPERATIONS

To kick off this discussion, we must first examine the backup software used to create and manage workstation-based backups. If you don't see your favorite backup application in our list below, let us know by sending us an e-mail at update@backupbook.com, and we'll try to work with the software's publisher of the software to cover it in our web-based and PDF-based update process. We've tried to work with as many vendors as we could, and selected the following packages basically because our trusty field editors have asked for them and the vendors were willing to work with us. Let's explore six different workstation-based backup software products:

1. @Backup, Internet backup service.

2. BackJack, Internet backup service.

3. Backup MyPC, created by VERITAS and now published by Stomp.

4. FWB ToolKit, created by Tri-Edre (and marketed as such in Europe), published by FWB.

5. NovaBACKUP, created and published by NovaStor.

6. NovaNet-WEB, created and published by NovaStor.

7. Retrospect Desktop, created and published by Dantz Development.

8. Retrospect Professional, created and published by Dantz Development.

We're covering both NovaBACKUP and NovaNet-WEB because NovaNet-WEB supports Internet backup and NovaBACKUP doesn't, which affects this section's destination media portion. We cover Retrospect Desktop and Professional because they used to be the same application, but Dantz has renamed the Windows version *Professional*, and there are some subtle differences in media supported by both.

That which you need to back up (your source)

What should you back up? I'd say every document that you've ever created, that's what—but that might not be practical. If you're like me—highly anxious about the material you create—you *absolutely know* what files are the most important to you, and you've created a filing system on your computer so that you can find those absolutely important files—whether anyone else understands that system or not. I'm not going to lecture you about what should get backed up—I'm merely going to suggest a few pointers:

Your Documents and Users folder, and all folders within it

On Windows 2000, it's called "Documents and Settings;" on Windows 98, it's called "My Documents;" on Macintosh OS X its called "Users;" and on Linux, it's the "Home" directory.

This folder *doesn't* hold programs, applications, or system information. It's the basic repository for all documents on your computer, hierarchically organized by the users assigned to the computer, and the individual directories and files beneath them.

If you're setting up a backup plan for a workstation with multiple users, back up the top level of this directory. If the workstation has only one user, you can probably get away with beginning with that user's home directory—although if you do that, you won't back up the Shared Library directory that exists on Linux and Mac OS X computers, nor will you catch some of the administrator directories on Windows 2000 computers. Depending on the applications and preferences set up, not having those directories' worth of data could be a very bad thing.

Project directories

This one's pretty self-evident: If you're working on a project, you've probably already created a project directory for it. If I were setting up an emergency backup plan, with only limited space, this is the directory I'd zero in on. While you're working on the project, you're going to remember the name of the directory that you're working in—you've probably even made short-cuts/aliases to the directory and placed them on your desktop for easier access.

Source selection methodologies

Once you know what you want to back up (and where the top-level directories are located on your drive), you need to tell the backup software application. Backup software packages call these directories the **source**. Different software packages employ different source selection methodologies, so, for your viewing pleasure, we've boiled them down to this list:

Source Selection	@Backup	BackJack	Backup MyPC	FWB Toolkit	NovaBACKUP	NovaNet-WEB	Retrospect Desktop	Retrospect Professional
Drag-and-drop interface				✔				
Standard OS browser interface	✔	✔	✔	✔	✔	✔		
"Home location" selectors							✔	✔
Pre-created selectors							✔	✔
Name/Path contains selectors				✔			✔	✔
Date selectors				✔			✔	✔
File name extension selectors			✔	✔			✔	✔
"Enclosing directory" selectors							✔	✔

Table 10-12. Source selection process

Drag-and-drop interface

The **drag-and-drop interface** is used only by Mac OS X backup software packages, as far as we can tell. For some reason, this type of interface doesn't work on or isn't offered by the Windows desktop backup packages. FWB Toolkit is a good example of the drag-and-drop interface. In the diagram below (see Figure 10-30. on page 321), you can see the source windowpane on the left and the destination windowpane on the right. The user simply drags the source directory into the left pane to select it.

Figure 10-30. FWB Toolkit drag-and-drop interface

Standard OS browser interface
Most of the Windows applications we've worked with use the standard browser interface—the same type of interface the user sees when working in the Windows environment. Below (Figure 10-31.) is the NovaBACKUP interface for selecting directories and files for backup:

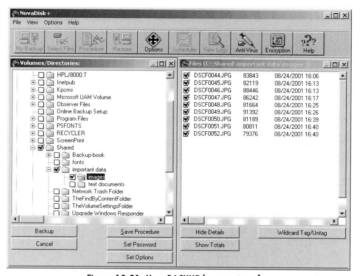

Figure 10-31. NovaBACKUP browser interface

Home location selectors
Only Retrospect (so far) has the ability to create *very* custom selectors for setting source directories and their files to be backed up. In the Retrospect environment, the user can select all files within the source directory to be backed up, or open Dantz' selector process to use the built-in special-home-user-folder selector for each operating system (shown in Figure 10-32. below).

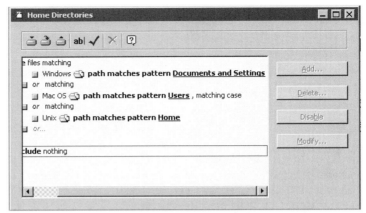

Figure 10-32. Retrospect's special selectors

Retrospect has a unique file and folder selection process, different than anything else we've encountered so far. However, this isn't the place to wax rhapsodic about details. We have, however, included an interview on the registered reader area of our website (repeat after me: www.backupbook.com) we conducted with Richard Zulch, co-founder and CTO of Dantz Development Corporation, wherein Richard explains the methodology behind the madness of his selection process.

Pre-created selectors Dantz has also created some pretty in-depth selectors (other than the Home selectors mentioned above). Users appreciate the ability to create custom selectors, save them, and then employ them in different backup scripts and schedules.

It would be even better if these custom selectors could be saved and then exported from one machine and imported into another—*that* would be a timesaving, value deal for many backup admins, who could then use that ability to create custom selectors for the organization and distribute them like largesse across multiple workstations. Richard, are you listening?

In Figure 10-33. on page 323, we show the depth of one of these selectors in the following dialog, which sets up the backup process to grab all files and folders *except* the cache folders for the most popular browsers.

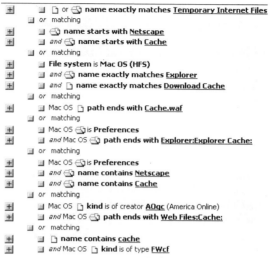

Figure 10-33. No cache files selector

Name or path-based selectors It's nice to be able to say "Please exclude files, *as a subset of what I've chosen*, based on this naming criterion;" i.e., "Back up my home directory, but please exclude the 'Boss is a turdball poems' directory." Of course, Retrospect has this ability because of their selector process, but it's not the only kid on this block—so does FWB Toolkit.

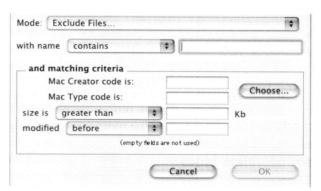

Figure 10-34. Exclude files selector

Date selectors FWB strikes again with the ability (shown in Figure 10-34.) to base file exclusion or inclusion upon modification date, enabling you to tell your backup software

doesn't have to be backed up each time—only the changed parts. If you're backing up video files or you're backing up over a WAN, this is almost a must-have because it manages the data throughput and delivery process so effectively.

 What do you need to know to make your selection? The problem for a lot of people boils down to this: They've selected a backup methodology and have run with it, only to find out during restoration that what they *thought* they were backing up, they *weren't* backing up. The best suggestion that Network Frontiers can give you is this:

Pick a method. Run a backup. Test the restore.

If the restore doesn't bring back what you're looking for, you have the wrong method—simple as that.

Special considerations

You need to think about four basic "special" considerations when picking your desktop backup software as shown in Table 10-14.

Special Considerations	@Backup	BackJack	Backup MyPC	FWB Toolkit	NovaBACKUP	NovaNet-WEB	Retrospect Desktop	Retrospect Professional
Open file backup			✔					
Backup system state (Windows Registry)	✔	✔	✔		✔	✔		✔
Backup privileges			✔	✔			✔	✔

Table 10-14. Source selection process

- **Open file backup** means that if you're running databases on your computer (which are always in the "locked, busy, or open state"), you won't be able to back them up if your backup software doesn't support backing up open files.

  Both NovaStor and Dantz offer open file backups with their more expensive products. However, what they seem to need to hear from you, the consumers, is that some of you might just be running local databases that you want backed up on your individual computers. So e-mail them and tell them that this is what you want. Both companies are very responsive to end-user requests.

- **Windows Registry** is a database of configuration settings in Windows 95/98/NT/2000 that holds configuration data about the hardware and environment of the PC it's been installed in. It's used to store information necessary to configure the system for one or more users, applications, and hardware devices. The registry contains information that's constantly referenced during operation, such as profiles for each user, the applications installed on the computer; the types of documents each can create, property sheet settings for folders and application icons, what hardware exists on the system, and which ports are being used. The Windows Registry is made up of the SYSTEM.DAT and USER.DAT files.

- **Backup privileges** or setting specific privileges for your directories, if you're backing up your workstation to a server, is important. However, if you aren't backing up your workstation's data to a server volume, don't worry about this, because privileges don't come into play in that case.

BACKUP MEDIA

Okay, you've figured out what you're looking for, from data selection through scheduling and special considerations. It's time to examine the available media choices (Table 10-15.).

Media Supported	@Backup	BackJack	Backup MyPC	FWB Toolkit	NovaBACKUP	NovaNet-WEB	Retrospect Desktop	Retrospect Professional
Attached or mounted volume			✔	✔	✔		✔	✔
USB drive			✔	✔			✔	✔
FireWire drive			✔	✔	✔		✔	✔
CD-R, CD-RW			✔	✔	✔		✔	✔
DVD-R, DVD-RW					✔	✔	✔	✔
FTP, Internet service	✔	✔				✔	✔	
Tape systems				✔			✔	✔

Table 10-15. Media supported

Attached and mounted hard drives

Mounted volumes/attached network drives are server share points that are either on your desktop (OS X) or are a part of your network neighborhood. This is an outstanding choice of media for most folks, because drive space on Network Attached Storage (NAS) boxes is *very* cheap and easy to manage. A lot of companies are going the route of backing up local user data to the NAS box and then backing up the NAS box itself to an offsite location (or using tape to achieve the same thing).

However, this won't do you any good if you're a notebook user sitting in the hotel in Pismo Beach while your server is back at corporate HQ in Ogunquit, Maine—unless your backup software has a web interface you can use to restore your files.

USB drives

USB (1.1 and 2.0) drives are great for small amounts of storage, but lousy for large amounts because of the 12 Mbps transfer rate of 1.1 and 400 Mbps transfer rate of USB 2.0. Files are backed up to the discs and the catalog is usually saved on the hard disk of the computer doing the backup. The drive shown on the right is the KanguruMicro USB (1.1) drive. It works on Windows, Mac OS X, and Linux without any special drivers,  and comes in capacities from 16 MB through 1 GB. However, the 128 or 256 MB drives are just large enough to handle whatever capacity you need—and not too large that you'll try to jam too much data onto them and slow down the backup process.

These drives are *great* for travelling notebook users (I'm raising my hand here as a road-weary warrior), as they fit into your pocket easily and have enough capacity to hold whatever presentation or project you're working on—I love taking these things with me when I speak at conferences. If my computer dies, all I have to do is find another computer somewhere with a copy of PowerPoint on it, plug the drive into the computer, and voilà! I'm in business.

 To take the greatest advantage of their plug-and-play capabilities, pair them with backup software that stores the files in native file format. Their only liability is that you have to convince the airport security that this is a computer hard drive—sure, buddy!—and not a high-tech lethal weapon.

FireWire drives

FireWire (also known as 1394) drives are about a gazillion times faster (and larger) than USB 1.1 drives, coming in at 400 Mbps for FireWire and 800 Mbps for FireWire 800. Files are backed up to the drives and the Catalog is usually saved on the hard disk of the computer doing the backup. My all-time two favorites are as follows:

Desktop-based FireWire drives should all be Maxtor. I wouldn't use other brand—seriously. I love them, and they're all SMART enabled (if you skipped that part of the book, go back and read *SMART precludes DUMB...* on page 112).

What are **Travelling FireWire** drives? Easy—iPod (there's one on the right). iPod is a portable FireWire drive that's both an MP3 music player *and* an outstanding storage device. I absolutely *love* my iPod, and never let it out of my sight: It's mounted on my desktop when I come in to the office, I back up my files to it before I go home, and I plug it into my MP3-capable stereo in the car as I drive. Because these little micro devices fit into the palm of your hand *and* hold up to 20 GB of information (cut that down to about 10 GB once you've downloaded your entire Elvis and Beatles collections onto it), you can pretty much store whatever it is you're working on in your iPod, and take it with you when you go. Its sole drawback? Unlike the USB, some FireWire devices require drivers for some computers, and therefore aren't as adaptable.

 Here's a product that fits into its own little category: **Road Warrior Backup Utility.** The ABS Plus from CMS (they must be into alphabet soup—I wonder if the founder was from the FBI or CIA?) is shown at right.

Its Express process is simple: Connect the 30GB ABSplus device to your laptop, using the supplied FireWire cable. Install the software from their CD, and then just let it run a full backup using their automatic method. On my computer, the full backup of almost 20 GB took 199 minutes, so you'll want to relax with a hot cup of joe and at least a dozen Krispy Kremes. Once the appliance has been set up, continued backups are a snap: Just attach the drive, and the software will begin backing any changed data to it. The device uses an incremental process, backing up only files that have been modified since the last backup. The automatic launcher initiates a backup of the entire drive in native file format, making the stored data accessible from any computer it's attached to (it runs in both Windows and Mac OS X mode). If the source computer dies, the ABSplus can simply be plugged into another computer that will recognize it as just another hard drive. For you rolling stones, this is a great utility because it's simple and backs up files in native file format.

Removable disk formats (Zip, CD-R/W, DVD-R/W)

Another type of block-addressable media is the **removable disk**, which comes in assorted varieties. There are magnetic removable disks, such as Zip and Jaz; and there are optical disks, such as CD-R/W drives and DVD-R/W.

Removable magnetic disks are very popular in large graphics networks and with pre-press professionals. I have one client who creates pages so big that only two of them can fit onto a single 750 MB removable Zip cartridge.

Zip drives

Zip drives from Iomega come in 100, 250, and 750 MB formats and are infinitely (okay, as close as you can get to infinitely) rewriteable. I have a few Zip 100 MB disks around and in use for more than six years. I wish I had hard drives that lasted as long.

Because Zip drives have their own format, they have to have their own drive mechanisms as well. These mechanisms can be connected internally on every Windows and Mac OS computer that I know of. They can be connected externally via FireWire, USB, and SCSI.

CD-R and CD-RW

Short for **CD-Recordable ReWriteable disk**, a type of CD that enables you to write onto it in one or multiple sessions. CD-Rs hold about 650 MB, and CD-RWs hold about 530 MB. One of the problems with CD-R disks is that you can write to them only once. The trouble with these disks? Once written to, they can't be overwritten. This makes them lousy standard backup drives but great archiving drives, especially if what's being archived has legal implications. Once files are written to the drive, they're locked and can't be replaced, so you've got a permanent record of the material on the drive. With CD-RW drives and disks, you can treat the optical disk just like a floppy or hard disk, writing data onto it multiple times.

Here's a helpful hint from Ken Lien at Kodak, a guy who knows a lot about writing data to CDs. CD-ROMs aren't as indestructible as you might think. Although data you archive to CD-R won't be damaged by magnetism, you still have to worry about light, temperature, humidity, and scratching, some of which can cause the thin gold reflector to flake off of the cheaper disks. Kodak's disks use a special organic dye recording layer and a scratch-resistant overcoat to combat this problem, and Kodak claims that its disks will be good for 100 years or more. How much data can you archive on a writeable CD? According to Kodak, about 240,000 pages of ASCII text. My book and all the reference material associated with it barely fits onto a single CD-R disk.

DVD-RW

Okay, there are four choices: DVD+RW, **DVD-RW**, DVD-R, and DVD-RAM. I'm discounting DVD-RAM totally because their size and format is different from the rest and can't be interchanged. DVD-R is like CD-R, and can't be rewritten once it's been written to, making it suitable for archiving but not much else. DVD burners generally write up to 4.7 GB on a single-sided DVD-R or DVD-RW, and up to 9.4 GB on a double-sided disk. DVD+RW currently uses single-sided 4.7 GB disks.

Can a DVD-RW drive read a CD-RW disk? Yeah, but only sometimes. The problem is that most CD-Rs are "invisible" to DVD laser wavelength because the dye used to make the blank CD-R doesn't reflect the beam. The common solution? The DVD device uses two lasers at different wavelengths: one for reading DVDs; the other for CDs and CD-Rs. The MultiRead logo guarantees compatibility with CD-R and CD-RW media.

 Use **Zip disks** for your day-to-day recordable media, skip CDs and go straight to DVDs for archiving. Zips are rugged, long lasting, and rewriteable. DVDs have the capacity you need. Simple as that.

CDs and DVDs make absolute sense if you have one of those computers with the CD/DVD-R (or RW) "superdrive" built in, or if you prefer optical media to tape media. CDs hold about 625 MB of backup data (more with compression), and DVDs hold almost 10 times that much. Files are backed up to the disks, and the catalog is usually saved on the hard disk of the computer doing the backup.

Tape formats

There are two basic types of tape recording formats: **linear** and **helical scan**. Why do you care? A thorough understanding of the market and the technologies is vital for mapping a strategy to handle your company's tape storage strategy. The choice of one technology over another is based on up-front price, ongoing costs, speed, reliability and capacity.

Linear tape technology uses a recording method in which data tracks are written in a linear pattern on the tape. The first set of tracks is recorded in parallel over the entire length of the tape. The recording heads are then repositioned and the tape direction is reversed to record the next set of tracks, again across the entire length of the tape, repeating this process in a serpentine fashion (Remember *The In-Laws*? The *original* one? Peter Falk and Alan Arkin are beyond compare!) until all data has been recorded. The major linear formats for data recording are DLT (normal, super, and DLT1), LTO (ultrium), and Travan (a great entry-level tape system).

Helical scan tape drives are based on a recording method in which data tracks are written at an angle with respect to the edge of the tape. This recording method delivers very high-density storage on small format tapes. While linear recording moves the tape at very high speeds across a stationary recording head, helical drives utilize a slow-moving tape and high-speed rotating drum containing the recording heads. While data rate performance is typically a function of the tape speed, helical recording produces effective tape-to-head speeds similar to linear recording, enabling acceptable data rates. The major helical formats for data recording include 4mm DAT (DDS), which is at the end of its lifecycle; and 8mm, consisting of Exabyte's Mammoth products and Sony's AIT (Advanced Intelligent Tape).

AIT (helical)

The AIT-3 offers customers 100 GB of native capacity and 12 Mbps data rate on a compact 8mm cartridge using Advanced Metal Evaporated Tape. Sony touts a 2.6:1 compression ratio for its AIT drives over the 2:1 compression ratio for every other tape format out there. The company attributes this increased compression to its ALDC (Adaptive Lossless Data Compression) technology. Sony's road map for AIT projects a doubling of capacity and throughput every two years. In addition to AIT-3 tapes, you can read and write AIT-1 and AIT-2 tapes on an AIT-3 drive.

Another speed claim is a 64 K chip in each cartridge that stores the tape log, so the drive can find the location of files by reading the chip. The payoff is a supposed average access time of less than 27 seconds. However, while writing this book, we've interviewed all of the backup software providers, and none are willing to write to this memory standard just yet, so this tape access methodology will have to wait for future acceptance.

DAT (helical)

DDS-4 is the latest incarnation of 4mm DAT technology based on the Digital Data Storage (DDS) standard. DDS-4 provides 20 GB of native capacity on a single DAT cartridge while boosting data rate performance to 3 Mbps. The fate of DDS is clear: No manufacturer has announced new products nor even intentions to proceed beyond the current DDS-4 version.

DLT family (linear)

This category includes DLT, SDLT, SDLT 320 and ValueTape 80. Super DLT has enjoyed the most widespread adoption and follows the most aggressive technology path, staying a step ahead of its two closest competitors, AIT and Ultrium. DLT has long been a corporate favorite thanks to its adoption by Compaq and its emphasis on servers in the market.

DLT The DLT8000 offers a native capacity of 40 GB and a sustained data rate of 6 Mbps, and is fully backward-read compatible with the installed base of DLT7000 and DLT4000 tapes.

Super DLT SuperDLT drives offer a native capacity of 110 GB per cartridge and a data transfer rate of 11 Mbps, while still providing the option for backward compatibility with DLT4000, 7000 and 8000 products. The current implementation of SDLT (SDLT320) has a capacity of 320 GB and a transfer rate of 32 Mbps, compressed. The compression ratio is 2:1.

DLT1 DLT1 and ValueTape 80 deliver the benefits of DLT technology at a fraction of the cost. Benchmark Storage Innovations' first product, the DLT1 drive, offers the same native capacity as DLT8000 (40 GB per cartridge) and a transfer rate of 3

Mbps for less than half the price of a DLT8000 drive. The ValueTape 80 uses the DLT Tape IV, a common older DLT format media with a 40 GB native and 80 GB compressed capacity, and can read tapes written by Quantum's DLT4000 series tape drives. The ValueTape 80 and the DLT1 drive, both from Benchmark, are targeted to customers with large installations of DLT4000 drives with DLT Tape IV media. DLT4000 drives have a native capacity of 20 GB and a compressed capacity of 40 GB.

LTO (linear)

Linear Tape Open (LTO) is the newest linear tape format on the market, the result of a consortium fromHewlett-Packard, IBM, and Seagate Technology. LTO consists of two formats: a high-capacity format designated Ultrium, and the Accelis fast-access design. The two formats use different physical tape cartridges and are not compatible. While Accelis is still included in the LTO consortium, no products that use it have been announced. Ultrium provides a native capacity of 100 GB per cartridge and up to 16 Mbps data rate. The LTO Consortium has indicated that the second generation of LTO Ultrium will be 200 GB per cartridge. The fourth-generation road map includes single cartridge sizes up to 1.6 TB compressed with a transfer capacity of 320 Mbps.

LTO has gained acceptance in the market because the idea of a consortium-based tape technology appeals to many, and the technology has been integrated into the designs of most automation companies.

Mammoth & VXA (helical)

Exabyte's Mammoth 2 and VXA (Mammoth on the high end, and VXA systems on the low end) is a helical scan format available with a native capacity of 60 GB, and a native transfer rate of 12 Mbps. This format has pretty much been eclipsed by the DLT and LTO formats. Exabyte has laid out a road map toward its Mammoth-3, which it says will sell for less than $3,000 and offer a compressed capacity of 625 GB and a compressed transfer rate of 60 Mbps.

The VXA-2, has a native capacity of 80 GB, 160 GB compressed, and transfer rates of 6 Mbps. VXA is targeted at companies with lower data capacity and transfer rate needs.

Travan (linear)

The Travan format was originally developed by Imation and is licensed to Seagate Technology. Travan NS (Network Series) is a value leader in tape technology for small office and entry-level server backup applications because Travan NS20 drives are available for less than $600 with 10 GB of native capacity and 1 Mbps data rate performance.

 Go with the LTO Ultrium format if you can—**but only** if your system has enough speed to handle it. It incorporates the best features of all of the existing tape technologies that we've reviewed here. Its multichannel recording, error correction capabilities, and scalability allow it to keep pace with future storage demands.

LTO's error correction codes (ECC), based on two levels of Reed Solomon ECC, are designed to automatically correct most cross-track errors. The drive can detect defective areas of tape. It also features a read-while-write capability that automatically verifies written data and rewrites data that has been written to a bad area of tape. Dual (redundant) servo heads adjust automatically for contraction/expansion of tape media. In addition, one servo head can maintain servo tracking if a servo head fails, or if a linear scratch to the media occurs.

And because there can be problems when a tape system tries to compress already compressed data, the LTO comes through again. An automatic, intelligent expansion protection feature switches off data compression—known as the **pass-through mode**—if it senses the data is no longer being compressed. This intelligence enables the average expansion of previously compressed data or otherwise uncompressible data to be reduced to less than 0.05 percent, compared to 12.5 percent with ALDC.

No wonder that such innovative and industry leading companies like Dell (PowerVault 110LTO) and Overland Storage (NEO LTO) offer LTO tape drives and libraries.

Basic media capacity and costs

Media Type		Basic Capacity	$100 MB	$1 GB
Hard Drives	ATA hard drive	60 GB	$0.20	$2.00
	Ultra 3 SCSI hard drive	60 GB	$0.86	$8.58
NAS	Iomega P415	720 GB	$0.78	$7.8
Portable Hard Drives	Kanguru USB	512 MB	$62.48	n/a
	ABS Plus	30 GB	$1.16	$11.60
	iPod 20 GB	20 GB	$2.47	$24.70
Write-once media	CD-R	650 MB	$0.06	$0.60
	CD-RW	650 MB	$0.15	$1.50
	DVD-R	4.7 GB	$0.10	$1.00
	DVD-RW	4.7 GB	$0.17	$1.70
	DVD+RW	4.7 GB	$0.15	$1.49
	Magneto Optical	640 MB	$3.53	$35.30
Rewriteable media	Zip	750 MB	$1.99	$19.96
	Jaz	2 GB	$4.33	$43.32
Tape Drives	QIC 2000C tape	250 MB	$1.32	$13.18
	DDS-2 tape	4/8 GB	$0.15	$1.48
	DDS-3 tape	12/24 GB	$0.07	$0.75
	DDS-4 tape	20/40 GB	$0.08	$0.85
	8mm tape	50 GB	$0.15	$1.59
	DLT tape	40/80	$0.14	$1.44
	AIT-1 tape	35/70 GB	$0.19	$1.93
	AIT-2 tape	50/130 GB	$0.15	$1.53
	AIT-3 tape	100/260 GB	$0.12	$1.25
	LTO	100/200 GB	$0.07	$0.75

Table 10-16. Basic media costs

Which application and backup media is right for you?

That's the big question that we can't answer for you—but we *can* help you with the decision process. On our website, you can download a spreadsheet that will help you weigh your decisions about the features you need, and then magically suggest a package for you. Basically, you set the desired weight of your criteria, and the spreadsheet calculates which product has the best individual feature sets (Figure 10-35. below left) and the best overall cost-performance ratio (Figure 10-35. below right) for your needs.

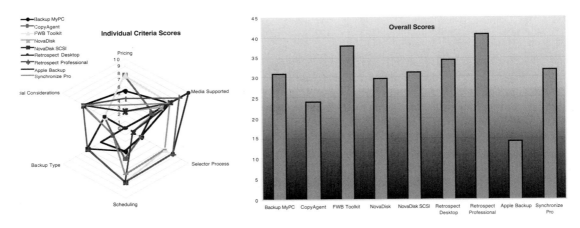

Figure 10-35. Decision support table

CHAPTER 11:
OPEN FILE BACKUP FOR DATABASES

Whenever you back up your data, rest assured that all you need to do is restore your files, and any lost items magically reappear. Right? Wrong. Many manufacturers of backup products "forget" to mention the cold, cruel reality: By default, you can't back up open files—files that are in use or just plain open during the backup process. You could leave, for example, your gorgeous Photoshop masterpiece open onscreen, fishing for your officemates' aesthetic approval; or a Microsoft Access document you're sharing with a coworker and don't want to bother to close. Because they can't keep track of midstream changes, the applications that own those documents lock them against writing by other users, and, as the ancient Greeks told us, hubris—and carelessness—go before a fall. To placate

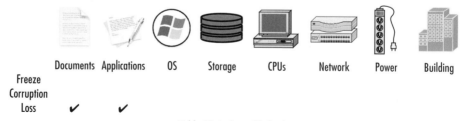

	Documents	Applications	OS	Storage	CPUs	Network	Power	Building
Freeze								
Corruption								
Loss	✔	✔						

Table 11-1. Open file backup

the backup gods, you must protect your end users and your organizational databases from succumbing to these kinds of problems. The good news? It isn't that hard to do.

THE MAIN THING

The Main Thing is that open documents fall into three broad categories:

1. Documents that happened to be in-use during the *exact* time of the backup.

2. Documents that are *always* open, like databases.

3. Hybrid documents like those found in mail servers (Exchange is the worst culprit here) that are part database and part regular document.

In this chapter, we walk through each of the above three scenarios and describe what's happening and why those actions thwart the normal backup process. We'll then cover the different variations of getting around those problems (if there are any) and the tools you can use to overcome the obstacles that open-file backups present to the backup administrator.

Special thanks...

I've got to say thank-you to Jean-Yves FockHoon at 4D for providing the information on 4D backup. Since we don't have 4D here in the office, his help was invaluable to us.

THAT WHICH YOU CAN'T DO NUTTIN ABOUT: IN-USE OR LOCKED FILES

Applications can be divided into two general categories: those built for group work and those built for individual usage. Most applications built for individual usage don't do anything special with their files when the user is working on them.

Take, for instance, Microsoft Word. When you open a Microsoft Word file, the document on the hard drive is read into the computer's RAM, and all of the changes made to the document by the writer are made in RAM until the writer hits the **Save** button or equivalent command-key combination. At that point, the data in the computer's RAM is saved back onto the hard drive. Word makes no attempt to lock the file as "in use" while the writer's working on it, so, if a backup occurs during the writing process, the file that loaded into RAM will be the same one that's backed up. If the user hits the **Save** button after the backup takes place, the newly saved document is not the one that is backed up—that honor goes to the previous version.

However, if the user just happens to hit the **Save** button at the exact same time that the backup software requests the file from the operating system, the operating system will tell the backup software that Microsoft Word is currently writing to the file, and that the file is in use. The backup system will then skip the file and go on to the next one in the list, reporting that the file was busy or locked when the backup occurred.

How often does something like this happen? Not very often with basic applications like Word; fairly often with other applications like bookkeeping programs such as QuickBooks, Great Plains, and others; and quite often with operating system support files like Preferences, which are regularly updated and generally messed with.

What can be done about this?

For your basic simultaneous save and backup operation—nada. It's just like the bus—no sense in getting upset if you missed it; just stand around and the next one will pick you up.

Same thing goes for those operating system support files. No sense in even trying, because the next backup will pick them up. But what about applications like bookkeeping tools, where the data is critical to the company?

Great Plains Small Business Manager  has a built-in backup and recovery management facility that works quite nicely, whether you use the stand-alone system or the hierarchical Commercial Headquarters system.

Intuit QuickBooks also has directly tied-in backup through NovaStor so that when the books are closed each month (or whenever the bookkeeper closes them), the software backs up the information not only to the C: drive, but to a keychain-sized hard drive called, appropriately enough, the Keyster.

Figure 11-1. NovaStor Keyster

Most other bookkeeping systems are based on SQL databases and therefore integrate their backup strategy into a more common open file–manager approach. We'll cover this throughout the chapter.

OPEN-FILE DATABASE BACKUPS

When you start looking at open-file backup, first examine what kind of software you're using. If you're running databases like SyBase, Oracle, mySQL, MS SQL or Exchange, you might be aware of the fact that databases are designed to run 24/7, all year long. They have a tendency to keep several files open simultaneously, and never shut down completely unless instructed to do so. Making a functional backup of a database while it's running is daunting, but not impossible. During heavy workload, the database has dozens or hundreds of files open, reading from one and writing to another. If you try a standard backup in a scenario like this, the backup software will miss more than a handful of files because they're in use. Furthermore, a standard backup will most likely grab files that are not up-to-date, as the database keeps updated information in a cache, and only at certain times does the database application update the primary database's tables. If you try to restore a database that you backed up in a regular manner, you'll be stuck with a database that is, at minimum, inconsistent, and more likely non-functional. Not a good idea, that. Even if you try to outsmart your database by starting a backup at 2A.M., when not a single sane soul is supposed to be at work, it'll fail—databases never sleep.

Quick review of database operations

Okay, we all know how databases work[1], so look elsewhere for a database primer—this is a database *backup* primer. In their simplest form, databases hold information in four basic locations:

1. The tables of information where most everything is kept.

2. The indexes of the tables of information that allow the lookups between records.

3. The transaction logs that the databases continually write to so that in case of failure, the tables and indexes can be repaired.

---

[1] If you don't, this isn't the place to find out. There are a ton of good database books up on Amazon; just search SQL if you need one.

4. The cache that sits in RAM on the database server.

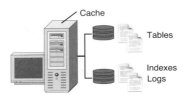

Figure 11-2. Basic database operations

At any given time, any one or all four of these places can be in flux with changing information. To back up a database properly, not only the information in the tables, but in the indexes and transaction logs must be preserved in a single **point-in-time snapshot**.

In this snapshot, each of the tables, indexes, and transaction log entries are sequenced in a manner that the database can understand. Every time the database writes information to these files, it maintains a write-order fidelity, keeping everything in order. Backing up file #32 out of sequence causes a failure if the database has to be restored using the backed-up information.

Solutions to this problem range from the simple to the *very* complex and should be based upon two factors: the amount of downtime that your database can withstand; and your budget. *AND I DON'T WANT YOU, THE BACKUP ADMINISTRATOR, MAKING THAT DECISION.* Get my drift on this one? Let's say that your users come to you, boasting, "This database can't *ever* go down, no matter what." So you decide to forego backing up the database and go straight into creating a synchronous volume replication on a mirrored server at a new service provider. (For the definition of synchronous replication vs. asynchronous replication, see *The tools* on page 514.) You do all your research, put all your plans together, and present the contracts to your CFO, who takes one look at the absolutely massive monthly cost and shoots you dead on the spot. Why? It turns out that this is a support cost center database, and not a profit-center database, and the CFO couldn't give a rat's patoot in the grand scheme of things if it was down for a couple of days.

If you don't want to start dodging bullets, when you plan your database backup method, answer three business questions:

1. How long can the database be "unavailable" on a regular basis in order to back it up?

2. If a disaster occurs, how much data in this database can be lost while still allowing the business to continue successfully?

3. What is the acceptable maximum amount of time you need to recover the data in this database post-disaster, while still allowing the business to continue successfully?

Now, Horschack, I know you're raising your hand, saying "Oooh oooh, *I* know the answer to that!" Here's why you don't want to give that answer. You want the business people whom this database affects to give that answer, so that you're out of the equation. If the business people say, "It can be down for four days" and it goes down for four days, *you* won't be the one they'll level their sights on, because you'll have their signatures on the document. Trust me, when people put their name (and their "good name," too!) on a statement, things—and people—suddenly become a whole lot more answerable for the inevitable disasters that occur.

That said, you need to follow two methodologies to protect the data that lives in databases. First: the backup and restore. This approach makes a copy of the data in the database and stores it in backup sets, as we discussed earlier (see *What's a backup?* on page 288). This approach (in its various forms) provides the simplest and least expensive way to gather and then protect your data. However, it also requires the longest time to restore the database (since the database has to be re-created from tape or disc) and causes the greatest amount of data loss in case of a disaster.

The second methodology uses replication instead of backup and recovery (we cover the basics of replication in *The tools* on page 514). Replication creates and then maintains as perfect a clone of the database as possible in some remote site that won't be affected by the same disasters that can befall the source server. In a replication environment, recovery time is negligible, the amount of data lost is a little less negligible, and the cost is anywhere from acceptable to astronomical.

Let's go through the backup methodologies first, and then move on to the replication methodologies.

If the database has one, use the built-in backup mechanism

There's nothing like the vendor's very own backup tool to back up a database they made the right way. Many of the smaller database servers, such as FileMaker and 4D (both support Ⓧ Ⓟ) have their own built-in backup systems. FileMaker's is very simplistic (as are its databases). At a certain time of day, you can tell it to make a backup copy of the database files. It obediently does so, writing all cached information to them. Once the files are on the drive, any backup software can then back them up to tape or other media.

4D Database Backup Ⓧ Ⓟ

From within 4D Server, you can perform a full backup without needing to shut down the 4D Server application. A scheduler comes with 4D Backup running with Server. It allows you to automatically program a full backup or a mirror. 4D Backup comes also with its own 4D language. This means that you can create your own process that will perform a backup or a mirror. You may load an existing project or build/choose the options on-the-fly and do it by yourself.

4D Backup comes with one single-user backup application and two plug-ins usable by 4D databases. The first one allows you to back up or restore your database. 4D Backup also supports simple data mirroring (replication) so that you can write the database to two simultaneous locations.

4D log for backup

This application helps you to integrate a log file when the database fails and becomes corrupted. As stated previously, 4D stores information for optimization issues in its memory. Let's say that you do have a running database—until a power shortage occurs. Well, you've just lost all information stored in the cache. When selecting 4D log, 4D will store each modification to the data file into this log file (*modification* means creation/modification/deletion of records). Then, after a crash, you just relaunch 4D Backup and integrate the current log file into the data tables. 4D Backup will show you what information is stored in the log file and whether it's been saved into the current data file or not. If the action has already been taken on the data file, it will be displayed as *disabled*. If not, it will be displayed as *enabled*. Thus, you can click on the **Integrate** button to integrate the changes that 4D Server didn't have time to save into the current data file.

4D mirroring 4D Backup also allows you to "mirror" an existing database by copying the 4D log files from the main server to a secondary server, and then reintegrating the data from the log files into the secondary server. 4D Server will send the current log file (every few minutes for example) to the mirrored database Step 1 (Figure 11-3.). 4D Backup running on the mirrored database will integrate the log file Step 2 (Figure 11-3.) to the current mirrored database and will back up this database after integration.

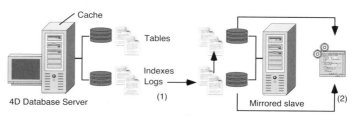

Figure 11-3. 4D Mirror and 4D backup integration

You could say that this was a very asynchronous type of transaction because of the lag time between the primary sending the log file and the mirror receiving and incorporating the log file. Depending upon how often the data was mirrored, if the source server dies, the current log file could be pretty small and you wouldn't lose that much data.

4D Backup requires all processes to release records before starting the backup. Only when all records have been released will 4D Backup perform its job again. Backing up the database might take a long time if the database is big. However, sending a log file to the mirror can be fast, especially if you perform a mirror frequently. Your job? To find that exquisite balance between emptying your wallet for replication and flushing your data down the toilet.

MySQL

The creators of the open source database MySQL are moving the application along the path of automatic backup and replication. Marten Mickos, CEO of MySQL, based in Sweden, told us that MySQL 5.0, due out by the end of 2003, will add advanced management tools such as data replication (from a master database) as well as speed improvements and other tools.

Starting in Version 3.23.15, MySQL *does* support one-way replication internally. One server acts as the master, while the other—you guessed it—is the slave. The master server keeps a binary log of updates and an index file to binary logs to keep track of log rotation. The slave, upon connecting, informs the master where it left off since the last successfully propagated update, catches up on the updates, and then blocks and waits for the master to notify it of the new updates[2]. With replication, you can get live backups of the system by doing a backup on a slave (as shown in Figure 11-4.) instead of doing it on the master, where you'll encounter open file problems.

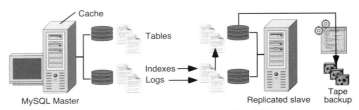

Figure 11-4. MySQL replication and then backup

Because MySQL tables are stored as files, it's easy to do a backup of a replicated database when no users are writing to it. To get a consistent backup, do a **Lock Tables** command on the relevant tables followed by **Flush Tables** command for the tables you're going to replicate. You only need a read lock, because this allows other threads to continue to query the tables while you're making a copy of the files in the database directory. The **Flush Table** ensures that the active index pages are written to disk before you start the backup. If you want to make a SQL level backup of a table (or the whole database), you can use **Select Into Outfile** or **Backup Table** in your SQL script.

 By doing your backup this way, you can run your server on a continuous basis and back it up, as well. The caveat, just as with the 4D approach, is that this isn't true *real-time* replication of data. There *is* a lag time, and the delta amount of data that was on the primary server when it went down will be lost (can you hear that gurgling, flushing sound?).

---

2.   If you're replicating a database, all updates to this database should be done through the master, as that will have the most up-to-date information.

Agent-based backups

If your database software doesn't have built-in backup, mirroring, or replication capabilities, you'll need a method to connect to the database and speak its language to back it up.

For this task, consider using **Application Programming Interface (API)**–based agents. API agents are software components that have been specifically written for a certain application or database. They hook into the API[3] of the application whose data has to be backed up—MS Exchange (which is database driven) or MS SQL, for example—and make sure that all files are being backed up and synchronized, even if they're in use during the backup. Because each backup server software packages calls these API agents something different (anything from plug-ins to add-ons, agents, etc.), we're going to settle on the generic term *plug-in*.

Backup Exec MS SQL agent backup 🔲

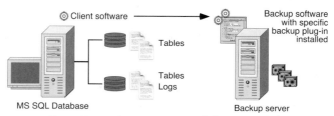

Figure 11-5. Backup Exec running with the MS SQL plug-in

VERITAS offers an optional MS SQL plug-in for Backup Exec that backs up open SQL databases. For this plug-in to work, the SQL plug-in must be installed on the backup machine and the remote client installed on the MS SQL server.

As the SQL plug-in is integrated into Backup Exec, you can make the backup of your SQL database(s) part of a regular network backup. Backup Exec saves data down to individual file groups and allows point-in-time rollback restores to a spe-

---

3.   This is where software developers describe "hooks" into their applications to let third-party developers add functionality.

cific point in time. During a backup wherein the database is live, the SQL plug-in caches changes to the databases and appends them to the end of the backup.

To back up an SQL server, click the **Backup Selections** tab in BackupExec's main window. From there, depending on whether the SQL server is installed locally or remotely, do one of the following:

- Click on the plus icon for local selections or the plus icon for remote selections (we've clicked on the plus icon for local selections as shown in Figure 11-6.).

- If your server is located in a domain, click the domain name, then select your server to see all databases available for backup.

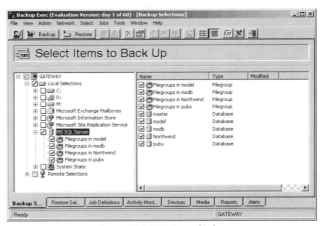

Figure 11-6. SQL Server backup

Several settings are available for fine-tuning the backup operation. Select **Options** from the **Tools** menu, and click the **SQL** tab. Then follow these methods:

- **Database**–Back Up Entire Database saves the entire database, including all tables and filegroups. Select this option whenever you've added or removed files from the database.

- **Log**–Back Up Transaction Log backs up only the data contained in the transaction log. After the transaction log has been backed up, committed transactions are removed. You need to save the complete database at least once before picking this option.

- **Log No Truncate**–Back Up Transaction Log is selected only when the database has a problem with continuing corruption. You can use this transaction log together with a database backup to restore the database to a point before it failed. Uncommitted transactions are rolled back.

- **Database**–Only Back Up Database Changes is an option that performs a differential backup of the database, which is considerably faster and smaller than a full backup. As this backup only allows for restores to a point in time, you should consider creating multiple log backups. This option is only available for SQL 7.0 or newer.

The options for a Consistency Check before and after backup and after restore are the following:

- **None** should be selected if you don't want to perform a consistency check—then go have your head examined, because that's Just Plain Silly.

- **Full check excluding indexes** checks the consistency of data pages and clustered index pages but excludes the indexes. This check runs faster than the full check.

- **Full check including indexes** performs a, yep, full check including the indexes.

- **Physical check only** (SQL 2000) performs a low-overhead check of the consistency of the database.

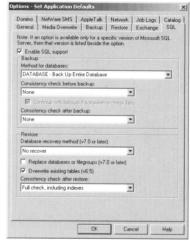

Figure 11-7. SQL backup and restore options

These are the Restore options:

- **No recover** restores additional differential or transaction logs.

- **Recover** is selected if the database and all logs have been restored. The state recovered brings the database online, and users can log in and use it.

- **Standby** is used during restore of transaction and differential logs.

If your database doesn't have the self-backup capability, and if you have a database that doesn't have any backup plug-ins available for your backup software, you can use an open file–manager application that intercepts the database's calls before they hit the system, and then passes those calls over to the backup software so that it can properly grab the files necessary to complete a backup operation. You can take two approaches to this open file–manager scenario; one by St. Bernard Software; the other by Dantz Development. We'll cover both.

St. Bernard Open File Manager

St. Bernard Software's Open File Manager is one of the few products to provide a viable solution for open file backups, and most backup software vendors have licensed their technology. St. Bernard's Open File Manager works on the principle of creating a file-by-file snapshot in order to present a stable point-in-time copy of a volume to the backup application.

Normally, database software sends information that it wants to write to the disk (whether that's table, index, or log file data) directly to the operating system. The operating system, in turn, writes the information to the disk, as in the left side of Table 11-2.

Table 11-2. Writing to a disk without (left) and with (right) Open File Manager

When a backup application wants to perform a backup, it notifies the OFM to ready the system for backup. From that point on, the OFM intercepts all reads and writes going to the file system. For each write, the OFM performs a Copy-on-write operation, wherein it makes a copy of the block about to be modified and stores it in a *diff* area within the volume, as shown on the right side of Table 11-2. For each read, the OFM checks against its database of 30+ backup packages to determine whether or not the requestor is a backup application. If the read request is from a known backup application, the OFM reconstructs a point-in-time copy of the volume by merging data from the source volume and the *diff* area, as shown in the left side of Table 11-3. If the read request is not from a backup application, the OFM passes the read onto the file system, as shown in the right side of Table 11-3.

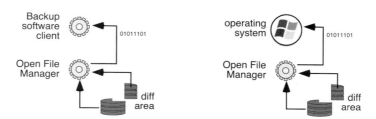

Table 11-3. Reading information to a backup client (left) and to the OS (right) with OFM

As described above, Open File Manager is compatible with the majority of backup applications and can be used as-is without too much customization. OFM consists of two components: the control component, which provides the graphical interface for configuring and distributing OFM software; and the system component, which is installed and controlled from the control component. If you use an administration server on your network, you might as well use it for the OFM control component. During the installation of the control component, the open file–protection service is installed, as well.

From the main window of OFM, you can browse your network and select other devices on which to install the system component through a standard Windows network browser. Select one of the PCs that has no open file protection yet and click the **Install OFM** icon. Remember that every system component has a separate license, so you'll need to enter a license key. And don't forget, once the system component is installed, it must be started, and the OFM service must be launched.

OFM can now be configured for each PC from the control component. With a right-click on a PC's name, you open the properties panel for each single PC. In the General settings, you can set the name and size of the log file OFM is allowed to write. The Volume Specific settings point to a drive—or drives—where OFM is allowed to store Preview[4] data.

Timing contains the settings for OFM to determine if the data is synchronized. The Write Inactivity Period is used to detect when the files on a system are in synchronized state. When modifications to a file are separated by a period of time greater than the WIP, the modifications are treated as unrelated, and the data is coherent.

Sync Timeout defines the time that OFM will delay a backup application's request for a data backup if the data is not synchronized.

Backup Inactivity Timeout is the time after which OFM assumes that a backup job is finished, after all backup activity has ceased. OFM then releases all resources and prepares for the next backup.

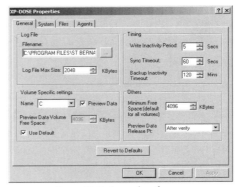

Figure 11-8. General preferences

The **Files** tab lists all files and directories that are to be ignored by OFM. Trying to manage the integrity of certain files, especially the systems paging file, is not useful and costs some system overhead. Other files—such as directories containing installation programs—might not have to be monitored, either. You can use the **Add** button to exclude files and directories, and subdirectories can be added by selecting a check box.

---

4.   OFM creates preview data of all open files during a backup operation while no partial transactions are pending. All changes that occur during this time are saved to the intended file while the original data is kept intact in the prewrite cache. When the backup application comes to a part that has been changed during the backup, OFM replaces the changed data with the original data. This ensures that all files have the same state they did when the backup started.

OFM comes with two different kinds of agents for the most common backup applications: application agents and login agents. Application agents allow OFM to log in to a PC and interact with the backup software in use. Application agents should be used when a component of the backup software—like a client or a control panel—runs on the PC. To disable the agent—and therewith interaction with OFM—uncheck the check box to the left of the agent's

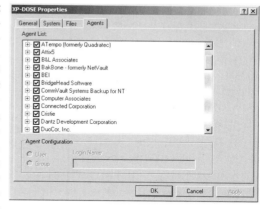

name (a list of agents is shown in the dialog at right). As application agents are compatible to each other, you can leave all of them selected. Login agents give OFM log-in rights for backup purposes when no backup software component is running on a PC, or if you just intend to copy files or a database from a remote PC. In that case, you must create a user account with all necessary access rights to the corresponding files, and enter this user account for the agent. Use the Remote System Backup agent for backup software that remotely backs up a PC, and use the Open File Copy agent for file-copy operations.

Performing a backup while Open File Manager is running

The following diagram (Figure 11-9. on page 356),depicts a backup of our main database server. During this backup, MS SQL was up and running, and users accessed the database for data updates and retrieval. As soon as the backup application[5] accessed the server, OFM started creating previews of the files the backup application requested for backup. During the backup process, OFM, logged progress on creating the previews and released the files in time for the backup application.

---

5.   This test has been performed using VERITAS NetBackup Professional with the MS SQL agent.

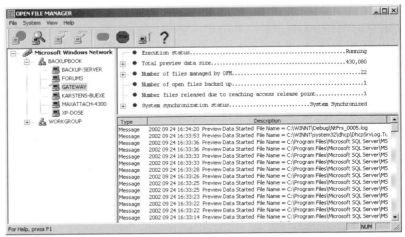

Figure 11-9. OFM creating previews

Retrospect Open File Backup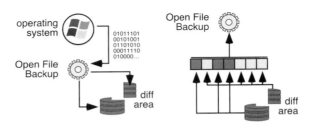

Retrospect Open File Backup is virtual duplication software that makes instantaneous copies of multiple volumes without using additional hardware. Retrospect makes use of a copy-on-write mechanism to create a point-in-time view of a volume. When the Open File Backup plug-in is installed, Retrospect creates a point-in-time copy of the volume being backed up, producing a consistent copy of data even if files are changing while the backup is in progress.

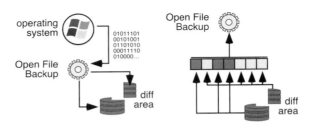

Table 11-4. Open File Backup creating a copy on write (left) and reconstructing a snapshot (right)

When the plug-in finds a period of inactivity on each of the volumes, it assumes that they're in a quiescent state and proceeds to create a point-in-time copy of each volume[6]. Before modifying any blocks on disk, after creating a point-in-time copy of the volume, Open File Backup agent copies old blocks before they get modified to the *diff* area in an unused portion of the disk. When the plug-in needs to present a point-in-time view of the volume to Retrospect, it virtually projects the *diff* blocks over the current blocks to re-create the point-in-time view.

Until now, this advanced technology has been available only to large data-centers. Dantz brings this Big Gun to us Little People via Open File Backup. The immediate benefits to businesses are:

• Reduces batch, background, and backup windows by hours per day—gaining several hours per day of uptime availability and user access to critical data

• Administrators can now back up line-of-business applications such as Exchange, SQL Server, and Share Point databases without shutting them down.

• Offers complete, consistent backup view across multiple volumes.

Retrospect's advantages

The Retrospect method of open file backup has a few advantages over St. Bernard's open file manager: Simpler setup, more thorough "catching" of information, and better performance.

Loss due to incorrect configuration Open file managers require the system administrator to configure groups of associated files together, requiring the system administrator to be intimately familiar with the application's data structures—a difficult task, as most enterprise-class applications write their data in many different locations and even distribute it across volumes.

Retrospect Open File Backup performs a volume-level system snapshot that's synchronized across multiple volumes, thus eliminating the guesswork of figuring out which files are related to each other—as well as loss of your data's relational integrity.

---

6. Actually, it relies on the file system being in a quiet state *or* the application being able to handle a crash—i.e., the restored data comes from a consistent point in time, as if the machine halted cleanly and suddenly. Databases tend to be well-designed for this, but el-cheapo applications aren't always up to the challenge of crash recovery. That's why Open File Backup tries to find a quiescent period to freeze the snapshot.

Some I/Os bypass the OFM

Many enterprise-class databases such as SQL and Oracle achieve optimized throughput by bypassing the file system to commit writes directly to disk. Since these writes don't pass through the regular file system, OFMs usually can't handle them, and provide low-fidelity database backups. Other writes, such as those to MFP, FAT, Directory, and Registry, also usually bypass the OFM.

Retrospect Open File Backup monitors the volume at a disk block level. Therefore, it's guaranteed to intercept all I/O going to the disk. Retrospect Open File Backup captures all the writes correctly, thus ensuring a flawless backup.

Performance impact

Open File Managers don't work at a true block level—they implement the copy-on-write algorithm by creating a *diff* area within the file-system volume itself. This causes a significant negative impact on performance, especially during backup, for two reasons:

1. Creating the *diff* area within the file-system volume means that all I/O through the different area has to go through the file-system layers, as well, thus slowing backups.

2. The OFM must intercept each read request and attempt to determine if it matches any known backup application from its knowledgebase. This process significantly slows any other applications that might share the CPU cycles with the backup application while a backup is in progress.

Overall, users may experience system slowdown between 50–70 percent when using competitive OFMs. Retrospect Open File Backup was designed for minimal footprint and maximum performance. Retrospect Open File Backup consumes less than 3–4 percent of CPU cycles when backup is in progress, thus making cycles available to other applications.

Retrospect Open File Backup stores the *diff* area outside the normal file-system volume in an unused area of the disk, greatly optimizing the data path when reconstructing point-in-time images.

Setup and config

Retrospect comes in three flavors: Professional, Single Server, and Multi-Server. The folks at Dantz figure that any computer running a database is a server. Therefore, they make you purchase either a copy of the single server or the multi-server, in case you want to run open file backup on multiple machines.

To work properly, the volume being backed up must be running Windows NT 4.0 Server or Workstation with Service Pack 6; Windows 2000 Workstation or Server with Service Pack 2; or Windows XP. To back up open files on a Windows XP computer, it must have an NTFS volume. If the volume being backed up is a client of the multi-server backup software, it must run at least Retrospect Client 6.0.

To check if you have Open File Backup installed properly, select **Window > License Manager** and ensure that Open File Backup is listed as installed for your software.

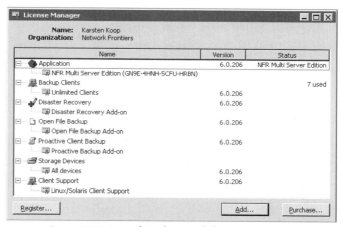

Figure 11-10. Open File Backup installed in License Manager

Once you've created your backup script, set some specific options for the Windows backups of open files. To do this, click the **Options** button within the backup script—doing so will present the Options window in Figure 11-11. on page 360. Think through the five different options, and then set as appropriate to maximize Open File Backup capabilities (and the chance that this will work correctly).

- **Back Up Open Files** allows Retrospect to copy busy files that could otherwise not be copied. It's on by default. If you're running a duplicate instead of a backup operation, this will be listed as **Duplicate Open Files**.

- **Protect Multi-Volume Datasets** will back up or archive applications that store files on more than one volume.

Retrospect Open File Backup agent coordinates creation of consistent point-in-time copies across volumes. The agent waits and looks for a period of inactivity on each of the volumes. If there is no disk activity, it assumes that they're in a quiescent state and proceeds to create a point-in-time copy of each volume. If a volume has ongoing disk activity, the agent won't create point-in-time copies for any other volume on the same machine, thus ensuring that the point-in-time copies contain consistent data.

If the Open File Backup operation includes multiple volumes, but none of the open file data spans multiple volumes (if your database resides on a single volume), make sure the Protect Multi-Volume Datasets option is off.

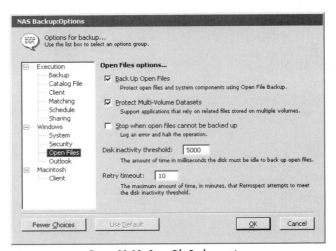

Figure 11-11. Open File Backup options

- **Stop when open files cannot be backed up** causes Retrospect to halt the operation if the retry timeout occurs or if the system configuration does not support Open File backup. When this option is off, Retrospect backs up or duplicates all other files (i.e., files that are not open). I would not suggest that you leave this check box on for normal backups wherein an open file backup is a part of the overall process. However, if you're creating a specific instance of an open file backup—in which you're backing up a single database volume or duplicating a single database volume, then, yes, *absolutely* turn on this check box so that you can get the error reports that note the volume can't be duplicated or backed up. Only with the first option, the dialog will read **Stop when open files cannot be duplicated** when you run a duplicate operation instead of of a backup operation.

- **Disk inactivity threshold** is the amount of time Retrospect waits for the source disk to be idle in order to proceed with Open File Backup. When the threshold is reached, Retrospect waits again until the retry timeout occurs. The default threshold is 5,000 milliseconds, but you'll play with this setting as you optimize your environment, scheduling, and Open Files options to maximize disk inactivity. Open File backup requires a period of inactivity on the source volume's disk (disk inactivity threshold) to accurately copy open files.

Schedule scripts using Open File Backup during off-peak hours.

Experiment with the disk inactivity threshold and retry timeout options to determine optimal values. A lower disk inactivity threshold increases the chance that it will be met, but also increases the possibility of data inconsistency. A higher disk inactivity threshold decreases the chances that it will be met, but, yes, also decreases the possibility of data inconsistency.

During Open File Backup, disable or stop applications on the source volume's disk that could increase disk activity, such as anti-virus software, disk defragmentation software, etc.

Once you've configured your backup or duplicate script, there's nothing much else to do other than look at your error log to ensure that your open file backups or duplications are humming along properly.

Remember: Retrospect checks to see that there isn't much usage on the disk before it begins its backup process. Therefore, with a heavy-use database, you're bound to get a great many errors, and the backup won't happen. With Retrospect, timing is everything: This is a great tool to back up or duplicate databases during their inactive time—usually late at night—but if your database doesn't have a daily lull, you could end up flushing about a day's worth of data down the drain.

Shut down, back up, restart

If you have *no means* to connect to the database and back it up while it's running, you're going to have to simply shut it down "for maintenance" every so often so that you can flush the log into the tables and then back it up. You can do this with simple workgroup databases, support system (where the support team actually goes home at the end of the day) databases, etc. It is, as the title suggests, based upon shutting the database down so that it writes its information to the logs, backing it up, and then restarting it. Define a time window in which the database won't be accessed, and then write a script that shuts down the database so that the backup cycle can kick in. After the backup process is finished, a second script restarts the database.

In a Unix environment, a cron job[7] can easily take care of this.

In the Mac OS X environment, you can create an AppleScript that takes care of this just as easily as you create the Windows scheduled task we'll show you below.

There's an easy way to do this in Windows. As you might know, Windows has a feature for scheduling tasks. If you combine this knowledge with the fact that you can create shortcuts for scripts that stop and start your database, you're getting warm. Here is how it works: First, create shortcuts for starting and stopping your database. You need to do this because the Windows scheduler can work only with "existing" programs—it can't execute scripts.

The shortcut for starting your database should point to the executable—mysqld.exe, in this case—and bear a descriptive name. Add any parameters that the database server needs to start—in the example that follows, we added the information that the database should start in stand-alone mode so that it can be shut down through the scheduler whenever necessary. It's also a good idea to start the application "minimized," as you don't want the database's console window staring at you all day. Click the **OK** button to close this dialog and create a second shortcut for stopping the database. Every database uses its own commands for starting and stopping, so you need to consult the manufacturer's manuals for the exact parameters.

---

7.   *cron* is a daemon (background program) that executes scheduled commands in Unix environments. Type *man cron* in a Unix console to obtain a detailed explanation.

Next, open the Windows Control Panels and double-click **Scheduled Tasks**, then double-click **Add Scheduled Task**. The wizard will guide you through the necessary steps, as follows. Select the shortcut you have previously created and click the **Next** button as shown in Figure 11-12.

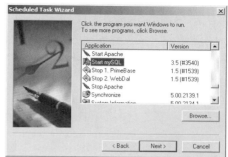

Figure 11-12. Select your shortcut

After you select the shortcut for starting the database, define when you want this to happen. Let's assume that your database is modified daily. In that case, you might want to schedule a stop and start for your database every day. Select the **Daily** radio button and click **Next**.

Figure 11-13. Start the database daily

Now, let's assume that you have a time window between 8P.M. and 5A.M. That would give you nine hours for the backup process. Believe me—some databases are so humongous that even 12 hours won't suffice. But as your database is fairly small, we'll grant the backup process two hours.

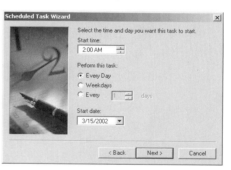

Figure 11-14. Set the time for starting

Set the start time for your database for 2A.M., click on the **Every Day** radio button and click the **Next** button to continue.

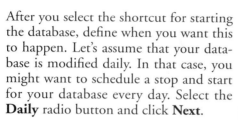

Next, Windows needs to know the password of the person who executes the program. If you're the administrator of this server, you have sufficient privileges to start and stop the database. If you're not the administrator or if you prefer to execute this program as a different user, check if that user has the right to start and stop your database by executing the start- and stop-commands manually. Click the **Next** button to finish this step.

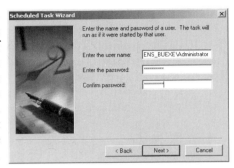

Figure 11-15. Set the Password

In this final dialog, select **Open the advanced options**, bringing up a dialog that lets you refine your settings one more time. If you're happy with your setup, just click the **Finish** button.

Figure 11-16. Finish the setup

Wait—it's not coffee time yet! You need to do the same thing one more time to create a shortcut for stopping the database. Schedule its execution for 12A.M. and define a backup schedule that saves your database during that two-hour time window. As a database usually doesn't come to a grinding halt when you stop it, you should leave a gap of a few minutes between stopping the database and starting the backup process. Voilà—you're free to satisfy your caffeine habit.

 When you use this approach, you're only backing up the data—at best—every night. If your database server dies during the day, you could lose up to a full day's worth of work. Time to ask the tough question: Are you willing to flush that much data down the toilet?

The second most difficult part of this approach is figuring out the length of the backup process. When you take throughput, the amount of data, and the number of tapes needed into consideration, you might find out that your backup takes longer than you've got. That's the moment when you have to rethink your backup strategy and start looking into alternative tape drives or backup methods.

My, that's a lot of flushing!

As you can see with each of these approaches to backing up live databases, you could be flushing a lot of data down the drain. If you're a company that relies on your databases, and your databases are running constantly with users hitting them 24 hours a day, none of these solutions will work well for you.

Instead, we recommend that you move to a system whereby you can either mirror your database to multiple storage volumes or replicate your databases in a live environment from a primary server to a secondary server. Replicating them from a live database server over to a standby server—and then backing them up—is a great way to make sure that you don't lose *much* data (we cover this in *Replication* on page 497). Mirroring your databases in a storage area network environment is a great way to ensure that you don't lose *any* of your data in case of a computer crash (we cover this under *Coupling storage virtualization software into a SAN* on page 477). Of course, you pay to play: With this method, you'll be flushing money instead of data down the drain, so you'll want to ensure that your business continuity cost-ratios can tolerate that loud sucking sound.

Chapter 12:
Recovering from operating system and application loss

If a virus corrupts your operating system, it can't be fixed by replacing this or that file. You can't go into the system to replace the infected files—doing so could fuel the virus, or worse: If this corruption was a back-door Trojan horse, it could activate an attack. You're left with three choices: Restore from the original disks, from backup copy, or from an imaged copy.

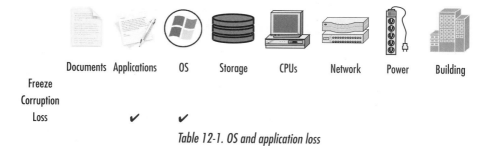

	Documents	Applications	OS	Storage	CPUs	Network	Power	Building
Freeze								
Corruption								
Loss		✔	✔					

Table 12-1. OS and application loss

We'll skip restoring from the original disks here, because that's just plain silly—and not as in funny silly. Silly as in "you've gotta be kidding me" silly. Installing the operating systems from original disks takes loads of original disk sets, many hours of downloads from Microsoft or Apple, and a great deal of time you could spend wisely in other ways[1].

In our continuum of fault tolerance through mirroring/duplication and backing up, recovering from application and operating system loss falls into either the mirroring/duplication category or the backing-up category of protection. You really can't create a set of spare parts (fault-tolerant protection) for your operating system or applications. They either break or they don't, and the fix process is to simply swap them out for good ones.

You can restore from a copy that you've backed up using your backup application. To do that, you first must a) boot your computer from some disk or partition that isn't corrupted, and b) access the organizational LAN where your backup is stored. Software like NTI Drive Backup, Retrospect, and VERITAS Bare Metal Restore create special boot disks that will launch the computer without a normal operating system. Once this **Emergency Recovery Disk (ERD)** has launched the computer, the normal restore process using the network-based backup software takes over.

Restoring from a backup has its good and bad aspects. It's the easiest method overall to incorporate into your organizational backup plan—but you probably haven't set up that plan to support parallel restorations instead of linear restorations. Although restoration of an operating system from tape for a single computer works just fine for most folks, what happens if the virus hit the department? You'd have to restore tens, maybe hundreds of computers at a single time. Linear restoration of multiple computers—even if it entails only the operating system—is exceedingly time-consuming and therefore very costly because of the amount of time many people would have to spend waiting to be restored.

If you do have backup software that supports parallel restores (backup software that can be web restore–initiated, driven by the client computer, or that supports simultaneous processes) you're in luck. You can then avoid the ERD and create a simple boot disk so that your computer can boot to an intranet-based software image that gives your computer enough horsepower to connect to your backup server and begin the restoration process. If you don't have backup software that supports parallel restores, use the disk cloning process of bringing your computer back to life instead of the backup and restore process.

---

1.   While writing this, I'm reinstalling Windows XP, which is proving my point: The Windows Update page found 21 critical updates and service packs. This will probably take about one day to fix.

For this process, create a standard image of a default drive so that many computers can be cloned very quickly. Utilities for creating images of hard drives and restoring PCs to their original state have come a long way since the XCOPY command. The idea is simple: When you have a hard drive in clean and working status, simply preserve this state for fast and easy restoration. You can do this on a computer-by-computer basis, or you can create a network-based drive image that can be used to clone multiple computers simultaneously.

In short, there are two main methods of operating system recovery: disk image creation and ERD creation. Disk images contain all the data of your hard drive partition; the ERD contains only enough information needed to boot your PC so that you can restore the rest of the data through some other means. Your choice depends upon your—and your users'—business needs.

And speaking of your users, while all your computers and operating systems might be the same, the human element is as individual as snowflakes. You may choose to image their computers' operating systems, but you can't ignore the "personality" or "flavor" they've added to their computers. There are some great packages out there that let you capture that personality, either as a part of or distinctly separate from the image, so that you can layer a person's "personality" back on top of a newly imaged drive or new computer with a new operating system.

While application loss is less dramatic, it's still troublesome to install applications from their respective CDs (Canvas has six CDs). You'll probably want to include standard organizational applications in your base operating system load during imaging. Some imaging tools allow you to layer applications on top of your basic operating system images, so that you can have a base image as well as an art department image, an admin image, etc.

Special Thanks to...

John Epeneter and Rhett Glauser at Altiris (especially John) who spent more time with us than you could imagine. Also Gidon Bing and Kathering Worthen from Symantec who walked us through all of the ins and outs of Ghost and where the product is headed in the near future.

THE MAIN THING

Here, the Main Thing is that you have options other than backing up your computer and restoring your computer in a traditional backup software manner. You can separate your operating system imaging from your user's applications and their "personality" information on the computers.

You can absolutely create a "universal image" of your operating system software and then use that image to blast out to tens or hundreds of computers at a time.

Then layer on top of that application packages by groups so that sales gets a different application set than does production.

And then layer on top of that the user's personality information.

This is all possible—if you plan carefully:

- Plan for the placement of your imaging servers so that all of the computers have access to them and the process of ongoing imaging and restoration doesn't bottleneck your network.

- Plan for additional TCP/IP addresses on your network for use in imaging and restoration of computers.

- Have a naming scheme for your computers and their associated disk images.

- Plan for the storage of your images on a server (we suggest a NAS box running the Windows 2000 SAK), because each image takes up about half the space of the original hard drive it came from.

- Put your images on a server that also has a CD/DVD burner so that you can burn emergency CDs or DVDs of images for recovery in the field if necessary.

- And last, have a file migration policy so that you know which computer files you should restore to an individual's computer and which ones you should restore to the server on which they originally belonged.

RESTORATION AND EMERGENCY RECOVERY DISKS

There isn't much theory here. If your hard drive completely dies and you have to restore to a new hard drive, it isn't going to have an operating system on it. Therefore, you need to install an operating system from scratch and then connect to your backup server and restore the rest of your data, or use your backup server's **Emergency Recovery Disk** operations to create a disk that lets you boot your computer just enough to connect to your backup server and restore everything at once. That's it for the theory portion of this section.

We've reviewed and liked two products in this category: NTI DriveBackup! and Dantz Retrospect's disaster recovery operations. Both tools are a subset of a disk backup operation (DriveBackup!'s operation is more of a snapshot-based drive imaging system); therefore, they're tied directly to their tool's restore routines and can't really be used in disk imaging.

NTI DriveBackup!

NTI DriveBackup! was suggested to us by one of our field editors who just happened to work for the company. It's a nice tool for both drive imaging and creating emergency recovery disks.

We'll skip the drive imaging portion of the tool for now and simply deal with their ERD creation process. Since it's such a quick and simple process, we'll cover it in its entirety.

Creating an Emergency Recovery Disk

NTI's DriveBackup! uses a simple wizard interface to move you through the three-step process of creating ERD disks. In the first step, select the destination device you'll use as the ERD. DriveBackup! supports writeable CD- or DVD-drives for this purpose. The disk image needs more space than fits on one CD media, so if you have the choice, go with DVD. Next, indicate whether or not your CD or DVD player is IDE or SCSI. If you use a SCSI device, you need a startup floppy disk for Windows 98 or ME.

Finally, select your source drive. The DriveBackup! software provides a drop-down list of mounted drives for you to choose from. Click the **Option…** button to set more options for this ERD, such as password protection, compression, and data comparison after backup. If you have not yet inserted writeable media, Drive-Backup! prompts you to do so. Once you have finished, label and number the CDs/ DVDs—just in case.

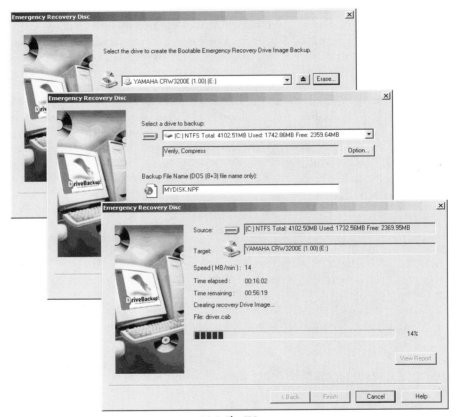

Figure 12-1. The ERD process

That's all there is to creating an ERD using DriveBackup! Because the software takes a snapshot of the system currently running, you won't need to remember where your Windows serials numbers are—or anything else.

Restoring the Disk image

To restore the disk in the event of a crash, insert the bootable ERD that you've created. DriveBackup! will boot into DOS and start the restore process.

Retrospect Backup Professional 🪟

Retrospect offers an option for creating an ERD as a separate election in their backup environment. Since their product is not ERD- or disk imaging–centric, creating the ERD or working with drive images is not its central theme. The Retrospect process is much different from that of DriveBackup! in three respects:

- You can create an ERD for only those devices you've already backed up;

- You must have the operating system installer CDs handy (for the serial number of the Windows operating system); and

- The software doesn't write directly to CD or DVD. You must first create an image file and *then* burn the ERD CD.

The ERD option is, by default, visible in Retrospect Backup Professional when you select Prepare for Disaster Recovery from the Windows menu, but to activate it, you must purchase a license for that plug-in and enter the license key. This works only if you've been backing up the computer's boot volume, including the operating system. Retrospect needs to create the ERD from data that has previously been backed up. Then you must locate the backup set you want to use for that particular volume on the computer, select a snapshot, and proceed with creating ERD instructions, or go whole hog and create an ERD CD. We'll proceed with the disk-image creation.

As with all of the software we write about, Retrospect uses a very easy-to-understand wizard process to guide the administrator through the ERD setup process. To create the ERD CD, Retrospect needs the installation CD of the operating system in use on the PC. The CD can be in the backup server's CD drive, or it can be a disk image located on the network, and accessed through the standard Windows Browser.

Because Retrospect first creates a local imaged file for the ERD creation, you must point it at a volume with enough space for building the software image of the

ERD CD or DVD. Retrospect writes the image files into that directory into chunk sizes that fit onto one CD each.

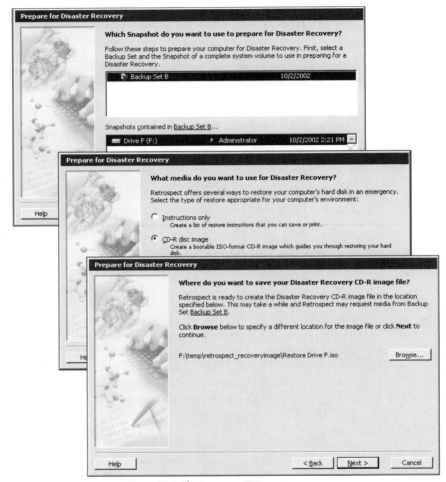

Figure 12-2. The Retrospect ERD creation process

After the image files have been created, use your preferred CD-writing application to write these ISO images to CD. You're now ready to complete the restoration.

Restoring with Retrospect

When you boot your downed computer, ERD installs a minimal operating system to get you going (that's why the pictures here don't look so great). After installation of the minimal OS is complete, your computer reboots and starts the Retrospect Disaster Recovery Wizard, connecting to the Retrospect server. Again, select the snapshot from which you want to restore (assuming that you have more than one volume on your drive, you'll have more than one snapshot to choose from). Retrospect will then start the restore process. After your hard drive has been restored, your computer will reboot into the state that you saved.

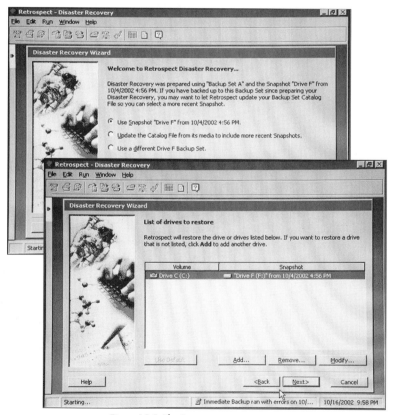

Figure 12-3. The Retrospect restore process

As you can see, this is a lengthy process, but can be run with multiple computers being restored in parallel, as long as the original backups were done to disk. Backups to tape are fine if you're restoring one computer at a time—but that just won't work in an organization that needs restoration of multiple computers in parallel.

For that situation, your best bet is to either back up your workstations to disk, or create disk images of the operating systems, key software packages, and save restorations for errant user data that isn't saved to the server. And, of course, you won't be tied to serial restorations if you move to disk imaging instead of using ERDs and then restoring from the ground up.

DISK IMAGING—UNDERSTANDING IMAGING BASICS

Remember your mother reminded you to wash behind your ears? Well, she was right: Starting with clean material is an essential part of creating a disk image, which then serves as a hard drive clone for restoration to the same PC or other PCs of the same caliber and type. That last part about caliber is important: Network environments have more than one type of PC and more than one type of operating system. Let's take, for example, our small print shop company, which has nine different classifications of computers.

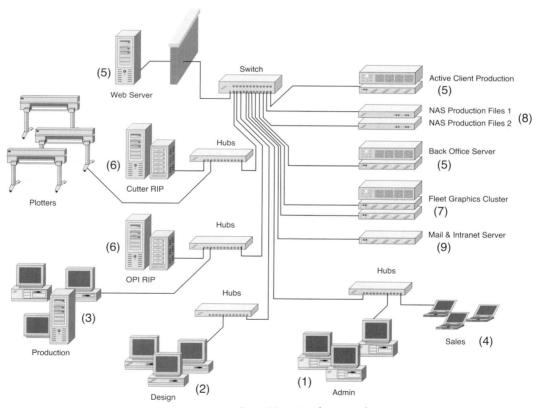

Figure 12-4. Print shop network

1. The admin group bought all of their PCs at the same time from the same Value Added Reseller (VAR), and they're all running Windows 2000 workstation software. These are prime candidates for disk imaging, as all of the computers, operating systems, applications, and drivers are the same.

2. The design group bought their computers at the same time, too. They're all Macintoshes running OS X—again, another prime set of candidates for disk imaging, as all the operating systems and most of the applications are the same.

3. The production group has a mish-mash of Macintoshes and PCs. Some of the PCs are desktops, and some are towers running Windows 2000. This is where it starts to get a bit sticky. A disk image for a Dell and a disk image for a Gateway can be different, depending upon the drivers in use. Only those production computers with the same operating system, manufacturer and drivers can be grouped together. Care will have to be taken when creating images for these systems.

4. The sales group has a mix of Toshiba Windows XP notebooks and Macintosh PowerBooks. Again, as with the production group, these computers must be grouped by operating systems and drivers.

5. A basic group of Windows 2000 servers act in capacities such as the web server, back office (Great Plains, ADP, etc.) server, and a production server that's also the Active Directory server. Since these computers all use the Windows 2000 operating system, they can be kept as a group and imaged for the basic operating system and Windows 2000 programs. Beyond that, the individual applications (such as Great Plains, Active Directory, etc.) must be reloaded from a restore from backup.

6. Two Mac OS X servers run Unix RIP software for cutters, plotters, and Arizona printers. Since both of these are server-class machines running OS X server software, they too can become a group with their own disk image.

7. A single cluster runs Windows 2000 cluster software for the shop's custom Fleet Graphics application and database. It wouldn't make any sense to create an image for these two computers because there are only two in this classification—it's easier to simply mirror their boot drives.

8. Two NAS boxes act as general-purpose file servers. NAS boxes run on a special version of Unix or Windows 2000 SAK. If they die, they can't really be im-

aged—they have their own version of an "image" burned into their internal setup.

9. Finally, there's the Mac OS X Xserve. It runs both the e-mail and intranet server. This must have its own image.

When imaging the operating system of Windows-based PCs, you can easily use a disk image for different PCs if their operating system and their hardware are the same. However, extra precautions are necessary when creating an image that will be cloned across different machines, as the disk image of an operating system contains the drivers for only the PC that it was installed on. In the OS X world, it doesn't matter whether the computer is a notebook or a desktop: The only difference is whether or not it's a workstation-class or server-class operating system.

 You also need to know a few things about how Microsoft licenses their operating systems (talk about Big Brother here). Beginning with Windows XP, Microsoft requires new customers of the retail version of XP and XP Professional to "activate" their software over the Internet with Microsoft. This product activation associates the installer software's media key with a specific computer's hardware configuration to ensure that the product key has not been used on more computers than it was intended for (namely, one). The activation code is basically a combination of the product install key plus a "hardware hash" derived from different components of the computer, along with a random value generated each time the installation ID is used. This information is then sent over the Internet to Microsoft, which returns a confirmation code to the computer, thus unlocking the operating system for use. *Can you get around this process?* The simple answer is yes and no. No, if you're trying to do something you shouldn't. Yes, if you purchase any of the volume "open" licenses from Microsoft. And since you can buy these licenses by the five-pack, there's no way an organization should be using the single-user versions anyway.

One more thing to remember, *disk imaging wipes out the hard drive completely and replaces whatever was there with the disk image's contents.* So when you clone a computer from a disk image, any applications or files left on the computer by the user are erased. With that in mind, within the disk image, you should include software that all users have, like MS Office, Star Office, or whatever you have standardized on. Whatever is loaded onto the computer you're going to image should stand as the reference PC for your department or organization.

And just to ensure that everything is hunky-dory, after you're done installing the OS, applications, and everything else, create your image and clone it to another PC (preferably of a different brand) to see if it works. Only then should you consider rolling out the image to tens, hundreds, or thousands of PCs.

One last note: Windows-based disk imaging applications can create an image of a hard drive or partition only when the PC is not running the operating system that you're about to copy, as the OS would otherwise be in use and files would be locked. Therefore, your PC will boot into some other operating system[2] and perform the imaging operation; then boot back into Windows when the operation is done.

Here's the disk imaging breakdown

With the nine distinct computer groupings, we have five different disk images to be created. The admin group's "white box" generic PCs and Production's Dells and Gateways need one image. The Macintosh OS X computers need another. And since the sales department uses XP-based notebooks, they, too, need their own image. The basic Windows 2000 servers need an image, and the Mac OS X server needs another.

Group	OS	CPU Type	Image ID
Admin		White box	
Production	Windows 2000	Dell tower	01
Production		Gateway	
Design			
Production	Macintosh OS X	Apple Desktop & notebook	02
RIP Servers			
Sales			
Sales	Windows XP	Toshiba notebook	03
W2K Servers	Windows 2000 Server	Dell tower/rack	04
Mail/Intranet	Macintosh OS X Server	Xserve	05

Table 12-2. Disk image groups

---

2. DOS or Linux

We've excluded the cluster, since none of the software that we tested images a cluster at this time. Knowing that you need five images is one thing—understanding how to create and manage those images is another.

Setting up your computers for imaging

Check out our website, www.backupbook.com, for a "living document" on disk imaging's best practices. Since these change often, we felt it best to offer that information in the fluid venue of the Web, rather than the permanence of paper. The software packages for disk imaging we tested create only an image of a whole partition or hard drive[3]; therefore the "static" data of a disk image should be kept in a separate partition or drive from the "dynamic" data that users work with. *In other words, you'll want to partition your drive to separate your operating system and applications from your users' data.*

Yes, I *know* you're thinking your users should be keeping their data on the servers. Yes, I *know* that you're grumbling that it's much easier to support corporate standards than it is to partition each of the drives before imaging them. However, what in the blazes are you going to tell the CEO when you have to image his or her assistant's computer and you wipe out the assistant's data—thus enraging the assistant and, by association, ticking off the CEO? I gotta tell ya, "Oops!" just doesn't cut it at times like that. Think about the people you have to work with and then shimmy around the fact that they probably aren't going to be following your IT-centric directions quite well. Grumble if you must, but partition their drives for *your* safety.

Figure 12-5. on page 382 shows our suggestion for integrating the use of disk images with your backup strategy: Keep the standardized PC installation on the first partition or drive and let the users keep their data on the second partition or on a file server. Keep the disk image updated and regularly back up the users' data. This is the most effective way to restore PCs in case disaster strikes. Alternatively (and not recommended by us), you can let the users keep their data on the system partition, but keep in mind that restoring a disk image completely erases the target partition. Without a separate backup of the users data, you'll be hosed.

---

3.   One exception: Clone'X for Macintosh lets you save the System Folder by itself, and the applications folder, if desired.

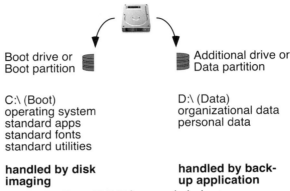

Figure 12-5. Disk contents by backup type

In a standard OS X, Windows 2000 and XP installation, this scenario creates a wee problem. By default, the Users (OS X) or Documents and Settings (Windows/XP) directory is located on the primary hard drive or partition. Thus, when users create data that they don't put on a server, that data will be overwritten when a drive image is restored. This is not a good thing. We recommend moving this folder to a different partition, possibly even to a file server that is backed up regularly if the users' computers are desktops—make that definitely a partition, on a notebook.

- Moving the Documents and Settings directory is easy: Right-click on the folder, select Properties, click on the **Move…** button, and select a destination on next logical drive or partition.

- In the OS X environment, first, copy the Users directory to the new location or hard drive. Then, use NetInfo Manager to edit the user information for the home (users) directory. The user's home directory must be changed from /Users/*username* to /Volumes/*partitionname*/Users/*username*.

Thinking through what to pack into your disk image

When the open road calls, you can follow one of the three schools of packing: the "Whatever fits in the overhead bin" school (usually too little), the "Let's hire 42 Sherpas to carry all the luggage" school (always too much), or the "I'll check the weather and itinerary and take what I need" school (just right). Of course, I'm of the overhead bin school and my wife is a distinguished graduate of the Sherpas-are-carrying-it academy. While that doesn't constitute a true crisis on vacation (though my wife might argue with me there, too), neither method is too effective when you're creating your disk image. Here, again, moderation is in order.

Local vs. centralized imaging

Disk imaging solutions come in two flavors: The small solutions, aimed at home users and small businesses, allow creating disk images per single PC. The big solutions provide centralized management of PCs and their disk images, allowing deployment of updates or restores across the network to multiple workstations at a time. Let's start small, beginning with the home editions, and then think big, working our way up to corporate solutions.

Space requirements   If you elect to put your disk images onto CDs or DVDs instead of storing them on a network server, you must think about how much space your image takes. The manufacturers of disk imaging applications claim that the compression rate of the disk image is between 50 and 70 percent of the original size. Our tests showed that, for example, an installation of Windows XP Pro and MS Office with a size of 1,561 MB was compressed to 921 MB, which fit onto two CD-R media—a compression ratio of 41 percent. If you want to make this media bootable, add another 350 or so MB, which just about fit on two media. Saving more data, and therewith using more media, is not cost-prohibitive, but easily adds up restore time.

Install from disk and then update your operating system

First, install your operating system and any of your utilities onto your hard drive. Then, go through the arduous process of updating all of the service packs and patches from the vendors. My OS X installation took 35 minutes for the base to install, and then another 35 minutes and 113 MB of downloads from Apple before everything was up to date. I had to install three different patches from Microsoft for their Microsoft Office installation.

Install your key utilities

Once you're done with the basic operations, it's time to install your key utilities. We suggest the following as a minimum:

- Backup software client for whatever backup software package you use;

- SMART Disk utility (SMART Tools for Windows, FWB SMART Toolkit for Macintosh);

- Disk defragmentation utility for your computer, such as Drive 10 for Macintoshes and Diskeeper for Windows); and

- Security remediation tools (such as Hercules from Citadel) for updating your security settings and patches.

Security test your boot drive

Next, security test your boot drive. Run Nessus or other other security test software (See *Testing (scanning) your network* on page 189) to discover any additional holes that need to be patched. If you use Hercules for immediate remediation, now's the time to do so.

Defrag your hard drive

Once you have everything installed, it's time to defragment your hard drive—*before* you create your image. If you don't, you will be creating a fragmented image, and every computer that you clone from thereafter will start life in a fragmented state—talk about going to pieces!

To put this into perspective, by the time I was done loading everything on our Windows 2000 clone and applying all of the patches and utilities, the drive had 7 percent fragmentation. Ouch.

Use SysPrep ⊞ to sterilize your install before imaging

Most modern disk imaging products support the use of the Windows utility Sysprep for sterilizing the rollout of Windows 2000 or Windows XP images. Sysprep is a disk image–based deployment tool that can be used to automatically sterilize (remove serial numbers and specialized drivers) or customize (add specialized drivers for devices that your organization has standardized on) within the OS setup during installation. The big plus for disk imaging products in supporting this tool is that Sysprep can be executed within the automated script they use for imaging. Without that level of integration, the user must run SysPrep, create the image, restart the computer, and then reapply all of the drivers and license codes that Sysprep deleted. It's much easier to click a check box in an imaging script and let the imaging software do all of that for you. We're talking about 20 minutes per computer of saved time here. Multiply that by the number of computers you have in your office, and you could probably warrant enough saved time to make a Krispy Kreme run!

If all your users had the same boring computer with the same boring Ethernet cards, video drivers, blah blah blah, you wouldn't need Sysprep. But if you live in the real world, you don't even come close to such a singular ideal. You have very different computers all over the place because you bought them based upon who had the best sale that week. Running Sysprep makes your Windows operating system image about as bland as borscht (unless, like Leopold Dilg, you like an egg in it). However, bland is good when you want to shove that same system out to 20 different computers made by seven different manufacturers. Making the image bland ensures that you aren't adding any special drivers to it that reside on the computer you're using as your base—drivers that don't necessarily reside on the rest of the computers in your office. So you make your borscht bland, shove it out there, and let the users add their own spices to taste. In addition, you can prepare the optional sysprep.inf file with information regarding the network environment, partition size, and much more. If your imaging system doesn't integrate Sysprep, here's what you need to do:

1. Download Sysprep from the Microsoft website to a directory of your choice.

2. In the console, select Sysprep Configurations from the **Tools** menu, name the configuration, click the **Create** button and point the console to the directory where you saved Sysprep.

3. From the **File** menu, **New > Image Dump** and click the **Sysprep** tab.

4. Select the Run Microsoft Sysprep check box and select the configuration that you've previously created in the console.

    The image dump you've created during these steps contains all possible driver configurations. After deploying the image to a new PC on the first run, the system will detect the Plug and Play devices and assign the according drivers and settings.

5. After you run Sysprep and the image is created (using your disk imaging software, which we'll cover in just a bit), don't let the imaging software extend the volume when applying the image to the target computer.

6. Finally, modify the sysprep.inf file to use the ExtendOemPartition key in the [Unattended] section in order to extend the partition to the full size of the target disk. Set it so that ExtendOemPartition = 1, which means to extend to the end of the disk instead of the 0 (do not extend) that's there to begin with.

HOME USER/SMALL BUSINESS DISK IMAGING OPTIONS

Clone'X Ⓧ

Clone'X is a nifty application from Tri-Edre that creates a clone of your OS X installation. You can use the clone as a backup in case your system gets corrupted or as a master system for further OS X installations on different Macs. Additionally, on request, Clone'X can save your applications folder so that a complete restore of the standard data (OS and applications) to your hard drive takes no more than an hour.

Creating a clone

When you start Clone'X, it requests the administrator's password to access and clone your System Folder. A user with no administrative rights can't use Clone'X to create a clone of the OS. Clone'X has two standard functions: cloning your system and restoring it.

Clone'X then lets you choose the system to clone and the destination it goes to, saving a clone of your OS to any mounted drive connected to your Mac as well as to CDs. During the creation of the clone, the system is compressed into a file that takes up approximately half the size of the original system. If you save it to CD and the file size exceeds the CD's available space, it splits the clone onto as many CDs as needed.

When creating your image, Clone'X asks if you want to save only the system or the applications, as well. It's a good idea to include the applications, as restoring a crashed system and your complete workspace takes only one step. At the current rate of OS X updates by Apple, it's a smart move to create a new clone of the OS after every system update—and keep the previous ones for awhile. Of course, this requires a useful naming scheme for the clones, so you'll want to ensure that you have a good naming convention.

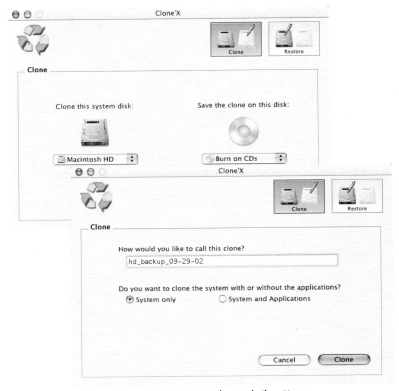

Figure 12-6. Creating a clone with Clone'X

After Clone'X has finished cloning your OS, it reports that the process has been successfully completed. You can now quit Clone'X and wait, smugly secure, for disaster to strike.

Restoring the OS

Because the makers of Clone'X figure that you'll make multiple cloned images, they include a list of all clones you've created when prompting you for a restore. This is a very good thing if you want to restore your hard drive to a certain version instead of only to the last previously saved version.

When you click the **Restore** button, Clone'X erases the System Folder on your hard drive and restores the system from the selected clone. After that operation is complete, simply reboot from your system disk and enjoy the freshly restored OS.

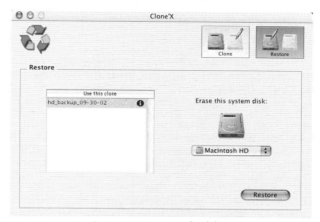

Figure 12-7. Restore to hard drive

Norton Ghost

Norton Ghost comes in two flavors: the single-user version (or five- and 10-packs) and the corporate edition. The biggest difference between the two? The corporate edition comes with the ghost client/server architecture that allows for rapid deployment of disk images to multiple PCs, while the home user/small business edition allows the creation of hard drive images for single PCs. Images can be created on the same PC on a different partition, on CD-R/RW, DVD-R/RW drives, external hard drives, Zip drives, tape drives, and mounted volumes. We'll cover the SOHO version here and the corporate edition later.

Creating a disk image

Ghost operates using a Windows interface, though for the creation of a drive image, it has to boot into DOS. Only when the PC is running from a separate operating system can Ghost create a usable image of the hard drive.

The creation of a disk image starts with launching the Ghost application. In the main dialog, click the Backup icon to enter the Backup Wizard. After a few innocuous screens, Ghost displays all available hard drives. Select the drive that you want to create an image of and select a destination for the image. Don't select the same partition on your hard drive that you're imaging as the destination, because that won't work.

When you use Ghost for the first time, it applies unique serial numbers to all hard drives in your PC for later recognition in case you need to restore an image. The destination file stands for a disk image file that can be located on any of the previously mentioned devices.

As I have chosen to create an image on CD or DVD, the disk image is created on the first empty media that Ghost finds. If Ghost has questions about devices attached to your PC (such as the USB version of the CD-R device we were using), you need to take the required action to make the devices accessible. For this reason, we suggest that you disconnect all USB and FireWire devices before you create your disk image, as you might not have the same devices connected over the lifetime of your computer.

Advanced settings… contains a boatload of settings that let you define your hardware and software environment for Ghost's optimal performance.

- When you click the User Files tab, you can define additional files or directories that you want included in the backup.

- In the CD Drivers section, you can choose if you want to have drive letters assigned to CD drives.

- The Compression tab offers three different rates of data compression: None, Fast, and High, where higher compression means a smaller disk image size while the creation of the image takes longer.

- The Virtual Partition Free Space option lets you define the default space being added when you create a virtual partition[4].

As with other Windows products, Ghost uses a graphical interface on DOS while creating the disk image. It reboots into Windows after the image has been created.

---

4.   A virtual partition is a bootable folder on your hard drive. You can store any files and utilities that you might need in case of a system crash in a virtual partition, and then boot your PC from there.

Finally, the summary displays the tasks that you've asked Ghost to perform. At this point, you're ready to go. If you need to make changes, this is your last chance. Click the **Back** button to make any changes, or the **Run Now** button to start the creation of the disk image.

Figure 12-8. Task summary

During the actual imaging, Ghost reboots your PC and starts in DOS, which leaves you nothing to do, so just let Ghost finish its work while you take care of that box of Krispy Kremes.

Ghost jumps directly into the disk-imaging process, searching for media in the drives to write the image to. If no media is present, you're prompted to insert the appropriate CD or DVD media for your drive. Depending on the amount of data that Ghost has to write, you're prompted for a new CD or DVD when the previous one is full. Label the finished media properly.

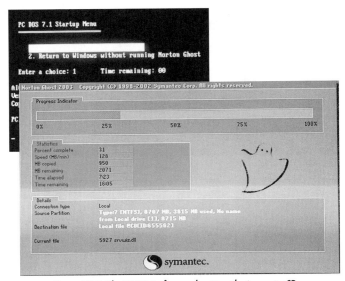

Figure 12-9. The DOS interface and writing the image to CDs

Restoring the hard drive

To restore your hard drive in case of loss or corruption, you must boot your PC to start Ghost and access your disk images. If your PC doesn't boot from the hard drive anymore, you need the emergency recovery disks that you previously created[5]. To continue with the restoration, choose the source partition from the image, and the destination partition or drive. If you have more than one hard drive installed in your computer, you can restore the image to a different drive. Remember that restoring a disk image completely erases the contents of the target drive or partition.

---

5. If you didn't create the disks, but have access to a similar PC, install Ghost there, create boot disks, and use them to boot your PC.

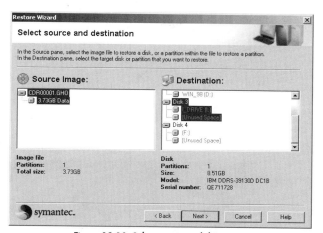

Figure 12-10. Select source and destination

The **Advanced Settings...** button in the next dialog lets you define additional settings for restoring your hard drive. Just select the correct version of USB or the correct SCSI driver. A summary of the items you're restoring and their destination is presented, after which Ghost will boot into PC-DOS and start the Ghost.exe application, which restores your hard drive to the same state as the image.

NovaStor InstantRecovery

NovaStor InstantRecovery does what its name promises: It lets you create instant recovery disks of your hard drive. IR uses Linux (instead of DOS) with a graphical interface as an environment for creating an emergency recovery disk and for restoring data from it. We cover this product in depth because it uses a wholly different process than Ghost. IR does not create bootable disk images; instead, you boot from the program CD, from which you start the backup and restore procedure.

Creating an Emergency Recovery Disk

IR starts up with a step-by-step character-based interface that first directs you to select the right driver for the graphics adapter in your PC. From the IR main screen, you can select one of the following options:

- **Backup** creates a backup of your hard drive or partition.

- **Restore** starts the restoration process.

- **Compare** compares the data on your hard drive with data on previously created backup CDs.

Clicking the **Backup** button begins creating a backup of your hard drive, allowing you to select the source and the destination for your data. IR automatically detects active partitions and connected CD- or DVD-writers.

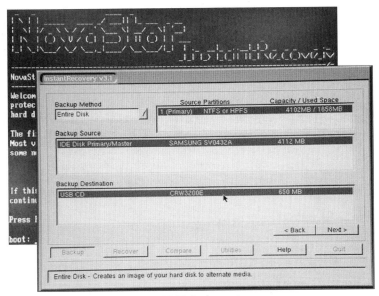

Figure 12-11. Backup options

IR offers few options for your backup disk image. Comparing the saved data with the original one is a good idea, as are the options for data compression and backing up only saved space. The backup should get a meaningful name, and if you want, you can protect it with a password. Let IR eject the disk at completion so you know when it's done, and perform a speed test before you write a CD for the first time. I trashed a few CD-Rs while ambitiously trying to use the maximum write speed. Insert a CD/R to begin the imaging process. IR then writes the data to the selected data to CD. If you have too much data to fit on a single CD, when it's full, IR will simply request a new one.

Restore/Recovery

Unlike other programs that allow you to boot from the imaged CD and then begin restoring from it, InstantRecovery must be booted from the program CD for restoring a hard drive. IR boots into its Linux interface, where you perform the hard drive restoration process.

Once you've clicked the **Recover** button to start the process, select the source for your backup and insert the CD containing the disk image. Not until IR has read the data from the CD will you be able to select the backup that you want to restore.

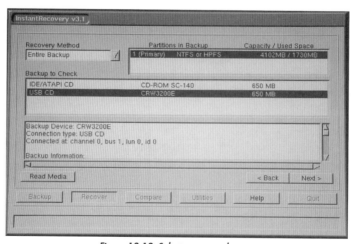

Figure 12-12. Select source and target

Starting with the first CD of your backup set, IR restores your hard drive; the time depends on the amount of data. In this example, IR took 45 minutes to restore 1.7 GB to my hard drive. While slow, it was still much faster than reformatting and installing from scratch.

NTI DriveBackup!

NTI DriveBackup! is a tool for creating disk images that also offers the option of creating an emergency recovery disk. As an additional feature, DriveBackup! provides file-level backup so that all backup tools are available in one package.

Creating a disk image is a straightforward process. First, select the drive that you want to back up. With a click on the **Option…** button, you can choose to verify your data after backup, to compress it during backup and to protect it with a password. You then select the backup destination and the file name. If you have more than one writeable CD or DVD drive attached to your PC, you can select all drives that you want DriveBackup! to write to. During the backup process, DriveBackup! requests new media when the current one fills up.

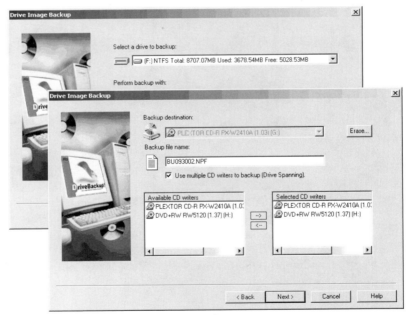

Figure 12-13. Backup in progress

LARGER ORGANIZATIONS & NETWORK BOOTING

In larger organizations that have servers (both to image and to use as network imaging platforms) and professional-class computers that can boot over the network, you have more choices. Because the products are more complex, we aren't going to get into the nitty-gritty as we did with the simpler ones—instead, we'll cover the process as opposed to the products, pointing out the individual products' differences in each step of the process.

Many backup packages we've discussed are source computer–based (as opposed to being driven by an external backup server). Thus, as long as they can boot, load their backup software, and access the place on the network where they've stored their backup files, they can initiate their own restoration. Other backup packages support multiple, parallel client restorations. Again, as long as the computers in question can boot and access the client backup software application, they can be restored in parallel. This capability eliminates the need for a full-blown ERD, because all they have to do is NetBoot and begin the restoration process.

Same thing with network-based imaging and cloning: There's no need to mess around with boot floppies or boot CDs if you can boot directly from the network and then immediately clone the computer with the network-supplied disk image.

For computers to boot from the network, two things must be in place. First, set aside a certain number of network addresses: the computers must have an address to access TCP/IP services. Second, and most obvious, your computers must have network-boot capability. All Macintosh computers have had this capability for quite some time: To bring up the NetBoot choices, simply restart while holding down the Option key. Windows devices must support PXE (Pre-Boot execution Environment) on their Ethernet cards and must have at least a network boot disk (or partition) available.

Setting up your network architecture

Creating a network-based boot and image install program for your organization depends on several factors. First, consider how your network architecture will impact what you're trying to accomplish. Figure 12-14. shows a simple network architecture with three basic parts: a public IP range in the DMZ where you'd be putting your web servers, etc.; a public IP range within the firewall, where you could put other computers with public addresses (such as your DNS servers, mail servers, etc.); and the rest of your network, which probably has private IP addresses (such as those in the 10.0.x.x range), with the connecting router acting as a Network Address Translator (NAT).

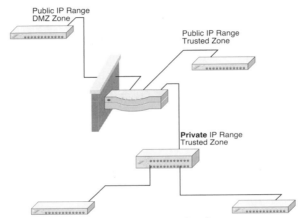

Figure 12-14. Simple network architecture

Client devices in the private range can initiate contact with other devices in the private range as well as devices in the public range. However, devices in the public range can't initiate contact with devices in the private range (hence the name *private*). Thus, if your network installs are pushed down to the client by the server, you must locate the server on your private range, because if it's located in the public range, it can't find the clients to push the software down to them. If you do put the key server in the private range and that server pushes files out to clients, it will be able to contact devices in both the private and public range.

Additionally, programs designed to allow the client to boot from the network and pull down the software must have different considerations. First, PXE boot servers should be placed on the same computer as the Windows 2000 DNS, Active Directory, and DHCP computer. Whichever package you end up with, the NetBoot or PXE computer, can be replicated across multiple servers at no additional cost, so multiple placements for the NetBoot server is a no-brainer. Since your workstations get their addresses locally, signing in to local Active Directory servers, we suggest placement in the private zones within each subnet. This allows you to have mirrored DNS in your AD environment, and it will localize the subnet's traffic related to network booting.

If your package has a console portion, make sure that the console is running on your private network so that it can reach everything in both ranges.

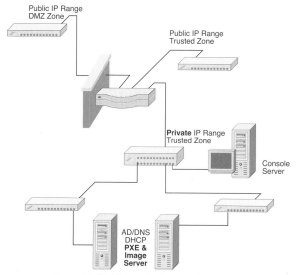

Figure 12-15. Placing the NetBoot/PXE Servers

By the way, this scenario also applies to the Apple OS X Server NetBoot environment.

 Now it's time to take a look at the tools and see how they operate in this environment. We'll check out the Apple NetBoot product first, because it's the simplest and only network-driven NetBoot and Disk imaging product. We'll then examine the Windows imaging and PXE products as a group, pointing out their similarities and differences.

NetBoot ⓧ

With this technology, Apple has included a powerful set of tools for managing Macs on the network in Mac OS X server. NetBoot is not directly visible as an application in OS X server; rather, it consists of a set of tools and server settings that provide server-based boot, install, and repair options for Macs. NetBoot enables Macs to boot from a server-based disk image instead of their internal hard drive. In a department or classroom setting, you can create a standard set of fonts, folders, and applications that are downloaded to each computer during the network booting process. In addition, you can set up a disk image that contains diagnostic tools to be used if a Mac can no longer boot from the internal hard drive.

Creating a NetBoot Image

To create a NetBoot image, you need the following: a Mac running Mac OS X Server on a network, the Network Image Utility application, the OS X installation CDs, and administrative rights on the server on which you're creating the boot image. If the Network Image Utility isn't installed, drag it from the admin tools CD into your applications folder on the OS X server.

In the NIU dialog, name the image and select Image Type NetBoot. Enter an ID for the image, which you can freely choose to facilitate image identification. To create an image that launches the Mac in a different language, choose your preferred language from the Default Language list. Enter the name and password of a default user on your network for this image.

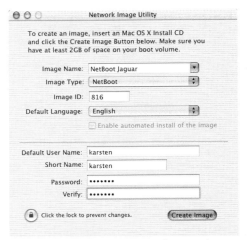

Figure 12-16. Creating a boot image using the Network Image Utility

After the disk image has been created, take a few more steps to make the image available to users on your network. Since the computers must have a TCP/IP address to find the server, set up your OS X server to work in conjunction with an existing DHCP server on the network (or it can serve as a DHCP server itself), or preassign spare static addresses. In the Image dialog, select the NetBoot and Net Install images that you want to make available for your users, and click the **Apply Now** button.

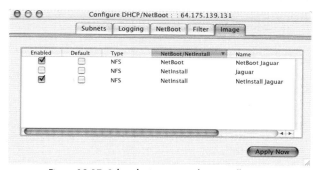

Figure 12-17. Select the NetBoot and NetInstall Images

NetBoot boots their Mac from the image while Network Install installs a fresh copy of OS X on the client machine. That's all there is to it for a Mac.

PXE in the Windows and Unix environments

 PXE support has been around for a long time (it was a part of the requirements for Windows 98). However, that doesn't mean that it's been employed by a lot of administrators. As a matter of record, not one of our hundreds of field editors actively worked with it as a part of their backup and disk imaging systems, and most were interested in learning more about it.

Pre-Boot eXecution Environment (PXE) is an industry standard–based system, relying on DHCP for doling out dynamic IP addresses and the TFTP (Trivial File Transfer Protocol) for moving necessary kernels of software from the PXE server to the netbooting computer. PXE uses the Dynamic Host Configuration Protocol (DHCP) following the PXE architecture for netbooting a client computer. When a PXE remote boot–enabled client computer starts, the client requests an Internet protocol (IP) address and the IP address of a PXE server by way of the DHCP protocol. The client computer receives an IP address, along with the IP address of the boot server that will service the client. The client is then passed the name of a boot image to request when contacting the boot server for initial service.

Unlike with the Macintosh computers, you must set up both a server component and a client component in order for PXE to work in the Windows world.

To image a workstation using Preboot Services, first determine if the workstation is PXE capable, and then make sure that PXE is enabled. PXE code is typically delivered with newer workstations (PC 99 compliant or later) on the NIC. PXE has been enabled on all Dell servers since 2002, and was installed on every Dell workstation we've bought in the last year or so.

 Ask your sales representative if your Intel-based computer or server is PXE compliant and then have that put in writing. Even though both Gateway and Dell stated that their devices have been compliant since 2001, some of the computers we've bought from them weren't.

As a matter of record, the Gateway server group saleswoman we spoke to didn't even know what PXE *was*, and had to go ask a technician, who then came back and told us that the box we had was compliant—even though it wasn't. We finally agreed to disagree, and now we get the last word, since we're writing the book. And guess what: The box I'm looking at is *not* PXE compliant.

Enabling PXE on a PXE-capable workstation

When PXE is enabled, it can prolong the boot process, so most NICs have PXE turned off by default. To enable PXE on a PXE-capable workstation, follow these steps:

First, enter the computer system BIOS and look at the Boot Sequence options. The PXE activation method for a workstation varies by manufacturer, but generally, one of the following methods is used:

- Some BIOSes have a separate entry in the BIOS configuration to enable or disable the PXE functionality. In this case, set the PXE Boot setting or the Network Boot setting to Enabled. The following picture is a bit fuzzy, but it shows the BIOS setup (hitting F1, F2, or Delete during the boot process) wherein I've tabbed down to the **Boot Sequence** and brought up the boot list.

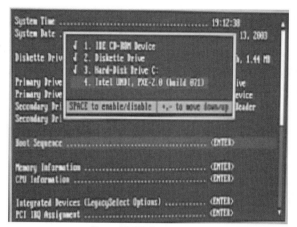

Figure 12-18. Boot sequence

At the bottom of the list you'll find the Intel NIC with built-in PXE. *Hint:* If your NIC card doesn't show up, *it* doesn't have built-in PXE. In that case, you'll need to create a netboot disk as described below. And since ours did show up, we've selected it to be a part of the boot sequence.

- Some BIOSes extend the entry that allows you to configure boot order. For example, you can specify that the system should try to boot from a diskette before trying to boot from the hard drive. The original order was to boot from CD, then floppy, followed by hard drive (and the NIC was disabled). The new order is to boot from the CD drive, hard drive, NIC for PXE, then the floppy. Always have the floppy first or last.

- If PXE isn't listed in the Boot Sequence options and if the NIC is embedded in the motherboard, enter the Integrated Devices section of the BIOS, which may have an option to enable PXE. PXE may be called by another name, such as MBA (Managed Boot Agent), or Pre-Boot Service.

Save any changes you have made and exit the system BIOS. Then reboot the workstation and you're all set.

If you don't have PXE enabled on your computer, you can find a network boot disk creation utility in many of the disk imaging products on the market today. This is the easiest way to get a network boot disk that's fully compatible with your imaging software. If you're feeling rather masochistic, you can create your own netboot disk by following the instructions we found at the AppDeploy.com website[6]. However, since there are some great tools on the market, we suggest that you use those.

Altiris Boot Disk Creator

Altiris Boot Disk Creator is a component of their Deployment Solution package. This tool provides a great interface for saving and editing your disks. However, to create the boot disk, you must supply a Windows 9x CD or a handful of files you can obtain from a Windows 9x computer.

PowerQuest DeployCenter

PowerQuest Boot Disk Builder is a component of their DeployCenter. I think this is the best of the three products we're reviewing here. It's a low-overhead MS-DOS alternative that provides support for auto-detection of multiple network cards. It also offers the greatest amount of free space for any customizations or additions you want to add as you go along).

Symantec Ghost Boot Wizard

Ghost Boot Wizard is a component of Ghost Corporate Edition. It doesn't provide support for supplying a password for automatic logon. To prevent you from using a second copy on another machine, Boot Wizard makes you specify a static computer name in the wizard.

Let's go through the process of creating a netboot disk using Ghost as our base model, covering differences in the other processes as we go. When you launch Ghost Boot Wizard, you can choose from five options to create a boot disk—though two of them are not actually "disks."

1. The first option creates a floppy disk that lets you boot into DOS and starts the Ghost restore routine with support for standard CD/DVD drives.

---

6. http://www.appdeploy.com/articles/bootfloppy1.shtml

2. Option two creates a boot disk that provides connectivity to a network drive containing your disk image on a secondary PC that is directly networked via an LPT, a USB, or a crossover cable. This is done so that you don't need to worry about assigning TCP/IP addresses, but is usable only on a very small scale.

3. Option three creates a boot disk that provides connectivity to a mapped drive containing your disk image on a PC on your network.

4. Better than a network-mapped drive is a PXE server that can handle multiple operations for booting, such as simply sending the boot files or running custom installation routines once the boot files have been set.

5. The last option allows you to actually install all the files needed for an emergency or maintenance boot onto the hard drive in an embedded partition or hidden partition. In case you're wondering, HP embeds XP Home into a hidden partition on the consumer computers it's been selling lately.

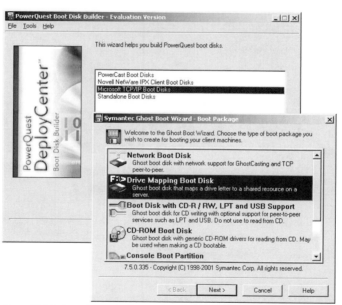

Figure 12-19. PowerQuest (background) and Ghost (foreground) boot disk options

The following table covers the five different boot disk installation options, noting the products that support those options.

Boot Disk Creation	Ghost CE	PowerQuest	Altiris
Boot & restore from CD/DVD	✔		
Boot & restore from mapped "no net" drive	✔		
Boot & restore from mapped "net" drive	✔	✔	✔
Boot & restore from PXE/multicast server	✔	✔	✔
Install Boot routine onto partition on drive		✔	✔

Table 12-3. Image creation

Next, choose the network card you're going to support on your computer. Power-Quest lets you select multiple cards, but Ghost and Altiris, limit you to one—although that "card" can be a multicard template (which means that you're actually selecting a wildcard). As usual, if your NIC isn't listed, in each of the packages, you may easily supply the driver to add it to the list, or, as in our case, select the multicard template.

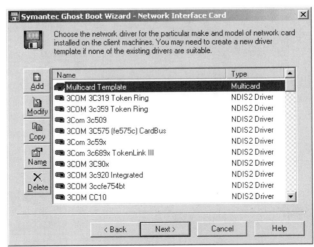

Figure 12-20. Adding network card drive interface

If you do choose the multicard driver, you can then select a group of drivers from the installed driver list. Multicard then examines which driver fits the actually installed NIC on your local computer.

Just because you're using a "multicard" or "universal card" driver doesn't mean that the software will support your card. As we were writing this, we bought a new computer from a manufacturer we kindly allow to remain anonymous. Instead of a standard Intel 100 Ethernet card, it came with a card that we had never even heard of. Nor had Ghost, PowerQuest, or Altiris Deployment Solution—none of the programs could boot with that card installed. When we went to the company's support website and entered our product ID, the card didn't even show up in the list. Five phone calls and two supervisors later (a total of three increasingly frustrating hours) they promised to send a NIC that they actually supported. After a week went by, a card showed up—sans any drivers, making it impossible to install. Another two phone calls and one more supervisor, who promised I'd have either a new card with drivers or at least drivers within a week. Today marked the end of the "week," and I haven't heard a thing.

The moral of this sad story is that you need to standardize on, and then *insist on* your NIC cards—and keep a few spares just in case some mega-company messes up and leaves you in the lurch.

If you opted for the network-mapped drive, you'll be prompted to add user name and password information to sign in and map the network drive. For some reason, the Ghost software didn't ask us for a domain password.

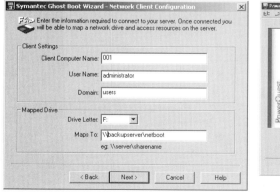
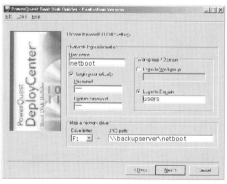

Figure 12-21. Network-mapped drive info for Symantec (left) and PowerQuest (right)

If you opted for the network boot drive (to work with a PXE/Multicast server) you must select the type of client software you want to include on the boot image. Some of the applications (such as Altiris' Deployment Solution) differentiate the types of files downloaded by their PXE server. You then must specify whether you're using a static IP address (not advised) or a dynamic IP address (that's the ticket). Altiris and PowerQuest asked if we wanted to connect to a Windows server versus a Novell NetWare server, and then even gave us the option of running IPX to communicate with the server.

Tell the software which drive letter in which to mount the floppy (I don't know why anyone would use anything other than *A*), and how many disks you want to create at once (think as many as you have computers here).

Network booting wasn't around in any of the last books we wrote, and I've got to tell you that it makes a heck of a significant difference in disaster recovery, making it much easier to recover troubled systems if those systems can boot over the network.

LARGER ORGANIZATIONS & NETWORK INSTALLS & IMAGING

 Okay, you've now got what it takes to create a network-bootable computer, which means that you have a computer that can find the network and determine where it should get its new software image. Guess what it's time to talk about? Yep, creating install images so that you can load your prefabricated installs onto your user's new hard drive; make that plural if your building gave up the ghost and you're re-installing groups of computers en masse.

Apple's Network Install ⓧ

Network Install gives you the means to create a server-based installation disk that can contain a new version of the OS, new applications, changed settings, or all of the above. If a Mac OS becomes corrupted, the user can boot the Mac from the network install image, which installs or updates the OS and reboots from the internal hard drive after the installation is finished. If you follow Apple Computer's directions, you'll create an image from CD, and the chances that the image won't have everything you're looking for are about 100 percent.

I created a NetInstall image using the CD, and once I had it loaded onto the target computer, I had about 113 MB worth of updates to perform on it! Ouch, that smarts! Nowhere in their manual do they tell you how to create a NetBoot or Net-Install image from an existing setup that you've already applied all of the patches to, but it can be done courtesy of Eric Zelenka and the great folks who write the tech docs for the AppleCare Knowledge Base[7]. We've put the whole detailed process on our www.backupbook.com website for you (it'd take too many pages here), so we'll just go over the basics now.

---

7.   This is adapted from AppleCare KnowledgeBase document keyword kmosxserver10.

Creating a network install image from an updated drive

First, create a partition or get a second drive to perform your clean installations. We suggest a second FireWire drive that you can have at the ready, or, if your internal drive is large enough, a partition will do.

Next, install your OS X software and follow the directions we set in *Setting up your computers for imaging* on page 381, so that your new image is completely updated and ready to go. Then restart the computer so that your new boot disk or partition is not the startup volume, but is accessible.

1. You'll need to open Disk Copy (it's in your Utilities directory within your Applications directory) and select **New > Image from Folder or Volume** from the **File** menu. Select your newly created boot partition or drive as the source of the image; then click the **Image** button and save the image somewhere other than the volume you're imaging.

Figure 12-22. Selecting the boot image

2. Once you've saved the disk image and the imaging process is completed, launch the Terminal application (it's also in your Utilities directory, in your Applications directory) and enter a few command-line strings to set up your install support files and descriptors. This must be done on the workstation and then on the server. While it might sound daunting, it's simple as pie.

3. In the OS X Server application, click the NetBoot tab to define if users should use NetBoot using a DHCP or a static IP-address, and then select the Net-Boot and NetInstall images that you want to make available for your users.

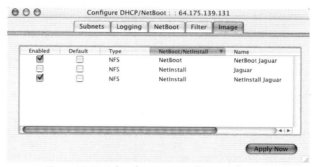

Figure 12-23. Select the NetBoot and NetInstall images

Now that both images, the NetBoot and the NetInstall, have been enabled, users can choose either of the two from the Startup Disk control panel. NetBoot boots their Mac from the image; NetInstall installs a fresh copy of OS X on the client machine.

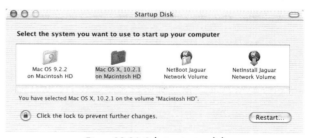

Figure 12-24. Select a startup disk

Package Creation   In addition to just creating an OS X installer disk image you can use two additional tools, PackageMaker and PropertyListEditor, to create application packages for distribution[8]. First, create the OS X installer image. Next, create a package of the application that you'd like to include. Now, mount the OS X image that you've

---

8.   To learn how to create packages, visit http://kbase.info.apple.com/cgi-bin/WebObjects/kbase.woa and enter "os x server" and package

created and open the file Packages.plist using the PropertyListEditor. Create a new package in the Package list under root and define it as Dictionary using the Class pop-up menu. Create a child labeled *packagename of type String* and enter the package name in the Value field. Create a second child labeled *required of type String* and type *Yes* in the value field. Repeat these steps for each package that you want to add. Save the updated property list and eject the image.

Altiris Deployment Solution, Norton Ghost CE, & PowerQuest DeployCenter

All three of these packages are tools for creating image files of partitions or hard disks as a way to clone networked computers, provide remote control for them, and even deploy software to them across the network. They differ, however, in their architecture and deployment on the network. The first three (I refer to them as "the big three") are somewhat the same in their deployment. VERITAS' system is more complex.

- Altiris Deployment Solution can run with the Deployment Server in stand-alone mode (with an integrated PXE server and imaging/cloning system) or as a part of the Altiris eXpress Notification Server Web interface environment that adds software delivery, help desk, inventory, and other solutions.

- Ghost CE runs on a server that controls the PCs on its network. The server tools allow client control, client installations, and the creation and distribution of disk images and software updates. The GhostCast Server is the central tool for imaging and cloning client operating systems and applications.

- Like the Altiris system, PowerQuest DeployCenter's console, ControlCenter ST, runs off a secure web server[9] in your company. ControlCenter lets you create or restore disk images of clients, reboot and shut down clients, run ImageCenter scripts, and deploy packages with software upgrades. Their system (ImageCenter, TaskBuilder, ImageExplorer, etc.), offers the same full gamut as the other two programs for creating, managing, and distributing images to computers across the network, as well as network management and control of those computers.

---

9.   DeployCenter uses IIS.

If you're wondering, while these programs might have started out as simple imaging products, they've become much more than that. The event wizard dialog from Altiris Deployment Solution says it all: They've become computer management *systems*, handling anything from simple computer imaging through mass-deployment computer migrations (moving, say, the Windows 98 My Documents folder to the Documents and Settings folder in 2000 and XP). These are very powerful applications. As you'll see in another section, they also have client backup capabilities that I've come to believe in fervently.

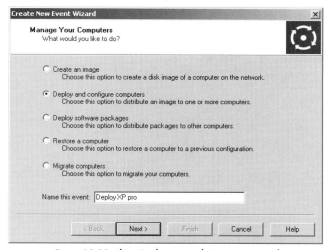

Figure 12-25. Altiris Deployment Solution event wizard

Managed workstation setup

Once you've installed your basic console and deployment server configurations for your imaging servers, it's time to set up your workstations: Your clients must have software installed on their computers for the imaging software to be able to manage them.

 When you're dealing with disk imaging, you're dealing with a concept of **managed computers**: taking either a point-in-time snapshot of either a "universal, virtual" computer (the **universal state**) that is pristine in its installation, applications, and preferences—or an ongoing snapshot process of individual computers (the **individual state**). Either way, your goal is to quickly and easily restore a single workstation or groups of workstations to either the **universal** or **individual** state they were in before disaster struck. Therefore, you must begin with some type of management and some business decision about which state your organization is willing to maintain and then restore.

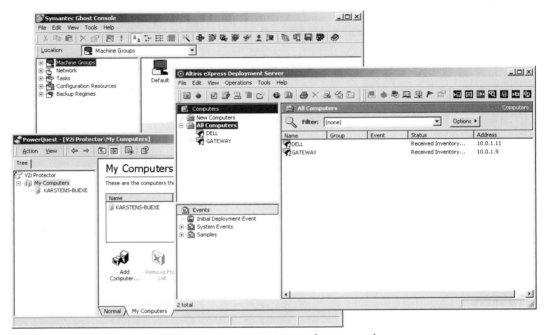

Figure 12-26. Deployment consoles

Starting from top and going around clockwise in the above diagram, we show the Symantec Ghost, Altiris eXpress, and PowerQuest interfaces for adding computers and then dragging and dropping them into groups—all pretty similar.

Defining your state groups In each imaging application's consoles, you'll find an area wherein you define the groups that your computers will fall into. In Table 12-2. on page 380, we covered the different groups of images that our sample company needed (Windows 2000 Pro, XP Pro, and Windows 2000 Server). That's one way to group your computers: by operating system. You can also group your computers by operating system plus the applications that you'll be installing on top of the operating system—just select whichever method works best for your needs.

Finding your computers
Each of the packages we tested uses the Active Directory domain system to find computers on your network and then add them to the list of available computers to manage. Using domain rules and privileges for installation across the network, your imaging console installs an application for remote control, allowing remote booting of the workstation into a proprietary disk imaging partition for loading a disk image or installing new software.

If necessary, you can expand the view of all of the active domains on your network (such as the top dialog found in Ghost) or work within a single domain (such as the bottom dialog using Altiris eXpress). When you've found the computers you're looking for, you must authenticate yourself as a user with administrative rights in your domain or workgroup to install the software.

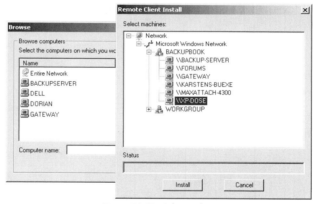

Figure 12-27. Select a client

Getting rid of the Security IDs (SIDs)
In Windows NT, 2000, and XP, a **SID** (**Security ID**) is a unique name assigned to each user and each workgroup. The NTFS file system requires certain security measures that may interfere with cloning. Windows 2000 runs most effectively on NTFS, and Microsoft doesn't want to compromise security any more than they do with the inadvertent bugs in their updates. Thus, the OS creates security identifiers (SIDs) during installation. Each workstation and user account on the network has its own SID. Every interaction with system security, which includes all disk activity on an NTFS system, requires these SIDs. The problem with cloning Windows 2000 systems (and Win NT systems) is the possibility of duplicating the SIDs themselves. If the SID is copied along with the drive image, two systems could have identical SIDs and the same permissions for network resources. This problem occurs primarily on networks configured as NT/2000 workgroups—not

those set up on a domain through a Windows 2000 Server platform—because the domain software controls the SIDs for the workstations and their users. Each time a user logs onto a domain, the domain server issues a unique SID to prevent any duplications.

Among the most beneficial of each of these products' features is the Multicast or PXE Server, which allows the simultaneous replication of a single disk image to multiple remote systems. An image file is typically an exact duplicate of a disk or partition, so the imaging application must include a SID generator or modifier for Windows NT, 2000, and XP systems. Typically, the imaging console's interface provides its own SID generator (as with Altiris SIDgen) or also allows Microsoft's Sysprep to be used for this purpose.

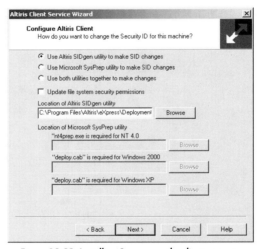

Figure 12-28. Installing Sysprep on the client computer

Imaging—the easy part

To image a computer, you must first shut it down and reboot it into whichever application's boot process you've loaded. Unlike Mac OS X computers, Windows computers can't be booted while they're live. The imaging process is considered a task, and depending on the application you're using, is called a **task** or a **scripted event**—even though it can also be done manually. You'll know it's running when the computer being imaged restarts into a fairly ugly-looking front end during the imaging process.

Adding additional applications

Adding individual files by copying or moving is one thing; adding entire applications is another animal entirely. Why? Application installations tend to put files *all over the place*—sometimes in hidey-holes where you'd never think to look.

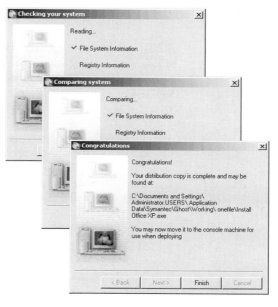

Figure 12-29. Ghost's Application Install builder process

Since our imaging "big three" are all adept at tracking, imaging, and managing a hard drive's every nuance, they can easily create a scripted methodology for examining a hard drive before an application is installed, and then re-examine it afterward—using that information to create an installation script for the application. Depending on the package, this is called an AI package, a RapidInstall package, or something else of that ilk. But, as The Bard told us, whatever you call it, a rose still smells as sweet, and here, the basic tenet also remains the same: You take a before-and-after picture of the computer and use the difference to create the install package. If you plan to use your imaging software to install software packages on the network, here are a few hints:

- Disable any programs running in the background, as they may be writing updated log files or other miscellaneous events that you don't want installed as a part of the new software package.

- If the installation process requires a restart, disable any programs that execute during the shutdown or restart process before you run the installation.

- Restrict the disks or partitions monitored by the installation manager program so that you don't track any errant information (such as a mapped network volume to which someone might be adding data).

VERITAS BARE METAL RESTORE (BMR) ⊞ 🐧

This one's completely different from anything else we've covered, so we're giving it its own mini-section. VERITAS BMR is a disaster recovery solution for UNIX and Windows servers designed for larger organizations and data centers. Combining several different technologies, it consists of four server application packages that can be run on one to multiple servers:

1. The BMR Main Server provides a management console for managing the clients, the other BMR servers, and the restoration process.

2. The Boot Server provides boot images for the UNIX clients—Windows clients must be booted from a floppy disk or CD.

3. The File Server holds all files that are necessary for the restore operation—**Shared Resource Trees (SRT)**, in VERITAS' parlance[10].

4. The NetBackup server runs NetBackup Professional to back up the clients and restore them when needed. If you already use NetBackup Professional, you can integrate BMR with it.

BMR enables fast, unattended restoration of a huge number of servers by combining several backup strategies into one product: Creating and providing SRTs is comparable to creating a disk image; providing a boot image is similar to the Net-Boot process; and finally, NetBackup is the VERITAS backup software package you use when running your regular backups—including the system state[11]. All these technologies run together in a certain order to restore a server when the system administrator issues that command.

---

[10]. SRTs are shared directories on the File Server(s) that contain a compilation of baseline system resources and tools for formatting drives and rebuilding the file system, as well as the NetBackup client software.

[11]. **System state** describes the machine's hardware and software configuration. Backing up the system state ensures that the machine can be exactly restored to its original configuration.

BMR recovery scenario

If a client restore is necessary, you need to prepare the client data for restoration using the Prepare to Restore function.

Make sure that the file server is available via NFS or SMB and open the Configure Client dialog on the BMR Main Server because the file server contains the SRT. From the list of available clients, select the client that you want to restore by clicking on its name. In the next dialog, select restoration of either the system disk alone or all disks. If applicable, enter the IP addresses of the main, file, and boot server. As opposed to a Unix client, on a Windows client, you must also provide the client host name and the network interface configuration. The BMR server creates a customized client-boot procedure and makes the SRT and the boot image available to that client.

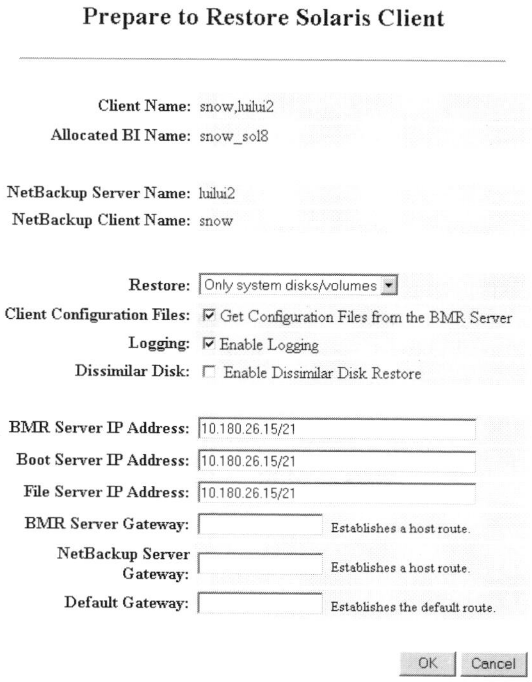

Prepare to Restore Solaris Client

Client Name: snow,luilui2
Allocated BI Name: snow_sol8

NetBackup Server Name: luilui2
NetBackup Client Name: snow

Restore: `Only system disks/volumes ▾`
Client Configuration Files: ☑ Get Configuration Files from the BMR Server
Logging: ☑ Enable Logging
Dissimilar Disk: ☐ Enable Dissimilar Disk Restore

BMR Server IP Address: `10.180.26.15/21`
Boot Server IP Address: `10.180.26.15/21`
File Server IP Address: `10.180.26.15/21`
BMR Server Gateway: `_____` Establishes a host route.
NetBackup Server Gateway: `_____` Establishes a host route.
Default Gateway: `_____` Establishes the default route.

`OK` `Cancel`

Figure 12-30. Preparing to restore the Solaris client

Restoring a Unix client using network boot

If you use a boot server on your network, you can boot Unix clients directly from the BMR Main Server over the network by providing the client with the boot server information upon restart. When the client starts up, use the necessary switches to boot it into bootp mode[12]. On request, enter the host name and IP address of the local machine, the gateway, the netmask, and the bootp server. The client now starts from the boot server, and you'll be prompted for the BMR server's IP address and port number. The automatic restore procedure starts:

- The client mounts its SRT file system from the file server and starts the core operating system.

- The client configures its disks, volume groups, and file system according to the metadata provided by the BMR Main Server.

- The client starts the NetBackup client and retrieves the complete backup from the NetBackup server.

- The client configures its boot record and configuration database.

- The client reboots itself.

- The client performs any necessary post-boot cleanup including deallocation of the BMR resources.

The scenario for a media boot, which applies mainly to Windows clients, is only slightly different in respect to booting the machine. When you boot a client from bootable media, BMR prompts you for the server's IP address and the BMR server port number. From there, the client takes the same steps.

Recovery of the rest of the information on each particular computer is accomplished through the standard process using VERITAS NetBackup Professional.

---

12. On AIX: When the LED displays 200, change the key position to *service* and press the **Reset** button. On Solaris: Terminate the boot process by pressing the Stop + A keys. At the prompt, type *N* and hit the Return key. On HP-UX: Press any key during startup to interrupt the start process, enter the command **boot** and hit the Return key.

PERSONALITY MIGRATION AS A PART OF IMAGING

 I thought that I'd throw this in at the end of the chapter for those occasions when your computer dies and you need to migrate the information on that computer to a wholly new computer. Instead of replacing the hard drive with a bigger one, you replace the whole computer. And if your computers don't die very often, you probably won't buy the same computer—mainly because the company probably isn't making them anymore.

To top it off, your new computer probably has a new (or upgraded) operating system, new cards, and new drivers for those cards. So instead of trying to force-feed your old computer's imaged operating system down your new computer's unwilling throat, you have another choice: Migrate certain aspects of the old computer to the new computer on top of the operating system and drivers that already exist on it.

This "personality transplant" package is also used in conjunction with imaging software for a full-fledged workstation-to–hard drive backup solution. This is done for reasons of speed, simplicity, and usability.

• The hard drive is imaged and stored on the server using an imaging system.

• Or the computer is backed up to some other source.

• The personality capture product is then layered on top of the imaging system or backup to collect and separate user-specific settings for applications, as well as user data located on the client computer.

• The computer's user-specific data (its "personality") can then be restored separately from the operating system data.

This appeals to us because of the nature of the separation between the capture of the computer's personality information and the capture of the operating system—straight backups simply can't separate the two. Trying to restore personality information from tape by weeding out each file is just plain nuts. Backups are great for restoring just about everything to the same type of computer with the same type of operating system—but restoring personality information is downright painful, if not impossible.

When migrating one computer to another or just plain old capturing the computer's personality, keep an eye out for these three areas:

• Desktop files (keyboard and mouse settings, etc.);

• Network information (TCP/IP address, DNS, printers); and

• Applications (associated files and settings).

Of these, desktop files and application specifications are the most important. Below are two screenshots from Altiris PC Transplant Pro that show both the desktop and the application settings that can be gathered.

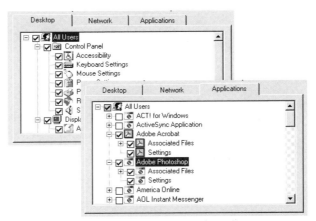

Figure 12-31. PC Transplant Pro from Altiris

The basic concept here? Create templates (based upon your corporate applications policies) for your user's types (however you organize your computers and your staff), and then apply those templates to the gathering and later re-dissemination of the files and settings within the template's purview back onto the computer that died or the user's new computer.

What steps does this type of automation replace? Tedious steps, that's what. Remember our little bit about borscht, and installing a bland version of the operating system and applications on all computers? Well, not everyone likes bland old borscht. Some folks like to put Crazy Jack's Hot as Hell pepper sauce in it for that eye-watering élan. And since we all have our own tastes (chaque a son gout!), you can expect folks to do the same thing with their computers. This person adds this desktop pattern; that one adds another. This one adds these hot-key combinations; that one adds little applets for calendaring. This process of salting a computer to taste wastes anywhere from one and a half to five and a half hours of each person's time. Multiply that by the number of folks in your office and you can quickly see the value of imaging and then replacing a computer's personality settings.

In the diagram above (Figure 12-31. on page 422) we show both the desktop and application settings within the PC Transplant Pro template, moving over certain files and their file types.

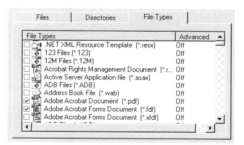

Figure 12-32. File types selected for moving

As you might suspect by this point in the book, we're big on policy here. And one of the elements of policy is that you just might want to set your transplant migration strategy to move certain file types to certain server folders, if the users haven't been doing that on their own. Policy pays.

 The best tools I've found so far for this application are PC Transplant Pro from Altiris and Personality Tranxport Professional from Tranxition. PC Transplant Pro can be purchased separately or as part of their Deployment Solution disk imaging tool. PC Transplant Pro is a stand-alone product that can be integrated into Norton Ghost; it also comes as an option with Connected TLM, an Internet backup solution.

Personality Tranxition Professional (PT Pro) ⊞ by Tranxition

PT Pro captures computer personality when migrating to a new computer or an existing one whose software environment is being updated. Other use cases include its utilization as part of regular backup routine because it preserves the user's operating system and application settings along with associated application data. PT Pro extracts user-specific settings from applications such as Microsoft Office, Lotus Notes, Internet Explorer, and many others, as well as all user data, wherever it may hide on the source computer. PT Pro then injects those settings and data into the target system, so that all data is copied over and all application settings are preserved, even if the target system has a newer version of Windows and/or the supported applications.

An engineering division of a very large manufacturing firm uses PT Pro as a regularly scheduled backup weekly task for disaster recovery (we're going to cover more of that later). The engineers constantly test their own products on their computers, requiring frequent system restores. After the computer is reimaged, user data and settings are restored with PT Pro.

PT Pro technology is also an option available with the Internet-based backup product Connected TLM (again, more on this later). Connected integrated the PT Pro migration engine into TLM, their backup product, to accommodate customers who want to preserve the user state for disaster recovery or for migration to new systems.

PC Transplant Pro 🪟 by Altiris

PC Transplant Pro can be used as a stand-alone product, integrated with Ghost and other imaging products, or used as a part of the Altiris Deployment Solution that integrates it with its own disk imaging system.

Since we've already covered PC Transplant Pro's features in this section, the best thing I can add is a story from DaimlerChrysler (one of my past ad agency's accounts). The DaimlerChrysler global field and technology team maintains and supports nearly 1,500 computers nationwide, more than 90 percent of which are mobile notebooks. When the company scheduled a deployment of new computers to every user in the U.S. during the first quarter of 2002, they had no existing solution that would transfer users' data and settings to a new Windows platform. The new computers were preloaded with Windows 2000 and many proprietary applications, and users couldn't afford to go without their computers and more importantly their data, so finding a suitable process to transfer existing Windows 95 data to the new operating system was quite a challenge.

For this purpose, DaimlerChrysler used PC Transplant Pro as a stand-alone application. Because most of the end users work remotely and never log into a server, the process couldn't be accomplished through a server deployment, so a PC Transplant Pro template that runs in their unique environment was developed. Individual notebooks received an auto-run CD, which automatically started PC Transplant Pro, running the specific template script. The files were then burned to a CD-RW drive and installed on the new notebook running Windows 2000. The data transplant ran without a hitch—with excellent results, and no additional training or downtime.

Chapter Appendix

Imaging capabilities

Table 12-4. outlines the imaging capabilities of each of the applications reviewed.

Image creation	Backup Now!	Bare Metal Restore	Clone 'X	Ghost	Ghost CE	Instant Recovery	NetBoot	Retrospect	PowerQuest	Altiris
Image whole partition	✔	✔		✔	✔	✔	✔	✔	✔	✔
Image operating system only			✔							
Image applications only			✔							
Create deployable packages					✔				✔	✔

Table 12-4. Image creation

Where your imaging application stores your disk images is just as important as the feature set included in imaging. For the future of imaging, look toward the Multicast PXE server implementations.

Image storage	Backup Now!	Bare Metal Restore	Clone 'X	Ghost	Ghost CE	Instant Recovery	NetBoot	Retrospect	PowerQuest	Altiris
CD/DVD	✔	✔	✔	✔		✔		✔		
File		✔	✔		✔			✔	✔	✔
Mapped Drive		✔	✔		✔			✔	✔	✔
Multicast PXE Server		✔			✔		✔		✔	✔

Table 12-5. Image storage

Table 12-6. on page 427 outlines the operating systems supported by the major imaging packages. By the time this book is ready for a new edition, I suspect that all of the packages will support the Mac OS X operating system, as it's growing in popularity and is no harder to support than any of the Linux operating systems.

Operating systems supported	Backup Now!	Bare Metal Restore	Clone 'X	Ghost	Ghost CE	Instant Recovery	NetBoot	Retrospect	PowerQuest	Altiris
Windows Server	✔	✔		✔	✔	✔		✔	✔	✔
Windows workstations	✔			✔	✔	✔		✔		✔
Mac OS X			✔				✔			
Linux						✔				✔
Unix (AIX, Solaris, etc.)		✔								

Table 12-6. Operating systems supported

Reading material

Macintosh NetBoot

http://www.macosxlabs.org/

PXE products

http://www.altiris.com/products/index.asp

http://www.Symantec.com/sabu/ghost/ghost_enterprise

http://www.bootmanage.de/us/index.shtml

Extending PXE to mobile platforms

http://developer.intel.com/update/archive/issue10/stories/top5.htm

PXE white papers

http://www.Microsoft.com/windows2000/techinfo/planning/management/remoteos.asp

Windows XP activation

http://www.microsoft.com/windowsxp/pro/techinfo/deployment/activation/default.asp. Deploying Windows XP using Windows Product Activation. (Nov. 2001)

http://www.microsoft.com/windowsxp/pro/evaluation/overviews/activation.asp. Windows XP Product Activation. Microsoft Corporation (June 2001)

http://www.microsoft.com/piracy/basics/activation/mpafaq.asp. Microsoft Product Activation: Frequently Asked Questions. Microsoft Corporation (Feb. 2003)

http://www.microsoft.com/technet/treeview/default.asp?url=/technet/prodtechnol/winxppro/evaluate/xpactiv.asp. Technical Details on Microsoft Product Activation for Windows XP. Microsoft Corporation (Jan. 2003)

CHAPTER 13:
HARDWARE LOSS

Hardware loss is due to only a few factors: The first is product death. Computer products die very early, or they have a long life, dying out as they age; there's no middle ground. The second cause of hardware loss is theft, and the third is building loss, causing loss of the equipment inside. We'll deal with the first two reasons in this chapter, and move on to building disasters in Chapter 14: *Replication* on page 497.

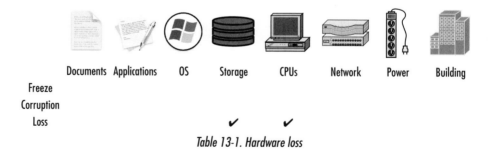

	Documents	Applications	OS	Storage	CPUs	Network	Power	Building
Freeze								
Corruption								
Loss				✔	✔			

Table 13-1. Hardware loss

In this chapter, you'll learn to plan your system for the event of failure, because failure *will* happen, and the only way to stop it from affecting your business is to build fault tolerance and redundancy through mirroring into your systems.

Fault tolerance begins with RAID

Ever wonder why you have a spare tire in your car? Probably not. But why not put a spare starter coil in there, or a spare distributor cap? Because they aren't as prone to wear out, that's why. Car makers know that to keep cars running they have to have an extra key ingredient—a spare tire. The first thing to "go" on a computer is the hard drive. You build redundancy into your hard drives by adding a **Redundant Array of Inexpensive Devices (RAID)** system that copies your data across multiple drives as it's being written.

And racecar owners know that they go to the race with at least two cars. If one car dies during qualification, they can turn to a second car. In case your computer dies (and not the hard drive), you too can have a spare handy. Building redundancy into your computers is accomplished through **clustering**, whereby you build two (or more) twin computers conjoined via a network heartbeat cable that monitors each device's health.

Fault tolerance can also be accomplished through replicating the data to a different computer reconfigured to take over for the primary, if necessary. We cover RAID and clustering in this chapter. We aren't going to tell you what combination of RAID, clustering, and replication you should be building for your system—the extra drives and spare server parts or preconfigured servers you'll need to have at the ready are really up to you. We'll give you some guidelines based on how we've seen it done, and you can take it from there.

One small definition before we begin: JBOD

You will see the term *JBOD* in this section used repeatedly. A **JBOD** is group of hard disks in a computer that aren't set up as any type of RAID configuration—they're just a bunch of disks. If your computer comes with two hard drives in it, and you haven't set up any RAID software, you have a two-drive JBOD configuration. JBOD has also come to be the term for the external enclosures that you put your hard drives in. The biggest difference between a JBOD enclosure and a RAID enclosure is that the RAID enclosure has a RAID hardware card built into it. If you want to set up a RAID array from the JBOD drives in your JBOD enclosure, you need to connect the enclosure to either RAID software or hardware running on the computer. We use *JBOD* to refer to either the drives *or* enclosures.

THE MAIN THING

The Main Thing to understand is that *failure will happen*. This isn't my 1970 Valiant (closing in on 223,000 miles on that magnificent slant-6 engine)—this is a server and hard drive. You need to plan for the inevitable: When drives turn up their toes, you must negotiate the warranty situation and design plans for spare drives.

How you configure your RAID system depends upon your business continuity needs. The systems we discuss in this section can run as little as $5,000 and as much as $50,000—so make sure you build something that makes good *business sense*.

Servers also go belly-up. You have four basic choices here, and all should be based upon your budget and needs:

1. Build a basic RAIDed server and back it up regularly. If any single component fails, obtain another component and restore the server if necessary. Hope like all heck that the building doesn't fall down.

2. Standardize your server types and build in extra RAIDed storage capacity and RAM so that if one server dies, another can temporarily do double-duty because you can restore the downed server's data to a secondary server's extra storage space.

3. Build a clustered server that gives you redundancy of RAIDed drives and the main server. This is a very failure-resistant system, and more costly and complex to back up and restore. Hope like heck the building doesn't fall down on top of this one, too.

4. Build a RAIDed server. Then build another mirror of the server, placing it off-site and a safe location. Replicate the data from the primary to the secondary server in case of server failure and building failure. Make sure that the pipes to the replicated offsite server are large enough so that if the primary goes down, users can continue working from the offsite server, if necessary.

Special thanks...

Connie Chronis of VERITAS, for getting me all of the information (and in front of all of the engineers) for my gazillion questions.

Matt Munger at StorCase, for all the custom product shots of the InfoStation. What a great box that is!

Mike Hall and Thuy Lowe from Adaptec, for answering my questions and helping me out with the RAID card section.

And special thanks to the folks at Dell, from Joe Marengi through Traci Reardon, Rhonda Gass, and Dixie Groll, who helped me out with obtaining hardware shots, computer information, etc.

UNDERSTANDING YOUR DRIVES FROM A BUSINESS CONTINUITY PERSPECTIVE

I'm not going to spend any time in this short topic area talking about drive performance issues such as spin speed, access speed, etc. Why? Because server admins care about all of that *right up to the point of failure*—and then they start caring about the business issues because the device's downtime is causing the company money and the CFO has become interested (in a bad way), as well. If you tried to talk to your CFO about the purchase of a drive that has a gazillion RPM rate resulting in the highest data access times, he'll yawn or slurp his espresso. You should, however, talk about warranty service and give your accounting folks the right capitalization and depreciation information.

Also, you'll want to *not* talk about the Mean Time Between Failure (MTBF) rate of your drives with anyone in accounting or finance in the organization, because more than likely they'll eat you for lunch. Why? CFOs have learned to investigate a device's warranty length and stated service life (as opposed to MTBF) as a much more analytic way of determining what the manufacturer *really* thinks of the drive. Drives, like most devices with moving parts, follow the "bathtub curve" lifespan model[1]: If they don't die very early, they follow a normal lifetime and then slowly wear out.

The normal service life of a hard drive is around three to five years, with SCSI drives usually outlasting EIDE/ATA drives. The service life is stated as five years, but the warranty life is around three years. What this should *scream* to you is that the manufacturer only *believes* the drive will last three years and isn't willing to *bet* that it will last the full five.

---

[1]. There's a great online reference to bathtub curves at http://www.itl.nist.gov/div898/handbook/apr/section1/apr124.htm, that states, "If enough units from a given population are observed operating and failing over time, it is relatively easy to compute week-by-week (or month-by-month) estimates of the failure rate $h(t)$. For example, if N_{12} units survive to start the 13th month of life and r_{13} of them fail during the next month (or 720 hours) of life, a simple empirical estimate of $h(t)$ averaged across the 13th month of life (or between 8640 hours and 9360 hours of age), is given by (r_{13} / $N_{12} * 720$)."

Your business responsibility for warranty repair

So what happens when it breaks? Here's the kicker: What many network administrators have in their hands is a drive component built by one manufacturer (like Western Digital), OEMed to another (like APS, LaCie, etc.) and sold to you by a third—your retailer or consultant. *Who* is responsible for repairing/replacing this drive according to the warranty, *what* are they going to be replacing it with, and *how* are they going to be replacing it?

I could cover about a gazillion opinions about who should *really* be responsible for warranty work, but it all comes down to the relationship between you and the place where you bought the drive. The *who* obviously isn't going to be the company you made the purchase from—even if that's where the buck will be spent again (through your future business) and therefore *should* be where the buck stops. The simple truth is, that's not how it works[2]. Let's look at three hard drives below (Table 13-2.): Seagate, Western Digital, and LaCie. Both the Seagate and Western Digital are made by their respective companies. LaCie doesn't make hard drives; rather, it incorporates OEM drive components from companies such as Maxtor or Seagate.

Product	Warranty	Manufacturer
Seagate Technology 40GB U Series 6 EIDE Ultra ATA 100 Hard Drive	3 Year	Seagate
Western Digital 40.0GB WD Caviar Ultra ATA 100 Hard Drive	3 Year	Western Digital
LaCie, Ltd. 40GB External FireWire Hard Drive	1 Year	OEM

Table 13-2. An example of three drives and their warranty repair

To get the down-and-dirty, I collared a sales rep who's sold us quite a bit of equipment and asked her how warranty work would be handled. Enjoy our verbatim exchange:

Dorian: If I buy a drive through you guys that has an *X*-year warranty, and the drive fails within that *X*-year period, how will replacement/repair be handled, and in what time-frame?

---

2. I have 28 pages of discussions on one of the hard drive bulletin boards on my desk regarding a single issue of how folks had to resolve a "double beeping" problem with a drive that wouldn't wake from Energy Saver Sleep mode. Some went to the retailer, some to the company that made the hardware the drive came in, and others had to go directly to the drive manufacturer itself. Ouch.

Value-added reseller: For defective products, if it's within 30 days of the purchase, it can be returned to us. After that period, you need to go through the manufacturer's warranty, whose policies may vary.

Basically, she's saying that if the drive dies in the infant period, we can go back to her, the reseller, and it will be replaced. However, from the 31st day to the end of the warranty (only one year, on the LaCie drive) we're on our own with the manufacturer.

The *what* part comes down to this: Almost nobody *repairs* drives when they break. It just isn't cost effective.—instead, they *replace* them. That means that you either get a new drive or a refurbished drive. How can you tell the difference? If you don't have the software to read the drive's "odometer," you can't—tell the difference, that is. Some manufacturers and retailers will tell you whether or not you're getting a refurbished drive; others keep their lips zipped. A special type of software— SMART[3]—can tell you a lot about your drive, and we cover it in detail in *SMART precludes DUMB...* on page 112. David Lethe of SANtools said this about garnering information about a drive's odometer:

> The hours are available on most SCSI & Fibre Channel disk drives, under vendor-specific log pages. You can find out such things as the date the disk was manufactured (either as a typical date, or a year, week number). Pretty much all models of Seagate drives, and maybe half of the IBM disks report them. As the total hours powered on is a vendor-specific thing and not an ANSI-defined feature, you won't get it on all disks.

> Obviously, it's a pretty useful feature, especially for people who *think* they're purchasing new disk drives. I put that feature in there specifically after my sister got burned buying a disk drive through mail order. It looked used; it had a few thousand hours on it.

> When a drive is refurbished from the factory, they reset the log pages, so the total numbers of hours is reset to zero. This really doesn't bother me, because if a drive is really refurbished by IBM or Seagate, for example, they really replace electronics and anything that would typically wear down during the new warranty period. What one has to avoid is buying a "refurbished" or "new" disk drive from a gray marketer. To many of those guys, *refurbished*

---

3. SMART (Self Monitoring And Reporting Technology) is an open standard for developing disk drives and software that monitor a drive's health and reports potential problems. It can also be used to tell you *much* more about the drive than most resellers know about it.

means they do nothing more than take a good cleaner to the outside of the case to make it look pretty.

Of course, not all gray marketers are this sleazy, but I advise you to get the serial number of the drive they're going to ship you, then check with the manufacturer to verify warranty. For Seagate & IBM, this can be done online, or via a phone call.

You should also know that some but not all OEM versions of these drives either have no warranty through the manufacturer, or it's degraded. As an example, eMachines buy Seagate disk drives for a very high discount. Part of this cost savings to eMachines is that they have to handle the warranty directly: Seagate won't fix, repair or replace the drive. You have to go through Seagate. When my father-in-law's disk failed, I contacted eMachines, and they said they would replace the drive for free—but I had to send them the whole computer, with the drive in it. I pay shipping out, they pay shipping back. It would take a few weeks, and they'd load a fresh copy of the O/S on that disk (but not attempt any data recovery, of course).

They told me they weren't set up to just swap out a disk drive. Even though I asked a supervisor, I had no luck. I don't know if this policy persists, but it was easier for me to just buy another disk for $100 and throw the old one away.

I don't blame eMachines or Seagate for this. You get what you pay for.

We get lots of e-mail from Seagate/IBM drive users who bought systems with Seagate or IBM disks in them, and the vast majority are no-direct-warranty serial-numbers.

While some folks don't want a refurbished drive, think of this: If they fixed your drive instead of giving you a new one, it, too, would be refurbished. The great news about the fact that drives are replaced? If your drive dies at the end of its life-cycle (and before the warranty is out), you'll probably get a better/larger/faster drive as a replacement. Why? Because companies that shipped 10 GB standard drives three years ago are now shipping 40 GB standard drives.

Now we come down to *how* to get your newly refurbished or newly new drive swapped out with the corpse you have on your hands. There are two basic methods: First, through the standard system, whereby you ship them the drive and they ship you a new one. Unfortunately, they have to *get* the drive from you before they send you a new one—read at least one week here. The second method is what I call the "mid-air" drive swap. While you send them your drive, they send you a new drive. This is usually accomplished over a two-day time period, expedited by urgent phone calls rife with debate. So in the best-case scenario, your post-mortem downtime is at least one work day and could extend up to one week. Let's return to that discussion with our VAR:

Dorian: How is repair or replacement handled?

VAR: Seagate and Western are both three years parts/labor and have advanced Depot Repair. Assuming the product is in stock, they could probably get you a replacement overnight.

With advanced Depot Repair, they wouldn't need to have the dead one first before [they] sent a new one out to you.—that's what Advanced or Express Depot Replacement/Repair means. We do the same thing. If something is deemed dead or defective within 30 days, we'll overnight you a replacement immediately if necessary.

For LaCie, I went directly to the source. They replied:

LaCie: We'd issue a warranty repair number. You're responsible for freight in to us. We normally get repairs turned around in one business day and we pay economy Federal Express back to you. Data is not covered under warranty. You're responsible for getting the data off of the drive if needed.

Such is the case for drives themselves. As David Lethe told us, some manufacturers, like eMachines, demand the entire computer if there's a problem with the drive. Apple Computer has the same policy: When I had problems with my desktop unit, they wouldn't accept the fact that I could take the drive out on my own—I had to ship the whole darn computer back to them so that they could replace the drive and get it back to me. In total, I was out that computer for about a week.

Your business continuity responsibility with regard to computers

As it is for drives, so it is for computers—basically.

Dell's warranty & replacement policy

The information below was taken directly from Dell's website[4]. I've chopped it into pieces to point out a few things.

> During the [90-day, or 1-4 year] period beginning on the invoice date, Dell will repair or replace products covered under this limited warranty that are returned to Dell's facility.

In other words, you have to send the parts back to Dell. That means that you'e out of pocket for the server while it's being fixed.

> To request limited warranty service, you must contact Dell's Customer Technical Support within the limited warranty period. Refer to the chapter titled "Getting Help" or "Contacting Dell" in your documentation to find the appropriate telephone number for obtaining customer assistance. If limited warranty service is required, Dell will issue a Return Material Authorization Number.

This means that you'll be calling them to say it's dead—and they'll ask you to check if it's dead. And while you play a game of solitaire on your laptop (because you can plainly *see* the device is dead), they go through a diagnostic, and, a couple of hours later, give you an RMA.

> You must ship the products back to Dell in their original or equivalent packaging, prepay shipping charges, and insure the shipment or accept the risk of loss or damage during shipment. Dell will ship the repaired or replacement products to you freight prepaid if you use an address in the continental United States, where applicable. Shipments to other locations will be made freight collect.

The warranty says *freight* shipping. A quick check of FedEx's ground shipping time estimator[5] shows that it takes four days to get from zip code (78682) in Austin, Texas, to my zip code (94402) in San Mateo, California. That means, at a minimum, you are out of pocket about a week for a downed server.

Can *you* afford to have your server out of commission for a week? I could. In fact, I can think of nothing more delightful than to ignore e-mail for a week, letting it all pile up in drifts at the mail exchanger over at Postini. My blood pressure would plummet, my house plants would thrive, and I'd even get a lot of writing done. However, don't count me as a part of reality.

---

4. http://www.dell.com/us/en/dhs/misc/policy_010_policy.htm#total_sat

5. http://grd.fedex.com/cgi-bin/rtt2010.exe?func=entry

PROTECTION AGAINST DRIVE LOSS = RAID

You can't stop drive corruption or loss. Unless, of course, you don't turn your drives on in the first place. But they might not be all that useful that way, would they? The easiest way to ensure a basic level of business continuity when one of your drives fails is to have the dead drive's data saved on *another* drive that you can quickly make "live." You do this by setting up a system of RAID drives.

RAID (Redundant Array of Inexpensive Disks[6]**)** is a method of combining several hard drives into one logical unit to provide speed (RAID 0), redundancy (RAID 1), or both (RAID 5). RAID's fundamental structure is the **array**: a group of drives arranged in a manner that increases their effectiveness. The number of drives, and the way the data is split between them, determines the array's effectiveness.

The RAID system's building blocks are the **physical drives** arranged into a logical array in order to create the **logical drive** (also referred to as a **volume**) that appears to the operating system, all managed by the RAID controller. The RAID controller has its own SCSI (or ATA) bus or buses. In Figure 13-1. we show a RAID card with a single SCSI bus and four drives (0 through 3) attached to it in daisy-chain fashion. While, in reality, you'd also have a terminator at the end of your SCSI daisy-chain, we've omitted it in our drawing.

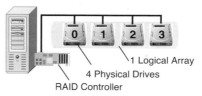

Figure 13-1. The basics of RAID

Once a set of drives (like the four physical drives in Figure 13-1.)has been combined into an array, the computer's operating system sees them as one large drive, and henceforth deals with the array rather than the individual drives.

---

6. The term was coined in 1987 by Patterson, Gibson, and Katz at U.C. Berkeley in their paper, "A Case for Redundant Arrays of Inexpensive Disks,"which can be found at sunsite.berkeley.edu/ Dienst/UI/2.0/Describe/ncstrl.ucb/CSD-87-391.

Why set up RAID? You may want to set up RAID for two simple reasons. First, you can use it to write the same data on two different disks at all times—a process called mirroring. If a device's hard disk crashes while mirroring information, you suffer only a brief inconvenience instead of an expensive and perhaps economically fatal loss of productivity for your users. You might also use RAID to improve data access performance through a process called striping, which allows your users spend less time waiting for a server to save or deliver their data.

RAID increases your system's uptime by providing uninterrupted access to your device's hard drives in case one of them fails. It does *not*, however, protect against all types of data loss—only against loss due to the failure or corruption of a hard drive. If a user deletes or overwrites a file on a RAID system, the file is just as gone as it would be on a single drive. In essence, you use RAID to:

- Ensure reliability in the case of a single drive failure;

- Provide greater system uptime through uninterrupted access if a single hard drive fails; and/or

- Increase system performance through multiple drives working in parallel.

Computer systems can utilize either software- or hardware-based RAID. Windows 2000, Unix, and Mac OS X computers all come with the built-in capability to combine multiple independent drives into a RAID configuration. However, this isn't a discussion for this section, as we're focusing on CPU performance issues, budget, scalability, etc. We will, however, cover both hardware and software RAID choices in this chapter.

Let's talk RAID

RAID is governed by international standards that correspond to the level of performance they offer. Let's go over the three most implemented methods: RAID 0, 1, & 5.

RAID Level 0 – Data striping

Striping is fundamental to RAID technology, providing larger volume formats and read and write speed increases by spreading parts of files across more than one disk, combining multiple drives into one logical storage unit.

The designation "0" is unintentionally appropriate, because that's exactly how much protection against data loss striping provides. This level has no redundancy. Striping combines two or more physical drives into a single drive array, partitioning the storage space of each drive into "stripes." Thus, incoming data from the operating system (in this case, three files A, B, and C) is split into discrete blocks, with the RAID controller now alternating the placement of each block between the numbers of drives in the array (A1, A2, etc.). By striping the drives in the array with stripes large enough so that each record falls within one stripe, most records can be evenly distributed across all drives. Our diagram (Figure 13-2.) shows files being striped in two blocks across both drives.

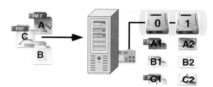

Figure 13-2. Striping

Advantages   Performance is improved by using the hardware in all these drives in parallel. Striping keeps all drives in the array busy during heavy load situations, maximizing the number of simultaneous I/O operations that can be performed by the array. Figure 13-2. shows how different files are chopped up and then the pieces spread across the striped drives.

Disadvantages   When any drive fails in a RAID 0 array, the entire array fails and the data is lost if it hasn't been backed up. What's striping good for, then? Operations that involve high data throughput rates like video editing, because both drives can be operating simultaneously to improve performance.

The best uses   Video editing and production, pre-press application, and any other application that requires high disk drive utilization.

RAID Level 1 – Data mirroring

Data redundancy can also be achieved through **mirroring**, a technique that puts duplicate data on more than one disk. To the operating system, both disks appear to be one. While this doesn't speed up the writing process, each individual drive can perform simultaneous, independent read operations. Mirroring thus doubles the read performance of a single non-mirrored drive. Below (Figure 13-3.) is a diagram showing how a single file is saved to *both* drives when they're mirrored.

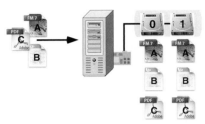

Figure 13-3. Mirroring

Advantages RAID 1 provides twice the read transaction rate of a single disk drive (the write speed is the same). It also offers 100 percent data redundancy: You don't have to rebuild your drives if one of them fails.

Disadvantages In a RAID 1 array, a failed drive reduces read performance to the level of a single drive (remember, the computer can read simultaneously from both drives when working), as data can be read only from the remaining drive. However, that's only part of the equation, as the failed drive must be removed and replaced, and the mirror set up all over again. Mirroring also carries the highest disk overhead of all RAID types, and is therefore very inefficient.

The best uses Accounting, web servers, or any other application that requires high availability.

RAID 10 – Striped mirrored array

Not to be confused with RAID 0+1, RAID 10 (10 or 1+0 are the same thing) combines RAID 1 and RAID 0 by striping data across multiple drives without parity *and* mirroring the entire array to a second set of drives. RAID 10 arrays are used in organizations that require unyielding availability and high throughput for data delivery. This is both fast and redundant, and requires at least four drives to implement.

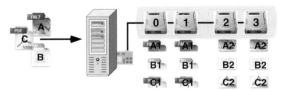

Figure 13-4. Striped Mirrored Array

Advantages This is an excellent choice for applications that need high availability and speed and don't need large scalability (because that would take a *lot* of drives).

Disadvantages With RAID 10, you're covered if one of the drives in a striped/mirrored set goes down. However, you're out of luck if both drives in the set (left and right drives in Figure 13-4. on page 442) went down. This is also very expensive, with high overhead and a minimum of four drives needed.

The best uses Database servers that require high levels of performance as well as high levels of fault tolerance.

RAID 0+1 — Mirrored striped array

Not to be confused with RAID 10, RAID 0+1 (01 and 0+1 are the same) combines RAID 0 and RAID 1 by mirroring data across multiple drives without parity, whose segments are RAID 0 arrays. This creates a very fast system that isn't as fault tolerant as a RAID 5 array.

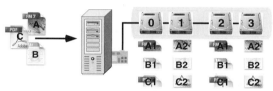

Figure 13-5. Mirrored Striped Array

Advantages This is great for high performance without maximum reliability, because the highest I/O rates are achieved through multiple striped segments.

Disadvantages Other than its costly overhead, a single device failure causes the entire array to become a RAID 0 array.

The best uses Anyone who has imaging applications or high-volume disk activity that can also afford potential downtime if necessary.

RAID Level 5 — Striped data with distributed parity

This provides both data redundancy through parity information and larger volume sizes/speed through striping and simultaneous input/output. RAID Level 5 is the best-of-both-worlds option because it provides striping for speed and also stores parity information about each file block on other drives for redundancy.

Why parity versus mirroring? Mirroring provides total data redundancy through ensuring that all files are written to at least two drives simultaneously. However, it comes with a high overhead, as mirroring takes up 50 percent of all drive space. Therefore, a better solution is to not store a complete copy on each drive, but instead to store parity information derived from the files themselves.

Parity is a method of calculating and distributing special bytes of information (called **parity data**) across multiple drives that can be used to restore original data in the event of one of the drive's failure. This redundant data takes up less space than mirrored data. How it works is pretty cool (OK, so the propeller on my beanie hat is spinning wildly): Let's use the example of the RAID 5 array below, with three drives in it for our *very simplified* explanation of RAID 5 and parity.

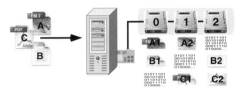

Figure 13-6. RAID 5 Striped data with distributed parity

As in Figure 13-6. a RAID 5 array is set up with a minimum of three drives. In this very simplistic explanation, let's say that the RAID blocks are set up to hold about half a file each (just to keep things simple). You'll notice that the Word icon, the first icon in the series, is cut in half and written to the bottom two drives, while a set of 1s and 0s representing the parity information is calculated by the RAID controller and then written to the top drive in the array.

The parity calculation is performed using a logical operation called XOR (known as eXclusive OR). Using your Excel spreadsheet, you can test that the OR logical operator is true if either of its operands is true (i.e., 1), and false, if neither is true (i.e., 0). However, the eXclusive OR operator is true *if and only if* one of its operands is true (i.e., 1). How does this differ from the normal OR? If both operands are true, XOR is false. Yeesh—but here's the thing to remember: Drives really only store a bunch of 1s and 0s. If you're writing information to a drive and then need to write that parity information, it looks like this:

Data to Stripe 1	Data to Stripe 2	XOR Parity to Stripe 3
0	0	0
0	1	1
1	0	1
1	1	0

Table 13-3. Striping & XOR parity

Why is this cool? Because if you look at the logic of XOR, you'll realize that an XOR performed twice in a row *reverts* itself. If we look at row two and do this calculation (0 XOR 1), we get 0 as the answer. Then, when we do the calculation again on itself (i.e., the answer XORed) (1 XOR 1), we get 0 again. Information being split between three drives in the RAID 5 array then separates two distinct bytes of data (D1 and D2) and uses XOR to create the parity (DP) byte (D1 XOR D2 = DP). So, in the Figure 13-7. the left drive data (part 1 of the file) represents 1, the middle drive data (part two of the file) represents 1, and the XOR calculation sets the parity bit at 0.

Figure 13-7. Creating the parity stripe (left) and reconstructing the parity stripe (right)

Now let's say that the left drive died, and you had to rebuild the data from the remaining drives on-the-fly for a user requesting the file. In this instance, XOR works by *reverse calculating* the information stored on the left drive from a combination of the remaining data and the parity data. As the table above Table 13-3. on page 444 showed, 0 XOR 1 = 1. So the parity information is used in the calculation, along with the remaining data to rebuild the lost data as shown below (see how Figure 13-7. left and right match the XOR rules?), *without* having to replace the lost or damaged drive.

In a RAID 5 system, parity information is alternated on different drives, striped into the array like any other piece of data, as shown in Figure 13-8.

Figure 13-8. RAID 5 Array with independent data and distributed parity

In this method, if any of the three drives dies, the RAID system can then XOR the other two together to create the missing third. However, recovery of this information takes longer than if it were mirrored because it must be restored from a *calculation* and not from physical storage space on the drive. So not only is the data striped across all drives; the parity is striped, as well.

Advantages   RAID 5 offers improved storage efficiency over RAID 1 because only the parity information is stored (as opposed to making full mirrored copies of data). Because of this, it takes three or more drives to create a RAID 5 array, with the storage capacity of only one drive dedicated to store the parity information. Therefore, RAID 5 arrays provide greater storage efficiency than RAID 1 arrays. In short, with a RAID 5 system that has three drives, you'll get the storage capacity of two. While not as fast as RAID 1 nor as redundant as RAID 10, it's a good, economical balance between the two.

Disadvantages   Because information is striped across all drives with parity information also stored in a RAID 5 array, when a drive fails, RAID 5 arrays amalgamate the requested data by threading the parity information in with the corresponding data stripes from the remaining drives in the array. Of course, to fix the problem, you must remove the failed drive and add a new one in its place (we cover that below, as well).

The best uses   RAID 5 systems are fantastic for file, application, database, web, intranet, and mail servers. This is your all-around most versatile system.

RAID 50 – Striped RAID 5 volumes

When you get to the level of needing more speed in your RAID 5 system, that means you need a RAID 50 system that stripes whole RAID 5 volumes. In Figure 13-9. we show how our incoming files (A, B, and C) are striped into four parts across the six drives in the RAID 50 array. When you set up a RAID 50 array, you probably want at least a two-channel RAID adapter card (like those from Adaptec), so that you have one RAID array on one SCSI channel and the second RAID array on the other SCSI channel.

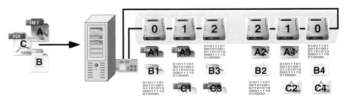

Figure 13-9. RAID 50 - two RAID 5s striped together

Advantages   The advantages here are speed and a *little* redundancy. By striping the data across two sets of RAID arrays on two different SCSI channels, you obtain a speed increase over writing to a single RAID 5 array. The other advantage is slightly more redundancy than a single RAID 5 system. In a RAID 5 system, if one of the drives goes out, you're okay. If two drives go out, you're hosed. In a RAID 50 system, you could lose one drive from each of the RAID 5 arrays and still be okay. However, if you lose more than one drive in either of the arrays, you're hosed.

Disadvantages   You've got the extra cost of the dual-channel RAID card and the extra cost of the parity drive in the second RAID 5 array as cost overhead. And you also need a box large enough to handle all of the drives. Six drives is the minimum number of drives for a RAID 50 array.

The best uses   If you need a really big volume on your system for imaging, post-movie production, or pre-press, this makes sense. Get a fast server with a dual or quad Adaptec RAID controller and hook up four external boxes' worth of drives into four RAID 5 systems that you then stripe together into one of the biggest RAID 50 volumes your users could imagine.

Which RAID is right for your reassurance?

You might think that the next logical definition herein would walk you through the steps of selecting a RAID system. Heck, seven years ago in our last book, when we wrote about RAID, that was the case, but things are different now. Because of the complexity of today's RAID environments, we've put off that stroll until the section on hardware failure, because you need to plan more than just a RAID setup—you've also gotta think about where to store the drives (internal to the computer or external in a RAID tower), how best to hook up to the RAID tower, and a host of other issues that revolve more around hardware failure than drive corruption. For now, you need to think through what happens when a drive goes bad—because your drives *will* eventually go bad, I promise.

What happens when a RAID component goes bad?

A failed drive must be replaced in a RAID array by physically removing the drive and replacing it. Adaptec, RAIDtec, and a number of other RAID controllers will rebuild the data for the failed drive onto the new drive or Hot Spare while the computer is operational, but Apple Xserve requires that the server be taken offline to rebuild the information.

RAID 1 arrays are rebuilt relatively quickly (the speed of your drive * amount of data), because the data is simply copied from the duplicate (mirrored) drive to the replacement drive.

In RAID 5 arrays, the data for the replacement drive must be assembled from the corresponding stripes and parity information of the remaining drives in the array. RAID 5 arrays that contain a large number of drives require more time for a rebuild than does a small array. And software RAID 5 arrays take even more time because they must calculate the XOR functions in rebuilding the data—let's just figure it's anywhere from two to four times *slower* than a RAID 1 drive. That said, remember that you can rebuild your missing drive while you're working, so, in essence, you won't lose much time at all.

Make sure you have a way of monitoring your RAID system for pre-emptive failure alerts. If you know a failure is going to occur, you can actively do something about it. Much of this information about pre-failure alerts comes in the form of SMART (for drives) and SAF-TE (for enclosures) monitoring.

Are there any limitations to backing up a RAID system and restoring it?

We get this question a lot, and it's a good one. Because of RAID's nature, there are no limitations to backing up an array. Remember, to the operating system, a RAID array is a single device, so when backing up a RAID 5 volume, your backup software doesn't care whether you have three or 53 drives in the array: It all appears as the same logical volume to the operating system, and therefore to the backup software.

As well as a good RAID system, you need SMART alert software installed and enabled so that if it detects a problem, the backup software kicks into high gear and begins backing up the array *before* the drive fails.

PLANNING A **RAID** SYSTEM TO COMBAT DRIVE AND SERVER FAILURE

Okay, get a cup of joe, a stack of paper, and a sharp #2 pencil with plenty of erasers. We're going to work through planning a RAID system for your devices. And no, the answer isn't always going to be "get a RAID 5 system." Other than budgetary limitations, you need to make two basic choices when deciding which type of RAID is right for you.

The first choice is the type of RAID itself, as explained in the table below. Hint: RAID 1 or RAID 5, if you want drive redundancy.

	RAID 0	RAID 1	RAID 10	RAID 5	RAID 50
Description	Data Striping	Disk Mirroring	Data Striping, Disk Mirroring	Data Striping with distributed Parity	Striping 2 or more RAID 5 systems
Min. # of Drives	2	2	4	3	6
Drive additions	Single	By Twos	By Twos	Single	By threes at least
Capacity†	S * N	(S * N)/2	(S * N)/2	S*(N-1)	N5*RA
Storage Efficiency†	100%	50%	50%	(N-1)/N	((N-1)/N)*RA
Availability	Low	Medium	Medium	High	High
Fault Tolerance	None	High	High	Medium	Medium High
+/-	High Performance High Capacity No redundancy	Redundancy of drives, fail over to a hot swap only in certain RAID controllers	High performance *and* drive redundancy	Balances performance, redundancy, & volume Databases are a perfect match	Increases volume size and speed over RAID 5 system

†S = Size of Drive, N = Number of Drives, N5 = the "width" of the RAID 5 dimension in the array, RA = Number of RAID5 arrays

Table 13-4. RAID types

Once you've made choice #1, you need to decide where to put your drives. If you want to use either RAID 0 or RAID 1, most computers have room inside the box for at least two to three drives. However, if you chose RAID 50, not a lot of computers have room for six drives—actually, I know of only one. I mean, you're talking about a server that's the size of a small, under-the-desk beer (or Coke) fridge here.

If you're talking six drives, you're talking the big Dell 1500 series box or an external hardware device such as Adaptec's DuraStor products. For example, in Table 13-5. on page 450 we show a couple of Dell PowerEdge servers. Notice how the boxes' physical girth increases as the number of internal drives increases. That Dell 1500 is one fat computer.

PowerEdge 500SC	PowerEdge 1400SC	PowerEdge 1500SC
3 Internal Drives	4 Internal Drives	6 Internal Hard Drives

Table 13-5. Three Dell servers compared

If you want to simply set up a RAID 1 through 5 system *and* you want all internal drives, use any of the Dell boxes above.

If you want to set up a RAID 10 system, use the 1400 or 1500. You've *got* to use the 1500 for a RAID 50 system, because the 1500 and up are the boxes that hold the six-drive bays.

On the left (Figure 13-10.) is an image of a Dell 2500 with its front bezel cover off to reveal its guts, showing only two of the four pull-out drives already installed in the upper drive bay.

These Dell boxes are outstanding for use with internal RAID because of these easily accessible, pull-out drives—if one of them gives up the ghost, you can pull it out and swap another one in its place with minimal effort and no screwing around (I'd better pipe down, or the Pun Patrol will lock me up). And the sheer joy of an easy swap can't be underestimated.

Figure 13-10. Dell 2500 Front with cover off

However, you've got some other options. You could choose an external RAID attachment that puts the drives *outside* the box. With this route, you could use the 500 *and* set up a RAID 50 system—it all depends upon the type of controller you want.

Software or hardware?

Some people sleep on beds as hard as granite; other folks cushion their every curve. As with mattresses, choice #2 is all about firmness: For your RAID controller, you can select soft or hard. The RAID controller provides the interface between your host computer and your disk array. A software-based controller added to the host's operating system must therefore rely upon the operating system and host computer's processor speed. A hardware-based controller *internal* to the host computer offloads the RAID controller's processes to the hardware PCI card. However, it's still somewhat limiting in configurability. A hardware-based controller *external* to the host computer (but connected through a Host Bus Adapter) offers the most flexibility, but, like a good night's sleep, it'll cost you.

If you're wondering which system is for you, here's a hint: Don't even *think* of building a six-drive RAID 50 array using a software RAID controller—the overhead would kill your CPU. Software-based RAID controllers are fine and dandy for either mirroring or striping of two drives internal to a computer. And once you start using more drives and RAID 5, you'll need a hardware-based controller. They come in two flavors: internal PCI cards and external, attached devices that connect to the PC through a Host Bus Adapter.

	Software	Internal Hardware	External Hardware
How it works	All functions are handled by the computer's CPU	Setup functions handled by CPU, RAID operating functions handled by RAID controller on card	Plugs into computer via PCI card or standard controller RAID operating functions handled by RAID controller on card
Benefits	Included with your computer's Operating System, or relatively inexpensive	Increased performance vs. software-based RAID More options for adding storage devices	OS independent High capacity Easier management

Table 13-6. Software or hardware?

The Case fer and agin software-based RAID

When I lived in Missouri while migrating from the military to work for PricewaterhouseCoopers, I quickly learned that many of the people there were either "fer" something or they were "agin" it—no middle ground with these folks. And mostly, they were "agin" everything. That about sums up my beliefs in software RAID: Unless you're deploying a software RAID implementation for a very simple, low-usage system, I'm agin it.

Most software-based RAID supports RAID Levels 0 and 1. Software RAID is implemented in the operating system kernel as a set of special software routines. Windows NT, 2000, most Unix systems, and Mac OS X all support software RAID. The benefits are cost and simplicity. The end user's cost for a software-based RAID controller is zippo, nuttin', nada—it comes with the operating system. Simplicity? You either set up the system through drive formatting or you don't—it doesn't take much effort to set it up.

Performance problems

However, you need to know that kernel mode components are at the mercy of the scheduler that pre-empts their operation as soon as their time period expires or a higher-priority task is scheduled. Even under the best circumstances, software-based RAID must share processor time with other software components currently running. The inclusion of ATA drives in most desktop computers is another telling point in the case against software RAID. When two or more ATA drives are set up internally to a computer, one of them is the master and the others the slaves. For maximum drive performance, we don't recommend that you use master and slave IDE drives in a RAID volume—use only master-master combinations.

Drive limitations

With RAID 1, the system must write the same information to both disks for every disk operation, and this dual write operation degrades system performance. Windows 2000 won't allow the operating or boot files to reside on a software-driven RAID 5 volume. And with a software-driven RAID 5 volume, you can't have a spare drive that can be automatically added to the array, should one fail.

As if that's not enough, here's a final problem: The RAID world, with the folks at Adaptec leading the charge, has finally figured out how to put multiple drives of different sizes into the same array. With software-based RAID (at least for the last couple of years), the smallest drive in the array sets the standard for the amount of data that can be utilized on the drive. But with the advent of full-capacity disk-array utilization[7], you can now have different drive sizes in the array—and overcome the RAID limitation of using the smallest drive as the size limiter. Here's a "hypothetical" to flush out my point:

A. Build an array of three drives

B. Have D1 = 20 GB, D2 = 60 GB, D3 = 40 GB.

C. *Without* full-capacity disk-array utilization, the standard limitation of all

---

[7]. Adaptec is one of the very few RAID vendors to offer this capability—just one of the reasons that we like them so much.

drives in the array is limited to 20 GB per drive, and the total array thus equals 60 GB (yes, I know, minus blah blah blah for parity).

D. *With* full-capacity disk-array utilization solution, the array equals 20 GB + 60 GB + 40 GB (minus blah blah blah for parity).

Advanced feature limitations With most software-based RAID, you can't utilize a hot spare drive to pick up the slack for a drive that fails, nor can you hot swap your drive if it fails. However, some products like SoftRAID for the Mac OS X platform or VERITAS Volume Manager do offer great features like a detachable third volume mirror that lets you break off the volume for backup purposes.

Hardware-based RAID — the professional's choice for speed

On to the hardware choices. Most hardware RAID solutions support Level 5, as well as Levels 0 and 1. A RAID controller card is simply a full- or half-length card placed inside the computer. Because a RAID controller manages the data on the disk array, it can (and does) perform many tasks, including—unlike a software-based controller—engaging the use of a hot standby drive in case a drive in the array fails.

With a hot standby drive attached, the RAID controller can kick it into gear automatically when it senses that a drive in the array is going to fail, allowing for unattended fault tolerance for servers placed in wiring closets, under desks, and more appropriately, in server rooms. If a drive fails, the hot standby is then added to the array. In the case of a RAID 1 array, the hot standby becomes the mirrored drive. In the case of a RAID 5 array, parity information is used to populate the drive. In the case of a RAID 0 array, you're SOL: Hot-standby drives don't work with striping.

Most RAID cards have ports for either external or internal drives such as this Adaptec 2400A ATA RAID board in Figure 13-11. on page 454. Some have both. You can also select RAID for ATA drives or SCSI drives (the card depicted is for ATA drives).

The four-channel Adaptec ATA RAID 2400A offers a microprocessor-based ATA RAID solution for devices with internal ATA drives. RAID 0, 1, 0+1, 5, and JBOD are supported, as well as online capacity expansion and background initialization. The card supports ATA/100 & ATA/66 drives and comes preinstalled with 32 MB of ECC SDRAM (expandable to 128 MB).

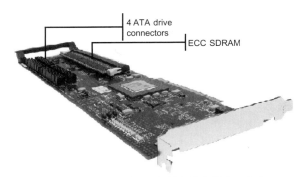

Figure 13-11. Adaptec 2400A ATA RAID board

Internal and external RAID

Hardware RAID controllers are not limited to PCI cards that can be added to computers. Hardware RAID controllers can also come as part of an external RAID storage enclosure. As a matter of fact, most external storage enclosures are called "JBODs," which is short for Just a Bunch Of Disks. The only difference between a JBOD and a RAID tower is that a RAID tower is a JBOD with a RAID hardware card built in. We'll cover the setups for when you should use internal RAID cards or when you should move to external RAID cards.

INTERNAL RAID SETUPS

Before we begin with the setups, let's walk through the process so that you get the details before we move on to the generalizations. To show you how simple it is to set up a RAID system, we'll use an Adaptec 2400A card and four drives stored in a Dell 2500. Before installing the 2400A, we plugged in two normal SCSI drives and mirrored them together as our boot drive, using the onboard SCSI controller and mirroring software that came with the operating system. Then we selected four Seagate ATA/IDE drives (much less expensive than their SCSI brethren) and the Adapatec 2400A four-channel RAID controller. Installing the card and drives was a simple plug-and-play setup that took less than five minutes.

When you first launch the Storage Manager Pro software that comes with the Adaptec card, it syncs through the system and displays a list of devices in the left windowpane and then the set of arrays in the right windowpane.

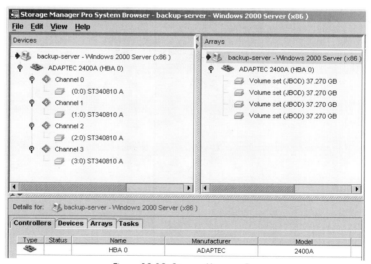

Figure 13-12. Storage Manager Pro

Notice that each of the drives (left in Figure 13-12.) is on its own channel: channels 0 through 3. And each of the drives themselves are set to SCSI ID 0 within their respective channels. If you had to daisy chain any of these drives in a row, they'd all show up as Channel ID:0 SCSI ID:0.

Since no RAID array has been set up yet, the volumes of each of the drives appear as individuals in a JBOD (Just a Bunch Of Disks) array—an array of drives connected together under the same controller. If we did nothing else, you could mount four 37 GB volumes on the computer and each would have its own channel for throughput.

Establishing
fault tolerance
To turn your JBOD array into a RAID array, determine the levels of fault tolerance that you need. Remember, **fault tolerance** is the system's ability to recover from a drive failure without interrupting access to the data through establishing a drive redundancy scheme. We can select a pair of drives and set up a mirroring scheme, or choose all four drives and set up a four-drive RAID array or keep one of the drives as a spare in case one of the RAID array drives conks out. If you *do* choose to use a fail-over drive, the controller puts it aside and, if necessary, automatically reconstructs the data from a failed drive (notice the singular article, meaning *one*) onto the spare. We'll use three drives in our RAID array and the fourth for the spare, as shown in Figure 13-13. below, in the Storage Manager Pro's array wizard tool that comes with the software.

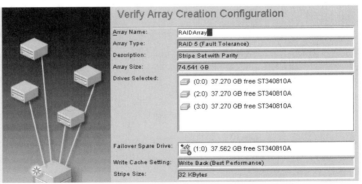

Figure 13-13. Array wizard in Storage Manager Pro

Once you've instructed the software to create the array, go return those library books that have been stashed in your trunk for too many months. You might as well, as it takes from five to seven hours to create the RAID array (ours took six and a half). When finished, the Storage Manager Pro window changes slightly.

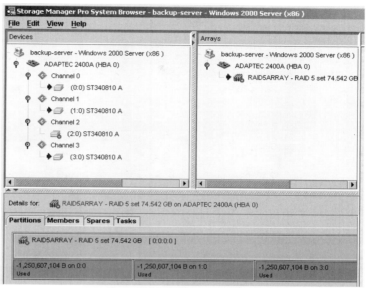

Figure 13-14. RAID array completed

Each active drive (on left in Figure 13-14.) in the array has an arrow next to it in the right side of the window. You'll also notice that the JBOD listing has been replaced by the RAID array.

Finally, take note of the size of the array in the right-sided windowpane. Remember, each of the drives held 37.27 GB worth of data. In a JBOD, the total storage space for the three drives is 111.81 GB. However, combined into a RAID 5 array, the total available space is now 74.542 GB, because each of the drives has to hold not only data,but parity information, as well (we covered this under *RAID Level 5 – Striped data with distributed parity* on page 443), thus reducing the array's overall volume.

Establishing your partitions

Once you've created your fault-tolerant array, you're ready to format and partition your drive so that it can be mapped to a drive letter and then mounted on the computer for use. By launching your **Computer Management** application and then selecting **Disk Management**, you can bring up the window that shows all of your currently mounted drives, their state of health (we're all healthy in this picture) and any unallocated drives such as ours, shown as **Disk 2** in Figure 13-15.

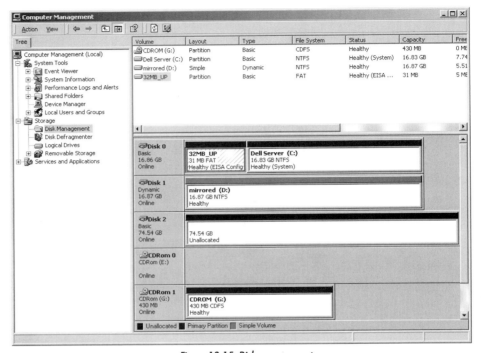

Figure 13-15. Disk management

From here, right-click on the drive's info window and opt to create a partition (or a couple of partitions, if you so choose).

Small systems

First, for a great many reasons, keep your boot drive separate from the rest of your RAID configuration. That said, let's walk through some typical applications that fit nicely with the Dell 500SC and a two-channel RAID controller card such as the Adaptec 3210S. The 3210S (Ultra160) offers high performance and scalability, making it a good pick for mid-range server environments that need SCSI drives with better performance and better SMART reporting. This two-channel card is ideal for uses requiring a high-performance RAID solution in which performance is paramount but cost is a consideration. The two-channel Adaptec ATA RAID 1200A provides optimal, cost-efficient data protection using ATA/100 technology for entry-level server and workstation markets.

RAID 0 for print server, Raster Image Processor (RIP), OPI server

For print serving in a high-volume print environment, RIPing jobs to high-end printers, or creating OPI files for high-end printing, performance is more important than redundancy because the original files are stored in another location and are sent to the print server only for print processing. If you're moving vast quantities of information, you're working in a sequential data–transfer environment that can be improved with a RAID 0 striping configuration.

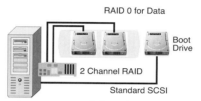

Figure 13-16. Dual Channel RAID 0 system

In the configuration in Figure 13-16. , the boot drive is separated from the RAID array on its own independant SCSI or ATA controller. Make sure you separate your boot drive channel from the rest of the RAID system. If either drive in the RAID array drive hangs, or hangs the RAID bus, it should affect only that particular channel. With the boot drive on a second channel, the server continues to run, and if you have your SMART system set up, you'll get the e-mail alert for data drive failure. Of course, if your boot channel or drive dies, you'll be busy restoring to a new drive.

Since there are two channels in this configuration, you won't need to daisy-chain the two RAID drives together in serial fashion to form the data array. Each of the drives (including your boot drive) will have its own SCSI or ATA channel, providing you as much speed as you can need (But, officer, I was only going 65...).

With a RIP or OPI server, I'd go with the more powerful SCSI drives and SCSI RAID controller (Adaptec 3210S) for the data drives because a *ton* of data is moving very quickly through these systems, working the drives harder than a dot-commer putting in 80-hour weeks at his failing startup. SCSI can handle a bigger load than ATA can.

When working with a normal print server, you can get away with ATA drives to lower your cost. I'd go with the ATA RAID controller for this instance (Adaptec 1200A) because the drives don't work nearly as hard, and you don't have to deal with a tsunami of data flooding the system.

RAID 1 for a small e-mail server, web server

E-mail and web severs require more redundancy than print servers. Therefore, for smaller e-mail and web systems, RAID 1 mirroring solutions work best. A dual-channel mirroring solution (with the boot drive off the internal channel) works best in this environment.

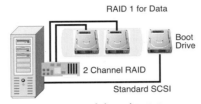

Figure 13-17. Dual channel RAID 1 system

As with the previous example, by putting the two data drives in the RAID array on different channels, the controller can access both hard drives simultaneously, increasing the write-time performance and allowing maximum performance for read operations (a large part of a web server's tasks). Again, to keep the server from hanging if the RAID SCSI bus hangs, we separate the boot drive from the RAID array.

Again, you'll want your boot drive off of the internal bus and separated from your RAID data channels for added throughput and in case the RAID bus hangs.

 Depending upon how hard the servers get hit, I'd go with the more powerful SCSI drives and SCSI RAID controller (Adaptec 3210S) for higher-volume servers and ATA drives and the ATA RAID (Adaptec 1200A) controller for lower-volume servers.

Medium-range systems

Any combination server, like Windows 2000 or Mac OS X, is a mid-range server to me. What makes it mid-range? It's probably doing a host of operations, like SMB file sharing, e-mail, Web, and FTP all rolled into one. At that level, you have more intensive drive operations, and you need a minimum of four drives in your server.

Windows 2000 or Unix mid-range server

Server operating systems, like Windows 2000 and Unix (including the Mac OS X server), utilize swap files to increase the RAM installed on the computer. The swap files are located on the boot drive of the server. Since you don't want swap file access on the same SCSI channel as data access, you need a way to separate these operations. You're now moving up to a Dell 1400 server platform if you want to handle four internal drives. Alternately, Xserve holds four drives as well, but supports only software RAID for its internal drives.

At this point, with four drives, you have several options. The easiest and most cost-effective is the standard onboard ATA or SCSI controller that comes with the computer for your boot volume. Since you have four drive bays internal to the server, you can set up a RAID 1 mirror for your boot drives to form a single volume. The swap files and boot mirror won't be a CPU hog, so there's no real reason to put these drives on a RAID card.

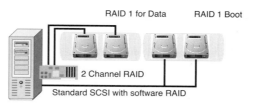

Figure 13-18. Windows 2000 server with mirrored data and mirrored boot arrays

Alternately, you could live dangerously and put all four drives on a single RAID card. The RAID controller you should be using at this point is a four-port controller like the Adaptec 3410S (for SCSI) or 2400A (for ATA drives). The setup for this system is shown in Figure 13-19.

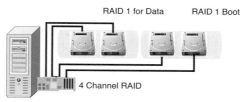

Figure 13-19. 4 Channel RAID card with two RAID 1 volumes

With one array configured for the data drives and one array configured for the boot drives, and each drive having its own SCSI or ATA channel, you're ready for performance. However, a RAID card failure or SCSI bus hang on the card could down your server. So just forget I wrote this and go with the internal volume and RAID card volume setup.

Alternate mid-range setup 2

Want an alternate setup to a dual mirrored system that provides for more data storage but less protection? Divide three drives into a RAID 5 system and use the fourth drive as the boot-and-swap file drive.

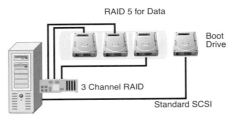

Figure 13-20. Windows 2000 server with RAID 5 array

In the first example, with two drives mirrored together in an array for redundancy, storage capacity is equal to only one of the drives. In the RAID 5 setup, storage capacity is measured as the size of two out of three of the drives (the third is used for parity). By moving to this configuration, you've effectively doubled your storage capacity compared to the previous configuration.

However, with boot drive failure, you're hosed. With RAID 5 drive failure, the server is slowed down because the files must be re-created from parity information until the drive has been replaced and the data rebuilt. However, using a three-channel RAID card does help improve data delivery speed throughout.

And you'll need that speed if you use this mid-range system as a database server. Database servers are laden with continuous indexing, reading, writing, and swapping of files. Whenever end users hit the database, both data files and index files are smacked simultaneously. Splitting the drive accesses throughout the array greatly speeds up the database access process, and the best way to do this is to put the database data on a RAID 5 array.

Da biggies

Now we're down to the final two configurations that fully utilize the Dell 1500 S servers' internal storage capacity. These mamma-jammas hold six internal drives, offering pretty much all the setup flexibility you need. Don't even *think* about using an ATA—you've just crossed over into the SCSI zone (apologies to the great Rod Serling).

Windows 2000 or Unix server battlewagon

The first of the two configurations for the battlewagon class server (those that can take a big hit and keep going) employs the RAID 10 array for data, as shown in Figure 13-21.

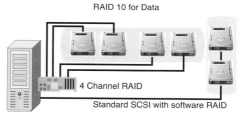

Figure 13-21. RAID 10 for data and RAID 1 for boot

Remember, in RAID 10, you have a mirrored, striped set of drives. While there are a lot of drives, this array's capacity is equal to only two drives. The other two drives in the bay comprise the boot drive array, which is set up as a RAID 1 mirror.

This system gives you the redundancy you need for the boot drive and RAID 1 speed for striping, along with a mirror's redundancy for the striped pair. You could lose one boot drive and one of each of the mirrored striped drives, and still keep going.

Battlewagon version 2 (slightly faster)

In another way to set up a system like this, utilize the hot-swap capability of a hardware RAID controller along with a RAID 5 array for data and a RAID 1 array for the boot drive as shown in Figure 13-22.

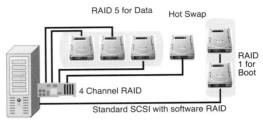

Figure 13-22. RAID 5 for data, RAID 1 for boot + hot spare

This configuration gives you the same setup for boot and the same storage capacity as the RAID 10 system (because two drives in the 5 array are used for data and one for parity). However, it's even faster, because you now have three drives in the data array with their own SCSI channel instead of two—now you're cooking!

Arguably, you could put four drives in the RAID 5 array for even more storage and a bit more speed, but why taunt Mercury? When one of the drives fails, the server will be degraded until you bring it down and replace the drive. With a drive set aside as a hot spare, you limit the server's "degraded" time to a minimum because the drive can be brought online by the RAID controller and rebuilt without having to take the server down and replace the drive. This type of setup is great for a mid-range database server as well as an applications server.

WHAT ABOUT EXTERNAL STORAGE?

Once you move beyond RAID's internal drive and PCI card setup, you need to have an external storage enclosure as well as the RAID controller and the drives themselves. This setup offers pluses and minuses. The pluses are attractive: hot drive swapping, additional space for hard drives, and upping the number of devices the RAID bank can connect to, so you can create such things as server clusters. The minuses? Like anything loaded with pluses, it'll cost you. Whether you decide on a combination RAID tower that fits a single server or a JBOD enclosure attached to a RAID controller for more configurability (such as server clustering), you need to know what to expect in regular JBOD and fault-tolerant storage enclosures.

Standard and fault-tolerant JBOD enclosures

Below (Figure 13-23.) is a graphic from Granite Digital, one of the better manufacturers of entry-level JBOD enclosures. These FireWire-based JBODs require software RAID for their setup. Each drive bay is removable and has a lock for security. They don't have dual power supplies, but each drive bay has its own fan.

Figure 13-23. JBOD systems from Granite Digital

At the most basic level, external drive storage enclosures are JBODs—an auxiliary case that holds "Just A Bunch Of Disks." However, most of these have evolved into fault-tolerant *systems* that incorporate one or more of the following features (to be selected based on business needs):

1. **Redundant, hot-swappable power** supplies are one of the key features that RAID manufacturers like to brag about. Some of the systems, like the Data-

Dock 7000 from MicroNet, have three power supplies that you can put in and take out. However, a quick call to a few friends who run global server facilities told me that since the advent of APC and good, clean power, they haven't had a single power supply go out in more than five years.

The biggest advantage of keeping your drive's power supplies in an external box? It takes the power load off the server. Like the control freaks among us (who, *me*?), drives are power-hungry, at times demanding more power than the rest of a server's system. Putting the power supplies outside the server box protects the server's power system and gives it a longer lifespan.

2. **Redundant, hot-swappable cooling** systems are another come-hither. These systems, unlike the power supplies, *do* go out; well, to be precise, they get old and noisy when the bearings start to wear out and therefore need replacing. All JBODs should have multiple cooling fans and systems that can be replaced without having to interrupt JBOD or server operation.

3. **Hot-swappable** drive **cases** or drives are another important factor. Look for four must-have features:

    A. **Latching mechanism**: Does the hot-swappable drive system have a latching mechanism on the front of the drive that locks the drive into place once it's in the box? You need either an electronic or physical system that clicks into place so that you don't accidentally pull out a drive while it's live and running.

    B. **Auto power sensing**: The drive system should auto-sense that you're about to extrude it from the system so that it shuts down the power and the drive spins down. You don't want to remove a spinning hard drive—it's like trying to juggle a gyroscope. Some systems will spin the drive down only if you first tell them to do so in the controller software system.

    C. **Security sensor**: In the best of worlds, you'll also have a security sensor so that once a drive locks in place; you can then secure the drive. Once the drive is secure, if it's removed, an alarm sounds or you'll be notified (see controller system, below) that it's being illegally removed.

4. **Extra drive bays** are necessary so that you can store additional drives for hot swapping, or add an AIT tape drive for backup purposes.

    A. **Hot spare** drive bays are also a factor. Remember, drives die. You're building a RAID system to protect yourself against losing the use of the server's drive systems when that sad event occurs—please, no flowers. Therefore, most JBODs allow you to have a drive designated as the "hot" or "warm" failover drive installed in the unit. If a drive in the active array dies, the RAID controller will be able to employ the use of the designated spare to add it to the mirror set or the RAID 5 array.

B. Some boxes allow you to add **AIT** tape drives instead of another hard drive for backups. While these tapes hold up to 100 GB in storage, most of the RAID 5 systems can carry a whole lot more, so even with a single AIT system, you're backing up only critical information on the system.

C. You therefore want at least **seven drive bays** on your JBOD to accommodate extra drives for hot swapping or tape subsystems.

5. **Control units** that monitor everything from power, through cooling status to drive status and even security. Some of these systems use proprietary reporting technology, and some rely upon the SAF-TE[8] standard (we cover that below in the SMART section) that monitors not only drives, but enclosures, as well. Here's what you really want out of your control unit when it finds something wrong:

A. **Audible and visual alerts** to tell you that *this* is the device having trouble. There's nothing worse in the world than getting paged that a RAID bank has problems, only to arrive in the server room to find it *full* of RAID banks that are, of course, unlabeled.

B. **SNMP traps** should automatically be sent out so that your custom network management applications, like OpenView, LANDesk, or LANsurveyor, are notified that there's a problem.

C. **E-mail and SMS** (to your pager—blueberry, mulberry, Mayberry, whatever) messages should also be sent notifying you that a problem is occurring. It should allow for a progression of e-mails, or at least different levels of whom to send to.

---

8.   SAF-TE (SCSI Accessed Fault Tolerant Enclosure) is the method by which SCSI-based storage devices, controllers, power supplies, and other components communicate their status (such as temperature, potential fan or power supply failures) to monitoring applications.

6. **Controller connections** should be variable. Some of the boxes come with RAID controllers as an integral part of the system; some of them come as simple JBODs that you connect to a RAID controller. That's really your choice, and we'll cover that below. Your other choice is whether or not to use Fibre Channel to connect your JBOD to your server, or Parallel SCSI to connect it to your server. Again, since that's a lot of questions, we'll cover that below, too.

Combination RAID Towers

Ah, it's nice to see that *something* is still around from the era of my first backup book. Combination RAID towers, like the DataDock 7000 (Beam me up there, Scotty!) from MicroNet, are what you can expect in your external RAID enclosure, and are shown in Figure 13-24. below.

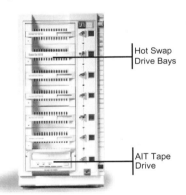

Figure 13-24. MicroNet DataDock 7000

The box's management software supports Macintosh OS X, as well as Unix and Windows 2000. Also, the box comes equipped with a bay that supports an AIT tape backup drive. While the storage capacity of the RAID tower eclipses that of the AIT drive, you can still use the AIT drive to back up critical data or to archive data from the server onto tape for long-term, offsite storage.

Basic configuration For this kind of RAID tower, you've got a mid-range server configuration with one RAID 5 array for data with a hot-swap drive in the device, ready to go in case of a drive failure in the array. Figure 13-25. on page 469 shows the typical setup (omitting internal drives for now). The host CPU communicates with the RAID system through a **Host Bust Adapter (HBA)**, also known as your standard **SCSI card**[9]. If you need to hook up to a SAN network or go longer distances, you can use a Fibre Channel card. The RAID system has its own RAID controller onboard (such is the case with the MicroNet system). The majority of the RAID controllers have a single RAID channel on board, so you've got just one SCSI or IDE bus.

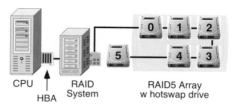

Figure 13-25. Basic setup for MicroNet RAID tower

This is a fine setup for a basic application server or mail server, but, because you're limited to a single bus, I wouldn't use it for high-performance systems like big databases or database-driven websites.

External JBOD storage enclosures + software RAID controllers

Hey, I know I'm pretty much against software RAID controllers—I've said so throughout this book. However, they often make perfect sense for small organizations—as a matter of fact, we use a software controller here at Network Frontiers.

External JBOD storage enclosures + internal RAID controllers

All-in-one enclosures are fine if you need only the speed of a single-channel SCSI or IDE system. But, if you need a dual SCSI sytem's speed and power, you'll want to separate your external JBOD from your controller. Of course, you'll lose the ability to have an integral AIT tape system, but you gain flexibility and speed (as the JBOD can be attached to other systems later).

The Storcase 9 and 14 bay InfoStation backplane enclosure[10] (see Figure 13-26. on page 470) is one of the best of its type. The InfoStation is available in one-, two-, and four-channel models (they can be upgraded from one up to four channels after purchase). These are JBOD boxes, but if you slap on an on-board RAID

---

9.   With other systems, like those from Granite Digital that use FireWire as a connector, you don't need an HBA.

10.   http://www.storcase.com/infostation/ifsii.asp?ml=1

controller, the enclosure becomes an SES-compliant RAID tower that can be used in single or clustered server environments. Through its InfoMon monitoring utility, the InfoStation also supports web-based chassis monitoring.

Figure 13-26. StorCase 14-bay InfoStation and drive carrier

The InfoStation's SCSI backplane is available for single-, dual- or quad-host interfaces, and fits perfectly well with the Adaptec SCSI RAID cards with single, dual, or quad channels. To really appreciate this system, look at its backside (Figure 13-27.)—everything is plug and play! InfoStation earns an A+ for ease of use.

Figure 13-27. Backside of a 14-bay InfoStation with power (top right) and blower (bottom right)

Each nine- or 14-bay rack mount InfoStation backplane chassis contains either one or two redundant, load-sharing, load-balancing, hot-swappable 650W power supplies, and four high-pressure, variable-speed blowers contained in two hot-swappable modules (two in each).

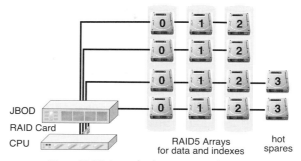

Figure 13-28. Large database server configuration

This system accommodates a RAID 5 array for a database's index files, two RAID 5 data arrays, and two hot spare drives to be added anywhere they're needed. Talk about loaded for bear—this is one big system, and about as big as it should ever get for an internal-based PCI-card RAID structure.

However, you still have two single points of failure: the server and the PCI RAID controller unit (if you're only using one of them). I'm not saying this isn't a good system: It's a very good system and a very good JBOD tower; of the specified JBODs, the one specified most often today. Yet, sometimes you need to build even more redundant systems.

External JBOD storage enclosures + external RAID controllers

Ratcheting up redundancy another level, we step away from using the RAID controller as an internal card to the server, moving it outside the server to either a RAID appliance or as separate hot-swap controller cards inserted into the JBOD. If it's internal to the server, you need a Host Bus Adapter card (or two for redundancy). To keep things in perspective, we'll use the same JBOD, the 14-bay InfoStation from StorCase. These enclosures are designed to support up to two optional InfoStation RAID Controller Modules for active-active failover operation. We show the module in Figure 13-29. on page 472, where you can see that it has two separate bins for the two RAID controllers.

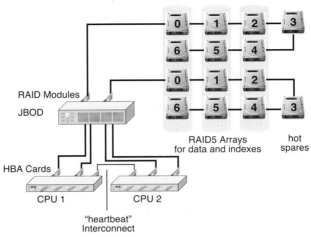

Figure 13-32. Dual servers in a RAID cluster

To create a clustered system, first ensure that each of the host servers has two Network Interface Cards (NICs), or one on-board network card with an additional network card for redundancy, as well as an Ethernet interconnect card for the heartbeat signal. Other than that, you need a cluster controller kit that fits the system you're using, as well as servers (Windows 2000 Advanced Server, various Unix servers) that support clustering, and clustering services software, such as Microsoft Cluster Server (MSCS). If you use the Adaptec system, you need the Adaptec Clustering Kit.

Active/Active RAID controller configurations operate in concert with each other,enabling fast data transfer between the RAID array and the host computer. Each controller in the configuration can serve information to a different host server while checking between them (through the heartbeat) to ascertain the other controller's "up" status. In the event of one controller's failure, the other assumes full-time status of responsibilities without any data loss.

Out There   Of course, to take advantage of your investment in the JBOD box, and if you don't need much storage, you can connect multiple clustered CPUs to the same StorCase InfoStation JBOD. When you connect two clusters, you effectively split the number of drives per cluster in half. Therefore, cluster one (on the left in Figure 13-33. on page 475) and cluster two (on the right, same figure) each has seven drives.

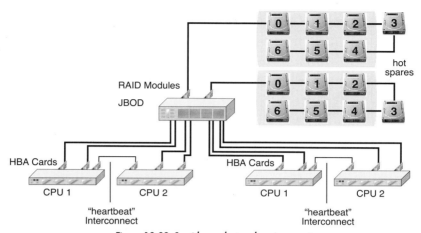

Figure 13-33. Semi large clustered environment

When would you use a system like this? Let's say that you're the IT director of a restaurant chain of 350 LobsterBurger restaurants spread from Ogunquit, Maine, to Pismo Beach, California. You've got a rack of four servers (the four in Figure 13-33. above) divided into two clusters. Cluster one on the left is your receiving system for all of the Point of Sale (POS) cash registers in each of your 350 stores. Each time someone orders a LobsterBurger, the information from the cash register (POS system) is fed into the store's server. Every 15 minutes, the store's server then batch uploads that quarter hour's worth of information to your POS management system. Since you can't afford to lose the data, you have it stored in a RAID 5 system. Since your server can't go down, you have it clustered.

Because you're at a franchise level, you run the Inventory Management (IM) and supply chain management (SCM) system for all 350 restaurants on the other two clustered servers. As the POS system is updated, the IM/SCM system culls information from the POS system for continual monitoring of your lobster stock, and your Just in Time ordering process is run on a daily basis for the freshest ingredients possible. Again, you want a RAID 5 to protect the data and a clustered server to ensure that it doesn't go down.

Single Point of Failure: Your budget.

The only thing more convoluted and more expensive is a Storage Area Network, or SAN. Wanna guess what we're going to cover next?

STORAGE AREA NETWORKS

Storage Area Networks (**SAN**s for short) can quickly get out of hand, price-wise and design-wise. However, I do concede that they have their place in the network storage hierarchy. A typical SAN is a network containing at least two servers that have access to a storage pool through an interconnection with at least one Fibre Channel switch (but usually two, to avoid having a single point of failure).

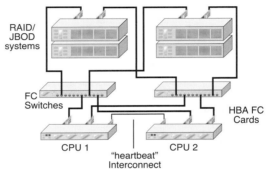

Figure 13-34. Small SAN

In Figure 13-34. we show a small cluster on a SAN setup. The two CPUs are attached to the LAN using standard Ethernet cards. Since they're in a cluster configuration, they share their heartbeat signal over an interconnect cable. They're connected to the **SAN fabric**, as it's often called (because it interweaves connectivity in the same way fabric interweaves threads) through either single or dual Fibre Channel cards. Here, we show dual cards per computer. Each card is then attached to a separate Fibre Channel switch. This can be a single switch, but we show two for redundancy. The switches then attach to the RAID/JBOD systems through Fibre Channel cards as well. Again, for redundancy, we show two HBA Fibre Channel cards connecting to the two FC switches. By setting up the system this way, either RAID system could go out, either switch could go out, and either CPU could go out. Chances are, if you build this system without your CFO's approval, *you'll* be going out. However, SANS offer many benefits that you can't get elsewhere. Their biggest advantage is superior connectivity between CPUs and storage. Every server on the network (or any storage device with enough intelligence) can address all the (other) storage devices on the network, for distances up to 10 kilometers. Storage resources scattered throughout a building, or several buildings, can be accessed for purposes of mirroring or clustering.

Coupling storage virtualization software into a SAN

As we've just discussed, SANs allow geographic separation of storage systems through Fibre Channel connectivity. This can actually be a very good disaster recovery tactic for some organizations with campus environments or short-distance metropolitan area networks (MANs). By coupling a SAN with volume mirroring through storage virtualization software like VERITAS' Volume Manager or Windows 2000 Logical Disk Manager (LDM), an administrator can create redundant data stores up to a distance of about 10 km.

Logical Disk Manager (LDM) is the result of collaboration between VERITAS and Microsoft. It's included with all Windows 2000 Server versions as a disk management snap-in to the Microsoft Management Console (MMC), and is designed for Windows 2000 environments with moderate uptime requirements or limited system administration resources available for configuring and managing storage.

VERITAS Volume Manager (VVM) is designed for heterogeneous environments requiring the highest availability. It supports heterogeneous storage management for HP-UX, AIX, Linux, Sun Solaris, Windows 2000 and Windows NT. It's not available for the Macintosh OS X platform (yet). Because of this heterogenous support, we prefer the VERITAS version of storage virtualization over any other vertical product's version. We also prefer it for its dynamic SAN management characteristics.

Heterogeneous storage management

Abstraction of physical disks allows you to work with storage equipment from multiple vendors, and to migrate volumes dynamically, giving you more equipment choices. Furthermore, you can better use the storage you have by creating and managing volumes more efficiently, thus saving on additional disk purchases.

Dynamic SAN management

Since VVM supports multiple dynamic disk groups, applications and data can be easily migrated from server to server in a SAN environment as a complete set. VVM also doesn't automatically try to import all of the storage resources that can be seen—this protects against storage being imported into multiple systems simultaneously. Finally, VVM protects SAN-based storage with the ability to designate dynamic disk groups as "private," which prevents other servers from accessing or importing these storage resources, thus protecting storage resources between servers by allowing administrators to partition storage and assign exclusive server ownership in a SAN or shared disk[11]. All of these features make VVM a valuable tool in managing any SAN environment.

Dynamic volumes

Before RAID came along, volumes and physical disks were pretty much one and the same. Then RAID taught us that we could arrange an array of physical disks into a logical volume. We now need to abstract that direction one more layer.

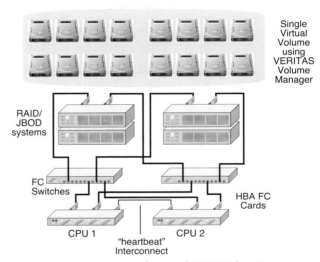

Figure 13-35. Dynamic volumes and VERITAS Volume Manager

For our purposes here, a dynamic volume in a SAN is an abstract storage object defined, created, and managed by a volume manager that operates as a layer within the operating system. Much like a SCSI or RAID driver, the volume manager intercepts calls relating to reading and writing to disk, and provides a mapping service that translates those requests into the appropriate physical locations on the disks. The required data locations are then passed to the disk driver. Since a dynamic volume is an abstract logical entity, it can start and end anywhere on a physical disk or in a partition, and be composed of space on physical disks on different devices. Storage virtualization makes it possible to better utilize your phys-

---

11. This is very important for the security of your environment and makes the creation and management of security policies much easier.

ical disks in a SAN fabric by creating any one (or combination) of the following dynamic volume types; Simple, Spanned, Striped Mirrored, RAID 10 (mirrored striped), or RAID 5. Pretty amazing stuff, if you ask me. Let's go through these one by one[12].

Simple volumes

A **dynamic simple volume** consists of a single contiguous region (or subdisk) on a single physical disk. Dynamic simple volumes can be extended or mirrored. When you extend a simple volume to a non-contiguous region in the same disk or onto additional disks, it becomes a spanned volume—but that comes next. In Figure 13-36. eight simple volumes in the SAN fabric (to focus directly on the logical volumes, we've omitted the rest of the picture). VVM intercepts a write to a volume, and the file is stored on a single drive, because in this scenario, each drive also represents a simple volume.

Figure 13-36. Dynamic simple volumes

Spanned and striped volumes

A **dynamic spanned volume** consists of two or more subdisks (single contiguous regions) on one or more disks, combining sections of unallocated space from multiple dynamic disks into one large volume. And, unlike other systems, in a SAN environment, you can span your volume across multiple JBOD enclosures.

The areas of unallocated space used to create spanned volumes can be different sizes (you don't have to use a whole disk, as shown in Figure 13-37.). Spanned volumes are organized sequentially—that is, VVM sequentially allocates space on each disk until that disk is full and then continues with the next disk until the volume size is reached. Up to 256 disks can be included in a spanned volume. Existing spanned volumes can be extended by the amount of unallocated space on all the disks in the dynamic disk group. However, after a spanned volume is extended, no portion of it can be deleted without deleting the entire spanned volume.

---

12. The following descriptions were "borrowed heavily" from VERITAS Volume Manager 3.1 for Windows 2000 User's Guide (2002).

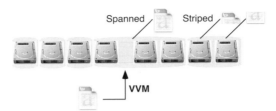

Figure 13-37. Dynamic spanned volume

 A spanned volume consists of smaller pieces of disk space from several disks, thereby making more efficient use of the disk space than is possible when a volume is limited to a single disk. However, spanned volumes are not fault tolerant (nor are they striped for speed). If one of the disks containing a spanned volume fails, the entire volume fails. However, a spanned volume *can* be mirrored.

Striped volumes differ from spanned volumes in that data is divided into blocks and spread in a fixed order among all the disks in the volume. Striping then writes files across all disks, so that data is added to all disks at the same rate. Up to 256 disks can be used in a striped volume. Striped volumes offer the best performance of all the disk management strategies. However, as with spanned volumes, striped volumes don't provide fault tolerance.

Mirrored volumes A **mirrored volume** (Figure 13-38.) is a fault-tolerant volume that duplicates your data on two or more physical disks. A mirror provides redundancy by simultaneously writing the same data onto two or more separate mirrors (VERITAS calls them **plexes**) that reside on different disks. If one of the disks fails, data continues to be written to and read from the unaffected disk or disks.

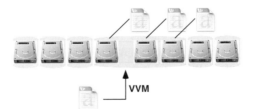

Figure 13-38. Dynamic mirrored volume

Now, here's the kicker: Unlike a traditional RAID system in which a mirrored volume equals two physical drives tied together in an array, a *dynamic* mirrored volume can be two, three, or *more* physical drives tied together in a dynamic array.

Here's why this is so great: When you create a mirror, the same drive letter is used for all plexes of the volume. If sufficient disks are available, you can create multiple mirrors for extra redundancy (up to the limit of 32 mirrors). Then you can break off a mirror to use for backup, data analysis, or testing without losing redundancy. Breaking off a plex from the mirrored volume doesn't delete the information, but it does mean that the split plex no longer mirrors information from the other plex or plexes in the mirrored volume. Instead, it's assigned a different drive letter than that of the original mirrored volume.

Figure 13-39. Split plex of a dynamic mirrored volume

While it's no longer part of the mirrored volume, the split plex retains its other volume layout characteristics. For example, if it came from a mirrored striped volume, the broken-off plex becomes a striped volume. To deal with a plex's unrecoverable error on a disk in a mirrored volume, you need to remove the damaged plex and then create a new plex on another disk to replace the damaged plex. When you want to use the space in a mirrored volume for other purposes, you can remove a plex and return its space to unallocated space. VVM lets you add a mirror to any kind of dynamic volume except RAID-5. You can extend any mirrored volume.

Mirrored striped, and RAID 5 volumes

VVM also allows you to have RAID 10 and RAID 5 dynamic volumes. Since these volumes are set up very much like the standard RAID 10 (page 442) and RAID 5 (page 443) systems we've already discussed, we won't go into detail about them here.

Providing for automatic volume growth based upon capacity

Let's go back to that POS/IM setup (see *Out There* on page 474). We're going to change the setup a bit this time, adding a bit more complexity, as shown below in Figure 13-40. on page 482.

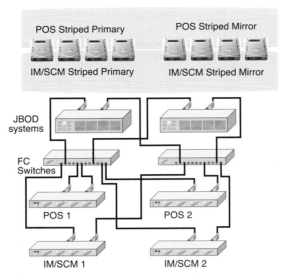

Figure 13-40. Dynamic RAID 1 + 0 systems

You've now decided that having both of your key server clusters in the same wiring closet may not be such a good idea, because the office where you' re running everything is in Ottumwa, Iowa (you know, by Pickwick and Bidwell), where electrical thunderstorms and tornadoes are all too frequent. Since you have two buildings within a block of each other, you've gotten rights for running a conduit between the offices that you've subsequently filled with fiber cable, and will split your clustered server system and JBODs of drives between two buildings to build a striped, mirrored system.

The left side of Figure 13-40. represents the primary server for both the POS system and the IM/SCM system, as well as one of the Fibre Channel switches and one of the JBODs. The right side represents the secondaries for each of the servers, as well as another FC switch and JBOD. Note that the drives (For space, we show only four each, but you could have up to 256) are set up much differently than in the original diagram (see Figure 13-33. on page 475), where two distinct RAID 5 arrays in the JBOD evenly split the number of drives. In this setup, we lay both sets of striped volumes over the same physical drives in the JBOD, and we then mirror those striped volumes to the second JBOD. When we deal with the second JBOD, you'll understand the method behind our madness. For now, we'll explain why we laid out the striped dynamic volumes this way.

When setting up your dynamic volumes, you can create more than one striped volume across the same physical media. For this example (see Figure 13-40. on page 482), we've created two dynamic striped volumes—one for each of the POS and IM/SCM databases. Each of these dynamic volumes is about 40 percent of the overall *total* physical disk space—leaving 20 percent of the total physical space open for use.

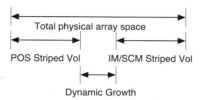

Figure 13-41. Setting up for dynamic growth

VVM has a script that automatically grows a dynamic volume when it reaches a certain percentage of capacity. With this procedure, you can conserve disk space on your servers. Space is distributed to users or database applications on an as-needed basis, and you don't have to be standing in front of the server to allocate the new disk space, since it's done automatically (based upon rules that you set). In our example, we set up a rule for growing the POS striped volume, the IM/SCM striped volume, or both when the Capacity Monitoring Threshold of 90 percent used space within the volume occurs. VVM's Capacity Monitoring function has two thresholds that trigger an alert: a Warning Threshold with a default setting of 80 percent of capacity; and an Error Threshold, with a default setting of 90 percent of capacity. When the Capacity Monitoring function sees that either of the volumes has hit the alert stage, it kicks into gear, launching an associated executable file (volgrow.cmd, FYI) that grows the volume. As long as space is available for the volume, volgrow.cmd will grow to meet it.

Which leaves only one ringing question: In this example, we've mirrored the first JBOD's striped volumes to the second JBOD—because striping doesn't provide any data protection, and somehow, that database must be backed up. Since we've already learned that Open File backups give up a lot of data (see *My, that's a lot of flushing!* on page 365), let's look into a better way to back up the databases you've already configured with VVM.

Replicating a database using VERITAS FlashSnap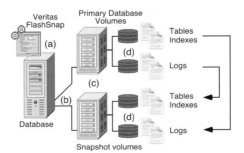

We've covered a few methods for creating backups of online databases already in *Open file backup for databases* on page 339. You can also perform a backup of a running database or file system by creating a snapshot of the data and storing it on a different volume. VVM's add-on, FlashSnap, coupled with a direct attached RAID system (we cover these types of RAID setups in *Standard and fault-tolerant JBOD enclosures* on page 465) or a SAN (which we've been covering) performs what's known as **point-in-time copying**, creating an exact mirror of a volume or partition for later use without disrupting production,. FlashSnap takes point-in-time copies of your mirrored database, "snapping" them off as remote volumes (hence, the second JBOD) that can be backed up and then reattached to the mirror on a regularly scheduled basis. If you need more real-time replication, skip this section and read one about synchronous replication that uses VVM plus VERITAS Volume Replicator (see *Current data* on page 509).

In Figure 13-42. we show a single database server running FlashSnap software (a) with two RAID banks (c) connected to it via either SCSI controllers or Fibre-Channel controllers (b). Each RAID bank holds the logical volumes (d) on which the database resides. FlashSnap creates a replica of the *primary* database volume onto the *snapshot* volume.

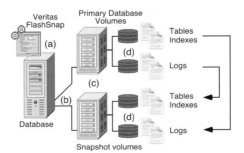

Figure 13-42. Point-in-time copying

FlashSnap features

FlashSnap offers a very flexible means for capturing an online image of data that is currently in use, be it a database or a file system. Once that point-in-time data has been moved from the primary to the snapshot volume, you can use the snapshot to perform maintenance tasks or backups to tape while leaving the primary data untouched. FlashSnap supports two kinds of point-in-time copying: volume-level solutions and file system-level solutions.

Volume Manager with FastResync

The volume-level solution is applicable when high I/O performance of the production server is critical. If you use this approach, add FlashSnap to VVM, because it utilizes the Persistent FastResync and Disk Group Split/Join features.

VVM allows taking multiple snapshots at the volume level. A snapshot volume contains a copy of the volume's data at the moment in time that the snapshot was taken. Once a snapshot is taken, since there are no active users of the replica database, it can then be used as normal for either read-only access or for backup purposes. FlashSnap uses a FastResync map to keep track of the changes on the primary volume. Or, if the volume and its snapshot get out of sync, FastResync maps and resynchronizes the volume with the snapshot. Only the changes are transferred to the snapshot, which makes synchronization very fast. FastResync comes in two flavors:

1. Non-Persistent FastResync stores the change maps in memory. If a system is rebooted, the information is not preserved and a full synchronization is required.

2. Persistent FastResync stores the change maps on disk to ensure that they survive a system crash.

File Manager with Storage Checkpoints

The file system–level is a better choice when your file system contains a small number of large files, and the data changes are relatively small. Use VERITAS File System[13] in conjunction with FlashSnap for this approach because of its Storage Checkpoint feature.

A Storage Checkpoint is a persistent image of a file system at any given time. Storage Checkpoints use a copy-on-write technology to reduce I/O overhead by identifying and maintaining only the file system blocks that changed since the previous Checkpoint was taken. Storage Checkpoints offers a number of advantages, including their persistence throughout reboots and crashes, and their ability to be immediately writeable by preserving the file system metadata, the directory hierarchy, and user data.

---

13. VERITAS File System is a high-performance file system that is optimized for database applications and data-intensive workloads.

Online database backup on the same host

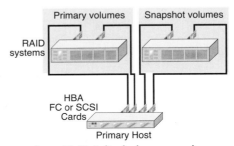

Figure 13-43. Online backup on same host

The illustration above (Figure 13-43.) depicts a database server using separate controllers to access the database and the snapshot volume. A lightly loaded host can handle the performance requirements of FlashSnap in addition to the database load. In this setup, File Manager and FlashSnap create and maintain snapshots of the database file system on the snapshot volume. At any time, a backup server can access the snapshot volume and save a backup to any writeable media.

Online database backup to a separate host

While the first scenario is great to ensure that the database itself is protected in case of an emergency (and also in an offline state so that it can be backed up normally), it doesn't provide much protection from losing the CPU, as well. With FlashSnap, you can also set up a dual CPU, making a point-in-time copy of the database to an off-host snapshot volume.

For this setup, we turn from a SCSI system to a Fibre Channel SAN. By moving to a SAN, we separate the two hosts and two RAID sets up to a distance of 10 KM. This is a great setup for a campus environment, where the Primary Host is in one building (along with its SAN fabric and RAID system), with the OHP (Offsite Host Point in Time) RAID set, along with its SAN fabric and OHP Host, in another building—remember our LobsterBurger restaurant franchise setting (see Figure 13-40. on page 482)? We had created two dynamic striped volumes within a dynamic mirrored volume, which encompassed two physically separated JBODs in two different buildings, with the primary striped volumes in one building and the mirror of the striped volumes socked safely away in a second building for disaster recovery.

Use the FlashSnap procedure with two servers, with the secondary server in the cluster to process the backup or other resource-intensive activities. That's what we're doing here: FlashSnap's Snapshot procedure automatically detaches the mirror of the striped volume, thus creating a new "snapshot" volume. It then "deports" this disk group from the original server (the primary) and imports it to the secondary server.

At this point, the secondary server performs a normal backup of the databases residing in the dynamic striped volume (in our case, both the POS and the IM/ SCM volumes will be backed up). Since the databases aren't online, they won't be susceptible to open file limitations during the backup process.

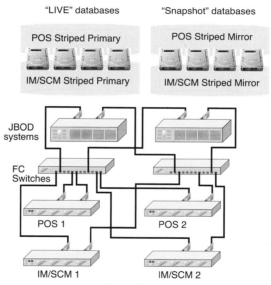

Figure 13-44. Online backup from a separate host

Once the volumes have been backed up, FlashSnap reattaches the mirrored striped volumes to the original disk set, once again creating a mirrored striped volume.

The only problems with this process? The striped volumes are without protection during the backup, and the backup provides only a point-in-time version of the data sets. You'll understand my hesitation about this once you read the chapter on Replication.

NETWORK ATTACHED STORAGE (NAS)

As redundant as a RAID 5 system, more expandable than a file server with **Direct Attached Storage (DAS)**, and less complicated (sometimes) than a full-blown Storage Area Network (SAN), here it is: the **Network Attached Storage (NAS)** device (or **NAS box**). A gazillion years ago, Novell, Microsoft, Sun, and Apple created their first servers to serve files for the organizational network; hence the term **file servers**. As time went on, these same servers became multipurpose servers, and file serving became just a very small percentage of their capabilities.

While the servers themselves are adding services, you can add another type of growth: the ever-increasing amount of storage space that seems to develop overnight on most networks[14]. With DAS, a storage pool is established for each server by adding those JBODs or RAID towers that we've been talking about and then configuring them for a certain percentage (usually around 40 percent) of extra space to allow for growth. DAS storage cannot be added easily to the storage pool without downtime: Each time you reset your RAID system, rebuilding the RAID structure can take as much as seven hours. As such, enough extra storage capacity for a DAS system must be established by planning for growth over the next several months or a year. If you business growth growth, figure in extra server downtime if that growth also means that you need more data space. With traditional servers, the storage and the server are one and the same.

NAS deployment separates the storage from the system. Instead of adding drives to a server—an arduous process at best—NAS boxes increase storage capacity by attaching more NAS boxes to a distributed file system or a SAN. Neither method is lengthy, nor do they disrupt day-to-day computing. All Iomega and Dell products use the Microsoft Windows 2000 Server Appliance Kit (SAK) operating system. Windows SAK's **Distributed file system (Dfs)** is a perfect feature for NAS boxes. Dfs is a service that provides integration of files and share points into one or more logical namespaces (such as NAS.backupbook.com) that eliminate the need for users to be aware of multiple physical devices (such as NAS1, NAS2, etc.). Dell takes this one step further in their top-of-the-line NAS boxes by deploying what they call "NAS over SAN," wherein the organization extends the

---

14.   Based on Merrill Lynch & Co. and McKinsey & Co.'s "The Storage Report–Customer Perspectives & Industry Evolution," (2001), storage capacity is estimated to be increasing, with workgroup applications growing in the annual growth range of 20–40%.

NAS device's storage capacity by attaching it to a fibre channel SAN-based storage array.

With NAS boxes, you get great *multiprotocol* file services without having to pay per-computer licensing fees, as you do with traditional server platforms. All NAS boxes support the common protocols you need and expect, including CIFS (Common Internet File System), FTP, HTTP, NFS (Network File System), and even AppleShare over IP.

Are they here to stay? You betcha. According to the folks we've been talking to lately at Dell and Iomega, the NAS equipment market has grown more than 12 percent, and is expected to accelerate in the next couple of years. High-end NAS products now come with several hundred gigabytes up to multiple terabytes of storage, multiprocessor CPUs, and capabilities that make them truly a part of any storage and business continuity plan. And, of course, they all come with either RAID 5 preinstalled for data or as one of the RAID options. Let's take a quick look at two leading NAS box vendors: Iomega and Dell.

The NAS box offerings we like

There are several NAS box vendors, but we like two best: Dell and Iomega—Iomega for a basic, all-purpose NAS box (and if you buy your equipment through VARs); Dell for a very complex system. Rotating clockwise from the top left of Table 13-7. , we have the Iomega P3400, the Dell PowerVault 725, the Dell PowerVault 775, and the Iomega P415. All four are top-flight NAS boxes that utilize the Windows 2000 SAK operating system.

Table 13-7. Iomega (left) and Dell (right) NAS boxes

The following two tables (see Table 13-8. on page 490) give you all the information you need to know about these NAS boxes. The first shows you basic information about capacity, etc., and the second focuses on backup and recovery information. In the first table, you'll probably notice that the Iomega P415 has the largest capacity of any of the other boxes listed—as of this writing, it has the largest capacity of any NAS box, period. As drive sizes go up, NAS box capacity rises with them (there's only so many drives you can put in a 1U, 1.75-inch-high unit). And, as drive capacities go up, cost per gigabyte of storage space in a NAS box goes down. Simple math; no ciphering necessary, Jethro.

Beyond storage capacity, we don't know of any other NAS systems offer hot-swap drives. While having a drive in hot spare reduces the NAS box's overall storage capacity, it balances that with increased availability should one of the drives die.

And speaking of drives dying, both vendors use the Ultra ATA drives in their NAS boxes. Dell offers Ultra SCSI in their highest-end unit, but also provides Ultra ATA drives in it. While ATA drives are great, they aren't SCSI and won't give you SCSI-drive lifetime, either, so you'll have to watch your drives carefully with a SMART alarm system come years two and three of their lifespan.

The larger 2U Dell 775 is the only NAS box that offers hardware RAID (which uses up one of the slots in the system). It's also the only one that offers NAS over SAN for expandability (we'll get to that in a moment).

Basic Info	Iomega		Dell	
	3400	P415	725	775
Internal Capacity	120 G	720 G	480 G	438 G
Hot Swap Drives	No	Yes	No	No
Drive Type	Ultra ATA	Ultra ATA	Ultra ATA	Ultra SCSI
RAID Type	0,1,5	0,1,5 + Swap	0,1,5	0,1,5,10,50
RAID Type	Software	Software	Software	Hardware
Extendibility	Distributed File System	Distributed File System	Distributed File System	NAS over SAN

Table 13-8. NAS breakdown

All four of the NAS boxes shown here support mirrored OS volumes. Some NAS boxes have enough drives so you can split off two drives to be mirrored for the OS and applications and have two drives mirrored for data. Since NAS boxes aren't OS powerhouses, don't turn them into high-end application servers. You can, however, turn them into very efficient backup servers for backing up client workstation data in a hierarchical storage model. With one NAS box as a "head" with a couple of others in a distributed environment or in a SAN configuration acting as storage, you've got yourself a great workstation backup solution. In the NAS-as-workstation backup server environment, only the Iomega device comes with its own multi-OS client backup software.

Backup Info	Iomega		Dell	
	3400	P415	725	775
Mirrored OS Volume	Yes	Yes	Yes	Yes
Journal File System	No	No	Yes	Yes
Block Level Snapshots	Yes	Yes	Yes	Yes
Mac/Win Client Backup	Yes	Yes	No	No

Table 13-9. Backup information for the NAS boxes

Extending NAS storage

You can extend the capacity of NAS boxes on a network with two distinct methods: First, by a simple distributed file system, and the second by making the NAS box a "head," or entry point to the Storage Area Network (SAN). While the distributed file system is much simpler and costs no additional monies, it doesn't provide the SAN environment's redundancy levels. However, while the SAN environment offers unlimited growth and unlimited redundancies, it empties your wallet faster than a teenager with daddy's platinum Visa.

Distributed file system

Distributed file system (Dfs) is a Windows 2000 service that allows a network administrator to set up several NAS boxes so that the users can locate files within the NAS system without having to know which NAS box those files actually reside on. Dfs accomplishes this by creating a logical, hierarchical view of file shares that exist on servers distributed in one or more domains such as two NAS boxes in a company's storage domain (NAS1.storage.myco.com, NAS2.storage.myco.com). The Dfs servers are responsible for maintaining this logical-to-physical-namespace translation table, and also for handing out physical server referrals to the users accessing this logical system. Using Active Directory, metadata configuration information is stored at the domain server. When looking up the Dfs NAS volumes, the Active Directory server points the user to the logical volume on the correct NAS box.

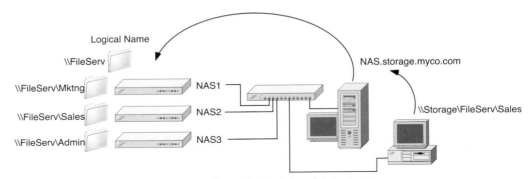

Logical Name

\\FileServ

\\FileServ\Mktng   NAS1

\\FileServ\Sales   NAS2

\\FileServ\Admin   NAS3

NAS.storage.myco.com

\\Storage\FileServ\Sales

Figure 13-45. Dfs through Active Directory

This makes it very easy to manage NAS volumes and add or move data. Dfs isolates users from the physical location of each share, assigning a permanent (logical) name to user shares that isn't dependent on the server name. In other words, when looking for information for a client's sales records, instead of typing in **\\NAS2\Sales** and then mounting a new server and typing in **\\NAS1\Mktng** when accessing the same client's marketing info, the user simply needs to know that all of the client's files can be found on \\FileServ, whether he wants to access sales, marketing, or administrative information.

As a result, the share name doesn't change when administrators move files around during such tasks as storage resource management, load balancing, and such, resulting in reduced administrative work and costs. We'll cover the idea of storage management later on in *Working with SRM (Storage Resource Management) software to eliminate cruft and reduce hardware needs* on page 713. For now, let's get back to the idea of keeping data safe on these NAS boxes through redundancy, which is what this chapter is about.

Another NAS box benefit is replication. To maintain this distributed system, servers in a Dfs hierarchy use the File Replication System (FRS) also integrated into Windows 2000. FRS synchronizes system policies, logon information for the system volume, and share points, and can even replicate entire NAS boxes. Since Active Directory information is replicated among all the controllers in a given domain, Dfs information and NAS contents can also be replicated for fault tolerance or across a WAN for business continuity.

While you *can* replicate certain volumes of a NAS box using FRS across a WAN, I suggest using one of two other products. The first, VERITAS Storage Replicator, is a robust Windows 2000 server–based replication engine that also runs on the

NAS box's SAK version of the OS. VERITAS Storage Replicator has many more controls for replication than does FRS, and is a much more robust solution. The other, simply called Replicator, is a much simpler solution than Storage Replicator. It too runs on Windows 2000 server and can run on SAK very easily. We cover both of these solutions in depth in *Replication* on page 497.

NAS on SAN

With the addition of Fibre Channel HBAs, Dell's PowerVault NAS line can now scale outward into a SAN. This gives Dell customers the ability to enter the mass storage arena through the NAS product line and expand into the SAN arena as their storage needs grow significantly—while maintaining their NAS front-end devices as an integral part of the system. Dell's PowerVault 750N and 755N NAS products offer the new SAN option, each with either 1 GB or 2 GB Fibre Channel paths to Dell/EMC SAN products such as the FC 4700, FC4500, and FC5300.

In the Figure 13-46. on page 493, we show the same type of virtual directory, but this one uses a SAN environment instead of multiple NAS boxes for storage. While this might look much like the same type of environment as the triple NAS boxes, the fundamental difference is that the data is now stored in a shared storage environment that can be accessed by other servers in the organization, more easily managed through a Storage Resource Management product such as those from Fujitsu-Softek or Overland Storage, and backed up more easily by a SAN-attached tape library such as the Overland Storage NEO (which we discuss in Chapter 18: *Organizational network backups* on page 655).

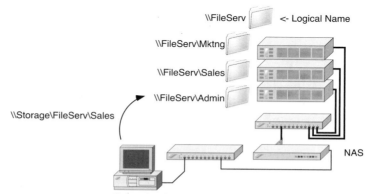

Figure 13-46. Dell NAS "head" attached to a SAN storage environment

WHAT IF YOU CAN'T AFFORD A CLUSTERED SERVER OR A SAN?

Some of us need the business continuity of a clustered server because we can't have our system down forever—but we don't have deep enough pockets for it. Now what? Well, *what* means more creativity instead of more money—it's called consolidation. And no, that doesn't mean anyone's getting laid off. It is the computer version of stuffing 20 pounds of manure into a 10-pound bag.

First, predetermine which servers in your office can go double duty in in a pinch. Let's say you have a setup like the one in Figure 13-47. below left (which is a real-life setup). This is a print shop; thus, also a job house. Everything is based on time and budget. While these guys can't afford to have a server down for long, they can't afford a fully clustered environment, either. Instead, we equipped certain servers with duplicate hardware and RAM capabilities, and specced each of them slightly more powerful than necessary, so in case of an emergency, one server can pull the load of two.

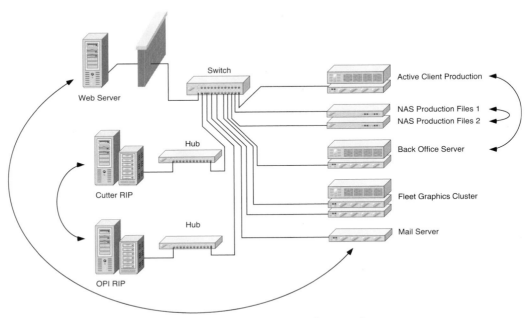

Figure 13-47. Print shop network

In the Figure 13-47. on page 494, we can double up the OPI and cutter servers. We cover just such a double-duty server configuration for doubling up the back office server with the active client production server in our Replication chapter, Figure 14-27. on page 531. Our NAS boxes were specced at twice the normal size for growth and for doubling up in case one failed, and the web and mail servers can swap, as well.

The only caveat, as you might have guessed by looking at the network picture, is that if we had to double up the cutter RIP and the OPI RIP, we'd probably cause a network bottleneck on the remaining network segment because twice the traffic would go through that leg of the network.

So the question remains: How did we know which to merge? The answer is simple, yet complex. About the time we began researching this book, Storage Resource Management (SRM) software hit the scene, promising that you can use it to monitor your devices in the hope of consolidating more processes (and groups of users' *stuff*) onto fewer computers so that you can grow your organization's computer usage without growing your budget. We cover SRM and consolidation in our network backup chapter, under *Working with SRM (Storage Resource Management) software to eliminate cruft and reduce hardware needs* on page 713. For now, hit the "I believe" button when I tell you that you can use SRM software to monitor the processes, bandwidth, and usage of your servers to create a consolidation plan, in case you lose one of them.

KEYBOARD LOSS

I had to add this, because we got it from a friend. Here's a step-by-step way to clean out spills on keyboards. Thanks to Daniel Knight of Ada, Michigan, for this great tip!

1. Shut down your computer ASAP.

2. Disconnect your keyboard and mop up the spill.

3. Drain your keyboard and bring it to a large sink (or bathtub, for home users).

4. Rinse your keyboard with tap water for several minutes.

5. Drain your keyboard.

6. Set your keyboard on edge and let it dry overnight.

7. Before you go home, call PC Connection and they'll have a new one for you in the morning.

CHAPTER 14:
REPLICATION

Replication is the process of automatically duplicating and updating data on multiple computers across a network—usually to a geographically dispersed location to fail-safe the data from building loss. The simple description of replication is that it moves data from source computers (those labelled "a" in Figure 14-1.) to destination computers (in this case, computer "b" in Figure 14-1.).

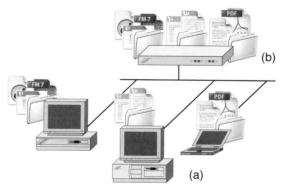

Figure 14-1. Basic file replication

As I said, that's the short version. It gets a bit more complicated when you implement the replication software, because at that point you have to know about three different variations dealing with the *source of the data*, *how often* that data is moved, and whether the data transfer is *synchronous* or *asynchronous*.

The source data for replication

The replication source data can either be individual files and folders, or whole volumes and partitions. Some products are purely file-focused and aren't used for backing up database volumes; other products are specifically designed with the replication of databases in mind, and therefore focus primarily on moving everything within the volume from point A to point B.

- If the replication process is file-based, the data is examined at the file level and then updated from the source to the destination either in whole or by using the delta block transfer method[1].

  File-based replication systems normally transfer the data from source to destination via any IP-based network. This means that these systems are outstanding for creating mirrored replicas in the organizational network or across the organizational WAN.

- If the replication system is volume-based, the volume is examined block by block, and the replica is updated by that method.

  Volume-based replication systems transfer the information from the source to the destination using either high-speed SCSI or Fibre Channel cabled systems. These systems are outstanding for creating mirrored replicas within server clusters, a campus network, or from one office to the next within a 10-kilometer area (using Fibre Channel).

Either way, replicated files on the destination volume are constantly updated with the changes made to the original files on the source volume so that an exact copy of each and every file targeted is continuously replicated and then available for use on the destination.

Because replication can be either file-based or volume-based, it's an ideal thread-in to network backup practices. It can be used to copy live databases for backup, to centralize data from multiple computer systems to a single computer system for easier backup, and for a host of other purposes.

How often do you want the data moved?

The next thing you need to know about replication is that you can move data in two ways: continuousy as it's written, or as a series of point-in-time snapshots.

File-based replication is normally *not* set up to move the data on a continuous basis from the source to the destination, because that just wouldn't make sense. Why spend the computer processes and network bandwidth to move a Microsoft

---

[1]. See *Delta block backup* on page 303 for more information on this method.

Word file that gets saved every 10 minutes while the user is working on it? At best, the replication software would have something to do every 10 minutes. Generally, documents just sit there until opened and saved. Therefore, file-based replication is normally set up so that the administrator can designate a regular schedule for when the replication should occur. *By setting up a normally scheduled replication process, an administrator can ensure that the data is consistent between points A and B.*

On the other hand, databases are usually accessed frequently, and therefore replication software that focuses on databases moves that data continuously between points A and B. As we stated in *Open-file database backups* on page 343, backing up databases using a point-in-time method causes you to lose a lot of data. Therefore, *allowing the replication process to run continuously will give the administrator peace of mind that the data is not only consistent, but current as well.*

Synchronous or asynchronous transfer

The last bit of replication that you have to come to grips with is how you're going to *move* your data from point A to point B. Moving the data can be done in two ways—synchronously and asynchronously.

The **synchronous** method is simple. When the replication process commences, all the data at the source that you've chosen to move is immediately sent over the network to the destination. If you're moving files during a point-in-time snapshot, this should cause no major problems, as it's handled like any other file transfer through the network. However, if you're trying to continuously move the contents of a database that's being hit hard with a lot of updates, and you're moving large blocks and huge amounts of data at a time, you're now outside the normal bounds of control that a network offers. Your replication system could easily cause your entire network's bandwidth to fill up and become congested during a synchronous transfer.

Therefore, **asynchronous** transfers were devised to curtail those sudden bursts of network traffic that continuous, block-based replication processes create. The asynchronous method of transfer establishes a queue at the replication server in which to hold data while maintaining a steady stream of network traffic between source and destination.

Your choice of using synchronous or asynchronous data transfers really depends on the information you want to replicate, how much change you're implementing to that information, how often that change comes (in lumps or gradually), and how big the network pipes are between source and destination.

THE MAIN THING

The Main Thing here is that you understand

- **Your business needs,**

  What happens if the data you're replicating isn't the most current? What's the cost of loss of a minute, hour, or day's worth of data loss? Would that cost more than the replication system, or are you trying to propose a replication system that has a price tag higher than the worth of the data you're replicating?

- **Your data transfer needs,**

  Do you need to move data in blocks or files? Do you need to move your data from one office to another office in the same building? Do you need to move your data to another city for it to be safe? You have to ask these questions before you can move on.

- **How often your data changes, and**

  If your data changes relatively often and you're trying to replicate a database, you might need to move to a block-based asynchronous replication process. If your database doesn't change often, or changes gradually, you can probably get away with a synchronous process. If you're replicating files and folders, you'll want to go with synchronous scheduled transfers.

- **The throughput available between your source and destination.**

  No matter which method you use, you need to understand your throughput and latency. Get a good set of network management tools and then manage your network throughput.

CURRENT, OR SIMPLY CONSISTENT DATA?

Choosing a replication system is a balancing act: You must weigh the cost of unavailable data against how much you want to spend. And you must grasp another balance—because it'll grasp your wallet one way or the other: the balance of **current** and **consistent data**. Replication helps you with both in the event of your computer's loss by moving that data to a destination that's usually at least a building away from the original source computer. However, the more current you want to keep your data, the more you must spend on connectivity infrastructure between your source server and your destination server. We mention that up front here because it's something that folks don't often think about, yet it could be one of the major cost factors you have to face in planning for replication. Let's start with consistent data and then work our way through to current data.

Consistent data

If the source server dies and the destination server must be made live, your data is **consistent** if the application using it on the destination can be successfully restarted to a usable state with data that's verifiable to a certain point in time—without any corruption (hearkening back to that "write-order fidelity" thing we've mentioned before). While this sounds easy, in practice it can get a tad complicated when you realize how some database transactions work while the replication process is going on.

Let's say that you decided that you're so darn cool you must buy one of the trendy hats at buttlecaps.com.

Consistent operation

1. You sign into the system (you've bought there before) and tell it you want to order a new buttlecap—in this way, you're telling the database manager running the store that you want to modify your purchase records.

2. The database software receives the request in the form of a Data Modification Language (DML) command to perform the update to your record. It then writes this transaction to its log.

3. Once you've entered all of the buttlecaps you want to buy, you hit the **Save** button, telling the database to commit your order to the system as a permanent change. The database enters this as another log transaction. If it's not

busy, it might update to the data table. If buttlecaps are going like hotcakes, though, it maintains your transaction in the computer's RAM until such time as it can write the transaction to disk. However, a write *never* occurs to the table space unless it's first committed to the log.

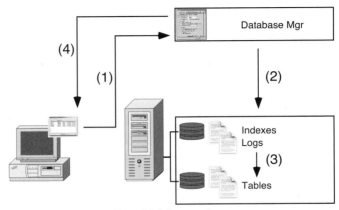

Figure 14-2. Data consistency

4. The database then replies to your computer's application, indicating that the write has been committed and telling it that it's okay to end the transaction.

As you can see from this simple example, the application on your computer is responsible for maintaining the transaction until it receives the commit from the database. That's only the first step in the process.

The database is responsible for maintaining the transaction (sometimes called the **redo**) log. Throughout the normal course of events, the database will checkpoint the log. **Checkpointing** means that all transactions still in memory are written to the disk's tables. After that, the transactions are cleared from the logs and the logs can be archived. In this way, the database maintains consistent data.

Crash and restore operations

Now that we know what a consistent operation looks like, let's examine what happens during a **non-consistent** operation—a fancy term for what happens when the database crashes. For that, we'll put you back in the seat of the user hitting the buttlecaps.com website to order a hat.

1. You've decided to update your buttlecaps order, thus telling the database manager that you want to modify your purchase records.

2. The database software receives the request in the form of a Data Modification Language (DML) command to perform the update to your record. It then writes this transaction to its log.

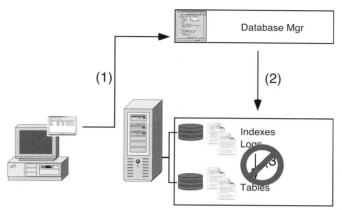

Figure 14-3. Non-consistent operation

3. However, before you can hit the **Save** button and commit your changes, the database server crashes. It won't matter now if you hit the **Save** button as often as you hit the down button in the elevator after a 10-hour workday. The database server isn't there to hear your urgent cries of "I want buttlecaps!" and sooner or later, your application times out.

The database must take several steps to return to a healthy, up-to-date state.

1. First, it must be restarted. This usually occurs after the angst und drang of everyone involved and after the database administrator has calmed down enough to get to the database server administration software and send the restart command.

2. When the database resumes operations, it performs a crash recovery, mounting the data tables in their pre-crash state—the instance of the last database checkpoint. This is called the database's **known state**: some time in the past between the points when the crash and the last checkpoint occurred.

3. Once the database is at a known state, it can then begin to "roll forward" through all of the log transactions and apply the actions to the database. This is the longest portion of time during the recovery process, and can take anywhere from a few seconds (highly doubtful) to hours. All transactions in the

log are committed. Any non-committed transactions (due to the crash) are "undone" in the database.

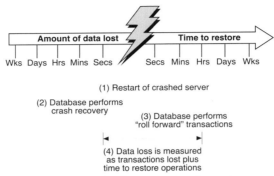

Figure 14-4. Database restoration after crash

4. That means that your buttlecap purchase won't be recorded. Had the **Save** button been hit before the crash, and the database received your order and entered the information into the transaction log, the transaction would be marked as committed. The end user would be able to see the record (remember, the server crashed before sending a response to the client app on the end user's machine) only if he or she re-signs in and examines the purchase history. *Data loss is measured as transactions lost plus time to restore operations.*

Of course, all of this depends on the database's ability to restart.

What happens if the database crashed due to a fire in the building that destroyed the computer? Or if the building fell down? Or, if you lived in my old neighborhood, where it's likely that somebody just came in and took the computer? Then there wouldn't be any computer to restart the database *with*.

Let's look at the restoration process rebuilt from a tape or disk backup of the data.

1. First, if your computer is gone, you must replace and reconfigure it. You can do this in less than an hour if you swapped in an existing computer and reloaded the software and setups from an imaged disk system.

2. Your next step: Layer on top of your image the data that was lost in your database. This could take anywhere from less than an hour to hours.

3. You're left with whatever data you had during your last off-site tape backup—up to a week's worth of data loss. That isn't good.

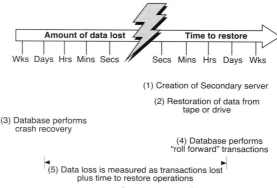

Figure 14-5. Database restoration from tape

4. Once your database is up and running, it must still go through the "roll for-ward" process (assuming that you've backed up the transaction logs, as well).

5. Your data and productivity loss spans a much greater time interval than it would have in a mere computer crash.

Which, of course, is why you've wisely chosen to replicate your data to an offsite computer. Let's walk through what happens during an asynchronous replication, and how it recovers in such a situation.

Asynchronous replication

In an **asynchronous replication** system, data is written first to the primary source and then to a source cache, which queues the data for transmission to the desti-nation as bandwidth allows. The queue acts as a buffer between the source and the destination, providing a much kinder replication environment for your network than synchronous replication does. When the writing application creates surges in the update rate, the queue grows. As the data is received by the secondary, the queue shrinks. This prevents the writing application from being bogged down waiting for data to transmit from the primary to the secondary.

However, in the event of an emergency, asynchronous replication is more suscep-tible to variances in data between the source and the destination. If the source dies before a transmission has been sent, or packets are delivered out of order, data is lost. If the source dies with a large buffer, the information therein won't be trans-mitted, causing a discrepancy between the information in the source and the information in the destination.

To handle this additional complexity, replication management software must be added as a layer between the database manager and the volumes being written to. Also, a replication journal that works with the replication management software must be created, and installed, with the replication manager in the receiving, secondary computer. On the receiving end, there should be no live database manager trying to access the replicated database—that would gum up the works. The diagram below (Figure 14-6.) shows the basic setup of the primary and secondary database, as well as the additional steps necessary for a transaction to take place. Let's walk through it.

Consistent Operation

1. You've decided to update your buttlecaps order; thus, you're telling the database manager that you want to modify your purchase records.

2. The database software receives the request in the form of a Data Modification Language (DML) command to perform the update to your record. Instead of writing the information directly to its transaction log, it passes the information to the replication manager, which writes the information to the primary server's replication journal.

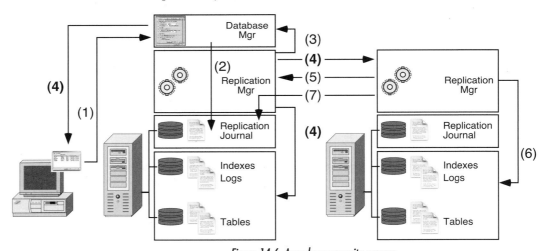

Figure 14-6. Asynchronous write process

3. Once you've hit the **Save** button, instead of the database manager writing to its transaction log, the Replication Manager again steps up to the plate, does the work, and tells the database application that the write is complete.

4. At this point, several things happen simultaneously. The database manager replies to the client that the transaction is complete. The replication manager writes the data to the primary volumes, and at the same time, adds the information to the outgoing queue to be sent asynchronously to the secondary host.

    At this point, more data might have been sent than the connectivity between the two hosts can handle. In this case, the queue begins to grow, creating a backlog on the primary server. We'll cover just how much backlog can grow in another section—for now, understand that only so much data can go through a pipe at one time. This isn't Wiley Coyote who turns on the spigot for the hose and watches a bulge go through—alas, real life is not nearly as colorful as a cartoon.

5. Upon receipt of the data, the secondary host sends a network acknowledgment to the primary host, stating that the data is present and in memory, ready to be written to disk.

6. The secondary host then writes the data to its local disks and sends an acknowledgment to the primary host.

7. Once the primary host receives the acknowledgment from the secondary host that the data has been written to local disk, it marks the write as complete in the replication journal.

In a database environment (whether that database is a simple MySQL system, a complex Oracle system, or the structured and incredibly complex file storage engine of a bookkeeping system), updates are made to various elements in a fixed-sequence methodology that can be spread over multiple directories, or even multiple volumes. If this data gets out of sequence, the database or bookkeeping system reject it. Any replication system that works in these environments *must* consistently safeguard the in-sequence writing of this data—VERITAS calls this **write-order fidelity**. This state can be achieved either through software (such as VERITAS' product) or through using asynchronous transfer mode (ATM) wide area networking, or a combination of both.

Crash and restore operations

Let's look at the process again—but this time, there's a hitch: The primary server dies in the middle of a transaction.

1. Let's say that you started the process as before, but you're expanding your TQ (trendiness quotient), and want to buy a different buttlecap for every day of the week.

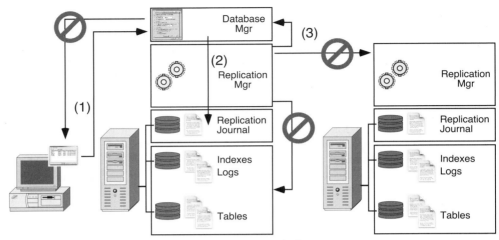

Figure 14-7. Death of a server

2. The replication manager starts to do its thing by logging the request into the replication journal.

3. It then passes the information back to the database manager that everything is hunky-dory. But before the database manager can send a reply to the client, or the data can be written to the primary storage volumes, or the data can be queued for sending to the secondary volumes, the unthinkable occurs: *The computer dies.* A massive typhoon has hit the Ogunquit office that housed the primary database, and the database is swept out to sea. Months later, some happy inhabitant of an uncharted island will have a dandy new coconut-smasher—but for now, let's return to civilization as we know it.

Since it has received no acknowledgment, the client computer will eventually either hang, or the end user will give up. You've now lost your primary server, along with any data in the primary server's queue. That's the bad news.

The good news? Restoring your system to productivity is *much* faster, because part of the secondary's job is to monitor the primary server's heartbeat (like all of us monitoring Cheney's to ensure that George doesn't take charge). If the secondary notices that the primary has missed a consecutive number of heartbeats and has lost contact, it immediately begins the recovery process, which is much like the recovery process of a server that has crashed. To the secondary, there is no loss of hardware—it doesn't need any imaging or data restoration from a backup operation. Here are the steps it takes, and the amount of your loss.

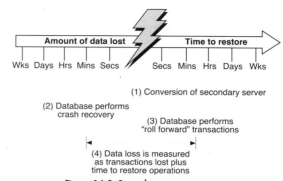

Figure 14-8. Secondary recovery process

1. The secondary senses the death of the primary and converts into active mode.

2. Even though this version of the database hasn't crashed per se, it still performs a full recovery operation from the last checkpoint.

3. It immediately begins to roll forward through the transaction logs.

4. The data loss consists of all of the information in the transfer queue on the primary computer (and which therefore hadn't yet been sent to the secondary), those transactions that were still live and not yet committed to the database, and the recovery time it took to switch the secondary from standby through live and the roll-forward operations. In essence, this could be anything from minutes to hours, but it sure beats having to restore the data from a backup and *then* begin whatever roll-forward process it can.

The only scenario that involves less downtime and less data loss is accomplished through synchronous replication. Caveat emptor here: Unless you have one heck of pipe from the primary to the secondary server, your system won't transfer a lot of data. I don't know what type of pipe it takes to run a synchronous replication for our servers over the WAN, but I do know that it would be expensive.

Current data

The obvious benefit of synchronous versus asynchronous replication is the reduction of data loss—but that benefit comes at a cost. Because of the complexity of the network connection, network management, and monetary considerations, a move from asynchronous to synchronous replication is ultimately a business decision.

In a perfect world, the secondary and primary hosts have almost identical information. If data loss is measured in minutes for the fastest possible asynchronous replications, it's measured in seconds for the synchronous system. The data lost in an asynchronous replication consists of those transactions that were pending, but not committed, as well as all of the data in the replication queue. The data lost in a synchronous replication consists solely of those transactions that were pending, but not committed. For this amount of data to be moved from the primary to the secondary, you need a very fast and wide connection. Let's explore synchronous replication in more detail.

Synchronous replication

In a previous chapter, we defined how the network protocol stack works, with its multiple layers speaking to each other (*The basics—a layered approach* on page 128). In a **synchronous replication** environment, the writing of data from the source to the destination is done at a very low layer in the protocol stack, so that the write update to the destination is acknowledged by the source before the operation is actually completed at the Application layer on the source. This must happen very fast, or it slows down the source's performance waiting for the data to be written. The synchronous method ensures that even if the source fails, the maximum amount of data has already been transferred to its destination.

Before you plan on deploying synchronous replication, you'll need to understand it and *y*our network's capabilities in the throughput and latency categories. In researching this book, we found out that roughly 32 percent of organizations recently interviewed by *InformationWeek* said that they had the network infrastructure to support high volumes of instantaneous data delivery[2]. For most of the world, synchronous replication is most effective in application environments that have normal LAN characteristics and low update rates within the data structure. It can also be deployed effectively in write-intensive applications, as long as a high-bandwidth, low-latency network connection is pervasive.

Current operations

1. You've decided to update your buttlecaps order—you're now telling the database manager that you want to modify your purchase records.

2. The database software receives the request in the form of a Data Modification Language (DML) command to perform the update to your record. Instead of

---

[2]. "How to build networks with zip—these technologies can help keep your network reliable and responsive," by R. Gareiss, *InformationWeek* (2002).

writing the information directly to its transaction log, it passes the information to the replication manager, which then writes the information to the primary server's replication journal (VERITAS calls this the Storage Replicator Log). *So* far, you've followed the exact same steps as you did in the asynchronous mode.

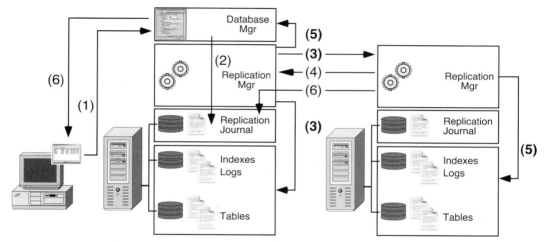

Figure 14-9. Synchronous replication process

3. In synchronous mode, this step consists of two simultaneous steps: The replication manager writes to the secondary host, and while waiting for the network acknowledgment from the secondary, it writes the information to the primary data volumes.

4. Once the secondary receives the write information and processes it in its kernel memory, even before it writes any data to its resident volumes, it returns a network acknowledgment to the primary.

5. In this step, more simultaneous processes occur. The replication manager on the secondary writes the data to its volumes. As soon as the primary receives the network acknowledgment from the secondary, it informs the database application that the write is complete.

6. As the write has taken place on the secondary's volumes, the replication manager marks it as complete in the replication journal. The database manager notifies the originating client that the transaction is complete.

The huge difference between synchronous and asynchronous modes? In synchronous mode, the primary writes data to its own drives while it sends the data to the secondary, and further, that write won't be acknowledged to the database manager until both primary and secondary writes are complete.

If a primary server crashes (or the building crashes down upon it) midway through the write phase (step 3, above) so that the write phase doesn't happen, the only real data loss consists of those writes that were about to happen, and any pending requests that might have been opened but were never saved or committed to the system. Let's go through the steps of a worst-case crash and restore operation:

Crash and restore operations

1. You started the process as usual: Deciding to boost your TQ, you want to buy a different buttlecap for every day of the week.

2. The replication manager starts to do its thing by logging the request into the replication journal.

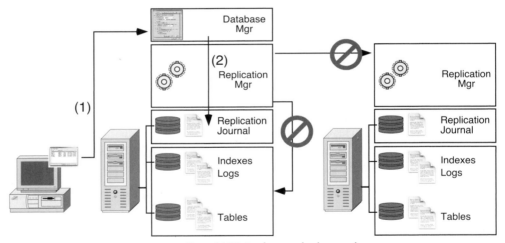

Figure 14-10. Synchronous database crash

3. Before or during the process of writing to the primary's volumes and sending the information to the secondary host —*the computer dies.* A massive tsunami has hit the Pismo Beach office where the primary database is located, and the building that housed the database collapses, washing its contents out to sea. On yet another uncharted island... well, you know all about arcane uses of flotsam and jetsam. However, the secondary database was housed across a fi-

ber link two blocks away, and neither the building nor secondary host sustained any damage.

Because synchronous systems are also usually tied in with clustered server management systems, you'll know within seconds that the primary has failed and the system will automatically jump into fail-over mode, bringing the secondary host to live status.

1. The secondary senses the primary's demise and transfers into active mode.

2. Even though this version of the database hasn't crashed per se, it still performs a full recovery operation from the last checkpoint. However, since the data is about as live as live can get, only seconds' worth of data isn't written to the secondary host's volumes.

3. It then immediately begins to roll forward through the transaction logs. Again, since synchronous operations are nearly simultaneous, there isn't much of a roll-forward log.

4. The data loss consists of all the information that was being written at the time of loss, those transactions that were still live and not yet committed to the database, and the recovery time it took to switch the secondary from standby through live and the roll-forward operations. In essence, this can be anything from seconds to minutes—and that's about as good as it's *ever* going to get.

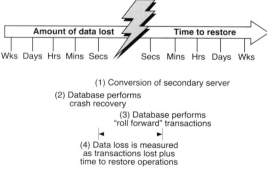

Figure 14-11. Recovery operations

THE TOOLS

The tools that we review here are all *replication-specific*. We also discuss (albeit in an oblique way) Retrospect's ability to duplicate information from point A to point B. However, since this application is not a replication-specific engine, we don't cover it directly in this section. It is, however, covered throughout the book, and duplication-specific information is covered in *Document and directory duplication* on page 277.

Replicator ⊛ Ⓧ ⦸

EverStor's Replicator is a server-based asynchronous replication engine that runs on Unix, Linux, Mac OS X, and Windows-based computers or Network Attached Storage devices. We think it runs best on NAS boxes or an Apple Xserve. This is one heck of a program, and we love it—it's easy to use and presents the user with a web interface for restoration. Replicator uses a three-step process to move files (it doesn't work with databases) from the client computer to its storage space. Replicator sits on top of the operating system.

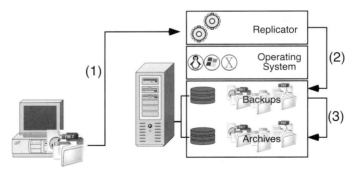

Figure 14-12. Replicator

1. Replicator pulls files from the clients at intervals set by the administrator. It can pull files through FTP or SMB.

2. Once it has the files, Replicator stores each of the client file sets in predetermined areas of the hard drive with permissions for access to those areas that are tied to each of the workstations.

3. Because Replicator is more than a duplication engine, it allows *N* number of versions of each file to be stored in its archive directory. So, if a file is being added during step 2, before it overwrites the present version, it archives that file according to the rules set by the administrator.

Machines

Machine is Replicator's term for an individual client computer. Each client machine managed under Replicator must have a separate machine definition. As system administrator, you can manage each of these machines individually or delegate responsibility to others.

Remember that part about naming devices that we talked about in the network corruption chapter (see *LANsurveyor* on page 153)? It definitely comes into play here, as machine names cannot be duplicated in the Replicator system. On Windows devices, you can find the device's name by right-clicking on **My Computer**, then choosing **Properties > Network Identification**.

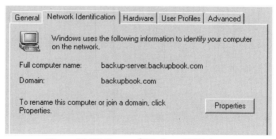

Figure 14-13. Name of Windows 2000 device

For Linux and Unix, the machine's name can be determined by typing the **Hostname** command at the command prompt in the terminal.

For Macintosh OS X users, select **System Preferences…** then click **Sharing** in the window to bring up the computer's sharing information.

Once you have the basic information in hand, you're ready to set up the device's replication parameters. Since Replicator provides a web-based management front end, you can set it up from any location and on any computer that has a standard web browser. It's pretty simple: Just add the device's name or IP address, the device's directory name for replication and archiving (usually the same name as the user device), how many iterations of the same file are allowed (they call this the *max number of archives*), and a log level for this user (if the user is having problems, you'll want to log it).

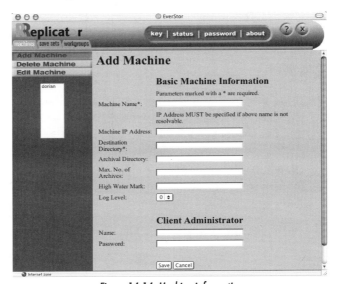

Figure 14-14. Machine information

It takes longer to figure out the device's name than it does to set up the device in the system.

Save Sets

Save Sets are defined for each machine, determining a set of files to be replicated, and how and when the replication is to be performed. The Save Set is the definition of the data to be replicated on each client machine. This definition includes the directory or directories to be replicated, those to be excluded (if any), the frequency of replication, and the maximum permissible levels of archival.

Since the Replicator product has no client software, the software uses SMB or FTP to access the local computer's source directory. FTP is the preferred method of setting up a share-point on a local Unix/Linux computer, and SMB, of course, is for Windows users. Mac OS X users can set up FTP share-points or SMB share-points—however, setting up an FTP share-point is much easier.

Figure 14-15. Save Set information

Workgroups

Workgroups consist of a group of machines managed by the workgroup administrator, and are used to delegate responsibility. The Replicator system administrator may designate workgroup administrators as responsible for groups of client machines. In a large organization, this can be a huge plus, but snce this is a logistical issue and has nothing to do with functionality, we won't cover it here.

 Replicator is a fine product for moving files from point A to point B. Because it doesn't use any software on the client source computer, it must have a very specific address (or a resolvable domain name within the network) to find the source volume. This makes it great for replicating general user directories, websites, and any other static file-based volume from the source to the backup destination.

It doesn't work, however, with any open files—so using it to replicate a mail server or a database server is out of the question. Any file that is not an open file can be quickly and easily replicated to the destination server where Replicator is running. And since it supports all major operating systems, we think it's great.

VERITAS Volume Replicator

Based on the VERITAS Volume Manager, VERITAS Volume Replicator (VVR) replicates volumes of data in real-time (either synchronous or asynchronous) to remote locations over IP networks. Why the plural emphasis (locations)? VVR can replicate one volume group to 32 secondary replication sites simultaneously (if you have enough bandwidth or your volume doesn't have a heavy change load). The ability to replicate entire volumes in this manner is an extremely robust storage-independent disaster recovery tactic. Unlike Replicator, VVR sits beneath the operating system, intercepting hard drive calls and routing them appropriately.

VVR follows roughly the same set of steps in both synchronous or asynchronous modes of operation.

1. As writes come in from the database application, VVR intercepts the call.

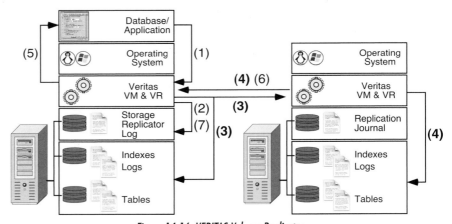

Figure 14-16. VERITAS Volume Replicator

2. VVR writes the change information to its Storage Replicator Log, so that if a crash occurs before the rest of the procedures is finished, the information is contained in its replication log and can be used for restoration purposes.

3. Once the write to the Storage Replicator log is complete, VVR sends the write to the secondary host (or hosts). In asynchronous mode, this data is written to a queue that then manages the sending of the data. In synchronous mode, the data is sent directly. At the same time, VVR writes the data to the primary computer's volumes.

4. On the secondary hosts, VVR receives the incoming write, processes it (putting the information into its kernel memory), and sends a network acknowledgment to the primary host.

5. In synchronous mode, once the primary receives the network acknowledgment from all of the secondary hosts that the data has arrived, VVR sends an acknowledgment of the write's completion to the application.

6. Once the secondaries have actually finished writing the data to their local volumes, they send a write acknowledgment to the primary.

7. Once the primary receives write acknowledgments from all of the secondaries, VVR marks the write as complete in the Storage Replicator Log.

Replicating databases as volume groups

Remember when we were talking about write-order fidelity (*Consistent operation* on page 501), how databases process the writing of information in a certain order, and how that order must be maintained in order to recover from a crash? Good—you were paying attention. Go grab a gold star and a Krispy Kreme. Now comes the part where you get to put all your diligence to use by planning out a VVR replication setup the correct way.

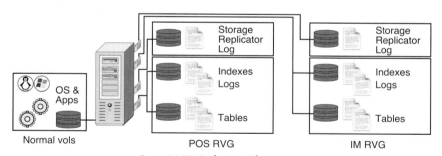

Figure 14-17. Replication Volume Groups

Let's say that you have a single large computer running both a POS database for your 30 stores as well as a second Inventory Management (IM) database for the same 30 stores. Each of these databases writes independently to its respective volumes and database transaction logs. To maintain write-order fidelity for each of the independent databases, you must set up independent **Replicated Volume Groups (RVGs)** for each database. An RVG is a group of volumes within a VVM disk group (Remember those? We talked about them in *Dynamic volumes* on page 478)—and all the related volumes are part of the same disk group.

Here are some tips for RVG setup:

- Separate each database into its own RVG, as we've done in Figure 14-17.

- For extra safety, make sure that you mirror all your SRL volumes, as well as all data volumes.

- Make sure that you name the volumes on all of your secondary hosts the same as those on the primary host's volumes. In a disaster situation, your secondary will become your primary and you'll want volume-naming fidelity if and when you have to map your drives over.

- Dedicated separate physical disks (with separate physical SCSI or FC controllers) to your SRL volumes, separating them from your data volumes. Ensure that your data volumes have separate physical disks and controllers as well.

Setting up the asynchronous RLINK

VERITAS calls the network connection between the primary and each secondary host a **Replication Link** (**RLINK**). The RLINK's attributes specify the replication parameters, whether synchronous or asynchronous, for the corresponding secondary host. If the amount of data sent by the primary is greater than the RLINK can handle, one of two things happens (other than your users start complaining that the network is pokey). In the synchronous replication mode, the primary server must wait until the writes are complete on the secondary server—and this could greatly impact the performance of your primary server. In asynchronous mode, the SRL queue grows until the change rate is less than the pipe size, and the queue can empty as the overflow gets sent to the secondary. Therefore, you must set up the data transmission link between the primary and each of the secondaries appropriately.

Below (see Figure 14-18. on page 521) is a graph showing the relationship between...

- The data pipe (ours shows a 100 Mbps network pipe);

- Normal network traffic (which doesn't amount to much here);

- The rate of data change taking place on the primary (that must therefore be sent across the data pipe to the secondary host); and

- The SRL that has to hold the excess data until it can be sent from the primary to the secondary.

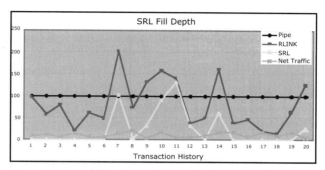

Figure 14-18. SRL fill depth as it relates to data flowing through an RLINK

The SRL begins to fill up with a backlog anytime that the amount of data that must be sent to the secondary is greater than the amount of data that can flow in the pipe at that time. *If the primary goes down with data in the SRL, that data is lost.* As you can clearly see in Figure 14-18. , wherein the fill depth of the SRL at points nine through 11 spike as the data rate mushrooms, a 100 Mbps pipe for this RLINK between the primary and secondary would be a bit small, even though there isn't much *normal* network traffic (think what would happen if the network traffic spiked, as well as the RLINK traffic?). In the diagram below (Figure 14-19.), we show an RLINK with even more traffic than before, but now the same traffic between the host and primary is running on a gigabit network instead of a 100 Mbps network. The SRL fill depth is never above zero because the pipe between the primary and secondary can easily handle the load.

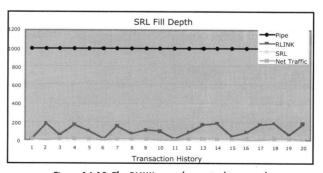

Figure 14-19. The RLINK moved to a gigabit network

Our suggestion? When you establish an RLINK between a primary and secondary host, build an RLINK-only network. By adding a secondary NIC card to both the primary and secondary host(s) and then routing that data directly to its own LAN or WAN, you eliminate any problems with LAN traffic snarls, give yourself a much cleaner path, and can easily monitor this network (with simple tools like CyberGauge from Neon Software, which we've mentioned throughout this book) to ensure that the data rates aren't soaring too high.

For heavy-use databases on a LAN, we suggest that you utilize a gigabit-switched network. For heavy use between a primary host and a secondary host over a WAN, we suggest that you create dedicated point-to-point connections (such as T1s, T3s, or better) between each device.

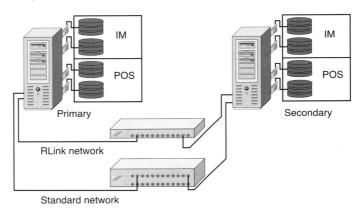

Figure 14-20. An RLINK network

Remember, this is key data, and you're creating a mirror through VVR to protect it. Don't foul up your protection scheme by cheesing out on the network connection—that's the least expensive part of the whole operation.

VERITAS Storage Replicator 🪟 🐧

VERITAS Storage Replicator is a file replication product that provides real-time replication for workgroup-level systems. It's ideal for consolidating the backup process to a centralized location within the Windows platform, or replicating databases from one point to another. Storage Replicator keeps an up-to-the-minute copy of specified volumes, directories, or files to allow for immediate recovery, by mirroring the source-file system writes to a destination server as they occur, operating with full fidelity on open files. Storage Replicator can be used to maintain real-time copies of databases stored in a safe location in a different part of the campus or in a remote location.

When replicating, Storage Replicator sends updates from the primary node on which the application is running, secondary or remote node. Replication is unidirectional (updates on the primary are sent to the secondaries, but access to the data at the secondary nodes is read-only while replication continues). If the data at the primary is destroyed by a disaster, the copy of the data at the secondary can be made write-accessible, and applications that were running on the primary can be brought up on the secondary. The secondary can then be used as the new primary for the writing applications.

Storage Replicator has three main components.

1. **Replication Management Server** software that holds the configuration data for the replication systems, controlling the beginning and ending of the replication process. This software drives the process and is the repository for all of the logs, alerts, and histories.

2. The **Replication Service Agent** is client software that is installed on every computer that is designated either a source or a destination. The Replication Service Agent must be installed on the same computer as the Management Server *if* that computer acts as either a host or a destination. Each Replication Service Agent is dedicated to a single Replication Management Server (to avoid conflicting jobs).

3. The **Console** is an application that provides a front end for information about the replication configuration and replication processes. It's great that VERITAS has separated the front end from the engine so that the administrator can remotely manage a replication server, or can have multiple copies of the console so that certain tasks can be delegated to subordinates who've installed the Console on their computers.

Storage Replicator ties all of this together into a "replication neighborhood" (with one server acting as the Remote Management Server for the whole neighborhood) and uses job management terminology to describe its process. A replication "job" defines the source and destination volumes, the data being replicated, the interval and scheduled duration of the replication, and a few specific settings that are germane to each replication process.

Storage Replicator works by placing itself in the computer's kernel stack just above the operating system in order to intercept the 64 k writes to the disk so that it can not only write the information to the primary host, but also to the replica destination. Because this is an asynchronous system, Storage Replicator simultaneously passes the incoming writes off to the operating system (2) and also adds the data to its replicator journal for processing and sending to the replication destinations (3). This works exactly the same whether files are being written to the drive or database writes are being performed.

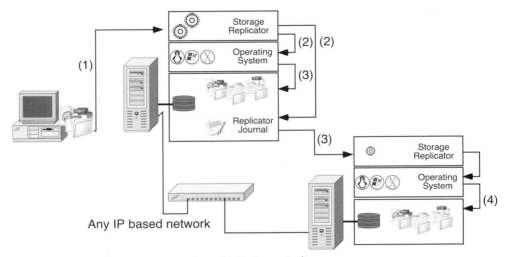

Figure 14-21. Storage Replicator process

Because Storage Replicator can replicate data over any IP network (that supports the throughput and latency necessary to accomplish the job), the primary source computer can be in one location and the replica destination can be elsewhere, such as the company hot-site, or another office or building. And because Storage Replicator works as the operating system is *writing to the disk*, live databases do not need to be shut down to be moved from point A to point B.

When a job is started, the source volume is not considered protected until each and every specified file has been replicated onto the destination and then checked to ensure that it is identical to the source file. We'll cover this in more depth below, but briefly, a synchronization phase is followed by a dynamic update phase. Storage Replicator first synchronizes a complete set of files between the source and the destination. Once the list of files has been synchronized, it then goes through the list to update any files to be replicated. For explanation purposes here, we'll walk through the process of creating a replicant database structure instead of a file structure, since the database structure is more volatile and specific.

Synchronization phase

When a replication starts, it synchronizes copies of files between the primary source and the destination replica, so that an exact list of all files targeted exists in both places. Therefore, the first step is to build an exact copy of the file structure on the destination computer. Any files that don't exist on the replica are copied from the primary to the replica. Any files that do exist are examined, and if changes are found, a new copy is transferred from the source to the destination (if the file is smaller than 1 MB), or the delta changes to the file are updated from the primary to the replica.

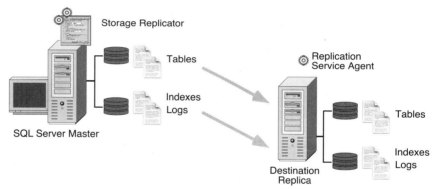

Figure 14-22. File synchronization phase

The only problem with this process is that since the database can be live with changes being made to it, as files are replicated from the primary source to the replicated destination, they can be out of date once they've hit the destination server because changes have been made to the primary copy of the file. At this moment, the dynamic phase comes into play.

Dynamic phase

The **dynamic phase** of replication tracks changes to the files as they are occurring on the source (remember above, where the Storage Replicator software intercepts the operating system calls to the drive? That's how it knows). Once synchronization has been completed, any changes to the primary files are then sent to the destination, updating the copies of those files on the replica.

To maintain write-order fidelity, the dynamic phase tracks the changes on the primary in the order they occurred, updating files on the destination file in the same order, thus guaranteeing the database's transactional consistency[3]. Once all of the files have been synchronized and then updated, the replication process is complete.

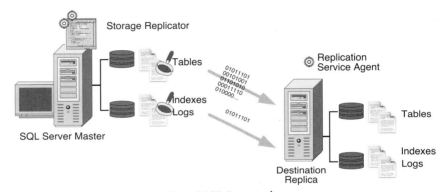

Figure 14-23. Dynamic phase

The ongoing process

At this point, the administrator has two choices. An ongoing, continuous replication can occur from here on out, or the replication process can be stopped and then restarted on a scheduled basis.

If the replication process is stopped and then restarted on a scheduled basis, further synchronization will take place, followed by the dynamic phase.

If the replication process is allowed to continue on an ongoing basis, only the dynamic phase will have to run, as the data will be moved to the replica destination as it is written to the primary source. During dynamic replication, Storage Replicator will continuously send changes on the source volume over the network

---

3. Storage Replicator is a *file replicator*, and as such doesn't understand SQL database tables, logs, etc. and therefore isn't used to move and reintegrate them. Instead, it replicates files ensuring write-order fidelity so that the data is a perfect match, and if necessary, can be run from the destination.

to the destination volume. In Storage Replicator, this happens asynchronously, using as little CPU processes on the source as possible. To do this, Storage Replicator's drivers record all the changes to each document and place them in journals.

Journaling

Because Storage Replicator uses an asynchronous replication process, the change can't be sent immediately from the source to the destination. Rather, a copy of the changed portion of the file is placed in a **journal**, transmitted over the network and written to a journal on the destination, allowing for temporary network bottlenecks. An inbound journal on the destination device that ensures all synchronization data (the creation of new files) is written first and then followed up with dynamic data.

Journal files are self-managing files that grow and shrink with the amount of data to be transmitted and then integrated into the destination. These journal entries are transferred across the network as quickly as the network allows (using as much bandwidth as allocated within the console of the software). Once arrived, each journal file will typically hold around 3 MB of data. Large job transfers can take up to several individual journals.

In planning for this additional space on both source and destination, take the amount of files being transferred. Add 10 percent for the addditional journal size. Journal files (on both source and destination) won't be deleted until after the journal has been marked as read by the software. Then multiply that combined number by a fudge-factor of 15–20 percent more for the total size you're going to need.

 If your network is up to speed (pardon the pun), you probably won't see a journal entry file on either source or destination. However, a total failure of the network connection between source and destination, or network corruption causing near-zero TCP Window problems on either one (See our *Low window size* on page 165 for more info), expands the source journal. High CPU contention or usage on the destination expands the journal on the troubled device and delays replication processes, causing potential data loss if the primary fails during that period.

Planning the Replication Link

Using the VERITAS RLINK estimating tool, we created a single RLINK between a primary and secondary host to replicate a 4.5 Gb database. The database changes by about 3 percent a day, and the 100 MB LAN is used to transport the data (with 10 percent traffic on the LAN).

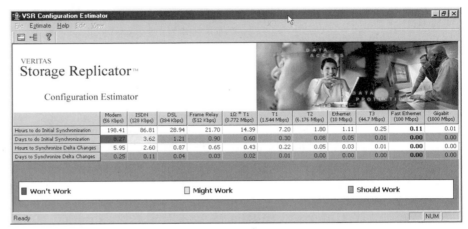

Figure 14-24. VERITAS Configuration Estimator

The VERITAS Configuration Estimator reveals that our computer will complete the initial synchronization in about six to seven minutes, and synchronize the delta changes even faster. Synchronizing over our T1 WAN connection takes almost seven and a half hours for the initial synchronization and about another half hour for the delta changes. Quite an improvement, I'd say!

USES FOR IP-BASED REPLICATION

You can employ several tactics to optimize IP-based replication. We've listed the applications that work in each specific instance in Table 14-1. through Table 14-3. to help you select the right software for the task at hand.

Live DB to standby DB replication

To maximize your database's uptime, perform a replication of your database to another SQL server running different SQL databases (and ignoring this one), or with the MS SQL software preinstalled but not running (standby mode). How does this maximizes uptime? If you replicate the data in a SQL server to SQL server mode, you can simply launch the standby server in case the primary fails completely, or you can map the standby server's drive to the primary's drive if the primary's drive fails.

In both low- and high-volume scenarios, you can use either Dantz Retrospect *or* VERITAS Storage Manager. However, you *can't* use EverStor Replicator, as it doesn't replicate open files.

Live DB to Standby DB	Retrospect	EverStor Replicator	VERITAS Storage Mgr	Storage Replicator
Low Volume Database	✔		✔	✔
High Volume Database			✔	✔

Table 14-1. Live DB to Standby-DB Replication

When replicating the database data from the primary SQL server to the standby, you can choose to replicate either individual databases or all the databases on the server . It epends on the importance of the information, and the amount of bandwidth between the two servers. When planning your SQL to SQL mapping, plan as if you were going to map the entire database set, just in case you need to do so later on. Therefore, make sure that your source directory and replication directory are the same for your SQL data.

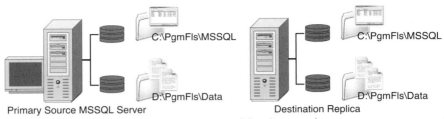

Figure 14-25. Mapping MSSQL and data directory information

Then, if your data volume on your primary source SQL server dies for some reason, you can map your replica drive over to the primary, and the database engine won't know the difference.

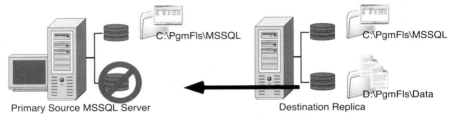

Figure 14-26. Remapping a downed volume

Or, in case of catastrophic failure, you can launch MSSQL on the replica server and have that act as the primary.

 Remember when we talked about not having the budget to create clustered servers and the fact that you might want to plan on doubling up your systems in the event of a failure (see *What if you can't afford a clustered server or a SAN?* on page 494)? Well, here, we show you how to implement such a system. Let's say that you can't afford a cluster, but also can't afford to have your database system down, so you set up your replication engine to replicate the database in your back-office server over to your normal database server. You then set up your database server to replicate its database over to your back-office server.

When setting up your servers to replicate to each other, you'll probably want to have separate partitions for each of your data volumes and your boot/applications volume. By setting up separate drive volumes and letters for each partition, when you replicate the information from the source to the destination, you won't overwrite anything. Also, you can *pre*-set up each local database application to access either data source. By doing this, if the the remote computer's data source goes down, you can ensure a smooth transition for bringing it live on the surviving computer system.

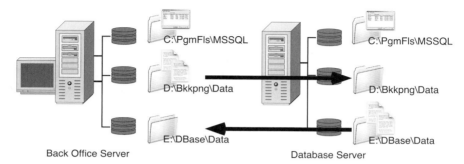

Figure 14-27. Double-duty server operations

You can also create a round-robin scenario using this method with two or three different database servers in different locations. Let's say that you have a home office, as well as two remote offices in Ogunquit, Maine, and Pismo Beach, California.

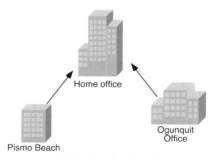

Figure 14-28. Round robin replication

You could replicate your home office to Ogunquit, Ogunquit to Pismo Beach, and then Pismo Beach back to your home office. This method allows very fast recovery of all of your servers, and ensures that *some* office will be up and running if a catastrophe strikes.

Live DB to file server replication

Storage Replicator can also be used to replicate live databases from their primary source over to a network file storage system (like a NAS box), so that they can be backed up using normal backup processes. This is considered a many-to-one replication, because many databases can be consolidated onto a single file server for backup centralization. In low-volume scenarios, you can use Dantz Retrospect's duplicate function and open file manager or VERITAS' Storage Manager. However, you can't use EverStor's Replicator, as it doesn't replicate open files.

By moving the databases off-host to a centralized location, you can make your backup processes much simpler because you won't have to worry about any other open file manager systems running on the SQL database server.

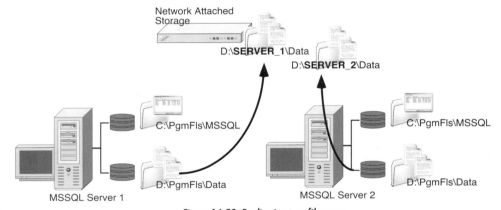

Figure 14-29. Replication to a file server

 In this scenario, when using both Retrospect and Storage Manager, if you use a regular file server as your destination, you can run the server software on that file server on another device, such as the backup server.

Live DB to File Server	Dantz Retrospect	EverStor Replicator	VERITAS Storage Mgr	Storage Replicator
Server software can be run from NAS box			✔	✔
Client software can be run on NAS box	✔		✔	✔

Table 14-2. Live DB to file server replication

However, if you use a Network Attached Storage (NAS) box as the file repository, Retrospect isn't the answer, because it requires a front end (that the NAS box really doesn't give you). Since VERITAS' console doesn't have to be on the server, you can run Storage Manager's Replication Server Manager software on the NAS box and the console elsewhere. Since EverStor's software would choke on a live database without an open file manager, we've excluded it from the list of candidates here.

File and directory consolidation

Replication can also consolidate information from many places to one, as shown in Figure 14-30. This allows the backup admin to run centralized backups of servers only, knowing that all pertinent data resides on the servers and that the workstations can be retrieved from an image, if necessary.

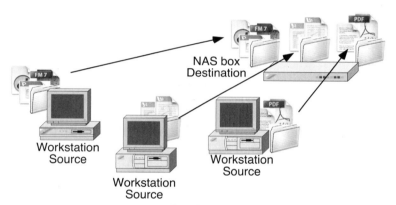

Figure 14-30. File and directory consolidation

Many corporations are geographically dispersed, but still need a centralized backup solution. In this case, how can you maintain local backup and archiving needs as well as a centralized backup solution without plunging into Administrative Inferno? Because this is an IP-based file replication scenario, you aren't limited to moving files and directories of information from single computers to a central server on your LAN—you can use this type of replication to move whole data sets from remote offices back to your home office through the use of the same tool. That means that you can, in essence:

- Consolidate reports on select computers from multiple offices to a single office;

- Consolidate application or file servers from remote offices to a central office for the purpose of centralized backup and recovery; and

- Create a tiered system wherein each remote office consolidates files onto a single server, and that server replicates itself up to the home office, where all of the data is then stored onto a backup tape system for history and long-term archiving and recovery.

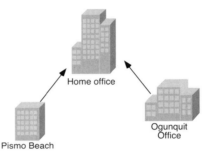

Figure 14-31. WAN consolidation

The only application limited in this regard is the VERITAS solution, as it has only Windows 2000 client software and won't work in a tiered environment. However, it does work for replicating one layer of servers up to the next layer. Each of the other tools allows all three operating systems to replicate their data from one place to the next.

File Consolidation	Dantz Retrospect	EverStor Replicator	VERITAS Storage Mgr	Storage Replicator
Windows Client	✔	✔	✔	✔
Mac Client	✔	✔		
Unix Client	✔	✔		
Allows multiple tier usage	✔	✔		

Table 14-3. File consolidation

CHAPTER 15:
DEALING WITH POWER LOSS

Don't re**volt**, get **grounded**, and learn **watts** up with your **ohm power grid**.

–Mitch Krayton, field editor

Boom, boom—out go the lights! The main power is down. Production can either grind to a halt or continue unabated as long as you have adequate amounts of secondary power planned for your office. Which will it be?

If this happens, how ready *are* you? If you're *very* ready, you can prevent corruption and know that when power resumes, everything—including the network—will be available. If you aren't ready at all, documents and database records will be corrupted due to unexpected shutdown, CPUs and storage devices will be irreparably damaged when the power surges back on, and the network will be unavailable since the network-dependent devices didn't restart in the right order.

	Documents	Applications	OS	Storage	CPUs	Network	Power	Building
Freeze								
Corruption								
Loss							✔	

Table 15-1. Power loss

While the computer industry has come to accept the shortcomings of power utilities and has made concessions such as longer power-glitch[1] and ride-through[2] times of up to 50 milliseconds, the devices that rely on power (that's all of them) must have a way to shut down and restart gracefully[3] when the power is going to run out. This magic is made through the deployment of an **uninterruptible power supply (UPS)** in conjunction with management software that facilitates communication between the computer and the UPS, sending the appropriate commands at appropriate times. In the best case, the UPS can keep everything up and running until power resumes. But at some point, it becomes cost-prohibitive to supply power through UPSes and sustain operation during lengthy power outages. At that point, you gracefully shut down and wait until the power returns. When that happy event occurs, your UPSes will sense available power, send a signal through the management application, and restart your devices in the right order. What a beautiful world.

Adding UPSes to your computer systems falls smack-dab in the perfect definition of fault tolerance. While you can't put a spare electrical utility grid on your block, you can attach your key systems to a UPS or add a power generator to your building in case the main system goes out.

Special Thanks...

Thanks to Dave Crago at Liebert, and Kristen Levy and Beata Wojciulewicz over at APC for walking us through all of the ins and outs of the UPS systems, as well as where UPS management is heading in the future. Also thanks to our field editor Mitch Krayton who forced me to re-write this chapter (again), making it much better.

---

[1] Fancy electrical term for nothing there—no power.

[2] The window of time that a device can sustain function without receiving power.

[3] There are two ways to shut down a computer. The first is through the standard shutdown procedure that closes all files, applications, unmounts volumes, logs off the user from any servers and from the system itself, and then turns the power off. The second way is either losing power or simply pulling out the power plug. The first is graceful. The second is not so—and not so good for a computer (duh).

THE MAIN THING

- UPSes are used for two tasks: To keep everything up and running until you move to a hot site, or to keep everything up and running until you can shut down services gracefully and restart.

- You can use one big UPS, many individual UPSes, or a hybrid of the two. Infrastructure costs to support a large UPS often outweigh the management time for multiple UPSes, especially with today's latest monitoring tools.

- Small to medium-sized businesses should not consider a UPS that attaches to a fueled generator. If you do require the 24/7 uptime that a fueled generator supplies and you're not mirroring your data to a different location, run your mission-critical applications from a hosting location—it's much more cost-effective.

- Devices fall into two categories: Those that make money (mission-critical) and those that don't. By herself, the IT manager can only guess at what is mission-critical to your busines—she must work with the head of production and operations to determine what needs to be up for how long, and with the CFO to determine when the cost of the UPS system exceeds the business loss during an outage.

Just a Story Five years ago, in Network Frontiers' B-grade office space, I was in love with our UPS configuration—those creeps at PG&E wouldn't fry *our* servers. Planning ahead and dealing with faulty utilities was all part of the entrepreneurial spirit in our loft offices. Flash ahead four years.

Now we're proud members of Corporate America, living large in an A-grade office space. We've got berber carpet, Aeron chairs, and Homaco racks out the wazoo. But, hey, what gives? The power still goes out at least once if not four times a month. This is the burden we all must bear as fiber is tunneled from block to block throughout our city streets—even Corporate America is not invulnerable (hear that, Halliburton?), and UPSes are as important today as they were back in our Top Ramen–and–peanut butter days.

TALK THE TALK—THE LANGUAGE OF POWER PROBLEMS AND UPSES

 Nothing new has happened in the world of power except one thing: There are a gazillion web pages explaining it. Here, we cover what you need to know before buying a UPS, as well as how to monitor power and tailor applicable alerts to your disaster recovery plan. If you want to know more, indulge your Inner Nerd at http://hyperphysics.phy-astr.gsu.edu/hbase/hframe.html. That site is just *so* cool.

What Can Go Wrong with your power

In a perfect world, you get clean power coming from the local power company and into your building in any of three capacities: two-wire 115-volt service, two-wire 230-volt service, or three-wire 115/230-volt service. This power is distributed throughout your building to electrical panels found at predetermined distances; most often in riser closets, since that's where the conduits run between the floors. From the electrical panel, the power goes to all sorts of outlets. The most common outlets are referred to as 208 and 110, and are configured as follows:

Figure 15-1. NEMA L6-30P for 208V and NEMA 5-15R for 110V

What comes out of these two plugs isn't always that clean, however. Below, we describe what can go wrong with your electrical power, and what you can attach between the electricity utility company and what your computer systems plug into. You have four basic choices for these power mediaries: surge suppressors, offline UPSes, line-interactive UPSes, and online UPSes. If you don't yet know the differences among the three UPS types, just read on—we'll cover those differences in great depth in this chapter. First, you need to understand power problems, and which power solutions fit which problems.

Blackouts **Blackouts** are a complete loss of power, worse than unplugging your computer, in that when the power comes back on, it causes a spike (see *Surges and spikes* on page

540). A significant drop in voltage (below 80 volts) can be considered a blackout as well, as most equipment won't operate below this level.

Blackouts	Surge suppressor	Offline UPS	Line Interactive UPS	Online UPS
No protection	✔			
Partial protection				
Full protection		✔	✔	✔
Transfer to battery power		✔	✔	
Full-time battery power				✔

Table 15-2. Blackouts

Sags A **sag** is just like a brownout (see below), but the power falls between 105 to 102 volts on 100-volt service and 210 and 204 volts on 220-volt service. Both sags and brownouts can be caused by utility companies attempting to negotiate peak load times and by the operation of heavy equipment, such as elevators, compressors, and shop tools. Sags happen within your building more than you think, accounting for more than 50 percent of all power problems.

Sags and Brownouts	Surge Suppressor	Offline UPS	Line Interactive UPS	Online UPS
No protection	✔			
Partial protection				
Full protection		✔	✔	✔
Transfer to battery power		✔		
Augment battery power			✔	✔

Table 15-3. Sags and brownouts

Brownouts A **brownout** occurs when voltage levels fall below 102 volts on 110-volt service and 204 volts on 220-volt service. Brownouts can be caused by too many users pulling power from the system. Mitch Krayton offers a story about "a client who had been getting power errors nearly every day at 4P.M. We came in and did all the normal tests in the equipment, and all the data equipment checked out fine. The error kept occurring, but we could find no reasonable explanation for it. While we happened to be chatting with the tenants next door, who coincidentally shared the same power line, you guessed it, they turned on their powerful burster (those old-fashioned devices that broke apart multipart forms printed on continuous feed paper). Yep, that was the cause of the brownouts." While your lights may only dim, your computers won't have enough power to sustain operation. Brownouts last anywhere from a fraction of a second to hours on end.

Surges and spikes

Surges and **spikes** are sudden and extreme increases in voltage. Lightning striking and going through the system can cause a spike (more than 1,000 volts). When a building's or electrical company's generator must produce an enormous amount of voltage to turn back on everything that turned off during a blackout, a surge (less than 1,000 volts) generally occurs. Also, switching off high-powered appliances, such as rooftop air conditioners, can cause a burst in voltage levels, a surge lasting less than a second. Surges and spikes turn perfectly useful computers into doorstops.

Surges and Spikes	Surge Suppressor	Offline UPS	Line Interactive UPS	Online UPS
No protection				
Partial protection		✔	✔	✔
Full protection	✔			
Clamp and divert energy	✔			
Suppresses energy		✔	✔	✔

Table 15-4. Surges and spikes

In the table above, the only device that provides full protection is the comparatively low-cost surge suppressor. We recommend that you plug them into the outlet and then plug the UPS into *them*, so that when a spike hits, the surge suppressor takes the brunt of it (and is usually wiped out completely). I've seen them blown completely out of the wall socket, lying helpless and gasping on the floor in the middle of the wiring closet. Don't waste any tears on them, though: A new surge suppressor is much less expensive than a new UPS.

Noise **Noise** is the general term for flaws in the electrical system that affect the quality of the power moving through the copper wires. Electromagnetic frequencies (EMFs) coming from elevator motors, HVACs in the ceiling, and other large apparatuses are the usual culprits, as well as poorly grounded electrical systems.

Noise	Surge Suppressor	Offline UPS	Line Interactive UPS	Online UPS
No protection				
Partial protection	✔	✔		
Full protection			✔	✔
Filters the noise	✔	✔	✔	✔
May oscillate between utility and battery power		✔	✔	

Table 15-5. Noise

One item of note: Like all bad things, a blackout doesn't come alone—it's accompanied by its friends: sag, surge, and brownout. A typical blackout is preceded by one or more sags and brownouts before the blackout occurs, and once the power comes back on, a surge comes in full force before the power settles down to anything resembling normal delivery. The following diagram, *Typical blackout cycle* on page 541, shows you what that cycle looks like.

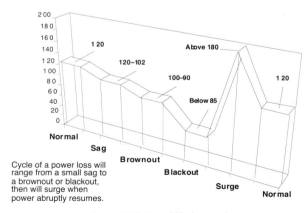

Cycle of a power loss will range from a small sag to a brownout or blackout, then will surge when power abruptly resumes.

Figure 15-2. Typical blackout cycle

Power primer

Get in contact with your Inner Nerd, recall that phun physics class, and embrace the power. If that embrace feels more like a stranglehold, hang in there—you need to know this stuff so you don't buy the wrong UPS.

Computer   UPS   Power Strip   Electrical outlet

Our premise in this basic exercise is that you want to connect a computer that draws 2 amps to the appropriate UPS plugged into a normal 120-VAC outlet.

Pipe size   Your 120-VAC outlet is like a pipe that delivers electricity at a certain rate. You can ignore the 120-VAC part of it (sort of) as long as you understand that somewhere behind that wall plate is a circuit (and circuit breaker) that provides x amount of amps. The electrical engineer who designed your building decided upon the amount of amps per circuit.

Your computing devices   Whoever built your computing devices decided how many amps the device needs to draw to run properly. In this exercise, we deal with a computer that draws 2 amps.

Volt Amps (VA)   When you plug your 2-amp computer into a 120-VAC power outlet, you get 240 **VA** of usage. Or in other words, Volts * Amps = VA.

Volts and amps and wattage   **Wattage** differs from VA in that wattage is time-averaged power flow, and VA is maximum power flow. If the computer were to draw its maximum power load 24 hours a day, VA would equal watts, but that's not the way it really works. Instead, during activities like startup and high disk usage, a computer uses the maximum amount of power available to it. But when the computer is lazing around at 4A.M., it draws very little power. So the amount of power that a computer uses over time is averaged to give us wattage, which is never more than the VA rating.

*Amps * VAC=Watts*   If you have a device that draws 2 amps of power plugged into a 120-VAC outlet, that's 240 watts if the computer is always drawing maximum load—but that's not very realistic. Practically, the actual power usage, watts, is generally lower than the maximum power usage, which is VA.

Power factor   The ratio between wattage and VA is **power factor.** Calculate $\frac{VA}{Watts} = Powerfactor$ both VA requirements and the watt requirements to get the power factor of the devices being served by a UPS.

Why is this important? Computer equipment has anywhere between a .6 to a 1 power factor. For example, a typical 1U rack-mount server with an attached rackmount JBOD with 10 drives in it might have a 456 VA, 328 watt, .625 power factor load.

To support all of the equipment you have plugged into it, the UPS must be able to supply both enough *maximum* power (456 VA) and enough *time-averaged* power (328 watts), and have a power factor greater than .625.

And this *is* important, because power isn't as stable as you think.

Inside a UPS

Time for more learnin'. Some stuff is obvious: There is a UPS and its batteries. But you also need to know about the UPS innards—a whole lot of parts. We suggest that you read this section only when you're poised to buy a UPS, so that you know what's in it and what isn't. Or, of course, if you're really, *really* bored or are an electrical engineering student and actually enjoy this kind of stuff, go ahead and read it now.—we won't snitch to the Nerd Patrol.

AC power

φ   **Alternating current** power is what your utility provides and what comes out of the UPS—all hail Nikola Tesla!

DC power

φ   **Direct current** power is the type of power that UPS batteries create after they receive AC power from the utility.

Rectifier and battery charger

This converts the power supplied from the wall outlet into DC current, which is used to charge the UPS's storage batteries and to power the UPS's inverter.

Inverter

The **inverter** converts the DC power into clean, regulated AC power, which is then sent to the computer equipment attached to the UPS.

Automatic Voltage Regulator

These come in many flavors, but all are continuously acting automatic excitation control systems. In addition to monitoring for voltage outside the acceptable range (**excitation**), they control the voltage of a generating unit such as PG&E, our utility, and are measured at the generator terminals such as the wall outlet or the power panel for hard-wired UPSes. In addition, AVRs suppress or enhance the incoming power before it hits your servers and hubs.

The key here is excitation. How much can your AVR withstand before the UPS literally gets fried? Stand-alone AVRs can have a range of 70–150 VAC for input and still keep the output at 105–130 VAC. The wider the range, the better the AVR and the better the UPS. And, as always, the better the anything, the more it costs.

Storage batteries

Storage batteries are lead acid or nickel cadmium cells that remain charged. For offline and nearline UPSes, the batteries remain in reserve until a power outage or brownout. For online UPSes, the power is drawn directly from the battery in all cases.

In the UPS system, while the power management software is the brain (and we all know that we can get by without too much of that), the batteries are the brawn: what ultimately keeps the computers up and running during times of power outages—and, more commonly, brownouts, sags, and surges.

The amount of "power time" remaining on batteries depends on how often they're used in the course of a given day. *It takes longer to recharge the batteries than it does to run them dry.* So if you purchased a UPS that you think will keep your systems up for a half hour due to battery power, think again. A typical outage cycle doesn't come abruptly—it comes after several sags, surges, brownouts, surges, and then blackouts (Figure 15-2. on page 541). The number of times the UPS's batteries had to kick in before the total outage ultimately determines how long the UPS can last during a total blackout.

Also, batteries eventually wear out. For offline UPSes (We cover all the different types of UPSes below in *UPSes Defined* on page 546, each discharge and subsequent recharge reduces the relative capacity of the UPS battery by a small percentage. The length of each discharge cycle also determines the reduction in battery capacity. A UPS battery can provide power over a large number of short cycles, or fewer cycles of longer duration. How soon the battery wears out depends on the capacity of the battery from the get-go, as well as how it has been treated: temperature, cycling, and loading. We've seen batteries last as little as a few years and as long as six years.

Don't be afraid to test your batteries—blinking lights have been known to lie. All UPS monitoring software tells you how long your batteries have to live. Once it gets down to the 20 percent mark, make sure you have new batteries on hand and swap them out.

If this is the type of system that's always drawing power directly from the batteries, it must also allow you to change the batteries without first shutting down the computer—unless, of course, you don't mind bringing the file server down to replace the batteries[4].

Bypass switch and control logic

The **bypass switch** is normally on for offline UPSes so the utility power can be sent directly to the computer systems. For these systems, the **control logic** system is the device that "decides" to switch from direct AC power to battery power. For online systems, the control logic detects when the incoming power supply has failed and alerts the device of trouble. No power switching is necessary, because the power to the computers is continually drawn from the battery system.

---

4.   The Symmetra by APC has hot-swappable components—pricey but nice.

Alarms and management interfaces

You can get information from the UPS in three ways. If you stand in front of it and wait, bells, whistles, flashing lights, and an LCD display will tell you what kind of power problems are being encountered. But, unless you care to spend all day in the wiring closet (please tell me you don't), there are better methods.

If you have one device per UPS that needs management, you can use the RS232 interface: a serial cable that can be run to the back of the server from the UPS. Your monitoring software will control just that—one device—since that's the only device that receives a signal from the UPS. However, many UPSes can connect directly to the LAN.

The best way of communicating is over the LAN, where the UPS acts as an intelligent device on the network[5]. Most UPSes and associated management software worth their salt use SNMP traps and integrate with SNMP management applications such as HP OpenView, Tivoli TME/10, and CA Unicenter. The UPS alerts the SNMP application or the devices that are running the shutdown applications that the power has switched to battery. Through the parameters set in the applications running locally on the server, the servers know that they must shut down within a given time-frame. In addition, either the UPS monitoring application or the SNMP software can page, e-mail, and/or give a low-voltage shock (just kidding) to the administrator so that he knows that the power has switched to battery. When the power resumes, hubs automatically come back online and servers can restart based on power or the presence of the LAN; i.e., the network, is available.

UPSes Defined

If you want the big picture on UPSes, the most useful definition can be found on Liebert's website (www.liebert.com) in their white paper, "The Basics of UPS Technology." Here, we'll cover the differences among the "big three": offline, online-regenerative inverter, and line-interactive UPSes. These are the most predominantly deployed UPSes in the field today.

---

5. That means that you're going to have to give it an IP address so that you can communicate with it.

Offline UPS

During normal operation, an offline UPS sends the incoming AC power directly to the computer while trickle-charging the battery system.

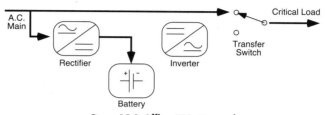

Figure 15-3. Offline UPS—Line mode

However, when the incoming voltage drops below a predefined VAC (enough to qualify as a brownout), a circuit in the UPS detects the fluctuation and switches the power source from the incoming utility power to the battery.

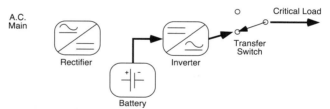

Figure 15-4. Offline UPS—Battery mode

The super-short (5–20 millisecond) power loss the computer experiences is called a **glitch**. That glitch can really mess up some of the computer systems, drop the phone lines on a modem, and cause other annoying problems. Additionally, offline UPSes provide very little protection from frequency variations, line noise, spikes, and brownouts. In other words, they provide absolutely 0 percent line-conditioning. So, what's good about them? They're cheap—about one third the cost of an online UPS.

You really have to dig to find a vanilla, offline UPS. APC (American Power Conversion) doesn't even sell them anymore, and all of the offline UPSes have some sort of enhancements; surge-suppression, "buck and boost" circuits, or AVR

(Automatic Voltage Regulators). I'd never buy an offline UPS for any device in my server room other than my icemaker (hey, we all like refreshing beverages).

Online regenerative inverter UPS

Online UPSes always provide power directly from the battery system to the computers, which means that when the power goes out, there isn't any switching and thus no switch-over time. These are the real McCoys.

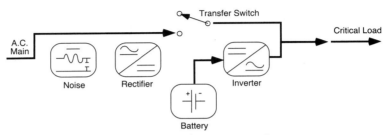

Figure 15-5. Online UPS—Line mode

These real McCoys are technically called **regenerative inverters** (or **double-conversion UPSes**) because they continuously filter the AC power to DC. Then, through a process that involves inverting AC power to DC power, they regenerate clean AC power for complete protection. This power is usually in a perfect sine waveform: The voltage is perfectly regulated and the frequency is stable. These UPSes offer the greatest degree of insurance against problems associated with power lines.

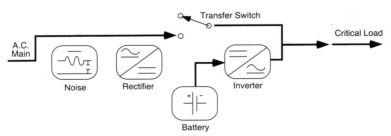

Figure 15-6. Online UPS—Battery mode

Most online UPSes are designed with an internal bypass switch that allows the inverter to ride through short-term overload and to supply power continuously in the unlikely event of inverter failure.

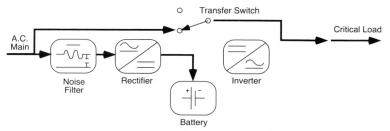

Figure 15-7. Online UPS—Bypass mode

Online UPSes do have disadvantages, including increased heat production, power consumption, and ticket price, but despite the fact that the inverter in an online UPS is always operating, their reliability is typically unaffected and you know exactly what you're getting.

Finally, if you're using a room-size or facility-size UPS that gets its power from the building power supply and supplies electricity to the outlets in the server room or facility, it's an online UPS. I've never seen a hybrid or offline UPS sized for whole server rooms or small facilities.

Everything else Between offline systems and online systems are a whole bunch of online wannabes. Look for terms like *line interactive, single conversion, load sharing, triport,* or *Ferro resonant transformers* in their descriptions.

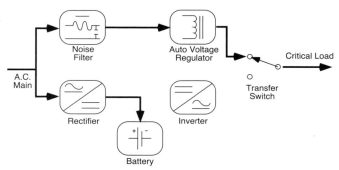

Figure 15-8. Line-Interactive UPS—Line mode

The addition of interactive design and the use of Automatic Voltage Regulators cause a UPS system to use a "ride-through" approach when converting the load transition from AC power to the inverter-supplied power.

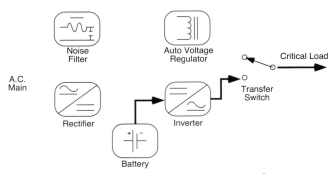

Figure 15-9. Line-Interactive UPS—Battery mode

Sometimes this ride-through approach doesn't work, and the UPS misinterprets a brownout as a blackout, thus kicking in the battery-supplied power. This can cause problems down the line if it happens a few times before a brownout. The batteries kicking in might dwindle their reserves to a point where they can no longer hold a sustained charge large enough to power the computer systems during the upcoming blackout. Thus, you have nothing—no batteries, no time, nada.

Sizing up UPSes

Some things are a given. If you're in North America, the power frequency (cycles per second) is between 50 to 60 Hz, and single or three phase. If you plug the UPS into the wall, you probably need a NEMA L6-30P wall outlet for 208 volts or a regular three-prong plug for 110 volts.

Figure 15-1. NEMA L6-30P for 208V and NEMA 5-15R for 110V

If you have a UPS that takes the 208 V outlet and you have only 110 V outlets, the UPS isn't going to work. So check your electrical distribution to ensure that you can plug your UPS into a power outlet before you buy it.

UPS size comprises two elements: the amount of current in VA and the amount of batteries in time. You need to get enough power in enough time to keep things up and running. The more power and battery time you require, the more you'll pay. If you think your load will expand, make sure that you can raise the amount of VA the UPS can provide, and check to see if you can add batteries to the system through external battery banks if you require additional battery-powered time.

UPS output

As noted above, UPSes have a power factor. If the power factor for the devices attached to the UPS is closer to 1 than the UPS's power factor, you must get a higher VA rating to accommodate that difference. For example,

- A typical 1U rack-mount server with an attached rack-mount JBOD with 10 drives in it has a 456 VA, 328 watt, .625 power-factor load; and

- A typical mid-sized rack-mount UPS has a 500 VA, 300 watt, .6 power-factor load rating.

While the VA rating is high enough, the wattage and power factor are undersized. Therefore, this particular user would have to move up to a higher-rated UPS. The right-sized UPS for this particular system must have a 650 VA, 390 watt, .6 power-factor load (the next size up).

In addition to putting out enough power, a UPS must tolerate less than favorable conditions. The following features help you to determine your UPS's robustness:

- **Regulation**–Even UPSes can provide fluctuating power, especially in unfavorable conditions. The ±% of regulation is the deviation from the desire voltage. If the power deviates too much, that defeats the purpose of the UPS—so the more deviation the UPS can handle, the better.

- **Transfer Time**–If you need to switch to battery, length of time is critical. The less time, the better.

- **Load Crest Factor**–This is the ratio of the peak power requirements to the average power requirements. The higher or bigger the peak (first number), the better. When you crank everything up to the top capacity, as in a restart, the UPS can support that 20 kVA draw that normally hums along at 7 kVA.

- **Overload/Over-Current Capacity**–While UPSes do have kVA ratings, many allow a buffer of overload for a certain period of time. The more overload and more time it can be tolerated, the better. But, again, you pay to play.

- **Transient Regulation**–As you're beating up your UPS and plugging and unplugging things, especially big things, there is fluctuation, just as noted in the first item. This is the amount of fluctuation when load is added and/or removed. The less the better.

Finally, make sure to do an inventory of all the plugs that will connect and check to make sure your space can tolerate the heat, weight, size, and noise the UPS creates. Silence is golden here—literally: Quieter UPSes cost more.

Batteries   Several things affect battery cost. It always takes less time to drain the batteries than it does to charge them, but the less time it takes to recharge the batteries, the better. The time that the batteries will run at full load is called **autonomy time**, and the good news is that the less load you have, the longer the batteries will run.

Monitoring   The UPS monitors two things: power and itself. Monitoring includes short-circuit protection, automated shutdown and restart after long power outages, monitoring and logging of power usage, performance metrics, and a display of the voltage/current on the line and of the draw of specific pieces of equipment. In addition, the UPS can have a direct relationship with the devices it's supporting. Small stand-alone UPSs usually have a single port that attaches to a single computer. When the power switches to battery, it can tell that one computer to shut down before battery power goes down. But to date, we haven't found a UPS that can tell multiple devices when to start up based on time duration—they depend only on "power available" and "network available."

WHICH UPS IS FOR YOU?

Wasn't that a whole lot o' learnin' for something just to keep the power on? Yes, but without that knowledge, you'd have the joyful experience of wasting your budget on a massive set of VEDs (Very Expensive Doorstops). CFOs who've just spent $30,000 don't take too kindly to hearing that there weren't enough batteries.

Offline, online, or line-interactive?

This is not a SOHO book. Don't buy offline UPSes.

You can approach UPS configuration in two ways. If you've got money to burn, go get a big online UPS, attend a couple of training classes, and power up your entire server room. Or, if you're like the rest of us, get a bunch of UPSes. These still throw off heat, but it'll be in your wiring room, where you already have HVAC to spare (right?). They'll take up space, but you have room at the bottom of each rack (right?). They take a bit of configuration—quite a bit—but there *is* a pay-off. With some creative planning, you can time the UPSes to shut down and start up automatically. Thus, if the power goes out, you don't need to start managing each box.

Question	Yes	No
Can you trade money (for a larger system) for management time (smaller systems)	✔	
Do you have a room that can support the HVAC and weight requirements of a large, single UPS?	✔	
Can all of your devices shut down in the same time frame?		✔
Can you afford an electrician who can install the online UPS?	✔	
The deployment of one large, hard-wired UPS is generally 4x the cost of buying a bunch of plug-in UPSes. Would you lose that much money if the plug-in UPSes failed?		✔

Table 15-6. Which UPS to buy?

If you answered *yes* where *Yes* is checked and *no* where *No* is checked, you should be looking at a room- or facility-sized online UPS. If you answered the opposite of the table, a group of line-interactive UPSes is the right solution for you.

DOING IT FOR REAL

There are several steps to determining the appropriate UPS configuration, duh. We'll use a very real-world example from the field.

Calculating load requirements

Load requirement refers to the number of power-drawing devices you want to hook up to the UPS. If you hooked up to your file server, this means the file server (CPU) itself, the monitor, the external hard drives, the tape drive, and anything else that depends on the server. If this is a WAN router, it also means the CSU/DSU. Get the picture? Don't forget to add those RAID banks you'll be buying in the next few months.

If you want to know where to get that information, simple: the vendors' websites and documentation. Below, we show three different portions of web pages for

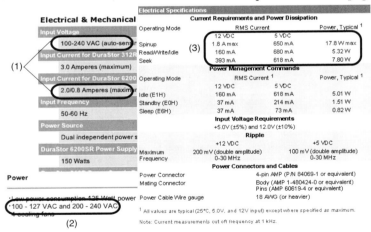

1. Adaptec Durastor JBOD enclosures

2. Dell rack-mount servers

3. Western Digital hard drives

If you already have the products, you can generally find out this same information in their technical documentation under electrical or mechanical specifications. The power needs of each device is listed in the user's manual under *watts* (the power draw) and/or *amps* (the current draw).

- The VA rating is calculated by multiplying volts and amps. Then, total the requirements for amps and then multiply that number by 120 or 240 volts (depending upon which you're using).

- If you know the wattage load for the system components, you can convert the watts to VA by multiplying the watts by 1.4.

- Or if you know the VA, multiply it by the worst possible power factor, .6. The UPS you select should be comfortably larger than the VA and watt rating you come up with.

UPSes perform best when the system that they're supporting draws less than or equal to 75 percent of their VA rating. Therefore, once all the other numbers are in, you should multiply the total by 133 percent. For example, if all the supported devices had a total rating of 300 VA, the UPS should have a rating of around 400 VA..

When deciding where to cut back (because your budget is now in the stratosphere), we also examined what devices wouldn't suffer—or cause us to suffer—if not connected to a UPS. First, all user machines that are not laptops will go down immediately. Thus, if a file server could shut down without corrupting files (remember, all users will no longer be connected), we labeled that non–mission critical. We put all of our backup servers in the same category: They simply restart where they left off. And secondary is just that—secondary. So our secondary DNS and our secondary ISP connection can go down and come right back up.

Why calculate by rack as well as by total? We may go for a rack-by-rack solution. Some folks may favor conformity with each UPS having the same rating. Sure, if you have the money versus the time to make sure you're not overloading, you can do that, but in the real world, you must pay attention to those dreaded two words: cost effectiveness. UPS pricing is not linear; i.e, a UPS that covers twice the power needs can be three time more expensive.

We also took note of our plug needs. Everything has a NEMA 5-15R except the big switch, which has a NEMA L6-30P. This is important for two reasons. First, if we supply UPSes for each rack, the UPS on the switch rack needs to have a NEMA L6-30P with input voltage of 208 V (remember, what goes in must be as big as what goes out). Second, there must be at least two, one for each switch power supply, NEMA L6-30P outlets on the UPS.

Alternative method The alternative measurement method for something this large is as follows:

1. Hire an electrical contractor.

2. Write a very big check for something the size of a VW beetle.

3. Go home, wipe the "I'm a moron and didn't do my homework and now I'm paying out the wazoo" stamp off your forehead, and start looking for another job.

Logistics and planning

As we all know, you can spend a gazillion dollars on backup equipment and software, but if you don't have a plan, forget it. UPSes require a full shutdown and restart plan for each duration of power outage. The parameters of this plan will also guide us on our shopping excursion.

Timing

Most calculators on UPS sites ask you how long you'd like your run-time. Let's consider a few things. First, when the power goes out, how long does it go out for? In our case, it's 10 minutes, or two hours, or days. Since 50 percent of our employees are on laptops, it would be nice if all services kept running for at least 15 minutes before shutdown, thus providing uninterrupted service for half the company. Plus, it would give the laptop users time to log off if the outage lasts more than a few minutes.

Next, it would be cost prohibitive to keep all of the servers up and running for two hours. Why bother when there aren't any users who will have power for that long? We'll set the system to shut down all services after 15 minutes of power outage; a.k.a., a graceful shutdown. However, we need at least two hours to get to the building on a weekend to make sure the network restarts properly. So, we'll keep the network up and running for two hours, letting it drop after that. When the power resumes, we'll be there to monitor the restart. You always want your network power to last longer than your server power in case your UPSes communicate with your servers via the LAN. Now that we have our parameters, we can do our plan.

Graceful shutdown and restart

The word *graceful* conjures up images of my IT director pirouetting from computer to computer. Pavlova he's not: Bursting with testosterone, he's galloping the 50-yard dash to the server room—not a shred of grace about it.

But we're not talking macho moments here, we're talking systems. As we discussed earlier, UPSes do two things: keep your system up and running until you can move the mission-critical operations to a hot site, or until you can shut down gracefully. A graceful restart ensures that hubs and servers are turned on in an order that results in all network operations (routing, internet access, security—got your attention?) functioning properly.

Hold the tutu, but do follow these networking rules of thumb when planning for a graceful shutdown and restart:

- Workstations go down and come right back up. So do printers. However, most workstations use DHCP; therefore, the DHCP server must be restarted before the workstations. Any workstations that sign into an Active Domain controller need that controller up and running before the workstation is up and running.

- Some printers (not mentioning any names here) grab the next available address if they can't find the DHCP server when they restart. For this reason, it's easiest to give your printers static IP addresses.

- Routers and switches usually restart faster than servers and workstations. However, some routers are configured for manual routes; others for dynamic routes. Any routers configured for dynamic routes, and that are dependent upon a certain hierarchy so they aren't "confused," should have special attention paid to the shutdown and restart process.

- Any device with SNMP or Wake-On-LAN can sense if the power is available and if the network is available.

So how is this all going to work?

Power goes out —Users

Half our users and all our printers immediately drop without power—and come up immediately when the power resumes. Did I mention surge protectors?

15 minutes later —Servers

Since we've converted to battery power, the UPSes have told all the servers running monitoring applications that we're running on battery power. After 15 minutes on battery power, our servers begin to shut down just as if we were standing in front of the machine and logging off properly. They'll restart when they sense that the network is available. It is important that IP addresses resolve from the DHCP server and that names resolve from the DNS server—that's why we wait until network services are available.

We can also let our external routers drop. In the event that power resumes in the next hour and 45 minutes, they'll simply come back online. Be ready for phone calls from those proactive types monitoring the other side of the router that faces outside.

2 hours later— Everything else

We've purchased UPSes with a two-hour run-time for our network serving servers (DNS and DHCP) and our internal hubs, LAN routers, firewall, and switches. When the power drops, these drop. With the two-hour window, someone from the staff over at the office will probably figure out what's going on and address it before the final shutdown due to total loss of power. When the power comes on, these start up right away. Your DNS server has a static IP address; thus, no mess to clean up if it starts prior to the DHCP server.

Shutdown, restart, and alert configuration

Most business-level UPSes have have some sort of management software. APC UPSes all come bundled with PowerChute Personal, Business Edition, or Enterprise edition. Liebert UPSes come with their own network management support that's also very good, but doesn't have as much support for the Macintosh platform as APC's software does. With both APC's and Liebert's software, you can manage UPSes through network management cards or through client-server software on computers attached to UPSes through USB or serial cables.

In other words, through a central console (either web- or Windows-based), you can connect to and manage all of the manageable UPSes in the network infrastructure, as well as all of the shutdown commands associated with those UPSes. You can use UPSes with network management cards to trigger the shutdown of any computer on the network by installing special shutdown software for Mac,

Unix, and Windows workstations and servers connected to the same network. When the network-able UPS triggers a shutdown event, it sends a shutdown signal to any computer it knows of—whether the computer is directly attached to that UPS or not.

 Your UPS monitoring software probably won't be able to send out notification through anything other than e-mail. Therefore, set up your UPSes so that when killer alarms trip, they send out SNMP MIB trap signals to your designated LAN management package, such as LANsurveyor from Neon Software, HP OpenView, or others with the capability to support direct-dial pager notifications.

We chose to have just one UPS do the paging since, if the power goes out, it goes out for all the UPSes. We do it on low battery for one of the UPSes that has a 15-minute run-time. That way we aren't paged for every power glitch, but we've got enough time to make a dash to the server room if we're on call. The setup and management screen for a network APC UPS is depicted below, with tons of notification events.

Status of Smart-UPS 1400 named RACK1

UPS status

On Line

Reason For Last Transfer To Battery:	Due to software command
Internal Temperature:	92.6 °F
Runtime:	53 Minutes

Utility power status

Input Voltage:
Input Frequency:
Maximum Line Voltage
Minimum Line Voltage:

Output power status

Output Voltage:
Output Frequency:
Load Power:

Battery status

Battery Capacity:
Battery Voltage:
Number of External Ba
Self-Test Result:
Self-Test Date:
Calibration Result:
Calibration Date:

About UPS

Model:
Firmware Revision:
Manufacture Date:
Serial Number:

Events	Log Event	Notify Users	Run Command File	Shut Down System
Battery: Discharged	✓	○	○	○
Battery: Recharged	✓	○	○	
Battery: Replaced	✓	○	○	
Battery: Replacement Needed	✓	✓	○	✓
Communication: Established	✓	○	○	
Communication: Lost while on Battery	✓	✓	○	○
Communication: Management Card cannot communicate with the UPS	✓	✓	○	○
Communication: PowerChute cannot communicate with the Management Card	✓	✓	○	○
Input Power: Restored	✓	○	○	
Runtime: Exceeded	✓	○	○	○
Runtime: Normal Again	✓	○	○	
SmartBoost: Activated	✓	○	○	
SmartTrim: Activated	✓	○	○	
UPS Overload: Corrected	✓	○	○	
UPS: On Battery	✓	✓	○	✓
UPS: Overloaded	✓	○	○	✓

Figure 15-2. APC's setup and web management screens

All UPS software offers a window of time prior to shutdown (assuming the UPS still has battery time). We set our servers to begin shutdown once the UPS determines there's enough power available for a safe shutdown. However, that works only when you have your UPSes all sized to have the same amount of run-time for the computers attached to them. If the lead UPS has a run-time of one hour and a smaller UPS (with a computer taking its shutdown cue from the main UPS) has a shorter keep-alive time, you'll l run out of UPS power before the attached computer gets the shutdown signal.

In addition to shutting down the operating system with your UPS software, you may need to shut down the application running on the server. This is especially true for databases, since if the server shuts down with an open record, that record could become corrupted. APC (plug, plug) does a wonderful job of keeping applications up-to-date for graceful shutdown of everything from Oracle to Lotus Notes; sorry, no FileMaker.

For our purposes here (and the way we suggest doing it in the real world), we'll go with only a couple of network-managed UPSes that we'll use to communicate with all other computers attached to "dumb" UPSes for shutdown purposes. We'll then place network shutdown software on each of the computers attached to any UPS. These computers will get their shutdown cue from the main UPS.

Prolonged outages

Get thee to a hot site. But before you panic, check your math to ensure that the cost of setting up and moving back are lower than the cost of being out of business for a day or so. Share the responsibility with the head of operations. And finally, know that you did everything you could to account for less than perfect power.

About that HVAC: If you don't have power, you don't have HVAC. This is reason #89b why you shouldn't have your equipment running when the power is out.

Shopping & setup

Let's walk through how we'd shop for, and set up, our print production plant. We've divided the plant into three floors. Starting from the top floor and working down, the third floor holds the sales staff, IT staff, executive offices, and the designer's area, along with the pre-press servers. The second floor is the production and accounting floor, with the CFO, the server room, two of the three main print plotters (these drive half of the company's total revenue), the OPI RIP and its associated Arizona plotter (the other half of the company's revenue), and, of course, the production workstations. Finally, the first floor of the company is dedicated to shipping, receiving, and the final jobbing stages for putting together the cut-piece banners, logos, and bus-sides that come out of the cutters and plotters. We've numbered each of the UPS placements, and will go through them one by one.

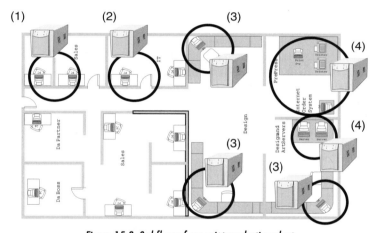

Figure 15-3. 3rd floor of our print production plant

1. Two of the sales computers are not notebooks: they're standard desktops with Celeron processors, 15-inch monitors, with external speakers, internal CD-RW drives, and an attached inkjet printer on each.

2. This is the IT staff room. Only one computer (running the network monitoring applicaitons) needs to continue running in case of a power outage. This computer also has a modem attached and a direct-dial phone line that doesn't need any external power. In a network-wide prolonged outage, this is the computer that will be sending out pages and SMS messages to cell phones or alternate e-mail systems.

3. These are the designer's stations. We've elected to put UPSes on them because if they had a power outage in the middle of working on a large client file, they could easily corrupt the file and the project. Therefore, each of the key designer's stations needs an individual UPS. Because each of these computers has a

21-inch monitor, external Zip drives, scanners, and the like, they consume more power than normal. And since these are *really* critical computers, we want to keep a close tab on the UPSes and have therefore requested that they come with network SNMP connections for monitoring purposes.

4. We've also put UPSes on each of the pre-press servers and printers as well as on the Internet ordering system feeder computer. Since the printers don't draw much power unless they're printing (all printing stopped when the power went out), we've figured on attaching them, as well. We've oversized the UPS for the Internet order feed computer because we want it to stay up longer than usual.

That takes care of the top floor. The folks not on UPSes will just be out of luck, but there won't be much for them to do anyway. Let's head down to the second floor and see what we have there.

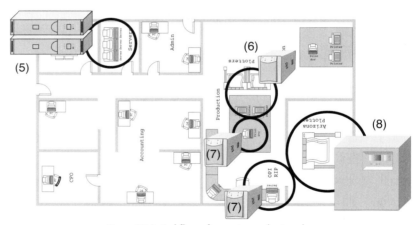

Figure 15-4. 2nd floor of our print production plant

5. The server room holds four Dell rack-mount servers (240 VA each), two DuraStor JBODs (200 VA each) with 12 Western Digital hard drives in each (324 VA total each), the firewall (110 VA), router (240 VA), a switch (127 VA), and various other stuff like tape drives, etc. (for about another 600 VA). We'll be splitting the sytems in two and mounting two rack-mount UPSes in here.

6. The plotters are the engines that cut the roll-fed magnets, plastics, contact paper, or anything else being die-cut for the clients. These two plotters are heavy-power drawing systems pulling down about 800 VA each. Therefore, we need a UPS that can handle at least 2200 VA.

7. The print and OPI servers that drive the plotters and the Arizona plotter are both tower models with external JBOD/RAID systems attached. Each one draws about 750 VA. Because we must monitor these closely, we need SNMP management hardware and software.

8. This is the Big Kahuna (see *The Big Kahuna* on page 564). It's the Arizona plotter that's the size of a Hummer, and it accounts for half of the company's revenue. This thing isn't just big, it's a major electricity hog as well, pulling down 9600 VA, (9 kVA). This thing sits in the room with the Arizona and handles that device.

Then there's the first floor assembly group (we've omitted the picture becuase there's only one computer tied to a UPS on this floor). Only the main jobbing PC (that tracks what finished sheets go into what packages and out to what clients) needs to keep running, so that whatever jobs are finished can at least ship out to the clients.

9. The jobbing PC is pretty small and doesn't take much, as far as a UPS goes.

The shopping list table for what we're building looks something like the one below, where we've compared the APC models and the Liebert models.

Group	VA/KVA	Net Comm	APC Solution	Liebert Solution
1 Sales	233*2		APC Smart-UPS XL 750VA * 2	PSA 650VA/390W
2 IT	220		Back-UPS 650V	PSA 500VA/300W
3 Design	460	✔	APC Smart-UPS XL 750VA	Interactive 1000VA/670W * 3
4 PrePress	299		APC Smart-UPS XL 750VA	PSA 650VA/390W * 2
5 Server Rm	2773	✔	APC Smart-UPS XL 3000VA RM * 2	Interactive 2200VA/120V * 2
6 Plotters	2128	✔	APC Smart-UPS XL 2200VA	Interactive 2200VA/120V
7 PServe	751	✔	APC Smart-UPS XL 1000VA * 2	Interactive 1400VA/950W * 2
8 AZ	9kVA	✔	Symmetra PX 10kW	Nfinity 4-16kVA
9 Jobbing	142		Back-UPS 650VA	PSA 350VA/210W

Table 15-7. Product selection and APC—Liebert comparison

The Big Kahuna

Because of this serious load, the Big Kahuna is hard-wired directly into the building's main power feed. The good news? We don't have to worry about distributing power from the UPS to multiple floors. The bad news? We must send out an RFP for something this bid. We have an example of what an RFP for UPS installation looks like on our website (shameless plug), www.backupbook.com. Not only will the VAR have to do the electrical work, she must install the UPS and train the team.

Guess what? The bids for work fell between $12,000 and $20,000. Even if the UPS costs less than $20,000, I have the HVAC unit to worry about, as well—have to keep that UPS cooled down. So already, we're looking at about $25,000. For that kind of cash, you want a Liebert UPS. Hands down.

Liebert is a wonderful company. I've never used anything but their product for HVAC. Their UPSes, big and small, are top-notch. If we have the money but not the personnel, we'll go with the Liebert Nfinity. Our power comes in as three phase; thus, it can support this size of UPS. This unit can expand up to 20 kVA, it's not enormous (size, sound, heat), and feature-by-feature, it's as good, if not better than the competition. The ballpark costs are $25,000 for two hours of run-time for 30 percent of our load and 20 minutes for the remaining 70 percent of our load. Why split the load? Space and money. If we were to go with the whole load at two hours, we'd need 15 battery modules. We were able to get by with six battery modules at about a third of the costs and the space. As it was, our batteries took up as much space and the UPS. There was no way we could support the size and weight of the additional batteries in our closet.

Communications & emergency shutdown setup

Because we have multiple network-managed UPSes on this system, we chose to set up a web-based management console on our IT staff computer, and SNMP MIB traps to communicate with LANsurveyor running on that computer. Again, we're running LANsurveyor on top of the UPS management software for emergency communications. UPSes can communicate only via e-mail servers, but when the network goes down, LANsurveyor can use the computer's modem card and straight-through dialer to access an outside line and send emergency pages. Think of it as an emergency communications channel for the emergency communications system.

Below is a communications diagram showing which UPSes are fully managed and fully monitored versus which UPSes are ignored. Each computer system attached to a UPS has at least network-driven shutdown software running on it and each takes its shutdown cue from the central IT console that monitors the UPSes. Just in case the UPSes miss their shutdown cue, LANsurveyor is also set to trap any UPS SNMP MIB's trigger alert and then send network-wide shutdown cues to any computer left standing.

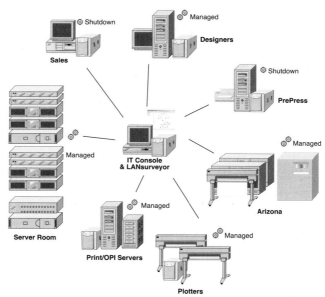

Figure 15-5. Fully managed system setup

QUESTIONS YOU SHOULD ASK

- Is there indication of load level, battery capacity, input volts, AC loss, low battery, overload, temperature problems, or squirrels chewing the cable? How often will the UPS need to be serviced?

- If the UPS is plugged into the server, can you change its batteries without rebooting the file server; i.e., do you have to shut down your computer before changing the UPS's batteries?

- Does the vendor offer training so that you can monitor the UPS and understand the procedures to rectify any problems?

- Can the file server be shut down automatically by the UPS, in an orderly way, in case of a prolonged power failure? Is this function included, or do you need to add the appropriate software?

- Can you test the UPS hardware on the network from a remote location? Is the UPS software network capable? If so, does it support more than one UPS across the network? If so, how?

- Is an automatic log of significant power events available? The more information garnered from the UPS itself regarding its operation, the better.

CHAPTER 16:
HIGH-AVAILABILITY NETWORKS

At the time we began this book, Network Frontiers was one of the 6,000 organizations in the San Francisco Bay Area to fall victim to AT&T's broadband network outage. It wasn't just a day's worth of outage, it was the entire system that they were OEMing from Excite going out of business, leaving us all in the lurch. Without secondary connectivity, many businesses were completely cut off from the Internet for up to two weeks as other carriers and AT&T were scrambling to fill the void.

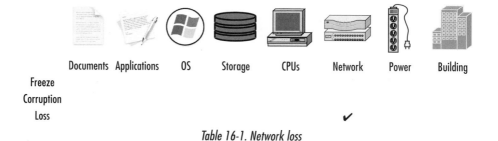

	Documents	Applications	OS	Storage	CPUs	Network	Power	Building
Freeze								
Corruption								
Loss						✔		

Table 16-1. Network loss

Our area isn't the only one to be affected by such mishaps. In July of 2001, a great part of the East Coast was troubled with a major slowdown of Internet traffic when a train filled with hazardous materials caught fire in a Baltimore, Maryland, tunnel. The blaze melted a mass of fiber optic Internet cables for almost every service provider on the coast, and it burned for two days—the cables couldn't even be repaired until the fire was out and the scene cleaned up.

How likely is this to happen to you? Take a gander at this table that shows each of the major service providers' days out of commission—and then start a-plannin'.

	2000 Outages	2001 Outages*
AT&T	27	24
BellSouth	30	29
MCI/WorldCom	8	10
Qwest	54	31
SBC	34	42
Sprint	8	11
Verizon/GTE	38	31

*This doesn't include the 9/11 attacks in 2001

Table 16-2. Network outages

In other words, not a single major carrier is exempt from outages. Your only hope is that if you have two of them, both won't go out at the same time.

Because of these types of outages, even the smallest of businesses in our area now have at least two distinct carriers and methods of connectivity. In fact, one of the basic tenets of redundancy is the establishment of both redundancy and route diversity—for the network and for key services.

- We have both broadband business cable and a normal T1 coming into the office from the north (broadband cable) and the south (the T1 Telco), just in case some idiot cuts a line with a trenching tool.

- We've hooked up with SaveTheMail for a redundant route for our mail service, and with Postini to scrub any incoming mail for viruses and spam.

- Our authoritative DNS is replicated at our ISP (SBC) on two different servers, and at SaveTheMail in case SBC goes down.

- And we can quickly replicate our web servers and begin hosting them within a day at any of the co-location sites in the Bay Area. We don't have them co-located because we don't rely directly on them for our revenue model. If we did, we'd have them offsite.

The Main Thing

The Main Thing here is that you establish a Service Level Agreement regarding your network, DNS, mail server, and other key Internet asset availability in your organization. Your team must know how long a server will be down and which levels of availability they can count on. This could be anywhere from a high of multiple business days (if you don't have redundant network connections) to a low of milliseconds in a high-availability environment. Here's the down and dirty differences among the three, using an e-mail server as the example.

Basic availability

Basic availability means that if the system falls down, you'll be able to restore it within hours (as long as you have all the necessary spare parts).

Backing up a mail server means backing up a system that is highly volatile. Microsoft's Exchange is even more volatile than normal Unix SMTP/POP/IMAP mail servers, in that its infrastructure is much more complex. When you back up your mail servers, at minimum, you'll need the following to ensure protection against hardware and software:

Some basic form of hardware redundancy like extra fans for the computers/hard drive JBODs, hot spare hard drives (or a RAID system), etc. (see *Standard and fault-tolerant JBOD enclosures* on page 465)

Once you've decided on your hardware and software setup, you must get your e-mail servers into your Intrusion Detection System (IDS) and network security plan. One of the hazards of e-mail servers is the directed virus, spam, and other attacks (see *Perimeter protection for your e-mail server* on page 228). You must also ensure that you've tied your server into your remediation system, as well (see *Immediate remediation* on page 197).

Establish an imaged OS and e-mail system that has been separated into two distinct volumes and two distinct images during setup. By separating the operating system image (and its updates) from the e-mail system's image (and its updates) you can quickly restore either one of them (see *Setting up your computers for imaging* on page 381).

On top of that, you'll need backup software that supports open file backup, or has a specific Exchange backup capability so that you can restore individual mailboxes rather than the whole server (see *Open-file database backups* on page 343).

Beyond protecting your hardware and software at the basic level, networking infrastructure must be available. You must have dual, redundant routes to the Internet as well as an offsite DNS server in your authoritative list so that if your network segments fall down, you can still communicate with the outside world through e-mail.

Advanced availability

Advanced availability is planning for complete failure of the hardware or software or network, along with decreased restoration time. Adding these options to the above protection plan decreases your restoration time dramatically.

To decrease restoration time vis-à-vis your hardware and software, you must have a "warm box" ready to go as a fail-over device in case your primary mail server falls down (see *Clustered servers* on page 473).

The primary mail server should be equipped with a "third mirror" hard drive system that allows you to break off the mirrored volumes of both the operating system and the e-mail server system so that you can reattach them to the "warm box" standing by.

A service with an outside backup mail provider such as SaveTheMail or Postini should be set up, so that as soon as your e-mail server is unreachable, it begins spooling the mail and then delivers it back to the server once it's back up (see *E-mail that doesn't go down* on page 594).

By adding the above options to your e-mail backup plan, you ensure that recovery is much quicker, and that clients never perceive you were down in the first place.

High availability

If you have **high availability**, your e-mail service is never down. If the main computer fails, a secondary computer is already synchronized, replicated, and running. If the network goes down, a second network is already running. If the building falls down and users are at home, they can still get to e-mail somehow, and send and receive their messages.

System-level protection has now moved to full clustering of the computers so that if a computer or a drive system fails, a duplicate is in place and running (see *Clustered servers* on page 473).

Regarding e-mail server level protection, the basic mail server is also clustered to a different computer in case the main computer is no longer available, *or*

The organization has signed up with a backup e-mail service provider that delivers a product that not only spools incoming mail, but provides a methodology for users to create outgoing mail and interact with incoming mail, *or*

The organization has integrated an offsite disaster recovery system that synchronizes with their mail servers in order to provide full-time redundancy of messaging services.

And if you're wondering...

We don't think that your network's availability should fall into the "basic" or "advanced" availability category. E-mail, maybe. But both DNS and the network itself should *always* be in the high-availability category.

A HIGH-AVAILABILITY QUIZ

Let's start with a quiz to segue into this chapter, which is about planning for the loss of your network, your data center, and your communications. You must ensure that the network connectivity out to your extended value chain (your workers, partners, and clients) can continue uninterrupted even if your primary servers or your primary network have all gone down.

Let's take the case of the common, ordinary data center or server room, such as one of those I've managed in the past, shown below. This is usually the epicenter of all things communication and network services for the organization. Have you ever thought of what could happen if you lost a couple of servers in this room, lost connectivity to the room, or lost access to the room itself?

Figure 16-1. Typical data center

When prequalifying your data center or server room as "highly important" to the company, ask yourself these three questions:

1. How many hours in the day are the computers in your data center actively used?

    If the y're used less than a full normal workday, then donworryaboudit. This isn't a full-time computing center for the organization, and you've probably got other fish to fry. You can ignore the rest of this chapter if you really want to.

If the computers in this room are being used *more* than a full day's workday (anywhere from 12 hours on up to the full 24), *then* you've got yourself a data center or server room worth really protecting and keeping live.

2. What does it cost your company per day, in lost revenue or other costs, for your data center or server room to be down?

An adjunct to the first question is the worth of the computing systems and information running within the data center or server room. Are these just internal files, or do these files form a production backbone in the organization? I have a client that has only 15 computers in the whole operation—with five in the server room driving his whole print production system and 90 percent of his business. Even though he's a small shop, that server room is mighty important. If all of the servers went down, he'd have to outsource the work and lose all of the revenue for those projects until the system was back online.

3. How many days of your data center, network, or server room being down can your company afford?

With all of the above said, how many days can the server room be out of operation? At True North, our data center housed all of the media buys for ad agencies strewn throughout the United States. The data center *couldn't* be down—one day of downtime equalled tens of millions of dollars lost. For most businesses, more than a month of downtime, or loss of 10 percent of their yearly gross revenue, will put them out of business.

The next set of four questions revolves around how quickly you can react to a key device or the whole data center or server room being down.

4. How many hours in the day is your data center or server room unattended?

If it's a server room, I think I know the answer—it's pretty well *un*-attended. If it's a data center, it should be well attended. But how well attended? Do you have staff around the clock? Do you have "outages" of staff at the four-, eight-, or 12-hour levels? Sometimes it's hard to get data center staff revolving 24 hours a day—not everyone wants to work the graveyard shift.

5. If the power goes out, on average, how many hours can your UPSes support the computers in your data center or server room?

   So let's say that folks aren't there and the power goes out. How long can your UPSes handle the load of their respective computers before they have to shut them down? Is the server shut down gracefully (see *Graceful shutdown and restart* on page 557), and are the failover replacement systems standing by?

6. Do you have smoke, temperature, water, power, computer and network monitoring systems set up to page and e-mail multiple contact points in case of an emergency?

   What about monitoring systems? We've talked about SMART alarms and computer-monitoring systems for freezes and crashes, but what about temperature alarms, water alarms, and network outage alarms?

   If the network or power goes out, how will you be contacted? Is it just you, or will multiple people in your organization be contacted? We ran a project once for BMW called CyberDrive. This was the world's most widely patched system, and it ran in two locations (Minneapolis and New York City). It had to be up and running 24/7 for almost a full month while hundreds of thousands of folks hit its streaming server content. We had pager systems set up for our key staff in both cities, backup staff in both cities, our VARs in both cities, and even select vendors and partners in both cities. While we went a little over budget, the system was always available.

7. If any of the key services in your data center or server room go down when you aren't there (including network access), once you're notified, how long would it take you to respond?

   Even though you have alarms and remote management tools out the wazoo, none of your tools will work if the power is out or connectivity is down. That means that somebody will be heading to the server room or data center. So how fast will you get to your site (or however you respond) if an alarmgoes off? What happens if the alarm goes off at 2:00A.M. on a Saturday (beer) night?

Your answers to these seven questions and the next three that follow determine your data center/server room risk factor. So let's get to those all-important last three questions, which elucidate what you'll be able to do when you get that dreaded alarm.

8. For redundancy's sake, have you set up additional *authoritative* DNS servers on your network segments outside your organization and outside of your data center or server room?

    More organizations than you'd think have their DNS servers locked tightly away in their server room or their data center for security, only to find out that if their network goes down, their company becomes invisible on the Internet (without DNS, nobody can find you). So the question becomes: Have you taken the precaution of setting up replicated authoritative DNS servers on network segments other than your primary network or your server room/data center?

    If yes, good for you—gold stars and Krispy Kremes all around. If not, stop reading any further and go directly to *The fourth rule of thumb: Get your DNS offsite* on page 588. Because if you don't set up a secondary DNS system before your network goes down, you'll be invisible to the world for at least three business days while DNS resets itself after you've reconfigured it.

9. For emergency communications services, have you set up a transferable e-mail system outside of your organization's network?

    Think of it: If your network falls down, if you lose access to your data center or server room, or the whole building is down and your e-mail system went with it, how will you mass-communicate with your organization? Setting up alternative e-mail systems is easy and inexpensive. For a simple system, you can use SaveTheMail, and for a more complex system, use the Emergency Messaging System from MessageOne.

    If you've set up an alternative e-mail system, you're well ahead of the game. If you haven't, waiting until your system goes down to set one up will be absolutely painful, so stop reading here, do not pass Go, and rush directly to *Moving to an external backup mail service provider* on page 599.

10. Are you the only trained data center or server room administrator who can re-DNS key equipment or coordinate setting the offsite equipment to take over as the primary systems?

    You may feel that being a solo operator makes you supercompetent, but unless you have help, you'll be in need of divine guidance. If I've learned one thing in life, it's that in a crisis, it's always best to have at least two heads thinking instead of one. Two heads (or more) can consult each other. One has no perspective, gets nervous, and tends to make mistakes. As Three Dog Night sagely informed us, one is the loneliest number. Find a friend, like a good VAR.

11. If your data center or server room facility will be out of commission for *n* day(s), do you have an offsite hosting facility pre-set up?

   That *n* day thing has to do with your answer to question 3, above (How many days can you be down?). Let's say that you answered "A week." Your server room floods and it's now day 3. You realize that come day 5 or 7, you aren't going to be back in business. It's time to make a decision to "cut over" to your offsite facility. Er... do you *have* an offsite facility? If you do (even something small, like a cage for hosting key servers), how quickly can you set up your servers?

   If you've been reading the book from front to back (yeah, I know, only insomniacs could do that) you'll have learned about replicating systems and clustering them over the WAN. If you're doing that, given the green light, you can bring your systems online relatively quickly. If not, you've got some work ahead of you. More on that below.

12. If something happens to your primary Internet access feed to the data center or server room, do you have a second, live feed already in place to switch over to?

   As I said in the beginning of this chapter, not having a second Internet access feed puts your company in great peril. If this is your situation, stop reading immediately and proceed directly to *The first rule of thumb: Always have two Internet providers* on page 578.

13. If the network on your primary VPN access point will be out of commission for *n* day(s), do you have a secondary VPN access point pre–set up at your offsite facility?

   Same deal with the *n* thing as above. I'm throwing in the VPN thing simply because I suspect you may not have thought of it yet. If you do have a VPN in your office, how did you set it up at the user's end for connectivity? Did you set it up (like some folks I know, Sean) with them hitting an IP address as the corporate connecting point? Or did you get clever and set it up as a DNS address (VPN.myco.com), so that the end user's home router or laptop can access the VPN through the DNS entry that can be changed to accommodate switching IP addresses? We'll get to the specifics of that in a minute.

If you haven't yet set up your organization's VPN up, you'll definitely want to get to *Adding a VPN for disaster preparation* on page 607 as quickly as possible. This is your green light: Run, don't walk.

The quiz online

The questions that we've been asking you are a part of our data center and server room disaster preparedness quiz. You can find the entire quiz online at our backup book website, where you can quantify your high-availability prowess.

http://www.backupbook.com/quiz1.html

Hit the website and take the quiz there. The worst score is somewhere in the 800s, and the best score is under 100.

If you're one of those folks that score in the 800s, do us—and yourself—a favor and e-mail us. We'll point you to various places in this book where you'd really better crack down and get going on your disaster preparations. We'll also hook you up with some offsite hosting companies and e-mail emergency companies like SaveTheMail or MessageOne.

If you're one of the folks who score really low, e-mail us and let us know that, too. We're always interested in learning from folks who really know what they're doing.

THE FOUR RULES OF THUMB FOR HIGHLY AVAILABLE NETWORKS

If you follow these four rules of thumb, you'll have highly available, hard-to-topple networks. Your system will become the "weebles" of networks: They might wobble, but they won't fall down.

The first rule of thumb: *Always* have two Internet providers

The first rule of thumb for network redundancy is to *always* have at least two Internet service providers. The adjunct to this rule? Ensure that they run their services to your organization on physically different cables.

Home offices

Home offices are at a disadvantage when it comes to service providers and having multiple cable runs to their offices. A typical city block has the telephone and broadband cables run under the street through conduit, with single feeds to each home. Those feeds normally carry both the cable and the telephone wires.

Figure 16-2. Typical city block

Thus, when some moron decides to trench on your block, both your phone and cable lines are at risk of being cut in half.

City offices

City offices, on the other hand, are quite different. Below is an aerial view of downtown Chicago, where my old office buildings used to be. The four thick lines in the picture represent the major cable feeds that went into the downtown area—two from the north (the left side) and two from the south (the right side).

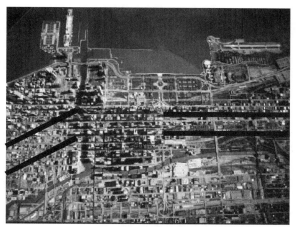

Figure 16-3. Inner-city feeder tubes

From those main feeder tubes, meshes of underground circuits were created with multiple sonnet rings of fiber cable connecting cables from AT&T, Sprint, Qwest, and others. Each of our buildings had at least two sonnet rings of cable that fed into different sides of the building. In my old office in Minneapolis, we literally had feeds coming in on each of the four sides of the building.

The real world

In the real world, when you're running your system, make sure that the cabling comes into your building through diverse routes. I talked to a guy the other day who was very satisfied that he had covered himself, running Covad's DSL service as his primary service coming in on one line and AT&T's service as his backup service coming in on another line. Except that, in reality, (he didn't know this) both lines were physically implemented on top of SBC's cabling infrastructure.

And, you guessed it, when some moron trenched through the street, both service providers were out for three days until the fix could be made to the physical cable.

This cabling from the service provider to your office is called **the last mile**. Make sure that your secondary service provider owns their own cable for the last mile, and that they use a different cable system than the cabling already connecting you to the Internet.

Questions for your Telco when creating interstate/city route diversity

Similar to rerouting traffic when an accident occurs, a redundant network's multiple routes provide an immediate alternate connection should any link in the network be cut. This redirection within the router happens in milliseconds; thus connectivity is neither lost, nor even interrupted.

The only problem in this scenario? While an organization *can* plan route and carrier diversity into their organization's premises, if they have multiple offices in multiple cities, they can't really plan route or carrier diversity between the offices because the carriers they're contracting with are also attempting to create route and cable diversity—therefore everything at a national level has become a mesh (No, I'm not slurring my words, honest, officer!). There are only so many rights-of-way that cables can be laid in. Because carriers lease each other's bandwidth, your best bet on a national basis is to work with a couple of vendors who can guarantee you route diversity throughout their network.

Ask your backhaul and backbone service providers the following crucial questions:

- Did the vendor construct the intercity and interstate routes, or did they buy the routes and cable-shares from someone else? Get a map route from both for proof and for checking against the news when you hear of a regional calamity.

- Are the circuits being planned fiber-diverse (collapsed ring) or are they route-diverse (geographical diversity)?

- How is reroute management handled in terms of congestion, reroute times, uptime, and throughput service level agreements?

- What is the Telco routing equipment failover plan, and what is the uptime service level agreement?

- If they do have a failover, what's their normal capacity, and what's the failover (doubled-up) capacity of the system? How close to 100 percent capacity will they be if they have a fail-over onto the circuit your system is on?

- What is the service level escalation plan, and can you test it? It's one thing to have an agreement on paper—it's completely something different to actually see the plan in place and working. By the way, when you test the plan, have your Telco's engineer and salesperson sitting next to you with their pagers and cell phones *off* so that they can't "help" the escalation process.

The second rule of thumb: Run your cabling in the building in a separate space

In any given building ,there's a place where the building cabling (called **intra-premises cabling**) connects to the cabling owned by the Telco provider. This place is called the **MPOP**, or **Main Point of Presence**. Sometimes, especially in smaller office buildings, the MPOP is simply a punch-down block that the cable comes in to. When this is the case, there really isn't much intra-premises wiring to speak of. The cable from the Telco biscuit is jacked directly into the back of the router's WAN port. And, since you have two different service providers, you also have two different routers.

Simple broadband operations

In the SOHO and small to medium-sized business market, you find either Netopia or Cayman (also by Netopia) routers, connected to DSL, ISDN, or broadband cable networks. However, this doesn't mean that you can't run dual Internet feeds to the company and put one of them on standby just in case your primary system fails. Although it's easier to do in a large-scale environment with a costly router that allows you to plug in two or more Internet feeds into the same box, it's just as doable at this level of the game.

You need a good firewall (we recommend SonicWALL), an extra hub if your router doesn't come with one (NetGear or Linksys will be fine), a Netopia router for your primary Internet connection and whatever other Internet-to-Ethernet gear your secondary service provider gives you for your backup Internet feed. We have an RCA cable modem with a standard coax cable going out to AT&T and the Internet, and an Ethernet cable that plugs into our hub. The network design is shown below in Figure 16-4.

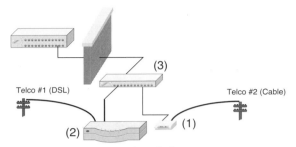

Figure 16-4. Basic dual route setup

1. This is your secondary Internet feed. Our diagram depicts a cable modem, but it can be anything. The secondary feed needs to tie into the hub (3) outside of your firewall (as does your primary router). The firewall should *not* be configured to point to it—it should point only to the Netopia.

2. This is your Netopia router, your primary Internet gateway that the firewall will point to. It has two Internet gateway pointers: one to the primary service provider, and the **backup IP gateway** to whatever other secondary Internet access device you've put in place. Below is an IP setup window as described. If the primary fails, the router redirects to the backup gateway.

Figure 16-5. Netopia setup config. with a primary and backup IP gateway

Larger organizations are somewhat more complex

In larger buildings, and higher-speed and more complex (bigger-budget) networks, life gets much more complicated. In this scenario, you have three parts to the intra-premises wiring system: the MPOP, the riser shafts, and the APOP. In a multiple-story building, intra-premises riser cable provides a two-wire or four-wire connection between points in a building where the Telco-owned facilities are utilized. This includes the building-type cable and associated terminations. Access to the intra-premises riser cable originates at the Telco's MPOP and extends to the **Additional Point of Presence (APOP)** where the organization's inside wire terminates. The basic schematic is shown at bottom left, and a real-world floor plan with both riser shafts is shown on the right for a building in Chicago that we worked on several years ago.

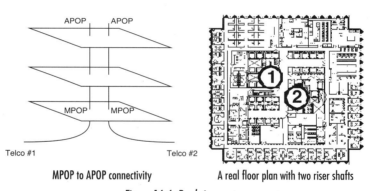

MPOP to APOP connectivity   A real floor plan with two riser shafts

Figure 16-6. Dual riser system

Are you guaranteed to have dual riser shafts and dual MPOPs and APOPs in your building? Not likely. Field editor Tom McBride relayed a story about a network he designed not so long ago. "When I designed Fallon's network for their new building, we had some very specific issues to deal with. In our initial assessment of the building, we discovered that only a single riser was allowed for running cable (they didn't plan on a second riser at all). So we built a second riser. Then we found out the building had only an MPOP and no APOP. So we built an APOP for our services only (this was a locked room that only Fallon and building maintenance could access). Finally, there was only one route into the building for Telco services, so we built a secondary to allow for diverse routing and access to a separate fiber ring served out of a separate central office." And this was all for a professional A-grade building that housed more than a thousand of Fallon's employees.

In these more complex systems, the MPOP probably has its own MUX[1] or IMUX[2] for controlling and bonding the multiple cable systems. In the diagram below, we show the complete system that goes with the floor plan of the office above. On the bottom are the two DS3 feeds that came in from the two Telcos (1). These feed into the MPOP and the junction box that provides an interface between the local loop and the organization's inside wire. Usually, this junction box is divided into two compartments: one containing the over-voltage unit (protector), buried service wire and drop terminals; the other containing the organization's inside wire, the inside wire terminals, and a modular plug that connects the inside wire to the local loop. From that point, each cable system runs up its own riser system into the APOP and then into the wiring closet, where it terminates into the MUX/IMUX (2). From there, it connects into the organization's higher-end Cisco router (3) and the backbone switch (4).

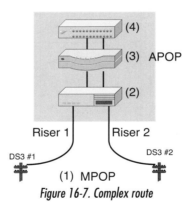

Figure 16-7. Complex route

---

1.   A **MUX** (**multiplexor**) is a device that merges several low-speed transmissions into one high-speed transmission, and vice versa.

2.   An **IMUX** (**inverse multiplexor**) is a device that breaks up a high-speed transmission into several low-speed transmissions, and vice versa. It's used to transmit LAN and videoconferencing traffic over lower-speed digital channels. For example, to transmit Ethernet over a T3 link, the 10 Mbps Ethernet channel is inverse multiplexed into multiple 64 Kbps channels of the T3 line.

The MUX/IMUX is used for the same reason that McBride used it at Fallon: "To allow for monitoring of the individual DS3s and allow for rerouting of traffic in the event of a failure. From the MUX, they went into an IMUX to allow for separation of services and bonding of T1s... This wasn't a cheap way to go; however, it allowed us to use AT&T's local service provision without ever running over Qwest's copper. We brought AT&T fiber links directly into our facility. This eliminated the finger-pointing problem when there was a service disruption." With both Internet connections feeding directly into the backbone router, you don't have to worry about boundary routing and when to decide to fail-over to the secondary ISP, because it's all automatic.

Scott McCulley, VP and managing director of technology operations for IPG, the world's largest ad agency, concurs with this type of design, and adds his own concerns about ensuring that your organization has direct management access to the Telco gear you're leasing or connecting with. "Make sure that your circuits are spread across two different pieces of equipment at the C/O and the MPOP in your building," he recommended. "We recently experienced an outage because both the primary and backup ISP circuits were terminated on the same Telco hardware in the building. This was hardware owned and maintained by the local exchange carrier, not the building, and not by us. By some freak of nature, or stupidity, the Telco gear was being powered by the tenants on the fifth floor, instead of common building power. When the tenants moved out, they used their 'think globally, act locally' mentality and turned off the power. It also removed power from our Telco gear. No worry, the UPS powered it for almost four days, until it gave up the ghost right in the middle of *our* day."

Here are a few more points for this type of design:

- Obviously, the only reason to run separate DS3s is to get them on separate fiber rings so that, if failure is outside the customer premise, the diverse route is truly diverse.

- The diverse route in the organization's facility is crucial during testing if the lines service an active business when the test is completed. This also enables the organization to determine if their own diverse route planning (the MUX and separate risers) works.

- With the type of design described above, you have one other consideration. Since DS3s are charged by the number of T1s active in the circuit, you may activate enough to carry only half your traffic (since you're load balancing the traffic across DS3s). This means that a failure of one decreases your traffic capacity by 50 percent. However, through careful negotiations, you may get your vendor to agree to an emergency response plan that allows you to call and have them activate the remaining T1s in the DS3 to allow for 100 percent of your traffic to be routed over the circuit that is up.

The third rule of thumb: Have fail-over firewalls

In a denial-of-service attack, a hacker hits your firewall so hard that it's completely overwhelmed and dies. If that happens, no traffic gets through to the other side. And if your firewall also provides the VPN security solutions to your remote sites, you're out of connectivity to those sites, as well. For this reason, we suggest that you don't employ a firewall on your router, but rather, put two *inside* your router and connect them in a high-availability manner. You can do this with Cisco or the folks that we really like, SonicWALL. A high-availability clustered firewall eliminates network downtime by allowing the configuration of two firewalls as a pair. In this type of configuration, the backup firewall monitors the primary firewall and takes over in the event of a failure.

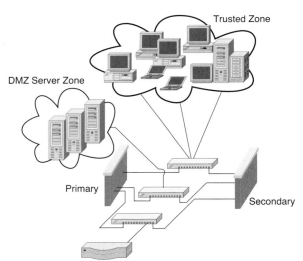

Figure 16-8. Dual, high-availability firewall scenario

All of the SonicWALL firewalls have built-in high-capability settings. To create a configuration like the one above (Figure 16-8.), you need two *of the same type* of firewall, and two additional IP addresses (they can be in the private range) assigned to the firewall pair for heartbeat monitoring purposes.

The primary and backup firewalls communicate with each other using a heartbeat signal at the specific heartbeat IP address. Because they use this address *only* for heartbeat purposes, it must be configured separately from the WAN IP, DMZ IP, and trusted LAN IP addresses. The interruption of this heartbeat signal triggers the backup firewall to take over operation from the active unit of the high-availability pair. The amount of lapsed time between the primary going down and the secondary taking over will be determined by the timing of the heartbeat signals and can be as short as six seconds or as long as 500 seconds. Configuration (at least with the SonicWALL products) is very simple and can be done on one screen:

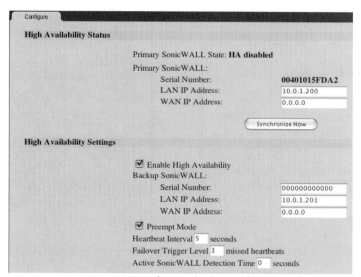

Figure 16-9. Configuring the clustered firewall

- You configure the first firewall as normal, and then add a second IP address for heartbeat monitoring.

- Give the primary the serial number and the heartbeat IP address for the backup firewall (which you haven't even turned on yet).

- Then set your heartbeat interval. In most cases, the interval is between three seconds and 255 seconds. This must correspond with the fail-over trigger value you set, as well.

- The fail-over trigger value tells the backup how many missed heartbeats should happen until it decides it's in charge and takes over.

From there, some firewalls also have "pre-emptive" measures that allow the primary, upon "coming back to life," to retake charge and put the secondary firewall into backup mode again.

The fourth rule of thumb: Get your DNS offsite

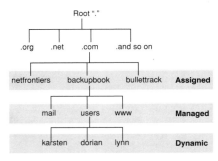

The world finds your organization (mail.youco.com, www.yourco.com, etc.) through domain name services. Domain name services run through at least a primary and secondary DNS server somewhere on the Internet. As a matter of fact, you can't set up only a single DNS server entry in any of the domain name registrars such as VeriSign. The simple reason for this is redundancy. If the primary DNS server is busy or fails, a secondary authoritative server can point the way to your company. DNS, which governs routing of all traffic on the Internet, contains billions of records, answers billions of queries and accepts millions of updates from millions of users on an average day. DNS is a hierarchy of servers, including 13 master "root" servers. On the lower end of the hierarchy, every organization that has a domain name depends on the reliability of its own DNS name servers to maintain an Internet presence.

According to an international study done by Men & Mice[3], 27 percent of all Fortune 1,000 companies have DNS configurations that put all their name servers on the same subnet, creating a single point of failure for the organization's zone (backupbook.com is a zone). That's just plain stupid, considering how, if DNS dies, your company simply vanishes from the Internet. To ensure robustness, name servers on different networks should serve the same zone. To provide optimal performance, a zone's name servers should be distributed throughout the Internet, as close to users and hosts as possible. Hence, if you have a company with

---

[3].   These are the guys who make the DNS management software that we so highly regard. The survey was an international survey that they conduct every year.

overseas presence, ensure that you have a DNS server in the same country that you have users.

And I don't get why this doesn't happen. First, a plethora of organizations are out there, wanting to host your DNS service, including (but not limited to); the registrar that sold you your domain name, your ISP, folks like SaveTheMail, and VeriSign.

Your registrar's tools

First, unless you're a large organization with a great deal of DNS changes or an integrated Active Directory/DNS system, I don't know why you're messing around with creating your own authoritative DNS records on your own server anyway. Domain registrars all have simple tools like the one below to manage your domain names. They're all web-based and very simple to use.

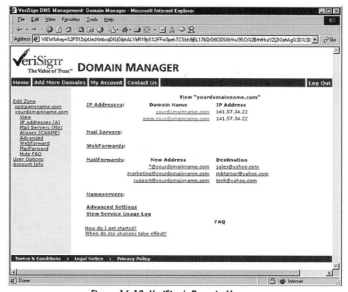

Figure 16-10. VeriSign's Domain Manager

Customer and domain name data is stored securely behind a firewall on an Oracle database. Zone data is generated from the database and transferred over a VPN to an extensive secondary name server constellation. VeriSign's server constellation receives 24/7 operational support from the same skilled operators and engineers who manage the .com, .net, and .org generic Top Level Domain (gTLD), arguably the most critical zones in the world. Services included are usually the big three, no matter who you go with if you don't choose VeriSign:

- Basic DNS Management capabilities, enabling your admin to edit IP addresses, Mail Servers, Aliases, and Start of Authority records.

- Advanced DNS Management capabilities, enabling your admin to edit name servers, responsible person, TeXT data, location, reverse DNS, and IPv6 Addresses.

- Configure User Options (Set Default for Mail Forwarding, Display Preferences, and Set Default Records for New Zones).

By using them, you know that if your network is down and not coming back up soon, you can rebuild your core servers somewhere else: Simply change the DNS info for them to the new location, and your business is "up and running" (at least in the eyes of the Internet).

VeriSign's High-Availability service

VeriSign's High-Availability service provides organizations with robust DNS support for Internet systems through their substantial investment in DNS infrastructure. In case you live in a cave, VeriSign name servers are located at locations around the globe and currently support the .com domains.

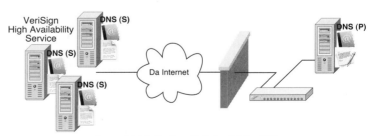

Figure 16-11. VeriSign High-Availability DNS

VeriSign's DNS High-Availability service offers an outsourced secondary DNS solution for organizations that want to maintain control over their zone data, yet don't want to incur the added expense of implementing and supporting extensive

DNS infrastructure. It allows a organization's zones to be hosted on VeriSign's global name server constellation as slave servers to the organization's primary DNS server. The organization retains complete control over the zone data by maintaining its own primary name server and using established tools and processes to update the zone files.

Your own organization as a DNS round robin

If you have an organization with public IP addresses for each site, you can use your own sites as your "DNS offsite" system. In the diagram below (Figure 16-12.) we have a primary DNS server in the top office and a secondary in the bottom office.

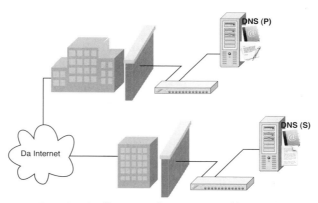

Figure 16-12. Offsite DNS with two separate public networks

Obviously, the more offices you have, the more robust your system is, if you utilize each office as a secondary. At True North, we had a round robin among New York, Chicago, Omaha, and San Francisco.

Setting up a round-robin operation is very easy, and there's only one tool on the market that we suggest you use to do it: the Domain Enterprise Suite from Men & Mice (Ⓧ 🏁 🐧). We say that here's only one tool for this because *there's only one tool for this*. Men & Mice is the only vendor providing solutions in every area of DNS, including DNS management, DNS diagnostics, DNS monitoring, DNS and Active Directory. The DNS Enterprise Suite works with a standard infrastructure such as BIND, and the Microsoft DNS Server, already in place in the enterprise. And for those dyed-in-the-wool Microsoft fans out there, Men & Mice have developed specialized versions of their products to solve the scalability, manageability and troubleshooting issues in an Active Directory environment (and trust me, at a large level, there *are* troubleshooting issues).

Setting up proper DNS management

If you haven't already set up DNS management on your servers for a proper round-robin system, configure your servers with the QuickDNS software. This means that you'll be provisioning your DNS servers, working with DNS records (new, change, delete). Think of the QuickDNS management module as a layer on top of a standard BIND or Windows DNS implementation.

In the first step, set up the software and the DNS servers in a proper round robin. Our scenario has three offices, along with a co-location facility such as SunGard, where key organizational computing equipment is kept.

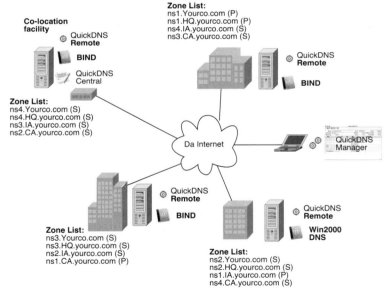

Figure 16-13. Round-robin DNS

This organization has four zones: the base zone (yourco.com) and three office-specific zones (HQ, IA, and CA). Each office can be set to manage its own zone through the use of QuickDNS Central's user authentication management tool.

We've elected to put the QuickDNS Central database at the co-location facility because it's the most secure. With QuickDNS Manager loaded on an admin's workstation, the admin can make configuration changes from any place on the Internet that can access the QuickDNS Central database.

From there, the HQ manager provisions data in both the top-level organizational domain (yourco.com) and the local-office domain (hq.yourco.com). The Start Of Authority (SOA) servers for the top-level organizational domain are spread across all three offices as well as the co-location facility. This is done in case any (or all) of the offices or their networks loses connectivity. As long as one of the authoritative DNS servers is alive, yourco.com can be found on the Internet. Each of the local DNS admins can then provision its own domain zone, and the other three servers will then act as slaves for that domain zone.

Staying healthy

Once the servers are up, you're not necessarily free of configuration problems—especially if Windows 2000 DNS gets hauled into the works. That's why the Enterprise edition of the software also includes DNS Expert and DNS Expert Monitor. DNS Expert uses standard DNS queries and zone transfers to scour your zones for logical and syntactic errors, and probe your name server for misconfiguration. It even finds subtle name server misconfiguration and zone data errors that can cause intermittent, hard-to-diagnose problems. The software can generate detailed explanations of the problems found, as well as links to pages on the Men & Mice website with information on fixing them.

DNS Expert Monitor is an automated version of DNS Expert. It conducts all these checks automatically, reporting the results via either the standard Unix syslog facility, the Windows Event Manager, or SNMP traps that integrate with HP's OpenView, IBM's Tivoli, or Neon Software's LANsurveyor.

By setting up your DNS in a round-robin fashion, you ensure that you can always be found on the Internet. By setting up your management station at your co-location facility, you ensure that admins who can reach the facility's Internet feed can re-DNS any devices they need to within the zones that they manage. And if you're smart about it and plan ahead, you'll have replicated or mirrored key pieces of equipment over to the co-location facility and can then make them the live version through a simple change in the DNS zone table.

E-MAIL THAT DOESN'T GO DOWN

There are a couple of choices you have when building an e-mail system that will survive pretty much any kind of downtime. Each of the choices involves interconnecting multiple systems into a single redundant whole. This is the case for both Exchange and Unix-based SMTP systems.

- The first choice is to build a very robust and redundant system yourself.

- The second choice is to buy a very robust and redundant prepackaged system from some organization.

- The third choice is to lease a very robust and redundant service from some organization.

Get the picture? Yep, you must have a redundant mail system, because if you don't, and your mail goes out along with your network or your building falling down, you'll lose the ability to communicate your disaster recovery plan. Plain and simple, the most important aspect of any company's infrastructure is communication—with your staff, with your partners, and with your customers. If you lose connectivity, you're dead to the world until it returns.

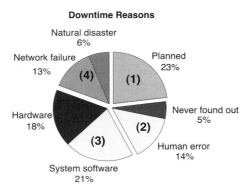

Downtime Reasons

Natural disaster 6%
Network failure 13%
(4)
Planned 23%
(1)
Never found out 5%
Hardware 18%
(2)
(3)
Human error 14%
System software 21%

At left are the four main groupings of reasons for downtime. The first grouping (23 percent of all downtime) accounts for planned outages for management or other reasons. The second grouping (a total of 19 percent of downtime) accounts for reasons we'll never figure out, and for human error. The third grouping accounts for hardware and software failures (39 percent of downtime) and the fourth group (19 percent of downtime) accounts for network and natural disaster failure—you can also count your building falling down in this category.

While you can't do anything about groups 1 and 2, which account for 42 percent of downtime, you *can* and *must* do something about the other 58 percent of the time. E-mail server backup, imaging, and replication can fix the problems with hardware and software failure. E-mail server backup, imaging, and replication combined with alternative mail-routing plans can solve the problems with hardware, software, and network failure, as well as natural disasters. Planning for three and four nets you a high-availability system.

But what does *high availability* really mean? As you can tell from the pie chart on the previous page, a highly available system has a few glitches because 19 percent of the time, problems that you just can't plan for will occur. Accept the inevitable: You're *never* going to hit zero downtime.

Establishing basic mail-server protection

The first step in building a high-availability e-mail system is getting to know its peculiarities. Basically, the world of e-mail servers boils down to Microsoft Exchange, Lotus Notes, and everything else. Both Lotus Notes and Microsoft Exchange are database-driven e-mail servers, which must be handled for backup purposes just like other high-use databases—especially Exchange. My best advice to you is to *really learn* about your Exchange database environment before you do anything else. There are a gazillion Microsoft Exchange books up on the Amazon website. That's your best place to start. Same thing for Lotus Notes. By comparison, everything else is a piece of cake.

Partition your drives & set up mirrors

Following our basic rules of mirroring (see *RAID 1 for a small e-mail server, web server* on page 460), set up your mail server so that it has the following partitions on different mirrored drives:

- Mirror your operating system drive as separate from the rest of your e-mail system.

- If you have an e-mail system like Exchange 2000 that has the ability to partition both public and user data into segregated units or storage groups, you need to do so. In the Exchange 2000 environment, each storage group shares a set of log files that should be placed on separate drives from the database files.

When segregating your storage group databases, align the size of each database with the sizes of your hard drives being mirrored. For example, if you're working with 40 GB hard drives, design your storage databases to be slightly less than an individual hard drive being mirrored so that you can break off a mirrored drive, back it up or replicate it, and reattach it to the mirror.

And if your e-mail system is database-driven and can support individual storage groups, set up individual replication requirements or backup and restoration requirements for each of the storage groups because each database in the storage group will share the same transaction log sequence.

You can set up your partitions and mirrors in two ways. In the first method, put all of your drives into a single JBOD/RAID array, mirroring your tables and then your transaction logs. This allows you to remove any of the drives in any of the arrays and replace them when necessary. This method does have a drawback: the single RAID card or single JBOD, either of which can fail.

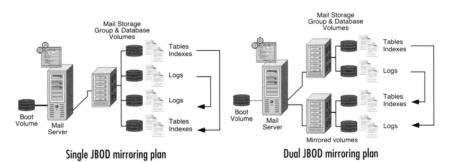

Figure 16-14. Two mirroring options

Alternately, you may set up your mirroring system on dual JBOD/RAID arrays, using either VERITAS Volume Manager software (⊞) or SoftRAID (Ⓧ), as well as dual Adaptec host bus adapters or Fibre Channel cards for connectivity. In this instance, moving to a software RAID configuration offers a few advantages:

- If you use SCSI cards, you must have both JBODs in the same room. If you use Fibre Channel cards, you can keep your data stores in completely different rooms (or buildings in a campus environment).

- Mirrored volumes to only two physical disks have an inherent limitation. VERITAS Volume Manager and SoftRAID introduce the ability to build *n*-

way mirrors that support up to a 32-way mirror. SoftRAID allows 16, but you'll never want it to get that high.

- Although a slight impact to write performance will occur, read performance will be increased through the ability to direct concurrent reads to all disks of the mirror simultaneously. The bottleneck is the SCSI or Fibre Channel bus in this scenario, but this performance increase should be effective with fewer than five disks in the mirror.

After you've set up your servers, test them for security

Before you image your servers and put them on line, test them for security and work out the bugs and holes. Who gets notified if the server is attacked? Which vulnerabilities and remediations should be set to automatic and which should be set to manual? Can the Intrusion Detection System (IDS) detect and report any attacks on this server? If you can answer these questions, you're ready to image your server and put it online. If you can't, go back and read *Corporate scanning with reporting* on page 192.

Imaging your servers

Once you've set your servers up with their basic operating system and data volumes, make sure that they're being imaged properly. We cover imaging extensively in *Disk imaging—understanding imaging basics* on page 377.

Setting up your backup software

As with imaging, we've covered open file backups in great detail in our earlier chapters (see *Open-file database backups* on page 343). Your choices are simple:

- Use an Open File backup tool to provide basic backup capabilities for the server.

- Use VERITAS FlashSnap (⊞) or SoftRAID (Ⓧ) to take apart your mirrored volumes and back them up, reattaching them to the mirror when complete (see *Replicating a database using VERITAS FlashSnap* on page 484).

- Use an Exchange-specific plug-in for your backup software if you want to be able to restore individual mailboxes versus restoring the whole storage group.

The best way to back up your e-mail servers and ensure that you're getting complete data is to use the snap-off mirror approach in the second bullet. VERITAS Volume Manager and SoftRAID both provide the ability to remount a mirror offline (mounted on the computer, but not as part of the mirror) to perform a backup. This is known as **mirror break-off**, and there are two primary scenarios for its usage:

1. One volume of a two-volume mirror can be broken off and mounted by itself, on the same host. This mirror can then be backed up to reflect a consistent state, representing an exact time. Post backup, the data on the mirror may be erased, and the disk space be used again subsequently for another backup.

2. A third-mirror break-off uses three mirrored volumes. The process is the same as in the first example, except that in this case, the mirrored volumes remain fault tolerant during the break-off because of the continued presence of two mirrored volumes while the third has been mounted for backup.

And you'll want to run whatever rotating backup script (see *Tape rotation methods* on page 651) that makes sense for your organization and gets your backup tapes off site.

Clustering your e-mail systems

Clustering provides redundancy, thus allowing either machine to be offline while the other assumes the duties of providing services. We've already covered the basics of clustered servers (see *Clustered servers* on page 473). The mail server cluster acts very much like the firewall cluster mentioned above (see *The third rule of thumb: Have fail-over firewalls* on page 586).

If you're using Microsoft Exchange, you can use the Microsoft Cluster Services (MSCS). MSCS ships with Windows 2000 Advanced Server and Windows 2000 Datacenter Server, and uses shared storage for both data and specific information about the services being protected. The cluster operates through a polling called a **heartbeat** (again, just like the firewalls), which determines the responsiveness of the other server in the cluster. When a cluster member detects that the other member is down, it assumes control of the services and name in short order.

The basic cluster can have mirrored volumes within the same RAID array, as shown in Figure 16-15. . Using FlashSnap with the cluster as a snap-off mirror volume takes more equipment and more effort. We've shown how to do that in (see *FlashSnap features* on page 484), and these steps apply to an e-mail server, as well.

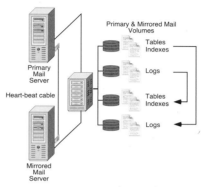

Figure 16-15. Microsoft MSCS cluster

You can't always trust building your own system—even if that system is a well-designed SAN infrastructure. As we wrote this book, we uncovered one case in which a national law firm's SAN cluster suffered a failure due to an esoteric hardware misconfiguration, leaving 2,000 attorneys around the U.S. without e-mail for about two days—at a cost of over $500,000 in lost billable time[4]. So even if you have the most robust system, that system must be robust *and* redundant. While you're building a second highly robust, redundant system, your budget is going to double or triple, depending upon how many redundant systems you buy. And while this is great for ensuring that your *server* doesn't go down, it doesn't do a darned thing for you if your *network* goes down. For that, you have to move your backup mail system offsite.

Moving to an external backup mail service provider

Think of SaveTheMail (STM) as a secondary mail server on steroids. In fact, that's what it is (well, actually it's just a combination of glucose and branched-chain-amino-acids, but who's looking?). The beauty part? It's not on your network. This is a great system for small and medium-sized organizations.

---

4. Because we don't want to heap insult upon injury, their name and address is withheld.

STM allows your users to check those e-mails from a browser on a network that works, such as the one at the local Starbucks. They can reply, compose, respond, or whatever from your organization's domain.

When the primary is back up and running, the system acts just like a good secondary and sends all of the mail you received during the outage back to the primary—untouched.

Administrating the system is insanely easy. For small organizations, you can enter individuals' names singly. For larger organizations, they'll coordinate a mail-box list dump with you.

Figure 16-16. SaveTheMail domain administration

You'll need to set an MX record for them at mail.savethemail.com. In your DNS system, create a setup that looks like this:

> *myco.com IN   MX10   mail.myco.com.*
> *myco.com IN   MX20   mail.savethemail.com*

Once your users have set up their accounts, you need only to pull the plug on your e-mail server to test the system. Insanely simple. After I remembered to put the period at the end of the domain name in the MX record (mail.savethemail.com versus mail.savethemail.com.), it took me about 10 minutes to set up the system and test it out. I spent more time talking to their guys about South Africa and safaris than I did configuring anything.

As we just said, this works great for small and medium-sized organizations. For larger organizations where you need to keep closer tabs on what's happening, and where you want to synchronize some of the current messages in case of longer outages, turn to MessageOne's Emergency Messaging System.

Moving to external, well-placed specialty hardware and software

Admin Console Home
User Administration
  User Information
  Users Sets
  Administrators
  Fault Alerts
  Transition Alerts
  Export
Additional Mailboxes and Aliases
Distribution Lists
Notification Status
Activation History

If you're a larger organization with multiple mail servers and multiple operational facilities, and you need an emergency messaging system that allows you to coalesce users and groups from various servers into a single emergency messaging plan, MessageOne has the answer. It's called the Emergency Messaging System (EMS), is based on Linux, PostFix, and Horde, and has three components:

EMS Infrastructure provides continuity of e-mail service while the primary messaging system is unavailable.

EMS SynchManager (SM) keeps the EMS infrastructure current with the primary messaging system—as long as the system you're synchronizing is an Exchange, Notes, or Groupwise server.

EMS RecoveryManager (RM) automates the reconciliation of messages from the EMS to the primary system after recovery.

The EMS system can be deployed as a software solution that resides in an organization's own designated emergency location or on hardware at co-location disaster-recovery facilities such as Sungard, HP, or IBM. Prior to an e-mail disruption, the EMS SyncManager replicates the company's mailboxes for each of the designated mail servers assigned to be protected.

Users' profiles are set for emergency notification (which includes cell phones, Yahoo-esque e-mail addresses, pagers, Blackberries, blueberries, raspberries, etc.) when their mail server goes down. This notification includes a web URL they can access for sending and receiving e-mail while their network or mail server is down.

Smart replication

One of the big differences between replicating a mail server and the EMS system is *what gets replicated*. In a traditional replication environment such as VERITAS' Storage Replicator, all data on the mail system must be replicated from point A to point B. That means that all of the hundreds of gigabytes of stored mail on the original mail server must be replicated to the offsite mail server in a one-to-one relationship. To maintain complete synchroniziation, this costs time, money, and bandwidth.

With EMS, the administrator and leaders in the organization make a business decision about which users will migrate to the EMS system in case of failure (1 and 2), and how many of the currently stored messages on the primary mail system will be synchronized with the EMS system (3). This winnowing process allows the administrator to cut back the number of users, as well as the amount of data synchronized (4).

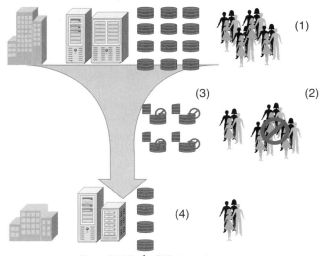

Figure 16-17. The EMS winnowing process

Therefore, the amount of data going over the WAN pipe to the replication center, as well as the size of the hardware and storage, are all decreased significantly. Or, of course, you can choose to leave everyone on the EMS system, along with all of the hourly e-mails from their fathers-in-law, and all the various and sundry sites they visit during the day. As if.

Once the system has been synchronized and the DNS records updated (and users are given a short bit of training on the interface), there's nothing more to do until an emergency happens.

Assigning users to your lifeboats

Using this listing of users, servers, and groups you've imported into the system, you can create "lifeboat groups" of users from any combination of servers, groups, lists, or individual user names, so that when a given server goes down (or group of servers, if you lose a building or campus), you can immediately notify and manage this list of coalesced users as a cohesive group.

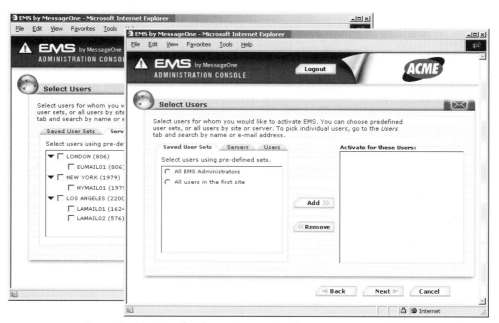

Figure 16-18. EMS interface for creating a coalesced emergency communications system

The screenshots in Figure 16-18. show two selection processes for activating users within the EMS system. On the left, the administrator can simply select any user who belonged to a particular mail server in a particular location (for instance, Los Angeles has two mail servers). The front right screenshot shows selecting users from pre-arranged groups (such as all administrators, etc.). The great thing about thiss? You can mix and match your groupings, adding users who might not be affected by a downed server or building, but nevertheless must be involved in the emergency communications process (such as the selected VARs who are coming to rescue you).

When the server goes Kablooey!

When your server, your network, or your building become inaccessible, one of two things happens. If it's a short outage, the EMS system simply spools the e-mail coming into it and then waits for the primary server to come back online, at which point it forwards the mail to the primary server. Or the administrator makes the decision that the server isn't likely to revive any time soon, and then activates the EMS mail service through the Web or via phone call.

Figure 16-19. EMS in active mode

Once the server moves from spooling operations into full-service EMS operations, it activates the user's preconfigured mailboxes (about a one-minute process) and begins the end-user notification through the various communication tools set up in the user's profiles. Each employee with access to the EMS system receives a message for the URL to access their e-mail over the Web. Figure 16-19. on page 604 shows the EMS console during the active mode of operations.

While the EMS system acts as the organization's primary mail server during the primary's absence, EMS logs and archives all traffic sent and received, for the legal record. This is a massive benefit that fulfills legal obligations for organizations that must track their e-mail usage at all times.

The recovery process

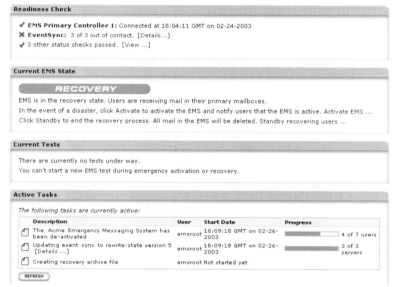

EMS in recovery mode

When the primary mail center has been reactivated, the EMS RecoveryManager kicks into high gear, and the EMS web-mail system is shut down. EMS-RM begins the migration of all e-mail from the backup system to the primary system. Any e-mail sent or received during the activation of the EMS won't be lost when the primary returns to normal.

During its deactivation, EMS generates archive files of all messages sent and received during its active lifespan. It then uses MAPI to connect to the primary mail server and restore mail directly to the user's mailboxes, preserving their read/unread and other status.

Once all data has been sent to the primary mail server, the recovery process is complete, and synchronization and standby mode return to operation.

 I can't emphasize how important it is to have an emergency communications process pre–set up and regularly tested. When all hell breaks loose, communication is the one thing that saves the day. Take the following advice to heart:

1. Set up the system early in your planning and test it regularly. Multi-channel communication—by phone, pager, and alternate e-mail, for example—increases the visibility of your disaster recovery plan.

2. Bring your partners into the picture early. If your vendors, VARs, etc., aren't up to speed during your plan's testing phase, think how poorly they'll perform when a real problem happens. During a disaster drill, a vendor once told me, "I'm too busy right now to conduct these emergency tests with you." I fired him on the spot, and went on to find a vendor who's still servicing that organization six years later.

3. Make sure that you've included all the right people in your "immediate emergency notification" group—and *excluded* the right people, as well. Don't Chicken Little this crucial process: While you need to test and communicate your plan, don't use it to impress too many higher-ups in the organization—they'll just become annoyed, especially if they get notified when a server simply fails and no building is lost.

4. Make sure that when the system goes down because of a catastrophic failure, you can quickly rebuild an offsite server. It's one thing to have an emergency communications system—it's another animal entirely to rely on it for any length of time. Re-establishing normal e-mail on your own servers (even at a backup location) shows the organization's leadership and staff that you're progressing in your disaster recovery efforts. E-mail is a high-visibility item. Normalizing e-mail after having to use an emergency communications channel is a real milestone that will bolster organizational spirits.

ADDING A VPN FOR DISASTER PREPARATION

Some companies have established Virtual Private Network (VPN) secure communication channels between their key offices and remote offices, home users, and notebook travellers.

As a quick review, remember that there are two ways to create a secure network in an organization. The first is to tie all offices together in a private switched frame relay or dedicated point-to-point network connections when building the organizational Wide Area Network (WAN).

The other method entails using the already existing Internet as the WAN, and then creating point-to-point secure "tunnels" in the Internet between each of the remote offices, home users, or travelling notebooks. These tunnels form the basis of the VPN, and are set up specifically within the firewalls, routers, or specific VPN software loaded on notebooks.

The key ingredient in your VPN is the **RADIUS (Remote Authentication Dial-In User Service) server**, a client/server-based authentication software system that centralizes the administration of user profiles maintained in authentication databases, thereby simplifying the process of supporting multiple VPN switches. The remote access servers act as RADIUS clients that connect to the centralized authentication server. When a notebook user or remote office router accesses the VPN router, the authentication routine is passed to a RADIUS server, which checks that the information is correct and then authorizes access to the HQ systems and network.

The way an organization sets up RADIUS servers and VPN access points and tunnels has a lot to do with how quickly and easily it can maintain a highly available VPN. When setting up the VPN for high availability, consider these three points:

1. Ensure that you have two RADIUS server—one at your central site and one at your offsite hosting facility.

2. Ensure that you allow each remote VPN routing device to have dual paths for Internet connectivity: one to your VPN gateway, and the other to the general Internet.

3. Ensure that the paths to your VPN gateway and your primary and secondary RADIUS server addresses are set up with a DNS entry instead of an IP address.

Typical setup

The diagram below shows a small three-point network between an organization's headquarters, a store in the field, and an executive's home office.

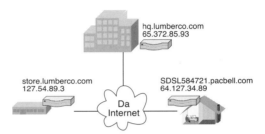

Figure 16-20. Small three point network

We've labelled each of the three points of contact with its domain name for that device (yes, even cable DSL equipment at home gets a DNS address from the service provider), and we've listed each device's IP address.

First, you must forget about using the IP addresses that you used to have, and get accustomed to using the DNS addresses instead. Why? VPN tunnels can go to only one place, and if that place does not respond, the VPN is dead. If you assign the remote routers a VPN IP address and your network dies, when you rebuild your network at some other location, you'll be assigned a different IP range than you had before, and all of those remote routers must be reconfigured with the new IP address. On the other hand, if you enter a DNS address into the VPN field and your primary network dies, you can build a new network somewhere else, simply change the DNS entry for your VPN router to the new address you were just assigned, and you're back in business with no reconfiguration at the remote router end. That's a good thing.

Next, think about where you're going to locate your secondary RADIUS authentication server, and remember what real estate agents tell us: Location is everything. A lot of folks put them on a different subnet in the highly secured data center or server room, but I don't recommend that. Instead, I strongly suggest that you move your secondary RADIUS server to your offsite hosting facility. That way, if something compromises your primary network, the one running at the off-site co-location facility can take over.

For these types of VPNs and remote-office firewalls we like the SonicWALL devices best. Below is a multi-part diagram of ways to set up the organization's VPN and RADIUS servers using the SonicWALL devices. Again, the DNS addresses are emphasized to bring home our point.

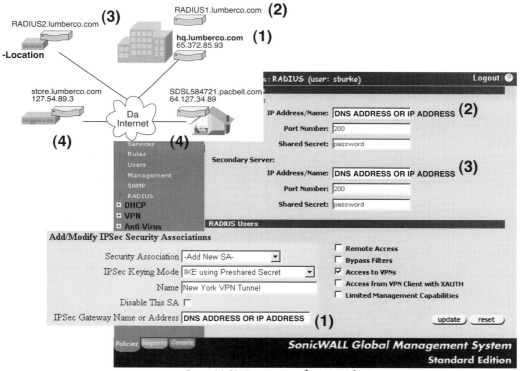

Figure 16-21. Proper setup of a RADIUS/VPN system

1. The DNS entry for the headquarters VPN router is depicted in the top left of the diagram, and the settings pane of the remote firewall is on the bottom. Each remote firewall device (the two number 4s in the diagram) must have a single VPN gateway address assigned to it. You can set either a DNS address or a numeric IP address, but we suggest the DNS address *always*.

2. When setting up the user profiles at the corporate management site, you'll want to set up two RADIUS servers in case one goes down. The first RADIUS server should be on your site and should be DNSed as such.

3. The second RADIUS server should be offsite, in case of a primary site outage of any kind.

4. And finally, your remote routers must all have a primary VPN tunnel gateway address, which should be the same DNS entry as we showed in item 1.

Ensuring that the remote routers support split tunnelling

VPN tunnels can be established between two sites in two different ways (and SonicWALL supports both):

1. By specifying that all traffic routes through the VPN gateway (the most secure for everyone); or

2. By specifying the remote site's destination network address ranges so that only traffic destined for these addresses goes through the VPN.

In the first scenario, when setting up the VPN tunnel to operate in the all-traffic mode, every packet bound for networks outside the remote organization's IP range is passed through the firewall and to the other side of the VPN gateway—even traffic destined for eBay. All remote locations must then route all of their Internet traffic through the headquarter's organization's network. If you want this, it's up to you, but we discourage it.

If you have an Internet outage at the primary site, not even web traffic at the remote sites can take place until either the primary is back in action, or a new primary has been set up. Remote organizations wouldn't be able to access the offsite DNS servers or offsite emergency e-mail servers for communications—they'd be dead in the water. By the way, that's not a good thing.

The second scenario is called **split tunnelling**, and, by default, a great many organizations set up their VPN tunnels this way. In this mode, each remote VPN firewall listens for traffic destined for the headquarters IP range. Any traffic destined for that range is then sent through the VPN to the headquarters gateway. All other traffic is sent on to the remote site's Internet router and passed on to the Internet in a normal fashion. In this scenario, a VPN outage at the corporate headquarters affects only traffic heading to the corporate headquarters or in the VPN itself.

If the headquarters loses total connectivity, at least each of the remote offices can still get to the Internet and the emergency communications infrastructure you've set up with your offsite DNS servers and your emergency e-mail systems.

For home users, companies like SonicWALL offer dual-zone firewall/VPN appliances. SonicWALL's TZX is a broadband firewall/VPN appliance with dual-zone connectivity: one for the "home" users on a home LAN that routes traffic directly to the Internet, and the other, the "work" zone that routes traffic to the organization's VPN settings.

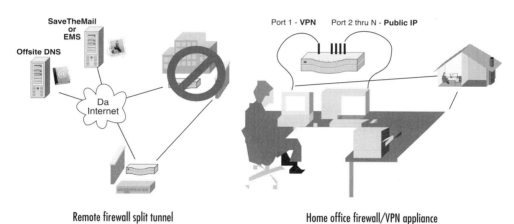

Remote firewall split tunnel   Home office firewall/VPN appliance

Figure 16-22. Remote office and home VPN setups

The most important thing to know about your VPN? Set it up so that individual device failure can't bring down your organization's communication abilities. While you need tight security, don't make it *so* tight that a single failure stops the company's communications.

CHAPTER 17:
BUILDING LOSS DOESN'T MEAN BUSINESS LOSS

The last time I checked, cannons and siege engines had pretty much done away with castles. Until the advent of this sophisticated weaponry, castles had steadfastly held their ground, protecting their innards from all attacks. Then cannons came on the scene and shot straight through their walls. Kablooey! Why should you care? Because until the last couple of years, most of us thought that as long as we had a building around our companies, and that building was secure, the company was secure. We put our company's production and informational nucleus into those buildings, and then protect the buildings themselves. But as others who have lost their buildings to fire, tornado, and other means have learned before us, it's more viable to protect a production process and the information needed to create that product than it is to protect and secure a building.

	Documents	Applications	OS	Storage	CPUs	Network	Power	Building
Freeze								
Corruption								
Loss								✔

Table 17-1. Building loss

Our good friends and close associates at WildPackets, a software company in California, learned that bitter lesson the day they found out their building burned to the ground. Here's a clip from the press release covering the devastating fire that occurred on July 15th at the WildPackets corporate headquarters:

> "Although saddened by the loss of so many memorabilia, including our recent trophies and awards for AiroPeek NX and EtherPeek NX, we are relieved that this occurred when no one was in the building," said Mahboud Zabetian, WildPackets' president and CEO. "WildPackets is already being rebuilt by employees who immediately began meeting in borrowed conference rooms, employee homes, parks and restaurants. We appreciate the countless offers of help from across the globe.

> "Good forethought and insurance meant that our software has survived the disaster thanks to the multiple offsite copies, and today, only one week later, we are moving into a new building. The network and phones are in place and over one hundred computers are being delivered over the course of the next week for our team, which is intact and will soon be getting to the point of 'business as usual.' We resumed product shipments on July 19th. We are working fast and hard to make certain there is no disruption of service to our customer and partner base," stated Zabetian.

What can you learn from this simple story of loss and recovery? When disaster strikes, a natural regenerative process happens—if you've prepared for it.

Emergency communication is the first post-disaster event to occur. Some form exists whether the company has planned for it or not. Even *uncoordinated* emergency communication spreads the news of the catastrophe throughout the organizational membership. Your best bet is to plan for it and manage it, even if you can't control it. As the folks from SunGard point out, "People can manage disasters; they can't control them." In WildPackets' case, the emergency communication was conducted by people standing outside of the burning building, using cell phones. In other organizations, emergency communication has been conducted through a pre-established emergency e-mail system, like SaveTheMail or EMS, which we've written about earlier (see *E-mail that doesn't go down* on page 594). Whether you plan for it or not, emergency communication *will* happen—so do plan for it.

As an adjunct to emergency communication, you must establish your **fallback security position** (a military term). This is the place where your remaining computers are reassembled into some kind of whole, you'll take stock of what you have, and then rebuild your process, information, or production system from there. In WildPackets' case, when Zabetian's core team met, they realized to their great relief that the full code of the software they'd been working on was actually distributed among their take-home notebook computers and work-at-home employees—they could continue working as long as they could communicate with each other. If an organization is smart enough to move DNS offsite and pre-install an organizational VPN that had been DNSed (see *Adding a VPN for disaster preparation* on page 607), a VPN can be re-created in a matter of hours, and any system prereplicated at an offsite hosting facility can be brought live and have its IP address changed to be the primary device that DNS points to. In effect, an emergency communication channel can be rerouted to close the hole left by a lost building.

In the next step, the leadership and emergency recovery team must ensure that as many client-facing systems as possible are brought back to life or moved from secondary to primary status. Fortunately, the WildPackets website (a primary means of sales and informational advertising) was hosted offsite, unaffected by the blaze. Larger organizations can begin with their key systems that are already replicated offsite. Properly integrating the offsite hosting facility into a building loss disaster recovery plan is the real ticket to moving forward very quickly. At this point, your key focus is to get whatever systems you have remaining up and running, kick your IT team into high gear, and prepare for the onslaught of coordinating the recovery process.

After these two steps, your natural tendency is to want to get working again. This is where you get to deal with people. They want to do something, *anything* to feel like they're helping to put the company back on its feet. To get things rolling, Zabetian's development and other teams met "in borrowed conference rooms, employee homes, parks and restaurants." Again, we return to that all-important key to fast recovery: integration with the offsite hosting facility.

There are two types of hosting facilities: those that simply have cages and rooms for computers, and those like SunGard, which also have "recovery room" office spaces attached so that your company's team members can have a sense of place to get together and regroup. This key phase of the organization's recovery builds morale and shows people that *something* is being done. Once everyone has accepted the disaster and is moving forward, it's time to re-establish the appearance of business as usual.

As Irv Fish, CFO of the famed ad agency, Fallon McElligott, told me, "The best way to show that you're back in business is to bill your clients. If your clients get a bill from you, they *know* you're in business again." He harped on this repeatedly when I was the CIO of the agency and we were working through our own disaster recovery plan. And he's right: If your organization is still decamped from your offices, the last stage before going to a permanent space is to organize into recovery rooms so that you can normalize your back office and billing systems. During those disaster-planning meetings at Fallon, Fish skipped all the inquiries about production, ad buying, and where to stash the 1,000-person workforce, instead asking that one question: "How soon 'til we bill?" Then, as now, I replied, "As soon as the systems are brought online, data is restored to new user computers, and those users hit the Print or Send key."

How long will that take for your company? I can't say for sure, but I know that happy day comes a lot sooner if you've pre-planned and are working with a company that can host not only your computers, but your recovery rooms, as well.

THE MAIN THING

Remember the Boy Scouts? Yep, the Main Thing here is their motto: "Be Prepared." Preparation helps you to take the following steps to categorize your staff and equipment to respond quickly to a building loss emergency:

1. Establish emergency communication systems *before* you lose the building, and then use those communications when the unthinkable happens. Immediately follow that with rerouting your pre-planned VPN. And follow that up with re-DNSing any surviving systems at your hosting facility.

2. Normalize your integrated and outward-facing systems as quickly as possible.

3. Normalize your production systems and group those staff members into recovery rooms of some sort to give them cohesion.

4. Normalize your back office and billing systems (and staff members in a recovery facility) to let the world know you mean business.

The Main Thing in all of the above is *planning for information availability*—whether through replication and normalization of hosted offsite systems or access to those systems by staff groups at special recovery rooms.

Special Thanks...

Thanks in this section goes to Jim Grogan, Weikai Chang, and Jason Fradin over at SunGard who read through the whole thing and helped a lot. A *real big thanks* goes to Judith Eckles at SunGard for her sharp eye and keen editing ability. Also a deep thanks goes out to all of our field editors who came back with *outstanding* tips on what should go offsite—things you probably haven't thought about.

WHAT GOES TO OFFSITE STORAGE

Everybody knows that you need to store your backup tapes and disks offsite (see *Tape rotation methods* on page 651). Everybody knows that, and most people adhere to *some* flavor of that principle. But too many companies at the small-business level don't adhere to it as well or as often as they should. Even WildPackets had a significant problem: Most of the company's tapes were onsite. This is simply courting disaster.

We all agree that you need to store your backup media offsite—now the question is, how much should go offsite, and how often? What do you store, and what don't you store? Without getting into arguments about information retention (which is a whole different category), let's create your offsite storage checklist.

Insurance will cover replacement costs only

If your systems fall down and you have insurance, you can buy new systems. How much insurance covers your loss depends on your individual insurance plan. But you'd better have a demonstrable data backup and offsite storage plan to show your insurance company. Without it, your insurance company faces undue financial risk leading to your organization's loss of business continuity insurance.

Depending on your insurance plan, coverage will range from replacing the lost backup systems so that you *can* restore, all the way to reconstructing data that has been lost through media salvage programs and organizations (see *Major surgery and DriveSavers* on page 273) or through manual data re-entry of that information backed up earlier into your data systems from the paper records you've retained.

What really *is* insured? The physical media and the salvage efforts—not the data itself. So make sure that you get the vast majority of your data offsite, so in case of disaster, you need only "tag" insurance to help you rebuild the trifles that might not have made it out of the building.

Legal and good business sense concerns

Your other responsibility is twofold: to your partners and your clients. And without getting into the nitty-gritty, let's say that at some level of integration with partners and online sales to your clients, you have a **duty of trust** to act prudently, a **duty of care** to preserve the organization's assets, and a **duty of good faith** to act in a way that is known to be right. These legal duties form a much broader scope than that which your insurance carrier requires—they also force your organization's hand to define what's critical and therefore should be stored offsite by answering three questions pertaining to each set of data within your purview:

1. Is the data stored on this system required to perform a critical business function?

2. Must the data stored on this system be maintained to satisfy a legal or audit mandate?

3. Is the data stored on this system a trade secret or at least proprietary to the company? Is it difficult, expensive, or impossible to reproduce?

To begin your definition of your mandatory backup and offsite policy, simply walk through your network and think of the three questions above when you review each system. If the answer to any of the three questions is *Yes*, the data on that system should be backed up and sent offsite.

Key systems files that you normally forget

The above was easy: Your tapes and disks need to go offsite. Your critical data needs to go offsite. But what about some of the key files that you have in the office that you aren't thinking about? Here's a list of killers that you might want to have go offsite, mostly contributed by our brilliant field editors.

Tape backup catalogs

Many of the tape backup systems that we use create a separate catalog of the files on the tapes. To restore the information on those tapes, the backup software must read the catalog. When creating tapes, these software packages create the catalog files on whatever drive volume and directory the administrator sets. *If the catalog is lost, the backup software must then re-create the catalog before it can access the tape again.* That statement's in italics because I just tried it this weekend with our writing facility's backup tapes. I moved the catalog and told my backup software to re-create a week's worth of backups (15 machines, including two servers)—which took 16 hours. Zabetian wasn't so lucky: WildPackets' tapes were in a fire safe and were slightly damaged by the water from the fire department. It took a week to restore the data, because not all of the information on the tape could be re-created. Make sure you take special precautions to back up your tape catalogs to CD or other means—and move those catalogs offsite along with the tapes.

Router, VPN, firewall settings files

Most firewalls, routers, and VPNs allow you to save the configuration settings files to disk. This becomes especially important when you work with a high-availability plan and need to re-establish your network presence at another location. If you have your settings files, you can re-DNS the firewalls and routers to your new location's IP addresses, load your settings files from your archive—and you're off to the races lickety-split. But hold those horses—first, you have to back them up and get them offsite.

The network map

Two of our field editors, Dave O. and Brandon Katz, suggested this one. Your network map must be saved offsite, along with any specific DHCP settings, addresses, etc. Sometimes, in rebuilding your network, you won't remember what connected to what, and not everyone who builds an integrated system remembers to put the DNS address of a connecting computer into a field instead of an IP address. As Brandon put it, "I've always found it helpful to create a diagram of the major systems in the network via Visio or some other mapping program. Include info such as IP, OS, Server HW, and server 'jobs'. This helps the IT staff re-create the critical systems from a map instead of from memory."

Think of it: If you don't have a historical map to refer to, how in the world will you remember the type of that device 10.2.1.173—you know, the one that connected and pulled reports out of your database? The folks at Technology Associates also suggested that you remember the Novell binderies, so that if you must reconstruct your Novell servers, you won't have to re-enter each and every user name and associated info.

Detailed system info

Along with the network map, Mitch Krayton pointed out that you must maintain copies of each device's serial number (and type), including any extended warranty and support agreements. That's not easy to do. I'm a Mac user and have one of the original titanium PowerBooks. I bought an AppleCare package way back when I purchased the computer, and I can't figure out the number. *Apple* can't even figure out the number. Everybody has a record of me buying the package, but nobody can figure out what the number is, so it's as if I tossed away that money at a race-track.

It's not just serial numbers and support packages: Hardware & disk configurations are required, as well, especially for Unix machines. Field editor John Shearer reminded me that "Building a Unix box requires a specific disk-partition layout to be in place before recovery can happen. Windows machines are easier, but you still need to know what hosts have how much disk capacity, how much memory, how many network interfaces, etc." And, as another field editor, Michael von Borstel, reminded me, make sure that you have user's passwords, as well, or when you restore the devices, you won't be able to access them.

And the software for the systems

Our field editor, Joe, from Columbia University in New York City, reminded me that "It's legally permissible to make one backup copy for archival storage. However, we found that not all CD writers will copy a CD correctly. Specifically, we found that the TDK brand Velocity series CD writers are 'immune' from the Hollywood-imposed 'do not copy copyrighted material' mandate when used with the Nero software and its latest updates." Your other option? Use an imaging tool to create network-load images of all of your applications, and then ensure that you have properly backed up your network imaging systems and properly recorded your application's serial numbers. And, as field editor Allan Kalar pointed out, don't forget to write down the serial numbers, as well.

Offsite staffing

Two more of our distinguished field editors (the aforementioned Dave O. and Mike Landman) suggested the same thing: Establish a good relationship with an outsourced IT company. Even if you do most everything in-house, after a disaster you'll need help, and it's always easier to find help if you have an established relationship. So use an outsourcer every once in a while to develop that relationship.

The foundation for all these techniques is truly the bottom line: You must have a well-documented restoration plan. You must know what gets restored in what order (we've already covered that) and by whom, because the net admin has his or her hands full, and probably coordinates with outsourced IT staff or "friendly organization helpers." The folks at SunGard also noted what they refer to as the "guru impact." If you're fortunate enough to have a very talented, specialized, well-trained team member, the plan must accommodate the possibility of that person's absence during the actual recovery and testing. If you want to see how well your plan works, do what the military does in training: They "kill" the leader and have a subordinate take over to run with the plan. Don't make the mistake of wishing on a star: If it's a good, well-communicated plan, anyone on the team can run with the ball.

And, of course, your all-important communications lists

These lists can be in the form of simple word docs, or as complex as a password-protected web page on your already-hosted offsite web server. As long as they contain the contact information you need in an emergency, you'll be fine. Among others, field editors Dan Gray and Pat Gallagher pointed out that if you don't have those offsite, you are sunk. This is where HR comes into the forefront. HR is the "keeper" of this information: Make sure to work with them to obtain the organization's alternate contacts, spousal information, etc.

But that's all *data*—what about the *systems*?

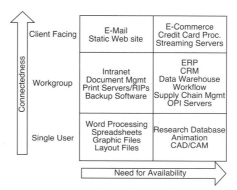

Figure 17-1. Connectedness and the need for availability

So far, we've discussed the fact that data goes off site. While getting the data offsite is very important, what we're missing is what happens to the staff when you lose the building. Let's go back—way back—to page 4, to re-examine that group work table we posted and are showing again in Figure 17-1. .

Starting with the top-left square in Figure 17-1. , we've covered the need for products like SaveTheMail and EMS. We've clearly stated that all revenue-producing websites should already be offsite (we don't know many that aren't), and the same goes for those systems in the top-right square (again, we don't know many that aren't already offsite).

In the bottom two squares, we deal with workstation backups (see *An overview of backup tool operations* on page 318) and open-file database backups (see *Open-file database backups* on page 343), and getting those documents into the normal flow of the backup and recovery cycle.

It's the two middle squares that should be gnawing at your craw. Not only do they represent important information to the organization, they also affect the organization's *group work* and *integrated systems*. Remember, *we work in a connected world*—we made that point quite clear on page 1. Information availability means maintaining the connection between an organization's critical business information and the people who need it to keep the business running. That's why you're probably feeling a little uneasy when you see those two squares. Again, we're going to refer to page 8 and our "When Kablooey! happens" charts. If all you had was a failure of any of the systems in the middle two boxes, or data corruption, you could easily scrounge enough parts to bring the system back up and restore the data quickly—and everyone will be happy.

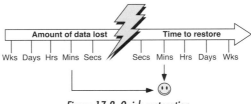

Figure 17-2. Quick restoration

But what happens when you lose the building? When that catastrophe strikes, you lose access to those extra parts you had lying around, and you lose the entire system, as well. When you lose the building, you have no system to restore to—*if* you didn't pre-plan to have a replicate of that system offsite already. In that grim event, your staff faces some major downtime, and must follow the organization's guidelines for downtime procedures—and no one will be happy.

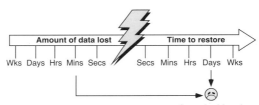

Figure 17-3. Minimum restoration time after a building loss

Not so long ago, a New York–based firm called David Michaelson & Company conducted a study of 200 organizations representing a broad range of industries, gauging their level of organizational information availability preparedness. The organizations surveyed stated that the average length of a major disruption was anywhere from 24 to 48 business hours, and that a loss of this length would greatly impact the organization. Now think about this: The Michaelson study found that, on average, it takes organizations "more than 50 hours to replace a failed processor, 80 hours to build a new network, and nearly four days (93 hours of work) to set up an alternate work facility if needed.[1]" Of those surveyed, 62

---

1. "Information Availability Assessment," by David Michaelson & Company (2002).

percent stated that there would be a major impact on staff productivity, 27 percent would lose revenue, and 15 percent would lose clients.

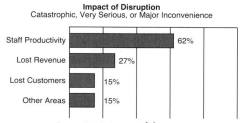

Figure 17-4. Impact of disruption

Here's the kicker: Only half of the companies studied had backup devices that they could restore to, and only a third of the companies had a hot site set up that they could use to "bring up" the backup devices and restore the data to them. And even though a third of the folks surveyed had hot sites set up, only 20 percent of the organizations had alternate networks set up or included provisions for facilities for displaced workers. Here's the problem with that: *We work in a connected world.* Some of the systems in that middle row of boxes need continuous connectivity to function correctly. Working for these systems means connectivity. Working for other systems listed in that row means *connectivity to people.*

So you must return to your network map and your systems and your staff and match up which systems need to stay connected and running because they're a part of an integrated system, and which need to be brought back along with a place to work as a group.

In short, you need to plan your **offsite hosted systems** and **offsite recovery-room** scenarios. For the purposes of this book, we'll look at your plans for integrated and client-facing systems (offsite hosting) and establishing emergency recovery-room facilities for a production system and a back-office system.

PRE-PLANNING OFFSITE COMPUTERS FOR INFORMATION AVAILABILITY

Throughout this book, we've discussed techniques for replication of critical systems. But until now, those techniques weren't put into perspective. In this chapter, we've stated that your organization's Internet presence should never be "down;" that, at minimum, you must have a constant DNS and e-mail presence for the basics of emergency communication at all levels. Given. But when we scratch the surface, we find a massive difference between replication and making information available for use; and between fault tolerance and disaster recovery.

VeriSign and other DNS service providers can make your DNS information available for use because they've already thought through software security measures, hardware load sharing (so that they don't have to dedicate individual customers to individual computers), and network access and security.

Both SaveTheMail and MessageOne have thought through these same issues, as well as load balancing, end-user communication, and, in the case of MessageOne EMS, synchronization of data and the legalities of log creation and archival.

Quite frankly, that's why they're in this business, and why they're the leaders in their field: They offer workable plans that sustain their customers' needs. If your organization decides that to provide highly available information, you, too, must do the same.

To begin, get out of your chair, take off your shoes, sit on the floor in the lotus position, put your hands on your knees with your palms up and your thumbs touching your middle finger, and repeat the following sentences 10 times: "There is more to disaster recovery than offsite tape storage. There is more to disaster recovery than imaging. There is more to disaster recovery than replication. It's all about making important information available to important people at all times." That's your mantra. And the crux of that mantra is the last sentence: "Making important information available to important people at all times."

Well and good, but let's return to planet Earth. It's one thing to restore a computer offsite or activate a replicated cluster pair offsite. It's something quite different to weave that restored or activated offsite computer into the fabric of your information architecture—especially if the main network that supported the fabric is dead.

Analyzing the "who" and "what systems" is the sizzle of your plan

Let's start with analyzing the people, because without people, there is no business. I call this the "sizzle" on the steak, because when presenting a plan to an organization's board, they'll get it if you talk about the people affected, but their eyes roll into the back of their heads and they start playing with their buttons if you begin by talking about computers and systems and data and other things they don't understand. What's sizzle composed of?

- Groups in your organization per se (the folks on your payroll)?

- Your suppliers?

- Your clients?

To help you get a handle on this, think of these important organizational systems and you'll get an idea of which groups of people tie into which groups of business systems.

- Business intelligence (no, it's not an oxymoron)

- Customer relationship management and sales force automation data

- E-commerce

- Enterprise resource planning

- Financials

- Inventory systems and supply chain databases

- Order entry

- Files created by "off-the-shelf" software or internally developed systems

Let's put this into perspective. Our example? A national lumber company with a main headquarters office and lumber stores all over the country catering to both the general public and contractors. The general public can purchase lumber goods in the store, at kiosks in the store (in case that particular store doesn't have what they need, but another does), or through the Web. Contractors can also order directly over the Internet through a special order-entry system. To round out this group, let's not forget the product suppliers, as well as the newspapers and media in which the lumber company advertises.

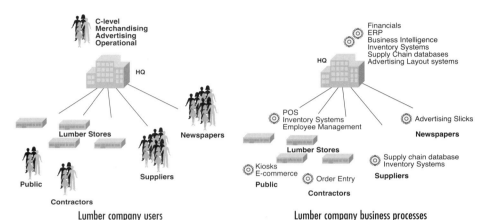

Lumber company users   Lumber company business processes

Table 17-2. Lumber company users and processes

The business processes and systems that connect this diverse group of people are highly integrated and require high availability.

External to HQ Group	System links		Internal Group
Public	Kiosk	Inventory Systems	Merchandising & Operational
	E-Commerce		
		Financials	
Contractors	Order Entry	Inventory Systems	Merchandising & Operational
Stores	Inventory Mgmt	Inventory Systems	Merchandising
	POS	Financials	Operational
	Employee Mgmt	ERP	
Suppliers	Supply Chain System, Inventory Systems & Business Intelligence		Merchandising
News/Media	Advertising Production		Advertising

Table 17-3. Linking business processes to users

Our table tells us that the inventory systems are tied to everything. Both the in-store kiosks (at least five in each store) and the e-commerce system (already hosted offsite) tie directly into inventory. The contractors' system ties directly into it. The inventory management system in the store's POS system ties directly into it. And, of course, the suppliers providing the products tie into it. The question now becomes: How long can the inventory be down? The answer is probably somewhere in the "less than an hour" category.

How about the financials? As items are ordered from the e-commerce system, batch uploads are sent every 15 minutes to HQ's financial reporting system. The POS system in the stores collects real-time data from the cash registers, uploading that information at 15-minute intervals, as well. Since the information flowing into the lumber company's financial reporting system from the POS system is one-way (each store's POS system creates its own daily reports and then forwards those reports up to the POS system at regular intervals), e-commerce/POS connectivity can be down for an extended period of time, and the information exchange can catch up when things are running smoothly again.

When it comes to store and employee management, however, communication between the employee management's payroll system and the ERP system must be pretty accessible. If a disaster strikes on the day that paycheck info is sent to the payroll company, one of two things will happen: Either a) an employee at HQ and an employee of the payroll company will be on the phone re-creating an automated process as manual for that week, or b) the paychecks will be delayed until the system is back up. At the minimum, an internal employee must have access to what should be sent to the payroll company so that the process can be done manually. Whether or not a computer sends the signal to the payroll company, somebody must be able to get to the records to send payroll.

With regard to the suppliers, their "business intelligence" window into how well their products are selling can be down for a certain amount of time. They'll understand a disaster, as long as they can track how much of their inventory is in the stores and use that information to manually predict future supply needs.

The newspapers that the company advertises in, however, aren't flexible at all. A Sunday paper goes out on Friday night (for Saturday delivery to supermarkets), period. If the ad slicks aren't ready for the run of press on Thursday, (which means that they're finalized and sent off on Wednesday afternoon), they aren't going in the paper on Friday, people won't be flocking to the lumber stores to buy anything on Sunday, and millions and millions of dollars worth of revenue will be lost. While the layouts might be composed with off-the-shelf software, the database-driven, highly customized client server system that drives this must be online and accessible for the art department, advertising group, and merchandising group that are all part of the production and approval process.

Let's summarize our findings. The inventory management system and the advertising production system must be high-availability systems. The supply chain system, the ERP system, and the financial system must be covered under advanced protection so that they can be brought back up within days. And the business intelligence system can be covered under basic availability, to be restored after the key functional systems are working.

Analyzing equipment and connectivity type is the meat of your plan

Now, let's examine the class of computers you're using.

- Mainframe computers

- Midrange computers (e.g., AS/400, RS6000)

- Departmental servers (e.g., NT, UNIX, Linux)

- PCs/Workstations

Let's go through our scenario above and start matching actual computers to the computer *systems* we've mentioned above in Table 17-3. on page 628, along with the emergency communications systems such as DNS, etc. Here, we'll touch briefly on the builds of these systems (sufficient to impart the drift of what you need to plan for), but we'll go into much greater depth in *Backup and availability plan—what type of backup should you run for your server?* on page 664. Here, we'll examine the staging of the server (i.e., what emergency recovery category they belong to, as explained on page 617), the access you need (Internet or associated office space), and how you might plan on getting data from your primary system to this system (replication versus restoration of data).

For our purposes, we'll have 11 servers: Three NAS boxes, two doubling up as dual-clustered servers, and the rest just plain old normal servers. You must estimate the total backup storage capacity that the servers need, as well as the duration of the full backups—both of these numbers are key for both backup and restoration planning. While we understand that not everyone performs full backups every night, we'll use full backups for this exercise. And while not everyone plans for full capacity, we'll use that, too, because that's how we plan, as our plans have to last three years and must therefore allow for growth without purchasing new backup gear.

Querying your network for some answers

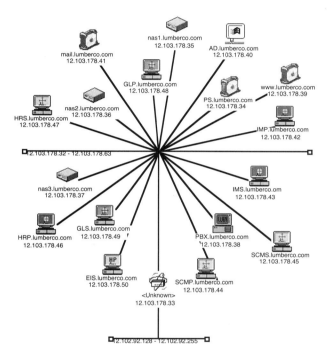

First, take a quick inventory of what you have and how it's connected to your LAN. The quickest, easiest, and least expensive method is to run LANsurveyor (W/M) from Neon Software. LANsurveyor is a wonderful network and computer analysis tool that we've written about throughout this book—and it won't cost you an arm *or* a leg. At left is a LANsurveyor map of your lumber company's network with only the servers showing (it's much larger with workstations and printers, so we omitted them). The two thick horizontal lines in the diagram are the subnet "networks" attached by the router (12.103.178.33). Each of the servers in the corporate network are listed here—even the offline" members of a cluster—as well as an admin computer.

Figure 17-5. Subnet map

While this is a nice picture of the devices, you must know more—such as storage capacity—about the servers than their network names and addresses. LANsurveyor also conducts analysis of storage space on each of the computers in the map. You can run a LANsurveyor report that lists the volumes for each of the each devices, as well as the volume's capacity and free space (from which you can deduce the capacity currently in use). For each of the servers you're backing up, gather:

*   Volume names and drive letter mapping, because these are important for setting up replication and for restoration purposes.

- Whether the volume functions as a boot drive, data drive, or both. This information helps you decide which volumes to image and which to back up.

- The total capacity of the volume, because this is what you plan your backup capacity for—not the capacity we're using right now.

Once you have this information, you can make some solid decisions about what to back up, what to image, how much capacity and how much time you need.

The raw numbers with backup info added

Once the basic information about the network connector for each volume[2] is added, calculate the backup duration as if you were running a full backup, because that same calculation will be used in planning your restoration times and windows[3]. Then, annotate your backup window for that device to determine its idle time. Finally, some systems need special backup software like open file support (OF), cluster server support (C), or replication (R) support.

Communications systems   First, you've got the four communication servers. The PBX server is an older device; hence it's on the 10 Mb network. The combination DNS and Web server is running on one box, and the other box is running the Active Directory, security, and proxy services. The primary DNS and web server is a Mac OS X server running BIND and Apache. The other DNS server is a Windows 2000 Server running Active Directory a third-party proxy server package. The LDAP and E-Mail server is running OS X Server with the integrated email and LDAP services.

The evening backup window for these devices begins when folks go home (for the PBX and security server), or when e-mail and web traffic die down for the night (somewhere between midnight and before the first meetings in the morning).

---

2.   Since you can have multiple network connectors per computer, no software in the world will tell you which application is running on which network connector and at what speed.

3.   If it takes two hours to back up a computer using a full backup method, it can take *no less* than two hours to restore that same computer. For simplicity's sake, we use the full-backup timings instead of attempting to calculate the extra time it would take to search out multiple tapes from a week's worth of incremental backups. Remember, the more incremental backups that exist for a volume, the longer it takes to restore that volume because of tape search time. But that's another story.

Because of the database nature of e-mail and the PBX, both of them need an open file manager for backup support.

Comms	Volumes	Function	Capacity	Net Type	Duration	Window	OF/C/R
PBX/Fax	(C:)	Boot	1 Gig	10 Mb	.2 Hrs	8 p.m. – 5 am	OF
	(D:)	Data	9 Gig	10 Mb	1.8 Hrs		
DNS/Web	Mac HD	Boot	5 Gig	100 Mb	.15 Hr.	12 am – 4 am	
	Data	Data	50 Gig	100 Mb	1.6 Hrs		
AD/DNS/Security Proxy	(C:)	Boot	5 Gig	100 Mb	.16 Hr.	8 p.m. – 5 am	R
	(D:)	Data	50 Gig	100 Mb	1.6 hrs		
LDAP/eMail	Mac HD	Boot	5 Gig	100 Mb	.15 Hrs	12 am – 7 am	OF/R e-mail is special
	Data	Data	150 Gig	100 Mb	5 Hrs		

Table 17-4. Communication servers

When you look at this table, remember all we've been harping on regarding high-availability information. When planning for building loss, there's not much you can do about your fax and PBX machines. If you have to work in a SunGard or other recovery room for a while, they'll let you use the system they have set up. If you can move to a new building quickly, you'll have more than enough time to buy a new phone system and restore your data to it. The DNS/web server combo here represents a working web server, not an e-commerce system (the e-commerce system is already offsite), so there's no special planning for this computer. However, the Active Directory/DNS/Security Management server should be replicated at your offsite facility. Using QuickDNS, you can set up your AD/DNS system to be a replicate of your internal system. Your RADIUS security system can be your secondary RADIUS server that you set up in your firewall/VPN devices (see *The third rule of thumb: Have fail-over firewalls* on page 586). If you use LDAP in your security structure, replicate that to your hot site, as well, because it will be key during that first restoration phase in which you re-establish your security systems. But if you use it only for internal directory purposes and not for security, don't worry about replicating it. However, your e-mail system should be set up to convert to either SaveTheMail or EMS, in case your building and primary mail systems are out of commission. You'll need e-mail immediately, and even the process of making a replicated system live is too slow for your emergency communication needs.

These systems allow you to establish emergency communication and a new secure communications infrastructure at your hot site. Without that communication and security infrastructue, you won't be doing much of anything on the Internet.

Inventory and SCM systems

Next, you must normalize your integrated and client-facing systems. In our scenario, the back-office integrated servers are quite extensive. First, there's the store operations Inventory Management (IM), Supply Chain Management (SCM), and Point-of-Sale (POS) clustered server suite. This is a four-computer cluster connected to two RAID systems. The four computers are set up in an asymmetrical cluster, with two servers as primary and two as offline secondaries—with all four servers connected in the cluster to the two RAID banks. The RAID devices are set up as a primary and a mirror. There are four database index-and-table volumes for each of the four key databases: IM, SCM, Parts, and POS. Each of the RAID volumes also has two additional database volumes reserved for replicating databases from the other RAID volume (through FlashSnap or Volume Replicator).

Remember, there is effectively no open window for these servers—for backup or restoration planning. While still functioning, they must remain active constantly, as the lumber yards are open 24 hours per day for the professional lumber clients who shop at any and all times.

If the building fell down and these devices weren't replicated offsite, it would take more than 15 hours to restore the data once new computer systems were put in place. That's way too long for the core business system to be down. Therefore, the systems must be replicated offsite. To back up these databases, you must ensure that you use backup software compatible with VERITAS' replication products, such as FlashSnap (in other words, stick with VERITAS backup software as well as replication software). And, yes, you'll need backup software with cluster support, as well, as these devices are clustered. You have your first candidate for offsite hosting.

Store Ops	Volumes	Function	Capacity	Net Type	Duration	Window	OF/C/R
	(C:)	Boot	5 Gig	100 Mb	.16 Hr.		
	(D:)	IM Index	10 Gig	100 Mb	.33 Hr.		
	(E:)	IM Tables	100 Gig	100 Mb	3.3 Hrs	No open window	
	(F:)	Parts Index	10 Gig	100 Mb	.33 Hr.		C/R
	(G:)	Parts Tables	100 Gig	100 Mb	3.3 Hrs		
	(H:)	SCM Reserved	100 Gig	100 Mb	—	N/A	
	(I:)	POS Reserved	100 Gig	100 Mb	—		
	(C:)	Boot	5 Gig	100 Mb	.16 Hr.		
	(D:)	SCM Index	10 Gig	100 Mb	.33 Hr.		
	(E:)	SCM Tables	100 Gig	100 Mb	3.3 Hrs	No open window	
IM/SCM/POS Apps & DBs	(F:)	POS Index	10 Gig	100 Mb	.33 Hr.		C/R
	(G:)	POS Tables	100 Gig	100 Mb	3.3 Hrs		
	(H:)	IM Reserved	100 Gig	100 Mb	—	N/A	
	(I:)	Parts Reserved	100 Gig	100 Mb	—		

Table 17-5. Store operations servers

That covers your back-end system that must remain open for business at all times. Since the system will be replicated to the hot site, its downtime will be minimal, which is a good thing, since this is the first system on the list that must be normalized in case of a building (and primary data center) loss.

Production systems

Then there are the production servers. Remember, production is the second system type on the list to be returned to normal. In our exercise, the lumber company must create advertising material each and every week. While they might not have to be replicated offsite, the restoration window for these servers is very short.

You have four of these servers: a print/OPI server and three NAS boxes that act as file servers for the whole office as well as house all of the production art, layouts, Point of Purchase graphics, and company ad inserts for the weekend papers. Two of the NAS boxes have been combined into a RAID 50 array, thus doubling the data volume's capacity. The Print/OPI server is a Mac OS X server. I bring this up only to thank all of the vendors who've finally come out with OS X client backup software in the past couple of years. Because of them, you can now rest assured that even your OS X devices are being backed up by your favorite backup programs.

The evening backup window for these devices occurs when the production staff goes after around 8P.M. and before they come back in at around 9A.M. Since these devices aren't used at all at night, there's no need for an open file manager. And

Production	Volumes	Function	Capacity	Net Type	Duration	Window	OF/C/R
Print Server/ RIP	Mac HD	Boot	20 Gig	Gig	.3 Hrs	8 p.m.	
	Data	Data	80 Gig	Gig	1.3 Hrs	9 am	
NAS Boxes	Data (E:)	Data	300 Gig	Gig	5 Hrs	8 p.m.	
	Data (E:)	Data	600 Gig	Gig	10 Hrs	9 am	

Table 17-6. Production servers

since the timing of restoration of these devices is second on our list, you'll have more than enough time to restore the computers from tape if necessary. In the event of an emergency, a good VAR can have computers and servers to you within one to two business days. Your organization's business decisions and restoration window determine whether or not you have a NAS box or set of NAS boxes in your hot site, ready to be populated with information.

Back-office systems

The final tier of normalization begins with the back-office servers. The heat on restoration times is not as intense for these devices as it is for the above-mentioned systems. Let's face it, operations guys order toilet paper for a living, and HR staff just muck around in your employment history (so shoot me for being biased). While both of these tasks are undoubtedly important, in our scenario they're not exactly crucial: They don't sell lumber, so they're the last groups to be normalized in an emergency offsite environment. You probably don't need to replicate any of these servers, but that doesn't mean you can ignore them. You'll definitely need to plan for acquiring new hardware to restore these systems, within the parameters of your game plan.

Let's deal with the Human Resources, scheduling, and payroll server cluster. This cluster isn't as complex as the first, as it has only two servers and two mirrored RAID banks. This is a symmetrical cluster with one computer running the HR system and the other running the scheduling and payroll system. The HR and payroll database is combined, and therefore only has two volumes (one for index and the other for tables). The scheduling system is a smaller database and has a single volume.

Very much like the production servers, these servers are hard at work when the office is full and then sit idle when the corporate executives go home for the evening. While there might not be an open file issue, it never hurts to use an open file manager when backing up a database. And, since these servers are clustered, we'll need cluster support, as well.

HR	Volumes	Function	Capacity	Net Type	Duration	Window	OF/C
	(C:)	Boot	5 Gig	100 Mb	.16 Hr.		
	(D:)	HR Index	10 Gig	100 Mb	.33 Hr.	7 p.m.	
	(E:)	HR Tables	100 Gig	100 Mb	3.3 Hrs	–	OF/C
HR/Scheduling Payroll Apps & DBs	(F:)	Scheduling and Payroll Dbs	20 Gig	100 Mb	.66 Hr.	8 am	

Table 17-7. HR servers

Rounding out the back-office server systems is the General Ledger (GL), Accounts Receivable (AR), and Accounts Payable (AP) server cluster. Again, this is a two-node sever cluster that shares a mirrored RAID bank. This system is asymmetrical, with all applications running on the primary computer. The HR server info goes for these servers, too. You'll need both open file and clustered server support in your backup management software package that handles these servers.

GL	Volumes	Function	Capacity	Net Type	Duration	Window	OF/C
	(C:)	Boot	5 Gig	100 Mb	.16 Hr.		
	(D:)	GL Index	10 Gig	100 Mb	.33 Hr.		
	(E:)	GL Tables	100 Gig	100 Mb	3.3 Hrs		
	(F:)	AR Index	10 Gig	100 Mb	.33 Hr.	7 p.m.	
GL/AR/AP Apps & DBs	(G:)	AR Tables	100 Gig	100 Mb	3.3 Hrs	–	OF/C
	(H:)	AP Index	10 Gig	100 Mb	.33 Hr.	8 am	
	(I:)	AP Tables	100 Gig	100 Mb	3.3 Hrs		

Table 17-8. GL, AR, and AP server cluster

Finally, you've got the Executive Information System (EIS) and reporting server. This is a single server with a single RAID bank for the database. Since this is a low-access system, the database index and tables are on the same volume. And because this server isn't clustered, all you need in your backup software package is open file manager support.

EIS	Volumes	Function	Capacity	Net Type	Duration	Window	OF/C
EIS/Reporting Apps & DBs	(C:)	Boot	5 Gig	100 Mb	.16 Hr.	6 p.m. – 8 am	OF
	(D:)	Data	50 Gig	100 Mb	1.6 Hr.		

Table 17-9. EIS and reporting server

The restoration window

 In this exercise, we used a total of four backup servers for our planning process. We did this to accommodate making our necessary recovery time frames as well as making our necessary backup windows each working day. We'll explain more about these backup windows in our *Backing up your servers starts with understanding them* on page 662. For now, just hit the "I believe" button and go with me on the fact that to achieve the desired backup and restoration windows, operations of this size need four backup (and restore) servers running concurrently .

All of the above planning does have a purpose: It enables you to act quickly and decisively in an emergency. Figure 17-6. on page 639 depicts the two-day restoration window you can achieve if you plan correctly and have a balance of backups and replication running. Figure 17-7. on page 640 depicts the extended time period you"ll suffer through if you haven't replicated the primary inventory management systems.

From these GANTT charts (Figure 17-6. on page 639 and Figure 17-7. on page 640), you can see that your lumber company faces a total systems restoration window of three or four days—as long as the restoration process runs 24 hours a day and you have enough equipment on hand to begin the restorations immediately.

A quick note about these two charts (Figure 17-6. on page 639 and Figure 17-7. on page 640): Yes, they show linear restorations from multiple backup servers instead of multiplexed restorations from a single or two backup servers. In our attempt to keep this book as simple as possible, we skip the arguments for and against multiplexing. Yes, it's much faster for backups—but it's much *slower* for restorations. This is all covered on page 679. For now, let's just say that this is the easiest way to represent our ideas of timing—and leave it at that.

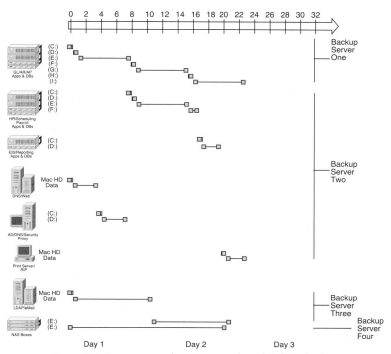

Figure 17-6. Restoration window omitting replicated IM/SCM databases

Back to our main point: If the team didn't plan for replicating key systems, even with four backup servers running concurrently, the restoration time would be a couple of days longer. What—and how much—data and systems you decide to replicate is up to you and your organization's business needs.

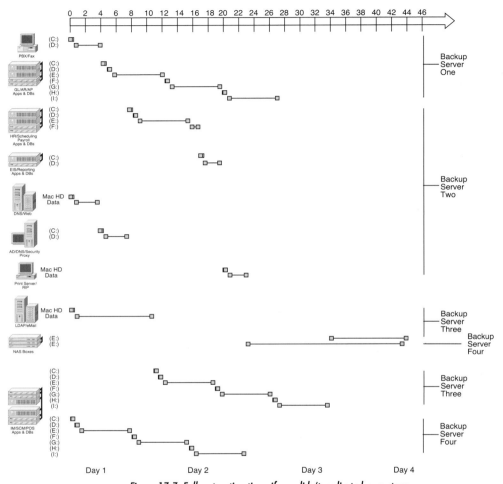

Figure 17-7. Full restoration time, if you didn't replicate key systems

What neither of these charts show is the time lag that you face if you don't already have an offsite facility with an prebuilt network that you can immediately tie into.

If you don't have a building to move into at least temporarily, add at least another four days to your restoration window. And if that building doesn't have a network preinstalled to accommodate the amount of people moving in, add at least another day or two. In our exercise, the production staff must create the ads for the Sunday papers. These ads must be at the plate-making shop by noon on Thursday. It takes up to two days to get the system running again—once a network is in place. If the building were lost on a Monday and there was a hot-site facility to house the displaced staff, they could be operational by Wednesday and have ads out the door by Thursday afternoon. However, if a new building had to be found with or without a new network being built, they'd never make it. The ads wouldn't run, and the company would lose a ton of revenue because the Sunday ad–driven traffic didn't materialize.

 Up to this point, we've explored hardware identification and replication planning for quick recovery times. This gets your key servers and information offsite, but it doesn't do a darned thing to make that information available to your end users. There's a bit of a difference between rebuilding computers to restore information and what you have to do to normalize access to those systems. The key is to figure out how your users are going to access those systems and that data, and where they'll be working when they do it.

Will your staff members access the systems and data remotely, each at their own homes? Or do they need to have some type of physical proximity to the systems or each other? Hooking up integrated systems into other integrated systems is one matter—establishing offsite parameters for teams that need access to each other as well as the data is something completely different. You'll be dividing your organization into a combination of people accessing your systems remotely, working at a remote recovery site, or sitting out a few innings of the game because there just isn't enough business need for them to get involved in an emergency situation.

We aren't going to get into arguments here about whether or not you should use reciprocal agreements for facility sharing, service bureaus, or any of the rest. Every choice has its pluses and minuses. We simply point out that to divide your equipment between full-time managed hosting and quick shipments or ready-to-go equipment at your hosting facility, you must plan user space there, as well. The best service we've scoped out for this type of hosting is SunGard. SunGard's managed hosting solutions protect and support your organizational mission-critical servers and applications in truly world-class hosting centers. Their solutions include redundant Internet access, 24/7 facilities monitoring, and access to an à la carte portfolio of managed services. These services help to ensure an uninterrupted business presence and the highest levels of performance, security, and reliability.

NORMALIZING ACCESS TO YOUR SYSTEMS WHILE HUNTING FOR NEW DIGS

When planning for normalized access to the systems in an emergency recovery state, you must examine the three major "ties that bind" that force your hand on where you're going to hang your hat in an emergency situation:

1. **Systems access or people access?** Re-creating access for integrated systems or client-facing systems normally means redirecting DNS queries to the offsite systems. It doesn't matter to a client or a database where the system sits as long as it has the same DNS address.

    However, production systems such as the ad production system for your lumber company require staff to meet together to create the product. This means that you need LAN access to the system, as well as access by the system to items like the inventory and pricing databases on the integrated systems you just brought back.

2. **Supply chain restrictions**—In our exercise, the production group must work with local service bureaus to make their plates and send them to local papers. Press checks take place at the press—and the press doesn't move. So you can scrap any plans that would cause this group to be moved outside of the geographical boundaries serviced by their production partners.

3. **Budgetary restrictions**—External sites fall into four broad categories of readiness, according to budgetary restrictions. The more "ready-to-go" the facility, the more it costs you.

    The utmost ready-to-go facility is the recovery-room scenario that SunGard offers. This facility is a combination hot site (see below) and space for end-user recovery, complete with office equipment, voice communications, call centers, and customer support functions.

- The most-ready option without space for users is a hot site with all the equipment and networks and replication procedures up and running all of the time.

- Less ready-to-go is the warm site, wherein you store equipment in case of an emergency. Once the emergency happens, you activate the networks, bring the computer systems online, and begin restoration procedures.

- The least-ready-to-go is the cold site. This is basically a room at a facility that has all of the necessary network connections, but no equipment. When an emergency happens, you move everything into this skeleton. This is what Zabetian ended up using because quick access to the other choices wasn't an option for WildPackets at the time.

  Site cost is one type of budgetary restriction, but not the only one. Relocating the displaced staff is also pricey. Let's say that you have two offices: one in Ogunquit, Maine, and the other in Pismo Beach, California. The CFO glibly says "Just use the opposite office as your hot site to keep the costs down." And then you bring up the fact that you must relocate staff to the other end of the country (airfare), house them (hotel bills), give them some type of food allowance (beer and Krispy Kremes), arrange daily transportation (car and van rentals), *and* you'll have to ensure that the secondary location always has enough additional trunk phone lines, network bandwidth (both LAN and to the Internet), and office space to sustain the sudden growth spurt an emergency will cause. With all of that in mind, an integrated hot site and recovery-room solution is worth looking at.

Now that I have your attention, let's run through what this plan might entail for the lumber company in our exercise. We'll use a few rules of thumb we've established here, namely that…

- Anything that *can* be accessed through the Internet or a VPN *will* be accessed through the Internet or a VPN; and

- The organization must have a recovery room integrated into the hot-site plan that will allow for staff work as well as staff meetings; and

- The restore order is communications, integrated and client-facing systems, production, and finally, back-office functions.

 For each of your key devices, you must know how people or other systems areare accessing it—through the Internet, a LAN, or a VPN connection. You must plan space for LAN users and access for VPN users. Devices that you consider "hot" should already be at your hot site and backed up through replication. "Warm" devices should be pre-ordered for fast-ship with your VAR so that you can get them by the next day. Devices earmarked "cold" can be ordered when Kablooey! happens.

Kablooey! just happened—get communicatin'

It's 2A.M. on a Saturday (Murphy never visits during the workday; only when you're sick, hung over, or Otherwise Occupied). You get the call that you've always dreaded: Your building is on fire. After dialing 911, your first step is to establish emergency communications such as e-mail and VPN remote access. Each of the

| System | Device(s) | Access | | | | | | Location Type | | | | |
		Internet	LAN	VPN	# User Spaces Required	Mtg Room Space Required	# VPN Users Required	Hot	Warm	Cold	Rec. Room	Geo boundary
Communications	e-mail	✔						✔				
	DNS	✔						✔				
	RADIUS	✔						✔				
	VPN	✔						✔				
	Emergency. Web	✔						✔				

Table 17-10. Emergency communications

devices listed in Table 17-10. below are accessed through the Internet, so you won't need any special user space, meeting rooms, or VPN access to the system. And each of these devices was listed as already at your hot site, so they're ready to go and you don't need to order anything at the moment.

If you use SaveTheMail, send an e-mail about what just happened to a predefined list of folks in your organization. If you use EMS, activate the system, which will then automatically send an e-mail to everyone in the list, giving them instructions on what to do next.

If you have an emergency website with your step-by-step business continuity plan running on it, you will have informed folks in that emergency e-mail about the site's URL and access passwords. You can point everyone to it so that they can take directions and get information from there.

 An up-to-date written plan, accessible via the Web, is critical in an emergency. However, when we polled most of our advanced field editors, they said that creating this type of plan was a royal pain. Because of that, we're working with Palo Alto Software to create a product called **Continuity Plan Pro** that will help you create, maintain, and publish your plan on the Web, in PDF and Word formats. We have a free version of the plan on the Web already posted for all signed-in readers, and we'll provide 30-day eval copies of the software as well.

Once you've sent your e-mail communications, reconfigure your DNS for your VPN router and RADIUS server so that the main router and main RADIUS servers are now the ones at the hot site. Then, folks at home will be able to access anything you run at the hot site as if it were at the main office.

And since you're partnering with the folks at SunGard and are planning on using their recovery-room office space, this is a dandy time to let them know that The Worst has happened, and that you'll soon be neighbors (with all due respect to the late, great Fred Rogers).

Communications are a "go"—get the engines running again

Once you've established communications, let the upper brass know that you're on top of the game and will be moving your critical hot site–replicated application servers, integrated systems, and client-facing systems from standby to full-time frontline operational status—basically the same thing as restarting the engines or switching to an emergency power plant. In our scenario, that means that you'll be

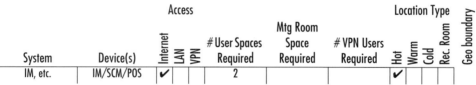

| | | Access | | | | | | Location Type | | | | |
System	Device(s)	Internet	LAN	VPN	# User Spaces Required	Mtg Room Space Required	# VPN Users Required	Hot	Warm	Cold	Rec. Room	Geo boundary
IM, etc.	IM/SCM/POS	✔			2			✔				

Table 17-11. Critical applications planning checklist

converting the Inventory Management, Supply Chain Management, and POS system from backup or standby to online status. In Table 17-11. on page 645, we can see that these systems are also accessed via the Internet, and therefore anyone can get to them from there. However, we've also added two user working spaces at the hot site's recovery room for this portion of the restoration process. It's important to have at least two staff members hanging out full-time where you have key equipment during an emergency. Think of them as your "advance party" who coordinates the rest of the restoration process and recovery-room access procedures—you know, putting out the welcome mat, baking a cake, and all that.

 Some folks overlook the fact that they hadn't been backing up these systems to tape when they were offline or standby systems. Therefore, you must immediately load your backup software onto these systems, give them the same name as the primaries, and add them to the tape backup regimen that you'll now be running from your temporary emergency hot-site location. Make sure that your offsite tape storage facility knows that it will be temporarily be picking up and dropping off tapes at your hot site.

At this point in the game, you have two staff members at the hot site. (Never have just one. Two folks can put their heads together when they get stuck—one tends to make fearful decisions.) You have your integrated, client-facing, and application servers running again. Next, it's time to deal with the production servers and some users. It's highly doubtful that you've thought of buying additional end-user workstations and placing them in your hot site. And it's just as doubtful that your users have all of their necessary equipment at home. That means that you must prepare a prearranged equipment list and prearranged fast-shipping plan with your VAR or vendor to be ready for the next step.

As our best-practices vendor, Dell has partnered with a company called Rentsys Recovery Services. Rentsys' platform of disaster recovery services focuses on one objective: providing Dell customers with fully configured Dell hardware, delivered anywhere in the continental United States within 24, 48, or 72 hours of notification. We think they're great because they allow three key ingredients in their service offering:

- **Full and partial plan testing programs** so that you can run periodic tests on your plan to ensure that it's up to date.

- **Built-to-Order configuration services** because we know that none of you will have "out of the box" solutions for any of your production crew.

- **Proprietary software installation** for the same reasons as above. We just know that you'll need specialty software loaded on your computers. Here's the kicker—instead of *you* reimaging each computer, you can send them your preconfigured images and the computers can be drop-shipped, ready for you to simply restore the My Documents directory with the user's personal data on it.

- In coordination with Dell, Rentsys delivers these computers **on time and ready to go**, and if you really need them to (and you decided not to partner with SunGard), they can even bring out one of their mobile facilities and set up the computers there.

Delivering the goods—bringing the production system back online

Communications are working great. Your integrated applications are humming along. You've contacted your favorite vendor or Rentsys, and you now have enough user workstations to bring up the rest of your production and back-office systems. Now, your focus is bringing production online. If you chose to replicate

System	Device(s)	Access			# User Spaces Required	Mtg Room Space Required	# VPN Users Required	Location Type				Geo boundary
		Internet	LAN	VPN				Hot	Warm	Cold	Rec. Room	
Production	RIP	✔			4						✔	50 Mi.
	NAS		✔		4	8	8	✔			✔	

Table 17-12. Offsite planning checklist

your NAS servers, they're already at your hot site, ready to go. However, if you chose to set the priority of these systems as "warm," you can count on server vendors such as Dell, working with SunGard, to have a proactive system ready for your business continuity needs. Server customers who have contracted for end-user recovery services at SunGard are provided with state-of-the-the Dell PCs either as replacement systems at the customer site or for use at a SunGard facility or in a Mobile Data Center. Another option, if available in your geography, is the Rentsys one we discussed earlier. Keep in mind, to achieve business continuity, you need to plan in advance, everything from your PCs to your servers to your NAS boxes need to be part of your pre-determined recovery plan. And don't count on Dell et al. to be able to quick ship all of the necessary replacement equipment, for instance Dell doesn't stock custom printers for immediate delivery—and your production group might need them. For these and other specialty items, find a good VAR to preconfigure a quick ship drop-off at the SunGard site.

Because you're setting up a LAN at your recovery-room site, you must coordinate with the site manager to set up the necessary networking equipment. Routers, switches, hubs, cabling—all of that can be precoordinated and ready to go when you are. In our exercise, Table 17-12. on page 647 shows that at the production stage, you'll need a total of eight workspaces, a meeting room for eight, and additional VPN capabilities for another eight. On your systems continuity plan website, you must let people know where they'll be working and how they'll access your systems. Whether they're work-at-home VPN users or recovery-room users, they must have clear, concise information about their expected tasks. Clear documentation is a key factor in your salvation and insured productivity.

Last call for overhaul —HR & back-office functions

By now you've gotten the hang of setting up systems, access, and temporary work-spaces for your users. It's time to add the back-office staff. When you start adding

| System | Device(s) | Access | | | # User Spaces Required | Mtg Room Space Required | # VPN Users Required | Location Type | | | | Geo boundary |
		Internet	LAN	VPN				Hot	Warm	Cold	Rec. Room	
HR	Sched. & Payroll	✔	✔		2	8	10		✔		✔	
Back Office	GL/AR/AP	✔	✔		2	10	10		✔			
	EIS/Reporting		✔			5	10			✔		

Table 17-13. Back-office planning checklist

the back-office staff, you start adding more "butts in seats" at the recovery room, as well as more folks to the VPN. Because this equipment is the last to be restored, you can either prearrange fast-shipping or you simply have your specifications ready to go with your favorite VAR.

By this time, you must also have as many users accessing your temporary network as you'll ever have—hence, the absolute necessity of monitoring and managing your network bandwidth to ensure that it's clog-free. The available bandwidth can be provisioned on a sliding scale if you're using a recovery-room solution like Sun-Gard. I can't vouch for other solutions, so, as part of your planning procedure, check their total bandwidth to the Internet.

Table 17-14. on page 649 shows the entire planning table in one shot: While this is very simplistic, with this type of information in hand, knowing what it will take to renormalize your systems in case you lose your facilities, you can now examine your backup plan to make all of the necessary adjustments I'm sure you need to make. For instance, by now, I'm sure that you've recognized your backup plan will need to cover...

- Replication of critical systems for any device that must be restored and nor-malized for access in less than one day from the time of the catastrophe;

- Consolidation of information so that recovery can be accomplished on fewer pieces of equipment than was originally running;

- Use of multiple backup servers so that critical systems can be restored in par-allel; and

System	Device(s)	Access			# User Spaces Required	Mtg Room Space Required	# VPN Users Required	Location Type				Geo boundary
		Internet	LAN	VPN				Hot	Warm	Cold	Rec. Room	
Communications	e-mail	✔						✔				
	DNS	✔						✔				
	RADIUS	✔						✔				
	VPN	✔						✔				
	Emergency. Web	✔						✔				
IM, etc.	IM/SCM/POS	✔						✔				
Production	RIP		✔		4						✔	50 Mi.
	NAS			✔	4	8	8		✔		✔	
HR	Sched. & Payroll	✔		✔	2	8	10		✔		✔	
Back Office	GL/AR/AP	✔		✔	2	10	10		✔			
	EIS/Reporting			✔		5	10			✔		

Table 17-14. Offsite planning checklist

- Separation of end-user workstation backups from server backups so that recovery efforts will be much cleaner and end-user recovery can run in parallel with server recovery.

As you can see by the overall chart, by the time you're done, you'll have at least 10 folks who have their butts-in-seats at your recovery room every day, you'll need meeting space for at least another 10 folks, and you'll have about 40 folks working from their home networks over your VPN. One way or another, you must be connected. So take the time to plan thoroughly, and then take the time to test your plan regularly.

One last note about your planning, your hot site, warm site, cold site, and recovery-room site. When your building falls down, you must rely on the strength of the disaster partners you've already chosen and tested your plan with. If, during this testing process, your disaster recovery partners don't live up to their service level agreements (SLAs), that's the time to immediately drop them like a hot rock.

If your partners don't live up to their SLAs in testing, they sure as shootin' won't live up to them when you have a *real* disaster.

Choose your partners wisely—and then trust what they promise you—*after* you verify it. As my ol' man used to say, "Put a load of crap in one hand and a load of promises in the other, and see which one fills up first. One stinks, the other's empty, and neither does you any good." Field editor Scott McCulley agrees with us about physical diversity, as well as holding DRP partners to their service level agreements:

> People need to realize that physical diversity is a very important DRP concept—especially after 9/11. Companies that can't afford two facilities in two cities should take advantage of the SunGard, Exodus, Level 3, or Qwest hosting options. They're a very easy way to get that redundancy. Just be *very* careful in the way the contract is written, and be *very* clear about expectations between parties. Most of all, hold them liable if they don't fulfill their end of the bargain. I've heard stories about servers "getting backed up," but the logs show hundreds of error messages. I'll bet that they were backed up, but probably couldn't be restored...

—and that would be a bad thing.

TAPE ROTATION METHODS

There are a lot of different backup methodologies out there. We'll present the most widely used here, even though we really don't believe in all of them. Whatever backup method you use, you have to keep one thing in mind.

1. Your backups are for restores, not for archives. If you want to archive a history of data, run an archive separate from your backups.

2. Your backup media is going to fail. No getting around it. It will wear out—and usually sooner than you expect. If you are running some elaborate scheme just to make your backup media last longer, then don't. Your scheme will probably cause you more headaches than simply buying more backup media.

Along with the definitions of full and incremental backups, we now introduce a new term; backup horizon. The backup horizon refers to how long data is kept on a backup set before the backup media is erased (recycled) and rotated back into the backup schedule.

Weekly cyclical rotation

Media: 3 Sets
Horizon: 1 Wk

The weekly cyclical rotation scheme uses three sets of tapes. We will name them A, B, and C. Each week begins on a Friday with a Full backup to the next set in

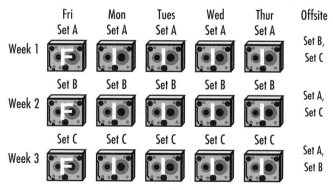

Table 17-15. Weekly cyclical rotation

line. As the week progresses, the tape set is kept onsite and in the tape drive or library so that backups can take place at any time during the week. While set A is in the computer, sets B and C are kept offsite. At the end of the week, the next set is brought onsite and the original set is sent offsite. This is a very simplistic rotational scheme, but at least it keeps tapes offsite at all times. The drawback? If the building burns down during the week, up to a week's worth of information can be lost. This scheme uses the least amount of media and as long as the building and tapes aren't lost, provides the easiest and most complete restoration possible because both the full and the daily incremental backups are on the same media set.

Son rotation

Media: 5 Sets
Horizon: 1 Day

No, we aren't talking about sending your tapes to orbit around the sun—we're talking about the first concept in the Grandfather, Father, Son rotation scheme. You can use the **Son rotation** scheme all by itself if you desire. The Son method

Table 17-16. Son rotation

creates a full backup each and every day. This is the simplest way to back up, but it requires the most time, since each and every backup is a full backup.

Father and Son rotation

Media: 6 Sets
Horizon: 2 Wks

The **Father and Son rotation** method uses a combination of full and incremental backups on a two-week rotation cycle. In this scenario, each week begins with a full backup. These full backups alternate between Set 1 and Set 2. Every Monday Set 3 is brought in and that day's incremental changes are backed up to Set 1. Every other Monday, Set 1 is "recycled." Every Tuesday, Set 2 is brought in and *that* day's changes are written to Set 2. Every other Tuesday Set 2 is "recycled." Repeat for Wednesday and Thursday. The Sons are only for a recent history (Oops, I deleted a file), but they're not kept past a week or two since they provide crappy complete restores. With Father and Son (as with Grandfather, Father, Son) you only get one valid complete restore point per week (the Friday full).

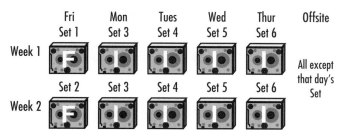

Table 17-17. Weekly cyclical rotation

 Some backup software products, like Dantz' Retrospect, cannot perform Father and Son rotation without "tricking" the software because of the way that they handle "normal" or "incremental" backups to tape. With Retrospect, the backup software examines the catalog for that tape set. And if the set has been recycled, then it will back up **everything** on the computer to that tape. In other words, when a tape is recycled by Retrospect, the very next backup is a full backup whether you want it to be or not. The trick is to have the Sons be part of the same Backup Set as the Father, with Automatic Skip to Blank Media turned on in Retrospect. Then Retrospect performs what are essentially incremental backups each night after the first full backup.

Grandfather, Father, Son rotation cycle

Media: 10
Horizon: 12 Wks

The Grandfather, Father, Son strategy rotates media in a way that allows each media to be used the same number of times over a 40-week period. This is the most difficult rotation cycle to administrate. This rotation cycle begins with a full backup on each Friday and continues with normal backups throughout the week, like all others.

This strategy is divided into 10 four-week periods. The same four sets are used Monday through Thursday throughout a given month, but then rotate within the scheme the next month. Each Friday, a different set is used for the full backups. Within a four-month cycle, all 10 tape systems have been rotated. Within a one-year cycle, all 10 tape systems have been rotated multiple times. This ensures that each set in the rotation scheme gets used the same amount of times over a 12-week period, and cycled in and out evenly over a 10-month period. Egads.

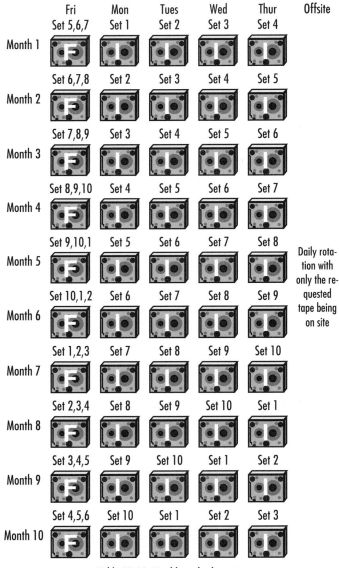

Table 17-18. Weekly cyclical rotation

CHAPTER 18:
ORGANIZATIONAL NETWORK
BACKUPS

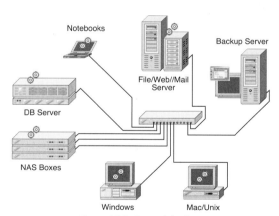

Figure 18-1. Network backups

So far, we've covered information loss, how to prevent it, and how to protect your-self through duplication, backups, and replication so that when failure and loss happens, you're ready to rebuild, restore, and resume operations. We've covered individual workstation protection, database protection, and server protection. But until now, we haven't addressed the holistic network environment. Here, you face the balancing act between dollars and data loss. A combination of replication, duplication, imaging, and backups must work in concert to create a comprehensive plan.

Your biggest challenge is the ever-increasing amount of data that you must protect running on top of a network that can cause bottlenecks during backup. Moving data from point A to point B takes time. How fast that data can move to some protected place is based upon the speed of the storage devices the data lives on, the size of the pipes that the data must run through, the speed of the tape drives and backup server, and the method of backups you plan to use.

Let's examine the small network depicted in the diagram that begins this chapter.

- We have a combination file, web, and e-mail server that has about 80 GB worth of data.

- All of the databases are in an attached RAID system and take up about 700 GB worth of data (the databases hold the item parts, as well as pictures of each item).

- There's a stack of three NAS boxes that hold 400 GB each.

- Then there are the network's Windows and Mac users as well as a cluster of notebook users (60 users in total) with around 20 GB each on their hard drives.

- That's a grand total of over 3 terabytes (3 TB) of data.

You aren't backing all that data up to a single backup server. You won't have time even if you used the whole weekend and evenings—*and* you wouldn't have a scrap of fun that week, either.

- If this were a 10BaseT network, the backups would run at 5 GB an hour. It would take roughly 614 hours to back up all of the data to a single backup server.

- If this were a 100BaseT network running at around 30 GB an hour, the backups to a single backup server would take about 102 hours.

- And if the backup were running to a single backup server over a gigabit network running at about 60 GB an hour, it would take around 50 hours.

So do you speed up the network, not back up some of the data, add more backup servers—or a mix of all three? It really depends upon your personal preference.

In the universe of backup operations, there are three schools of thought about *what* to back up, two schools of thought about *how* to back that information up, four schools of thought about *where* to put the backups, and four general types of scheduling. Two elements form a common thread throughout all these theories: First, there's a backup server that connects to remote client software running locally on either servers or workstations that then runs the backups over the network. Second, there will always be more data to back up than time to back it up in for a single backup server. Let's go through each of these schools of thought here in short form and see how folks have dealt with this over-abundance of data and under-abundance of time.

"What to back up?" theories

The three schools of thought about backup come down to the "everything" school, the "nuttin' but the server" school, and the hybrid school. In more business-like terms, they're described as follows.

1. The **Back up everything** school espouses installing either a single or multiple backup servers throughout the organization tied to groups of workstations and other servers (such as mail, file, database, etc.), and then backing up all of the data to tape or other means.

2. **Back up only the data on the servers** is the other swing of the pendulum, wherein the only devices that get backed up are the servers. The workstations are ignored.

3. **Back up all data on servers and only "important" data on end-user devices** is the hybrid, or middle-of-the-road school of thought. While the other two scenarios are dead simple in their approach, this school of thought requires backup administrators to define what "important" means to each end user, choose a method of locating this important data, and then back it up.

"How should you back up your data?" theories

This is really an extension of the "what to back up" school of thought. There are two methodologies for backing up computers:

1. **Back up all of the data** on the computer in one fell swoop—which means backing up the operating system and applications, as well as the documents. This is great if you want to ensure that the end user gets his computer back in *exactly* the same shape it was before it crashed. That could be a good thing—or it could be a bad thing (especially if the drive looks like some I've seen).

2. **Create a disk or file image** of the operating system, or operating system and applications, and then back up only the user's data. This is great if you want to speed up the restoration process, but it leaves the computer "sterile," and some users might want to take an inordinate amount of time "junking it back up."

"Where should you put your data?" theories

1. First, there was **tape**. Enormous, gigantic spools of it. Then it came in a nice little box. Many of the backup software companies still treat backups like managing a collection of tapes—even though they purport to support disk and Internet backup, as well.

2. Then came **disk-based** backups, because drive prices were going down and drive sizes were going up. Disk-based backups are faster for restores than tape backups, but you can't really shove racks of disks out the door and over to the offsite tape vault.

3. To hybrid disk-based **virtual tape systems**, or as Quantum calls them, enhanced backup systems. We'll touch more specificaally on this later in the chapter, but since its a new concept to some of you, I thought we'd mention it here.

4. Then came (and went and came back again) **Internet** backup (which actually backs up to disk, but in some other location). Internet backup is great for getting certain quantities of data and certain databases or files offsite. However, I haven't found an Internet backup solution yet that allows me to back up my 300 workstations and 9 terabytes (9 TB) of data over the Internet each night.

5. And now we've got IP-based replication of whole servers, databases, etc., so some organizations back up all of their servers in office A over to office B over their WAN.

"When should you back up your data?" theories

I haven't read many arguments about when to back up your data—just different schedules for different types of users, workstations, or servers.

1. **Continuous** backups, or rather replications, are usually the order of the day for key databases.

2. **Daily** backups are what a great deal of folks run on normal servers and even workstations.

3. **Weekly** is about how often servers get a "full" backup of all data. This is done to ensure that the backup operations don't interfere with the production operations that the servers (and the documents on them) support daily.

4. **Catch as catch can** is the keyword for backing up notebook computers. I know one particular managing partner whose computer doesn't get backed up very often at all (since she's never in the office).

Theories, schmeories—it's all about phased restoration

Here's the O-fficial Network Frontiers *übergreifende* [1] on all of these theories: Pick whichever one you want to espouse for backups, as long as you can do the following when catastrophe hits:

1. Establish emergency communications via e-mail, a password-protected web server, and phone list.

    And then immediately establish (or switch to) an emergency VPN connected to your hot site and get your offsite DNS servers ready for new IP addresses of replacement servers.

2. Normalize integrated and outward-facing systems and functions now running from the hot site.

---

[1] Von Karsten, dem resident Teuton at Network Frontiers, explains that *übergreifende* means a bracketing, and in the way we use it, an all-encompassing theory.

3. Normalize user intensive production systems and access to them at the hot site or through VPNs to users' homes.

4. Normalize your back-office systems and functions, and establish access to them at the hot site or through VPNs to users' homes.

5. Consolidate whatever data you need for these emergency systems into as few boxes and storage spaces as possible, so that you don't overwhelm yourself during the restoration process.

6. Back up your key end-user workstations (i.e., the ones that connect to the servers and systems mentioned above) so that they can be restored concurrently with the servers and you can restore multiple workstations in parallel.

Whether that timing is hours, days, or weeks from start to finish, the restoration order we've covered is roughly the same for everybody. You must be able to restore your systems in a four-phase approach, within budget, within your organization's time frame, and at whatever temporary workgroup hot site or users' homes your organization sets up.

THE MAIN THING

The Main Thing is to back up all the data that you can as often as you can, and make sure you *get the bloody backups offsite before something happens to them!*

Remember, your shining moment occurs when everything at the company is rushing to Hades in a handbasket, Kablooey! exploding all around you. That is precisely when you need to call upon your well-practiced backup and recovery plan.

So—get it together.

Understand your data.

Understand your systems and how they tie into the company's business.

Plan your backups for a four-phased recovery and restoration plan.

Then test your system regularly and, finally, relish the fact that you are prepared.

Special Thanks...

This chapter was a toughy. I couldn't have done it without the help of Rebecca Gonzalez and Dave Kenyon over at Quantum, Rob Turk and Rich Miller over at Exabyte, and J. Cloyd and Jim Moody at Overland Storage. Special thanks go out to Richard Zulch and Pat Lee over at Dantz who walked me through *a lot* in this chapter. Kudos and much thanks to all of you.

BACKING UP YOUR SERVERS STARTS WITH UNDERSTANDING THEM

I won't tell you to get to know your inner server, even though you're now staring

Server backup and recovery profiles	Awareness			Backup & availability plan						Loss Recovery Phase
	Load Intensity	Data Change Rate	Open File Propensity	Cluster	Image & forget	Consolidate Data	Replicate Data	Replicate System	Host Offsite	
Audio/Video servers	H	M	H	✔					✔	
Backup & Imaging servers	M-H	M-H	L					✔		2
Chat, Forum, IRC servers	M	M	H		✔				✔	
Combination (OS platform) servers	M-H	M	L-H		✔					‡
Database servers	L-H	L-H	H	✔			✔			2/4
Directory & Security (RADIUS, other) servers	L-M	L	L					✔		*
File Transfer servers (FTP, file sharing)	M	M-H	L	‡	✔					‡
File Storage devices (NAS, NAS on SAN)	M	M-H	M		✔	‡				‡
Groupware servers	M	M-H	H					✔	‡	3
Integrated Application servers	M-H	L-H	L-H	✔				✔		2/4
List servers	L-M	M	L-M		✔					2
Mail servers	L-H	M-H	M-H					✔		*
News servers	L-M	M	L		✔					
Print& OPI servers	L-M	H	L		✔					3
Proxy servers	M	M-H	L		✔					3
Voice & Fax communication servers	M-H	M	L		✔					
Web servers	L-H	L-M	L	✔					✔	

* You had better replicate these devices offsite and make them live *before* anything happens

‡ With these servers, it really depends upon your own organizational workflow

Table 18-1. Server profiles

at a server table that you must internalize. I won't tell you to align your server's chakras, either. What I *will* tell you is that your servers will react to backups based on certain characteristics—most of which are listed in that table you just skimmed—er, studied so carefully. I'll also tell you that the first order of business in your organization is to protect your servers, because while individual workstations might be important to individual users, servers are important to the organization as a whole. But you don't back up a server by installing software and pushing the "Backup Now" button—there's a bit more to it than that.

Each server type has its own unique backup and recovery needs. Some servers are 9-to-5 creatures, lying dormant all night, allowing you unfettered access to back them up. Other servers are 24/7 animals, that will no sooner allow you time to back them up than a loan shark would allow you time to come up with a missed payment. We know this because we've made a study of the nature of servers when it comes to backups. However, because of the dreaded Page-Count Monster, we had to cut the in-depth 30-page analysis of each server type's backup nature down to that single table you see on page 662. If you're a registered reader of the book (meaning that you've signed up at our website and given us the ISBN number on the back cover), you can access all of the 30 pages or so that we've posted there (www.backupbook.com), and can even suggest further information if necessary. For now, let's leave it at the fact that you must understand two general categories of information about your servers: their backup awareness factor and their availability factor. Ignoring either one of these factors will result in data loss or loss of time during restoration.

Server awareness

Three issues with backing up servers can cause data loss during the backup process: The load density of your server, the rate of change of the data that lives on your server, and the propensity of the files on your server to be "open" and therefore not backup-able. We've rated each server type in Table 18-1. on page 662 with a ranking of low (L), medium (M), or high (H) probability of being affected by load, change rate, or open files.

Load intensity A server's **load intensity** affects the processor's ability to handle multiple system requests. If this is a high-load intensity server and you try backing it up at one of those peak times, the backup process is going to run *much* slower than normal simply because the server doesn't have enough juice to run both at the same time. Let's take audio/video servers (the first one in the list) for an example. When users access video servers, the servers are streaming information to the user at very high bandwidth rates. This clogs the process, the disk access, and the server's network cards all at the same time. Running a backup on top of a heavy processing load of a video server causes major performance problems.

Data change rate
The rate at which data changes on your servers is another factor in backup performance. Let's take the case of a static web server. Once you've backed it up during a "full" backup, not much is going to change, and the rest of the week, your incremental backups will be insanely fast because almost no files are being modified, so they don't need to be backed up on the server. But then there's the e-mail server, which changes information minute-by-minute, affecting its database files. This is a great example of a high-change rate server. Each and every incremental backup of this server creates a lot of information being backed up, and therefore creates the need for more backup space on the tape or database backup system you're using. If you don't plan for a sufficiently high rate of change, you'll run out of storage space on your tapes or file-based backups during the middle of the week. If you're not an attentive backup administrator, or if you have your notifications turned off, you won't notice that these devices aren't being backed up, and will therefore lose data. That is not good.

Open file propensity
Let's go with the web server versus e-mail server comparison again. With a static-page web server, the files aren't open. They're HTML files that just sit on the hard drive, get sucked into the RAM cache before being sent, and then take up space. Backing them up is a snap. The e-mail server is the complete opposite. You can pretty well guarantee that somebody, somewhere will send or receive e-mail any time you try to run a backup. You can't say to the organization, "Okay, gang, let's not communicate, so that I can back up these drives." Files in the process of being sent or received have the "open" state assigned to them, and are therefore skipped during backup execution. If they're skipped, they aren't on the tape. And if they aren't on the tape, they don't get restored. That is not good.

Backup and availability plan—what type of backup should you run for your server?

Your server backup and availability plan should have several categories. Deciding whether or not you want to cluster a server (see *Clustered servers* on page 473) depends upon hardware availability needs at your location, and isn't an overall backup scheme. Beyond hardware availability lie several decisions you must make regarding the permanency and availability of your server's data.

On one end of the spectrum, you create an image of the server's OS and software and ignore the data (see *Disk imaging—understanding imaging basics* on page 377). Print servers fall into this category, because you don't want the data in flux on the print server. All you care about is the operating system, font list, color match list, and print server software—all of which you can image.

The other end of the spectrum? Replicating both the hardware and the data of the server so that you have an identical match in both hardware, software, and live data resident on the server (see *Replication* on page 497). If imaging is a do-it-and-forget method, replication is a continuous-flow process.

Between the two extremes, you have data consolidation (taking 100 GB of garbage and fitting it into a 50 GB drive) and backup. How you consolidate your data, and what data you choose to consolidate, is an ever-increasing aspect of an organization's network backup process. But before we can get to consolidation, let's first cover the basics: deciding what types of backups to perform for each server, creating a windowed backup schedule that doesn't interfere with network operations, server loads, or user's work routines, and setting up your network, backup servers, and tape libraries for high-speed network backups.

Image and forget, full, incremental, or differential backups...

Without going into great detail about the differences among full, incremental, and differential backups (for a refresher, see *Incremental backups (a.k.a. normal backups) to tape* on page 296), we need to cover which type of servers should generally receive which type of backup treatment. I say *generally* because we can provide you with only a rule of thumb, as only you can understand how the server operates in your arena. This is important because the type of backup you choose determines the backup window, amount of tape, and restore time for that particular server.

Image and forget Let's start with the servers you can create a disk image of and then forget when it comes to backing up: the servers in which the software is consistently unchanging but the data is constantly flowing through without having to be retained. The two most likely candidates for this classification of backup are:

- Print & OPI servers

- Proxy servers

Full backup candidates   The candidates for backing up in-full each time are those servers that must be restored completely and as quickly as possible. These usually have many daily incremental changes, such as new files and file modifications. Database servers are prime candidates, because they have that unique combination of many daily changes and are usually needed back as fast as possible.

- Backup and imaging servers
- Chat, forum, and IRC servers
- Database servers
- Groupware servers
- List servers
- Mail servers
- Voice and fax communication servers

Incremental backup candidates   Incremental backups give the administrator a "history," or "snapshot" to restore from—which is good because people tend to do bad things to good files, and sometimes the administrator needs to restore a couple of files from a backup four days ago. However, incremental backups take much longer to restore after a complete computer loss than full backups—and much more space.

- Audio/video servers
- Combination (OS platform) servers
- File transfer servers (FTP, file sharing)
- File storage devices (NAS, NAS on SAN)

Differential backup candidates   Differential backup candidates are those servers that need to be brought back as quickly as possible, and that don't have many daily changes—or the daily changes don't equal a huge amount of storage space. This is a trade-off blend of the "rollback" option of a historical backup process and the speed of a full backup process.

- Directory & security (RADIUS, other) servers
- Integrated application servers
- News servers
- Web servers

Some special items of note when backing up clustered servers

Another part of server awareness during backup planning is the special alertness you must have when dealing with clustered servers. So far, we've been talking about backing up the ever-changing user data on the servers. While user data on the server is important, you must do more than just backing up the data to restore a failed cluster, such as the Microsoft Cluster Server (MSCS). MSCS comes in two-node (Advanced Server) and four-node (Datacenter Server) setups, either of which provide fail-over of application and system resources in the event of hardware or software failure. If a primary node fails, the surviving node(s) provides continuous access to the systems. But what happens when a complete cluster fails? If you didn't take the appropriate steps to back up several different configuration items such as those for the storage system and the individual nodes' settings, you're hosed. Toast. SOL. Your next job will be as a bunghole sniffer[2] or paper-clip realignment specialist, because they sure won't let you anywhere near high-availability servers anymore.

Does your backup software support clustering?

Not all backup software supports clustering. Backing up a cluster's and node's system state data is essential for cluster recovery, because it includes the cluster configuration data, the state of each of the shared resources, and the quorum logs. The cluster configuration is stored in multiple places within the cluster—on each node and on the quorum device, as well. Microsoft has added special APIs for backing up these files; hence backup software that supports clustering includes a special plugin to perform these actions. Some software does, and some software doesn't.

If it doesn't have specific support for clustering, does it at least back up the system state data? If it doesn't do that, you can at least use the Windows Backup Utility to back up the cluster's quorum log files to a special partition or area on the drive. Of course, if you do that, you'll need to use the CLUSTERS utility found in the Windows 2000 Resource Kit to reintegrate the logs during the restore process—which is about as much fun as yanking out your nose hairs.

---

2. Get your mind out of the gutter. A *bunghole sniffer* is the person who sniffs the wine barrels to ensure that they've been properly charred before the wine goes in. I just *had* to use that somewhere.

You've got a third choice, though: Use the Microsoft Cluster Tool as an integral part of the cluster backup process. This utility backs up the configuration of the cluster to a file that can be used in the restore process. You'll use the cluster tool to back up the state of the cluster in case the cluster becomes corrupted. As long as you back up a "good state" once, you don't have to make another backup until you change the cluster's parameters.

If you're using the Dell servers, you can use the Dell OpenManage Cluster Assistant with ClusterX to back up the cluster configuration to a file. Not only does this back up the cluster's configuration, it also backs up any of the linked DLL libraries that aren't a part of the standard MSCS installation. We like the ability to separate the normal backups from the cluster configuration backups using this tool, because it also provides SNMP alerts to the administrator for audits, cluster events, uptime statistics. and an overall view of all managed clusters.

Don't forget your disks

Disk signatures are very important to clusters. MSCS just won't bring a drive online into the cluster if the disk signature doesn't match what was previously stored in the registry. For this, you can again turn to your Windows 2000 Server Resource Kit for another utility: DumpConfig, which gathers the configuration (partitions, file systems, each disk's signature) of all disk drives attached to the clustered system and writes that information to a file. If a DumpConfig is created prior to a drive failure, the information in the file can be used to set the signature on the replacement disk to the signature MSCS is looking for.

You aren't done with server plans until you've done the paperwork

When we asked our field editors about the critical information they needed during an emergency, a great many of them came back with this bit of wisdom: "Document the heck out of the system." And that wisdom goes double for a clustered system. Here's what you need to have written down or in a database about your clustered nodes so that you can return them to the same state they were in after a cluster failure:

1. Hard drive, SCSI ID, and volume details

2. Operating system version, service pack levels, and "hot fixes" applied

3. Hard disk types, sizes, RAID configurations and volume details

4. All software installed and upgrade versions

5. RAM and various cache settings applied

6. PCI slot assignments and card and driver versions

7. LUN assignments for each server connected to a storage system (especially in a clustered environment)

8. Firmware updates for any specific hardware

9. Cabling schemes and network identification information

SETTING UP MULTIPLE BACKUP SERVERS AND WINDOWED SCHEDULES

When planning for server backups, you're really planning for server restoration. You can plan for the restoration of individual servers if they die, or you can plan for the restoration of your servers if, say, the building falls down and you have to restore them en masse. Many people don't take into account what an en masse restoration entails: think multiple backup servers and parallel restorations instead of a single backup station handling all of the restorations. *The object of the game is to restore as quickly as possible*[3]. So, clearly, when planning for en masse restorations, you must have a distributed backup architecture. Where do you draw the dividing lines and how do you handle the backup processes?

Another reason for having multiple backup servers? Handling your backup window time slots. Remember, each server has a window in which backup opportunities are the best, so you'll need to plan your backups during that window. In the planning stage, we always list the backup window for each device. This helps to plan the backup schedule and organize which servers can be paired with other servers to maximize the number of devices per backup server that fit into the backup window. If your backups run longer than your available backup window, you have two choices: Not to back up all of the data or to add another backup device and rebalance your backup schedule so that you can back up everything. I'd go with the latter if I were you.

 A third reason for having multiple backup servers? For restoration's sake, you generally want to ensure that you have no more than 50 to 100 backup sessions per backup set, and don't want your backup set to run more than five tapes. The reason for the five-tape limit is that each tape you add to a backup set also adds the chance that Mr. Murphy will visit, and one of the tapes will conk out on you. Why 50 to 100 sessions per backup set? The backup software must begin linearly at the front of each tape and then progress through each of the sessions for that computer until it has restored all the data from the beginning session to the final session for each computer. The more sessions you have, the more time it takes. If five tapes and 50 sessions are best, 10 tapes and 100 sessions should be your outer limits.

---

3. Please read that sentence again so that you understand it. It is your mantra.

Using our lumber company example from page 628, let's work through the backup planning exercise. Below are a couple of backup charts that show the backup windows and delineate how we'd take a stab at creating backup scripts to accommodate each of the server's volumes within the correct backup window, meet our maximum tape and session limitations, and minimize the amount of backup servers needed to accomplish the job. This first chart shows the evening backup windows and depicts how the computers and backup servers can be arranged to fit everything in.

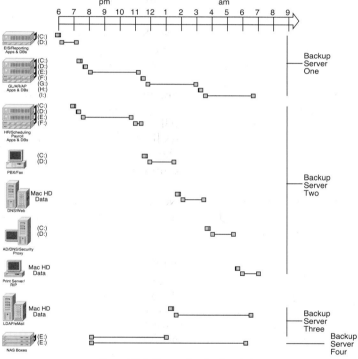

Figure 18-2. Server planning by window

Taking into account incremental daily changes

Okay, we've arranged the servers so that they can be backed up in a backup window that fits their in-use schedule and allows a full backup within the window. So, what happens to capacity if we plan for a full backup once a week and then incremental sessions the rest of the week? When you plan for incremental changes, you must estimate how much data changes per server. While this is never exact, over a 10-year period of looking at backup logs, we've found that you can expect:

- Housekeeping servers like DNS, security, proxy (minus the cached files), and Active Directory, will have anywhere from 1–2 percent change;

- Workstations also change anywhere from 1–5 percent;

- Data servers experience around 10 percent incremental change;

- Database servers have around 20 percent incremental change; and

- E-mail servers experience around 25 percent incremental change.

Taking into account this much incremental change, will the chart hold up against our 10-tape and 100-session maximum on backups? You betcha. For the most part, we're under five tapes, and the only backup server that approaches the maximum on sessions is backup server two.

Server	GB Capacity		LTO Tapes @150 GB		Sessions	
	Full	Incremental	Full	Incremental	Full	Incremental
One	345	413	3	3	9	63
Two	400	442	3	3	12	84
Three	455	518	3	4	3	21
Four	300	330	2	3	1	7

Table 18-2. Backup checklist

Since you're such a wide-awake reader, you've probably noticed that the large back-office system is missing from the above chart. That's because *there was no backup window* at all—since the lumberyards are 24/7, so must the POS and IM databases be available 24/7. Therefore, we've excluded it from the previous chart and have created another chart to show these backups because they must be handled a bit differently.

Since these are key databases and this is a clustered system, we've ensured that all of the servers and storage are handled by the VERITAS Volume Manager. This means that we can add FlashSnap to the mix for backing up the databases, as well. With FlashSnap added, we can script the system to automatically break off the mirror of the databases first thing in the morning, and then create a tie-in script with VERITAS' NetBackup to back up the databases. Once the databases are backed up and the NetBackup script is finished, the database volumes are added back to the original mirrored system in the Volume Manager architecture. With this type of scripting in place, we can utilize two of the already existing servers. We'll choose backup server three and four for this exercise.

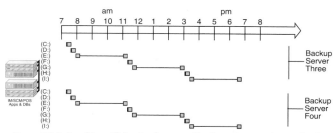

Figure 18-3. Breaking off the databases and backing them up during the day

Because we have two "standby" servers in the cluster, we can use those servers to be the backup conduit for the daily database backups. That gives these two servers a daily purpose to serve in addition to being standby servers, and it allows us to reduce the number of overall backup servers by two, thus utilizing as much of the 24-hour day as we can for backup purposes.

But what does that do to the number of tapes and sessions for backup servers three and four? It adds nine more sessions to the full backups on backup server three, bringing to the total sessions to 84—still within the limit. How about maximum tapes in the set? Backup server three goes slightly over the halfway mark with six sessions, so we're under our maximum limit. We're cleared for go at this point.

	GB Capacity		LTO Tapes @150 GB		Sessions	
Server	Full	Incremental	Full	Incremental	Full	Incremental
Three	680	788	5	6	12	84
Four	525	605	4	4	8	56

Table 18-3. Backup maximums

If you don't feed your tape drives fast enough, they'll stop for a shoe shine

While it might sound like I'm being funny here, I'm not. To ensure that your backups are going smoothly and you aren't actually adding to your backup time by designing your backup architecture the wrong way, you must understand a couple of characteristics of tape backup. We've talked about the effects of throughput and latency before in terms of general backup practices. Now it's time to talk about latency and throughput in terms of how they affect what's happening to your backup tapes.

Each backup tape type writes data to the tape at a certain speed. SuperDLT, AIT, and LTO write at about 16–20 MB. Simple enough. Now you need to add to that the fact that these tape drives also *compress* the data as they're writing to the tape. Taking into account that tape drives compress the data as it comes and before it's written to the tape, you must feed data to the tape drives at about a 3:1 transfer rate; i.e., if your tape drive can write at 20 MB, you must feed data to it at 60 MB.

Most streaming tape systems today use the **helical scan** method of writing to tape. Helical scan uses read/write heads embedded in a drum rotating at high speed against the tape, which then "streams" past the heads very slowly. As the device writes to the tape, the read head is positioned so it verifies each "frame" of data after writing the frame. Because the tape continually streams at a low speed under the tape drive heads, a constant source of information must flow to the tape drive. When the drive runs out of information to write to the tape (1), it must stop the tape (2), which takes a foot or two of actual tape; rewind the tape to a point *behind* where it left off (3); stop again (4); then start the tape stream again (5), so that it's up to speed by the time it reaches the last point on which it wrote data. The process looks like the circular motion of a shoe shine.

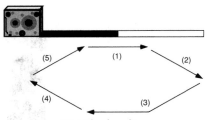

Figure 18-4. The shoe-shine process

The point here? It's not a good idea to get the fastest tape drive possible. It's a *better* idea to match the write speed of the tape drive with the feed speed of the systems being backed up. If you need the fastest, biggest tape drive available, design your backup network, your backup throughput, and overall design to accommodate the write speed of the tape drive—which brings us into the realm of discussing your network topology in regard to tape backups.

Other than directly connecting backup storage devices to each server that you want to back up (which is really inefficient), there are three main methods of connecting backup systems in a networked environment:

1. Running the backups directly on the LAN wherein the backup traffic runs on the same cabling system as the normal traffic.

2. Adding a high-speed "backup network" to the normal LAN so that the backup runs at top speed and backup traffic bypasses the normal LAN. You could also add multiplexing[4] to allow you to back up more servers simultaneously.

3. Attaching the backup libraries to the same SAN that's running the rest of the data center storage equipment.

Each method has its own merits and drawbacks. Let's take a quick look at each. For each of the scenarios below, we'll use four backup servers as previously discussed. We'll back up to LTO tape, and we'll use the Overland Storage NEO 2000 tape library as our backup device. We chose the NEO because we love Overland products, and further because it supports multiple SCSI or Fibre Channel connections, has two magazines that hold 15 LTOs each, and has two drive mechanisms. Therefore, we can attach two of these babies to our four backup servers and have four simultaneously running backups.

Figure 18-5. Overland NEO 2000 dual-drive, dual magazine library

---

4. This is also called **multistreaming** or **interleaving**, but we call it multiplexing. Multiplexing allows multiple streams of data from one or more clients to be simultaneously written to a single tape drive.

If you're wondering what happens if you run out of capacity on one of these, here's the other reason that we recommend this product: expandability. When you begin building your LAN tape backup plans, make sure you have room to expand your tape library. We chose the Overland Storage NEO series to discuss here (and for many of our own clients) because it supports the Distributed Robotic Architecture (DRA). When using tape libraries that support DRA, you can build modular, expandable systems by merely stacking multiple libraries together, creating a massive, modular library system. In so doing, if one of the libraries fails, the failure affects only that unit and not the total tape backup system.

Below is the back end of one of the NEO 2000s. Notice that the system has a pull-out power supply, pull-out drive mechanisms, and, as you can see on the right side of the picture, additional slots. These slots can be used for expandability into SAN stacking modules in a DRA architecture.

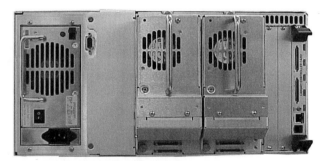

Figure 18-6. Rear view of a NEO 2000

In the DRA architecture, once more than one tape library is stacked, each additional library can become a slave (driven by the master), or you can add one of the libraries to the stack, making it a standby in case of module failure. This standby device can be configured as a standby master, monitoring the master tape library and standing at the ready to take over if necessary.

Backing up over the LAN

Adding the four backup servers (grouped in twos with their respective NEO libraries) to the network backbone switch is the oldest method we know of adding backup servers. Other than the four backup servers and the two tape libraries, you don't have to do anything special to the data center network to add backup services.

Of course, when adding backup servers to the normal network, make sure that the backup servers are attached at the highest level of the network's backbone. You wouldn't want the servers off on a spur, forcing traffic to go through several hubs, switches, or even routers. Each time your backups begin going through routers and multiple switches, you begin adding time to the backup process because you're adding latency.

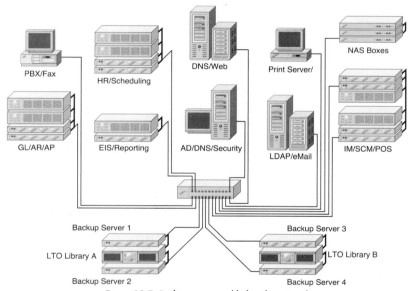

Figure 18-7. Backup servers added to the network

And with four backup servers running simultaneously each night, make sure when you add them directly to the network that you add them on a switched backbone, or at least have a switched network segment that routes the traffic between the four individual backup servers and the computers they're simultaneously backing up. Think of it: If the backup servers were all on the same hub, they'd have to divide the network's total bandwidth by 4. That would defeat the purpose.

Creating a separate sub-network for backups

Another method for running backups is to create a sub-network *just* for backups and management traffic. While this might be pretty hard to do for backing up servers strewn throughout the corporate facilities, it's relatively easy in a data center environment because of proximity and the open wiring architecture of the data centers. In the diagram below, we've segregated the backup servers onto their own switch and have run a second set of cables from each of the servers being backed up over to the backup sub-network (the dashed lines).

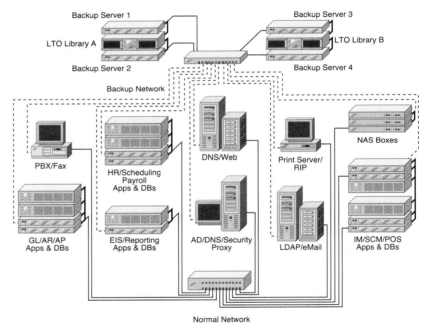

Figure 18-8. Separate sub-network for backups

The additional costs are the gigabit Ethernet switch and each of the gigabit Ethernet cards that you must install into the servers being backed up.

The benefits are many. The backups won't have to run over the standard network, and therefore you won't have to worry about normal traffic interfering with the backup traffic. You can install the fastest network cards in each of the servers being backed up, and therefore improve the speed over the normal network speeds. And, if you do run a separate backup-only network, you can also reduce the number of backup servers, tune your system, and use multiplexed backups. Multiplexing allows multiple streams of data from one or more clients to be simultaneously written to a single tape drive. This means that you could set up your backup server so that it has multiple NICs to allow multiple simultaneous clients to send their data to the server at once, so that the backup server can interleave the incoming data onto the tape backup system. How many simultaneous clients you allow to back up at once is determined by your backup software, the speed of your backup server (having multiple processors, multiple "peered" NICs, and SCSI connectors for the tape drives is a must), and the speed of your tape drive system (and whether or not it allows you to simultaneously write to multiple tape drives in the system).

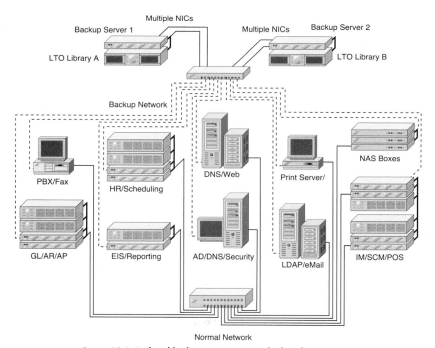

Figure 18-9. Reduced backup servers in a multiplexed environment

How does multiplexing work? In this discussion, we'll cover how multiple backup clients simultaneously write data to a single tape drive. When multiple clients send simultaneous data streams to a single tape drive, you need a method for managing and writing the incoming data. There are two basic methods: **file interleaving** and **block interleaving**. File interleaving writes file 1 from source 1 to the tape drive, buffering incoming files from other sources while this occurs. Once the file has been written to the tape, it then writes the next sequential incoming file. Figure 18-10. shows three backup sources interleaving their files onto a single tape. The only difference between file interleaving and block interleaving? Block interleaving writes data to the tape in 32 K chunks. Block interleaving is better than file interleaving in that if the tape encounters a very large file, it doesn't have to handle it all at once before accepting data from the next computer. Instead, it simply splits the large file into multiple blocks, therefore accepting data more evenly from each of the incoming computers.

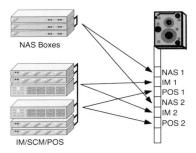

Figure 18-10. Multiplexed, interleaved backup

Multiplexing is great for speeding up backups because it ensures that the tape drive is *always* running at its maximum speed threshold. However, it's not so great for restorations because it spreads the same amount of data from a single computer over a greater amount of tape. During restoration, the tape must find the first chunk, read it, jump to the next chunk, read it, and so on. In an e-mail conversation, Rob Turk, one of Ecrix' engineers in Europe, shared this information with me:

> Multiplexing is no more than a stop-gap measure to allow multiple clients to fill the bandwidth of a high-performance tape system. It's a nice way to optimize the backups, but it's a complete disaster for restores. The biggest mistake in sizing a backup system is to look at backup requirements alone. The sole reason for doing backups is the ability to restore. Therefore, the restore requirements are way more important. You have to ask yourself how much time is allowed to bring back the data during a restore. In a worst-case scenario, using a high-performance HP/IBM LTO-2 tape drive (30 Mbps native transfer speed) and 16 multiplexed clients means that each client

stream will only have to supply 2 Mbps. Provided the network infrastructure and backup server can handle the load, the LTO-2 will zoom along, streaming, and all clients will happily supply this data rate. Say it takes eight hours to complete all jobs.

None of the backup packages on the market today can run multiplexed restores. They all schedule restores in a queue. Each job is matched against a tape and that tape is loaded into the next available tape drive, read and demultiplexed. Only the stream that is relevant to the job is used; all other streams are discarded.

When restoring all the data to all systems, each client gets its data back at a measly 1/16th of the backup rate. One in 16 blocks of data is part of "his" stream. Effective restore rate: about 2 Mbps. Each tape must be read 16 times (once for each stream), so now it takes 16*8= 128 hours (over five days!) to fully restore all systems. I'm sure that's not what the customer had in mind when she bought her top-notch drive... She could have had the same backup performance but 10 times better restore performance had she used 10 low-cost Exabyte VXA-1 (3 MB/s native) tape drives. In many cases, it turns out that using more tape drives is a more effective way to guarantee both backup and restore requirements than to start multiplexing. Those tape drives can be of lower performance (read: cheaper), but overall you'll have a better performing restore platform. As a bonus, having more tape drives also provides better redundancy against hardware failures."

If you're multiplexing, you can count on adding 50 to 100 percent to the restoration time over that of the backup time for each device multiplexed. I'd rather have more backup servers than a slower restoration time. However, if you *are* going to use multiplexing, keep these thoughts in mind (other than a multiprocessor CPU and tons of RAM) on the backup server:

- Don't multiplex more than eight backup sources simultaneously.

- Ensure that each backup source has its own data pipe on your switch and a corresponding NIC on the backup server.

- Ensure that you're running either dual high-speed SCSI or multiple Fibre Channel cards to your tape backup system.

Backing up in a SAN

The only better idea I have for the backups than creating a sub-network for them to run on works only if you use a Storage Area Network (SAN) in your data center's server farm. If you've decided to attach your storage to your servers through a SAN, you could run the backups over the Fibre Channel SAN instead of a gigabit Ethernet. This would provide the maximum amount of throughput, but would also be the most complex method. As discussed previously, when multiple computers back up across the network to a single tape library, they transfer the data across that network to a single backup server that has connectivity to the tape device. On a SAN, each server can have equal access to the same tape device. Because each machine on the SAN directly communicates with the tape device, transfers speeds are equivalent to having a device locally attached to the server's PCI bus.

In the diagram below, we show a small SAN with redundant fibre switches connecting each of the servers on the left with the storage farms on the right. Because the Overland NEO tape libraries and others like it can be connected to a SAN, and because most enterprise-level backup software can run backups over a SAN, this becomes a real option. We've kept the four backup servers in place because we need four restore servers running simultaneously in case of building loss and we're faced with restoring everything in the data center as quickly as possible. Remember, each backup server can restore only one device at a time from tape.

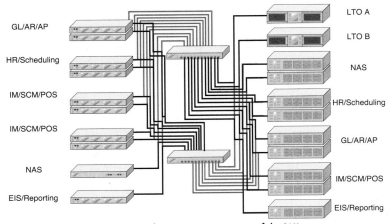

Figure 18-11. The tape system as a part of the SAN

While the obvious drawback of running backups over a SAN is the SAN's complexity, this method offers some benefits. If you remember, in our scenario, we have four computers used in clusters, set up as secondaries without much to do until the primary fails. By using these devices as the backup servers while they aren't busy, we can avoid the overhead of four additional backup servers. The only drawback is that devices such as the DNS servers, web server, and e-mail server aren't a part of the SAN; therefore backing up those devices must be done over the normal network or through a much smaller sub-network used for backups. Because this is a SAN environment, the NAS boxes can be reduced by two, with one of them being the NAS "head" for the NAS storage on the SAN (using the Dell NAS over SAN boxes).

Remember to examine your full backup path and then adjust as necessary

In these different scenarios, setting up your tape backup system is a blend of having the right throughput on both the sending and receiving ends. Now that I think of it, also having the right blend of throughput on the network layer, as well. To make this a little easier to think about, we've created a table for you to peruse (Table 18-4. on page 684) at your leisure. Hopefully, by looking at the pointers we've listed below and the table we've listed there, you can you then go back and examine your own network and make whatever changes you feel necessary. If you need to brush up on tape speeds and types, see *Tape formats* on page 333.

Volumes and the data-set size

How much data you push through the pipe from your volume to your tape does affect throughput and tape sizing needs. You need to understand three basic data set factors: your total data-set size, your data-set changes, and the compression factor for your data set.

Total data-set size   This is one of the easiest pieces of information to obtain. It's a combination of knowing the total number of files you have on any given volume and the average file size of each of those files. The average file size can be determined by dividing the volume's used space by the number of files listed for the volume.

Data-set change factor   Once you know your total sizes, figure out how much will change each day. Again, this goes back to your total path throughput planning. If you have a ton of little

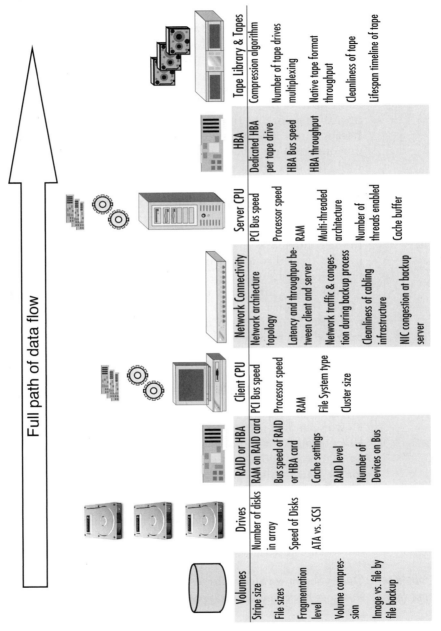

Volumes	Drives	RAID or HBA	Client CPU	Network Connectivity	Server CPU	HBA	Tape Library & Tapes
Stripe size	Number of disks in array	RAM on RAID card	PCI Bus speed	Network architecture topology	PCI Bus speed	Dedicated HBA per tape drive	Compression algorithm
File sizes	Speed of Disks	Bus speed of RAID or HBA card	Processor speed	Latency and throughput between client and server	Processor speed	HBA Bus speed	Number of tape drives multiplexing
Fragmentation level	ATA vs. SCSI	Cache settings	RAM	Network traffic & congestion during backup process	RAM	HBA throughput	Native tape format throughput
Volume compression		RAID level	File System type	Cleanliness of cabling infrastructure	Multi-threaded architecture		Cleanliness of tape
Image vs. file by file backup		Number of Devices on Bus	Cluster size	NIC congestion at backup server	Number of threads enabled		Lifespan timeline of tape
					Cache buffer		

Table 18-4. Data flow in backup path

Full path of data flow

files (8 K or so) that change often, you'll be sending large amounts of small streams of data to the backup server. If your backup tape drive is an LTO, you'll be under-feeding it. If your backup tape drive is a VXA-1 or early DAT, you'll be fine. However, if you have a groupware server wherein the art-database changes, you'll be sending massive quantities of large chunks of data to the backup server and you'll *want* the power and speed of the LTO.

Volume and file compression

Part of the speed ratios of your tape backup devices depends on their ability to compress the incoming data. Tape drives can compress incoming data at 2:1 and 3:1 ratios, but only if that data is not *already* compressed and only if it lends itself well to compression schemes.

- **Database** and **application** files have varying structures and contents, and also contain both text and numeric data with large amounts of redundancy. All of this improves the effectiveness of hardware compression at the tape drive.

- **Graphic** files are usually stored in some type of compressed state by the application that creates them, or by the method that they were saved to disk (like the compression ratios achieved by JPEG). The problem with precompressed graphic files is that they inflate during hardware compression at the tape drive.

- **Text** files have a *lot* of redundancy, a *ton* of redundancy, are *very* redundant (Get it? Funny? Okay, fine, just ignore my mordant wit). This redundancy (there I go again; stop me, please!) allows them to be very tightly compressed by the tape drive.

Volume structure

More likely than not, one of the biggest bottleneck areas in the full backup path is the volume structure on the client disks. Consider three factors in this area: partition placement, fragmentation, and logical structure.

Partition placement

The outer regions of a disk have faster access times than the inner regions of the disk. Therefore, if the drive can be partitioned, make sure that the data partition is the outer region partition and the inner-region partition is for the system files, because the files change more in the data partition.

Fragmentation

We've covered fragmentation in an earlier chapter (see *How bad can the fragmentation get?* on page 98). Fragmentation causes an access pattern that requires frequent seeks between portions of the disk causing overall throughput rates to decrease dramatically. Regular defragmentation will allow the computer to be backed up as fast as possible.

Logical structure The logical structure of the volume affects both performance and reliability. RAID0 volumes will provide faster read throughput for backups, but slightly slower restores. RAID5 systems will provide even faster reads but much slower restores (by a factor of 2 sometimes). Also, the number of physical disks in the logical array (the more the better) affects both read and write throughput speeds.

Disks

The native speed of the disks (this is a product-by-product measurement) in both throughput and seek times, whether or not the disks are SCSI versus ATA, and the disk's buffer size all affect the throughput of the disks.

For instance, the 40 GB, Ultra 320 SCSI Seagate Technology Cheetah 10K.6 has a 320 Mbps transfer rates, 4.7 msec. average seek time and 8 MB buffer. Compare that to the 40 GB, ATA IV Seagate Technology Barracuda that has a 100 MB/sec. transfer rate, 9 msec. average seek time and 2 MB buffer.

RAID and HBA attachments

The speed, RAM, and cache size of the RAID card or Host Bus Adapter (HBA) will affect the throughput.

The number of devices in serial attachment on the RAID or HBA bus also affect throughput. The fewer devices per bus, the better. Having 4 ATA drives on separate buses versus having them connected in master-slave serial fashion provides an incredible throughput jump.

If the RAID system is software based, all performance will be slower than if it's hardware based.

The client CPU

The overall processor and bus speed of the client CPU, the amount of RAM, the operating system, and whether or not the client is "in use" all affect throughput. In testing here, a 500 MHz computer runs at about 1/3 the speed of a 1 GHz computer. We don't know why, but that's the way it works. And high CPU process screensavers running during the backup can slow down the process.

The marriage of the OS and bus

Multithreaded operating systems—mainly UNIX systems and multiple channel peer-to-peer buses—offer the maximum throughput on the client computers. Backing up the Apple Xserve is twice as fast as backing up a Dell server of the same ilk.

Network connectivity

Network connectivity is broken down into three subcategories that you need to be aware of:client connectivity, network architecture and health, and backup server connectivity. Do you have PCs with a 10 MB Ethernet card? Are you trying to run a gigabit Ethernet network over CAT3 cable? Is the client computer on a hublet connected to another hublet connected to the wiring rack hub?

Client connectivity

What type of network connection does the client computer have? What speed does the connection run on, and is the network connection through a peer-to-peer PCI-based NIC, or motherboard-based NIC? Does the client connect over the cabled network or over one of the WiFi networks (which you might want to check often with your notebook users)?

Speaking of notebook users, how mobile is the client? Are you backing up the client from segment A of the network one day, segment G the next, and from a hotel room in Pismo Beach the third day? Where the client is located on the network and the client-to-backup server latency and throughput have huge impact on the backup speed.

Network architecture and health

What is the network architecture like? Are you backing up directly over the LAN? If so, how healthy is your LAN? When was the last time you ran a cable scan? How much traffic is present during the backup process? Is there any way that you can move the backups to a separate "backup-only" network, as we've discussed in this section?

Backup server CPU

Everything that we said about the client CPU goes for the backup server CPU. This should be one of the fastest machines on your network, and definitely must be faster than the clients it's backing up. Too many companies I've visited have had out-of-date backup servers trying to run fast backups to high-speed tape-drive systems. A great backup server is a multi-NIC, multi-HBA, tons-o-RAM, multiprocessor, multithreaded computer. Think "Tim the Toolman" when building your backup server. Ooh, ooh, ooh!

Server HBAs

You should have one dedicated HBA per tape drive on your backup server. Ensure that it's at least three times faster than the tape drive you're writing to.

Tape libraries and tapes

Here's the scoop: *DO NOT JUST GET THE FASTEST TAPE DRIVE OUT THERE!* Make sure to go through everything that we've written above and match your tape drive to your overall throughput. Take into account the ability of the tape drive to compress the data that gives you at least a 2X speed factor. Then set up your tape system to match the overall data flow throughput.

More tape drives and backup servers are much better than a single large backup server that can write faster than you can send it data.

What happens if you look at Table 18-4. on page 684, make all of your changes, and still decide that you have so much information you won't be able to back it all up in your nightly backup window—*and* you've also ruled out multiplexing to speed up the process? At this point, you have three choices. First, you can add additional backup servers and associated tape systems to your plan. That's a choice, all right. Alternately, you can move in the same direction as Dantz Development's Retrospect backup software, which has chosen not to follow the multiplexing and interleaving pack. Instead, they've created a backup server channel system that is most impressive. *Or,* you can back up to disk in a different way than you might have tried before. One of our field editors turned us on to a great product from Quantum that creates a *virtual* tape library, substituting disks for actual tapes. Sounds kind of strange, but in reality and practical application, it's very cool. The point here is that you *do have choices* you can make to help your backup process.

Why backup channels and less expensive, and slower drives might be a good path

Retrospect allows multiple simultaneous backups—not to a multiplexed tape drive, but instead to individual multiple tape drives. Let's say that you want to back up the e-mail server, DNS server, web server, and PBX server to the same backup server. The e-mail server is your exchange system, and while it might not be the fastest server on the market, it does have a lot of data that needs to be backed up, with lots of small changes every day. Ditto for your PBX server. Then there's your DNS server and your web server. These two servers are also not the world's fastest, but they don't have a lot of changes. With a single Retrospect backup server and either two single-drive tape libraries or one multiple drive tape library, you can "channel" your e-mail and DNS server to back up to one tape drive, and your PBX and web server to back up simultaneously to another tape drive. Two perfect tape libraries for this type of high-capacity and mid-range speed

Figure 18-12. The Exabyte Autopak 1x7 (left) and 430 (right) tape libraries

level backups are the Exabyte VXA-2 tape libraries shown above. The AutoPak 1x7 is our personal favorite for your basic Mammoth or VXA tape library. It has seven cartridges and a single tape drive with a SCSI-2 LVD interface. The throughput is about 6 MB/s. You could hook two of these up to the single Retrospect backup server to serve both backup channels, as described above, or you could hook up the 430-tape library (it's a 5U rack-mount system) with two tapes drives in it, with one drive serving one backup channel and the other serving the other backup channel. Either way, you match your tape system performance to your throughput performance, and that's a very good thing.

Once you've honed your end-to-end throughput to your particular needs, focus on honing in on the most appropriate data to back up for your backup plan. What you decide to back up is your next priority in your plan.

If you want to multiplex, at least do it to disk (sort of) with the Quantum DX

If you aren't using Retrospect and have to multiplex because your software automatically supports it, or you simply want to take advantage of the shorter backup windows that multiplexing affords you, we have the perfect hardware solution for your needs. A couple of our field editors suggested that we examine two devices from Quantum: the DX30 and DX100. The Quantum DX series of backup devices are **Virtual Tape Library (VTL)** products that *emulate* a tape library, but are in fact a **RAID system** of very fast ATA hard drives. The DX family provides high-speed disk-to-disk backups, alleviating the problem of tape shoe-shining and therefore allowing the administrator to configure up to six simultaneous multiplexed streams. And since the multiplexed streams are *to disk*, even though the DX systems read the backup file linearly, the multiplexed restores are 10 times faster than tape restores. In other words, it's as fast as it could be, and you never have to worry about restoration slowdowns caused by multiplexing (while gaining the shorter backup window advantages of multiplexing).

Figure 18-13. DX30 showing disk arrays, controller, and tape emulation (left) and a real one in a rack (right)

Figure 18-13. above shows an actual DX30 (right) with its front bezel cover off, with the controller unit on top and the RAID system on the bottom (you can add two more of those RAID systems for added space). On the left is my version of a schematic, showing how the controller unit separates the actual drive arrays from what the backup software sees. What the backup software sees is what it would expect to see from a six-drive tape library. Below, in Figure 18-14. on page 691 we show a screen from VERITAS NetBackup running a backup to a 30 tape robot. That 30 tape robot is actually the DX30. To VERITAS NetBackup (the VERITAS products, Legato's Networker, Computer Associates, and others currently support this drive set.), it is a tape library with 30 tapes in it.

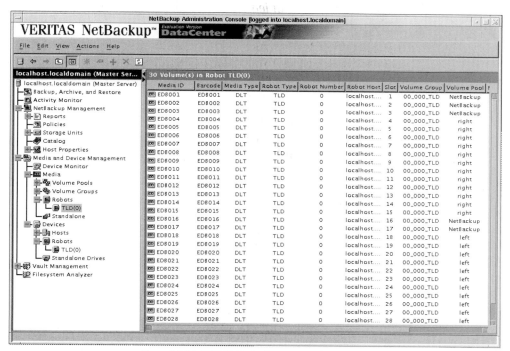

Figure 18-14. VERITAS NetBackup connected to a Quantum DX30

How it works Think of these DX systems as a two-part component set: a controller and the disk array(s). Utilizing software that resides on the controller, the DX series configure the disk arrays to look like a set of tapes and tape drives in a tape library. This allows zero configuration on the part of the backup software, as it now thinks that it's writing data to the DX in tape format and utilizing the standard media management schema (which is sized to fit the storage capacity of the specific DX system in use). The DX30 controller (1U in size) and disk array (3Us in size, with 24 ATA drives in the array) are a combined unit and have all the features you'll find in a mid-tier or enterprise system: SNMP, SES, RAID 5 or 10 arrays for the drives, dual cooling and power, etc.

The usable capacity of the first drive array in the DX30 is 3.2 TB (roughly equal to about 16 LTO tapes, given compression ratios). Two additional arrays (of 4.3 TB each, because they can hold more data) can be added to the system to bring the total expanded storage capacity up to 12.4 TB (or 64 fully compressed LTO tapes).

That's about where the comparison of a RAID 5 drive capacity of a disk array and the DX system virtual tape capacity stops—but remember, kids, this is a book, and books are frozen in time the moment the press slaps ink onto paper, so by the time you read this, the capacity will probably have grown faster than the weeds in my back yard.

For one thing, using ATA-based drives usually *isn't a good thing* for fast backups. When reading and writing the small chunks of data that incremental backups create, ATA drives are much slower than the speedy SCSI-based drives in high-end RAID arrays. However, ATA drives are lightning fast when they are used for sequential I/O large block format writes. Because the DX family emulates a tape versus a drive write, the write's "personality" is changed to the large block format that works great for the ATA drive-base. A regular RAID array just can't do that.

When a backup software application (or an operating system, for that matter) writes to a RAID stripe, it has no idea of the optimal method to write the data; therefore the stripe size can be mismatched with the size of the data block being written. This mismatching causes more CPU overhead, using more space than is necessary. In the DX series, the controller running the tape emulation software is also tuned to match the disk array; therefore it can more precisely match the stripe sizes of the array and use fewer CPU processes during the operation. That's one smart controller!

To the server, it's a tape drive

The DX30, for example, emulates an ATL P1000 tape library that has between two and 80 cartridges of tapes per array and two to six installed DLT7000 tape drives (whether you have one or three RAID systems attached). The DX30 system is set up to split the RAID 5 arrays into a two-LUN configuration, with half the number of emulated tapes per LUN. And although it emulates that tape drive type, it will be *much* faster than an actual tape library—around two times faster for multiplexed backups and 10 times faster for multiplexed restores.

Here's something that all of us with expanding waistlines would love to be able to do—expand capacity based on what we want to have today. What in the world does that mean? Simple, really: The total size of each of the tapes in the library is bound only by the size of the *entire* array. You could have two *very* large tapes (1.7 TB per tape), or you could have 80 tapes of 47.5 GB each. Try that with a real tape—*not*. This is a great advantage for tape backup software packages that won't stretch their catalogs throughout multiple tapes.

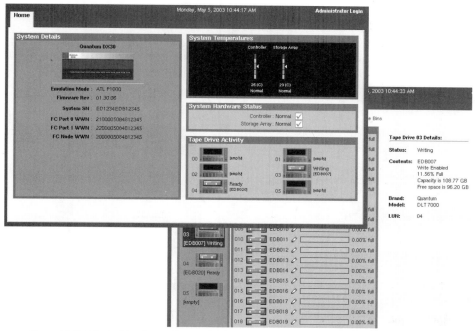

Figure 18-15. The DX30 software showing the drive setup (top left) and the virtual library (bottom right)

For disaster recovery purposes (as well as for archiving), data can be moved to real tape cartridges using the backup server's cloning or duplication functionality. A typical network configuration for the DX family houses the system within at least a "mini-SAN" comprising the DX backup unit and a traditional tape library connected via a 2 Gbps switch to the backup server as shown in Figure 18-16. on page 694.

This gives the system the maximum throughput between it and the backup server that it needs, and allows it to connect directly to the tape library within the same SAN architecture. With its high data transfer rate, ability to migrate virtual tapes over to physical tapes during non-backup window hours of operation, and its ability to scale, these DX systems from Quantum are very, *very* attractive for backup administrators who want to multiplex their backups for speed.

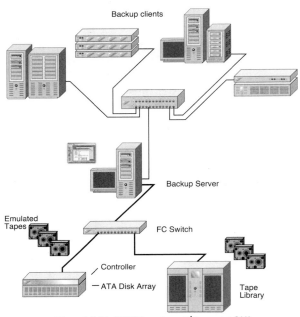

Figure 18-16. DX30 in action within a mini-SAN

What does this really get you? No cigar, but you do get a faster backup process, a faster restore (compared to tape multiplexing), and no tape shoe-shining. You can also better utilize the existing tape library because you can utilize the system during your backup window much more productively, and then move the virtual tape backup off to *real* tape during the backup server's normally idle time period.

Here's what you really, *really* get: You get to back up to disk. A disk array that is *protected* through RAID 5 or 10. A disk array that isn't going to fail at 2:00A.M., leaving you with a sick report of "backup didn't happen because we either ran out of tape or lost a tape to a media failure." *That's* what you get—and that's plenty.

But, if that's not enough for the tough sells among you, you get even more: a great hierarchical storage management system for backups. You get to have both tape and disk backups. You get something "in the middle" of your tape system that allows you to migrate data offsite, or have it onsite and highly available. And that gets you the biggest boon of all: peace of mind.

FINDING THE IMPORTANT DATA—WHAT'S *YOUR* STRATEGY?

So far, we've covered the creation of a backup plan that takes your servers' backup window into account. We've covered the necessary network architectures you'll need for a multi-server high-speed organizational backup plan. Now it's time to focus more closely on what you're backing up and how you can rid yourself of some of the extraneous data you don't want.

I don't normally open with a story this long, so please indulge me this one time. I recently spoke with Richard Zulch, CTO of Dantz Development, about the contents of hard drives. Richard had read an article by Martha Stewart about how best to organize one's closet. Martha said that it isn't about the size of the closet—it's about organization; more closet space simply means more "stuff." Below right, I show a picture of one of Martha's organized closets. This picture comes from the Martha Stewart website,[5] and it shows how nice and neat everything *can* be in a closet. Ha! Big, fat, hairy chance in reality there, Mattie.

Table 18-5. Reality vs. Martha Stewart

On the left in Table 18-5. on page 696 is a *real* closet. Mine, as a matter of fact. You'll notice the shoes (Yes, that *is* a bunny slipper on the bottom right) are nicely piled up, and the T-shirts on top are stacked sideways to make it easier getting them off the shelf. I have T-shirts dating back to trade shows before I met my wife. I claim that I keep them for posterity's sake, but my wife claims that a great deal of stuff in my closet probably doesn't fit anymore, and that I only keep it in the vain hope that some day, I'll lose enough weight to fit back in.

Let's call the "stuff" that my wife thinks I should get rid of *cruft*, or *dreck*. A certain amount of this cruft or dreck seeps into one's closet over the years. If you were Martha, you'd throw it out every spring. If you were me, you'd look for a house with more closet space—which brings me back to the point of this segment.

Fortunately for us, storage manufacturers give us more and more closet space for the cruft and dreck of our computer files every year. When I wrote my first backup book in 1994, the average hard drive size was a couple of hundred megabytes— somewhere around the size of the applications and files within my Microsoft Office directory of today (384 MB). As the drives have gotten bigger, I've learned to better organize and keep more stuff—er, cruft. I actually have about 4.6 GB of applications (89 total application folders) on my computer. However, day in and day out, I use Photoshop, Canvas, Microsoft Office, Eudora, Dreamweaver, Screen Catcher and Explorer. But I sure wouldn't part with the other 82 applications.

Now, multiply that philosophy by 250 people in a medium-sized organization, and you've got more cruft than you can think of. Multiply those ever-expanding storage bins we call hard drives and what you end up with is a storage problem that becomes a backup administrator's nightmare.

If you back up only the important stuff, you must have a strategy. Your strategy must have several tactics, as well, such as a regular inventory method, a data classification method, some selection methodologies, a training method, and a reporting method (you must always have a reporting method in organizations). Since reporting is specific to each organization, I'm going to ignore that part. However, the rest is germane to everyone.

---

5. To find the article, go to http://www.marthastewart.com and search on *closet*.

Create a storage inventory

You can go fancy here, or you can go simple—but what you must do is create an inventory record of the devices that you have, and then list, for each of the devices:

- How much storage space is being used?

- Whose data lives there?

- How does this data support the business?

A great many storage management packages are available on the market today. I'm not going to go into them all because they vary widely in what they do, and they seem to change daily. I'm simply going to return to my references to LANsurveyor and the map it creates along with the very simple table that it can export[6]. You can easily use LANsurveyor to map out your network and create a spreadsheet for each and every volume of data that resides in our organizational LAN/WAN structure. However, there is no tool in the world other than communication and common sense that can identify how the data supports the business. That's a staff function.

Let's return to the server table, adding desktop and notebook computers, as well, and this time, let's take an inventory-esque look at the data that resides there, and see if we can classify what's stored on the server. We can think of four basic data classifications (if you know of any more, contact us and let us know):

1. **Service** data is mission critical, directly affecting the ability of the business to deliver its products or services. In the case of our lumber company, service data could range from the advertising department's weekly Sunday paper ad inserts (that generate considerable foot traffic in all of the stores), through the active inventory system that each of the store kiosks uses and is key for the SCM database that constantly updates the suppliers.

2. **Internal** data is the opposite of service data. Internal data affects the workings of the company, but since it doesn't have a public face, it won't directly make the company look bad if it's lost. Corporate reports, e-mail storage, and day-to-day file servers all fit into this model.

---

6. We've used this application throughout this book to document and report on various networked computers. It's a very utilitarian tool.

3. Then there's data that you must have around by law or contract, which we call **retained** data. In our example, the inventory history database that contains historic records for parts, prices, pictures and sales data is retained data. While it's there and available and must be kept around, it isn't accessed much and doesn't change at all.

4. Of course, we couldn't forget **cruft**. Cruft is the stuff that's there, but you don't remember what for, or why. Nevertheless, it's there, it's real, and it grows. Cruft and retained data share two characteristics and have one major difference: they're neither accessed often nor changed. The difference between retained data and cruft? Retained data can be pointed out specifically by contracts or law, and cruft is just sort of "there."

It's pretty easy to figure out the service, internal, and retained data breakdowns for servers such as the NAS boxes, e-mail server, and HR database servers. Each of these three are highly structured for users and groups and definite usage reasons.

- File servers are usually organized by group, project, or functional area. With easy-to-use storage quota management software, cruft is kept out of a great deal of these servers by simply putting a limit on how much the user can store there.

- Most organizations that require maintaining historical client files or records set up special areas of their file servers earmarked for that information. It's more than likely that whatever is in there is good data and not cruft.

- E-mail servers can fall into the category of internal data that doesn't need to be retained (other than for very specific legal reasons) and are mostly internal facing.

- Databases don't have cruft, other than records that should be purged. And databases are usually either mainly client facing or internal facing, so they too are easy to classify.

- When you get down to the level of desktop and notebook computers, life can get a tad ambiguous. Notebook computers are less ambiguous than desktops because (ostensibly) notebooks are given to end users who travel to meet with clients; therefore, notebooks should contain client-facing data. However, looking at my own organizations over the past 15 years, I'd say that only about 30 percent of a user's notebook contains service, or client-facing data. The rest is a combination of internal data and *cruft*.

Device Type	Volume	Group	Used Space	Service	Internal	Retained
NAS Boxes	Data (E:)	Multi	165 GB	30%?	70%?	10%
	Data (E:)	Advertising	360 GB	100%		
LDAP/eMail	Boot (C:)	IT	2 GB		100%	
	Data (D:)	Multi	90 GB	20%	80%	
HR/Scheduling Payroll Apps & DBs	Boot (C:)	IT	2 GB		100%	
	DBs (D-F:)	HR/HQ	80 GB		100%	100%
Desktop w/ removable media	Int (C:)	IT	1 GB each		100%	
	Ext (D-?:)	?	@ 10 GB	10%?	90%?	
Notebook	Multi (C:)	?	@ 10 GB	30%?	70%?	

Table 18-6. Data classifications on servers

The question then becomes, other than server data, how do you identify that which is service related, internal, and should be retained—and then separate and dump the cruft?

In Mac OS 9 (sorry, Windows users, we'll get to you in a second), it was very easy to identify mission-critical files and folders. The user simply selected the file or folder in question and then applied a "Finder label" to the item(s), thus changing the color of those items and identifying them differently to the system. Backup applications like ArcServe, FWB Backup, and Retrospect then set filters to back up only files and folders labeled Essential.

But that's gone in OS X, and never really existed in Windows. So I asked our distinguished group of field editors for a good way to "tag" files and folders as critical—or should the users be encouraged to simply put those files and folders in a "critical" directory to make it easy to back them up? Here's the general consensus:

Painting the target

Before the military had GPS-based bombs that could be programmed in Cincinnati to automatically hit a target in Singalor, Uzbekistan, they had to paint the target by hand. **Painting the target** is a military term that refers to a process whereby a local soldier near a target who is familiar with it points a laser guidance system onto the target, thus illuminating it for an incoming bomber. This guidance system provides pinpoint accuracy for the bomber to release a weapon that's guided onto the target by the painting device. We use the term here to describe the process of moving from the theoretical discussions of "Okay, this is what I want to back up" down to the nitty-gritty of identifying and locating the information—painting the target—for the backup software to find the information and back it up while ignoring nonessential information. In smaller organizations, painting the target is more of a hands-on approach than it is in larger organizations, only because larger organizations can afford to employ Storage Resource Management (SRM) software to automate the process, similar to the way the GPS software automates the guidance system of the newer bombs.

Specially marked packages

I call this one the **specially marked packages** approach[7]: The backup administrator suggests that users mark their files and folders with special characters to denote that the file or folder is an Essential item and should therefore be backed up. The figure below shows my application of this philosophy to the directory that holds the contents to this book. I marked this directory with three asterisks (using the Shift-8 key combo).

Backup_Book***

Figure 18-17. Special characters in an item's name

---

[7]. This tidbit contributed by Sean Greathouse, Sid Hughes, and Ed.

If I tell my users to mark their files and folders with three asterisks for all information that should be protected in a disk-to-disk backup for immediate retrieval, I need only to set my backup filters to include any item with those characters.

Once the items are no longer Essential, the user can remove the three asterisks, and the backup system (running the essential backups) will ignore the folder.

Special directories

Another way to mark Essential data is through putting that data into a special directory in the user's system[8]. As field editor Doug Nomura put it,

> While the "Finder label" in pre–OS X was a useful tool, we never used it in our enterprise setting. We knew at some point a user wouldn't label his data as critical (and it would be), and inevitably something bad would happen (and it would). During high-throughput data production environments, users don't have time to worry about labels; also, they start to save data all over the drive.
>
> We heartily encouraged users to save into "critical folders" on their machines or, even better, on the file server.

Field editor Tony Abruzzese added that (in his academic environment):

> I generally look at anything in a "Home," "Documents" or "Users" folder as being critical. Other places would include any directories in which applications/services store user data. Depending on the OS, user account info might be included. In an NT Domain system, account info is already backed up on the BDCs. On Linux- or Unix-based systems/servers, you may need to back up the files holding user account information.

Table 18-7. on page 703 shows your standard directory structure for Windows 2000 and XP users on the left, and Mac OS X users on the right (there wasn't really much of a structured system for Mac OS 9 users, so we'll ignore them here).

---

8.   Contributed by Thierry Rolland, Leon, Doug Nomura, Tony Abruzzese, and Kip Tobin.

I've taken the liberty of marking directories that are the same on both platforms with a dual-arrow (<>).

Windows		Mac OS X
Local Hard Drive (C:)		Local Hard Drive
\Documents and Settings		\Users
\Dorian (or any other user)	<>	\Dorian (or any other user)
\Desktop	<>	\Desktop
\My Documents	<>	\Documents
\Shared	<>	\Public
\Favorites		\Library
\Start Menu		\Movies
		\Pictures
		\Sites

Table 18-7. Standard directory structure

Here's what's in the matching directories by default:

Desktop   The Desktop is the same on both Windows and Mac OS X. It contains everything that you put onto your desktop. Aliases don't show in Windows, but they do in Mac OS X.

Now, I know that most of us like to clutter up our desktop. You should see Karsten's (and I thought Germans were supposed to be neat and tidy!),—it's as bad as my *real* desktop. However, Network Frontiers hasn't fallen prey to Martha Stewart's organizational obsession, so we'll ignore that one.

Shared/Public   Empty by default. This is supposed to be the user's shared folder.

Unless users are employing their own computer as a local file server for others in their workgroup (and we recommend against that for all but the smallest of offices), putting Essential files here shouldn't be the ticket.

My Documents/
Documents   Contains by default two folders: My eBooks and My Pictures on Windows and "user data" folders for Mac OS X. All Office applications point to My Documents by default when you hit **Save as...** in Windows as well as in Mac OS X.

This leaves a lot of room for leverage here. If we go with the "critical folder" theory, a simple directory structure for both Windows and Mac OS X users looks like the table below. We've added directories (folders) for Essential, Hot, and In Progress items within the My Documents/Documents directories.

Windows		Mac OS X
Local Hard Drive (C:)		Local Hard Drive
\Documents and Settings		\Users
\Dorian (or any other user)		\Dorian (or any other user)
\Desktop		\Desktop
\My Documents		\Documents
\Essential	<>	\Essential
\Hot	<>	\Hot
\In Progress	<>	\In Progress

Table 18-8. Special backup directories

Targeting known file types

The final method of identifying critical information that we'll discuss here is to simply get a handle on all of the types of filename extensions that are already attached to your documents—and back up those files that have matching extensions. While filename extensions might be new to the Mac OS X community, the Windows world has worked with three-letter filename extensions all along.

For example, this book was primarily written in Microsoft Word. Word attaches a ".doc" three-letter extension on all of its text files. It attaches a ".dic" for dictionary files, ".rtf" for Rich Text Files (a standard formatted-text interchange format), and so on. Get a handle on all the filename extensions that a particular application uses and ensure that you back up all of them. Take the filename extension .alf, for example. Here's the listing (so far that I've found) for the applications that claim the extension:

- Abacus Law File
- ALF Logic File
- AdventNet Look and Feel Standards
- Aventail Connect License File (AVENTAIL.ALF)
- VPCom Remote User Configuration File
- LANDesk Client Manager Configuration File

- ACT! User Logon Tracking

- Cadence Ambit BuildGates

How will your Mac OS X computer know which application to launch when you launch an .alf file? The Finder works in conjunction with Launch Services to determine the extensions that are known to the system. Known extensions can be those within an application's search paths (as in Word, where you tell it where to put certain files), or the Finder associates an extension with an application that had previously launched the file with that extension.

The easiest way to tell which applications append which filename extensions to which documents is to watch what the application is doing when it saves a file. If the application appends .ppt to the file, you can pretty well be certain you are using Microsoft's PowerPoint. If it attaches .cdd to the file, you know you're using the new ConceptDraw[9].

Knowing the different filename extensions can be very beneficial to you as a backup administrator. Why? Because you can use this information to create different backup filters for your backup policies. Let's say you want to back up all of the different Photoshop files that your users might create. Table 18-9. on page 706 shows file format types for the files that Photoshop creates, along with their Macintosh and matching PC/Unix filename extensions.

Let's say that you want to set up your backup program to back up any type of Photoshop file that you or the artists on your network create. To capture each and every possible variation of files, you must know what the corresponding filename extensions are, as in the list above. Once you have a handle on these, you must then communicate that to your backup software, which we cover in *Painting the target* on page 701.

---

9. If you *really* want to know which extensions belong to which applications, check out the Network Frontiers website. Our filename extension database lists more than 6,500 different extensions to date.

		Macintosh	PC/Unix
Format	Type	Creator	Extension
Bitmap	BMP	8BIM	bmp, rle
EPS	EPSF	8BIM	eps
GIF	GIFf	8BIM	gif
JPEG	JPEG	8BIM	jpg, jpe
PCX	PCX	8BIM	pcx
PDF	PDF	8BIM	pdf, pdp
DCS 1.0	EPSF	8BIM	C, M, K, Y, eps
DCS 2.0	EPSF	8BIM	eps
PICT resource	SCRN	8BIM	rsr
PICT	PICT	8BIM	pct, pic
PIXAR	PXR	8BIM	pxr
PNG	PNGf	8BIM	png
Photoshop 2.0	8BIM	8BIM	n/a
Photoshop native	8BPS	8BIM	psd, pdd
Photoshop raw	User definable	8BIM	raw
Scitex CT	..CT	8BIM	sct
TARGA	TPIC	8BIM	tga, vda, icb, vst
TIFF	TIFF	8BIM	tif

Table 18-9. Photoshop type and creator (Mac) vs. extension (Windows).

Separating the cruft through active use

When you're creating your backups, the easiest way to separate those files that have become cruft is to target active files—files that have been in use recently through being accessed or modified. Windows and Unix file systems have three key data-sensitive file flags: creation date, latest modification date, and last accessed date. You could very easily combine a selector of the file types mentioned above, and then add to that selector that you want to back up only those files that have been active within the last x days (our cutoff is 90 days). If this is interesting to you, you'll love the planning tool in LANsurveyor. You can select your devices and create a Backup Profiler (that's what they call it) report that displays files that were accessed or modified within the last x number of days.

We've abbreviated one of their exports from our network to fit here. The report is based upon file type and activity within the last 120 days, showing the total space, and how much of that was active. We then added our own audit information about whether the files are service, internal, retained, or cruft (we think that MP3s, music files, are all cruft). The active amount to back up is shown, as is the amount that we'd skip over since it's cruft.

File Extension	Total GB	Active GB	Flag (S/I/R/C)	Cruft GB
doc	810	110	S/I	700
fm	86	81	I	4
LOG	46	2	I	42
mp3	150	118	C	150
ppt	82	24	S/I	0
xls	29	11	S/I	18

Table 18-10. Active files by extension

From our figures here, we could afford to lose about 80 percent of the documents in this report if they weren't backed up. Since that would save backup time and backup storage, it makes a good argument for going through all of these gyrations to determine what's important to back up and what's not.

Now that we've covered what you need to know about separating the craft from the cruft, let's discover how you do it. You can use two basic methodologies: The first is for SOHO and SMB (small to medium-sized business) networks, and involves creating file selectors in your backup software based on the file types and reports generated with programs like LANsurveyor. The second methodology is for medium- to enterprise-sized businesses that can afford SRM (Storage Resource Management) products that can automate the process on a much larger scale and can integrate with backup software products.

CREATING SPECIFIC SELECTORS IN YOUR BACKUP SOFTWARE TO ELIMINATE CRUFT

At this point, we need to get more specific. In the SOHO and SMB realm, the world divides into two camps: those who must protect OS X computers and those who don't. Dantz Development's Retrospect is the only backup software we know of that allows you to a custom selector that delineates among universal information (such as the triple-asterisk method), Windows information, and Macintosh information.

To set this up in the Retrospect application (Windows only, but it can back up all three OS platforms), click **Configure > Selectors** to bring up the default selectors window. To create a custom selector, click the **New…** button and give this custom selector a name. In our case, we called it "Essential Directories." Once you've clicked the **New** button again, click the **Add…** button in the window to create the first of your four custom selectors.

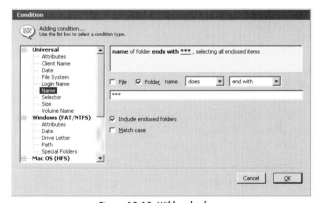

Figure 18-18. Wildcard selector

The first selector that we suggest you create is the Wildcard selector, ***, a **universal selector**, which, in Retrospect parlance, is one that can apply across all three (Win, Mac, Unix) platforms. And since all three platforms allow users to add three asterisks to the end of folder names, this qualifies as a universal selector. Set up the criteria so that it reads "**name** of the folder **ends with** <u>***</u>, selecting all enclosed items."

Include enclosed folders to ensure that you capture everything in the folder, not just the top-level folder and its files.

The next folder you need is the **Documents** folder for Windows users. Retrospect pre-identifies this as a *Special Folder*, and it can be selected from the **Windows > Special Folders** list.

Next, add another item to your list: s the Mac OS X **Users** folder. Dantz hasn't gotten around to making this a Special Folder as of this writing, so you'll have to use the **Mac OS > Path** selector. Set the selector to read "Mac OS **path** of folder **contains** <u>Users</u>, selecting all enclosed items."

You now have a special selector of your own to use when creating your backup scripts. You can now create custom selectors, save them, and export them to your other backup servers. We'll post all of the custom selectors that we and our field editors create or update on our backupbook.com website. They're free for downloading in the Registered Readers section.

File extension selectors in Retrospect

We chose Retrospect for our example because it's the easiest backup software that we know of that allows the user to create a special file-set selector that can be saved and reused over and over again. To access this feature, select the **Special** tab; then the **Selectors** button.

A dialog with all of the current selectors in it will appear. Since you're creating a new selector, click the **New** button and give your selector set a name such as "Photoshop." After you've named your new selector set, you'll see a window like the one below that allows you to add filters for both inclusion and exclusion filters.

Click the **blue arrow button** below the **Include** filter. When you do so, a pop-up with several choices appears. For our purposes here, you'll want to select the **File Name** filter. In the dialog below, we've set the file name filter to read "**file name** ends with .pct". To make sure that you back up all the different types of files that Photoshop can create, add a "file name ends with" type of filter for each and every filename extension in the mapping list. The dialog below shows how we've added multiple filename extensions (the completed list is too long to fit here) for our Photoshop filter.

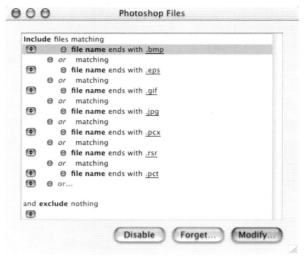

Figure 18-19. Partial Photoshop Files filter list

How do you know if this works? In Retrospect, you can test your filter by selecting the **Check Selector** menu item in the **Selector** menu (or by typing CMD-T). You'll be asked to choose a test volume, and Retrospect will run the file selector on that volume, producing a list of all files that your selector would choose to back up. As with the other selectors from Retrospect, you can save these as well and you can find updated ones on our website.

File extension selectors in VERITAS NetBackup Professional

VERITAS NetBackup Professional has a straightforward but powerful way of selecting all files that Photoshop can create for a backup. In the client, click the **Properties** button as a first step to create a selector for the files. Then click the **Backup (Primary)** button, which brings you to the file and directory selector. Notice that in the upper window, **All directories** is not marked for backup. If the files that are to be backed up are scattered all over the hard drive, you might as well select **All directories**. If the situation is more orderly, point NetBackup Professional to the actual images directory. To add a path, click on the **Add Path…** button that opens a selector window so that you can browse your hard drive. Click the **Add** button to add a directory.

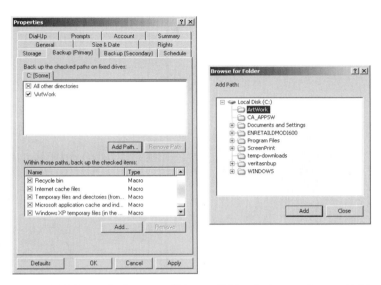

Figure 18-20. Setting the directory and file types (left) and selecting a directory (right)

Next, you'll need to select the file types that you want to back up. Remember that Photoshop can save in about 20 different file types distinguished by filename extension. To select these extensions, you must put them into NetBackup Professional. In the lower half of the window, click the **Add** button to add the extensions. In the Add Rule dialog, enter all extension names from .bmp to .vst by typing the name and hitting the Return key. This is a very quick process, taking only about two minutes. Once you're finished, NetBackup Professional displays the full list of files and the according directory(s) to be backed up on the next run of the backup script. Note that in the lower window, **All other files** is unchecked. This ensures that only the Photoshop files are being backed up.

File extension selectors in NovaDisk +

NovaDisk doesn't offer the NetBackup Professional's file selection options. File selection is manual, and must be done before each backup, as NovaDisk doesn't check for new files of the same type. NovaDisk's only method of selecting files by their extension is its wildcard function. Click on the **Wildcard Tag/Untag** button, and a dialog pops up (Figure 18-21.). Here, enter the file extensions that you want to select. But, beware, this selection only works in the current directory; it doesn't include subdirectories.

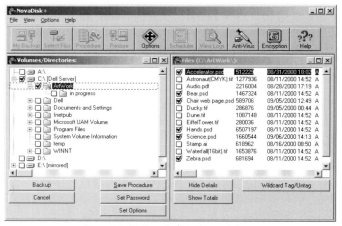

Figure 18-21. NovaDisk & Custom Selector

WORKING WITH SRM (STORAGE RESOURCE MANAGEMENT) SOFTWARE TO ELIMINATE CRUFT AND REDUCE HARDWARE NEEDS

Storage Resource Management (SRM) tools were designed to help larger organizations maintain their expanding storage requirements as well as plan for future requirements. They help to determine issues such as which users utilize the most storage space on the network, how best to partition storage in a SAN, and now, with their integration with backup management tools, they can deal with backing up the craft and dumping the cruft.

SRM tools provide a central view of the physical storage resources (such as RAID drives, tape libraries, SAN space, etc.) and an overall view of the logical space (volumes, files to include file name extensions, specialized directories, etc.). Of all of the storage space on your network, do you know who's using what space, what they're putting there, and how much space you have left on *each* of your drives?

Before the advent of SRM, though we had all become connected and begun to work in a connected world, we had no tools to view or manage our connectedness. In a connected world, resources can no longer be managed as individual components in isolation from the whole. The promise of SRM is the view of, and ability to manage data and storage as a part of the connected whole. And that's important, because we work in a connected world.

At present, SRM tools focus on data policies that invoke both consolidation and migration, partially due to the rapid rise in storage space. In addition, medium-sized to large businesses must plan for and manage their storage space to allow best use of the space they have, and to migrate files to tape or offsite in case of a disaster. Because the cost of storage and network bandwidth are decreasing, the real cost is now in data management.

Think of it: At first, all data was on the mainframe. Then LANs and servers came out, and it was all on the server. Now, with the advent of NAS boxes and SANs, the data can be *anywhere*. How do you back up only the most necessary information? How do you exclude information you don't want? How do you consolidate your backed-up information so that it can fit within the constraints of the equipment you've placed at your hot site or recovery room? SRM tools can help.

SRM tools fall into approximately 11 different categories to handle ever-more complex data-management needs. Some of these categories aren't relevant in a backup management environment—some are. Some SRM tools have all of the categories; others won't. We provide this table so that you can examine the potential offerings and see what fits in your backup and disaster-planning environment.

Category	Description	Backup Application
Asset Management	Tracks and keeps records of all physical storage systems	Useful for disaster plan documentation
Backup Window Planning	View your backup timeframes in a GANTT chart for adjusting your scripts and allocated time slots	A must
Capacity Management	Creates real-time or historical reports about physical media storage usage or logical storage usage	Can be used for tape capacity planning
Chargeback	Used to "bill" departments and end users for storage capacity utilized. Usually creates more paperwork for the company and is really "funny money"	None
Configuration Management	Allows the administrator to determine "best practice" consolidation of logical storage across physical storage media	Great for hot-site and recovery room planning
Data Migration	Tied to configuration management, allows the wholesale or very specific consolidation of data across the system onto discrete logical structures	Great for hot-site and recovery room planning
Events Management	They tell you when something's amiss	Whatever...
Performance Management	An overall view of how things are ticking	Whatever...
Policy Management	This is your rule set for managing logical storage space across your physical hardware. It can be tied to configuration management and data migration	A must for consolidation during backups and for disaster recovery plans
Quota Management	This ties into, and enforces, policy management	None
Removable Media Management	Maintains the historical records of on- and off-site tape, removable HDs, and optical media management	Great for tracking your moveable media *if* it ties into your backup server software

Table 18-11. SRM categories

Starting with asset management views

A great place to start planning with an SRM system is by examining what you already have, and how well you are using it. Below is a charts from Overland Storage's Overland SRM product (one of two products we really like). This chart offers an overall view of the gigabytes of data in use by servers in the organization. It is interesting to note that the last five servers in the list all have the same amount of physical storage as the second server in the list (which is 90 percent full). Just looking at in-use storage versus total storage is a big plus for many organizations.

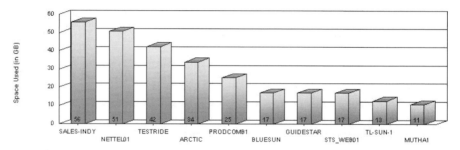

Top Systems by Total Space in Use

Figure 18-22. Top systems report from Overland SRM

Storage Profiler from Tek-Tools shows the same type of report, but enables you break it down into the *types* of storage on your network, such as Direct Attached Storage (DAS) on your servers, Network Attached Storage (NAS) for your various NAS boxes, and Storage Area Network (SAN) space spread throughout. This is a great type of visual breakdown of what you've got and where you've got it.

Enterprise Storage				
Type	**Hosts**	**Total**	**Used**	
DAS	102	1,411 GB		44.62%
NAS	1	82 GB		13.93%
SAN	2	5,014 GB		1.93%
Total:	**105**	**6,508 GB**		**11.34%**

Figure 18-23. Storage Profiler overview chart and table

More detailed than the overall view, the SRM software can quickly drill down into each of the systems and examine the files by their filename extension type (which we've already discussed as being pretty important), as well as by other means. Figure 18-24. shows the breakdown of one volume (3CPO) on one of the servers (System 3CPO) of the servers. While this shows EXE, DLL, SYS, and LOG files (hey, it's a database application server, okay?), the same type of report can be created for any of the special filename extensions that you deal with.

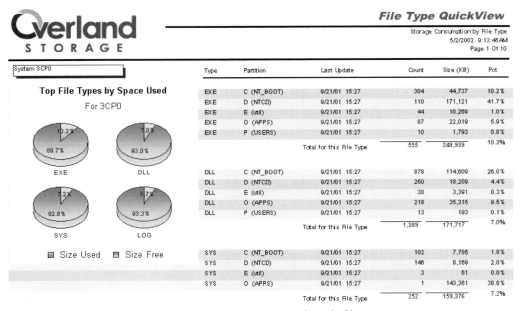

Figure 18-24. Server volumes by file type

This gets to be real handy when you want to examine directories with special markings, such as the ones we discussed in *Painting the target* on page 701. By combining special directory listings and file types, you can get very specific information about your systems. You can then use that information to consolidate your data before backing it up.

> If you think you might be ready for storage consolidation, go to our website (www.backupbook.com) and take the storage consolidation readiness quiz. A score of 50% or more suggests that you should make the move to invest in an SRM solution.

Again, jumping to another application to look at the data, you can view it by the owners of the data, as well. At right, this report from Storage Profiler breaks down marketing, accounting, and a couple of other groups. You can exclude all data from accounting or other groups that didn't have to be recovered during the recovery room phase or your offsite restoration plan.

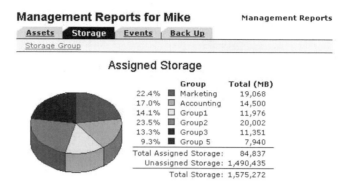

Management Reports for Mike   Management Reports

Assets | **Storage** | **Events** | **Back Up**

Storage Group

Assigned Storage

	Group	Total (MB)
22.4% ■	Marketing	19,068
17.0% □	Accounting	14,500
14.1% □	Group1	11,976
23.5% ■	Group2	20,002
13.3% ■	Group3	11,351
9.3% ■	Group 5	7,940

Total Assigned Storage: 84,837
Unassigned Storage: 1,490,435
Total Storage: 1,575,272

Assigned Storage Usage

Group	Size (MB)	Current Usage	Rate
Marketing	19,068	38.70%	0.45%/day
Accounting	14,500	27.80%	-0.21%/day
Group1	11,976	47.15%	-0.11%/day
Group2	20,002	24.77%	0.05%/day
Group3	11,351	23.95%	-0.69%/day
Group 5	7,940	30.88%	0.07%/day

Figure 18-25. Data by owners

Using SRM to streamline your backups

Once you have a handle on where your organizational data lives on your system, you've still got to fit that data into an organizational backup window.

For backup administrators, the real plus of SRM occurs when you can couple the information you've found in the overall reports into a **policy management plan** that allows you to automatically script your backup software to select to back up only the volumes, directories, and file types that fit the policy, and then squeeze those volumes, directories, and file types into a backup window that fits the needs of the organizational users and servers. Figure 18-26. on page 718 shows what one of those windows looks like. This is the Tek-Tools Storage Profiler application's view of a backup summary, depicting a GANTT chart of what the backup window looks like for the various client volumes being backed up from that particular backup server on that particular day (Tuesday). Not only can it provide the basic timing information, it also offers real-time status of successful backups. Figure 18-26. below shows the backup window for a single tape drive attempting to back up multiple servers with multiple volumes in a multiplexed environment (hence you see bigdaddy, tdettmer, and starfish interleaved during the process). The open backup window for these servers was between 10:00P.M. on Tuesday and 4:00P.M. on Wednesday—during the break in their production schedule. If the GANTT chart had gone beyond 4:00P.M., we would have had to reduce the amount of data being backed up (using a filter) or the amount of servers being backed up.

Backup Summary

■ Client Successful ■ Client In Progress
■ Client Failed □ Client Exceeded Backup Window

Backup Cycle: Tuesday ▾

Client	Backed Up (MB)	Duration	Throughput (MB/sec)	Level	10:00 PM ▼ Backup Window 4:00 PM
tdettmer	0	1 sec	0.11	Unknown	
tdettmer	0	1 sec	0.49	Unknown	
bigdaddy	24	0 sec	0.00	Unknown	
bigdaddy	224	2 min	1.84	Unknown	
starfish	18,007	4.9 hr	1.02	full	
bigdaddy	1	5 sec	0.17	Unknown	
bigdaddy	14	14 sec	1.01	Unknown	
starfish	327	8.4 min	0.65	Unknown	
bigdaddy	245	2 min	1.99	Unknown	
bigdaddy	224	1.8 min	2.06	Unknown	
bigdaddy	1	6 sec	0.14	Unknown	
starfish	223	2.8 min	1.35	Unknown	
starfish	1	9 sec	0.09	Unknown	
starfish	13	18 sec	0.73	Unknown	
starfish	790	15 min	0.88	Unknown	
bigdaddy	804	9.2 min	1.45	Unknown	
bigdaddy	0	0 sec	0.00	Unknown	
bigdaddy	14	49 sec	0.29	full	
bigdaddy	224	3.2 min	1.17	full	
bigdaddy	1	46 sec	0.02	full	
bigdaddy	0	1 sec	0.00	full	
starfish	769	23.8 min	0.54	full	
starfish	13	29 sec	0.45	full	
bigdaddy	0	0 sec	0.00	full	
starfish	223	5.9 min	0.63	full	
starfish	1	13 sec	0.06	full	

Figure 18-26. Backup summary in Storage Profiler

When we began this book, we talked with organizations like Fujitsu-Softek and VERITAS about their SRM solutions partnering with backup software products. To be honest, we didn't like their answers. Fujitsu partners with Legato, and VER-

ITAS partners with, well, VERITAS. The products that we like are the ones that partner with *everybody*. We know that Overland Storage partners with BakBone and a few others. We know that Tek-Tools works with Legato, ARCserve, and a few others. Make sure you pick an SRM tool that integrates with a backup software package you like. Again, we turn to the Tek-Tools Storage Profiler product's view of multiple backups running from the ARCserve backup server in Figure 18-27. This depicts a live organization-wide view of the backup process as it runs across seven different ARCserve backup servers.

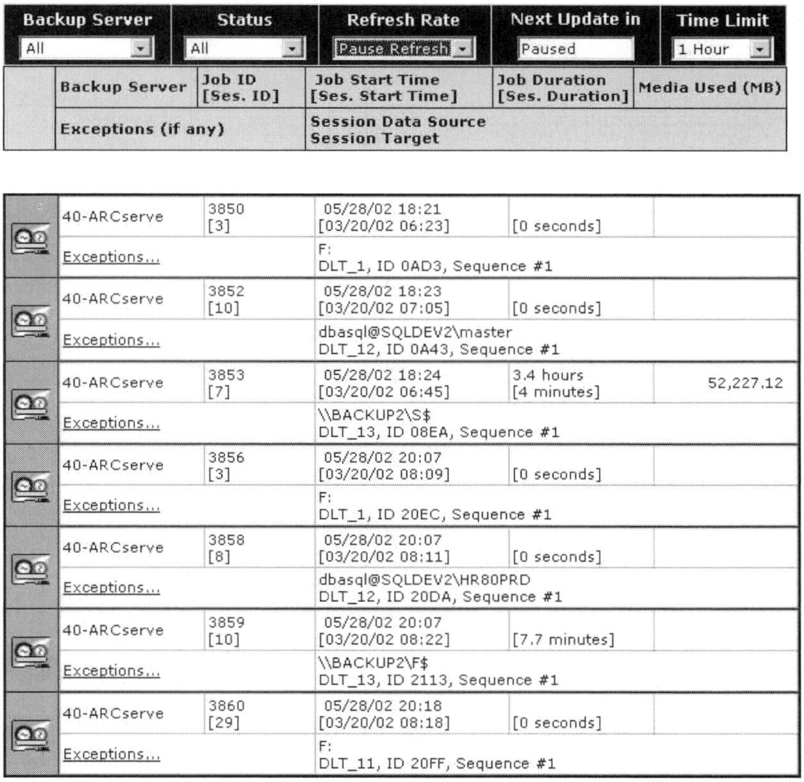

Backup Server	Status	Refresh Rate	Next Update in	Time Limit
All	All	Pause Refresh	Paused	1 Hour

	Backup Server	Job ID [Ses. ID]	Job Start Time [Ses. Start Time]	Job Duration [Ses. Duration]	Media Used (MB)
	Exceptions (if any)		Session Data Source Session Target		
	40-ARCserve	3850 [3]	05/28/02 18:21 [03/20/02 06:23]	[0 seconds]	
	Exceptions...		F: DLT_1, ID 0AD3, Sequence #1		
	40-ARCserve	3852 [10]	05/28/02 18:23 [03/20/02 07:05]	[0 seconds]	
	Exceptions...		dbasql@SQLDEV2\master DLT_12, ID 0A43, Sequence #1		
	40-ARCserve	3853 [7]	05/28/02 18:24 [03/20/02 06:45]	3.4 hours [4 minutes]	52,227.12
	Exceptions...		\\BACKUP2\S$ DLT_13, ID 08EA, Sequence #1		
	40-ARCserve	3856 [3]	05/28/02 20:07 [03/20/02 08:09]	[0 seconds]	
	Exceptions...		F: DLT_1, ID 20EC, Sequence #1		
	40-ARCserve	3858 [8]	05/28/02 20:07 [03/20/02 08:11]	[0 seconds]	
	Exceptions...		dbasql@SQLDEV2\HR80PRD DLT_12, ID 20DA, Sequence #1		
	40-ARCserve	3859 [10]	05/28/02 20:07 [03/20/02 08:22]	[7.7 minutes]	
	Exceptions...		\\BACKUP2\F$ DLT_13, ID 2113, Sequence #1		
	40-ARCserve	3860 [29]	05/28/02 20:18 [03/20/02 08:18]	[0 seconds]	
	Exceptions...		F: DLT_11, ID 20FF, Sequence #1		

Figure 18-27. Storage Profiler's network-wide backup monitor window

Planning, managing, and viewing backups as a part of storage management is one of the best uses for SRM software that we've found.

WHAT ABOUT WORKSTATIONS?

You're now nearing the end of this book. You've just finished a discussion of backup this and image that; replicate this and archive that. And while we might have spent a chapter on document loss, we didn't really deal with backing up the users' workstations in a networked environment.

Adding workstations to your nightly tape backup window is all but impossible for any organization beyond 50 computers—either there isn't much to back up, or there must be a great many backup servers.

 Network Frontiers doesn't believe in backing up workstations to tape systems in a networked environment. Maybe, *maybe* you can get away with it if you have five to 10 workstations and one server. However, any organization that must restore a great deal of workstations after a building loss will really suffer if it must restore one workstation at a time from tape. It just doesn't make sense.

So what's the alternative? Back up the workstations in the following manner:

1. Image the applications and operating system.

2. Create a "selector" to back up everything *but* the imaged data to a disk-based backup system.

Why do this? Here are several reasons, any one of which should make you switch:

*   Disk-based backups can be restored in parallel through connecting multiple "temporary" backup servers to the same disk location, whereas one backup server can be connected to only one tape system.

*   Disk-based backups are at least 200 percent faster than tape-based backups. Tape-based restores are usually 25 percent slower than tape-based backups. But disk-based restores are *faster* (by 25 percent, oddly enough) than disk-based backups.

*   Disk-based backup software like EVault's InfoStage, NovaStor's NovaNet-WEB and Altiris' Client Recovery Solution can run with public IP addresses, and users can then schedule and run their own backups from any place on the planet with an IP address.

The methods of disk-based network backups

- Backups are either initiated by the client (**push**), the server (**pull**), or *both*. This becomes very important if your client happens to move around the Internet. If the backup software is pull only, it tends to look for the client in the last place it saw it, and ignore it if it isn't there anymore (meaning that it moved to a new IP address). Push-based backup software can back up from *any* IP address to *any public* IP address, or any *private* IP address *within its own subnet*. We'll ignore all pull-only software in this book.

- What gets backed up is either sent across the network on a file-by-file basis, a block-by-block basis, or a delta-bit basis (we've covered this in-depth in our Document Backup chapter).

- When the files are moved to the file server, they're placed there in their native format, stored as an image file, or stored within an SQL database.

Here's how the different software products break down:

Disk-based backups	EVault InfoStage	Iomega Automatic Backup	Altiris Client Recovery	NovaNet-WEB	Dantz Retrospect	Symantec Ghost CE
Windows client	✔	✔	✔	✔	✔	✔
Mac OS X client	✔	✔			✔	
Unix/Linux client	✔		✔		✔	
Push based	✔	✔	✔	✔		✔
Pull based	✔		✔		✔	✔
File-by-file backup		✔			✔	✔
Block-by-block backup	✔					
Delta-bit backup			✔	✔		
File-based structure		✔			✔	
BLOB file structure				✔	✔	✔
SQL-based backup	✔		✔			

Table 18-12. Disk-based backup software

Iomega Automatic Backup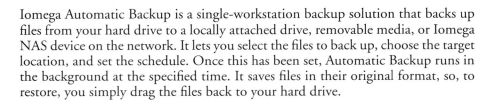

Iomega Automatic Backup is a single-workstation backup solution that backs up files from your hard drive to a locally attached drive, removable media, or Iomega NAS device on the network. It lets you select the files to back up, choose the target location, and set the schedule. Once this has been set, Automatic Backup runs in the background at the specified time. It saves files in their original format, so, to restore, you simply drag the files back to your hard drive.

EVault InfoStage

Our field editors chose EVault InfoStage as their single favorite block-level disk-based backup software. This product is designed for medium and large-sized organizations that require fast, cost-effective data protection. The EVault InfoStage server can be installed on any Windows 2000 or better server, and operates best with a RAID5 drive array. The client software is all IP based and runs on most operating systems that we know of.

EVault InfoStage store the data on the server in an interesting manner. All files are formatted in a System Independent Data Format (SIDF) that negates operating system version obsolescence by enabling files from earlier OS versions to be restored to later versions of the OS, vice versa, and even to a completely different OS. Throughout the backup process, the data is encrypted before it leaves the client computer and isn't decrypted until the keyholder enters the pass code.

NovaNet-WEB

NovaNet-WEB is a TCP/IP-based backup solution that gives corporations an easy-to-set-up solution for backing up their users' data to a disk-based backup. Users connect to the NovaNet-WEB server and create their own backup sets and backup schedules. The NovaNet-WEB server receives the user data and saves it in a folder structure on any mounted volume. The data is encrypted and is decrypted only upon restore.

Altiris Client Recovery Solution 🪟 🐧

Altiris CRS is a server-based solution for automatically creating snapshots of client computers and managing the snapshots as disk-based backups on the server. CRS is highly centralized so that a systems administrator doesn't have to visit a client PC even once. Everything from installing the client software and taking snapshots to restoring a PC can be executed from the CRS server console. The process of taking snapshots is both server and client driven. To keep the amount of data low, CRS maintains the disk-based backups in an SQL database and can therefore omit redundant files (even among multiple computers), transmitting only the delta changes of a file after the initial snapshot. In other words, it's insanely fast, with the smallest "storage space footprint" of any of these products. Snapshots of a hard drive or of single files and folders can be taken. A predefined exclusion list exists on the server, which can be modified by users—if the administrator grants them that right.

Symantec Ghost CE 🪟

In addition to creating images of hard disks and partitions, Ghost also provides a backup functionality for PCs on the network. To enable the Ghost Console to perform a client backup, the Ghost client software must be installed on the PC. By creating a backup regime, you can define backup schedules and settings for incremental backups for each single PC. First, Ghost performs a baseline backup that captures the whole disk. You can then set the interval for incremental backups until the next baseline backup is performed. Ghost saves the backed-up files of each PC into one file on the server storage. Symantec recommends doing one baseline backup every five incremental backups.

Dantz Development Retrospect 🪟 🐧 ⓧ

Dantz' Retrospect disk-based backup hasn't yet matured to our liking, but we've included it because they do offer it as a part of their tape backup application and backup strategy. This is a file-by-file backup method with some very strong filtering capabilities. The files can be stored in a single BLOB file (which gets very large very fast) or as a set of proprietary files within a folder structure. What we do like is the speed of the backups and restores. What we don't like is the pull-only mechanism of the backup process, and the way Retrospect manages file "history." Their current strategy is to treat all backups as if they manage sets of tapes instead of logical units of data. Since they're predominantly a tape company, it "works for them." However, it doesn't work for us. The sooner they get with the program, the better, because overall, this is one of the bright shining stars we've seen in the backup world.

The products in action

All of the products reviewed take more or less the same path to create a disk- based backup. Altiris and NovaNet-WEB require some server setup. The rest start with the selection of data, proceed to the creation of a schedule, and end with setting of filters. We will cover all but the Dantz product here, because all setup is done as a part of Retrospect's server scripting routines.

Setup

NovaNet-WEB can be run as a service to your users or even paid subscribers. Therefore, each account requires server setup before the user can access the system. After the applications have been installed and the server has started up you need to create users on the server. First, start the NovaNet-WEB Backup Server Configuration Manager by clicking on the Start menu, going to Programs, then to NovaNet-WEB Backup and select the manager application (that's about as long as its name). Each user needs a distinct user name. As the text in Figure 18-28. on page 724 shows, the account name must be an existing user on this computer—even better, on a Primary Domain Controller—so don't just make up a name, because that won't work.

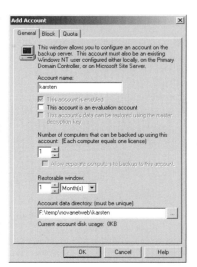

Figure 18-28. NovaNet-WEB new account dialog

Altiris backs their clients up to a database, so the server software must first be installed. It requires Microsoft Windows 2000 Server and Microsoft SQL 7 or 2000. When the server's up and running, the product offers three methods for the client installation: letting users run the installer from a server directory, using SMS for distribution of the package, or letting the users log on to the web server that runs on the CRS server and having them run the installer. We took the browser approach. When clients have installed the Altiris client software, they show up in the server console. They can now be managed from here, and never have to be touched by an administrator. You can give the users rights to manipulate settings like file exclusion or the snapshot scheduling, or you can be very restrictive. For management purposes, computers can be grouped by recovery period, etc.

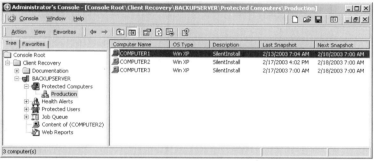

Figure 18-29. Altiris server console

Both NovaNet-WEB and Altiris Client Recovery allow the administrator to set the file-retention duration for each client being backed up. In the Altiris' Rollback Data window, you can define the file types to be excluded from restoring when a user initiates a rollback. This option applies only when the user chooses to restore system and application files, and is not found in any other software. In the Space Management window, you can define when data is to be deleted from the server. If you wish to delete certain files earlier or keep them longer, you can add them to the exception list.

Figure 18-30. Space management settings

Selecting the source containers

Each program starts with selecting the source "containers" for the backup. A container can be a whole volume, a directory (and all of the subdirectories within it), or just a file. Below is the NovaNet-WEB interface, which is much like the standard Windows browser. Most of the disk-based backup tools we've worked with use the standard Windows interface for selecting source containers.

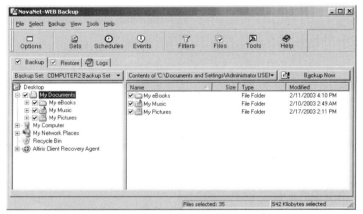

Figure 18-31. The NovaNet-WEB directory selector

The only non-standard tool is the Iomega product. For each folder that you want to back up using that utility, click an **Add Folder...** button, highlight the desired folder within a file selector window and click the **OK** button. This is a bit tedious, but it gets the job done.

Filters

Each of the products apply backup filters by filename extension, entering special codes for directories, or a combination of both methodologies.

Creating a schedule

Some of the products allow a single backup schedule per day, and others allow for multiple backup schedules per day. In the Ghost CE application, you can create multiple schedules for a PC by checking the **Show multiple schedules** check box. Each additional schedule appears in the drop-down list in this dialog.

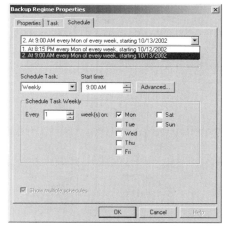

Figure 18-32. Schedule the backup

Network setup of your disk-based backup server

Your disk-based backup server needs special considerations for setup. Of course, it should have its own UPS—that goes without saying. Additionally, you might want to add a few more items:

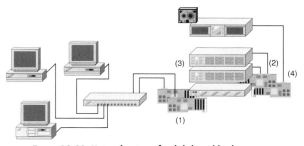

Figure 18-33. Network setup of a disk-based backup server

1. Make sure you have at least two of the fastest Ethernet cards that you can get for the server. Load balance your cards and your access to the server with a

network load balancer, and then set up as many simultaneous client backups as your network pipes and your server can handle before it hits a bottleneck.

2. Don't go running any software-based RAID systems for this puppy. Make sure that you run the fastest RAID card with the biggest RAM cache your backup server can handle. If you're backing up to a RAID10 system or mirrored RAID 5 systems, have two peer-to-peer PCI cards or a very fast dual-bus PCI card.

3. When you back up to your disks, run a RAID5 system with an extra hot-swap drive, or for even more protection, a RAID10 system. For extra protection you connect one of the RAID5 systems via Ultra SCSI locally to the server and the other across your campus using a Fibre Channel card.

4. Attach your tape backup system directly to this server so that you can restore it quickly. Or, if you're using disk-based backup programs like EVault, you can use a duplicate of the backup server in another location and then back up this server to the duplicate across the campus Ethernet or Metropolitan Area Network fiber connection. Whichever method you choose, ensure that you have a connectivity card *specifically for the backup of the server*. Don't daisy chain your tape system off of your RAID PCI card, and don't use the same Ethernet card that accepts incoming client data for your MAN-based backup efforts.

Once everything is set up...

Once your client disk-based backups are up and running, and your SRM system or filtering system is reducing your backup workload and running your network-based backups—it's Krispy Kreme time! Go out. Pig out. And pat yourself on the back, because if you've gotten this far and implemented even one fourth of what we've advocated, you've done a *massive* amount of work. While things are humming along without incident, you may wonder what all the fuss was about—but when disaster strikes, you'll *know* that all your preparation was worthwhile.

Remember, if you ever need help, we're just an e-mail away. If you have any questions about anything you've read, e-mail us at support@backupbook.com. We'll try to help in any way we can.

CHAPTER 19:
LAST THOUGHTS...

This book is finished. You've made it to the end. I hope that while you were curing your insomnia, you actually learned something. I'll tell you what I've learned: Even though this book is finished, this is really *just the beginning* of your, and my, education. To that end, ensure that you sign up for our **update service** at www.backupbook.com when you register your book. When new products, topics and updates come up, we'll be sending out the info to our readers. And I *know* that our field editors will be keeping us updated on what's new.

One of our field editors, Mitch Krayton, sent me an e-mail as I was putting this book "to bed," saying, in essence, "Hey, check out this cool product"—from a company called Chaparral Network Storage. They've been making the internal parts for most of the RAID and other high-end storage systems that Adaptec, Overland, and others use. Mitch told me about their newest product line, which sounded so intriguing that I got hold of one of their Vice Presidents, Cooper Cowart, and picked his brain. After I got done with the messy bits, I found this fact: the world of storage is changing even faster than I thought it was. So, for this wrap-up, I thought I'd talk about the *future now* for a few pages.

Heterogeneous volume virtualization

Heterogeneous means having unlike, dissimilar qualities. When you think of network storage volumes, if you're like me, you tend to believe that you've got Unix volumes, Windows volumes and Mac OS volumes. Each of these volumes, as we've described in *What's put where on your drive* on page 264, have their own unique structure. While a lot of us build Storage Area Networks (SANs) to house our storage and allow multiple servers to tie into them, not all of us are quite at the point of building storage systems that connect to multiple heterogeneous servers. If Chaparral has their way, we'll be able to do just that, and with very few configuration headaches. Their RIO RAID appliance is a modular, SAN-ready, Fibre Channel–based, fault-tolerant storage controller.

Each RIO appliance can scale to manage 36 TB of drive space, with 128 LUNs per appliance, thus giving the servers that access it 128 unique data volumes. And each appliance comes with two 2 Gbps Fibre Channel data gates. These on-board data gates allow this device to act both as a RAID controller *and* a direct-attach SAN storage volume. Figure 19-30 on the left shows the mechanical architecture of the RIO; on the right, it depicts the RIO configured to create its own SAN: two Apple Xserve rack-mount servers connected to the RIO, as well as a pair of clustered Windows servers. Wondering what's so futuristic about this example? The *way* that it's configured, and the services that it brings to the table.

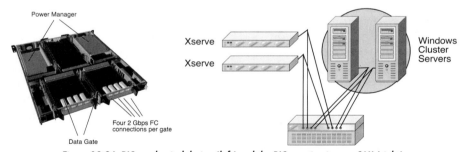

Figure 19-34. RIO mechanical design (left) and the RIO creating its own SAN (right)

Provisioning for the RIO storage architecture is done through Chaparral's RAIDAR Administrator Plus web-based console. RAIDar PS manages the various RIO devices through a web-based JAVA console. You can manage multiple RAIDar PS servers and all their physical and logical resources, as well as end-to-end reporting and diagnostics, because RAIDar PS generates SNMP messages and is integrated with Tivoli, HP, and CA management consoles. Figure 19-35. on page 731 shows a screenshot from Chaparral's web-based management application, showing the various RIO storage arrays and one of the RIO hardware devices.

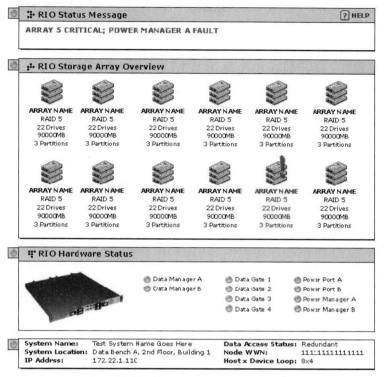

Figure 19-35. RIO RAIDar PS management window

To make things even easier—and a first for any storage company—Chaparral has made their RIO RAIDar administration tool Rendezvous compliant, so that it works with the OS X environment. I know that you Windows guys are saying "So what?" or "What is Rendezvous?" so I'll clue you in as to why this is the *future now*.

Rendezvous lets you create instant networks of computers and devices just by connecting them to the same network. In other words, this is a zero-configuration environment. Chaparral has added Rendezvous to the RIO system to enable them to be added and removed from SAN fabrics without configuration. Think of it: When was the last time you heard *that* about a SAN device? And since we know that the folks in Redmond eventually follow suit and then claim victory for things that work, I suspect that before this book goes into a second edition, we'll have a zero-configuration SAN setup for Windows, too—and Chaparral will probably be leading the way.

The benefit of heterogeneous storage management

However cool Rendezvous is, coolness—nor configuration flexibility—isn't the real benefit to administrators that heterogeneous storage management offers. The real boon is more efficient use of storage resources and the capacity for across-the-board server consolidation. Chaparral has separated the data from the operating system and shown us all that high-end servers aren't the only ones that can play in the SAN world, because while the Xserve is a solid server, it is definitely mid-tier. By doing this, Chaparral has made our jobs as backup administrators and disaster recovery planners easier by allowing us to separate the data so that we can image the servers and then forget about them, so that we can focus on managing the data and securing it. Do you want to mirror it? Okay. Replicate it? Fine. Run backups from it so that the data passes from the storage devices on one point of the SAN switch to the backup unit on another? Okay. To me, heterogeneous storage management is The Future—now.

Chaparral is leveraging the fact that we work in a connected world. They're leveraging the fact that most organizations today have high-end, low-end, and every-thing-in-between data storage needs. And, by providing storage as a totally separate entity from the server, they're offering an easier way to preserve data.

As I said in the beginning of this book, it's all about the work that people do. None of what we've written in this book will change the world—but the data we're protecting can.

So, keep it safe, keep it secure, keep it backed up.

We—Dorian, Lynn, and Karsten, the humble authors of this book—want to thank you very much for spending time with us and our thoughts. We truly do appreciate it. If there's anything more you want to know, or anything that we haven't covered, let us know. Drop us a line to say "hi" and tell us how you liked the book, or even what you didn't like. And if you really want to get involved, become a VAR supporter or a field editor. You can get ahold of us through www.backupbook.com.

Numerics

A

CONTINUITY PLAN PRO, SYSTEMS CONTINUITY PLANNING SOFTWARE

Network Frontiers has partnered with the award winning Palo Alto Software, makers of Business Plan Pro, Marketing Plan Pro, and other business planning software, to bring you **Continuity Plan Pro**. When the plan counts, rely on Continuity Plan Pro to smooth the process of plan creation and get your team on the same page. **Continuity Plan Pro** is the most advanced systems continuity-planning software available in its price category. No other systems continuity-planning product compares with it's functionality and flexibility.

- **Help at Every Step** with instructions and examples to build your plan quickly and easily.

- **EasyPlan Wizard®** guides you through every step from start to finish.

- **Most Complete** with everything you need to define your systems continuity plan, set schedules, create personnel and restoration plans, and defend the funding you'll need.

- **Powerful collaboration tools** which enable you to work efficiently and effectively with your team to create an impressive plan that you can post on the web for colloboration while building the plan, use in emergency communications when all heck breaks loose.

If you need help creating your systems continuity plan, if you want a tool to walk you through the steps and help you get down to the nitty-gritty of what you *really* need to do to support your organization in a crisis, then you'll love this product.

Orders can be taken at http://www.paloalto.com/store/, or by calling them at (800) 229-7526.

We are proud to provide this software product to students, faculty, and accredited academic institutions at greatly discounted prices.